RAGGED MOUNTAIN PRESS

GUIDE TO OUTDOOR SPORTS

GUIDE TO OUTDOOR SPORTS

*All You Need to Get Started Camping, Dayhiking,
Backpacking, Mountain Biking, Sea Kayaking, Canoeing,
River Running, Cross-Country Skiing, and Climbing*

Edited and written by Jonathan Hanson
and Roseann Beggy Hanson

RAGGED MOUNTAIN PRESS
CAMDEN, MAINE

International Marine/
Ragged Mountain Press

A Division of The McGraw·Hill Companies

10 9 8 7 6 5 4 3 2 1

Library of Congress Cataloging-in-Publication Data
Hanson, Jonathan.
    The Ragged Mountain Press guide to outdoor sports : all you need to get started camping, dayhiking, backpacking, mountain biking, sea kayaking, canoeing, river running, cross-country skiing, climbing, and mountaineering / edited and written by Jonathan Hanson and Roseann Beggy Hanson.
        p.   cm.
    Includes bibliographical references (p. 328) and index.
    ISBN 0-07-052114-X (pbk.)
    1. Outdoor recreation.   2. Outdoor recreation—Equipment and supplies. I. Hanson, Roseann Beggy. II. Title.
GV191.6.H36   1997
    796—dc21
                                                            96–54239
                                                                CIP

Questions regarding the content of this book should be addressed to
Ragged Mountain Press
P.O. Box 220
Camden, ME 04843
207-236-4837

Questions regarding the ordering of this book should be addressed to
The McGraw-Hill Companies
Customer Service Department
P.O. Box 547
Blacklick, OH 43004
Retail customers: (800) 262-4729; Bookstores: (800) 722-4726

This book was typeset in Adobe Garamond, Frutiger, and Helvetica

A portion of the profits from the sale of each Ragged Mountain Press book is donated to an environmental cause.

The Ragged Mountain Press Guide to Outdoor Sports is printed on 60-pound Renew Opaque Vellum, an acid-free paper that contains 50 percent recycled waste paper (preconsumer) and 10 percent postconsumer waste paper. ♻

Printed by Quebecor Printing, Fairfield, PA
Design by Carol Gillette
Production and page layout by Janet Robbins, Deborah Krampf, Mary Ann Hensel
Edited by Jonathan Eaton, Daniel Flanagan, Tom McCarthy

Unless otherwise noted, photography by Jonathan and Roseann Hanson
Unless otherwise noted, all illustrations and photography in Chapter 5, River Running with Inflatables, *by Jeff and Tonya Bennett*

To our parents—Patricia A. Mauler, and Charlie and Terry Beggy—for telling us to go play outside (and giving us real freedom to do it).

And to the next generation of outdoor sports enthusiasts. We hope you will adopt and protect our fragile and precious wildernesses.

CONTENTS

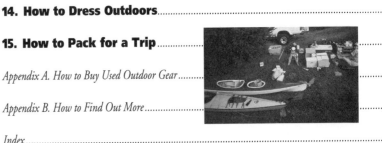

ACKNOWLEDGMENTS

The idea for this ambitious work came from Jonathan Eaton of Ragged Mountain Press, and we are grateful for and humbled by his confidence in our ability to put his idea to paper. We hope we "did good" by his confidence; any errors or shortcomings herein are strictly our responsibility. In addition to serving as a top-quality editor for the project, Jon was also a delight to work with, was always available for our questions, and listened to our concerns. We wish to thank him for those attributes, so rare in editors today.

This book would never have come together without the cooperation of the other Ragged Mountain Press authors who generously gave permission to adapt and excerpt their works, and who provided excellent editing and advice:

Zora and David Aiken, *Simple Tent Camping*
Jeff Bennett, *The Complete Inflatable Kayaker* and *The Complete Whitewater Rafter*
Jerry Cinnamon, *Climbing Rock and Ice*
Annie Getchell, *The Essential Outdoor Gear Manual*
Michael Hodgson, co-author, *The Dayhiker's Handbook*
David Seidman, *The Essential Wilderness Navigator*
Chris Townsend, *Wilderness Skiing and Winter Camping* and *The Backpacker's Handbook*, Second Edition
An incredibly knowledgeable and talented group of writers and outdoorspeople, we thank them all wholeheartedly.

Katie McGarry, April Emery, and Janet Robbins at Ragged Mountain Press proved to us that working on a book can be both professional and fun. We are especially pleased with their individual talents in helping to make this a fine book—Katie for her infectious enthusiasm and creative ideas, April for her cool and calm advice rising above a sea of differing opinions, and Janet for her outstanding production talents. We'd also like to thank Carol Gillette for her outstanding design.

Many friends and colleagues provided invaluable consultation on chapter drafts while we compiled this book. In particular we want to offer deep gratitude to Terri Gay, of Tucson, who edited the climbing chapter and offered some good suggestions for "top five" destinations, and Tom Furgason, of Tucson and Grand Canyon, who edited the river-running chapter. John Shepard and Cheryl Poll gave excellent technical reviews of the canoeing chapter, and Cliff Leight did wonders with the mountaineering section. Thea Ulen, now of Tucson, provided great trip ideas in Minnesota; Washington's Tom Derrer offered great tips on perfect canoeing in the West. Outdoor writers Chris Paige, of Missoula, and

Bob Howells, of Los Angeles, provided good ideas for several "top five" destinations, and environmental educator Lucia Sayre, of Tucson, offered great advice on the children's chapter.

Invaluable help with the mountain biking photographs was provided by Cameron Hintzen, of Tucson. And Full Cycle, of Tucson, and Scott Bicycles came to the rescue when we had a bike breakdown in the middle of shooting.

Chris Cunningham and Karen Matthee at *Sea Kayaker* magazine helped get the whole ball rolling by recommending us to Jon Eaton at Ragged Mountain Press. Much thanks!

And finally, none of this would have been possible without Frank Hestand, our UPS delivery driver, who never failed us, come flood or lightning or just dang hot weather (without an air-conditioned van). He often came two and three times a week to our remote house 50 miles from Tucson—through a locked gate, and five miles up a washboarded and sometimes washed-out dirt road, even when we were out of cold lemonade.

INTRODUCTION

Go Play Outside!

Remember when your mother got so fed up with kids in the house—the noise, the clutter, the TV—that she'd fling open the back door and order: "Everybody out! It's a beautiful day—go play outside!"

She was right—there was so much to do: ride bikes, sled down snowbanks, scale hills, float in creeks, climb trees, go exploring, watch birds, catch tadpoles, and chase lizards. . . .

Fortunately, the fun doesn't change when you grow up—the only differences are the scope of your playground and the price of your toys: mountain biking, hiking, climbing, river running, mountaineering, cross-country skiing, and backpacking are some of the activities you can enjoy today as a grown-up. Everyone should take Mom's advice and go play outside.

Why? For one thing, good health. Studies show, for example, that people who walk outdoors regularly have stronger immune systems than people who jog regularly. That's good news. And don't forget the value of mental health, too—a good hike or climb or mountain bike ride is like health food for the brain.

Another reason to play outside is to forge and renew connections to wild places. The more people there are who understand the value of undeveloped, protected land, the better off will be both the land and the human race. People and the land are irrevocably tied together—everything we do affects the land, and the land continuously affects us. So playing outdoors is about more than just getting from point A to point B or bagging peaks, and wild places are about more than just being playgrounds for humans. It's all about remembering that humans and wild places and other animals are all part of a web, and each needs the others to endure.

But how can millions of outdoor enthusiasts playing in our wildernesses possibly do anything but harm them? We can start by making sure that the activities we do are low-impact—and a good way to do that is to make sure we know what we're doing when we venture forth with a mountain bike or climbing gear or a backpack. In fact, a good way to start is with a book such as *The Ragged Mountain Press Guide to Outdoor Sports*—which will tell you everything you need to know to get started safely and soundly, for both you and the wild places you visit, in a wide range of outdoor sports.

The Ragged Mountain Press Guide to Outdoor Sports is a how-to book for anyone interested in pursing outdoor activities, including:

Hiking	Backpacking
River running	Sea kayaking
Canoeing	Climbing
Cross-country skiing	Mountain biking

If you've never hiked a trail before, you can use this guide to get going.

If you're an avid hiker but you'd like to get into backpacking and long-distance trips, you can use this guide to go farther.

If you're an accomplished cross-country skier or mountain biker, but you'd like to try backpacking or river running, you can use this guide to jump between sports.

And if you're just getting back into your favorite outdoor pursuits after starting a family, you can use this guide to go with your kids.

Part One contains eight chapters, each covering a different sport (as listed above), including:

- A brief history of the sport
- Current trends and the range of activities included
- What gear you'll need, including an "essential start-up kit" with minimum cost
- Basic and advanced techniques
- Tips on what you can expect first time out
- Sport-specific fitness and health information
- How to find places to go
- Gear care and repair advice
- Expert tips
- A "kid quotient," rating the sport for kid-suitability and offering tips on getting kids started
- Further resources

Part Two comprises the general skills everyone needs to adventure outdoors. Map and Compass Magic (Chapter 9) offers an introduction to navigation both naturally and with map and compass. Chapter 10, The Art and Joys of Camping, tells you everything you need to outfit and operate a camp from a car or a boat or a pack high in the mountains miles from any road. To keep you well fed, Camp Cookery and Adventurous Fare (Chapter 12) informs not just about stoves and cooking, but also about kilocalorie needs and what foods are best to keep you well-stoked on your outdoor adventures. Chapter 13, Safe and Sound Adventures, offers tips on dealing with the hazards of outdoor travel as well as how to travel with the least impact. Half-Pint Adventuring (Chapter 11) is all about introducing kids to the outdoors. *The Ragged Mountain Press Guide to Outdoor Sports* wraps up with How to Dress Outdoors (Chapter 14) and How to Pack for a Trip (Chapter 15).

Appendices A and B, respectively, tell you How to Buy Used Outdoor Gear and How to Find Out More about the resources available for outdoor adventures.

The Ragged Mountain Guide Press to Outdoor Sports offers the outdoor enthusiast so much in one package: eight sports, a thorough treatment of outdoor skills, and informative treatises and lists.

Lots of cross-referencing chapter-to-chapter ensures that you will learn everything you need to know while exploring a new sport. Expert tips interspersed throughout broaden your knowledge, and the photos and illustrations make sure you see what fun is in store around every page.

Before you gear up to go play outside, however, there's one more word of advice Mom just might have for you today: be an outdoor advocate, not just an outdoor adventurer. Join sport-affiliated clubs as well as conservation organizations. And don't just send a check—vote, keep informed, and do some on-the-ground stewardship. Green groups are great, but also look to social services—there are lots of inner-city kids who would benefit, for example, from your new-found knowledge of the outdoors. And remember that clean air and clean water are important for our wildernesses and our cities.

People and the land are inextricably laced together in the web we call Nature. Without one the other can't endure. So get going, have fun, be safe, and do your part to protect our wildlands, or some day we won't have places left where we can go play outside.

RAGGED MOUNTAIN PRESS

GUIDE TO OUTDOOR SPORTS

Chapter 1

DAYHIKING—*Wonderful Walking*

"A good walk requires . . . endurance, plain clothes, old shoes, an eye for nature, good humor, vast curiosity, good speech, good silence, and nothing too much."

—Ralph Waldo Emerson

Walking in the Wilds

Of all the outdoor pursuits profiled in this book, hiking is perhaps the only one that comes naturally to just about everyone. In the mists of prehistory, before we made planes and cars and bikes and canoes and kayaks, when we wanted to go somewhere, we walked. Some atavistic hiking gene must hang on in most modern humans, because for so many of us, hiking triggers feelings of belonging and well-being. The mountains, deserts, forests, canyons, and jungles of long ago were all just the background of our comings and goings as we foraged and hunted for our families, but when we enter those landscapes today, many of us feel like we've really come home—we've not forgotten our roots.

Fortunately, today we forage in supermarkets and our time hiking in the wilds can be devoted to full enjoyment of the place itself, instead of finding dinner for six mouths back at the cave. Hence we have witnessed the evolution of hiking as a "sport"—one that can take many forms:

Basic: The most basic dayhiking involves throwing food, water, and a first aid kit into a simple pack and exploring any place that interests you for however long you like.

Intermediate: Moderate, or intermediate, dayhiking involves a little more planning, over distances of a few miles and more, probably with a specific goal in mind; the pack will be a little more substantial in design and will contain more food and accessories to cope with being outside all day.

Advanced: Hiking more than 10 miles in a day, over steep or rugged terrain, and carrying a well-honed backcountry dayhiking kit in a contoured daypack constitute advanced dayhiking.

If you've never hiked before, the best way to start is to find a like-minded friend or two, read the tips in this chapter for starting out, and then go for it. (Until you're an experienced hiker, it's best not to hike alone.) Hiking with others will expose you to lots of different gear and technique preferences—invaluable to any beginner. If none of your friends is game, see if there are any hiking clubs or informal hiking groups at your local recreation center.

As your hiking experience grows, you will probably meet others with whom you can gradually explore more and more adventurous endeavors—topping your first

FIRST TIME OUT

How far can I hike in a day? How long will it take me? What is the definition of *steep*? Each hiker will have a different answer to these questions, but there are some good general rules for beginners:

- *Hiking on level ground* with a light load, with moderate elevation gain: expect to cover 2–4 miles per hour at a steady pace.
- *Hiking on uneven, steep ground (ridges and mountainsides):* expect to cover 0.5–1 mile per hour.
- *Hiking cross-country (bushwhacking):* expect to cover 0.5–2 miles per hour depending on terrain.
- *Add approximately 1 hour for every 1,000 feet of elevation change.* For example, if you hike 4 miles per hour, a 4-mile hike with 2,000 feet of elevation change might take you as long as 3 hours.
- *Take note of elevation gain in relation to distance traveled.* A trail that climbs 1,000–1,500 feet in over a mile may be considered moderate, while one that zooms up 1,500 feet in half a mile may be considered steep.
- *Don't overdo it.* Turn around when you begin to feel fatigued (or preferably before), since at that point you're only halfway into your hike.
- *All beginners should stay on trails and use maps.* Don't venture off-trail on your first hikes—that's the way most people get lost.

See Chapter 9 for navigation and map-reading tips, including how to determine steepness and estimate distances.

Hiking with others creates friendships, and you can learn from their gear choices and hiking techniques.

14,000-foot peak in Colorado (called a fourteener), wading chest-deep down a slot canyon in Utah, or traversing a cliff-wrapped beach on the Olympic Peninsula. You can also opt for a trip with an adventure travel company—the price can be a little high, but think of it as tuition and it's a bargain indeed.

Or you may be perfectly happy ambling down a trail for a few miles and enjoying lunch under a gently spreading oak before taking an afternoon snooze.

Whatever type of hiking you do, it will be tremendously good for you. Studies show that people who walk regularly have stronger immune systems than do people who jog regularly. And the wonderful thing is that hiking is not a sport you outgrow as you age. Hiking improves with age—or perhaps it's age that improves with hiking.

A number of tips and some of the information in this chapter were adapted from The Dayhiker's Handbook, *by John Long and Michael Hodgson (Camden, ME: Ragged Mountain Press, 1996).*

What You'll Need

The beauty of dayhiking as a sport lies in its simplicity: you don't need much to get out there. In fact, a good rule to remember is Keep It Simple—your gear, your hikes—until you're pursuing advanced dayhiking goals such as canyoneering or alpine trekking.

All you need for your essential starter kit is footwear, water bottles, first aid kit, map and compass, and a pack to put them in. Of course, in theory you can do without all those things, but think of this: early people had callused feet, drank water they found (no matter what condition), knew how to administer first aid with natural resources, could navigate by memory and constellations, and used an animal hide to carry jerky and a flint fire starter. If you can do all that—then happy hiking, and the outdoor retail industry mourns your loss. The rest of us need a little help, however.

THE ESSENTIALS—A DAYHIKING START-UP KIT
- Trail footwear ($45–$200)
- Daypack or fanny pack ($20–$175)
- Hiking socks X 2 pairs ($5–$14 per pair)
- Water bottles X 2 ($0–$5)
- First aid kit ($10– $45)
- Compass and map ($10–$50)
- *Minimum cost, essential hiking kit: $90**

ADD-ONS
- Hat
- Possibles kit (see sidebar, p. 12)
- Synthetic hiking shirt
- Hiking shorts
- Pull-on pants
- Pile jacket
- Rain gear
- Hiking vest
- Insoles
- Gaiters
- Trekking poles or hiking staff
- Altimeter

*The essentials list above is intended to give you an idea of minimum start-up costs, from scratch, for moderate entry into a sport using new equipment. Other options include borrowing gear from friends or renting from retailers, YMCAs, or church activity clubs, as well as buying used gear—see Appendix A.

The rugged mountains of the Southwest are a dayhiker's heaven when sturdy boots and durable clothing are worn.

Footwear

When first getting into dayhiking, most people spend quite a lot of energy and thought on footwear, which is a good thing. Good footwear can make or break a hiking experience. But before charging off to find the Perfect Hiking Boot, you need to know its most important attribute: fit.

Once upon a time, back when hiking boots were called "waffle stompers" (and for good reason—they weighed a ton and were fitted with heavily lugged rubber soles), buying a pair of boots meant a trip to the corner outdoor shop, where you piled on thick ragg wool socks, stuck your foot in a rock-hard all-leather boot, and performed the "fit test." This meant shoving your foot all the way forward in an unlaced boot; if you could slide a couple of fingers behind your heel, a good fit was declared and you were sent off with a pair of 10-pound monsters and a can of beeswax. And "breaking in" meant not breaking in the boot so much as breaking in your feet to the boot (a painful process of blistering and callusing that, if you were lucky, eventually did the trick—if you didn't give up and try lawn bowling instead).

A revolution was launched when Nike and other athletic shoe companies introduced lightweight fabric-and-leather hiking boots, and today we have a dizzying array of boots and shoes to choose from when we head to the outdoor shop. But whether you have 10-pound monsters or featherweight approach hikers, you still need a great fit. Getting a good fit today is easier than it used to be, but it's still a challenge. Some good tips to go by:

- Find a service-oriented specialty outdoor retailer, with a well-trained and knowledgeable staff. The outdoor industry today is full of superb training opportunities in the footwear sector, such as the fit clinics given by Asolo boot company's Phil Oren, a legend in the outdoor industry. If a salesperson tries the old "stick your finger behind the heel" routine, head for the door.

DO I REALLY NEED BOOTS?

For easy to moderate dayhiking, many people do great with running shoes. Just pay attention to your feet: if they hurt after a day out, you might need footwear with a little more support. If you are prone to stumbling or twisting your ankle, opt for more sturdy shoes than running shoes. And make sure they have a pattern on the soles for gripping—definitely don't wear smooth-soled court shoes even on easy hikes.

For advanced hiking, such as canyoneering or alpine trekking, you would do best with footwear made especially for hiking.

To maximize your hiking boot fit, you might want to try some different lacing techniques:

◆ *Double-hitching:* Wrap the laces two or three times around each other in between eyelets or hooks as you pass them over the instep; this will allow you to adjust the tension of the lacing both above and below the triple wrap.

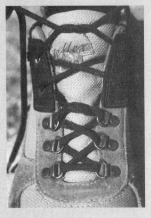

To tie a double-hitch, wrap the laces as if for a bow (shown), then tuck one more wrap for extra grip.

◆ *Alleviating pressure points:* You may encounter a pressure point or hot spot on the top of the foot, along the instep (a common problem for people with high arches). You can alleviate the pressure by tying a double hitch below and above the trouble spot, leaving the pressure spot untied or loosely tied.

◆ *Maintaining tension:* If you have trouble keeping your laces tight while you're tying the bow at the top, try this: if your boots have hooks, wrap the lace around each hook "backwards" once before moving up (called a mountaineer's lace); if your boots have eyelets, throw a double hitch at the top of the row, which will hold the lacing taut as you tie the bow.

Mountaineers's lace above a double hitch.

• In general, trail footwear, like all shoes, is built around lasts or footforms that are low, medium, or high in volume. Knowing the "volume" of your foot is invaluable, since that will determine what type of last to look for. The best way to learn how to recognize volume is from a well-trained boot fitter (see p. 5). Once you get the hang of it, you can usually spot a likely boot or shoe candidate on the shelf.

• Find an outdoor retailer that has good fitting aids, such as incline boards to test-fit for downhill walking or boards with rocks imbedded in them to test ankle support. Ask if you can test the shoes around your house for a few days and return them if the fit feels wrong.

• Bring your hiking socks (see the section on p. 8 on selecting good hiking socks) to every boot-fitting session; sock thickness will affect how boots fit.

• A well-fitted trail shoe will fit like a comfortable glove: snug (but allowing you to wiggle your toes freely), with no bagging or bunching.

• Go for comfort, not fashion. Turn a blind eye to those beautiful blue wonders with purple laces and let your toes choose their favorite model. They'll thank you later (besides, all trail shoes eventually end up looking like something the cat dragged in).

Fit might just be the easy part once you decide on a type of footwear for hiking. The choice is difficult because the variations are baffling. Hiking boots range from low-cut, leather-and-nylon lightweights with well-tractioned soles to over-the-ankle, all-leather heavyweights with heavily lugged soles, as well as everything in between. "Approach shoes," which have become popular lately, look like running shoes on steroids—or the offspring of a running shoe and hiking boot. And you can always choose aggressively soled running shoes or hiking sandals.

Before you buy, think about your intended goals:

• Where will you hike? For easy trails in temperate forests, running shoes or light boots will do nicely. For the Pacific rainforests, think about Gore-Tex lined boots or hiking sandals. Or for the rocky and thorny Southwest, a pair of midweight, all-leather boots might offer the best protection.

• What kind of walker are you? If you have bombproof ankles and the agility of a mountain goat, less-

BOOT TREATMENT TIPS

Leather is hydrophilic; it will absorb most any wet stuff like a sponge. Once leather becomes wet, moisture quickly travels from pore to pore by pumping action (as the boot flexes) and from fiber to fiber by wicking, or capillary action.

Even though leather is one of the most durable and resilient materials known, once wet it stretches and weakens; as leather dries, it shrinks and becomes brittle. Leather is skin, plain and simple. Unlike skin, however, leather no longer has natural lubricants and protective coatings in steady service—unless *you* supply them, that is. The key to long life for your leather boots is to maintain the leather's natural equilibrium with lubricants that provide water repellence.

The type of leather conditioner you choose is less important than how you apply it. Simply slathering on boot goop won't protect your boots. A great amount of damage occurs when wax is applied over dirt, which gets worked into pores and weakens the leather. *Thorough leather treatment begins with a clean boot.* A stiff brushing under the faucet will remove old wax and dirt. A well-known Seattle cobbler recommends thorough washing inside and out with Woolite.

- Break in new boots slightly before treatment.
- Boots should be very dry before conditioning (unless you're applying a water-based treatment).
- If you plan to seam-seal boots, do so *before* waterproofing the leather and allow the sealer to cure completely before treatment.
- Remove boot laces and meticulously work in the dressing with your fingers, paying special attention to overlapping seams and folds around tongue gussets, where most water penetrates.
- Allow dressing to cure completely, preferably overnight, before wiping off excess with a lint-free cloth (chamois or PackTowl). At this point you may wish to apply a second, thin coat of goop, depending on the condition of your boots.
- Set freshly treated boots in a sunny window or apply moderate heat (from a woodstove or hair dryer) to warm and soften the conditioner. Then polish or buff the boots to seal the dressing—that is, to create a hard, smooth finish.
- If the boots feel sticky even after 24 hours, the dressing has not cured and will pick up dirt rather than protect the boot against it. Rewarm and buff the boots until any excess conditioner is removed.

On seamsealing: Apply a thin line of urethane sealant on clean, dry seams *before* weatherproofing, to seal and protect seams. First, clean along the seams with water and a stiff brush. After allowing it to dry, buff the seam with denatured alcohol to remove any residual oils and ensure a successful bond. The best way to achieve a clean, consistent bead of sealer is with a syringe. Allow full cure time before applying leather treatment.

For an excellent discussion of breaking in, cleaning, treating, and repairing hiking boots and other gear, see Annie Getchell's The Essential Outdoor Gear Manual *(Camden, ME: Ragged Mountain Press, 1994), from which this excerpt was taken.*

structured footwear such as running shoes or hiking sandals are tailor-made for you. If you are prone to twisted ankles and stumbling or have knee problems, stick to footwear that offers good support and toe protection. One thing to remember is that good support doesn't mean high, over-the-ankle tops. Those certainly help, but you'll get the best ankle support from a combination of a stiff sole and a good heel counter (the cup around the back of the heel). Obviously, no one type of footwear works for everyone. The only rules to go by are to get a good fit and to choose footwear whose soles are relatively stiff and have aggressive tread for traction. Lots of people have hiked the Appalachian Trail or Pacific Crest Trail in Keds hightops, but even more people have been airlifted out of the Grand Canyon with bleeding, blistered feet or broken bones from a bad slip.

Types of hiking footwear include, from left to right, all-terrain sandals, canyoneering shoes, low-top shoes, lightweight nylon-and-suede boots, midweight all-leather boots, and heavyweight all-leather boots.

Socks

You've spent lots of time picking the perfect footwear, so don't just grab a pair of cotton athletic socks from your dresser and head out. You'll be asking for lots of trouble. Why? Cotton absorbs water like a sponge, but it doesn't dry out very quickly. Remember how your skin gets soft and puckery after a few hours of swimming? When it's in this delicate state, it's easily torn or blistered by friction. Feet get pretty hammered when we hike, so it's a good idea to dress them well.

Fortunately, socks are pretty simple these days. Some choices:

- *Sport blend socks.* Recent innovations in sock "technology," if it can be called that, will make your toes dry and happy. These socks are blends of nylon, olefin, acrylic, wool, or Spandex spun very densely, usually thicker in the heel and toe. The idea with ultradense padding is that it's not thick but offers more cushioning than a sock twice as thick but loosely woven. These are truly great socks, though pricey. They are worth the cost, however, and seem more durable than the old, cheap ragg wool socks.
- *The two-sock system.* The traditional way of socking it is to use a heavy ragg wool sock over a thin silk or synthetic liner sock, usually polypropylene, Cool-Max, Capilene, or other fiber that wicks moisture away from the skin. Many people still swear by this method. Experiment to see what works for you.

Socks, like boots, should fit snugly but not constrict your feet. When buying new boots, bring your favorite hiking socks along (socks can affect the fit of a boot by as much as one whole size). When buying a new type of sock, bring your boots along and try them out.

Many hiking socks these days are blends of nylon, olefin, acrylic, wool, or Spandex spun very densely, usually thicker in the heel and toe.

Insoles

Relatively new additions to the outdoor retail industry are custom and specialty footbeds, or insoles, tailored to hiking. Hiking boots, like running shoes, come with slightly sculptured foam insoles. Some people will hike their whole lives without replacing their footwear insoles, but many people benefit greatly from replacing these foam wafers with custom-formed footbeds made from a sandwich of cork, plastic, and foam or with off-the-shelf footbeds made from nitrogen-impregnated neoprene or other materials.

Whatever footbeds you choose, make sure you try them in your boots before buying them, because they will alter the fit. Ask your hiking companions what works for them before taking the plunge—some custom-formed footbeds cost nearly $100.

Packs

After footwear and socks, the next most useful piece of gear for dayhiking is something in which to carry your stuff—a daypack or fanny pack.

Concerning daypacks, Michael Hodgson wrote in *The Dayhiker's Handbook* that "no matter how large it is, you will fill it." This is an excellent observation to keep in mind when choosing a pack: don't buy too big, but don't buy too small, either, or you'll overstuff it—which will cause it to carry poorly.

As with choosing boots, before you buy a pack you will want to identify what type of dayhiking you will be doing most. Simple hiking? Simple pack. Long day-hikes? A more structured pack to carry the load comfortably. Daypacks come in three basic structural types: *simple* (one-size pack bag + padded shoulder straps + webbing antisway hip belt); *supported* (one-size or sized pack bag + back stiffener + padded and/or contoured shoulder straps + webbing or padded antisway hip belt); and *structured* (sized pack bag + back stiffener and shapeable stay + padded, contoured and sized shoulder straps + padded weight-bearing, sized hip belt). They range in volume from around 1,000 cubic inches to 3,500 cubic inches or so.

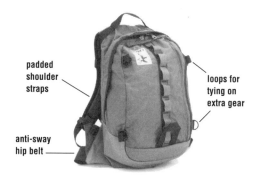

Simple daypacks are lightweight, and offer padded shoulder straps and webbing anti-sway hip belts.

Structured daypacks offer shapeable back stiffeners, padded hip belts that are sized, and perhaps sized shoulder harness lengths as well.

HOW TO PACK A PACK

The cardinal rule of daypack packing is Thou Shalt Not Overstuff. Overpacking a daypack will cause the pack bag to round out, or "pickle-barrel," which throws off the structural dynamics of pack fit and load-bearing ability and also causes fatigue and pain. Good structured and supported packs will have a padded polyethylene sheet integrated into the back of the pack bag so it resists the pickle-barrel effect. Keep these other rules in mind when filling up your pack:

1. Put soft and lightweight items in the bottom and outer back areas of the pack; these include rainwear or fleece, light first aid kits, spare socks, etc.
2. Put water and other heavy items (water filter, books, etc.) in the high-middle area of the pack, close to the body; i.e., keep weight in the middle and close to the center of gravity. You don't want your pack creating a heavy pendulum-effect that can swing you off-balance or wrench your lower back.
3. Put medium-weight or fragile items, such as food or a camera, in the top area of the pack—but not on the outside, where they are vulnerable to a fall or a dropped pack.
4. Take care to pack sharp items so that they do not rub against the pack bag and create holes. The outer lower area of the pack bag is under the most stress and thus the most vulnerable to wear and tear.

A good rule of thumb for choosing a pack is to keep it *simple* (around 1,000 to 2,000 cubic inches) for short, easy hikes; but the more advanced type of hiking you do, the more *supported* or *structured* pack you will need (1,500 to 2,500 cubic inches). Most serious dayhikers will be carrying a substantial amount of weight and will want comfortable shoulder straps; some kind of frame sheet, or back stiffener, to resist the "pickle barrel" effect (see sidebar); and a hip belt that properly snugs the frame sheet closer to the back, further transferring the load where it should be.

So getting the right-size pack is crucial. If you hike a lot in the Southwest, where water is scarce, remember

HOW TO WEAR A PACK

Most of us just slog a daypack on our backs, blindly pull a few tabs, and take off up the trail. That's okay for a simple pack, but if you want optimum performance from your structured or supported daypack, try following these steps.

After the pack is packed but *before* you put it on

1. Loosen the harness straps at the top and bottom.

2. Firmly tighten the load-compression straps on the back of the pack (*not* the load-stabilizing straps that join the harness and the pack bag).

3. Drape the pack comfortably over the shoulders.

4. Lightly pull in the lower tabs of the shoulder straps; this is a temporary adjustment that you will fine-tune later.

5. Snug-in the hip belt so that it comfortably cups or rides slightly above the iliac crest (the bony part) of the hip bones.

6. Now readjust the lower tabs of the shoulder straps so they are comfortably snug but never tight.

7. Adjust the load-control straps of the upper shoulder straps so they are finger-tight—never overtighten. If overtightened, they will pull the frame-sheet out of proper contact with the back; if undertightened, they will allow the load to shift and sway.

8. If there are any snugger straps joining the harness to the pack bag, such as at the hips, adjust them finger-tight.

Good pack fit includes properly draped shoulder straps, shown here. Advice from professional outdoor retailers can be invaluable.

No matter what type of pack you buy, good pack fit means a pack that hugs your back and has a slim profile that doesn't restrict the movement of your arms or throw you off balance. If you have a hard time finding the right pack fit because you just don't fit the "average person" mold for which most daypacks were built, a number of daypack manufacturers offer supported and structured packs with aluminum stays that can be custom-shaped to your body, as well as sized, removable (interchangeable) hip belts.

Fanny packs are another popular option for dayhiking. Fanny packs that have water bottle holders built in to the sides seem to make the most sense, since they leave the main pack free for plenty of gear. Look for fanny packs with padded lumbar pads and antisway straps, as well as accessory straps so you can strap a jacket on the outside (but don't hang heavy stuff off the back of a fanny pack—it could throw you off balance). Consider using a small fanny pack in tandem with a daypack; wear the fanny pack with the bag turned to the front, for fast access to lip balm, Swiss Army knife, compass, sunscreen, or snacks.

Fanny packs carry a surprising amount of gear. Look for models with side pockets for carrying water bottles. This hiker is prepared for potential creek crossings.

Clothing

You can learn a lot about outdoor clothing by observing what is worn by people who work all day in the field. In the Southwest, for example, almost all field biologists

that for a dayhike you'll need to carry a minimum of 4 liters of water, which weighs about 8 pounds; add to that your essentials and your gotta-haves, and your pack weighs 20 pounds. If you hike a lot in cold and wet weather, you will need a larger pack to accommodate outerwear. The best strategy is to take your hiking kit with you to the retail store to load up prospective packs (don't forget to fill the water bottles). Everyone likes to carry different stuff—pick the pack that fits and feels the best with your stuff in it.

working in the summer in rugged canyon country wear long pants and long-sleeved shirts for sun and thorn protection, a wide-brimmed straw hat, and, very often, gaiters over their boots for creek crossings and to keep grass seeds and burrs out of their socks. You don't see them in tank tops, shorts, and sandals, that's for sure.

Dressing for dayhiking is pretty simple: go for comfort and function, and remember that light weight never hurts. Be smart about the terrain you are traversing: if it's rugged and thorny, wear tough pants and long-sleeved shirt; if it's humid and hot, wear synthetic or cotton blend shorts and shirt; if it's humid and cold, wear synthetic pants, top, and fleece jacket. Always prepare for the worst possible conditions. Cotton is comfortable, until it gets wet, so most savvy outdoorspeople opt for modern synthetics: nylon and polyester treated to wick moisture. Brushed nylon feels soft as silk—you'll never know it's synthetic, until it dries quick-as-a-wink. If you don't like the idea of clothing made from nonrenewable resources, linen is an excellent warm-weather fabric, and silk and wool are very efficient in the cold.

For most conditions except winter, a good hiking outfit might consist of a pair of shorts or tights and a shirt made of moisture-wicking and quick-drying fabric such as Supplex, Capilene, or Coolmax; carried in your pack as insurance against weather variations would be a pair of synthetic pull-on over-

To keep warm when cold-weather hiking, cover your head and wear good insulating clothing.

pants and a midweight underwear top or light fleece jacket. If there is the slightest possibility of cold temperatures, always carry lightweight gloves and a knit cap. Likewise, for hot, sunny conditions, always opt for a sun hat. (For more on layering to get the most out of your outdoor clothing, see Chapter 2, p. 39; for a thorough

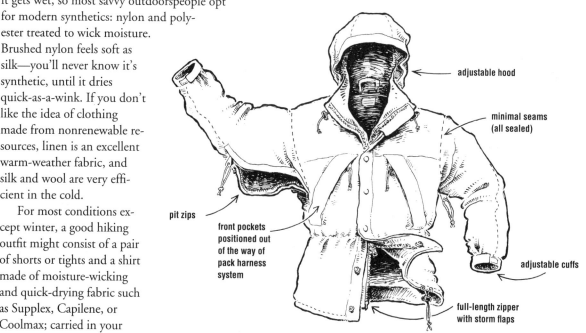

adjustable hood

minimal seams (all sealed)

pit zips

front pockets positioned out of the way of pack harness system

adjustable cuffs

full-length zipper with storm flaps

MIKE CLELLAND

A good rain jacket or poncho is nearly essential for comfortable dayhiking. This jacket has an integrated hood, slanted pocket openings that can be accessed while wearing a pack, and a long length to protect the hips.

discussion of outdoor clothing and fabrics, see Chapter 14, p. 299.)

Like Crusaders searching for the Holy Grail, outerwear manufacturers are always looking for the Perfect Outerwear Fabric: watertight as rubber yet breathable as cotton. But the Holy Grail remains elusive. In the mean- time, there are many excellent outdoor fabrics—laminates such as Gore-Tex, coatings such as Ultrex, and microfibers—but none is perfect. One might be more waterproof than breathable, another the opposite. All perform very well in moderate conditions; none is going to perform perfectly in extreme conditions. Don't expect too much and you won't be disappointed.

Essential Hardware

Now that you've got your trail footwear and a good pack, are you ready to go? Not quite—a few more items should be considered essentials because they are important for hiking safety. (See Chapter 13, p. 289, for a few more items you might add to a "personal essentials" kit to carry with you on all outdoor adventures.)

Water bottles: Just about any plastic water bottle will do, but if you want leakproof security, invest in some good outdoor bottles, such as those made by Nalgene (which have a guarantee). Remember to carry *at least* 2 liters per person, per day—more in hot weather.

Compass: Along with a map of your destination, a compass will save your hide if you lose the trail (make sure you know how to use your compass; see Chapter 9 for a discussion of navigation). A basic compass can be had for less than $10.

"Possibles" kit: Early American woodsmen carried small leather pouches called possibles kits, which contained everything they needed to survive in the event of any possibility. Every hiker should have one. (See sidebar for a list of typical contents.)

First aid kit: For dayhiking you need only the essentials. Make your own or purchase one of the small prepackaged kits made just for hiking. Some must-haves: precut molefoam, 2nd Skin (see sidebar on first aid, p. 285), assorted bandages and sterile pads,

A possibles kit might contain (clockwise from upper right) a space blanket, unbreakable signal mirror, length of cord, seam sealer/glue, quarter for a phone call, mini flashlight, pocket knife, compass, energy bar, repair kit with needles, thread, etc., and waterproof matches.

antiseptic swabs, tweezers, Extractor snakebite kit, and painkillers. Add-ons: antibiotics, antihistamine, tincture of benzoin, Ace wrap, SAM splint, adhesive tape, compress. Peruse a catalog from a specialty outdoor first aid manufacturer such as Adventure Medical Kits—you can customize your own first aid kit with their minikits, including items for treating dehydration, road rash (bike accidents), and the needs of children.

And Yet More Stuff

Walk into any outdoor retailer and you'll see the vast array of accessories available to augment your hiking experience. Here's some of the cool stuff that really does come in handy:

Hiking staffs: There are two ways to go—single hiking staffs or two trekking poles. Choose the former for more casual hiking and for additional security on descents, a pulling aid for ascents, or a monopod for a camera—a hiking staff can be a really useful tool and

---

SNOWSHOEING

Don't let a little (or even a lot) of snow slow down your hiking in winter. Snowshoeing has enjoyed a renaissance of late, with new models of lightweight and streamlined showshoes hitting the outdoor stores every year.

Unlike cross-country skiing, for which you must learn basic and intermediate skills before you can head off into the hills, snowshoeing is as simple as walking. Following are some snowshoe purchase and use tips from Michael Hodgson, coauthor of *The Dayhiker's Handbook.*

Snowshoes are simple to use. Your shoe or boot is held securely to the snowshoe using a combination of toe holster and heel strap—called a "modified-H" binding—which is relatively easy to get on and off, even with gloved fingers.

The narrower profiles and lighter weight of today's alloy snowshoes allow the user to walk or even run normally (compared to the older and wider wood and rawhide models)—in fact, they are very popular for running and cross-training, and even mountaineering. Plan on spending around $200 to $250 for a modern snowshoe and binding package. Wood-and-rawhide models are about $100 with bindings. Insulated bindings (for those really cold days) and heel cleats (for days when even a surefooted snowshoe wants to act like a ski) are available on many models.

In general, the old school of thought was that the longer and broader the snowshoe, the more buoyancy provided and therefore the more weight it could support. With that in mind, fitting wooden and laced snowshoes was done by comparing snow conditions with the size and weight of the individual and the gear being carried. More weight and softer snow meant longer, wider snowshoes. High-performance demands and recreational use have changed the picture somewhat. The most important considerations are the snow conditions and whether a person is hiking solo or in a group. A solo hiker will need a shoe in the range of 9 x 30 inches or 10 x 36 inches for breaking trail. When hiking in a group, however, trail breaking is shared, making flotation less important, so a shoe in the size range of 8 x 25 inches is appropriate. If you plan to run and use snowshoeing as a form of cross-training for aerobic benefits, you will want to purchase the smallest, lightest shoe possible.

If you are at all uncertain about how you will use the snowshoes or what size is best for you, don't buy for a while—rent them. Many retail stores offer demo rentals, as do many ski resorts.

Once you have your snowshoes, no other gear is required. Standard hiking boots, or even running shoes if you are seeking a workout, are all the footwear required. Dress in layers as you would for skiing, but be prepared to peel down to the minimum since snowshoeing can work up quite a glow. If balance seems to be a problem, or you just want an additional security blanket to keep from falling in the white stuff, opt for ski poles; one in each hand will offer four-point stability in awkward conditions.

A few basic techniques can make your initial foray a little easier:

- When climbing, keep your weight over the balls of your feet.
- Traversing a slope is more difficult but can be accomplished by either "sawing" or "kicking" the uphill edges of your snowshoes into the snow.
- Heading downhill, keep your weight over the balls of your feet and be conscious of digging the heel cleats into the snow. Lean back and you will "butt-slide" all the way down, for sure.
- Stick to ungroomed hiking trails—ski trails are for skiers only. Foot and snowshoe traffic should be kept off to the side of any established ski trail, so as not to ruin the trail for those sure to glide along later.

Hiking staffs are used to help pull up steep inclines, for additional security on rough trails, to alleviate knee stress on downhill sections, and as monopods for cameras.

knee-saver. Make your own from natural resources, or go to an outdoor retailer for a lightweight aluminum staff. Trekking poles, a European favorite, are gaining ground in the United States. For endurance hiking, use them to enhance your performance (for more on double poling technique, see the Walking Lessons section, p. 16).

Altimeters: An altimeter is a barometer: it reads the atmospheric pressure. After you set it properly to a known elevation, an altimeter will tell you on a dial or digitally exactly what elevation you have climbed or descended to (give or take 50–100 feet, depending on the model). Used with a map, an altimeter can help you extract yourself from the backcountry in the dark or during a storm (learn how to use one before you leave home). You can also use an altimeter to predict changes in weather—an incoming low-pressure system will cause the needle to fall, for example.

Hiking vest: Sure they look nerdy, but vests with a bunch of pockets on them can be very handy hiking accessories, especially if you choose to use a fanny pack. You can stash in the vest items you always want at-hand: camera, lip balm, knife, map, field guides, handkerchief, sunglasses, gloves, and so on.

Food and Drink

Think of a dayhike as a fluid process: pleasant, steady walking, endlessly interesting scenery, and frequent snacking and drinking. Don't think in terms of *breakfast, lunch,* and *dinner* breaking up the day; make it one long meal made up of a series of snacks. Your body will perform much better this way, as long as you're feeding it the right stuff.

Buck Tilton, director of the Wilderness Medicine Institute in Colorado, recommends that a hiker's diet should contain about 70 percent carbohydrates, 15 percent fat, and 15 percent protein. Furthermore, if you eat a high-carbohydrate diet for several days prior to hiking, you will double your glycogen stores and increase your trail performance by up to three times.

Good carbo foods for the trail include dried fruits, bagels, muffins, rice cakes, energy bars, and cookies. For protein, make sure you're getting some beans, cereals, nuts, or meats. And for a little fat, add cheese, butter, meat, or some nuts. Beware of consuming too much of your carbohydrate quotient in energy bars (also known as "power bars"), which often contain a lot of high-fructose corn syrup. Digesting this form of fructose requires a lot of water—at least three times as much as does fructose from fruit juice or rice dextrin. (See Chapter 12 for a more in-depth look at nutrition outdoors.)

> *"Whatever grub you settle on, never hike till you are hungry. Stop every hour or so for a snack and water."*
>
> —John Long, *The Dayhiker's Handbook*

Your body will lose tremendous amounts of water when you hike, even if you don't feel hot (any aerobic activity burns water in the body). Drinking plenty of water is actually more important than eating food, since without adequate water your body cannot metabolize

Hiking is easy if you remember a few tips: warm up a little first, use good posture, and take it slow if you experience any pain or fatigue.

nutrients efficiently. To avoid dehydration (which leads to thirst, fatigue, headaches, and eventually disorientation), drink a *minimum* of 2 liters of water per day, preferably 3–4 liters (a liter is a bit more than a quart). Drink frequently (about a cup of water every half hour), and don't wait until you're thirsty—by then, you're already getting dehydrated.

Unfortunately, you need to assume that all the free-flowing and lake water in the backcountry is undrinkable—microorganisms such as *Giardia* and *Cryptosporidia* live in water just about everywhere, and they can make hikers very ill. Carry all your water with you, or carry iodine tablets or a water filter. See Chapter 13, p. 284, for more on water treatment.

DRINK TO YOUR HEALTH: WHAT ABOUT SPORTS DRINKS?

If water is good for you, then sports drinks—high-carbohydrate and electrolyte-rich supplements such as Gatorade, Ultrafuel, Recharge, and others—should be better, right?

As usual with most physiology questions, there are two camps. Many experts say that if you eat correctly before, during, and after sports activities, you should not need sports drinks to make your body function better. They say plenty of water is the best sports drink.

Other experts are big fans of sports drinks, which the body absorbs more readily than water and which contain sugars in a form the body can use quickly. Just don't use sports drinks as your only fluid replacement; always drink at least a liter or two of water in addition to sports drinks. Your body needs pure water to eliminate waste buildup.

Walking Lessons

You really don't need any special instructions to hike: just point yourself down the trail and put one foot in front of the other. The rest comes naturally. Following are some tips to make your hiking more enjoyable.

Basics

- *Warm-up*: Warming up for hiking can help you avoid stress injuries. The best kind of warm-up for all activities is simply performing very low-level repetitions of what you will be doing during your activity. Stretching alone should not be considered a warm-up; it can be part of a warm-up, but take care—many people stretch too far and too aggressively and end up injuring themselves.
- The best warm-up for hiking is to start out hiking very slowly; if you know the trail is going to climb very soon after the trailhead, do some gentle step-ups on rocks or logs before you start. Windmill your arms a little. Walk around the trailhead area with exaggerated, long steps and then tiny steps. Relax, take it easy, and your body will do the rest.
- *Walk balanced:* Stand tall, swing your arms naturally at your sides, and make sure you're not bending forward too much at the waist. Take care not to lock your knees. Use common sense and you'll do fine.
- *Use your upper body:* When ascending, use your upper body to help your knees—as you step up, press down on the uphill thigh with your hands and use your arms and legs in tandem to lift your weight.
- *Small steps:* In general, remember that small steps are easier on your body than big strides. This is especially true when going downhill, when you should take care to keep your knees bent.

Advanced Techniques

Poling: Trekking-pole manufacturers claim that poling reduces impact to the body from walking by up to 250 tons per day. To get the most from trekking poles, use them like you would when cross-country skiing—alternating arms (the forward pole is on the opposite side of your forward leg), swinging, planting, and pulling forward as you hike swiftly. For hikers who want to make time and distance, trekking poles provide an excellent tool. Use downhill ski poles (trekking poles should be a little higher than your elbow) or look at adjustable models just for hiking at outdoor retailers.

Speed and endurance hiking: Called fastpacking or power hiking by some—a combination of hiking and trail running—this is an extremely efficient, challenging, low-impact way to cover a lot of backcountry ground. Experienced fastpackers can cover 20–35 miles in a day. Sometimes the trips are overnight, sometimes in-and-out. Experts recommend carrying not more than 10 percent of your body weight while fastpacking, so you really need to think hard about what to carry. Most fastpackers carry their essentials in specialty fanny packs, such as those made by Ultimate Direction, a pioneer in fastpacking gear. If you want to get into it, check around with your local hiking club, Sierra Club, and running clubs to see if there are any groups specializing in fastpacking.

Happy Canine Hikers

You work all week while your ever-faithful best friend waits patiently at home. Then it's The Weekend, and time for hiking, or backpacking, climbing, mountain biking, or river running.

But while it's easy to indulge in the happiness of our pets, there are commonsense health, safety, and wilderness-impact precautions for humans that tend to be overlooked for our pooches.

- *Water.* We religiously filter our own drinking water in the backcountry, but we let our pets drink directly from streams or ponds, even in cattle country. Dogs are just as susceptible to the *Giardia* parasite as humans, and they suffer the same symptoms: intermittent diarrhea, vomiting, and loss of appetite. Treatment is difficult, but there is an easy solution, one that's covered a bit more in detail later in this section: keep your dog on-leash. It's hard to do—they have so much fun blasting over hill and dale—but you can avoid all sorts of problems, including diseases from waterborne parasites, if Fido stays with you.
- *Dehydration, heat stroke.* Dogs can also suffer dehydration and heat stroke, so make sure they drink water as often as you do, and don't overdo sun exposure. If your dog shows signs of dehydration or heat stroke—weakness, eyes rolling back, tissues dry—immerse him in water if possible, or pour water over his chest and throat.
- *Vaccinations.* It goes without saying, but your dog should have all the proper vaccinations before venturing outdoors: rabies, distemper, parvo, corona, and others. Consult your veterinarian about proper

vaccines, as well as the need to guard against heartworm at your destination.

- *Aches and pains.* Make sure your dog gets weekly exercise in addition to her weekend gonzo outings, or she'll be very sore—if you have a training program to stay in shape for hiking or mountain biking, include Spot.
- *Skunked.* A full hit of skunk spray will have an immediate and painful effect on your dog. If hit in the face, your dog will probably be temporarily blind, and he will foam at the mouth. Get him washed up as soon as possible. Traditional stench removal attempts involve tomato juice, diluted lemon juice, or vinegar (mix 1 to 10 with water, and wash, always being careful of the dog's eyes). There is also a product called Skunk Off, an odor eliminator/neutralizer. It's nontoxic, biodegradable, and it reportedly works "in minutes." Look for it at camping stores.
- *Porcupine quills* and *thorns.* It's best to have a veterinarian remove porcupine quills; the dog will be in a lot of pain and may be hard to handle. If you must do it yourself, use pliers (multi-tools are indispensable) to grasp each quill and work it back out with a steady, twisting pull. Cutting off the quill ends may help; they're hollow and, with ends cut, more flexible. Apply antiseptic to each puncture wound to ward off infection. The same applies for thorns.
- *Foxtails.* Red brome and other grasses put out nasty seeds called foxtails. These dart-shaped burrs can get into your dog's ear and puncture the eardrum, causing extreme pain and disorientation. During foxtail

All dressed up and ready to go: this canine hiker has all his essentials, including a comfortable walking harness, leash, packs with bowls and some dog biscuits, and current vaccinations.

season, inspect his ears at every rest stop and pick out any seeds. If you suspect foxtails deep in your dog's ear, you need to get to a vet, so they can be removed under anesthesia. (Foxtails can also puncture skin elsewhere on a dog's body and cause infections, so groom carefully each night.)

- *Permits.* Before you pack Fido off into the wilderness for a weekend of fun, check with the land management agency for its rules on dogs. In some places, such as wildlife refuges, dogs may be banned entirely, and nearly everywhere on other public lands dogs must be leashed. There are many, many good reasons for this. See below.

- *Leash.* Your dog is much safer leashed up with you. Running free can lead to encounters with skunks, porcupines, bears (which might just get *you* into some serious trouble), or snakes. Cuts, scrapes, and broken bones can also be avoided. Also, many studies show that dogs are very disruptive to wildlife, most especially in roadless backcountry. One study in the Rocky Mountains showed that during lambing season, bighorn sheep experienced extremely elevated stress levels when a dog approached them, surprisingly much higher than when a natural predator such as a fox or coyote approached.

- *Doggie gear.* There is some really useful outdoor gear for dogs out there, but it can be hard to find. Some great dog gear includes packs (fit the pack so that the weight—never very much—is supported on the dog's sides, not on his backbone), booties for snow, fleece jackets, PFDs, fluorescent collars and vests for hunting season, portable kennels, and field canteens and bowls. For the best selection of gear, check out the hunting catalogs, such as Dunn's (800-223-8667) or Cabela's (800-237-4444). Another excellent source of pet products is Doctors Foster and Smith (800-826-7206).

For more on pets in the outdoors, see *Simple Tent Camping,* by Zora and David Aiken (Ragged Mountain Press, 1996), and for good health information, see *Emergency First Aid for Your Dog,* by Tamara S. Shearer (Columbus: Ohio Distinctive Publishing, 1996).

Where to Go?

Now is the fun part—getting out in the backcountry. Your choices are as varied as the terrain, and you are limited only by how far you want to drive for a dayhike and your own level of experience.

Your local outdoor retailer should have dozens of guidebooks on hiking areas close to you. Talk to the sales clerks to see if they can recommend hikes for beginners or for kids.

Is there a national park, state park, county park, national forest, Bureau of Land Management wilderness area, or wildlife refuge near you? If so, call to see if they have hiking trails; most also print their own maps, which they make available free or at minimal cost. Look in the government pages in your phone book, under Department of the Interior and Department of Agriculture for federal agencies, and under Parks for your county and state governments (see also the resource listings in Appendix B).

With so many hikers venturing forth into the wilds, we all need to practice no-impact hiking. Before you go, read the section To Protect and Explore, p. 296.

If you've always wanted to try desert hiking, or alpine trekking, see Chapter 13, and refer to *The Dayhiker's Handbook.*

Health and Safety

Staying safe means being prepared for the backcountry. This means being fit and healthy, learning basic navigation and first aid skills (see Chapters 9 and 13), amassing the hiking essentials, and having a safety plan—*before you leave your house.*

A safety plan for dayhiking must include

- Knowing the shortest evacuation route at any point during your hike

---

**PUSHING THE ENVELOPE:
GRAND CANYON IN 24 HOURS**

The ultimate dayhike might just be the famed Rim-to-Rim-to-Rim hike in the Grand Canyon. Participants begin this loosely organized (officially unsanctioned) event on the South Rim and descend 4,460 feet and 9½ miles on the Bright Angel Trail to the Colorado River, then up the Bright Angel 5,816 feet and 14 miles to the North Rim . . . then—you guessed it—they *turn around* and go back to the South Rim, all within 24 hours. That's 47 miles and 10,276 vertical feet.

Word is that the Park Service has put the stops on any club-sponsored rim-to-rim-to-rim hikes, but the Canyon beckons.

TOP 5

CLASSIC NORTH AMERICAN DAYHIKING TRIPS

Olympic Peninsula, Washington

Glacier National Park, Montana

Cascade River State Park, Minnesota

Acadia National Park, Maine

Grand Canyon, Arizona

DENNIS WELSH

St. Mary Lake with Wild Goose Island in foreground. Glacier National Park, MT.

- *Bright Angel Trail, Grand Canyon, Arizona.* Any trail in the Grand Canyon might just be classic, but the Bright Angel drops down 4,460 feet and 9½ miles to the Colorado River at Phantom Ranch—an advanced and stunning dayhike.
- *Hoh River, Olympic Peninsula, Washington.* This dark and lush trail offers a rare bit of temperate rainforest in North America: big trees, big ferns, and amazing, old-growth, Pacific Northwest forest.
- *Hanging Gardens Trail, Logan Pass, Glacier National Park, Montana.* Beginning at the crest of the Going to the Sun Highway, the Hanging Gardens Trail is a path and boardwalk that winds through very delicate alpine meadows to a stunning overlook of Hidden Lake (a cirque lake cupped by the high peaks of Glacier NP). Company might include mountain goats.
- *Acadia National Park, Maine.* Here's a chance to explore a pristine and awesome patch of New England's rockbound coast. More than 120 miles of trails for all levels of hiker, including 1,530-foot Cadillac Mountain.
- *Cascade River State Park, Minnesota.* In classic lake country near Lutsen, here are trails that follow both sides of a twisting gorge as the Cascade River cuts its way to Lake Superior.

☞ KID QUOTIENT

Dayhiking is perhaps the best way to get kids out exploring the wilds. From babies to teens, dayhiking is great for kids of all ages.

☞ Pack babies in commercial kid carriers sold at outdoor retailers. Look for a comfortable harness for you and a well-padded sitting area for the kid (no bare metal or rough spots anywhere they can touch). Other must-have features include a safety belt, a sturdy "kickstand" (although you should never leave a child unattended in a carrier), and a storage compartment for formula and diapers. Good options would be a sun and/or rain cover.

☞ Until kids are in their teens and getting into more advanced adventures, they don't need special equipment. Tennies with grippy tread will work great for years and won't bankrupt you when feet grow a size a month. However, if the terrain warrants better footwear, look at kids' hiking shoes at outdoor retailers.

that is no more than a half-mile or so from the car for very small kids (up to age five), or no more than a couple of flat miles until they're older than about eight. If you make it too demanding, they won't want to go again.

☞ Kids must eat and drink just like adults when hiking, so take lots of fun foods you know they'll eat—cheese sticks, M&M's, dried fruit, peanut butter and crackers—and lots of fruit juice.

☞ For safety, dress kids in bright colors in case you need to search for them, give them a whistle and tell them when to use it (only in an emergency!), and discuss what to do if *you* get hurt.

☞ Sun protection is a must, so use sunscreen formulated for kids.

☞ Be more circumspect with bug repellent. Most contain the chemical DEET, which for children and some adults can be toxic in a deadly way if used too heavily for too long (even a few days in a row). To be safe, it's best to use repellents without DEET, such as Permanone, which can be applied to clothing.

(See Chapter 11 for more tips on adventuring outdoors with kids.)

☞ Kids' daypacks are sold at outdoor retailers; carrying their own lunch or jacket (keep it very light) makes kids feel like they're real hikers, so consider indulging.

☞ Always pack a change of clothes when hiking with kids— it gives them the freedom to play in the creek or build mud castles.

☞ Go for quality, not quantity. Plan a hike to an interesting destination—a pond, creek, or wildlife viewing area—

- Leaving your itinerary and estimated time of return with someone at home
- Keeping a list of who to call should a rescue of one of your party be necessary
- Making a contact list of next-of-kin for everyone in the party
- Designating a trip leader and backup leader who take responsibility for rescue
- Having a prehike group discussion about the safety plan

Cellular phones, which are becoming more prevalent in the backcountry, make good rescue tools if you can get reception and know how to direct rescuers to your position; but you should never rely on electronics in place of being prepared, and of knowing self-help and standard rescue procedures.

Where Can Dayhiking Lead You?

Remember, you can hike just about anywhere. On your next business trip, throw your essential hiking kit in your suitcase and plan an extra day exploring an easy trail. Call ahead to an outdoor store or government park for advice.

How about planning your next vacation as an overseas dayhiking trip? "Rambling" is very popular in the United Kingdom and its former colonies. A few examples are the fantastic long-distance trails, such as the South Downs Way in England and the Milford Track in New Zealand, which offer B&B accommodations en route. Peru, Africa, Hawaii, Switzerland, France—choices for hikers will keep you busy for a lifetime. (See Chris Townsend's *The Backpacker's Handbook,* Second Edition, for more on adventure travel.)

For some people, dayhiking will naturally lead to backpacking. Moving deep into wilderness with all your supplies on your back for two days or two weeks can be a very rewarding experience. See Chapter 2 for information about how to start backpacking.

Further Resources for Dayhiking
Books

The Dayhiker's Handbook, by John Long and Michael Hodgson (Camden, ME: Ragged Mountain Press, 1996). This lively guide provides all the information you need on hiking all over the world—and right at home. In addition to gear and technique tips, the authors give advice on specialty hiking in deserts, mountains, snow and ice, jungles, canyons, forests, and coasts. Among the gems in this book are John Long's humorous, self-deprecating, and intelligently written stories about his many hiking explorations around the globe and in his own backyard.

Periodicals

Walking Magazine, 9-11 Harcourt Street, Boston, MA 02116; (617) 266-3322.
Outside, 400 Market Street, Santa Fe, NM 87501; (505) 989-7100.

Organizations

The organizations listed below provide excellent periodicals as membership benefits: American Hiker, AMC Outdoors, *and* Sierra.

American Hiking Society, 1422 Fenwick Lane, Silver Spring, MD 20910; (301) 565-6704; amhiker@aol.com.
Appalachian Mountain Club, 5 Joy Street, Boston, MA 02108; (617) 523-0636.
Sierra Club, 85 Second Street, Second Floor, San Francisco, CA 94105; (415) 977-5500.

Other Resources

Appalachian Mountain Club Huts, AMC Reservations, P.O. Box 298, Gorham, NH 03581; (603) 466-2727.
Also, see Appendix B for more outdoor resources.

"In time, I learned to let my feet make the decisions, and they were usually right."

—Alex Shoumatoff, *In Southern Light: Trekking Through Brazil and Africa*

Chapter 2

BACKPACKING—*Footloose Freedom*

"Only by living in the wilderness 24 hours a day, day after day, do I gain a feeling of 'rightness,' of being with instead of against the earth, the deepest contentment I have found."

—Chris Townsend, *The Backpacker's Handbook,* Second Edition

SPORT FILE
Couch potato quotient: 2 (couch to backcountry requires moderate fitness)
Coordination factor: 2 (can you walk and chew gum at the same time?)
White-knuckle rating: 1 (very relaxing)

The Journey Begins

In answering his own query, "Why backpack?" in *The Backpacker's Handbook,* author Chris Townsend explained, "The heart of backpacking lies in the journey, the desire to explore a world beyond our everyday lives, and in so doing explore ourselves. Until comparatively recently, most journeys were like this, because the known world extended little beyond one's hometown. Now, with modern communications and mass transportation, most so-called journeys consist of nothing more than the mechanized moving of bodies from one place to another, a process so sanitized and safe it precludes any sense of adventure or personal involvement. Only when I shoulder my pack and set out into the wilderness do I feel a real journey beginning."

The rewards of backpacking are great—the self-contained freedom, the pleasure of moving through miles and miles of wilderness with your household on your back, perhaps the only human venturing afoot for 50 square miles. But isn't it difficult? All that weight on your back, suffering sore feet and a hard bed at the end of a day?

According to Townsend, a veteran of 15,000 miles exploring the world with a pack on his back, backpacking isn't difficult, but it does require both physical and mental preparation. Three things permanently kill most ambitions to turn from dayhiker to backpacker: setting off unfit, being ill-equipped, and having unrealistic expectations.

You don't need to plan to the nearest yard how far you will walk every day or to choose every campsite weeks in advance; rather, you should know what your desired goals are and assess the extent of your capabilities in light of those goals. Beginning backpackers who set out to carry 65 pounds 25 miles a day through steep, mountainous terrain just about guarantee exhaustion, frustration, and disappointment unless they are extremely fit and know beforehand that they're capable of performing such strenuous activity.

Like dayhiking, backpacking can be as simple as walking a few miles to a secluded campsite and enjoying a night under a canopy of sweet-scented pines, or as advanced as traversing a 100-mile trail over several weeks through spectacular alpine country. Nearly anyone can enjoy backpacking—from babies in backpack carriers to grandparents well into their golden years. The only requirements, to avoid the three pitfalls described above, are to be fit, to attain adequate gear, and to prepare in advance.

Much of the information in this chapter was adapted from The Backpacker's Handbook, *Second Edition, by Chris Townsend (Camden, ME: Ragged Mountain Press, 1997).*

FIRST TIME OUT

When you backpack, you will be moving considerably slower than when you dayhike; the hiking speeds listed on p. 3 should be cut about in half.

For a first backpacking trip, choose a relatively easy trail, preferably one you know from dayhiking. Get an early start so you'll have plenty of time for rest stops, and don't obsess on proving you can plow ahead great distances. Stop around midafternoon, so you can take your time finding the right tent site and making dinner while it's still light.

Some backpacker's Rx tips: take along some pain relievers in case you have some surprised muscles in the morning, and make sure you have plenty of moleskin or molefoam to cover sore spots on feet or hip bones (never wait until sore spots become blisters to administer first aid).

The sense of total freedom you feel when carrying all your household needs on your back is one of the best reasons to backpack.

carry 50 pounds comfortably or make a leaking rain jacket waterproof. The right equipment can make the difference between a trip you want to repeat and a nightmare that will make you shudder every time you see a pack. You don't need to charge out and buy all the latest-and-greatest gear—just take the time to learn a little about current equipment choices and outdoor fabrics, and you'll be way ahead of the game.

What You'll Need

The essence of backpacking is simple: you carry all your daily needs on your own back. Think of it as a very distilled version of your house packed into a backpack—bedroom, bathroom, kitchen, and roof—and you get the picture. That may sound daunting. Isn't it outrageously heavy? Many years ago, it was—before metal, nylon, and plastic technologies helped designers refine packs, sleeping bags, tents, stoves, and cookware into lightweight and functional backpacking components. A very comfortable backpacking setup these days will weigh around 35–40 pounds or less. (See sidebar on common gear weights, p. 38.)

A Simple Start

If you've dayhiked but never backpacked, it's best to start simple and learn how to do it gradually, because unlike dayhiking, backpacking requires a few special skills that can easily be gained during simple outings. With a little experience, you will also begin to customize your own backpacking gear outfit and skills, because one of the most attractive aspects of backpacking is its affinity for individuality. Most of the other sports discussed in this book, such as sea kayaking, climbing, whitewater paddling, and cross-country skiing, require a certain degree of adherence to equipment, skills, and techniques that are relatively set because of safety concerns—you wouldn't take a sea kayak down a Class IV rapid any more than you would use racing skis on a backcountry ski tour or try to climb a rock face using gear you had modified out of manufacturer's specs. But once you meet a few basic safety requirements before setting out on a backpacking trip—such as first aid resources and adequate clothing, food, and shelter—the whole wilderness is your backyard, and you are only limited in your gear and technique experimentations by your own desires and skills.

But while experience and technique will be the keys to your best backpacking experiences, no amount of outdoor skill will make an inadequately designed pack

◆ **EXPERT TIP: PACK FIT**
In terms of comfort, only your boots are as important as your pack, so take the time to find a pack that fits.

The Pack

The heart of the backpacker's equipment is the pack. Tents, boots, stoves, and rainwear may be unnecessary at a given time and place, but your pack is always with you. It must hold everything you need for consecutive days of wilderness travel but still be as small a burden as possible. To fulfill this role, a backpacker's pack must be more than the bag with shoulder straps that is adequate for dayhikes.

Modern internal frame packs feature adjustable back systems, sternum straps, top tension straps, side tension straps, triple-density padded hipbelts, and lumbar pads.

Ever since aluminum frames and hipbelts were added to packs in the 1940s and 1950s, designers have tried to make load-carrying as comfortable as possible.

WHAT ABOUT BOOTS?

In their book, *Backwoods Ethics*, Laura and Guy Waterman pose this thought: "Grandma Gatewood, the fabulous woman who hiked the entire 2,000-mile Appalachian Trail three times—the first time at age 67—wore sneakers. If Grandma Gatewood could hike 2,000 miles in sneakers, does Joe Athlete really need heavy boots with lug soles?"

It would be a great disservice to suggest to beginning backpackers that they can wear Keds-style sneakers for carrying even moderate loads over uneven terrain. Something of a resistance movement to heavy boots arose around 30 years ago, the result of painful experiences with the old over-weighted monsters. But the footwear choices for today's backpackers are wonderfully varied, from light but supportive leather-and-nylon hybrids to all-leather medium-weights that offer excellent protection and support but weigh substantially less than the old style, thanks to new sole and leather-tanning technologies. Beginners should opt for a comfortable pair of supportive and protective boots until they learn if their feet can tolerate less-substantial shoes under the extra weight of a pack. (For further discussion of trail footwear and fit, see Chapter 1, p. 5.)

Hiking boots are available in a wide range of materials and styles, including this medium-weight leather boot that sports a water-repellent, zippered cover over the laces.

External-frame packs are still popular, but they have largely been superseded by more-streamlined packs with internal frames. Most backpacks today have adjustable back systems, sternum straps, top tension straps, side tension straps, triple-density padded hipbelts, and lumbar pads. The modern pack suspension system is a complex structure that requires careful selection and fitting.

If fit is the most important factor in selecting a pack, the second most important should be size. Make sure you buy a backpack that will hold all your stuff in all seasons during which you are likely to be backpacking (cold-weather gear will add substantial bulk and weight to your outfit). Overstuffing a too-small pack is not the way to achieve a comfortable carry. Some experienced backpackers feel that if you go on trips ranging from summer overnighters to winter through-hikes, you would better off with more than one pack—say, a 5,500- to 8,000-cubic-inch pack for long hikes in remote wilderness and winter expeditions and a 3,500- to 5,000-cubic-inch pack for summer weekends and lightweight trips. Most people start out with a moderately sized pack, in about the 4,000- to 5,000-cubic-inch range.

◆ EXPERT TIP: TRY BEFORE YOU BUY

Confused about what size or type of pack to buy? Most good outdoor retailers not only rent a variety of quality backpacks but also offer rent-to-own programs. Usually this means deducting the cost of a rental or two off the retail price of whatever pack you end up buying after your "test drives." So, you can compare external and internal frames, as well as different types of pack bag features.

An Innie or an Outie?

The suspension system is the most important technical feature to consider when choosing a pack—it supports the load and is the part of the pack that comes in direct contact with your body. A top-quality, properly fitted suspension system will enable you to carry heavy loads comfortably and in balance. An inadequate or badly fitted suspension will cause you great pain. As with boots, time is needed to fit a pack properly (see the section on fit criteria, p. 10).

To hold the load steady and help transfer the weight from the shoulders to the hips, the pack needs some form of stiffening. For loads of under 30 pounds, a simple, stiff, foam-padded back is adequate; for higher loads, a more rigid system is needed. In the past, the gear packed inside a pack provided this rigidity; but these old designs required so much care in packing that they were very awkward to use, and they have all but disappeared. All packs designed for heavy loads now have frames.

There are two frame-types: external, in which the pack bag is attached to a frame by straps or clips; and

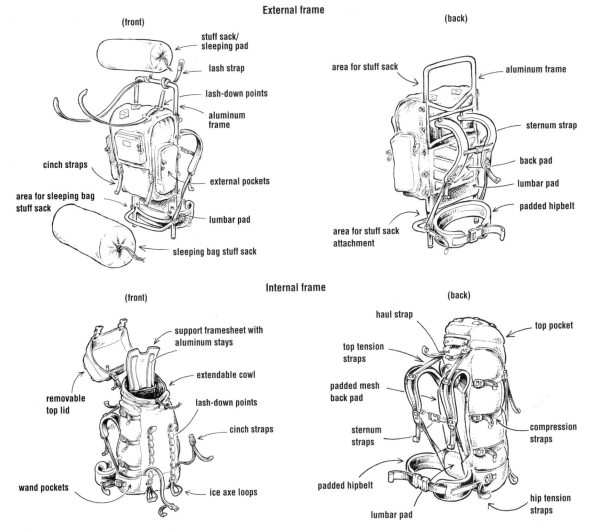

Key features of external- and internal-frame packs.

internal, in which the frame fits inside the fabric of the pack, often completely integrated into it and hidden from view. Currently, more internal-frame pack models are available, although external frames still have a following, especially among those who walk mainly on trails in forested and gentle terrain.

The debate centers on which frame best supports a heavy load and which is the most stable on rough ground; the answer used to be external for the first and internal for the second. Today, however, new designs and materials have made the distinction less clear-cut.

For most purposes, many experienced backpackers prefer internal-frame packs, which are more stable than

all but a few externals, easier to carry around when you're not on the trail, less prone to damage, and comfortable with medium-weight loads (30–45 pounds). If you carry more weight than that, pack choice becomes more critical, since only the very best of either type will handle really heavy loads properly.

The external frame has been around since the early 1950s. New designs introduced in the late 1980s and early 1990s have ensured it will yet be around for many years. The traditional frame is made of tubular aluminum alloy and consists of two curved vertical bars to which a number of crossbars are welded. These nonadjustable frames come in three or four sizes and have padded shoulder straps and hipbelts, plus backbands and frame extensions. External frames are easy to fit, as the weight transfers directly through the rigid frame to your hips—a vast improvement over earlier, unframed packs. Their rigidity makes it easy to keep the weight close to the center of gravity, enabling you to walk upright. Another argument for external frames is that because they stand away from the back, they allow sweat to dissipate, unlike internal-frame packs, which "hug" the body—although when working hard, most people will sweat no matter what type of pack they carry.

External frames have balance and stability disadvantages, however. Because of their rigidity, external frames do not move with you; on steep downhills and when crossing rough ground they can be unstable, which can make walking difficult or unsafe. Some new external-frame packs mimic the advantages of internals while avoiding the disadvantages, principally through modifications to the frame and the use of flexible plastic instead of rigid alloy. But externals are still bulkier than internals, making them awkward for plane, car, or bus travel and difficult to stow in small tents. (Their bulk also makes them more susceptible to damage, especially on airplanes.) It's worth noting, however, that externals usually are considerably less expensive than internals.

The basic internal frame consists of two flat aluminum alloy stays running vertically through the pack's back. This original design, introduced in the late 1960s by Lowe Alpine Systems, addressed the instability of external-frame packs on rugged terrain and the difficulty of designing a frameless pack to carry a heavy load comfortably. The bars or stays are usually parallel, though in some designs they form an upright or inverted **V**.

Many internal frames now have flexible plastic framesheets as well as stays, to give extra rigidity to the pack and prevent hard bits of gear from poking you in the back. There are many variations on the framesheet/parallel stays theme, using aluminum, carbon fiber, thermoplastic, Evazote, and polyethylene.

Whatever the style, internal frames are lightweight and conform to the shape of the wearer's back, allowing a body-hugging fit that provides excellent stability. A few packs come with prebent stays that can be bent further, fine-tuning the frame to your particular shape.

Because internal frames move with your body and allow the weight to be packed lower, they are excellent for activities during which balance is important, such

THE ESSENTIALS—A BACKPACKING START-UP KIT

Suggested gear list for a nice 22–35 pound solo backpacking setup for mild-to-moderate subwinter conditions:

- Pack, 4,500 to 5,500 cu. in. ($90–$375)
- Tarp, solo ($10–$20)
- Sleeping bag, three-season ($95–$300)
- Closed-cell foam sleeping pad ($10–$15)
- Trail footwear ($45–$200)
- Hiking socks X 2 pairs ($5–$14 per pair)
- Stove and fuel canisters ($40–$65)
- Quart pot with lid ($15)
- Cup ($0–$10)
- Kitchen accessories: pot grabber ($1–$3), spoons ($0–$3), matches/lighter ($1), towel or PackTowl ($0–$10)
- Quart water bottle ($0–$5)
- Gallon water bag ($10)
- Flashlight or headlamp and spare batteries ($10–65)
- Compass and map ($10–$50)
- First aid kit ($15–$50)
- Basic camp repair kit ($10–$50)
- Knife or multi-tool ($15–$75)
- Iodine pills for water purification ($5)
- Toilet paper and trowel ($3)
- Waterproof jacket ($45–$300)
- Fleece top or jacket ($45–$150)
- *Minimum cost essential backpacking kit: $485**

ADD-ONS AND TRADE-UPS

- Hat
- Possibles kit
- Solo tent, three-season
- Self-inflating sleeping pad
- Cookset with 1½- and 2-quart pans, lid
- Altimeter
- Water filter
- Synthetic hiking shirt
- Hiking shorts
- Pull-on pants

pack

pad

stove and pots

sleeping bag

boots

*The essentials list above is intended to give you an idea of minimum start-up costs, from scratch, for moderate entry into a sport using new equipment. Other options include borrowing gear from friends or renting from retailers, YMCAs, or church activity clubs, as well as buying used gear—see Appendix A.

as rock scrambling, skiing, and hiking over rough, steep terrain. A disadvantage of this characteristic is that it can lead to a forward lean to counterbalance the low weight. Careful packing with heavy items high up and close to the back is a partial answer, but the design and quality of the pack may prevent this.

BACKPACK CARE AND REPAIR TIPS

With a Speedy Stitcher (a hand stitcher that has a strong needle and a built-in thread spindle) and some sticky-backed nylon patches, you can fix just about any pack failure in the field. But take some wise advice from outdoor veteran Annie Getchell, author of *The Essential Outdoor Gear Manual*: before you head out, take time to inspect your pack. Then repair it *before* you leave.

1. *Zippers.* Because zipper problems usually are slider-related, you should always have a spare slider if you use a panel-loading, zipper-dependent pack. (This is less of an issue with top-loaders.) If after replacing the slider, you determine the zipper needs replacement, send the pack away! The tedious, technical task of replacing a pack zipper requires heavy-duty machinery and experience. Clip back and heat-seal any snagging fabric threads with a lighter or soldering iron. Use a garden hose with a powerjet attachment to clean out any grit, or try a stiff brushing in the tub or sink.

2. *Straps.* Straps rarely break; rather, they pull out from seams. Watch for any cuts or abrasions that may cause a failure. If an important strap does break, you can cannibalize another from your pack (a compression strap, for instance) and splice it in by stitching or with ladderlock fasteners from your repair kit. To reattach a pack strap, use a Speedy Stitcher. Start from the outside to determine the correct placement. Pin the strap to secure the angle. Turn the bag inside-out to expose the seam, then close with several lines of stitching. If there's enough length, anchor the pack strap tail to the body of the pack for added security.

3. *Fasteners and hardware.* Polycarbonate buckles and sliders commonly fail—especially vulnerable is the female side of a 2-inch hipbelt buckle. Cold makes these plastic parts brittle, so if they get stepped on or tossed onto a rocky surface, *hasta la vista*, baby. Usually you can manage to keep the buckle functioning with a wrap of duct tape to hold the split together. For that matter, consider protecting the hollow half with a duct-tape jacket *before* it breaks. Always pack matching spares for crucial parts.

4. *Fabric and coating.* Look for signs of abrasion, punctures, fading, stains, dirt, or mildew. Add a patch of nylon tape to create a protective, slippery surface. Any sticky stuff, such as klister wax from skis or food debris, should be removed as soon as possible, or it will attract dirt and, ultimately, mildew.

5. *Seams and stitching.* Look at all visible stitching on the main pack body to check for any broken stitch lines—touch these up immediately by hand with a stitcher. Run a bead of urethane seam sealer along the stitches of wear-prone seams to protect them.

Specialty Packs

Travel packs: A travel pack is a cross between an internal-frame pack and soft luggage. To protect it from conveyer belts and other travel hazards, the harness system is covered by a zippered nylon flap, making the pack much easier to handle without all that webbing spaghetti hanging off. Technology has brought travel packs up to par with most good internal-frame backpacks in terms of comfort and ability to carry loads, so travel packs are an excellent choice for the overseas backpacker.

Packs for women: Many pack makers are recognizing that at least half, if not more, of their customers are women. And they are finally acknowledging that because women's bodies are different—in general, shorter torsos, narrower shoulders, and proportionately wider hips—properly fitting backpacks for many women should have different harness qualities than those for men have. A man's pack worn by a woman usually is too long, leading to instability and overweighted shoulders; has too-wide shoulder straps

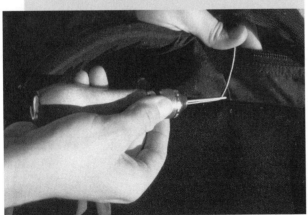

A Speedy Stitcher is a versatile tool for repairing packs, tents, and other camp accessories made of fabric.

DENNIS WELSH

Women's bodies are different from men's, and properly fitting backpacks for many women should have different harness qualities than those for men.

◆ EXPERT TIP: PURCHASING A PACK

When looking for a backpack to purchase, consider these key features:

◆ *The fit.* A poorly fitted pack can give you sore shoulders, hips, and back, and can be very unstable.

◆ *A well-designed hip belt.* A good hip belt should support up to 90 percent of the pack weight without chafing or causing sore hips.

◆ *Curved, padded shoulder straps* with top tension/load-lifter straps to take pressure off the top of the shoulders.

◆ *A frame/frame sheet* to help transfer the weight to the hips and prevent lumpy gear from poking you in the back.

◆ *A capacity and design suitable for the gear to be carried.*
A small pack for summer weekends doesn't need ice-axe loops, ski slots, or room for a four-season sleeping bag, but a pack for a winter ski-backpacking trip does.

◆ *As light as possible for the weight to be carried.* About 10–15 percent of the total load weight is good.

Before you try on a potential pack, test-load it with at least 35 pounds of gear (most stores will have items available for this) and loosen all the straps. The next stage is to put the pack on and do up the hip belt until it is carrying all the weight and the upper edge rides about an inch above the top of your hipbone. Next, adjust in the hip belt stabilizer straps. Finally, tighten the shoulder straps and pull in the shoulder stabilizer straps so that the shoulder straps rest at a point roughly level with or just in front of your collar bone, at an angle of between 25 and 40 degrees. If the angle is smaller than that, the harness needs lengthening; if larger, it needs shortening. The aim is to achieve a back length whereby most of the pack weight rides on the hips and the pack hugs the back to provide stability.

Adjusting a backpack properly requires two steps after adjusting the harness: 1. Put the pack on with all the straps loosened and cinch up the hip belt. The top tension straps should be at an angle of 25 to 40 degrees. Note how the shoulder straps wrap the shoulders. The top of the frame should be 1½ to 2 inches above the shoulders, and note that the top tension straps are tight but not tugged all the way in to the body. 2. The top of the hip belt should ride about an inch above the top of the hipbone. Tighten the side tension straps to pull in the load around the hips, for maximum stability.

that slide off; and has a large, gaping hipbelt. Look for manufacturers that offer women's models or interchangeable, sized hipbelts, and shoulder harnesses.

The Roof over Your Head

A backpacker needs shelter from cold, wind, rain, insects, and, in some places, sun. The kind of shelter you need depends on the terrain, time of year, and how Spartan you are prepared to be. Some people like to sleep in a tent every night; others use one only in the worst conditions. Shelter choices include bivouac bags, tarps, and tents. Some trails, such as the Appalachian Trail, offer shelters or huts for backpackers, but for most North American backpacking, plan on carrying your own shelter.

Bivouac (or bivy) bags offer the simplest way to cope with weather changes. This is a waterproof "envelope" into which you slip your sleeping bag when the weather turns wet or windy. More-sophisticated designs have short poles at the head to keep the bag fabric off your face. The least-expensive bags are made from nonbreathable waterproof materials such as plastic or "space blanket" metallized fabrics. These are light—from 4 to 12 ounces—but they're suitable only for emergency use, because they keep in all your body moisture. Breathable bivy bags, such as those made from Gore-Tex, work very well.

Tarps are useful for creating cooking or sleeping shelters, especially in parts of the world where the presence of bears means that you shouldn't eat or store food in your tent. Another use for a tarp is as an awning for your tent, providing a large undercover cooking, storage, and drying area that also allows you to leave your tent door open in rain with no danger of leakage.

Tents provide more protection from the weather than do bivy bags, as well as space to sit up, cook, eat, read, make notes, sort gear, play cards, and sit and watch the world outside. Of course, a tarp provides more space for the weight, but it doesn't give the same protection against windy weather or, especially, biting insects.

Selecting the right tent isn't easy. They come in all shapes and sizes, and few stores have the space to display many. Salespeople at a good store should be prepared to erect a tent you are considering buying, so you can have a look at it. Good advice from a salesperson and careful study of catalogs and magazines will help you narrow the field. But it's useful to have an idea of the type of tent you're looking for before you go shopping:

When and where will it be used? If foul weather is common where you plan to backpack—the Pacific Northwest or high Rockies, for example—plan to look for a top-quality, sturdy tent. Tents are rated *three-season* (spring through fall) and *four-season* (winter). The latter are designed to handle the weight of heavy snowfall and the stress of high winds.

How many must it sleep? While most backpacking-weight tents are one- or two-person, if you plan to backpack with young kids, you will need a larger tent (they are heavy, but the rainfly, poles, and body can be split up among the adults' packs).

How critical is weight? If you are walking long distances or traversing tough terrain, you will want the lightest shelter possible.

How do you feel about the color? This may seem trivial to a beginning backpacker, but veterans who have spent days on end waiting out bad weather can attest to

violent reactions to strange colors (it's different for everyone). Also, consider if you want to carry "loud" colors into the wilderness.

Is the shape and design attractive? Consider how you are going to use your tent, and where. If you are going to be packing through areas where campsites are marginal or nearly nonexistent, you probably will want a freestanding tent design. If two people will share the tent, is it wide enough? If you are tall, make sure your head and feet are not cramped.

Price and personal choice are important. This will be your home on many wilderness nights. You may cringe to fork out a little more money for a better-quality tent, but you'll appreciate it in the field.

TENTIQUETTE

Annie Getchell, author of *The Essential Outdoor Gear Manual*, offers these tips to keep your home-away-from-home in great shape:

- Establish "house rules," such as no footwear to be worn inside the tent, and always roll up and secure door flaps so they don't lie in the mud. Meticulous campers might carry a scrap nylon "doormat" to curb tracking.

- Before packing up each morning, remove the fly and drape it upside down to dry the inside. Make sure the tent body is also dry. Pull up the stakes and lay the tent on its side to let the floor air. Before removing poles, open doors completely and shake out any debris.

- NEVER store a wet tent. If a tent is soaked when stuffed in your pack, remove it as soon as possible and set it up to dry. Even a little morning dew can cause mildew in a few days. Once mildew is established in dark, star-patterned splotches, coatings begin to delaminate.

- In rough terrain or during extended trips, consider using a groundsheet to minimize abrasion to the tent floor. The cloth should never protrude from the perimeter of the tent, or water will puddle under the floor. Sleeping out on just the groundsheet is also a nice option for clear nights under the stars, when a tent isn't really necessary.

◆ **EXPERT TIP: KEY FEATURES TO LOOK FOR IN A BACKPACKING TENT**

◆ *Easy pitching.* Check for minimum stakes or freestanding design (although *all* tents should be carefully staked out).

◆ *Shock-corded aluminum alloy poles* that can be quickly fitted to the tent via clips or wide sleeves.

◆ *Waterproof, UV-resistant fly sheet.*

◆ *Uncoated inner tent* to allow condensation to escape.

◆ *Good space-to-weight ratio.*

◆ *Insect net doors.* (When the mosquitoes or black flies are abundant, this is more important than any other feature.)

◆ *A roomy vestibule,* for cooking and storage. While this is not absolutely necessary, once you've used a tent with a vestibule integrated into the fly, you'll find you won't want to do without.

As a rough guide, look for at *least* 30 square feet of floor area in a three-season tent for two, and 30 to 35 square feet or more in a winter tent. For solo use, 25 to 30 square feet gives plenty of room. The width for twosomes should be at least 54 inches at the widest point; for soloists, 36 inches. The length for each should be 7–8 feet, longer if you're taller than 5 feet, 10 inches.

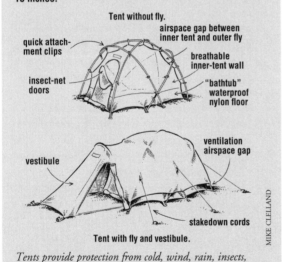

Tents provide protection from cold, wind, rain, insects, and, in some places, sun.

A Good Stake-out

Whether you choose a tarp or tent, you will need stakes and guylines. Long, heavy steel stakes aren't necessary. Round alloy stakes hold well in most soils; for softer ground, carry a few 6-inch alloy **V**- or **T**-stakes (skip plastic, which can chip when pounded with a rock).

Stakes are easy to misplace, so take two or three more than needed to pitch the tent, and keep them in a small nylon stuff sack packed with the tent. Be very careful pounding in stakes with rocks—always wear eye protection and tap firmly rather than pound heavily, to avoid smashed fingers.

Depending on the design, tents need anything from two to a dozen or more guylines to keep them taut and stable in a wind, though more than 10 is too many for a tent that will be pitched daily. Most tents come supplied with a full set of guys, but only some have the main ones plus attachment points for others. It pays to attach these extra guys, because they're usually needed in a storm; but don't overtighten your tent, either—that causes more stress than it relieves.

For information on campsite selection, setting up camp, and camping safety, see Chapter 10. For a discussion of pretrip contingency planning, see Chapter 1, pp. 18 and 20. For a discussion of snow camping and snow caves, see Chapter 10, p. 263.

✓ **EXPERT TIP: USE CHECKLISTS**

When, where, and for how long you go will determine what you carry for any walk. You need to know about the weather, the terrain, and the environment, and you should prepare for the most extreme conditions you may encounter. From a complete list of all your gear, weights included, distill a shorter list for the trip at hand (see sidebar on weights of common backpacking gear, p. 38). Add about 2 pounds of food per day, factor in water weight (8 pounds per gallon; minimum requirement about a gallon per person per day), include any personal gear, and you'll have the total load weight.

At this point, seasoned backpackers review the list again to see if anything can be left out or replaced with a lighter alternative.

See Chapter 15 for master lists you can use to create your own trip lists.

The Bedroom

Whether you sleep out under the stars, in a tent, or in a bivy bag, you need to keep warm at night. For most people this means using a sleeping bag and sleeping pad—your bedroom set. Beginning backpackers commonly underestimate the importance of a good sleeping set—not only for comfort, but more importantly, for critical insulation between you and the cold ground, which will steal heat from your body. Your sleeping set is a good place to splurge on weight: safe backpacking starts with a well-rested backpacker.

Sleeping Bags

A sleeping bag traps warm air, to prevent the body from cooling down. In general, the sleeping bag must allow perspiration to pass through it while it retains body heat, which means that both insulating fill and shell should be breathable. If you intend to sleep out in your bag without shelter, you also need a wind-resistant bag with a quick-drying shell, or a bag with a waterproof/breathable shell.

Choosing a sleeping bag is much easier than choosing a tent. There are far fewer designs, although many models. The biggest decision is which kind of insulation or fill to go for. The ideal material would be lightweight but very warm, low in packed bulk, durable, nonabsorbent, quick-drying, warm when wet, and comfortable. Unfortunately, this ideal doesn't yet exist, so compromises have to be made in terms of which properties are most important—determined in part by when and where you'll camp, and what shelter you'll use. The basic fill choice is between synthetic fibers or goosedown.

Down. The lightest, warmest, most comfortable, most durable sleeping bags use down as fill. Down bags are the best choice when weight and bulk are critical factors, since nothing comes anywhere near down for compactness and low weight combined with good insulation. Down, the fluffy underplumage (not a true feather) of ducks and geese, consists of clusters of thin filaments that trap air and thus provide insulation. No synthetic fiber has down's insulating ability. But down must be kept dry, as it loses virtually all its insulation when wet, and it's very absorbent, so it takes a long time to dry. Drying a down bag in bad weather is practically impossible—only a hot sun or a machine dryer can do the job. There-

> **◆ EXPERT TIP: THUMBS UP FOR DOWN**
> Though initially more expensive, in the long run down costs less. One company that makes both down and synthetic sleeping bags estimates that with average use, a down bag will last 12 years, a synthetic one only four years.

fore, keeping a down bag dry means packing it in a waterproof bag and always using shelter when it rains.

Synthetic. Synthetic fills cost less than down, are easy to care for, and resist moisture. They are not, however, "warm when wet," as some manufacturers claim—nothing is. What matters is how fast something dries, and synthetic fills dry fairly quickly, since they are virtually nonabsorbent. Because the fill doesn't collapse when saturated, much of its warm-air-trapping thickness is retained. Compared to a wet down-filled bag, a wet synthetic one will start to feel warm in a comparatively short time, as long as it's protected from rain and wind. You can't sleep outside in a storm in a synthetic-fill bag and stay warm, however. Reviews suggest that Primaloft is the most water-resistant synthetic.

The disadvantages of synthetic fills are short life, less comfort compared with down or pile, and more bulk and greater weight for the same warmth compared with down. However, the new synthetics are lighter, more compressible and perhaps more durable than earlier fills.

Many people, especially those who use external-frame packs, like to strap their sleeping bags under the packbag. But however sturdy your stuff sack, this leaves your sleeping bag vulnerable to rain, dirt, and damage. It's best to pack your bag at the bottom of the lower

> **◆ EXPERT TIP: SLEEPING BAG LINERS**
> One way to improve the warmth—and cleanliness—of a sleeping bag is to wear clothes in it. A liner accomplishes the same but adds a little weight to your outfit. Liners are available in cotton, polypropylene, silk, fleece, and coated nylon. Cotton is not recommended because of its weight, absorbency, and slow drying time. Polypropylene liners make more sense—a typical one weighs 16 ounces, which is still heavier than a set of polypro underwear. Fleece liners can uprate a bag for colder conditions, but a fleece suit is more versatile. Silk (at 5 ounces or so) is really light and low in bulk—the best choice for a bag liner.

A comfortable backpacking setup includes a good shelter, room for the camper and her gear, and a sheltered cooking area.

CHRIS TOWNSEND

◆ **EXPERT TIP: KEY FEATURES TO LOOK FOR IN SLEEPING BAGS**

◆ *Fit.* One that is too tight will be uncomfortable; too much room can lead to cold spots. A few manufacturers are marketing bags for women.

◆ *An adjustable, shaped hood.*

◆ *A tapered shape* for efficient insulation.

◆ *A shaped foot box.*

◆ *A two-way zipper* for ventilation.

◆ *A filled draft tube* behind the zipper, to prevent heat loss.

Another feature you will want to take into account in a bag is the measure of its loft—the physical thickness of the insulation and thus the measure of its warmth. For a discussion of loft, see Chapter 10, p. 259.

What about cleaning the bag? A veteran outdoor retailer once said, "Don't clean your bag until it can walk in on its own." Although a little extreme, the basic advice is good: don't overclean your sleeping bag. Handwashing is always best for either down or synthetic fills. Buy soaps especially for down or synthetic sleeping bags and follow the directions. Most outdoor retailers offer bag cleaning services.

Outdoor gear guru Annie Getchell has this to say about dry cleaning: "Not! Dry cleaning processes employ ethylene-based solvents that are harmful to down and synthetics. Even the 'Stoddard Process,' often touted as better for down products, uses distilled kerosene. Most down garments and bags sport a 'Dry Clean Only' label simply to prevent careless machine washing, even though the solvents are harmful to both down and synthetic fills (as well as to shell fibers)."

compartment, in an oversized waterproof stuff sack. Ordinary stuff sacks usually aren't waterproof—the seams aren't sealed. A cheap alternative is to pack your stuffed bag inside a heavy-duty garbage bag or waterproof nylon sack liner. When packed in an oversize stuff sack, the bag can mold to the curve of the pack around the lower back and hips and fill the corners.

Sleeping Pads

The insulation of a sleeping pad under a bag is needed to prevent body heat from seeping into the ground when the bag's fill is compressed by weight.

"Three major factors govern choice of gear: performance, durability, and weight."

—Chris Townsend, *The Backpacker's Handbook,*
Second Edition

Pads also provide cushioning. In summer weather, some hardy souls manage without a pad by putting clothing (and even their packs) under their bags, but most people use a pad year-round.

The two types of sleeping pad in general use for backpacking are *closed-cell foam* mats and *self-inflating, open-cell foam* pads. (Air beds and covered, open-cell foam, popular for car camping, have just about vanished among backpackers.)

Closed-cell foam. Closed-cell foam pads are lightweight, inexpensive, and hard-wearing, but very bulky to carry. Although they are efficient insulators, they don't add much cushioning. These pads may be made from either pressure-blown or chemically blown foam; the first are warmer, more durable, and resist compression better than the second, but they look identical and manufacturers rarely tell you which is which. The synthetics they're made from don't affect performance—Evazote (EVA), Ensolite, and polyurethane are commonly used. Closed-cell pads come in different lengths, widths, and thicknesses. You can save a bit of weight and bulk with three-quarter-length pads (about 57 inches). A three-quarter-length, four-season, pressure-blown pad weighs up to 9 ounces. Because of their bulk, closed-cell pads are normally carried on the outside of the pack, wherever there are convenient straps; but take care where you place them when hiking in brushy areas.

Open-cell foam. Cascade Designs introduced the first self-inflating pad, the Therm-a-Rest—and most veteran backpackers swear by them. The polyurethane-waterproofed nylon shell of these pads is bonded to an open-cell, polyurethane foam core that expands when the valve at one corner is opened; a few puffs of breath help. Once the pad has reached the desired thickness, the valve is closed to prevent the air from escaping. The Therm-a-Rest provides astonishing comfort and warmth. Although heavier than a closed-cell foam mat, a Therm-a-Rest is much less bulky and can be folded and packed down the back of the pack, where it is protected from damage. Therm-a-Rests require care, though; don't throw one down on the bare ground and sit on it without checking for sharp objects that might puncture it. If you're going tentless, always carry a groundsheet to protect your pad. In case the pad does spring a leak, a repair kit containing patches, glue, and a spare valve is available. Finding a pinprick-size leak can be difficult, however—the pad must be immersed in a creek or pool and inspected for bubbles, the way one finds leaks in rubber inner tubes.

Pillows

For a pillow, try a fleece or down top packed in a stuff sack. Some people actually use their boots, but those who prefer more comfort can choose from among a number of lightweight pillows available. Inflatable nylon or down-filled pillows can be found in many outdoor stores. They weigh 4–15 ounces, take up very little room when packed, and can greatly enhance your night's sleep.

The Kitchen

Food plays a large part in how much you enjoy the outdoors. The possibilities and permutations are endless, so your diet can be constantly varied. Wilderness dining has two extremes: gourmet eating and survival eating. Gourmets like to make camp at lunch time so they have several hours to set up field ovens, in which they bake cakes and bread and cook multicourse dinners. They walk only a few miles each day and may use the same campsite for several nights. Survival eaters, on the other hand, breakfast on a handful of dry cereal and a swig of water. They are up and walking within minutes of waking, and they pound dozens of miles every day. Lunch is a series of cold snacks eaten on the move; dinner consists of more cold snacks or a freeze-dried meal "cooked" by pouring hot water into the packet. Most people, of course, fall somewhere between these two extremes.

Outdoor retailers stock a wide variety of freeze-dried and dehydrated foods for backpacking. These usually come in foil packets in quantities allegedly suitable for two people—although, depending on the maker and the two diners, sometimes a packet amounts to merely a generous helping for one hungry backpacker. Vast improvements have been made in the last few years in the dried-food market, including a trend toward natural foods. And remember that you don't have to eat only dried foods (actually, few can afford it—freeze-dried dinners are five times the cost of regular food); many backpackers take along dried vegetables and meats to

With a little planning and ingenuity, camp cooking can become one of the great pleasures of backpacking.

concoct delicious stews or omelets with fresh ingredients, or dried fruits to make desserts.

Another new arena in the backpacking-foods market is "bakepacking." Several manufacturers make lightweight pot-hoods and pot inserts that work like ovens. These manufacturers also sell their own dried mixes, to which you only have to add water to bake up yummy dinners such as pizza or desserts such as chocolate cake. You can also adapt grocery store mixes to the same purpose, but you should experiment at home first.

The only limitations to backpacking dining are how much food weight you are willing to carry and how much pretrip preparation you are willing to invest. And the only rule to go by is to make sure you provide yourself with a proper diet to feed your hardworking body, in sufficient quantity. (See Chapter 12 for more on camp food, cooking, and energy needs.)

Cooking Sources

Sitting around a campfire on a cold evening is, for many people, the ideal way to end a day in the wilderness. In many areas, however, badly situated and constructed fires have left scars that will take decades and more to heal, and too many trees have been stripped of their lower branches, or even hacked down, to provide fuel. Even collecting fallen wood can damage the environment if not enough is left to replenish the soil with nutrients and provide shelter for animals and food for insects and fungi.

Treat fires as a luxury, and ensure that they have minimum impact on the environment. Landowners and managers may ban fires in certain areas—for a few dry weeks when the fire risk is high, or for decades if a damaged area is being left to recover. In national parks, fire permits may be needed, and you may be required to carry a stove. Such regulations may seem restrictive, but they prevent further degradation of popular areas. Fires, officially permitted or not, are inappropriate in some areas, anyway. They shouldn't be lit at and above the timberline or in deserts, because of the slow growth rate of trees and woody plants and the need for soils there to be replenished by the nutrients from dead wood. (See Chapter 13, p. 296 for information on minimum-impact adventuring, and Chapter 10, p. 247, on how to build leave-no-trace campfires.)

Small, single-burner stoves negate the need for campfires for cooking. A stove also ensures that you can have hot food and drink quickly whenever you want or need it.

There aren't many stoves to choose from, but the differences among them are significant—most notably, in the types of fuel used and how the fuel canister is connected to the burner.

The availability of fuel in the areas you visit may determine which stove you carry, especially on a long trek during which you need to resupply fuel every week. The choices are solid fuel, liquid fuel (alcohol, kerosene, white gas, or automobile gasoline), and pressurized gas cartridges (butane or butane/propane).

Solid-fuel tablets and jellied alcohol, available under various names, aren't efficient enough to be worth considering. Fuel for alcohol stoves, which can be expensive and hard to find, is available in most countries under various names, usually including the words *alcohol* or *spirit* (denatured alcohol, rubbing alcohol, or marine stove fuel in North America; methylated spirits in

> ◆ **EXPERT TIP: KEY FEATURES TO LOOK FOR IN STOVES**
> ◆ *Good heat output.* A stove must be capable of bringing water to a boil under the most horrendous conditions you are likely to encounter.
> ◆ *Weight.* It must be small and light enough to carry.
> ◆ *Simplicity.* It must be simple to operate, especially in difficult conditions.
> ◆ *Stability* is important too, particularly with stoves that will be used with large pans.

Britain). Alcohol is the only fuel not derived from petroleum, which makes it more environmentally friendly than other fuels. It's also the only one that burns unpressurized as a liquid, which makes it a safer fuel. It's clean, too, evaporating quickly if spilled. For these reasons, it's a good fuel to use any time you'll be cooking regularly in the tent vestibule. Alcohol is not a hot fuel, however—it produces only half as much heat as the same weight of gasoline or kerosene. A quart of alcohol lasts only a little more than a week with simple cooking, which makes it a heavier fuel than others to carry on long trips. White gas is probably the most efficient stove fuel, lighting easily and burning very hot—a quart lasts at least 10 days. Sold under various names—the most common being Coleman Fuel, although MSR White Gas is becoming increasingly available—white gas is available in outdoor, sporting goods, and hardware stores; often, especially in towns near popular parks or wilderness areas, it can be found in supermarkets. Whatever form it comes in, this is a volatile fuel, igniting easily if spilled, and its use requires a lot of care.

Because they burn pressurized fuel, all white-gas stoves can flare badly during lighting, so great care is needed if they are to be used in a tent vestibule. Some white-gas stoves have built-in fuel tanks; other, newer models use fuel bottles. Both types operate best when the tanks are at least half-full—they should never be filled totally, since the fuel must have room to expand or you won't be able to pressurize the stove fully. Built-in fuel tanks are usually quite small—1/3- to 3/4-pint capacity—which means they may need refilling every few days. If you run out of fuel while cooking, you must wait for the stove to cool down before you can refill it. A good strategy is to get in the habit of refilling your tank each morning before packing up for the trail.

Light, clean, simple-to-use cartridge stoves are used by the majority of backpackers—especially those who don't undertake marathon treks or head deep into the winter wilderness. The fuel of choice is liquid petroleum gas stored under pressure in a sealed cartridge. Pure butane, the most common version not so long ago, has generally been replaced by butane/propane mixes or by isobutane, at least for backpacking. Because of the low pressure in the cartridges—necessary because their walls are thin to keep the weight down—butane won't vaporize properly in temperatures much below 40 degrees F at sea level, making it a very poor performer in cold weather. As the cartridge empties and the pressure drops, the burning rate falls until a point is reached at which the heat produced won't bring water to a boil. Cartridges can be warmed with the hands or kept warm by storing them inside clothing or sleeping bags.

Cartridge stoves are best for solo or duo use, because the cartridges cool as they release fuel, so that running a stove over a long period—often necessary for group cooking—leads to a much more rapid performance drop than does running it in short bursts. For the same reason, cartridge stoves are less efficient at melting snow than are stoves that run on other fuels.

Cartridges come in two types: those with a self-sealing valve that allows you to remove the cartridge at any time, and those that must be left on the stove until empty. The latter results in a tall structure that isn't very stable, especially with large pans; an optional stabilizing base helps. Although the pan supports fold away for packing, the fact that the cartridge cannot be removed makes these stoves inconvenient to carry. The advantages of resealable-cartridge stoves are so great that they should be the only choice for backpackers. An added advantage of resealable cartridges is that it's possible to change cartridges before the one in use is empty, which could be useful if you're trying to boil water in very cold weather. The more than

25 makes of cartridges available worldwide all have the same size thread and valve.

In the past, ministove fuel cartridges were not refillable or recyclable. Recently, however, at least one manufacturer has begun offering recycling services, via outdoor retailers, for its cartridges. Ask your local shops about recycling services for canisters; if they don't yet offer the service, urge them to.

◆ EXPERT TIP: STOVE SAFETY

All stoves are dangerous and should be used carefully. The most important safety point is never to take a stove for granted.

Before you light a stove, always check that attachments to fuel tanks or cartridges are secure, tank caps and fuel bottle tops are tight, and controls are turned off. Carefully study and practice the instructions that come with all stoves, especially kerosene and gasoline models, before heading off. When you're cold, wet, and tired, and it's half-dark and you desperately need a hot meal, it's important that you can safely operate your stove almost automatically.

Cooking Accessories

Cooking while backpacking can be a lot of fun—especially because you will be ravenously hungry and will appreciate food much more. Once you get your basic stove and pot set, you'll want to have a few accessories that do wonders to improve the ease of single-burner cooking:

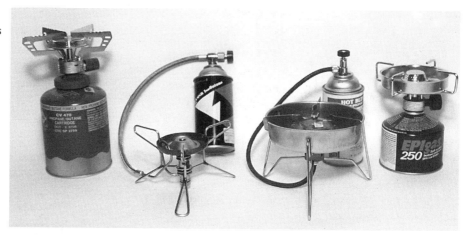

Cartridge-fuel stoves are very popular because they are simple to use (no priming) and the fuel is clean and convenient. Fortunately, many stores are now offering recycling services for empty cartridges.

By adding a backpacker's oven, such as this Outback Oven by Cascade Design, you can hugely increase the variety and tastiness of backpacking food.

Windscreen. All stoves need a windscreen to function efficiently. There are several windscreens on the market, from roll-up aluminum to larger, rigid, aluminum alloy models; some stoves come with wind screens.

Heat exchangers and diffusers. Recent stove accessory innovations include heat exchangers and heat diffusers. The MSR XPD Cook Set with Heat Exchanger consists of two stainless-steel pots with frying pan/lid and pot grabber, plus a corrugated aluminum collar for the pots meant to reduce boiling time by directing more heat up the sides. Traveling Light makes an aluminum windscreen/heat exchanger, called the Tutu, that comes in two sizes, as well as a ribbed stainless-steel heat dispersion plate, the Scorch Buster. Similar products designed to optimize ministove efficiency are available at outdoor retailers, but also look at hardware stores with good housewares sections for heat diffusers and other gadgets.

Pots and Pans

Most likely your backpacking kitchen will evolve over time as your food tastes and cooking needs change, your outdoor cooking skills increase, or you decide you hate cooking and go no-cook.

The most basic cook set will be a pot, a spoon, and a cup. Some people get to be real whizzes at one-pot cooking (see Chapter 12, p. 279), and if you're going solo, you can eat right out of the pot, so cleanup is a breeze.

A step up would be a pot with a deep-sided lid that can be used as a frying pan or double boiler. Multipot

sets that nest for packing are best for more than one person and for multicourse meals. If you backpack in a cold climate, you will appreciate having an extra pot in which to boil water for a hot drink while you make dinner.

The next question is which metal to buy. Aluminum cooksets are by far the least expensive and lightest; they heat evenly, without hot spots, and conduct heat quickly, making for fast boiling times. However, aluminum pits, scratches, and dents easily, which makes it hard to clean and can taint some foods with a slight metallic flavor. Some experts have expressed concern

---

HOW MUCH DOES IT WEIGH?

Honing your backpacking outfit to lower the weight will do wonders for your endurance as well as enjoyment. Some sample weights, in ounces, of common gear:

Pack of 4,500–5,500 cubic inches (90)

Three-season boots, size 9½ men's (40)

Sleeping system. Tarp, solo (20); groundsheet (10); solo tent, three-season (64); three-season sleeping bag (48); closed-cell foam mat (9); self-inflating sleeping pad (14)

Cooking gear. Multifuel/white gas stove (16); foil windscreen (2); 1-quart pot with lid (8); cookset with 1½- and 2-quart pans, lid (26); 1-pint stainless steel cup (4); mini pot grabber (1); plastic bowl (3); dish cloth (0.5); two spoons (2); matches/lighter (1); 1-quart water bottle (5); 2-quart water bag (2.5)

Safety and camp gear. Headlamp and spare batteries (6.5); candle lantern and three candles (10.5); compass and whistle (1.5); maps (4); first aid kit (4.5); repair kit (4); altimeter/watch (1.5); knife (1); iodine pills (2); water filter (11)

Personal gear. Wash kit (2); toilet paper (2); toilet trowel (2); sunscreen (2)

Clothing, summer. Synthetic T-shirt (4); fleece top (16); shorts (6); synthetic long johns (4); summer-weight trousers (12); windproof top (12); waterproof jacket (16); overpants (8); warm hat (2); sun hat (4)

Clothing, winter. Synthetic zip-neck shirt (8); fleece top (20); windproof fleece (for wet/cold) (25); down top (for dry/cold) (20); synthetic long johns/pile pants (8); long pants (24); waterproof/breathable jacket (28); waterproof/breathable pants (20); warm hat (2); windproof pile-lined cap (4); liner gloves (2); warm gloves/mitts (4); shell gloves/mitts (5)

about the adverse effects of ingesting aluminum. Stainless steel is easy to clean, noncorroding, scratch-proof, tough, long-lasting, and doesn't taint food. Unfortunately, it's significantly heavier than aluminum and also conducts heat more slowly, leading to longer boiling times. Two new cookset materials that have just come on the market perform excellently. An aluminum/stainless-steel combo called either Duossal or Inoxal is lighter than stainless steel, although not as light as aluminum, but it heats exceptionally quickly. Titanium is lighter than Inoxal, and the latest pans are made of this material. The cost is about double that for stainless steel cookware, but titanium doesn't pit, scratch, or taint flavor, and it cleans easily.

The Closet

When the clouds roll in, the wind picks up, and the first raindrops fall, you need to know that your clothing will protect you from the coming storm. If it doesn't, you may have to stop and make camp early, crawl soggily into your tent, and stay there until the skies clear. At worst, you could find yourself in danger from hypothermia. While its prime purpose is to keep you warm and dry in wind and rain, clothing also must keep you warm in camp when the temperature falls below freezing, and cool when the sun shines.

The Layering System

As if keeping out rain while expelling sweat and trapping heat while preventing the body from overheating were not enough, clothing for backpackers also must be lightweight, durable, low in bulk, quick-drying, and easy to care for, and it must perform in a variety of weather conditions. The usual solution is to wear several light layers of clothing on the torso and arms (legs require less protection) that can be adjusted to suit the conditions and activity.

The *layer system* is versatile and efficient if used properly, which means constantly opening and closing zippers and cuff fastenings, and removing or adding layers. Layers should be added on legs, hands, and head in severe conditions.

A typical modern layer system consists of the following:
1. An *inner layer* of thin, synthetic wicking material that removes moisture from the skin.
2. A thicker fleece *middle layer* to trap air and provide insulation.

3. And finally, a waterproof/breathable *outer layer* shell to keep out wind and rain while allowing perspiration to pass through.

Alternative or additional layers include
- A thin shirt or sweater over underwear.
- A windproof shell for dry, windy conditions.
- A down- or synthetic-insulation-filled garment for camp and rest stops in cold weather. If the weather will be wet as well as cold, another fleece jacket could substitute here.

On trips during which a wide range of weather conditions could be expected, the layers might include thin underwear, medium-weight shirt, warm top, windproof top, waterproof top, and insulated top—six layers in all.

How many layers you plan to take on a particular trek depends on the conditions you expect. The best rule is to take clothing that should keep you warm in the worst likely weather. If in doubt as to what is enough, take a light, insulated vest, or an even lighter vapor-barrier suit, just in case. (For a thorough discussion of outdoor clothing, fabrics, and their functions, refer to Chapter 14.)

Closet Organizers

For carrying clothing, nylon stuff sacks are ideal, especially for compressible down- and synthetic-filled items. Stuff sacks weigh from 1 to 4 ounces, depending on the size and thickness of material—thin ones are fine for use inside a pack. Experienced backpackers carry spare clothing in a stuff sack in the lower compartment of the pack; down jackets are stuffed in their own stuff sacks inside a larger one for extra protection. Dirty clothing can ride in a plastic bag at the very bottom of the pack. Rainwear and clothing that may be needed during the day (windshirt or warm top) shouldn't be put in stuff sacks; along with headware and handwear, they must be quickly accessible, and so should be packed in an outside pocket if possible.

Other Necessities and Niceties

Numerous small items can make any backpacking trip more safe and enjoyable. Some are essential, some merely enhance your stay in the wilderness.

Light. You'll need one light for walking and one for camp. A walking light will do for camp use, but not vice-versa. Handheld lights are cheaper and lighter than headlamps, and buyers have a much wider choice, but a *headlamp* is far more useful, because it leaves both hands free. Walking is also easier with a headlamp. Whatever flashlight or headlamp you use, it's wise to carry spare batteries and bulbs. However, batteries are heavy, expensive, and polluting; to minimize their use, try using candles around camp for times when you don't need direct light. The short stubby candles that weigh up to 7 ounces when new and burn for 10 to 30 hours, depending on their size, are great because they're self-supporting. Never bring a candle into the inner tent or stand it on a groundsheet, of course. Candle lanterns protect the flame from wind and can be hung up so that the light covers a wider area.

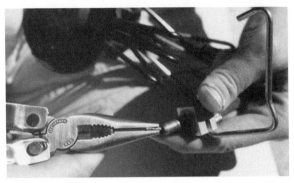

A multi-tool such as a Leatherman is indispensable for fixing things like stove fuel lines.

A headlamp allows you the freedom to cook or do camp chores with your hands free. Choices include lamps with battery packs on the belt, or on the headband.

Repair kit. It's an unusual trip on which something doesn't need repair, or at least tinkering with, so a small repair kit in a stuff sack is an essential item. Although the contents will vary from trip to trip, the weight should hover around 4 ounces. Repair kits for specific items, such as the stove and the Therm-a-Rest (available at outdoor stores), should travel in this bag, along with backup items such as waterproof/windproof matches. A very handy item is waterproof, adhesive-backed, ripstop nylon tape, which patches everything from clothing to fly sheets. Also packed in the repair bag should be a small sewing kit, some lengths of nylon cord, and a selection of rubber bands. A length of shock cord tied in a loop makes an extra-strong rubber band. Any detachable pack straps not in use also end up in the repair bag. (For a list of other items to include in a repair kit, see the description of a hiker's "possibles kit," Chapter 1, p. 12.)

Knife or multi-tool. A classic Swiss Army knife by Wenger or Victorinox, or a multi-tool such as a Leatherman or SOG, is worth its small weight in gold. Keep the blades sharp.

Watch. It's tempting to leave your watch at home when backpacking, but unfortunately a watch has its uses, even in the wilderness. It's helpful to know how many daylight hours are left when you must decide whether to stop at a good campsite or push on. When the sun's visible, you can estimate time fairly accurately, but on dull, overcast days it's almost impossible. A watch with a built-in calendar also helps keep track of the days, something that can be confusing on long trips. Checking your watch when you stop for a break may also help get you moving again, especially when you realize that the intended "couple of minutes" has somehow become a half-hour. If your watch has an alarm, you can set it to wake you up for morning starts. There are also wristwatch/altimeter combos that also have date and alarm functions.

Binoculars. Binoculars are practical for scouting the trail or the country ahead, and for checking out whether that dark lump under the tree you're approaching is a mossy stump or a bear. Good backpacking binoculars are around 8-power with 21 mm objective lenses and weigh around 6–8 ounces, if you can find them that light.

Thermometer. Backpacking expert and author Chris Townsend includes a thermometer among his essentials,

---

◆ EXPERT TIP: TRY AN UMBRELLA
If you backpack in forests and places where strong winds are uncommon, consider using an umbrella instead of your rain jacket (but do bring your jacket, for really stormy days). It's a wonderful break from confining, sound-deadening hoods. Small umbrellas are best for hiking—under 13–14 ounces, and around 30 inches long closed and 38–40 inches in diameter open.

When packing up, keep your pack well balanced side-to-side, and keep heavy items a little higher and placed closer to the back.

if only for its entertainment value: "My immediate finding, reinforced whenever I camp with others, is that it's never as cold as people think."

Packing Your House

Where you put gear in your pack depends on the sort of hiking you are doing and which items you are likely to need during the day.

For walking on level ground on well-maintained trails. Heavy, low-bulk items should be packed high and near to your back, to keep the load close to your center of gravity and to enable you to maintain an upright stance.

For any activity where balance is important, such as scrambling, bushwhacking, cross-country hiking on steep, rough ground, or skiing. Heavy, low-bulk items should be packed lower for better stability, though still as close to your back as possible. Women tend to have a lower center of gravity than do men, and they may find packing

◆ **EXPERT TIP: SAMPLE PACKING**

Chris Townsend, author of *The Backpacker's Handbook,* has a system for packing his pack:

LOWER COMPARTMENT

1. First in is the sleeping bag (in an oversized stuff sack inside a pack liner), to fill out the corners and enable an internal-frame pack to wrap around the hips.
2. Spare clothes (in another stuff sack), and rainwear, which pads any unfilled spaces and is accessible if it rains.
3. A bivy bag, if carried.

UPPER COMPARTMENT

4. Tent poles slide down one side of the upper compartment next to the back, and if they are very long, through the cutaway corner of the lower compartment floor.
5. A Therm-a-Rest mattress, folded into three sections, goes down the back of the pack, where it is protected from abrasion and anything piercing the pack (an unlikely event). This procedure also ensures that hard objects can't protrude into the back, which can be a problem with packs that don't have a plastic frame sheet.
6. In the bottom of the top compartment rest cooking pans, stove and fuel, and small items such as candles, boot wax, and repair kit; the heaviest items (such as full fuel bottles) go close to the back.
7. Because of its weight, the food bag (or bags) is placed toward the back of the pack.
8. In front of the food bag(s) go the tent, separated into two stuff sacks, and camp footwear.
9. The top of the pack is reserved for books, spare maps, and a windbreaker or warm top.

THE LID POCKET

In no particular order, the lid pocket receives hat, neck gaiter, gloves, mitts, writing materials (in a nylon pouch), tube of sunscreen, camera accessories bag, insect repellent, thermometer, and any small items that have escaped packing elsewhere.

SIDE POCKETS

Into the side pockets go water containers, fuel bottles or canisters, food for the day, tent stakes, headlamp, first aid kit, and items that didn't fit into the lid pocket or that were overlooked.

(Some people line their backpacks with a heavy-duty plastic garbage bag before they pack up, which is not a bad idea if you expect a lot of rain.)

PUSHING THE ENVELOPE: WALK THROUGH TIME
In the early 1960s, Welshman Colin Fletcher became the first known person to walk the entire length of the Grand Canyon National Park. Fletcher dropped down into the western reaches of the Grand Canyon at Hualapai Hilltop and proceeded to walk to Point Imperial, a journey of two months and many hundred miles (it's nearly impossible to tell, with sinuous route, backtracking, and side trips) through millions of years of geologic history. Not once did he "surface" above the rim (although he was resupplied with three airdrops).

in this way leads to a more comfortable carry for trail hiking, too.

However you pack, keep your pack load stable. The items you'll need during the day should be accessible, and you should know where everything is.

Moving Your House

Walking is very easy. Walking in the wilderness with a pack isn't quite so simple: with considerable weight on your back, you have to find your way, perhaps in dense mist or thick forest; cope with terrain, which may mean negotiating steep cliffs, loose scree, and snow; and deal with hazards ranging from extremes of weather to animals. However, walking in the wilderness is relatively straightforward as long as you are reasonably fit, learn a few basic skills, and know a little about weather and terrain.

Fitness—Laying the Foundation

Your outfit is totally honed. Now what? Backpacking requires fitness. You need aerobic, or cardiovascular, fitness to walk and climb all day without your heart pounding and your lungs pleading for air. Without muscular fitness, particularly of the legs, you'll be stiff as a board and aching all over on the second day out. Also, if you set out unfit, the likelihood of injury from strains and muscle tears is much greater.

Achieving fitness takes time. Those people who claim they can get fit over the first few days of an annual backpacking trip usually suffer during most of the walk. With a little preparation, they could enjoy every day.

The best way to train for carrying heavy loads over rough terrain is to carry heavy loads over rough terrain—what sports trainers call "specific training." Al-

though this isn't always practical, it's surprising what you can do if you really want to, even if you live and work in a city.

At the very least, spend a few weekends getting used to walking with a load before setting off on a longer trip. Walk as much as possible during the week—including up and down stairs. Brisk strolls or runs in the evening help, too, especially if hills are included. In fact, hill running is probably the best way to improve both your aerobic fitness and your leg power in as short a time as possible.

Coping with Terrain

As long as you stick to good, regularly used trails, you should have no problems with terrain, except for the occasional badly eroded section. However, don't assume that because a trail is marked boldly on a map, it will be clear and well-maintained. Sometimes the trail won't be visible at all; other times it may start off clearly, then fade away, becoming harder to follow the deeper into the wilderness you go. Trail guidebooks and ranger stations are the best places to find out about specific trail conditions, but even their information can be inaccurate.

Off-Trail Travel

People who never leave well-marked trails, feeling that cross-country travel is simply too difficult and too slow, are missing a great deal. The joy of off-trail travel lies in the contact it gives you with the country you pass through. The 15- to 20-inch dirt strip that constitutes a trail holds the raw, untouched wilderness a little at bay. Once you step off it, the difficulties you will encounter should be accepted as belonging to that experience. You can't expect to cover the same distance you would on a trail or to arrive at a campsite before dark. Uncertainty is one of the joys of off-trail travel, part of the escape from straight lines and the prison of the known.

Learning about the nature of the country you're in is very important. Once you've spent a little time in an area—maybe no more than a few hours—you should be able to start interpreting the terrain and modifying your plans accordingly. Surveying the land ahead from a hillside or ridge is useful when possible—for which purpose binoculars are well worth their weight. A good strategy is to climb a hill, if possible, to survey the next day's route. (See Chapter 9 for information about cross-country navigation.)

Steep Slopes

Traversing steep, trail-less slopes is tiring and puts great strain on the feet, ankles, and hips. Climbing to a ridge or flat terrace, or descending to a valley, is preferable to traversing a slope for any distance.

In general, treat steep slopes with caution. If you feel unhappy with the angle or the ground under your feet, retreat and find a safer way. Backpacking isn't rock climbing, although it's surprising what terrain you can get up and down with a heavy pack if you have a good head for heights and a little skill. *Don't climb what you can't descend* unless you can see that the way is clear beyond the obstacle. And remember that you can use a lightweight rope for pulling up or lowering your pack if necessary. However, it's unwise to drop packs down a slope, as they may go farther than you intend.

Talus Slopes, Boulder Fields, and Scree

Slopes of stones and boulders, known as *talus,* occur on mountainsides the world over, usually between the timberline and the cliffs above. Trails across these features are usually cleared and flattened, though you may still find the going tricky. Balance is the key to crossing rough terrain—a walking staff is a great help (see Chapter 1, p. 13 for more on walking staffs). Cross large boulder fields slowly and carefully, testing each step and concentrating on firm footing. Unstable boulders, which may move as you put your weight on them, easily can tip you over. The key to good balance is to keep your weight over your feet, which means not leaning back when descending and not leaning into the slope when traversing.

You may go crazy scrambling over the smallest stones, known as *scree.* The trick is to keep moving. Some people like to run down scree—a fast way to descend—but this practice damages scree slopes so quickly that it should no longer be practiced; too much scree-running turns slopes into slippery, dangerous ribbons of dirt embedded with rocks. Be very careful if you can't see the bottom of a scree slope—it may end at the edge of a cliff. Because other parties may be crossing below you, if a stone does start rolling, you should shout a warning— "Below!" or "Rock!" are the standard calls. If you hear one of these calls, *do not look up,* even though you will be tempted to. Stop and crouch, covering your head as best you can, until the rockfall danger has passed.

Water Hazards

In many areas, major hazards are presented by unbridged rivers and streams. Water is more powerful than many people think, and hikers are drowned every year fording what may look like relatively placid streams. If you don't think you can cross safely, don't try. If no logs, boulders, or other structures present a crossing, wading a stream or river may be the only option; use a hiking staff to steady yourself, and unclip your waist belt and sternum strap in case you fall and need to get out of your pack fast. Whether you prospect upstream or downstream for a potential ford depends on the terrain.

(For tips on traveling in alpine and desert terrain, see below and also Chapters 13.)

Before you head out backpacking, or any other outdoor activity, you should know how to use map and compass (see Chapter 9) and be prepared with first aid knowledge and self-help skills (see Chapter 13).

Using a staff for support, and carefully choosing rocks on which to step, is one way to cross some creeks.

CHRIS TOWNSEND

TOP 5

CLASSIC NORTH AMERICAN BACKPACKING TRIPS

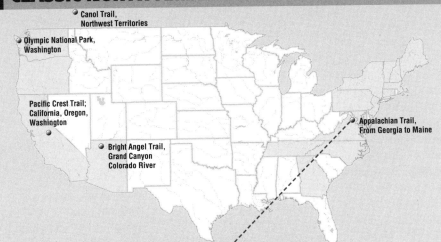

Canol Trail, Northwest Territories

Olympic National Park, Washington

Pacific Crest Trail; California, Oregon, Washington

Bright Angel Trail, Grand Canyon Colorado River

Appalachian Trail, From Georgia to Maine

DENNIS WELSH

Tackling a hill on the Appalachian Trail.

- *Appalachian Trail*. From Georgia to Maine, this is a classic Eastern trail; en route, huts provide an extra touch of comfort.
- *Pacific Crest Trail*. Stretching along the spine of the West Coast's Sierra Nevada, this is the legendary stomping grounds of conservation giants Muir and Brower.
- *Bright Angel Trail, Grand Canyon*. Descending into millions of years of geologic history to the Colorado River in this legendary canyon ranks high on any backpacker's "best" list.
- *Olympic National Park*. The coastal trails in this mystic rain forest of Washington state provide an experience not equaled anywhere else in the United States.
- *Canol Trail, Northwest Territories, Canada*. A backpacking trip into the heart of Arctic "barrenlands" country is a top challenge for any backpacker, and a lifetime experience.

Planning a Trip

Common reasons for failure to complete a backpacking trip include heavy packs, sore feet, exhaustion, overly ambitious mileage goals, and unexpected weather, terrain, and trail conditions. To avoid many of these pitfalls, read the accounts of other hikers, check guidebooks for information on weather and terrain, and study the planning guides that are available for popular trails.

In its simplest form, planning means packing your gear and setting off with no prescribed route or goal in mind. This procedure works well in areas you know well—such as favorite dayhiking trails. Usually, a little more planning is required.

Information Overload

There is no such thing as too much information, but it's easy to have too little. Guidebooks, maps, and magazine articles all can provide information on where to go, and an increasing amount of information is available on the Internet. Videos and CD-ROMs can also provide information (and inspiration). Once you've selected an area, up-to-date information can be obtained from the land managers—the National Park Service, the Forest Service, the Bureau of Land Management, or state land agencies.

For the initial route planning, use small-scale (1:250,000) maps covering large areas before purchasing the appropriate topographic maps and working out a more detailed line. But remember that cross-country routes may be impassable on the ground or that a far more obvious route may show itself, so don't stick rigidly to prehike plans.

Permits

Don't neglect to find out about permits. Most areas don't require permits, but many national parks and some wilderness areas with easy access do. The number of permits issued may be severely restricted in the most popular places, making it essential to apply for permits long before your trip. If you want to backpack popular trails in some national parks—Grand Canyon, for example—you need to apply for a permit many months in advance and must be flexible about your route. Whatever you think about limiting numbers by permit, it means that even in popular areas you won't meet too many people. There remain vast areas of less-frequented wilderness where permits aren't needed and even the most crowded summer trails are usually quiet out of season.

"Do not break into this cabin except in an emergency. If you do not come to the mountains prepared, you do not deserve to be in them."

—sign on a wilderness outfitter's backcountry cabin in the Canadian Rockies

---

THE LONG HAUL

Author and 15,000-mile backpacker Chris Townsend talks about long-distance backpacking:

"A surprising number of hikers set off each spring for Mount Katahdin, Maine (the northernmost point of the Appalachian Trail), or the Canadian or Mexican borders on the Pacific Crest Trail or Continental Divide Trail, with little or no previous backpacking experience. This in itself ensures a high failure rate. A gradual progression—an apprenticeship, in fact—should precede a multi-month trip. Before attempting one of the big three, try hiking a shorter but challenging trail, such as the John Muir, Colorado, or Long Trail. My first solo distance hike, a 17-day, 270-mile trip along Britain's Pennine Way, followed several years of short, 2- to 5-day trips. Two years later, I made a 1,250-mile Britain end-to-end hike. Then, after another 3 years of shorter trips, I set out on the Pacific Crest Trail. I still made lots of mistakes, but I had enough knowledge and determination to finish the walk. If it had been my first distance hike, I doubt I would have managed more than a few hundred miles.

"Preparation for a long trek doesn't mean just dealing with logistics—knowing where to send food supplies, where stores and post offices are, how far you can realistically walk per day—it also means accepting that at times you will be wet, cold, or hungry, and the trail will be hard to follow. Adventures are unpredictable by definition. Every long walk I've done included moments when ! felt like quitting—but I've always continued, knowing the moment would pass. If the time ever comes when the moment doesn't pass, I'll stop. If backpacking isn't enjoyable, it is pointless. Completing the trail doesn't matter—it's what happens along the way that's significant."

☞ KID QUOTIENT

There's no doubt about it: backpacking with kids is challenging, but the rewards are so high, it's worth trying. The tips in Chapter 1 on dayhiking with kids all apply equally to backpacking—especially to keep it short and simple.

At how young an age can kids be taken backpacking?

Many people take babies into the wilderness in child carriers (as long as they are old enough to hold their heads up on their own), and have great success using a roomy tent as a "playpen." The most challenging age is the toddler—small enough to carry in a child carrier, but mobile and curious enough to really keep a parent hopping around camp. At around four or five years of age, a child becomes too heavy to carry in a carrier but is able to walk far enough that you can enjoy weekend outings away from the crowds. Closer to nine or ten, children can carry special kid-size backpacks, which will add immensely to their experience—the pleasures of self-sufficiency are even more intense for children.

Most parents learn to backpack successfully with their kids by trial and error, developing strategies that work for their families but may not work for others. However, all will give you the same piece of advice: Start young! Don't wait until your kids are addicted to weekend television or shopping mall cruising to "force" them out into the wilderness. If you make it a regular family outing, backpacking and wilderness exploration becomes a part of their lives—and maybe TV will seem alien to them (well, it's worth hoping). Some tips for beginning backpacking with kids:

☞ Several good books for parents who want to introduce their kids to the outdoors are well worth the small cover price in the priceless experience they offer. Try *Wilderness With Children* by Michael Hodgson *(Harrisburg, PA: Stackpole Books, 1992).* Older kids (about 8 to 14) will enjoy their own how-to guide, *Kids Outdoors* by Victoria Logue, Frank Logue, and Mark Carroll (Camden, ME: Ragged Mountain Press, 1996), which includes sections on backpacking and woodland skills.

☞ Dress kids carefully outdoors and they'll have more fun. (You don't like being wet and cold, so why should they?). It's tempting to use whatever clothes are lying around the closet, because kids outgrow stuff so quickly; at the very least, make sure they have good urethane-coated rainwear and a fleece jacket, as well as several pairs of mittens and a couple of hats.

☞ Look for used kid's gear and clothing: try putting a Want Ad in the bulletin of your local hiking group or Sierra Club.

☞ There are two schools of thought on tenting: everyone sleeps in one big tent, or the kids get their own shelter, pitched close to Mom and Dad's. The total weight may be nearly the same, although if you choose the one-tent option, smaller kids can share double sleeping bags with the adults, cutting weight considerably. Many kids will enjoy the thrill of having their own tent, but there may be some scary moments when animals investigate or call around camp late at night.

☞ Make sure everyone, even small kids, knows the safety rules and plan before an emergency happens.

☞ During a backpacking outing, kids will need things to do—they're not so inclined as adults to lounge around reading the latest John Grisham novel. Until your kids get the knack of exploring or building forts or castles on their own, have a few activities planned—a short hike, fishing, swimming, collecting pine cones, or whittling sticks.

☞ Get kids involved in the cooking—it's fun and helps occupy them at times when they're likely to be getting cranky. Plan early dinners, too, so that all the eating and cleaning can be finished before it gets too dark to see. Enjoy marshmallows over a small fire when it gets dark.

☞ Have only one goal: fun! Uptight, goal-oriented parents are detrimental to a successful family backpacking outing.

(See Chapter 11 for more tips on adventuring outdoors with kids.)

Not so long ago, in many national parks and wilderness areas you could camp legally only in specific sites that were nearly always crowded and were well-known as food sources to local wildlife. Many areas now allow you to camp where you like, which gives far greater freedom. Where good campsites are few, such as the Grand

CHRIS TOWNSEND

The Pacific Crest Trail is one of North America's legendary through-trails, stretching along the spine of the Sierra Nevada for hundreds of miles.

Canyon, campsites are restricted in the most visited areas, although backcountry camping is allowed elsewhere in the park by open permit.

Where Can Backpacking Lead You?

Like moving from dayhiking to backpacking, a logical progression from backpacking for a weekend or week at a time is to extend your trips longer and farther. For many backpackers, the ultimate trip is through-hiking a long trail such as the Appalachian or Pacific Crest. Some people might bite off a few hundred miles of these legendary treks, or go for the entire length—1,000 miles or more, taking months on end.

If long-distance through-hiking appeals to you, start by reading narrative accounts of the trails that interest you. If you don't know about many of the long-distance trails, subscribe to walking or backpacking magazines, which often feature accounts of these trails.

(See Appendix B for a listing of booksellers that specialize in outdoor narratives and guidebooks.)

Mountain Hiking and Beginning Mountaineering

The definition of just what mountaineering *is* can span an enormous range of activity, from a steep hike up a rocky crag to an oxygen-assisted, technical climb up the vertical face of an 8,000-meter Himalayan peak. Certainly, any ascent that is likely to require the assistance of crampons, ice axes, and rope techniques, and that involves significant elevation gain, exposure, and the possibility of snowy or icy conditions, can confidently be called mountaineering.

As a novice, you can take mountaineering one facet at a time, first learning high-elevation mountain hiking techniques in summer; then progressing to nontechnical routes using crampons and ice axe, along with basic rope work; and finally, after accumulating much experience, graduating to full-on alpine assaults, perhaps hiring a guide to tackle glaciers and steep headwalls.

For our purposes here, we offer only a brief introduction to the equipment and skills necessary to move through the high mountains. Mountaineering, and even mountain hiking, require skills best acquired through expert instruction.

JAMIE BLOOMQUIST/OUTSIDE IMAGES

By using crampons, ice axes, and ropes, experienced backpackers can begin exploring high mountains.

Equipment

Boots. Mountaineering boots are made from leather or injection-molded plastic. Some mountaineering boots are built in a single layer; others are actually two boots in one—a light, insulating inner boot and a heavier, stiff outer boot. Some double boots offer a choice of liners to suit different conditions.

All mountaineering boots are designed to provide firm support for the foot and ankle, with a rigid sole to shrug off sharp-edged talus, kick into hard snow, and provide a stable platform for crampons. Often the sole will be slightly rockered to make the approach hike more comfortable. Plastic boots sometimes incorporate a hinged joint at the ankle for the same purpose.

If you're just starting out with mountain hiking, there's little point in buying a 5-pound pair of double boots. Look for a midweight pair in leather, suitable for crampons.

Ice axe. The standard ice axe designed for general mountaineering consists of three parts: the head, shaft, and spike (shorter ice tools designed for vertical ice climbing have the same parts but are much more variable). The head, consisting of a long pick on one side and an adze on the other, is normally made from chrome-molybdenum steel (also known as chromoly), a light but very strong alloy; the shaft can be aluminum, carbon fiber, or titanium. A leash, attached through a hole in the head of the axe, will prevent you from losing your axe if you slip.

The spike is driven into ice or compacted snow to aid climbing or provide security while standing. The most important use of the ice axe is for self-arresting. The pick is used to bite into the slope for self-arresting during a fall. (See p. 50 for a description of self-arrest technique.)

The adze is used to chop footholds in hard, steep snow or ice. The spike gives the shaft purchase on a slick surface when used as a staff, and the entire shaft can be plunged into the slope for a self-belay when footing is treacherous. (See Chapter 6 for more on technique.)

The average length for an all-around axe seems to be between 65 and 75 centimeters; use your own height to determine where in that range you should buy.

Crampons. Crampons are magic traction devices on ice and slick, frozen snow. Their sharp points bite into the surface, providing tremendous traction. Stamped from chromoly, crampons can be one-piece, to provide rigid support for vertical ice climbing, or hinged in the middle, to help walking. For general mountaineering the hinged style is a good compromise, as it will perform well in mixed conditions.

Crampons must attach to your boots with complete security. In addition to general sizing, most crampons adjust to match the length of the boot sole exactly. Some crampons attach with straps; others use a steel wire bail that clips to the front of the boot sole, plus a cammed toggle that cinches to the heel, with a security strap to ensure the cam stays put. The latter crampons are called "step-ins" and require boots with a distinct shelf on the sole or a groove designed for the bail. Easy to put on and take off, step-ins are a good choice for mixed rock-and-ice climbs.

Clothing. The attire you need to face mercurial mountain weather conditions needs to be versatile. The key word is *layering.* By wearing several light layers rather than one heavy one, you can adjust your insulation level and don or shed weatherproof barriers as the conditions and your level of exertion dictate. Chapter 14 offers a comprehensive guide to assembling a high-performance outdoor wardrobe, with information on fabrics, laminates, and design, as well as the layering system.

Mountaineers and mountain hikers should always have with them several pairs of gloves or mitts, and glacier glasses. Head protection is mandatory, and good gaiters, if your waterproof pants don't include integrated snow cuffs, are also a good idea.

When choosing mountain clothing, keep this in mind: The Scottish have a saying, "There is no such thing as bad weather, just bad clothing." You could add this footnote to it: It doesn't matter how good your clothing is if you don't have it with you.

Safety gear. Your backpack should contain a full complement of safety equipment, including first aid kit, altimeter, map and compass, personal safety kit, bivouac gear, water, food, stove and fuel, a snow shovel, and a rope with a water-resistant finish ("dry" rope).

See Chapter 13 for a discussion of high-elevation safety and health, including important information on elevation sickness, and tips on essential personal safety gear. Appendix B lists good sources to help you find mountaineering and wilderness first aid courses, which are essential for any high-mountain adventures.

> *"Having once tasted the pleasure of living in high, solitary places with a few like spirits, I could not give it up."*
>
> —H.W. Tilman, "When Men and Mountains Meet," in *The Seven Mountain Travel Books*

Basic Mountain Travel

The essential rule for traveling in the mountains is lifted right out of the Boy Scout handbook. If you're prepared for the worst the mountain could throw at you, you'll not only be safer, you'll enjoy yourself much more. Since the difference between bringing nothing at all and carrying a full day's load of proper equipment is only about 25 pounds, there is little excuse to be caught without something you need. See the Basic Mountain Hiking Checklist, below.

Moving on Loose Rock and Talus

All mountains start to crumble even as the forces of their birth begin to push them above the surrounding plains. This erosion manifests itself in rocks that suddenly roll out from under you as you move up the mountain. Since true mountaineering begins about the place that smooth trails stop, you're often going to find yourself moving up loose slopes that are too gradual to

---

✓ BASIC MOUNTAIN HIKING CHECKLIST

For a full day of nontechnical mountain hiking, on a route that might include snow and ice but doesn't require roping up, here is a basic checklist to include in your pack, in addition to wearing the proper complement of clothing listed above.

- Outer-shell jacket and pants (if not worn)
- Spare gloves or mitts, and hat
- Crampons
- Ice axe
- Spare glacier glasses
- Food
- Water
- First aid kit, including sunscreen and lip balm
- Compass
- Altimeter
- Map
- Headlamp, preferably with twist-on switch
- Spare batteries
- Swiss Army knife
- Waterproof matches, and/or lighter
- Personal safety kit (see Chapter 13, p. 289)
- Useful Extras
- Short insulating pad
- Collapsible snow shovel
- Helmet

---

require belaying but steep enough to result in a nasty tumble after a misstep.

The keys to avoiding accidents are deliberation and caution. Never put your full weight on any rock or ledge that could crumble without testing it first. This involves a two-part move to each step—a tentative push downward with the foot, while keeping the center of gravity over the back foot in case the foothold gives way, then a committed step on to the forward foot.

On talus—the piles of loose rocks that build up at the bottom of steep slopes—there are often *no* really secure footholds, and extreme caution must be taken when moving over the surface. See p. 43 for tips on crossing talus and scree slopes.

Moving in Snow

Traveling on snow is a never-ending lesson, because the medium itself is so variable. A fresh snowfall can result in several feet of loose powder impassable to anyone not wearing skis or snowshoes; several days later the same surface might be slick and hard as ice, requiring crampons and ice axe to negotiate. One warm spell can turn the whole slope to mush.

On the other hand, snow tends to be pretty homogeneous in whatever state it happens to be. The climber is lifted above loose boulders and talus; sharp gullies and dips are smoothed over. And descending through snow can be much faster than walking down a dry trail.

Read the cold-weather section of Chapter 13, on alpine conditions, for advice on avalanche precautions and emergency bivouacking in snow. A mountain hiker should be constantly attuned to avalanche conditions.

Stepkicking. Snow that has had a chance to settle and compact will often stabilize into a firm, frozen crust with a resilient underlayer. Purchase on the crust will be tenuous, even on a shallow slope, but by breaking through to the surface below a climber can gain good traction.

On a shallow slope, stepkicking really consists of just stomping your boot firmly into the snow. As the slope steepens, the toe of the boot will be used to kick into the crust and form an actual step. Make sure that the step slopes into the side of the hill, to provide a secure platform, and is deep enough to support the ball of your foot. As much as possible, use the weight of your boot to break through the crust, to save energy. As the crust thickens, you'll need to put more force behind the kick. If several people are traveling together, the leader will kick steps in which the rest of the party can follow single-file, saving much energy on their part. In this case, it is the leader's responsibility to choose the best route.

As the slope approaches 30–45 degrees, it becomes easier to move up it diagonally rather than straight up the fall line. This is when your ice axe becomes very useful as a self-belay device, increasing your security. Grasp the head of the axe as you would a cane, with the palm of your hand over the adze, and plunge the spike and shaft vertically into the slope above you, leaning on it as you stepkick up to its level, then repeat the process. Remember to watch for avalanche-prone areas while traversing a slope.

The rest step. Stepkicking is hard work, even for a very fit climber. Add the minimal oxygen you've got to get by on, and any overenthusiastic attack on the slope will soon leave you gasping. The solution is a slow but steady progression, called a rest step, which climbers use on the very highest Himalayan peaks.

The rest step takes advantage of your strongest balance point to allow your body a short rest period. As you initiate a kickstep, your lower leg is locked, all your weight resting on it. Kick into the slope and anchor your boot, ready to step up onto it. Then, *stop*. Take a breath, or two or three, depending on the elevation and your condition. While you are doing this, your weight is supported on your locked lower leg, while the upper leg is consciously relaxed, allowing it a rest before it has to raise your body up another foot. By concentrating on synchronizing your breathing with your movements, you can adjust your pace to allow steady progress.

Descending in snow (plunge-stepping). In snow that provides ascent via stepkicking, descending is easy. You essentially perform the opposite maneuver you did on the way up, except you face downhill and use your heels to gouge steps. This involves much less exertion than ascending, because your full weight is behind each step; with your leg locked, the heel of your boot usually breaks through the crust readily and stamps a secure platform. The hardest part is committing yourself fully to each plunge, because if you lean back too much, your boot will bounce off the crust and throw you off balance, causing you to fall.

If the slope is simply too steep to permit walking down in this fashion, you again use your ice axe as a self-belay, by reaching below you and planting it in the snow, then stepping down to it with your face to the slope. This is essentially reverse step-kicking.

Of course, the best, and most fun, way to descend snow is by glissading, which can be described as a controlled slide. In soft snow, you simply sit down and use your butt as a sled, controlling speed with your ice axe, the spike of which is trailed in the snow behind you like a rudder. If your speed increases beyond comfort, dig in deeper with the axe, but resist the temptation to suddenly plunge your boots into the surface, which could result in an instant end-over-end flip. Also, keep a firm hold on your ice axe to help avoid puncture wounds.

In general, be especially conservative in using glissading—it's hard on your clothing, and if you're not careful you could glissade right off a dropoff you didn't remember. Never glissade while wearing crampons.

Self-arrest. Unless you're both incredibly cautious and incredibly lucky, there is going to come a time when traction fails you, and you find yourself sliding down the mountain out of control. This is when your ice axe earns its living.

In a self-arrest, you use the pick of the axe as both a brake, to slow and stop your downward plunge, and a rudder, to orient you properly with your head pointing uphill. The self-arrest is possibly the most vital skill a mountaineer can learn, as it can save not only your life but the lives of anyone roped to you. Accordingly, you should practice and master the technique under controlled conditions—on slopes with safe run-outs—before you actually need it. Be sure to practice on both your left and right sides and in any position you might fall—feet first, head first, face up, face down—since as you traverse slopes you switch the axe from hand to hand.

A self-arrest starts with a proper grasp on the ice axe. With your strong hand, grip the head of the axe above the shaft, with your thumb wrapped around the base of the adze and the pick projecting out the bottom of your hand. With your other hand, grasp the shaft just above the spike. If you are sliding down the slope on your back, use your strong hand to press the pick into the surface just above your shoulder. Do not plunge the pick in all at once, or it can be torn from your grasp, but press quickly and firmly to slow your descent as soon as possible. The adze will be pointed toward your shoulder, the pick away from you, and the

One of North America's most popular mountaineering destinations is Washington's Mt. Rainier; this is the top of Gibraltar Ledges.

CLIFF LEIGHT

shaft held across your chest. As you lean on the pick, arching your back to transfer weight on to the tool, it will dig in and start to slow you. Roll toward the axe, right over on top of the shaft, pressing the pick in more and digging in with your boots to assist slowing you. Be sure the spike does not dig in and trip the axe out of your grip. You should stop face down in the snow, on top of the axe, facing uphill.

Even if you accomplish this maneuver smoothly, the axe is likely to jerk and yank as it digs in. Hang on tightly! Your strong hand will take most of the strain.

On the face of it, this seems like an insane thing to try with a tool that has three sharp ends. But by controlling the head with your strong hand and grasping near the spike with your other, you can direct the operation with a surprising degree of safety.

You can self-arrest from nearly any position. If you are sliding headfirst, you need to plant the pick off to the side, so you do not slide directly down on it. The pick will swing you around.

The key to a successful self-arrest is to *immediately* grasp your ice axe in the proper position and get the pick into the snow. Hesitation allows precious time to pass, with a resulting increase in the speed of your slide, making slowing down more difficult.

One very probable source of confusion occurs in a sudden slip during an ascent, while using the axe in a self-belay stance. The reason is that the head of the axe is held *the other way around* for self-belay—with the adze under the palm to spread the load as you plant the spike. You must instantly switch the head so the your thumb is under the adze for a proper grip and safe self-arrest. Practice this switch while you are practicing the arrest sequence, by first grasping the shaft with your weak hand and then turning the head the right way. If it is not uncomfortable for you, you can also self-belay with your hand already in the self-arrest position on the head.

Required reading for mountain hikers and beginning mountaineers should be *Mountaineering: Freedom of the Hills,* edited by Don Graydon (Seattle: The Mountaineers, 1991), 5th edition. Also include *Climbing, The Complete Reference,* by Greg Child (New York: Facts On File, Inc., 1995); *Ice World,* by Jeff Lowe (Seattle: The Mountaineers, 1996); and *Hypothermia: Death by Exposure,* by William W. Forgey, M.D. (Merrillville, IN: ICS Books, 1985). The resources section of Chapter 6, Climbing, provides contact information for several mountaineering organizations, which can help you find schools.

Further Resources for Backpackers
Books
The Backpacker's Handbook, Second Edition, by Chris Townsend (Camden, ME: Ragged Mountain Press, 1997). Be the beneficiary of Townsend's several decades and 15,000 miles of backpacking experience. A friendly and informative book that's not afraid to list favorite brands and divulge tried-and-true tips. Much of this chapter was adapted and excerpted, with permission, from *The Backpacker's Handbook.*

Periodicals
Backpacker, 33 East Minor Street, Emmaus, PA 18098; (610) 967-5171. The name says it all.

Outside, 400 Market Street, Santa Fe, NM 87501; (505) 989-7100. Though not exclusively devoted to backpacking, *Outside* has excellent gear reviews and the coverage tends to be more worldwide than that in other outdoor magazines.

Organizations
Several of the organizations listed below include excellent periodicals as membership benefits: AMC Outdoors *(Appalachian Mountain Club),* American Hiker *(American Hiking Society), and* Sierra *(Sierra Club).*

American Alpine Club, 710 10th Street, Suite 100, Golden, CO 80401; (303) 384-0110.

American Hiking Society, 1422 Fenwick Lane, Silver Spring, MD 20910; (301) 565-6704; amhiker@aol.com.

American Mountain Guides Association, same address as American Alpine Club, above; (303) 271-0984.

Appalachian Mountain Club, 5 Joy Street, Boston, MA 02108; (617) 523-0636.

Appalachian Mountain Club Huts (AMC Reservations), P.O. Box 298, Gorham, NH 03581; (603) 466-2727.

Sierra Club, 85 Second Street, Second Floor, San Francisco, CA 94105; (415) 977-5500.

Schools

Colorado Outward Bound School, 945 Pennsylvania
  Street, Denver, CO 80203; (800) 477-2627.
National Outdoor Leadership School, P.O. Box AA,
  288 Main Street, Lander, WY 82520; (307) 332-
  6973.
Contact the American Mountain Guides Association,
p. 52, for a complete listing of their members in your area.

Other Resources

See Appendix B for more outdoor resources.

*"Take nothing for granted. Not one blessed, cool mountain day, or one
hellish, desert day, or one sweaty, stinky, hiking companion. It is all a gift."*

—Cindy Ross, *Journey on the Crest*

Chapter 3

SEA KAYAKING—*One with the Sea*

"The kayak . . . represents a means of man becoming at one with the rhythms of the sea; and as a means of transportation, it represents a singular image of freedom."

—David W. Zimmerly in *Qajaq: Kayaks of Siberia and Alaska*

SPORT FILE

Couch potato quotient: 2 (couch to coastal kayaker requires moderate fitness)

Coordination factor: 2 (pretty intuitive)

White-knuckle rating: 3 (if only for the slight shark potential)

Harmony with the Sea

Probably no other outdoor pursuit can exceed the breadth of experience available in sea kayaking. In a sea kayak you can glide silently across a lake at sunset, or potter about a harbor watching seals and seagulls. The next day you can load up the same boat and head out on a multiweek expedition along the Alaskan coast, through the fjords of Chile and Argentina, or around Great Britain—or Australia. Office workers in seaside towns commute in sea kayaks; others have crossed oceans in them. Grade-school children paddle sea kayaks, as do octogenarians. Paraplegic kayakers have participated in major expeditions. You can learn the basics of sea kayaking in a few hours, then spend years refining your technique and expanding your horizons.

No other craft is as intimate with the water. Experienced kayakers can play in conditions that send powerboats running for cover. Yet, with its shallow draft, a kayak can explore estuaries and tidal flats, and its responsiveness allows pinpoint maneuvering among rocks and reefs. And this union with the sea is uninterrupted by the smell and noise of internal combustion, or the constant attention that a sailboat demands.

Some people never carry more than lunch in their kayaks, but most models are capable of carrying 200 or more pounds of gear. Even a fully loaded kayak glides through the water with a minimum of effort, and at the end of the day you can relax in the comfort of a well-equipped camp. In fact, with a single boat, you can vary your activities immensely:

- Daytripping
- Surfing/playing
- Touring
- Extended expeditions

Sea kayaking is a thrifty sport. If you demand the best, you can spend thousands on a new, high-tech Kevlar kayak and carbon-fiber paddles; however, a few hundred dollars can put you on the water in a solid used kayak. And whatever you invest, kayaking gear is very durable: many 15- and 20-year-old boats are still afloat.

What bad things can you say about a sport that is easy to learn, is inexpensive to invest in, is environ-

FIRST TIME OUT

Sea kayaking is an intensely experiential sport. The perspective of a coastline gliding by just yards away, of dolphins or seals playing within paddle reach, of open sky and distant islands, is so overwhelming that distance becomes unimportant. Still, to properly plan an outing, whether daytrip or weeklong tour, you need to have some idea of how much water you can cover.

- The sea kayak is so efficient that even a first paddle can cover several miles. In fact, you should keep a few things in mind when just starting out on open water. If your destination takes you downwind, or if you're helped along by a tidal current, remember that the return trip will be *much* harder. Try to make the return trip the downwind leg, or time the tide to ride the current back as well.
- Round-trip afternoon paddles of 4 or 5 miles are usually no problem for a novice in calm water. With experience, you'll be able to cover 10 to 15 miles a day with ease in the right conditions—even with a loaded boat. If you are exceptionally fit, 25- to 35-mile days are within reach. And veteran paddlers have recorded days of 50 and even 75 miles, usually because conditions demanded it. Several years ago, two experienced kayakers who were circumnavigating Iceland found themselves off an exposed shore in conditions too rough to land. They simply had to continue paddling into the evening and through the night, while icy breakers pounded the shore. By the time they fought their way to a harbor, they had been paddling for 22 hours—and had covered 106 miles.
- Don't try this at home.

mentally friendly, has unlimited possibilities for adventure, and will keep you in shape to boot?

What You'll Need

It takes exactly four items to get started in sea kayaking: a boat, a paddle, a spray skirt, and a life jacket. Although there are many more accessories you can add—and some you definitely should—with those four basics you'll have everything you need to learn the techniques and experience the freedom of the sport.

The Boat

When most people think of kayaking, they picture helmeted figures in tiny craft bouncing down whitewater rivers, continuously capsizing and rolling back up. We've forgotten that the sea kayak was the original kayak. For millennia, the Inuit tribes of the Arctic regions hunted and explored in kayaks fashioned from wood or bone and covered with the skins of marine mammals. Our modern permutations may be made from space-age materials, but if you took one back in time an early Inuit hunter would have no trouble recognizing it.

Fifteen or so years ago, when the modern boom in sea kayaking was in its infancy, choosing a boat was easy—there were only about a dozen models from which to select. As the sport has grown, so have the choices. Not only are many new companies manufacturing sea kayaks, but they are designing ever more-specialized models. There are short, broad daytrippers; long, stiletto-like performance boats; and full-on expedition kayaks. You can choose a traditional kayak with a cockpit or an open sit-on-top boat. Plus you can pick from a variety of materials, from plastic to fiberglass to Kevlar, as well as frame and fabric folding boats. So how do you narrow all that down to one kayak?

Unless you have really specific goals in mind, it's best to start with an all-around sea kayak. You want a boat that will be friendly to learn in but responsive to your increasing skills. It should be handy enough to take out for daytrips, but able to swallow a couple hundred pounds of gear for when the wanderlust strikes. It should combine good straight-line stability with decent maneuverability—plus a fair turn of speed. Finally, it must fit you well enough to become an extension of your body. Fortunately, there are many boats that fill all these requirements handily.

Types of Kayak

Sit-in or sit-on-top? The traditional kayak has a fairly deep hull and a cockpit you sit in, with a sprayskirt that fastens around your torso and the cockpit rim to keep out spray and splash. A more recent design is the aptly named sit-on-top kayak. This type of boat has a shallow hull, with an open cockpit and a molded-in seat with channels to drain the water that inevitably gets in.

THE ESSENTIALS—A SEA KAYAKING START-UP KIT
- Boat ($1,300–$4,000)
- Paddle ($130–$320) (need two)
- PFD ($40–$75)
- Spray skirt ($50–$125)

Minimum cost essential sea kayaking outfit: $1,650*

ADD-ONS FOR DAYTRIPS
- Hat
- Sunscreen
- Water bottles
- First aid kit
- Paddle float for self-rescue
- Bilge pump
- Dry bags
- Deck bag
- Wet suit
- Deck compass and charts
- VHF radio and/or weather radio

*The essentials list above is intended to give you an idea of minimum start-up costs, from scratch, for moderate entry into a sport using new equipment. Other options include borrowing gear from friends or renting from retailers, YMCAs, or church activity clubs, as well as buying used gear—see Appendix A.

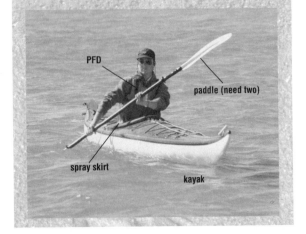

PFD

paddle (need two)

spray skirt

kayak

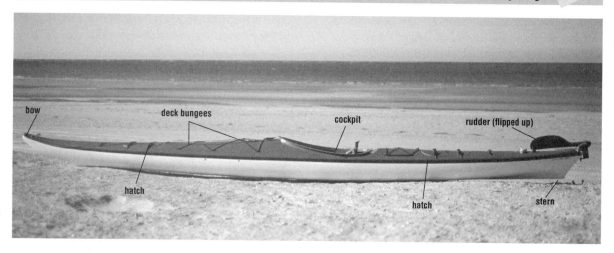

bow

deck bungees

cockpit

rudder (flipped up)

hatch

hatch

stern

ONE SEAT OR TWO?

If you're going to be paddling with a partner, don't underestimate the seriousness of deciding on taking one boat or two. Some couples can paddle a double kayak in complete harmony; others—even though they get along perfectly on shore—become sniping, whining, mutinous polecats if stuck in the same boat. The only way to be sure which type you are is to try a double first. You might be surprised.

Double kayaks have several advantages. They are significantly faster than singles, and less expensive than two singles. They are usually quite stable, and thus confidence-inspiring for novices. On the other hand, a double usually hasn't the gear capacity of two singles, and one 90-pound boat is often harder to deal with than two 60-pound boats.

If you do decide on a double, pay attention to the distance between the cockpits. On most doubles under 20 feet in length, the cockpits are close enough that the occupants need to synchronize their paddling to avoid whacking the blades together. On longer doubles, especially those with an extra cargo compartment between the cockpits, no synchronizing is needed. The extra compartment also provides valuable additional flotation.

The sit-on-top kayak is extremely user-friendly. Since you sit right out in the open, there is no spray skirt to worry about. If you fall out of the boat you can just climb back on—no Eskimo rolls or fancy rescue techniques are necessary. This feature makes sit-on-tops great for swimming, snorkeling, or even scuba diving (some models have attachment points designed to hold a scuba tank).

On the other hand, you are always fully exposed to wind and water in this type of craft. In any but the calmest conditions, you will be constantly wet paddling a sit-on-top. And although many models have watertight storage compartments, the volume doesn't approach that available in a traditional kayak—so touring is difficult. As a result, sit-on-tops are mostly used for casual daytripping, although a few radical models have been designed for extreme paddling in surf.

People who choose to invest a bit more effort during the learning stage will benefit from the outstanding versatility of the traditional sea kayak. With a spray skirt protecting your lower half, the traditional kayak offers a dry ride even in choppy conditions (of course, in warm, calm weather you can leave the skirt off and splash as

Double kayaks are faster and a little more stable than singles, but they require good communication between paddling partners.

much as you like). Storage capacity is excellent, and sea-worthiness is unbeatable. Also, traditional kayaks come in a wide variety of sizes and hull designs, so you can match the boat precisely to your needs and be sure of a proper fit.

Construction Materials

The next big decision you'll face is what material your kayak should be made from. This might largely be determined by your budget.

Plastic. Plastic sea kayaks—that is, those made from rotomolded polyethylene—are the cheapest: new, expedition-equipped examples (with rudder, front and rear bulkheads, and deck bungees) start at around $1,300. Yet in many ways plastic kayaks are the toughest of all. You can bounce them off rocks with apparent impunity, and there is no brittle gelcoat to worry about scratching. However, continued abuse will roughen and fray the plastic under the waterline, substantially increasing drag and thus slowing the boat. Polyethylene is also subject to ultraviolet deterioration. And a plastic boat's hull can take a crooked "set" if stored improperly or cinched down too tightly on a roof rack, which will warp the hull and adversely affect the handling until the material slowly recovers its proper shape. That said, a plastic boat will go anywhere any other sea kayak can, so if your budget so dictates, don't hesitate to choose one.

RECYCLABLE BOATS

Two types of polyethylene are used in rotomolded kayaks: linear and crosslinked. Crosslinked polyethylene is theoretically a bit more impact-resistant and durable. But its structure means that it cannot be remolded, so it cannot be recycled, and patching is extremely difficult. Linear polyethylene kayaks can be recycled, and hot patching—that is, heating the material to weld a new piece of plastic in—is a bit more practical.

Fiberglass. Fiberglass is the material of choice for most sea kayaks, and with good reason. Fiberglass is light, very strong, and extremely attractive. Field repairs are easily made with duct tape or a fiberglass patch kit. The useable lifespan of fiberglass is virtually unlimited, and even the gelcoat that gives fiberglass boats their smooth finish and color is easily protected with automotive-type wax. Dragging a fiberglass boat over rocks will scratch the gelcoat but affect overall performance very little (still, it's a practice to avoid when possible).

Fiberglass kayaks are more expensive than plastic models—fully equipped examples start at about $2,000—but the investment is worth it. If you can't decide between the two, keep this in mind: many people start out with plastic kayaks and then move up to fiberglass, but hardly anyone buys a fiberglass boat and later trades for plastic.

Kevlar. Kevlar is lighter and stronger than fiberglass, and even more expensive. Manufacturers that offer both materials typically charge a $400–$500 premium for Kevlar. The weight savings is not spectacular—a 55-pound fiberglass boat might weigh 47 or 48 pounds in Kevlar—and that savings diminishes proportionally once the boat is loaded. The difference is most noticeable when you carry the kayak to the beach or load and unload it from a roof rack. If you frequently kayak alone or are small in stature, the savings might be worth the cost. Of course, if you're a confirmed tech-weenie the choice will be easy.

Polycarbonate alloy. Recently, a new material for sea kayaks has been introduced. Eddyline Kayaks was the first to formulate a polycarbonate (a type of plastic) alloy that can be molded into hulls and decks. This new material is said to be stiffer, lighter, and more abrasion-resistant than polyethylene, and it has the look of very well-finished fiberglass. The cost of a polycarbonate alloy sea kayak slots neatly in between that of polyethylene and fiberglass kayaks. If early indications hold true, polycarbonate has a promising future as an affordable but good-looking and durable material for sea kayaks. It's also recyclable.

Fabric-and-frame. If your sea kayaking plans include far-flung destinations such as the coast of Chile or the Scottish lochs, consider a folding kayak. These amazing boats fit into one or two duffels and can be checked on airlines as excess baggage, then assembled into a seaworthy craft in about 20 minutes.

Folding kayaks are more complex than hard-shell boats, and the individual frame pieces are more prone to breakage. Since folders lack watertight storage compartments, much more attention must be given to flotation and gear protection (any water that gets in the cockpit can slosh through the whole boat). Folding boats tend to be a bit slower than the equivalent hard-shell design. And the best expedition-ready folding kayaks *start* at around $3,500. Fortunately, they are very durable if cared for properly—many 20-year-old folding boats are still being paddled. And with a folding kayak your choice of destinations is limited only by your imagination.

There are two approaches to folding-kayak construction: the traditional *wood frame, canvas deck* designs and the high-tech *aluminum frame, cordura deck* models. Actually, both are perfectly functional— it's more a question of esthetics and hull design than performance. The aluminum and nylon designs tend to be slightly lighter for their volume, but they lack the rich warmth of varnished wood.

Folding kayaks, which travel as excess baggage and can be assembled from bag-to-kayak in about 20 minutes, offer unlimited adventures worldwide.

✓**KAYAK MATERIALS PROS-AND-CONS CHECKLIST**

Plastic (rotomolded polyethylene)
 Pros: inexpensive, resistant to abuse
 Cons: ultraviolet deterioration, flex, abrasion reduces speed
Fiberglass (fiber-reinforced plastic or FRP)
 Pros: strong, light, attractive, durable, repairable
 Cons: gelcoat scratches easily, higher price
Kevlar
 Pros: very light and strong
 Cons: high price, harder to repair
Polycarbonate Alloy
 Pros: inexpensive, but stiff and abrasion-resistant
 Cons: unproved durability
Fabric-and-Frame
 Pros: go anywhere, store anywhere
 Cons: very high price, complex frame

Boat Design and Dimensions

So far, the choices you've made could be decided from your living room. Now it's time to go shopping.

If at all possible, you should visit a waterfront sea kayaking shop that offers boats you can paddle on-site. Nothing can replace actually paddling a kayak for getting a feel for how it fits and responds. Even if you are an utter novice, you'll be able to tell if the seat is comfortable, if the boat feels tippy, or if the cockpit is too wide. Consider taking a basic sea kayaking class before you shop; just a day or two of instruction will give you a lot of insight as to how the boat should feel.

If you can't paddle the boat, at least sit in it on the showroom floor for as long as possible. Pay attention to how the seat fits your bottom and how the backrest supports your back. If you start to squirm within 10 minutes, try another boat—remember, it won't get *more* comfortable after a three-hour paddle. At least one manufacturer has introduced a nylon seat cover into which different thicknesses of foam can be placed on the back and sides, to custom-fit the seat. One thing to keep in mind: it's not a good idea to pad the bottom of the seat more than minimally. Raising the center of gravity on a kayak by even an inch will affect its balance.

These days, most sea kayaks come equipped with foot-operated rudders. You should be able to brace your knees against the underside of the deck while working the pedals with your feet, and the pedals should slide easily.

◆ **EXPERT TIP: PURCHASING A SEA KAYAK**
Some features to look for when shopping for a kayak:

◆ *Front and rear bulkheads.* These watertight partitions isolate the cockpit from the front and rear sections of the boat, creating compartments that provide both storage and flotation in the event of a capsize. In the past, many sea kayaks came with rear bulkheads only, so ensuring adequate flotation in the bow was difficult. This feature doesn't apply to folding kayaks, which have no bulkheads at all.

◆ *Well-secured hatches.* The hatches protect the integrity of the storage compartments. They should strap down tightly—bungees won't hack it.

◆ *Flip-over rudder.* Although not vital, a rudder that flips over and stores on the rear deck when not in use is less prone to catching wind or waves—or shins.

◆ *Deck compass.* Even if you only plan on daytrips, a compass is handy. For touring it is indispensable.

So—what size boat do you need? The typical sea kayak—one that will fit into our "all-around" category—will be between 15 and 18 feet long and 22 and 25 inches in width, or *beam* in nautical terms. Boats of this length will be handy enough for short trips but big enough for longer ones. A kayak less than 22 inches wide will likely be pretty tippy for a first boat; much wider than 25 inches is getting bargelike.

The boat's beam is one of the most important parts of fit. Beginners tend to worry about capsizing, and there's no doubt that a wider boat is generally more resistant to tipping over—but only in calm or moderately choppy conditions. When the waves start kicking up, you need to be able to lean the boat into them with

body English, and a boat that is too wide for you will be hard to lean. Also, a too-wide kayak is like a multihull sailboat: it's stable in small stuff, but if a big wave ever knocks it over, it's just as stable *upside down.* For this reason, you should concentrate on fit when shopping for a sea kayak, not some pre-determined measurement.

WILL IT TIP OVER?
Kayakers talk about two kinds of stability—initial and final. Initial stability refers to the amount of rocking motion you experience sitting in the boat, or the ease with which you can rock the boat by swinging your hips. This characteristic is determined by the cross-sectional shape of the hull—a rounded hull rocks more, a flattened one less. Most beginners feel more comfortable in a boat with a lot of initial stability; however, it's actually better to put up with some rocking, since the boat will be more responsive to your movements.

Final stability is the big one—it occurs when you lean and lean, and suddenly you're watching fish instead of birds. It's not necessarily connected to initial stability; a kayak can have a lot of both, a little of both, or any combination. The best hulls will respond to your body English but resist tipping more and more the farther you lean in either direction. If you can practice with a helper in a pool or lake you can determine where the "point of no return" is on your boat. Most sea kayaks are very forgiving—you can lean a lot farther than you think before the boat goes over. And once you learn some basic boat-handling skills, you'll be able to extend that limit even more.

Beginners are often surprised at how far you can lean in a kayak before it tips over.

As a *very* general rule, consider the following rough guidelines:

- A person 150 pounds or over should feel comfortable in a kayak with a 23- or 24-inch beam.
- If you are under 5'5", or weigh less than 150 pounds, you might feel just as stable with a 22- to 23-inch beam.

Of course, nothing is hard-and-fast, and hopefully you will be able to compare several boats.

Fashion Considerations

Some people are happy with whatever color boat happens to be in stock. To others the selection of just the right shade might be the most important choice they face. The kayaking market caters to the latter personality with a rainbow of colors, plus fades, spatter jobs, metal-flake, and even clearcoats that let Kevlar fabric show through.

For safety's sake, consider a bright-colored boat. Yellow and red decks show up well against water, while it's surprising how greens and blues and teals disappear from even a short distance away.

If you're buying a fiberglass or Kevlar kayak, stick with a white or off-white hull (the underside). Some manufacturers like to mold the hull the same color as the deck, but scratches in colored hulls are much more obvious, and harder to repair.

Since rotomolded boats are usually one color top and bottom, you can't put a white hull with a red deck. However, since the color is molded into the plastic, hull scratches aren't as obvious. One thing to keep in mind: if you paddle in warm weather, a white plastic boat, while seemingly a good choice, actually lets in *more* heat, since the material is so translucent. You'll be cooler in a colored boat.

A final tip after you purchase you sea kayak: check with your home-state transportation department for rules on registering personal watercraft. Many states require that you register all boats over a certain length, whether they have motors or not. At least you won't have to worry about a smog test.

The Paddle

Next to the kayak, the paddle is by far your most important piece of equipment. That might sound trite—obviously you won't get far without a paddle—but keep in mind that the paddle also represents weight you must

---

> ### STORAGE TIPS
> Annie Getchell, outdoor gear expert and author of *The Essential Outdoor Gear Manual,* offers these hints for properly storing your kayak:
> - If you use a rack, support the kayak directly beneath the bulkheads.
> - Hanging from grab loops is okay, but with plastic boats it tends to increase hull rocker (the curve of the boat from bow to stern) over time.
> - Stand plastic kayaks on end, bow on the ground. This is how manufacturers warehouse new boats, and so should you—if you have the headroom. If not, rack the boat on edge, where sharper hull curves support the weight of a plastic hull with negligible deformation.
> - Store with hatch covers off. This prevents your kayak from becoming a giant petri dish for mildew inside the hull.

constantly lift and swing. As with the boots on a hiker's feet, every ounce makes a difference. Yet the paddle is subjected to considerable force when you lean on it to brace or power through a wave. So stay away from the aluminum shaft/plastic-bladed cheapies. You'll be glad you invested wisely.

Construction Materials

Fiberglass. Hand-laid fiberglass paddles are the standard for quality, strength, and lightness in sea kayak paddles. A good two-piece fiberglass paddle will usually weigh between 33 and 38 ounces and will be comfortable to use all day. Prices start at around $160. If you don't mind dealing with a paddle that's always 7 feet long, you can save money and a little weight by ordering a one-piece model. But you'll have to decide in advance whether or not you want to paddle with feathered blades (see sidebar on feathered vs. unfeathered blades, p. 62).

Graphite. Graphite is stiffer than fiberglass, so the paddle manufacturer can use less of it to achieve the same rigidity. Those thin blades, however, will not be as rugged as fiberglass, so pushing off rocks and planting the paddle upright in the sand should be avoided. But a 25- or 26-ounce paddle feels like a magic wand, and over the course of a long day can really make a difference. If the thought of a $300 paddle makes you wince, consider ordering graphite blades on a fiberglass shaft. This combination saves weight at the ends of the paddle ("swing weight"), where it's most important—and also saves about $50.

FEATHERED OR UNFEATHERED?

It is much easier to learn to kayak with an unfeathered paddle. As you can see from the photograph, the blades of an unfeathered paddle are in line with each other, which makes it easy to plant each blade correctly in the water when you've got a lot of other things to think about.

The blades of a feathered paddle are at an angle to each other, usually close to 90 degrees. The biggest advantage to this setup is that the blade that is out of the water is parallel to the surface, so it is less affected by wind (a paddle blade, particularly a broad one, makes an annoyingly effective sail at times). The disadvantages are that you have to remember the attitude of each blade—although that will become automatic in time—and that you have to rotate one wrist with each stroke to orient the paddle properly, which can lead to tendinitis. Also, if a feathered paddle gets away from you in a wind, it can "helicopter," spinning through the air for an amazing distance before plunging into the sea.

Most two-piece paddles can be assembled either way, so you can start with an unfeathered paddle and experiment later.

Wood. Quality laminated-wood paddles start at around $130, making them a good choice for the budget-conscious. At 38 to 40 ounces, weight is reasonable, too. Many companies offer exotic laminations or beautiful inlays of marine animals on the blades; these, of course, cost more. A good feature to look for on a wood paddle is a solid fiberglass or fiberglass-reinforced blade tip. This is where most abrasion occurs, and if water gets into the grain of a wood paddle, rot can weaken or ruin it.

Shape and Sizing

Width. Blade width is an important variable on a sea kayak paddle. A wide blade—7–8 inches—offers more surface area, and thus more power and firmer bracing. But it can be tiring to use all day, and the risk of tendinitis and muscle strain is increased. A narrow, 4½- to 5-inch blade is easier on your arms and won't catch the wind as much when conditions deteriorate. Some paddles split the difference with 6- or 6½-inch blades.

Shape. Most paddles are made with asymmetrical blades: the bottom edge of the blade curves toward the tip more gradually than the top edge does. This slightly more efficient design supposedly reduces "flutter," the tendency of the blade to wobble as it is pulled through the water.

Length. The overall length of the paddle, while it makes a difference, is not critical for most people. If you're between 5'6" and 6', a 240-centimeter paddle should suit. If you're big, try a 250 or even 260. If you're small in stature or paddling a narrow boat, you might like a 220 or 230. A too-long paddle can sometimes strain tendons and joints.

A Word on Spare Paddles

Always—*always*—carry a spare paddle. If you're on a major expedition and your only paddle breaks or is lost in a storm, you will be in serious danger. If, on the other hand, you're out for a lunchtime jaunt in a crowded harbor and you have to dogpaddle your kayak to shore in front of three tour boats and the Hobie sailing club, you'll probably *wish* you were alone in a storm.

It's tempting to economize on the spare paddle. However, all kidding aside, if you do lose your main paddle it's likely to happen in bad conditions—exactly when you don't want to rely on inferior equipment. So grit your teeth and buy two paddles of good quality. Some kayakers buy a narrow-bladed paddle for the main and a wide one for the spare. That way they can switch as conditions or mood warrants.

PFD

The PFD (personal flotation device) is another item you should never leave shore without. Like "just driving to the store" without a seatbelt, "just paddling around the harbor" without wearing a life jacket is an invitation to a freakish accident.

You can get by with an inexpensive, slab-sided water-skiers' PFD, but you'll be much more comfortable with a model designed specifically for sea kayaking. These incorporate sewn-in channels of foam for greater flexibility, often have a flip-up bottom to prevent interference with the spray skirt, and have large arm holes for freedom of movement. Many include pockets to hold emergency signal flares. Buy as bright a color as you can stand; red or yellow are probably the best for visibility. (For a discussion of the U.S. PFD rating system, see Chapter 4, p. 91.)

Some paddlers use inflatable PFDs, with a carbon dioxide cartridge triggered by a pull ring. These are very comfortable to wear, but if you capsize into very cold water, or hit your head going under, you could become disoriented, or even unconscious, and be unable to trigger the inflator. Also, any number of leaks can develop in an inflatable life jacket without your knowledge, even if you check it regularly. So most paddlers stick with the foolproof, if bulky, foam PFD. (For tips on PFD care, see Chapter 5, p. 119.)

Spray Skirt

The spray skirt provides both safety and comfort. It prevents water—whether drips from the paddle or breaking waves—from getting into the cockpit. The deck of the spray skirt has an elastic edge that fits snugly over the rim of the boat's cockpit. The chest tube of the skirt fits around your torso, held up either by elastic or by shoul-

Put on your spray skirt and make strap and chest-tube adjustments before climbing into the boat. Once in the boat, fit the skirt to the cockpit rim (starting at the back is usually easier).

der straps, or a combination of both. At the front of the spray skirt is a large release loop, sometimes called the rip cord, that allows you to quickly yank the skirt free of the cockpit in the event of a capsize.

The least expensive spray skirts are made from coated nylon and work just fine for most uses. The deck of a nylon skirt is prone to sagging, however, which often results in pools of water and a slow, steady drip into your lap. Other spray skirts are made from neoprene, which stays taut but can be somewhat confining around the chest. All-neoprene skirts are good for rough water and cold conditions, since they provide some insulation.

The best all-around touring skirts combine a taut neoprene deck with a comfortable nylon chest tube. They are, of course, more expensive, but you get the best of both materials.

Many spray skirts have a pocket sewn into the chest tube, where you can keep sunscreen and other incidentals. The skirt will be made to fit your boat's cockpit rim size; if you order from a custom maker, you can specify the height of the chest tube as well, ensuring a perfect fit—in addition to a palette of colors.

SPRAY SKIRT CARE AND REPAIR

No matter what type of spray skirt you opt for—nylon or neoprene—it will get blasted by sun and salt, and must be treated like the delicate and critical garment it is. Regular rinsing with fresh water is essential.

Suspenders on a nylon skirt are not a fashion statement—they serve to tension the fabric so water won't puddle up and leak through the seams. Seamsealing may be necessary. Treat the coated nylon as you would a tent or shell garment to maintain water-repellency.

Because neoprene is also one of the materials most quickly damaged by UV, try to minimize the amount of exposure time. Don't use your skirt as a travel or storage cover—invest in a nylon fabric cockpit cover.

—from *The Essential Outdoor Gear Manual,* by Annie Getchell (Ragged Mountain Press, 1996)

Other Necessities and Niceties
Bilge Pump
Rest assured—water *will* get into your cockpit now and then (the inside of a boat is often called a *bilge*). It might just be a few teaspoons, but a rough crossing could leave several gallons sloshing back and forth. Whatever, you need a way to get it out.

Some sea kayaks, especially British designs, come equipped with built-in bilge pumps, operated by a hand lever either just behind the cockpit or right in front of it. The advantage to a built-in pump is that it's always there, ready to work, and you only need one hand to operate it.

You can also buy inexpensive, portable, plastic pumps that resemble a piece of water pipe with a spout and a T-handle sticking out of one end. These work best two-handed—not a problem if you're on the beach but difficult when you're bouncing around offshore (the option is to hold it between your legs and pump with one hand). The advantage is that portable pumps can be used in different boats, and are also usable if water gets into the cargo compartments.

An alternative is to use a simple plastic drink pitcher with a handle to scoop the water out. The old sailor's axiom, "The best bilge pump is a scared human with a bucket," is true—you can remove impressive amounts of water in a short time. The downside when you're afloat is that you have to remove the spray skirt to use the pitcher; if it's rough you're likely to find yourself working at a deficit.

Whatever system you choose, you should also keep a large sponge in the boat to soak up the last dregs.

Dry Bags and Boxes
"Watertight compartments." "Leakproof hatches." "Waterproof bulkheads." These are all optimistic terms—water can find its way into the storage areas of even the best kayaks. So it's always advisable to protect your gear further by storing it in watertight containers.

Dry bags. Dry bags not only keep your stuff safe, they provide backup flotation if a hatch cover or bulkhead comes loose. But they are subject to a lot of abuse—abrasion against the inside of the hull, stress from cramming them through hatches, and so on. So inspect them frequently. Most pinholes can be repaired with seam sealer. Don't buy dry bags in large sizes, because they are harder to pack into the confines of a

kayak's ends; a mixture of medium and small bags works better. Since bags come in many colors, you can code them for easy identification of the contents—yellow for clothes, blue for food, red for sleeping accessories, and so on. Transparent bags make organizing even easier, but the clear material is not as durable as coated nylon or PVC.

Dry boxes. Several companies make small dry boxes (roughly the size of a big bathroom tissue box). These are very handy for first aid kits, tools, spare parts, and incidentals such as notebooks, spare batteries, and flashlights.

Deck Bags
Although it is inadvisable to store gear on deck—it adds windage, throws spray, and could come loose in rough conditions—there are always a few small things you want handy. These could include a water bottle, a map, snacks, sunscreen, a camera, and binoculars. You can use a regular dry bag for these and stow it under the bungees on the deck in front of the cockpit, but a proper deck bag does a better job. It straps down more securely, and has a zipper for easy access.

Most deck bags, while made from coated nylon, are not meant to be completely waterproof. However, since the gear inside is protected from the worst of the elements, you can often get away with a simple zip-top bag to protect a camera or binoculars. A couple of deck bags on the market go the whole way, with a waterproof, dry-suit-type zipper. These are very expensive, but if you are a serious photographer who needs instant access to expensive and moisture-sensitive camera gear, they are worth the price.

Safety Gear
Never paddle without a few essential safety items—they're cheap, take up little room, add almost no weight, and could save your life.

Whistle. The most basic item is a loud whistle, to alert fellow kayakers to trouble—either your own or theirs. A plastic whistle costs a couple of dollars and can be tied with a short cord to your life jacket, where it is instantly accessible. Try it, though, and you'll be surprised at how short the range is—it's strictly for alerting nearby companions.

Flares. Pocket flares, such as the Skyblazer type, grab attention much better for real emergencies. These little handheld, waterproof cylinders contain a small rocket flare that reaches an altitude of 150 feet or so, then goes off with a bang. Two or three fit easily into the pocket of most PFDs, and they should stay there permanently. For situations in which you might need to signal planes or powerboats, heavier ordnance is called for. Smoke flares produce a cloud of bright orange or red smoke and burn for several minutes. Parachute flares are the really big artillery: they send a rocket-powered flare several hundred feet into the air, where it deploys a parachute and floats slowly back to earth. At night such a device can be seen for miles.

Mirror. More humble, but amazingly effective if used properly, is a signal mirror. Pilots have reported seeing the flash from a signal mirror from as far as 20 miles away in broad daylight (which, of course, is the only time they're useful). The easiest ones to use are the kind with an aiming hole through the center. Read the directions and practice with the mirror in your front yard; you can annoy the neighbors to no end.

Radio. Many sea kayakers carry a handheld, marine VHF radio, with which they can directly summon assistance. Radios are useful as long as you are in an area with VHF traffic. Keep in mind that the range of VHF is fairly short—20 miles is a practical maximum.

Additional items you will want to include with your kayaking outfit are a first aid kit, charts if you are unfa-

Assorted safety equipment includes a VHF radio (left), a whistle (on zipper pull), flares, and an unbreakable signal mirror (right).

> ◆ **EXPERT TIP: A KAYAKER'S TOOL-AND-SPARES KIT**
>
> Sea kayaking equipment is blessedly simple. The most complex components on the kayak—in fact, probably the only moving parts—are the rudder and associated foot pedals. So a small tool kit, properly equipped, should be sufficient to handle any need:
> - ◆ Duct tape
> - ◆ Screwdriver with multiple tips
> - ◆ Small adjustable wrench
> - ◆ Small Channelock pliers, or multi-tool
> - ◆ Wire cutters (some multi-tools have this feature)
> - ◆ Spare rudder cables and fittings
> - ◆ All-purpose glue/seam sealer, such as SeamGrip
> - ◆ 50 feet of nylon cord
> - ◆ Spare buckles/fittings for hatches

miliar with the area, and, if you are daytripping, a "possibles" bag. For first aid kit recommendations, see Chapter 13; for a description of a possibles kit, see p. 12. Sea kayak charts and navigation are covered beginning on p. 77.

Clothing

Sea Kayaker magazine frequently publishes accounts of kayaking accidents. Some of these mishaps result in nothing more than an embarrassed paddler; some, though, have much more tragic results. By printing such stories, the magazine keeps its readers alert to the causes—and preventions—of potentially disastrous situations. (*Sea Kayaker's Deep Trouble*, published by Ragged Mountain Press in 1997, is a collection of these accounts and analyses.)

Review of these accidents makes it clear that most resulted from one or two very simple failures on the part of the kayaker: paddling without a life jacket, or paddling without proper clothing. The dangers of going without a life jacket are obvious, but few people realize how important clothing is to safe kayaking.

It's easy to stay out of trouble if you just remember a simple rule: *dress for the water temperature.* (River runners—see Chapter 5—follow the "120-degree rule:" If the combined air and water temperatures equal less than 120 degrees F, don wet suits, dry suits, paddle jackets, and booties to stay warm. You can always peel off layers during the trip if you get *too* warm.)

Water conducts heat away from your body about 100 times faster than air. An air temperature of 60 degrees feels no more than chilly, but immersion in 60-degree water can result in hypothermia in a short time—and kayakers in northern coastal areas often paddle in 50- or even 40-degree water. Therefore, no matter what the air temperature is, you should dress as though you were going swimming. If you're in Baja in late summer and the water temperature is 80 degrees, that might mean shorts and a T-shirt. But in colder areas more specialized clothing is needed.

Outerwear and underwear. The minimum protection you need in cool water is some sort of synthetic underwear, such as Thermax or Capilene, with outerwear—waterproof or water-resistant jackets and pants—layered over that. If you submerge, the underwear alone will very slightly slow the loss of body heat to surrounding water, by retarding the circulation of the water close to your skin. Waterproof or water-resistant shells and pants with tight-sealing wrists and cuffs will further slow this circulation. The advantage to this wardrobe is that it is "normal" clothing that can be worn on shore and ventilated easily when the air temperature rises. For coastal trips and mild-to-brisk conditions, it works well.

Several manufacturers make jackets or anoraks specifically designed for sea kayaking, with good freedom of movement in the shoulders, big pockets, and good sealing around the wrists and hood. The pants that go with them have properly waterproofed seats to resist water pooled underneath.

For the Cold

Wet suits. For crossings or colder conditions, better insulation is provided by a wet suit—whether just a jacket, a farmer john (a one-piece body suit with tank-style shoulders and long or short legs), or a full suit (jacket and pants). As its name implies, a wet suit won't stop you from getting wet, but it traps next to your skin a layer of water that quickly warms and retains heat. A wet suit top will provide good protection for your vital core area in chilly water; a full suit is suitable for all but the coldest waters (below 40 or so degrees). A two-piece wet suit, consisting of a farmer john plus a jacket, is versatile paddling wear for most cold-water situations, since you can wear either or both as conditions dictate. Wet suits also come in different thicknesses. A 3-millimeter

suit is fine for cool water and allows good freedom of movement; a 5-millimeter is better for colder water. Tip: buy wetsuits made for kayakers, rather than scuba divers, for their greater range of motion.

Dry suits. The maximum protection you can wear in a kayak is a dry suit. Logically, the dry suit is designed to be completely waterproof, with latex seals at the neck, wrists, and ankles. An insulating layer of synthetic

In cold water conditions, safe paddlers will wear a farmer john wetsuit with full leg coverage, a synthetic fleece midlayer top, and a waterproof paddling jacket over everything.

underwear or fleece is worn under the suit for warmth. Properly insulated, a dry suit provides protection even in very cold water. However, a dry suit must be zealously guarded against even the smallest leaks, and the seals at the extremities can tear. Dry suits are, at best, difficult to get on and off, with their awkward waterproof zippers normally placed on the upper back. And they turn into effective saunas on a warm day, with no possibility of ventilation. Lastly, they are very expensive—the best Gore-Tex models (which allow some body moisture to escape) can run over $500. As such, they are most suited to serious expeditions or frequent paddles in icy water.

Extremity protection. Gloves are very important to the sea kayaker, since your hands are always out in the open and often wet. Thin neoprene gloves are good for chilly conditions; they combine insulation with dexterity. Thicker gloves can be worn when it's colder (it's a good idea to have a spare pair, since it's easy to lose a glove). An alternative is a synthetic fleece glove, with a Gore-Tex or coated nylon overglove for layering.

For really cold paddling, many kayakers use "pogies," which are neoprene mittens that attach to the paddle itself with hook-and-loop tape. You slide your hands into the pogie to grasp the paddle shaft. You can still wear gloves with pogies, doubling your protection.

Most of your body heat escapes through your head, so it makes sense to protect it well. A simple fleece headband might be enough to keep your forehead and ears warm when it's mild, but you'll want a full cap as well as a good hood on your jacket to button up when it starts to blow.

Cold-weather footwear can be approached from either of two directions. If you like keeping your feet dry, you can wear high rubber boots and thick socks, risking a soaking if you step in too deep or have to wet-exit. Otherwise, neoprene booties will keep you warm, if not dry.

Some Like It Hot

Kayaking in hot weather (and warm water) requires a different approach. Here your priority is protection from the sun. A broad-brimmed hat with a retaining cord is a good place to start. Long-sleeved shirts of lightweight cotton or fast-drying Supplex nylon stay cool while protecting your constantly exposed arms from sunburn. Since your legs are mostly covered by the boat, shorts are the way to go. Sport sandals are practically *de rigueur* for warm-weather paddling, although if you're going to be around rough rocks you might consider water shoes instead, with mesh uppers that protect your feet but drain water quickly.

Transporting Your Boat

Sea kayaks are probably the single most awkward piece of outdoor gear to move around. Fortunately, modern sport roof racks have kept pace with the demand for safe, sturdy carriers.

If you don't have far to drive to get your boat to the water, you can use an inexpensive type of rack which consists of shaped-foam blocks that strap to the roof of your vehicle. For longer distances, though, invest in a high-quality rack with proper kayak saddles. Watching a couple of $2,000 boats cartwheeling down the freeway in your rearview mirror would definitely make you regret scrimping. No matter what you use, it's a good idea

to back it up with a line tied from the bow of the boat to your front bumper (but don't overtighten—the flex between the car and boat could damage your boat).

There is also the matter of getting the kayak from your car to the water. If it's not far, you can carry it, especially if you're with a friend. For longer distances, several companies manufacture small two-wheeled carts that strap on the stern (rear) or under the cockpit of the boat, taking most of the weight on fat little tires. The cart then folds and can be carried inside the kayak or strapped on the rear deck.

(See Chapter 15 for further resources for transporting outdoor gear.)

Getting on the Water

The essence of sea kayaking technique is simplicity itself. You sit in the boat and pull your paddle through the water first on one side, then the other. Assuming your boat has a rudder, to go left you push with the left foot, to go right you push with the right foot. To stop, paddle backwards. That's it.

Well, okay—there are some nuances to consider. But the point is, basic paddling technique is a very natural action.

Although you can teach yourself, you should consider taking an introductory paddling course. The advantage is that an instructor can point out glitches in your technique or offer suggestions to improve your efficiency that otherwise might take you months to discover

Sea kayaks can be safely transported to your ocean destination on commercial roof racks for cars. Specially designed, rubber-padded saddles cradle and securely hold boats even at highway speeds.

by trial and error. An instructor will also ensure that in your enthusiasm, you don't neglect safety procedures.

Launching

Your first few outings should be in a very sheltered harbor or lake. You don't want to deal with waves pounding the shore for a while yet. Pick a beach with a very gentle, sandy slope into the water. That way you can rest your kayak so the bow is already floating and the stern is just about to. The rudder should be retracted at this point so it doesn't drag.

Step into the spray skirt and pull the straps over your shoulders, then put on your PFD (some people like the PFD under the spray skirt; it makes little difference). At this point you will resemble a rather goofy ballerina. Step into the cockpit, keeping your weight in the center of the boat. Slide down in until you're seated, then make sure the rudder pedals are adjusted properly—remember, you should be able to brace your knees under the deck while working the pedals (in a rudderless boat, you will still have foot braces to adjust).

Reaching behind you with both hands, hook the rear of the spray skirt over the rear edge of the cockpit, then work forward on both sides at once. When you get near the front, don't be surprised if the whole thing snaps off—that happens to everyone. Make sure the release loop is out before you hook the front of the skirt over the front edge of the cockpit. The spray skirt should fit tightly over the cockpit rim, so that a wave can't wrench it loose, but you should be able to yank it off with the loop without much effort. For your first paddles you should err toward easy removal, for peace of mind.

Now you're ready to launch. If your kayak has a "paddle park"—two cleats right in front of the cockpit behind the deck bungees—you can balance the paddle across the boat on the cleats, then pull a loop of bungee back over the paddle and hook it under the cleats to secure the paddle reasonably well. Otherwise, just balance it across your spray skirt.

Lean down and push the boat into the water with a hand on either side, as if you were a seal: push and scoot, push and scoot. Some paddlers push with the paddle on one side and a hand on the other; this technique is easier and puts the paddle in your hand already, but it is hard on the blade.

As soon as the kayak is afloat, take a couple of strokes to get it into deeper water, then drop the rudder. Now you have steerage and can point in the direction you want to go by pushing with either foot. It will seem touchy at first—the hardest part will be going straight—but you'll develop a feel for it.

Basic Strokes

Sea kayakers use a different paddle stroke than that used by whitewater paddlers—long and shallow with the paddle kept low, rather than short and deep with the paddle held high. For sea kayaking, you want to conserve energy, moving the boat as efficiently as possible. Try to take long strokes, planting the blade in the water ahead of the cockpit and pulling it well behind you. Keep the paddle low to the water; the blade in the air shouldn't rise above your head. This not only conserves energy, it helps control the paddle in wind. The blade in the water needn't dig too deep, as long as it's completely submerged. Continued practice will reward you with a smooth stroke that doesn't splash water around.

The paddle can be used to steer the boat as well—after all, many kayaks have no rudders, and rudder parts can break. It's a good idea to learn to maneuver with only the paddle even if you have a rudder.

If you paddle only on one side of the kayak, it will turn in the opposite direction. You can combine this action with a push on the rudder to turn more quickly than is possible with either rudder or paddle alone. Even more effective is to extend the paddle well out to one side and take an extra-long stroke, the paddle describing a wide arc through the water. This is called a sweep stroke. You can also steer with the paddle by trailing it in the water behind you, with the blade perpendicular to the water. The boat will turn to the side the paddle is on.

Landing

When you're ready to land, you can take one of two approaches on a flat, calm beach. One is to paddle as hard as you can straight for land (sandy beaches only). Often the boat will hit with enough momentum to slide partly out of the water, allowing you to step out stylishly with utterly dry feet. Of course, this technique is abrasive on the hull. Also, if the shore is too steep you can wind up with your bow in the sand, your stern in the water and the middle of the boat in the air. In this case the boat will instantly rotate and dump you unstylishly on your side.

A better way is to approach the beach slowly at an oblique angle, so when your bow makes contact you are nearly parallel with the shore and can step out on the dry, or at least shallow, side. Just before the boat contacts the shore, raise your rudder so it won't drag or bend. Brace the paddle across the cockpit, with one blade on land, to steady the boat.

You can also step out into shallow water while the boat is still completely afloat. But be careful to keep your weight completely centered. The best technique in less than a foot or so of water is to remain seated while you pull your legs out of the cockpit and straddle the boat. Lower your feet and raise your butt until you are standing, still astride the boat, then step over and pull the bow to shore.

Leaning, Bracing, and Other Techniques

If all you ever do is paddle around the duck pond in the park, you probably won't need any more instruction than you've just had. Sooner or later, though, the sea will call. To experience broader horizons, you'll need to learn more about handling your kayak.

Leaned Turns

At first, your natural tendency is to keep the kayak straight upright in the water. As you gain confidence, though, you can take advantage of the built-in characteristics of the hull to make the boat respond more quickly to your input.

When you turn while riding a bicycle or motorcycle, you lean into the turn: that is, you tip the bike the direction you want to go. The instinct is to do the same in a kayak—but in this case, instinct is wrong. The underwater shape of a kayak is such that it will turn more quickly if leaned *away* from the direction of the turn. If you want to turn right, rock your hips to lean the boat to its left. Note that your torso stays upright through this maneuver; only the boat leans, so you maintain your stability. Combining a push on the rudder with a lean and sweep will turn any kayak with alacrity—in fact, some kayaks will turn faster with the rudder *retracted,* using just a lean and sweep. The reason is that if a rudder is pushed too far over, it "stalls," assuming such a severe angle in the water that it acts more like a brake than a rudder.

Bracing in Waves and Wind

If you sit upright in your kayak, place one blade of your paddle flat on the surface of the water, and push down, you and the boat will tip in the opposite direction. Conversely, you can rest the blade on the water, then tip yourself and the boat *toward* it—right to the point of capsizing—and lean sharply on the paddle to right yourself. The water provides a surprising amount of resistance to the paddle blade. Bracing, as this technique is called, helps you keep your kayak upright in rough water or wind. When bracing is combined with a variation of the leaning technique described in the last section, the paddler can safely negotiate very choppy seas.

An empty kayak floating on the water, with waves coming at it from the side, will tip to follow the slope of each wave as it passes underneath the boat. As the crest of the wave passes, the boat tips the opposite way down the back of the wave. As the waves get steeper, the kayak tips more and more until, when the face is near vertical and the wave is breaking, the boat capsizes.

But a paddler sitting in the boat can use simple hip movements to lean the boat *into* the passing wave, an action that actually keeps the boat level with the horizon. It's a complex response to describe but will soon become automatic. You can practice in calm water by rocking the boat back and forth with your hips, while keeping your torso upright—like hula dancing sitting down.

In sculling, you move the paddle blade quickly back and forth across the water's surface in a figure eight so that it planes on the surface in both directions. With practice you can support a kayak at the verge of capsizing for as long as you like.

In small chop, leaning alone is enough to maintain balance. When waves coming from the side get bigger, the best way to maintain control is to lean into the wave and brace with your paddle on top of or even into the face of the wave. If you try to brace on the opposite side of the boat from where the wave is coming, the paddle will try to dive under the boat and pull you over with it. Remember to always lean and brace *into* the wave.

The process should become instinctive with enough experience. The only tendency to guard against at first is the involuntary *"AH! I'm about to get wet!"* reflex that can cause you to lean away from a big, sloppy wave.

Sometimes a quick brace isn't enough. If you lean on the paddle for more than a moment it will start to sink. The solution is *sculling.* You move the paddle blade quickly back and forth across the water's surface, rocking it in sort of a figure eight so that it planes on the surface in both directions. With practice you can support a kayak right at the verge of capsizing for as long as you like by sculling.

Sometimes a strong wind can be blowing even though there is very little wave action. When paddling across the wind, try to keep your profile as low as possible: lean forward and keep your paddle stroke even closer to the water than normal, to prevent the wind getting under the blade and flipping it over your head. You can lean sideways into the wind, as you would a wave, but don't lean too far—if a sudden lull comes . . . *kabloosh.*

Paddling directly into waves or wind is a slower but much safer method than paddling broadside to them. A wave coming straight at you will lift the bow, roll under you and then tip up the stern as it passes. Big waves can roll partly over the boat, slapping you on the chest with a big dollop—but that rarely causes problems. The biggest risk in very steep waves is that the bow will pitchpole; that is, the bow will bury itself in the trough of an oncoming wave and the whole boat will be driven underwater, often capsizing. Shift your weight backward when in the trough to help the boat ride up the face of the wave, then shift forward again immediately to ride over it.

Waves coming from behind act a little differently. Pitchpoling in following seas is uncommon, but you do need to be prepared for a broach, which occurs when a wave suddenly swings the kayak sideways 90 degrees, so you find yourself engulfed broadside to the wave. Some-times it is impossible to avoid a broach, such as when the wave is steep enough that it lifts your rudder blade completely out of the water. Broaches often occur when landing through surf. The proper response to a broach is to lean into the wave immediately and brace strongly. You will be carried along sideways in a welter of foam and noise. As the wave passes, you can quickly rudder and sweep to regain your course.

Landing or Launching in Rough Seas

For a beginning sea kayaker, the best way to land through surf is not to. If possible you should look for a harbor or protected cove. If there is no alternative, the best technique is to sit just outside the breaker zone and watch the waves, which usually come in series of several large waves followed by smaller ones. Once a large set has passed, paddle strongly toward shore on the back of the last big one. You want to balance right on the top of the wave, with its breaking front just off your bow. If you can paddle fast enough you can sometimes get all the way through the surf line before the wave outpaces you. If not, continue to paddle like mad as the next wave comes up behind you. As it overtakes you, your boat will often surf on the face, speeding toward land. If the kayak broaches, you might still be carried on the wave for a good distance, even all the way to shore. If the waves passes, turn toward shore again and paddle hard to catch the next wave. Once you have practiced surf landings they can become downright fun; in fact, kayak surfing is a sport all its own.

Beware of dumping surf. This happens when the beach is steep and waves only curl and break within the last few feet of shore, often with heavy, shocklike sounds. Dumping surf is very dangerous to land (or launch) through, and should be avoided at all costs.

Launching through surf is usually easier than landing in it. You should still count wave sets to find a slack period (much easier to do when the waves are coming at you), then paddle your boat straight out through the break, powering through each wave, first leaning back to let the bow ride partly up the wave, the leaning forward and punching through the top of the break. When launching, you can look for a spot in the surf where the waves are spilling smoothly into foam rather than curling and falling over. It's much harder to determine this when landing, since then you're only seeing the backs of the waves.

Falling Over

Many people sea kayak for years, even through major expeditions, without capsizing. Paying attention and using bracing and leaning skills will greatly reduce the chances of an unexpected spill. But there's always that sneaky wave waiting to come up and surprise you. Everyone who takes to the water in a kayak should be familiar with what to do if the horizon suddenly turns wrong side up.

Wet Exits

Capsizing a kayak is like jumping off a high dive. Once you've done it, you realize it's not so bad.

Of course, you wouldn't want to fall off a high dive by accident, so the best strategy is to step up and deliberately throw yourself over the edge. Likewise, a good way to prepare for an unexpected kayaking mishap is to deliberately practice capsizing. Once you've experienced being upside down in your kayak under controlled conditions, the fear of the unknown will recede. You'll then feel confident and relaxed when learning more-advanced procedures, from reentries to Eskimo rolls.

A wet exit from a capsized kayak involves releasing the spray skirt, rolling out of the cockpit, and coming to the surface next to the upside-down boat. This maneuver is performed the same way whether you are practicing in a pool or have just had a sneaky wave knock you over offshore. When first practicing, try to wear a diving mask, which will keep water out of your nose and let you see what is going on clearly. Later, you should practice without the mask, to increase the realism. Likewise, you can try it without a spray skirt once or twice, but dealing with the spray skirt is really the crux of the whole procedure.

Whether pool, lake, or harbor, practice in water about waist- to neck-deep. Try it in someplace too shallow and you'll surface with a faceful of mud. With your PFD on, sit in the boat as if you were paddling, with the spray skirt fastened (release cord out!), and the paddle in both hands. Take a breath, and lean over until the boat capsizes. It might be harder than you think, but once past a certain point, the boat will fall over and come to rest hull-up. At this point you will be hanging upside down in the cockpit, still holding the paddle. With your strong hand, grab the release cord of the spray skirt and yank firmly to pop the skirt loose. Now grab the cockpit rim with the same hand, and tuck-roll out of the cockpit. The buoyancy of your PFD will pop you to the surface next to the boat. It is important to hang on to both the paddle and the boat; in windy conditions either item could easily be swept away from you (if you ever find yourself out of the boat in wind, stay on the downwind side of the boat so it can't be blown out of your reach). A useful device to add to your boat is a commercially produced webbing loop called the Kayak Safe, which bolts to the front of the cockpit and acts as both a sure-fire spray skirt release and a handle with which to keep hold of the kayak.

Getting Back In

It's significant that the chapters in sea kayaking books dealing with "getting back in" are often titled "Rescues." A capsize in warm, calm water is no big deal—any of several simple techniques will have you back in the boat in minutes. But the same situation in a cold, stormy sea is much more dangerous. Keep this in mind when you practice any kayaking skill—once you master a technique in sheltered water, try it in rougher conditions, too.

Assisted Rescues

If you're paddling with a friend and have to wet-exit, the easiest recovery technique is the assisted reentry. The empty kayak is turned upright (if possible the bow or stern can be lifted before righting the boat, to pour out any water; otherwise the paddler will bail out the boat after reentry—although oftentimes a capsize will not necessarily add much water to the cockpit). The assisting paddler positions his or her boat directly alongside, usually bow-to-stern, and pointing into any oncoming seas. The assisting paddler steadies the empty kayak by grasping the cockpit rim, while the person in the water climbs in from the opposite side. The assisting paddler provides counterforce to the weight of the reentering person. The two kayaks form a surprisingly stable platform, even in rough water, if the boats are pointed into the waves. If a third kayak is present, it can be positioned on the other side of the assisting boat to stabilize the procedure further.

The paddler who is reentering must at all times stay as low as possible, to avoid recapsizing. The best technique is to pull your upper body onto the deck just behind the cockpit, then slide your legs into the cockpit so you are lying face down looking at the stern. Slide down until you can rotate into the seat properly.

Paddle Float

For the solo paddler, the most useful piece of reentry equipment is the paddle float. This is an inflatable collar that fits snugly over a paddle blade. A kayaker in the water places the paddle float on the paddle and inflates it with two or three breaths. The paddle is then braced across the deck of the kayak just behind the cockpit, with the floated end forming an outrigger. The paddler can then scramble into the cockpit while holding on to the paddle, in a manner similar to that described in the assisted reentry. Several sea kayak models now come with bungee

A float will turn a paddle into an outrigger, to steady the boat for solo reentry.

arrangements, or even grooves in the rear deck to position the paddle shaft firmly for greater stability.

The paddle float reentry can be mastered quickly in calm water by anyone of reasonable strength. With practice, it is also effective in choppy conditions.

Other devices available to assist reentries range from dual, inflatable sponsons that fasten to either side of the cockpit, to CO_2 charged bags that inflate with the press of a button. Many of these aids are useful under certain circumstances, but it's important to remember that as complexity increases, so does the chance that something will fail. Also, the longer it takes to set up a rescue, the greater the chance of hypothermia and resultant disorientation.

Sometimes it's better not to try to reenter the kayak. If you capsize while landing through surf, it is generally safer to grab on to the carrying toggle at the bow of the boat and let the surf carry it in stern-first with you following (*never* leading). Do *not* put your hand all the way through the carrying loop; if the boat is rolled again your hand could become trapped or injured. Better to let the boat go if you have to; it will likely precede you to shore anyway.

Eskimo Rolling

This has become a somewhat politically incorrect term—"Eskimo" was originally a derogatory reference meaning "eater of raw meat"—but the chances of getting everyone to call it "Inuit rolling" are slim to none.

Some early Inuit kayakers wore tight-fitting spray skirts that were *lashed* to their cockpit rim—if they capsized, there was no way out of the kayak; they had to roll back up or die. This must have provided a good incentive to develop bombproof technique.

Many modern sea kayakers paddle for years and never learn to roll: some have thoroughly practiced alternative reentry techniques; others simply toss a paddle float in the cockpit and figure it'll never happen to them. There is a mystique about rolling—an assumption that it's an arcane, difficult skill to master. But the assumption is wrong.

Nearly anyone can learn to Eskimo-roll in calm water in one day, given proper instruction. With just a little diligent practice, the technique can become second-nature even in heavy seas. Perhaps the most important benefit is the sense of security and self-reliance the skill imparts. There is no quicker or simpler way to right a capsized kayak than merely to flick it back upright with a practiced sweep of the paddle, never leaving the cockpit or loosening the spray skirt and often shipping no more than a few ounces of water into the boat.

A proper roll results from technique, not strength, so physique is no handicap. The sequence of moves is in itself simple, as you can see from the diagram on page 73, but knowing exactly how to time each move to result in a smooth recovery is difficult to portray in pictures. Many kayak stores offer inexpensive classes in rolling; once you have been coached through a few rolls, it's easy to practice on your own.

Of the many, many different types of Eskimo roll, as well as dozens of arcane variations, the easiest and most versatile is the screw roll. Starting from the capsized position, you brace firmly into the boat with your knees, and with the paddle reach to the surface on one side of the boat as far forward as you can. (1) Orient the far blade so that it planes across the surface of the water like a hydrofoil as you sweep it around and back. (2) The downward force of the paddle, combined with the buoyancy of your PFD, will bring your head and torso up to the surface. (3) At this point instinct will tell you to get

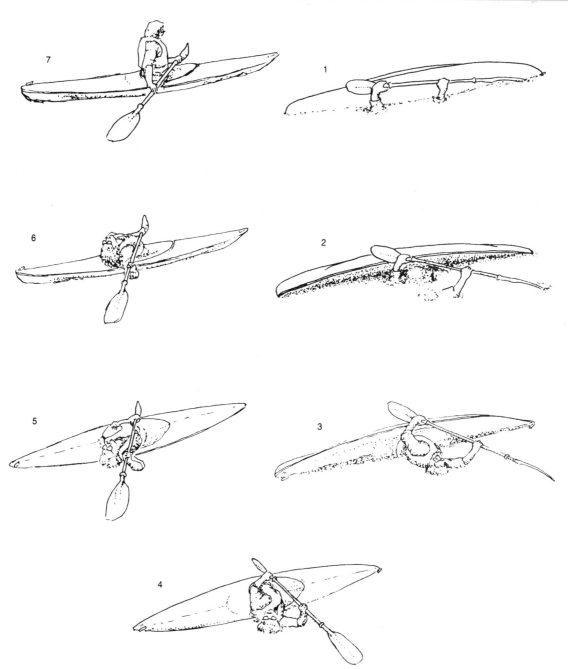

The Eskimo roll. See text, pages 72 and 74, for explanations of each step.

ANDY SINGER

your upper body out of the water, but the proper tactic is to leave your face just clear of the surface, and with your hips flick the boat sharply upright while still sweeping and leaning hard on the paddle, which should now be at almost a right angle to the boat. (5) Once the kayak "turns the corner," it will pop back upright; just as it does so, you can use the momentum and the final end of the paddle's sweep to lift your upper body back upright. (6) At the end of the sequence you should be leaning well backward in the boat, because the paddle will be behind you; this keeps your weight low until you can reorient and brace if needed. (7) Simple, huh? It will be, eventually. So effective is this technique that many experts can roll using only their hands.

A couple of variations in technique can assist a roll. For example, many people can roll while maintaining their normal grip position on the paddle shaft. However, you can shift the paddle away from you so that you have more leverage during the sweep, grasping the near blade with one hand. You can also perform the roll in two parts, first lifting your head to the surface to breathe and get oriented while sculling with the paddle, then completing the roll.

Touring

It is perfectly possible to enjoy sea kayaking without ever carrying more than lunch with you. But the real forté of the craft lies in its ability to cover miles of coastline swiftly and silently, tucking into hidden coves or tiny islands for the night, then gliding away through the dawn to explore the next bay or estuary. Since even a small sea kayak can easily carry 150–200 pounds of

Kayak touring introduces you to all kinds of places, from the British Columbian forests to the rocky islands of Baja, shown here.

gear, you can stay out—in style—for weeks if the opportunity is there.

Touring Equipment

If you backpack, you already have everything you need to camp with a sea kayak. The gear used by backpackers—compact single-burner stoves and cooksets, lightweight tents and sleeping bags—lends itself perfectly to kayaking. All you need to add are dry bags. If you haven't backpacked or done other lightweight camping, the backpacking (Chapter 2) and camping (Chapter 10) sections of this book will help you select the right gear and explain campsite selection and techniques.

When packing the dry bags for the trip, keep in mind how you'll be utilizing the contents. For example, rather than loading all your underwear in the bottom of a bag, then all your shirts, and so forth, load each day's clothes together in a layer. You can often do the same with meals—or at least separate them into breakfast, lunch, and dinner bags.

If you've never packed a kayak before, it's very helpful to do a trial run at home. This will help avoid the frustration of standing at your launch site with a stuffed kayak and three leftover dry bags. When you do get to the beach, load the boat as close to the water as possible, to avoid dragging the loaded hull over rocks or gravel.

Just as a backpacker needs to distribute the load a certain way in the pack to optimize balance, so does a kayaker need to distribute it properly in the boat. Surprisingly, a properly loaded sea kayak is *more* stable than an unloaded one, and less affected by crosswinds as well. The main rule: Keep weight low and centered. Heavy items, such as water bottles, should be placed in the front of the rear compartment, or the rear of the front compartment, and on the centerline of the kayak. Lighter stuff can go toward the ends. A rolled tent in a narrow dry bag, for example, is a good item to stuff into the bow, where not much else will fit. A sleeping bag in a dry bag can go behind it, or you can stuff that in the stern. Similarly light objects should go in next, then the heaviest gear in the places nearest the center. Reducing weight in the ends of the boat makes turning easier.

As much as possible, load items in the reverse order in which you'll need them. Setting up camp will be the last thing you do each day, so having the tent and sleeping bag buried is no handicap. Lunch fixings and extra clothing layers should be more accessible.

TOP 5

CLASSIC NORTH AMERICAN SEA KAYAKING TRIPS

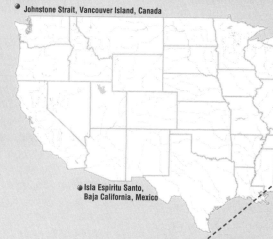

Glacier Bay, Alaska

Johnstone Strait, Vancouver Island, Canada

Maine Island Trail

Isla Espiritu Santo, Baja California, Mexico

Everglades, Florida

JAMIE BLOOMQUIST/OUTSIDE IMAGES

Exploring a rockbound cove along the Maine Island Trail.

- *Johnstone Strait, Vancouver Island, Canada.* Having a pod of orcas surface 50 feet from your kayak is an unparalleled thrill. Sheltered passages between forested islands heighten the appeal of this area.

- *Maine Island Trail.* Islands, inlets, rocks, and inns; the Maine coast allows you to choose nature or Northeastern hospitality, or mix the two any way you want.

- *Glacier Bay, Alaska.* An awesome seascape bounded by towering mountains and the unimaginable forces of flowing rivers of ice, which calve building-size chunks into the water in towers of spray.

- *Isla Espiritu Santo, Baja California, Mexico.* Paradise under a benign winter sun. Austere desert flora provides a surreal backdrop to clear, warm water. Diamond and velvet skies wheel overhead at night.

- *Everglades, Florida.* Like the womb of the world, the incredible fertility of this drowned land-scape fills every cubic inch of water and land with life.

It's vital to make sure the load can't shift. For most of us, this isn't much of a problem, since it is human nature to take as much stuff as will fit. If, by some chance, you have room left over, you can fill empty dry bags with air to take up the space (and ensure adequate flotation).

It's a good idea to keep sharp edges or corners of dry boxes and such away from the hull, where they could either gouge the hull or create a hard spot where exterior abrasion will be exacerbated.

When the boat begins to fill up, it's tempting to lash a few things on deck. Don't. Anything you put up there will catch wind, throw spray, and adversely affect your center of gravity. During a capsize, such items could come loose and interfere with a roll or rescue. The only things that should be on deck are your spare paddle and, if you choose, a deck bag that can hold charts, snacks, water, a camera, and such safety items as a VHF radio, flares, and a paddle float. The spare paddle should, if possible, be carried on the rear deck, with the blades toward the stern. Take an extra loop of bungee around the shafts, near the cockpit. This will help secure the paddle halves against waves, while leaving them easy to retrieve. Even in calm conditions, secure everything as if you were paddling out in a hurricane.

A helpful hint: Make a diagram of your loading arrangement, and keep it handy. A diagram makes it much easier to replicate loading after unloading the kayak for the night.

Coastal Cruising

Whatever you do, don't fall prey to the "We need to be *here* by tonight, and *there* by tomorrow," approach to trip planning. Not only do rigid schedules take the fun out of discovery, they are a significant cause of accidents, when people push too hard or try to continue on through deteriorating conditions.

Especially for your first few trips, make sure you paddle a coast with plenty of safe landing spots, so you can pull in quickly if weather or fatigue threatens. Look for sheltered routes, as well as benign weather windows—skirting the Oregon coast in January is definitely out as an introductory weekend excursion.

Paddling a loaded kayak for the first time, you'll immediately notice the increase in stability and a reduced sensitivity to crosswinds. The cost of the added mass is diminished maneuverability and slower acceleration. Give yourself plenty of room for turning and stopping.

◆ EXPERT TIP: FIELD REPAIR OF HULLS

With a big roll of duct tape you can fix anything short of a kayak broken completely in two—and even that might not be out of the question.

To repair an abrasion hole, a split, or even a major crunch on a fiberglass kayak, clean the hull and let it dry thoroughly. Run strips of tape lengthwise on the hull to cover the damage, overlapping each strip and extending beyond the hole several inches in each direction. Round off the corners of the tape strips; this will help prevent peeling.

For polyethylene boats the procedure is more complex. Annie Getchell, author of *The Essential Outdoor Gear Manual*, recommends warming the hull if possible (even just in the sun), then sanding around the damage and cleaning with alcohol. Apply a thin coat of marine contact cement, such as Sea Bond or HydroGrip, to the area; when it is almost dry, apply a duct tape patch over the cement.

Coastal paddling is fun because you can divide your attention between the sea and the land, watching seabirds, dolphins, and ships, then eagles, trees, and rock formations. Depending on surf conditions, you can sometimes skirt within yards of shore, but watch closely for submerged rocks, and keep one eye out to sea for any larger-than-usual wave sets. Always give yourself margin for error.

If there is surf, the water will be calmer farther offshore. If waves are being driven against a cliff, they often rebound far out to sea, creating dangerously random waves called clapotis. As you paddle, keep watch well ahead of your position so you can alter course if need be.

Landing a loaded boat is similar in technique to landing an empty one, but remember that the potential for hull damage is greater with all that extra weight—it's best to avoid the "how far can I shoot it up the beach" approach.

When you stop for the night and unload the kayak, make sure—make *really* sure—it (and your camp, for that matter) is above the highest possible tide line. Even then, it doesn't hurt to tie the bow to a tree. Also be sure that the kayak's hatches are fastened down and the spray skirt is inside one. The paddles should be either taken apart and placed down in the cockpit or laid under the curve of the hull, to prevent wind from picking them up.

Several years ago four men were camped on an island in the Sea of Cortez, with their two folding double kayaks lying high on the beach. One night a wind Baja residents call an *elefante* came roaring from the peninsula across their island. As they huddled in straining tents, they heard a *thump*, then a *thump . . . thump, thump thump thump*. Investigation revealed that the wind had picked up one of the 90-pound boats and cartwheeled it into the sea, never to be seen again. After waiting futilely for several days for another party to come by, the four men managed to return to the Baja mainland in the remaining kayak.

Navigation

Route-finding for coastal kayak trips has one huge advantage over both open-water navigation and cross-country route-finding: however lost you might be, at least you know *you're on the coast!*

That might sound flippant, but it's essentially true. Think about it—if you stay away from crossings and archipelagos, you can only be somewhere along a single, though possibly convoluted, line on your chart. The only error you can make is being farther up or farther down the coast than you think you are.

Because nautical charts were designed for use by people cruising in powerboats or sailboats, for whom

false information could be disastrous, they tend to be highly detailed. Although much of the information in charts can be overkill for the sea kayaker, it never hurts to have more information than you need, so a good nautical chart of your paddling area is highly recommended. The flip side is that charts often lack good land detail, so if you like to hike inland or pick your camp-

Paddling with whales, such as these pilot whales in the Sea of Cortez off Baja California, is one of the greatest thrills of sea kayaking.

sites ahead of time, you'll want a topographical map as well. Tip: Store your charts and maps in a waterproof, clear-plastic chart holder, such as those made by Ortleib, or seal them well with special liquid map sealer, available at outdoor or map retailers, and stow in your deck bag.

Chapter 9, on map and compass use, will provide you with some basic route-finding skills. But nautical charts differ significantly from maps, so it's helpful to study a chart in advance.

The most basic information a chart provides (beyond telling you where the land ends and the ocean begins) is the depth of the water. This might not seem like important information when you're in a boat that only draws 3 inches—but water depth can affect other things, including currents, surf, and the temperature of the water itself. For example, picture a narrow channel open at both ends, 100 feet deep at one end and 20 feet deep at the other. If a tidal current flows through the channel, the result is a large amount of water trying to move through a small space, and there is only one way for that to happen—the current has to flow faster at the shallow end, sometimes dangerously fast. The same thing can happen in a channel of consistent depth but varying width. Charts often note such spots, even listing speeds of currents.

Make sure you note if the depths on your chart are in feet or in fathoms. If it's the latter, multiply by six to get feet.

A useful companion to the chart is a tide table, which will tell you when the high and low tides will occur, as well as their range—good information for convenience as well as safety. For example, a chart and tide table might warn you that if you land in a particular bay at high tide, you will have a 400-yard portage to the water at low tide.

Areas that receive a fair amount of recreational boat traffic are often covered by "cruising guides," books that provide much detailed information about water and weather conditions, harbors, even fishing and diving possibilities. These books are useful to kayakers as well—if only to warn you away from spots that might be overcrowded with smelly power boats.

Whatever chart you choose, wherever you go, just remember the most important navigational tip: go where you'll have fun.

> **◆ EXPERT TIP—DON'T CONFUSE YOUR COMPASS**
> A deck-mounted compass is a worthwhile option on your kayak. It's the easiest type to use while underway, and some can even be lighted for night or low-light paddling. Be careful, though, to keep large metal objects as far from the compass as possible, or you might get false readings. This especially applies to items in the deck bag. Experiment with such things as cameras and binoculars to see if the compass needle swings when you put them in the bag. If so, you may have to store them elsewhere.

Where to Go

In the world of sea kayaking, the best source of where-to-go information tends to be word of mouth. Clubs and kayak shops, as well as sea kayaking web sites on the Internet, provide lots of fodder for trip planning, especially if you want to avoid the crowds that flock to "hot" destinations touted in guidebooks.

National sea kayaking magazines, such as *Sea Kayaker, Paddler* and *Canoe & Kayak,* are good sources for adventure trips, and regional publications, such as *Wave-Length* in British Columbia and *Atlantic Coastal Kayaker,* are great for weekend and daytrip ideas, especially for gleaning such important tips as areas that are overcrowded or dangerous. (For contact information, see the resources section at the end of this chapter.)

Gather as much information as you can about an area from kayakers, retailers, sailors, charts, guidebooks, and the Coast Guard. Check on such necessities as permits or registration, the nature of other boating and shipping traffic, what areas are private property and should be avoided, and what the local kayaking-use scene is like. For example, in the exceptionally popular Johnstone Strait of British Columbia, where friendly resident orca whales frolic alongside boats, there is so much competition for campsites that some professional kayaking outfitters actually try to lay claim to "their own" beaches for the entire summer. Many altercations are reported when private boaters try to explain that the beach is public property.

If tropical waters beckon, or you fancy a trip through the canals of Europe, there are a number of good adventure travel narratives. One to look for is Maria Coffey's wonderful book, *A Boat in Our Baggage.* This account of her trip with her husband around the

Kenai Fjords National Park, Alaska

world with a folding kayak is guaranteed to get your wanderlust juices flowing. The *Complete Folding Kayaker* will help prime you for travel with a boat in *your* baggage. (For more book information, see the resources section, below.)

☞ KID QUOTIENT

Children love boats. They seem especially attracted to kayaks—perhaps because kayaks are small compared to a lot of other types of boats, and thus not so intimidating. Sea kayaking is a wonderful sport for children, but they should be self-sufficient in the water, with good swimming abilities, before coming along.

Always make sure kids wear proper life jackets at all times, even just *near* the water—choose the high flotation style that supports the head while floating—and safe clothing appropriate to weather and water temperature.

The child should know how to swim, or at least have experience floating in the water wearing their PFD. That way if there are any unexpected dunkings it won't be an unfamiliar and frightening event.

Outings with young children should be limited to very sheltered waters, close to shore.

Several models of double kayaks with center compartments can be used as triples, with the center hatch converted to take a seat. These are perfect for carrying children—but in the event of a capsize, the child must be capable of self-rescue. Don't count on your own ability to be able to help the child—you'll be busy enough on your own, or could even be injured or otherwise hampered.

Many people put young children in the seat with them in a single; this is an unsafe practice, because you both could be trapped in the cockpit. Likewise, putting a child in the rear compartment of a single eliminates the flotation in the rear of the boat, which is also very unsafe. Even the triple kayak sacrifices flotation in the center compartment.

These cautions shouldn't scare you off from including your children in the sport. It's just common sense to be sure your child is as ready as you are for any situation that might arise.

Older children can take advantage of kayaks and paddles made especially for them. This is when the real enjoyment starts, since no child loves anything better than a little bit of independence. The only problem arises when they start outpacing mom and dad!

(See Chapter 11 for more tips on adventuring outdoors with kids.)

Where Can Sea Kayaking Lead You?

What is there beyond daytripping and touring?

Adrenaline junkies gravitate to surf kayaking, usually in custom-made or specialty kayaks. Surf kayakers wait to head out until conditions arise that have the daytrippers scrambling for shore. There's even a loose club or group of kayakers in northern California called the Tsunami Rangers, whose exploits in the region's murderous rock gardens and caves have anointed danger-kayaking with cult status.

Long-distance sea kayak racing is also gaining popularity. Do you fancy an Iditarod for kayakers? Each year paddlers race for 30 days from Chicago to New York City, across four of the five Great Lakes, through the Erie Canal, and down the Hudson River to Battery Park at the southern tip of Manhattan Island. The winners make big money (recently the top four all made $10,000 or more, with first place taking $25,000). For more information, contact the American Canoe Association, 7432 Alban Station Blvd., Suite B-226, Springfield, VA 22150-2311; (703) 451-0141; acadirect@aol.com; www.aca-paddler.org.

If you are interested in pursuing high-performance kayaking, you might want to check out the video *Performance Sea Kayaking: The Basics . . . and Beyond* (Performance Video and Instruction, Inc., Durango, CO; 970-259-1361).

Further Resources for Sea Kayaking
Books

The Essential Sea Kayaker, by David Seidman (Camden, ME: Ragged Mountain Press, 1992).

Eskimo Rolling, by Derek Hutchinson (Camden, ME: Ragged Mountain Press, 1994), 2d edition.

The Complete Folding Kayaker, by Ralph Díaz (Camden, ME: Ragged Mountain Press, 1994).

The Whole Paddler's Catalog, edited by Zip Kellogg (Camden, ME: Ragged Mountain Press, 1997).

A Boat in Our Baggage, Around the World with a Kayak, by Maria Coffey (Camden, ME: Ragged Mountain Press, 1995).

Periodicals

Sea Kayaker, 7001 Seaview Ave. NW, Suite 135, Seattle, WA 98117; (206) 789-9536.

Atlantic Coastal Kayaker, P.O. Box 520, Ipswich, MA 01938; http://www.qed.com/ack/.

Folding Kayaker, New York, NY; (212) 724-5069; rdiaz@ix.netcom.com.

Canoe & Kayak, 10526 NE 68th, Suite 3, Kirkland, WA 98033; (206) 827-6363.

Paddler, P.O. Box 1341, Eagle, ID 83616; (208) 939-4500.

Wave-Length, RR1 Site 17 C49, Gabriola Island, BC V0R 1X0 (604) 247-9789; http://www.island.net/~wavenet/.

Sea Kayaking Organizations

Trade Association of Sea Kayaking, 12455 N. Wauwatosa Road, Mequon, WI 53097; (414) 242-5228; http://www.viewit.com/wtr/TASK.html.

North American Paddlesports Association, 12455 N. Wauwatosa Road, Mequon, WI 53097; (414) 242-5228.

Conservation Organizations

The Cousteau Society, 870 Green Briar Circle, Suite 402, Chesapeake, VA 23320; (757) 523-9335.

Sea Shepherd Conservation Society, P.O. Box 628, Venice, CA 90294; (310) 301-7325; nvoth@igc.apc.org; http://www.seashepherd.org.

Surfrider Foundation, 105 Ave de la Estralla, Suite 1, San Clemente, CA 92672; (800) 743-SURF, (714) 492-8170; http://www.sdsc.edu. (Works toward international protection of waves and beaches.)

Centre for Marine Environmental Initiatives, Fisheries and Marine Institute of Memorial University of Newfoundland, P.O. Box 4920, St. Johns, Newfoundland A1C 5R3; (709) 778-0648; cmerits@gill.ifmt.nf.ca.

Center for Marine Conservation (CMC), 1725 DeSales Street NW, Suite 600, Washington, DC 20036; (202) 429-5609.

"The fastest and most dangerous of waters which are treacherous terrors even to the largest sailing boat or motor craft can be conquered by the shallow-draughted kayak."

—Derek Hutchinson in *Sea Canoeing*

Chapter 4

CANOEING—*The Voyageur Mystique*

"Boats are for work; canoes are for pleasure."

—John Boyle O'Reilly (1888)

Historic Waterways

Canoeing allows you to reach deeply into the past to touch its history. If you wish, you can buy a handmade birchbark canoe virtually identical to the ones paddled by pre-Columbian Native Americans and adopted by the French Voyageurs and other explorers. And you can paddle that canoe along many of the historic watercourses that opened up our continent to those early adventurers.

True, a birchbark canoe is a pretty rarefied work of art today, but you can also find beautiful wood-and-canvas or all-wood canoes that retain a strong connection to tradition yet are still perfectly efficient. Many people even make their own—few things in our world are as satisfying as launching a boat you have crafted yourself and heading out with a load of supplies for a week or two of solitude and exploration.

On the other hand, you might be attracted to the latest aerospace renditions of the craft and the outer limits of the sport: polyethylene or Royalex whitewater canoes designed to challenge the most demanding rapids. Either extreme, or anything in between—you'll always enjoy the fulfillment of paddling a craft that becomes one with its pilot and harkens back so strongly to its past.

Canoeing can be divided into three broad categories.
- General daytripping on lakes or rivers
- Extended touring and expeditioning
- Whitewater river running

For each of these categories, certain models work best. Between these categories there might also be some overlap of capabilities, of course, such as larger daytrippers that can easily be used as extended touring canoes, and there are offshoots of each category as well, such as flatwater racing boats, and short and wide children's models.

Some people know what kind of canoeing they want to do from the start and buy the boat for their needs; others learn with a general-use boat, then buy a more specialized model as their interests develop.

Canoeing is an easy sport to learn. Touring and general-use boats are reassuringly stable; in a couple of hours you can be paddling proficiently. Years later you will still be refining your technique in a never-ending, enjoyable quest for perfection.

Some of the information for and excellent technical review of this chapter were provided by canoeing experts Cheryl Poll and John Shepard.

What You'll Need

Romance aside, it's probably not a good idea to start out with a $3,000 replica birchbark canoe. Canoes made from materials much more forgiving to novices start at around $600, and it's possible to pick up sound used examples for less. Olympic-class slalom racing aside, canoeing is still a relatively low-tech sport, so you don't have to worry that your boat will be outdated by next year's equipment revolution.

The Canoe

To the inexperienced eye, a canoe is pretty much a canoe. Oh, it's easy to tell a long one from a short one, and a wood one from a plastic one, but that's about it. The details of hull configuration are what set apart a twitchy whitewater canoe from a solid daytripper.

General Canoe Design

It's difficult to pin down a "typical" canoe, since there are thousands of variations possible in each hull. But the basic parameters are pretty simple.

Length. This is the most obvious variable, and one that contributes significantly to the overall character of the boat. Solo whitewater canoes designed for quick handling can be as short as 12 or 13 feet, but a tandem model designed for extended wilderness touring might be 18 or 19, even 20 feet long.

Note that overall length differs from waterline length. An 18-foot boat with plumb stems—a bow and stern that drop straight into the water—will have a

---

THE ESSENTIALS—A CANOEING START-UP KIT

- Canoe ($600–$2,500)
- Paddle X 2 ($20–$225)
- PFD ($40–$70)
- Bailer and sponge ($0–$5)

Minimum cost essential canoeing kit: $695*

ADD-ONS

- Hat
- Map and compass
- Water
- First aid kit
- Dry bags
- Float bags
- Portage packs
- Boat repair kit

*The essentials list above is intended to give you an idea of minimum start-up costs, from scratch, for moderate entry into a sport using new equipment. Other options include borrowing gear from friends or renting from retailers, YMCAs, or church activity clubs, as well as buying used gear—see Appendix A.

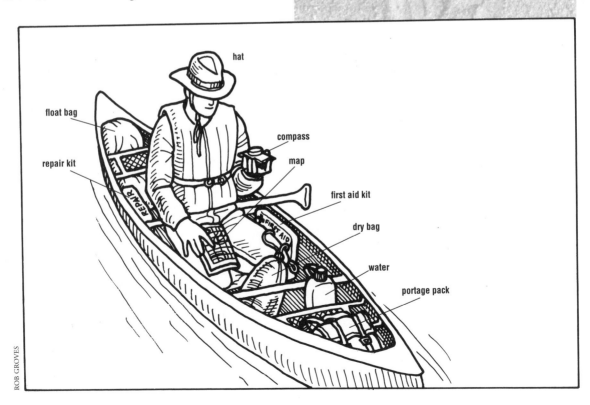

ROB GROVES

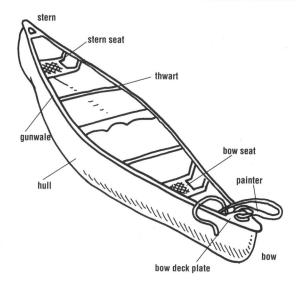

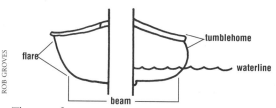

The parts of a canoe.

ROB GROVES

line, when the canoe is carrying the ideal load for which it is designed. Finally, the molded beam is measured at the widest point across the gunwales, not counting the exterior rail.

Cross section. Look at the canoe from one end. If the hull curves up gradually so that the widest beam is at the gunwales, it is said to be flared. If the hull is fat near the bottom, then curves inward to the gunwales, it is said to have tumblehome. A flared hull deflects waves a bit better, and feels more stable as you lean the boat sideways—in fact, you probably won't capsize until water is pouring over the sides. A boat with tumblehome feels more tippy at first, but it paddles more efficiently than a boat with a flared hull.

The cross section of the bottom of the hull can vary tremendously as well. It can be nearly flat, gently arched, noticeably V'd, or a combination of any of these. Although a nearly flat bottom feels very stable in flat water, and for that reason is often the preferred hull shape for waterfowl hunters and fly fishers, it is difficult to handle in waves because it doesn't respond to your body movements. An arched hull is just the opposite— tippy-feeling, but very responsive in rough water. A V hull attempts to combine the two characteristics. Usually, the manufacturer will match the hull cross-section to the intended use of the boat, so it won't be a vital choice you need to make. A typical all-around canoe will likely have a rounded V bottom, which is stable but reasonably responsive.

Rocker. The line along the bottom of the hull of the boat, from end to end, is called the keel. The amount the keel curves up toward each end is called rocker.

Rest a canoe on its keel on a flat floor and try to look underneath it from the side. On a touring canoe, which is designed for good directional stability for long paddles, the keel will contact the floor for most of its length,

longer waterline length than an 18-foot boat with either raked stems, which curve under to meet the waterline, or recurved stems, which curve back to the waterline and back again at the top (the classic canoe profile).

Beam. The width of any boat is referred to as its beam. On a canoe, the beam can be measured in three places. The maximum beam is measured at the widest point of the boat, period. The waterline beam, as its name suggests, is the widest measurement at the water-

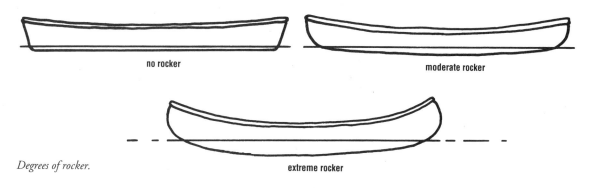

Degrees of rocker.

no rocker

moderate rocker

extreme rocker

ROB GROVES

only rising near the ends. This boat has a straight keel, with little rocker.

Now look at a canoe designed for whitewater paddling. Only a couple of feet in the center of the hull will rest on the floor; the ends will curve up noticeably, like a banana. This boat, designed for quick turns, has considerable rocker. The straighter the keel, the more the boat wants to travel in a straight line, which is known as tracking. Also, as a boat is loaded with gear the ends sink deeper into the water, further assisting tracking by putting more of the keel underwater.

Materials

The first canoes were products of the forests, which were themselves products of the abundant water that flowed through and around them. The ancestral canoe, a simple hollowed-out log, was probably the first boat. Some variation of the dugout canoe, as it is called, can be found in nearly every primitive culture with access to trees and water. The ancestors of the modern Polynesians carried the dugout to its ultimate form—huge oceangoing craft with outriggers.

When the first Europeans landed in North America, the Native Americans of the Northeastern forests had perfected their own canoes suitable for the broad rivers and huge lakes that formed a natural highway system crisscrossing the region. Using as a hull material the astonishingly pliable bark of the birch tree formed around steambent ribs of cedar or other woods, they fashioned a lightweight yet rugged craft that would remain state-of-the-art for hundreds of years. Although modern materials finally supplanted the birch, the shape of many current touring canoes scarcely deviates from the ghostly silhouettes that preceded them along the forested waterways of the northern United States and Canada.

Wooden and wood-and-canvas canoes. Wood-framed canoes (usually ash and cedar) with canvas hulls, popular in the early part of this century and still offered by many manufacturers, have a lot to recommend them. They are very beautiful, very quiet to paddle, and are straightforward to repair—in fact the entire hull can be renewed, if necessary. For touring on flat rivers or lakes, wood and canvas canoes are perfectly efficient, and they retain a tangible connection to the earth. Wood-and-canvas canoes are, at least theoretically, environmentally sound products made from renewable resources. Like any other natural product, they must be maintained with care, but they are very durable if looked after properly.

The ribs for wood-and-canvas canoes are usually steam-bent over a metal form. Longitudinal planks are fastened to the ribs with copper clinch-nails that, as they are pounded through the wood, bend back on themselves when they hit the metal form and "clinch" the ribs and planks together. After the frame is removed from the mold, seats and thwarts are added, and then the boat is covered with stretched canvas. The material is smoothed with a filler and then painted to provided a smooth, glossy, surprisingly tough surface.

A similar mold can be used for wood-hulled canoes. In some designs, thin strips of wood are glued together over the form without ribs; others use a ribbed substructure. The boat is then sheathed in clear fiberglass cloth, which lets the beauty of the wood shine through but adds structural rigidity and keeps water from penetrating the grain, where it would quickly cause rot. If care is taken with the application of the fiberglass sheathing, these boats can be surprisingly light in weight.

A few canoes are still being made entirely of wood, using ribs and frames to which planks are fastened, either edge-to-edge or overlapping, like clapboard house siding (the latter technique, called lapstrake in shipbuilder's terms, is used on many kinds of wood boats). Like birchbark canoes, all-wood canoes are more exquisite showpieces of the boatbuilder's art than are everyday boats, although they are perfectly functional.

Where wood and canvas don't shine is on whitewater, or anywhere they could be subjected to bashing against rocks or other abuse. Although structurally rigid, wood frames and hulls are sensitive to severe impact damage. For such abusive treatment you need a canoe made of more resilient material.

Aluminum. Shortly after World War II, the Grumman company, saddled with a sudden surplus of aluminum, introduced a canoe made from material formerly intended for aircraft and other implements of combat. Virtually corrosion-free, lightweight, and extremely strong but affordable, aluminum canoes brought the sport within reach of a new generation of paddlers. Aluminum canoes remain a great buy, and they are virtually immortal, barring a catastrophic crunch. Many outfitters and rental companies use aluminum canoes because of their indestructible nature and low price. When retirement finally does arrive, the whole thing can be recycled.

Perhaps aluminum's biggest drawback is esthetic. Particularly when contrasted with a richly organic wood counterpart, an aluminum canoe looks like the appliance it is. This impression is magnified by the dull clanking that emanates from any aluminum boat while on the water, as paddles knock the sides or cargo shifts against the hull. Aluminum is hot to the touch in summer and cold in winter, and it can reflect annoying glare back to the paddlers' eyes.

Also, although it is much more resistant to bashing than wood, aluminum is not an ideal material for a whitewater boat. The metal tends to "stick" to rocks, increasing the chances of getting hung up in a tight spot. If holed, it is difficult to repair without actually riveting on an aluminum patch—although boats so patched lose virtually none of their structural integrity.

As a result of this durable but utilitarian nature, plus the fact that aluminum cannot be formed into complex hull shapes, most aluminum canoes are designed as general-use boats, suitable for casual paddling and touring.

Fiberglass and Kevlar. A more recent innovation in canoe construction than aluminum, fiberglass was introduced in the mid-1950s. A very tough and durable material, fiberglass (or FRP—fiber-reinforced plastic) is easy to mold into the curves necessary for a sophisticated canoe hull design. It can be formed to hold a hull shape by itself, with minimal reinforcement and trim, or layered over an interior wood frame of ribs and planks—a delightful and practical marriage of old and new.

Fiberglass itself is made from glass fibers which are impregnated with plastic resin. Inexpensive fiberglass boats are made with chopper guns, which blow resin and chopped-up fibers into a mold. In general, such boats can be either light or strong, but not both. Also used in inexpensive boats is fiberglass mat, a very coarsely woven fabric with a necessarily high resin content. Better fiberglass boats are made with finely woven fiberglass cloth, which facilitates a light *and* strong layup. It's easy to see the difference between the fine texture of cloth and the random, matted appearance of chopped glass or the coarse appearance of mat.

The technique of laying fiberglass involves working with fairly toxic resins, thus making major repairs messy, albeit easily accomplished by an owner. However, virtually any fiberglass mishap can be repaired in the field with duct tape, which adheres tenaciously to fiberglass and can securely cover truly horrifying holes for the duration of a trip.

Kevlar is similar to fiberglass in the way it is constructed (although no one would dream of blowing Kevlar from a chopper gun), but the material is both lighter and stronger, as well as significantly more expensive. Kevlar cloth itself is nearly 50 percent lighter than fiberglass cloth, but after the resin is added, an all-Kevlar boat will weigh about 25 percent less—still a significant savings. Many manufacturers add Kevlar reinforcements to high-stress or high-wear areas of fiberglass boats, such as the bow, stern, and keel, to gain strength while keeping costs down.

Fiberglass boats are normally finished with a layer of gelcoat, a thin, hard (although somewhat brittle) top coat into which the color is molded. Kevlar boats are sometimes topped with nothing but a clear coat to show off the golden weave of the material, although more commonly they will have gelcoat finishes in order to protect them from scratching.

Fiberglass and Kevlar boats are extremely sturdy and hold up well to the rigors of touring, including rough landings and the occasional encounter with a rock. For years fiberglass was the material of choice for whitewater use as well. But recently, advanced plastics have proven to be superior for situations in which rock and canoe frequently have differences of opinion.

Royalex. Royalex is a heat-set laminate consisting of a foam core bonded on both sides to ABS (acrylonitrile butadiene styrene, if you must know), and fused to an outer vinyl layer that is impregnated with color. The resulting material is incredibly tough and requires very little maintenance, can be bounced off rocks time and time again with little effect, and is very competitive with other materials in cost. Royalex is versatile enough to be used in everything from expedition canoes to serious whitewater boats. It has an agreeably smooth surface that slides off rocks satisfactorily, and it can be sprung back into shape after a near-total pretzelization around a boulder. Many companies are making derivatives of Royalex (with derivative names as well), seeking to match or improve on the qualities of the original.

ROYALEX AND ITS EVIL ENEMIES

Annie Getchell, author of *The Essential Outdoor Gear Manual*, offers the following tips on caring for a Royalex canoe.

- *The sun.* Although it's tempting to store something as care-free as a Royalex canoe outside, nothing could be worse over the long term. UV radiation will eventually fade and weaken the vinyl outer skin, so protected storage is crucial. Rack the canoe indoors, or at least under a shed roof. Regular applications of 303 Protectant will also help maintain the color and resilient qualities of your ABS hull. If you must store your boat outdoors, see that any scratches exposing ABS layers are filled or painted to protect against UV damage.

- *Careless adhesive use.* Solvents such as acetone and those in contact cements can seriously damage Royalex laminates. If using acetone to etch a surface for adhesion, apply it sparingly, don't rub too hard, and allow it to evaporate completely before attempting a bond. Use denatured alcohol whenever possible. Never touch a prepared surface with your hands—even momentary contact practically guarantees that the bond will fail in that spot.

- *Below-zero temps.* Royalex has a high shrink coefficient and will expand and contract significantly between a hot August day and a winter night when temperatures dip below zero. Many Royalex canoes feature wood gunwales, which contract at a radically different rate; this difference can create pressures great enough to crack the laminate. These "cold cracks," which may be up to 5 inches long, must be repaired by removing rails entirely and patching the interior with Kevlar structural patches.

- When preparing your Royalex boat for hibernation, loosen the screws that secure the gunwales by backing them out several turns. Longer deck screws should be completely removed to open outer rails and separate decks from the hull. Come spring, dab a bit of penetrating oil into each hole, then replace and tighten screws.

Molded polyethylene. Although inexpensive, polyethylene canoes are quite tough—many whitewater models are made from this material, which slides off rocks and resists gashes very well. It is not nearly as rigid as fiberglass, however, so a reinforcing structure must be added to the boat, or the polyethylene stiffened with a foam core.

Polyethylene shares with Royalex a sensitivity to ultraviolet light and should be cared for as described in the Evil Enemies of Royalex sidebar. Older polyethylene boats should be checked carefully for minute radiating cracks around stress points, which will indicate that the boat is near the end of its service life. As it ages, polyethylene hardens, becoming brittle sometime between 7 and 12 years of age. Older polyethylene boats in very cold climates have been known to shatter after an impact (such as dropping off a roof rack).

Other Features

Seats. The classic canoe seat is lovely, woven cane, which is sturdy, breathes well, and is resilient enough to be very comfortable. But like any other natural material, cane must be maintained, which in this case means a yearly varnishing. It is one of those tasks you can look at as a chore or a relaxing experience, depending on your frame of mind. Even many modern Royalex canoes have cane seats (and wood gunwales), to lend a touch of tradition to an otherwise space-age craft.

Other natural canoe seats have been made from rawhide or from wood. Canoes made from synthetic materials often have synthetic seats as well—aluminum in the case of aluminum canoes, plastic for the space-age boats. Plastic seats can be molded to comfortable shapes, but they need drain holes if water pools in them with regularity.

Some touring canoes have seats mounted on sliding rails. This allows fine-tuning of weight distribution in the boat, especially when loading camping gear.

Canoes designed specifically for whitewater paddling use an entirely different seating arrangement. Most touring canoeists sit in their boats these days, but whitewater paddlers still kneel astride form-fitted foam saddles that lower their center of gravity in the boat, firmly anchor the boat to the paddler, and allow the use of body English to lean and even help completely roll the canoe. The saddle supports your butt and has grooves for your thighs to grip, as well as a strap arrangement that holds the knees firmly to the boat hull but can be released instantly in the event of a capsize. Although a saddle lacks something for long-distance comfort, the control a good saddle gives you over the canoe has to be experienced to be believed.

Gunwales. Many modern canoes have aluminum or vinyl-covered aluminum rails on the gunwales. Aluminum is light and maintenance-free, but doesn't hold up well under heavy abuse. Some canoes have wood gunwales—and for reasons beyond mere esthetics. Wood rails (mostly ash or spruce) are very resilient, resistant to impact damage, and easy to repair. But, like cane seats, they must be maintained. Varnish isn't recommended, since it lacks the necessary flexibility. Better is an oil such as Deks Olje, which penetrates and restores the wood, and protects against rot and fungi.

Thwarts. These are the crosspieces that connect the gunwales. They are necessary to add structural rigidity to the boat, and are *not* intended as seats. When carrying lots of gear, thwarts are used as lash-points for dry bags and equipment, not just for security in the event of a capsize, but also to keep things from shifting, especially in rough water.

Portage yoke. There inevitably comes a time when you just plain run out of water under the boat. If you're lucky, the longest stretch you'll ever have to carry your canoe is between the car and the lake. But on many extended wilderness trips, portages between rivers or lakes are essential to the route. The portage yoke enables you to balance the canoe across your shoulders and carry it with some degree of comfort, although nothing can

keep you from reeling like a drunken sailor when carrying a canoe in a high wind.

Painters. It's a very good idea to have lengths of line attached to the bow and stern of the canoe. These can be used to tie the boat while stopped, but they are vital for rescuing a boat stuck on a rock, or for lining the canoe through rapids. Painters should float, so polypropylene (preferably brightly colored) line is best. The minimum length for a painter on a recreational boat is 10–15 feet; 25 feet is better for one that will be used in whitewater. The painters should be kept coiled and tied down with a bungee or Velcro, so they can be immediately retrieved but won't come loose in a capsize and cause a tangling hazard.

Which Canoe?

Now it's time to put all this arcane knowledge to use and select a canoe that will suit your needs.

Will you be paddling solo or with a partner? A tandem canoe is generally longer than a single, although the lines can blur—a tandem whitewater model might be shorter than a single wilderness tripper, for example.

An idealized all-round canoe, suitable for tandem paddling but manageable for one person, and designed for general paddling, might be around 16 feet long, and 34 or 35 inches in beam, with slight rocker at the ends. If you plan long trips with two people, a 17-foot canoe could be more suitable for your cargo needs; if you're a solo adventurer, 16 feet or less might be closer to ideal. Whitewater canoes will be a couple of feet shorter in both solo and tandem models. Beam will vary proportionally with length, and with model *and* manufacturer. A canoe designed for wilderness touring will be deeper, for carrying more gear, than an all-around boat. Just keep in mind the averages, so you can question with authority someone who tries to sell you an 18-foot canoe to paddle by yourself or offers a highly rockered 14-footer with saddles and thigh straps for your honeymoon cruise to the Boundary Waters.

Your choice of materials will be influenced by several factors. If your idea of proper boat storage is a couple of sawhorses behind the shed, buy an aluminum canoe and forget it. If you take care of your stuff but use it hard, Royalex or a proprietary variation might be your best bet. It will stay looking good with a minimum of attention to the hull and rails but shrug off normal abuse with ease.

CARING FOR CANE SEATS

Cane seats can quickly degenerate into pain seats if you neglect their seasonal varnish requirements. The cane becomes brittle with exposure and either pulls from its seating or fractures with the slightest pressure.

Unseated cane can be worked back into its groove and encouraged to stay there with epoxy. Don't bother trying to reweave a broken section; replace the webbing once you've punched through part of the cane.

Most modern cane seats are constructed of prewoven panels, which are easy to replace. If you store your canoe outside for the winter, unscrew the cane panels and store them inside the house.

(Care tips are from Annie Getchell's *The Essential Outdoor Gear Manual*.)

TRADITIONAL GEAR FOR YOUR TRADITIONAL CANOE

If you succumbed to the beauty of a wood-and-canvas or all-wood canoe, you'll want to equip it with accessories that complement its traditional materials and lines.

Several companies offer lovely, hand-woven ash baskets that fit across the thwarts of the canoe, matching the bottom profile. Also available are traditional woven pack baskets for portaging your gear.

Another approach to portaging is the Duluth Pack, a canvas-and-leather freight hauler in production since 1911. The Duluth Tent and Awning company makes several styles, along with many other traditional but useful canoe accessories.

Modern nylon tents are light and efficient, but it's hard to beat the comfort of a big, solid, canvas wall-tent. They're a bit bulky and certainly heavy, but many offer standing head-room, and if properly tied down, they will stand through just about anything. The smaller Baker style canvas tent, with a front that can be opened up into a porch awning, works well and can be heated easily with a fire in front or with a collapsible wood stove.

Finally, anyone with a traditional canoe should really own at least one big, thick, red-and-black checked Mackinaw jacket.

If you are cost-conscious, you will be naturally attracted to polyethylene, which will serve you well, especially for boulder-bashing (although its ultimate value might be questionable, given its limited service life and the difficulty of repair).

Techno-weenies, of course, argue that a canoe can never be too light. Your choice will likely be an all-Kevlar boat that dances as lightly on the water as a fallen autumn leaf, with a hull so thin as to be translucent.

Finally, the romantics among us will toss thoughts of practicality out the window at the sight of gleaming wood ribs and a well-faired canvas hull. Yet with the aid of a few tools and some craftsman skills, a wood or wood-and-canvas canoe can be a long-lived workhorse. When you've retired to more genteel pastimes, you can hang it from the ceiling of the cabin as an *objet d'art* and gaze fondly at it from your overstuffed chair.

The Paddle

A canoe paddle is possibly the single most elegant transportation tool ever devised, and it has certainly changed less in essence in its many-thousand-year history than any other artifact. The traditional canoe paddle is still fashioned from a single piece of wood, although we now use band saws and power shapers instead of flint axes and obsidian scrapers.

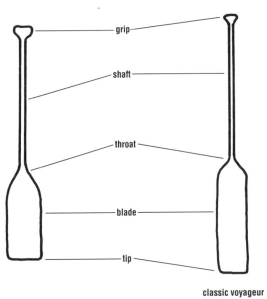

grip
shaft
throat
blade
tip

ROB GROVES

classic voyageur   laminated wood   fiberglass or plastic blade with aluminum shaft   bent shaft

Paddle types.

Materials. Inexpensive wooden paddles are fashioned from one board, but using only one type of wood forces compromise—if it's tough enough to resist abrasion at the tip, it's likely to be heavy; if it's light, it might not be tough enough, and so forth. The easy solution is to laminate different woods, applying each at the right point to utilize particular qualities. That the result also is beautiful is often just a bonus, although a maker can choose laminations to accentuate appearance as well as function. Some wood paddles are reinforced with fiberglass tips or fiberglass-covered blades. Others combine a composite shaft with a wood blade.

Synthetic materials used for paddles include fiberglass, Kevlar, and really exotic fibers such as carbon or graphite (a form of carbon) with foam cores. Fiberglass is a good mid-price choice; it blends excellent strength with reasonable weight. Carbon/foam paddles offer the ultimate in strength-to-weight ratio, but be cautious—many are designed for racing purposes and sacrifice durability for fanatical ounce-paring.

Recently developed thermoplastic technology is seeing use in paddles as well. Thermoplastic construction combines a plastic matrix, such as nylon or polyurethane, with fibers of carbon or silica-boron, in a heat-setting process that produces a very strong material.

The least expensive paddles usually combine a fiberglass or plastic blade with an aluminum shaft. Although these can be adequately strong, they are often heavy, and the shaft is not very pleasant to grip unless wrapped with thin foam or tape.

Design. A canoe paddle is designed to be gripped with one hand around the lower shaft and the other grasping the end of the shaft, which is shaped to provide a comfortable and secure hold. Wood touring paddles usually have what is called a pear grip—a gentle, rounded swell. Other paddles have a T-grip, which is a little more secure in rough water and allows you to use the paddle turned either way.

Blade design varies between touring and performance paddles. For long-distance use, you'll want a fairly small blade, which reduces your effort per stroke and is less affected by wind. A rounded tip is easier to paddle efficiently and splashes less. If you're going to be paddling for hours each day, you want as light a paddle as you can afford—another reason to go with a small blade.

For whitewater paddling, where you need more power, a wide, tulip-shaped or square-edged rectangular blade offers more surface area for acceleration and bracing. Unless you're a professional and don't have to buy your own paddles, look for stout blades with protected tips and a stiff shaft, even if there's a slight weight penalty.

Bent-shaft paddles, which cant the blade forward at a slight angle to the shaft, are a bit more efficient than straight shafts at straight-line propulsion, since the blade stays closer to vertical in the water toward the end of the stroke (so you're still pushing the water instead of lifting it). But they are trickier to use in advanced turning strokes, and can be a hindrance in rough water, where, for example, you might want to use the back of the blade to brace. It's better to start with a straight-shaft paddle and to experiment once you gain proficiency. If you carry a spare paddle for touring (a must), you can take one standard paddle and one bent-shaft, and switch as conditions mandate. A recent development in bent-shaft paddles is the *double* bend—an angled blade plus an additional bend in the shaft to locate the wrist at a more natural angle.

The length of your paddle is important but not critical. An old rule is that if you stand next to the paddle it should come up to just under your chin. For most people this is somewhere between 54 and 60 inches. A bent-shaft paddle is usually a few inches shorter.

PFD

Your life jacket, or PFD (personal flotation device), should be worn any time you step in the boat. In fact, federal law requires that there be one life jacket for each person in a canoe or kayak (although, ironically, the law does not require you to be *wearing* it). The kind of PFD you buy will depend on the type of paddling you do.

All PFDs sold in the United States must conform to a type rating, which goes from I to IV. A type I life jacket is intended for offshore use, with over 22 pounds of flotation and a buoyant collar designed to turn an unconscious person upright in the water. A type IV is a simple throw-ring or cushion. The type III jacket is the kind most paddlers use. It combines good flotation (minimum 15.5 pounds) with better freedom of movement than the bulkier models offer. Fifteen pounds of flotation might not seem like a lot, but keep in mind that the average adult only weighs about 10–12 pounds while in the water. Unless you are large and heavily muscled, the minimum type III flotation will suffice to keep your head safely out of the water.

Some type III PFDs are made with slabs of foam covered in nylon. Others use channeled foam, which is a little more comfortable and flexible. When you shop, make sure you get the right size—it should be snug but allow nearly unlimited movement of your arms and head. Various adjustment straps on the PFD will allow you to custom-fit. Remember that when you are in the water, the PFD will attempt to float while your body attempts to sink, so the jacket must not ride up around your head. Some models are equipped with crotch straps to prevent such slipping.

Keep safety in mind when you choose the color. You might prefer to blend in with the surroundings while you're paddling, but in an emergency situation you'll want to stand out. Red, yellow, and orange are the best colors for visibility.

Remember that the nylon covering of any PFD will eventually deteriorate in sunlight. You can extend its life by paddling only at night—or do the next best thing, which is to keep it in the shade when it's not on you. (See Chapter 5, p. 119, for tips on care of PFDs.)

Other Equipment
Flotation Bags

Unlike a kayak, a canoe is open to water coming over the gunwales—an obvious problem when tackling serious rapids. The solution is fitted flotation bags, which occupy the bow and stern, essentially filling the entire space with air. This accomplishes two closely related things—it provides flotation and prevents the boat's becoming sluggish from several hundred pounds of water sloshing back and forth. Flotation bag setups for tandem canoes can include a center bag. Of course, the bags eliminate cargo space in the boat, so they are mostly used for daytrips on whitewater.

Bailer

About $1.99 will buy you a perfectly efficient bailer—a half-gallon plastic drink pitcher with a stout handle. If that seems like too much to pay, cut off the bottom of an old bleach bottle and take a canoe trip with what you saved. Don't forget to tie the bailer to the canoe

A handy extra is a really big sponge to soak up the last dregs. It can be stuffed inside the bailer.

Clothing

A good rule to remember for canoeing attire is, Dress for the water. Paddlers get into trouble when they wear shorts and T-shirts because it's 75 degrees in the sun, while forgetting that the water in the lake they're crossing is 50 degrees. This doesn't mean you should bundle up in a dry suit every time you head out; it does mean you should pay attention to the conditions and your route. A tour along the shore and a long crossing might call for different degrees of protection. (River runners, see Chapter 5, follow the "120-degree rule:" If the combined air and water temperatures equal less than 120 degrees F, don wet suits, dry suits, paddle jackets, and booties to stay warm.)

Wilderness tours require a good layering system. A close-fitting underlayer of Capilene or polypropylene, which inhibit heat loss even when wet, is a good start, followed by light outerwear and insulating or waterproof garments, as needed.

Whitewater canoeing demands considerably more serious clothing. A wetsuit top is the minimum for chilly water; a farmer john, which combines leg and torso protection, is one step up; followed by a full wetsuit.

Another option is a dry top, sort of half a dry suit that prevents water entry with latex gaskets at the neck, waist, and wrists. For ultimate cold water, a full dry suit, with an insulating underlayer of fleece or pile, gives complete coverage. (For more on wet suits and dry suits for whitewater, see Chapter 5, p. 119.)

If both water and weather are warm, clothing selection loses its immediacy, but keep in mind sun exposure. A lightweight, long-sleeved shirt and a broad-brimmed hat, together with sunscreen for any uncovered skin, are essential.

Your choice of canoeing footwear will depend on whether or not you plan on getting your feet wet. For touring, if you're certain of your balance and the proximity of convenient landing and launching sites, you can wear walking shoes if you choose. The next option is rubber boots, which can help save your canoe's hull. How? Simple—you won't be tempted to ground the boat so often to avoid soaking your shoes.

Sandals, of course, are great in warm weather, and the new generation of water shoes, which offer more support and protection than sandals but can still be dunked, are excellent for both splashing and hiking.

Transporting

A canoe is a bulky thing to attach to a car. Fortunately, the parallel gunwales of canoes provide a sturdy support to carry the weight of the boat. A canoe is normally carried upside down, with the rails resting on pads or L-shaped gunwale supports attached to the crossbars of a roof rack. If you own other outdoor equipment such as a bicycle or kayak, you can use a commercial rack system that allows you to switch fixtures for different gear. Otherwise, you can make your own rack from commercial rack clamps, such as Quick-n-Easy's, and some strong wood bars. The homemade approach, however, will only work if your vehicle has standard rain gutters. If not, you'll need towers designed for your particular model, from a company such as Thule or Yakima.

Whichever system you use, install the bars as far apart as possible front to rear, to spread the load better and minimize side forces from crosswinds. The straps across the boat should be quite snug but not torqued down enough to distort the hull. It's always advisable to use bow and stern lines tied to the front and rear of the vehicle, both for extra security and to prevent wind from lifting the ends.

(See Chapter 15 for further resources for transporting outdoor gear.)

Storage

How long your canoe lives will depend to a great extent on how you store it. This can be summarized in one word: *inside.*

No matter what material your canoe is made from, it will stay in better shape if you can store it in a garage or workshop, or at least under a roof. If it has to be kept in the open, rig a tarp over it, using a rudimentary framework to keep the tarp from touching the hull.

The canoe should rest upside down, with its weight evenly supported on the gunwales. Weight distribution is especially important for canoes made from either natural materials or polyethylene, both of which can warp and take a set.

If your canoe gets stored for the winter, try to nag yourself into doing maintenance *before* storing it, not the following spring. Oil or varnish the wood, depending on which it needs; paint or touch up the canvas hull; and repair any gouges in the laminate. On Royalex

---

WOOD RAIL CARE AND REPAIR

Regular maintenance of wood rails is important to prevent rotting, splitting, or even cracks in the canoe's hull caused by the shrinking of dried-out wood.

At least once a year, apply a penetrating oil to the rails, after a light sanding with fine sandpaper (mask the hull to prevent scratching). Deks Olje brand oil is recommended because it contains fungicides and soaks deep into the wood. Varnish is not compatible with the constant give and bend of canoe rails, and it will soon crack off.

Apply several coats until the wood stops soaking up the oil. After allowing a couple of days for drying, wet-sand the rails using oil and 400-grit (very fine) sandpaper, which will result in a satiny smooth topcoat. This procedure can be used for any other nonvarnished wood on your boat.

For more great tips on canoe care and repair, see Annie Getchell's *The Essential Outdoor Gear Manual.*

---

hulls, don't forget to loosen the screws holding the rails to the gunwales, so the hull is free to shrink and expand. (See sidebar, p. 88, on Royalex care tips.)

Canoeing Lessons

Getting started in canoeing is like playing chess—you can learn enough in an hour to have fun, then spend the rest of your life mastering tactics and nuances. There's rarely a period of frustration involved; each time you go out you'll learn more, become more smooth, and gain more confidence.

Single or tandem? Canoe technique varies depending on whether one or two people are paddling. It's actually easier to learn with two: with one person paddling on each side, the boat will naturally go fairly straight, while a single paddler will have to change sides regularly to maintain a course. Turning and ferrying (moving the boat sideways) also are easier with two paddlers. The following sections will distinguish between tandem and solo technique when there is a difference.

Sitting or kneeling? Originally, all canoes were paddled from a kneeling position. Modern whitewater canoes are still designed this way, with foam saddles to add control and comfort. Recreational and touring canoes, however, have regular seats, which offer better long-term comfort. But the presence of seats doesn't mean a canoe *can't* be paddled kneeling. When rough conditions threaten, the paddler can slide forward off the seat to kneel in the boat, while still sitting back against the seat to brace. This position significantly lowers the paddler's center of gravity in the boat and contributes to greater control.

Basic Strokes
Launching

If you're learning on your own, you'll want a quiet body of water—a lake or very slow river—with a gently sloping beach with enough privacy so you won't be rushed when launching.

It helps if you can launch the canoe with the boat parallel to shore, just barely floating. When you climb in, remember to step in the *center* of the boat, to keep it from tipping. Keep your weight low at all times. You can brace a paddle across the gunwale to the shore to steady yourself. Use the same technique for embarking at a dock. Statistically, most nonwhitewater capsizes happen in shallow water, when participants are getting in or out of the canoe—the least dangerous, if definitely most embarrassing, situation.

Forward Stroke

The basic propulsion stroke comes so naturally that it hardly needs explaining. Nevertheless, there are a few tips that will increase your efficiency.

The instinctive tendency is to hold the paddle diagonally across your chest, so that the blade enters the water at an angle. A much more effective stroke is gained by planting the paddle nearly upright in the water, as close to the boat as possible. (1) This accomplishes several things: it gets more of the blade in the water, resulting in less wasted energy; also, the closer the paddle is to the centerline of the keel when pushing, the less the boat is turned to one side or the other; finally, a vertical paddle describes more of a straight

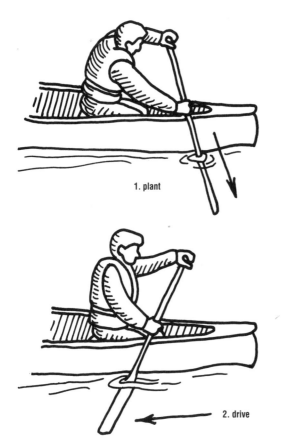

1. plant

2. drive

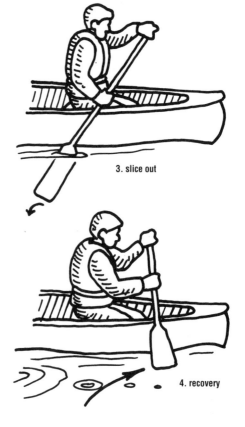

3. slice out

4. recovery

The forward stroke. See text, above and page 95, for explanation.

ROB GROVES

line through the water, parallel to the keel, further helping to keep the boat straight.

Even if you master an efficient stroke early on, the boat is still going to turn away from the side you're paddling on. If you're with a partner in a tandem boat, the way to remedy this is to paddle on opposite sides. If you're alone, you'll still have to switch sides occasionally.

Your back and shoulders should do more work than your arms in paddling. Much of the power of an effective stroke comes from driving the upper arm, rather than pulling with the lower. (2 and 3) Keep your back straight while you paddle and you'll almost automatically use more of your upper torso strength to power the canoe.

Learn to feather your paddle on the recovery portion of the forward stroke (while the blade is in the air—4). Turn your upper hand so that the thumb points forward and the paddle blade slices horizontally through the air. This makes the paddle much easier to control in a wind.

Finally, use a fairly short stroke in a canoe. Once the paddle gets behind you, the blade starts lifting more water than it pushes. Lean forward as you plant the blade so it enters the water upright, draw it back to keep the blade close to vertical, then lift it smoothly out shortly after it passes your hips. You don't want robot-like motions; you want a liquid flow of effort, so don't try to compartmentalize the stroke.

Turning

If you paddle on one side of the boat only, it will gradually turn toward the opposite side. When you wish to turn quickly, throw your efficient forward stroke out the window. Now you *want* the blade to describe an arc. Plant it close to the hull in front of you but sweep it out in a wide arc that ends close to the hull again, but behind you. This arc acts in three separate ways on the boat. While the blade is sweeping away from the hull in front of you, it is pushing the bow away from the paddle, the way you want to turn. The center of the stroke is far from the keel, further pushing the boat into the turn. And the end of the sweep essentially pulls the stern toward the paddle, which simultaneously pushes the bow the desired way. (See illustrations on p. 96 for this and subsequent strokes.)

When you become comfortable with the feel of the canoe, you can further assist your turns with leans. If you're turning left, for example, by sweeping the paddle on the right side, lean the boat to the right as well—that is, away from the turn. Leaning the canoe lifts the ends

out of the water, reducing the length of the canoe in the water—and a shorter boat turns faster.

Draw Stroke

Sometimes you want to move the canoe (or one end of it) straight sideways. If you're paddling solo from near the center of the boat or paddling tandem, reach straight out and plant your paddle in the water with the blade parallel to the canoe. Draw the paddle toward you, and the canoe will move to meet it. If two paddlers, one in the bow and one in the stern, use draw strokes on opposite sides of a stationary boat, it will spin in place. While under way, single or tandem paddlers can use draw strokes to alter the heading of the boat or to adjust the attitude of either bow or stern.

Although you need to be careful not to capsize by leaning too far out to plant the paddle, once you begin pulling, the forces involved actually work to keep the boat upright.

Pry Stroke

The pry is essentially the opposite of the draw. Plant the paddle in the water angling *under* the boat, then use the side of the canoe as a lever to pry the blade outward, which moves the boat the other way. If you need to repeat the pry stroke, the most efficient technique is to leave the paddle in the water but twist it 90 degrees, so the blade slices through the water on its way back under the hull.

Don't extend the pry stroke so far that your paddle winds up levering off the gunwale, or you'll push the boat down more than sideways. Be careful not to pinch your lower hand between the boat and paddle shaft. You can also perform a pry stroke using as a fulcrum your lower hand instead of the boat.

When tandem paddlers want to move the boat sideways, one can draw on one side while the other pries on the opposite side; thus both paddlers aren't leaning out one side of the boat.

Sculling

Sculling accomplishes a sideways boat movement similar to the draw stroke. You plant the paddle as you would for a draw stroke (although it needn't be as far out), but instead of drawing it back toward you, you describe a back-and-forth figure eight with the blade, angling it each way so the face of the blade (the side toward you)

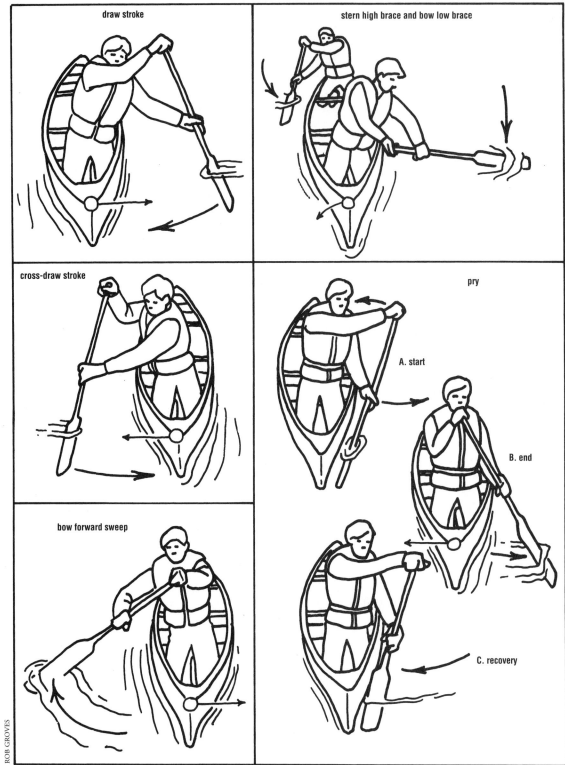

draw stroke

stern high brace and bow low brace

cross-draw stroke

pry

A. start

B. end

C. recovery

bow forward sweep

ROB GROVES

pulls the boat sideways. The path of the paddle in the water should be parallel to the boat hull. It's a difficult movement to describe on paper but easy once you try it.

Back Paddling

This might seem like an obvious one, but it's amazing how often technique goes down the drain when a grizzly bear or waterfall appears around the bend—paddles begin flailing impotently against the water. An effective backstroke—whether to slow or stop the canoe or actually to back up, should be as powerful and efficient as your forward stroke.

A really strong backstroke begins when you twist your torso to reach behind you, planting your paddle well back with the knuckles of your top hand pointing the direction you came from. Draw the paddle forward, keeping the stroke parallel to the keel, until the paddle is next to you, then quickly rotate the blade 180 degrees, until your top knuckles face the front of the boat, and finish pushing. The paddler in the bow, who is now essentially the stern paddler, might have to add a pry at the end to keep the boat straight.

Solo Propulsion Strokes

Solo paddling is perhaps the only aspect of canoeing that can be aggravating to a beginner, since the boat always seems to want to turn when you want to go straight. This tendency is accentuated if you are paddling from the middle of the boat, near its widest beam, where your stroke is necessarily farther away from the centerline of the keel. Paying attention to your propulsion stroke, as outlined in the previous section, helps a lot, but you'll still have to switch sides to

maintain a reasonable course. Two different strokes are used by solo paddlers to reduce the need for frequent switching.

J Stroke

The J stroke is important for both solo and tandem paddling if you want to travel in a straight line. It combines a standard propulsion stroke with an abbreviated pry stroke at the end, which kicks the stern back into line. It is most effective if you are paddling from the stern of the boat, since your pry stroke will apply the most leverage there. Take a normal stroke, but just at the point where you would normally be lifting the paddle from the water, twist the paddle and give a little outward pry with the blade. Your upper hand will turn so the thumb points forward, and your lower wrist will rotate inward. The blade should turn so it is completely perpendicular to its normal position on the propulsion stroke.

The J stroke is also used by the stern paddler in a tandem canoe to make small adjustments to the course. A strong paddler in the stern can use it to compensate for a wandering tendency produced when a weaker paddler is in the bow.

C Stroke

The C stroke works well from the center paddling position. It's especially useful when getting underway, since this is the time when the canoe has the least directional momentum and will try hard to turn.

Initiate the C stroke by planting the paddle ahead of you, about a foot away from the hull. Draw the paddle in and back, so that it sweeps slightly under the hull (the shaft will be angled well outward toward your

The J stroke.

ROB GROVES

upper hand now), then push it out from the hull in a strong J stroke as it sweeps behind you.

This stroke accomplishes the opposite of the sweep you use to turn—it first pulls the bow toward your paddle, then kicks the stern away, counteracting the normal forces of a solo propulsion stroke. Once you are under way, you can use a less pronounced C motion to maintain course.

Techniques for Rough Water and Currents

Waves can kick up on all but the smallest ponds, and a lazy river can get boisterous just beyond that bend. Once you've mastered the basic strokes, you'll want to know a few tricks.

First, read the section on basic hydrodynamics in Chapter 5 (p. 121), which will give you an idea of how moving water behaves. You won't become an expert river runner overnight, but you'll start out with a big advantage if you know the basics of hydrodynamics.

Bracing

Most canoes are very stable, even in bouncy conditions. But they *can* capsize, especially if you just sit there and let it happen. If the boat starts to tip, the proper response is a brace.

Bracing exploits the considerable force that results when you push straight down on the surface of the water with the face of the paddle. A *low* brace is accomplished by slapping your paddle blade flat against the surface, so that the shaft and your hands hit the water too. A quick, forceful slap is better than a push, since you don't want the paddle to completely sink beneath the surface.

A *high* brace looks like a draw stroke: the paddle is held vertically with the blade parallel to the boat and is drawn quickly toward the side of the canoe. A high brace is useful for situations in which you need to combine a brace with a maneuvering stroke. You can combine a high brace with a wide sweep, for example, to support the boat while turning.

You can also brace by sculling—in fact, with sculling a canoe can be held right on the edge of capsizing for as long as you like. The sculling brace is the same as the sculling draw stroke, except that the blade is held almost flat on the surface while being rocked back and forth in a figure eight to keep it planing and support the boat.

Sideslipping

You and your partner have learned to carve razor-sharp turns on the lake. Now you're trying a river for the first time, paddling downstream on a pretty quiet section, and you see two boulders in line with each other, one downstream from the other. Using your newly honed skills, you attempt to turn across the current to go between them—but something unexpected happens. As the bow of the canoe slides behind the upstream boulder, it suddenly slows and turns upstream, while the stern continues to travel downstream despite your efforts to line everything up. Before you know what happened, your canoe is bearing down sideways on the downstream rock. Uh oh.

You fell victim to the eddy behind the first boulder, an almost stationary patch of water out of the main current. Your bow slowed as it entered the eddy, but the stern was still out in faster-moving water.

One solution to maneuvering across the current in these situations is to sideslip. You and your partner use a draw/pry stroke to move the boat sideways while it remains pointing downstream, thus minimizing the effects of different currents—which can be caused by many things besides a boulder sticking out of the water. Remember that while sideslipping, the canoe is moving diagonally downriver.

Ferrying

Ferrying, as its name implies, is a technique for quickly moving a boat across a river. Like judo, it uses the force of the current to your own ends.

Back ferry. Suppose you and your partner are paddling downstream when you see a diversion dam ahead, or some friends on the opposite bank—or, you realize you're headed directly toward Niagara Falls. With a few backstrokes, you slow the boat in the water, so the current is moving past you. With either a draw or pry stroke, the bow paddler sets the canoe at about a 30-degree angle to the current, with the *stern* pointing toward the side to which you wish to go. Both paddlers backpaddle, holding the canoe at roughly the proper angle, and the current will carry the boat across the river. You have essentially used the entire boat as its own rudder. The back ferry works best with touring canoes, which have long keel lines that help grip the current. If the current is not moving very quickly, a back ferry can move you virtually straight across the current.

You can use a back ferry to enter a calm eddy as well. As the stern enters the slow water, the current will actually help the bow swing in after it. Watch the edge of the eddy line; often it extends at an angle from the source, and you must increase the angle on the canoe slightly to enter it properly.

Forward ferry. The forward ferry is a more aggressive paddling maneuver than the sideslip or back ferry, but in practice may actually be easier to do. It is similar to the back ferry, except that the canoe is pointed upstream and the stern paddler turns the boat so the bow is pointed in the desired direction of travel. Depending on the speed of the current, a forward ferry can carry you straight across the direction of flow or, if the river is moving fast, at a slight downstream angle.

Using Eddies

Even on fairly slow-running rivers, it's valuable to have places to pull out of the current, to check the map, scout conditions on the next stretch, or just take a break. But if the difference in current speed is substantial between the eddy and the main flow, it can be tricky to swing in to the lee of the boulder, island, or whatever is forming the eddy. If you don't catch it just right, you'll be swept below the calm water and forced either to frantically paddle upstream or to look for the next available eddy.

Eddy-in and Eddy-turn

Aim for the eddy from upstream and try to time your approach to just miss the boulder. To do this, of course, you'll have to aim *upstream* of the rock, since the current will be carrying you along. Only practice and experience will hone your aim and timing. It's better, of course, to miss the eddy than to collide with the boulder if you're not certain of the line.

The second the bow of the canoe enters the calm water, the bow paddler should lean out, plant the paddle in the calm water on the boulder side of the canoe, and perform a deep draw stroke to pull the bow toward the rock. At the same time, the stern paddler should do a draw on the eddy side of the boat, to pull the stern into the slack water as quickly as possible and to line the canoe straight upstream. The canoe should be leaned into the turn. The result, if timed right, is a nearly stationary boat pointed upstream right behind the boulder. (Once the turn is completed, both paddlers should con-

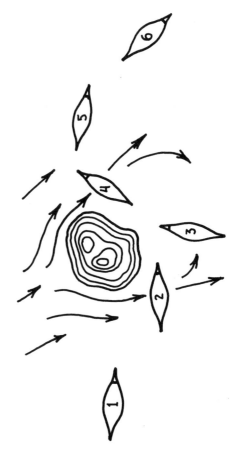

Enter the eddy: 1. Drive forward. 2. Cross the eddy line at 90 degrees and lean. 3. Pull up into the eddy. Peel out: 4. Drive up the eddy. 5. Cross the eddy line at 90 degrees and lean. 6. Hold lean.

tinue forward-stroking, in order to prevent the boat from slipping out of the eddy.)

The solo technique is identical, except you must lean and sweep the boat into the eddy in one powerful move, if possible.

Peeling Out

When you want to resume paddling downstream, you should leave the eddy with as much alacrity as you entered it. Allow the canoe to drift straight back from the boulder for a few yards, then paddle strongly toward the side of the boulder that lies across the top of the eddy line. Turn sharply toward the eddy line and drive through it, with both paddlers sweeping to turn the boat downstream, while again leaning into the turn—this time downstream. You don't want the canoe to stall in the unstable water at the edge, where it could begin drifting downstream still broadside to the main current.

Rescues
Capsizing

Sooner or later, if you push your limits at all, you're going to capsize—especially if you're running rivers. It's usually no big deal—in fact, it's a good idea to get used to the sensation, and to practice what to do afterward. That way, when an upset happens unexpectedly it won't feel like a disaster.

If you haven't figured it out beforehand, your first capsize will convince you of the value of tying in all your cargo. When practicing, you'll want to begin with an empty boat; however, for maximum real-world effect add some inert cargo later to simulate the load you might be carrying if you plan on touring.

There's certainly no trick to capsizing a canoe—just lean far enough and over it will go. Pay attention during these exercises, though—it's a good idea to be familiar with the limits of your craft. You can combine a session of envelope-pushing bracing practice with capsize management.

Always concentrate on hanging on to your paddle. Make it utterly instinctive, so that even after an unexpected capsize in rough water you will surface to find it still clutched in one hand. In a real-world capsize in river rapids, you should immediately get upstream of the canoe, if you are not already. You don't want to get caught between a swamped canoe and a rock. If you have to ride through a rapid without the boat, face downstream and keep your feet up in front of you to cushion any collisions with rocks. If conditions aren't dangerously rough, you can grab one end of the canoe or the painter to help it ride through the rapids (but *never* put your hand through any loops or lines in which you can become entangled). Your body will act as a drag to keep the boat parallel with the current and lessen the chances of rock collisions.

Back to practice—the first recovery technique you should try is simply dog-paddling the swamped or over-turned canoe to shore, since in most wilderness situations you'll be able to do the same. Once in shallow water you can right and empty the boat.

However, you might at some point be caught far enough offshore that you need to reenter the canoe from deep water. If the canoe is upside down, your first task is to turn it over—but the trick is to turn it over while scooping the least amount of water into it as possible. A maneuver called the Capistrano Flip accomplishes this well.

If you're paddling tandem the flip is much easier. First, both paddlers secure their paddles, usually by wedging them under the thwarts in the boat. Then both duck under the canoe, where there is usually a trapped air pocket. The paddlers face each other, each holding the canoe by the gunwales, and lift one edge of the boat to try to capture as much air as possible under the hull. Then, at the same instant, both give a mighty kick and a push, breaking the boat free of the surface and flipping it back upright. Often only a little water will remain in the boat after this move. A solo paddler will have to accomplish the flip from the center of the boat, and will likely scoop up more water in the process. If the boat is loaded, this maneuver is much more difficult; often even two paddlers cannot lift the boat while flipping, and more water will remain inside. However, properly dry-bagged gear helps displace water in the boat and, while heavy, actually adds buoyancy.

Reentry

Two paddlers in the water on either side of a canoe can usually get back in without much trouble. One can hang off the gunwale to balance the weight while the other clambers in. The one who gets in can then lean to the other side while the remaining person reenters.

A solo paddler faces a more difficult task. If the canoe has enough water in it that the gunwales are close to the waterline, it's possible to scoot over and into the boat. If so much water remains in that the canoe is awash, the paddler can either rock the boat from the side to slosh out a good deal of the contents, or push down on one end, which will encourage the water to flow down the length of the boat and out both sides. Neither of these actions will get most of the water out of the boat, but either might give it enough freeboard to regain a little stability. The paddler can then bail once he or she is inside.

Assisted Reentry

If another canoe is present when yours capsizes, the situation is much easier to handle. If the assisting canoe is positioned so it forms the head of a "T" with the capsized

lift

pull

flip

return

swimmers climb in

The assisted reentry.

boat, the rescuers can lift up on the end to right the boat and dump out the majority of the water. If the assisting canoe is pulled alongside the empty boat, the rescuers can steady the gunwale while the paddlers in the water take turns climbing in. A movement called the scoop will help here: the empty boat is tilted so the gunwale is almost under water next to the swimmer, then the rescuers literally scoop the person with the edge of the boat, depositing him or her in the bottom like a big fish.

Fitness and Health

You don't have to be in spectacular shape to begin canoeing. By simply adjusting your goals, you can accommodate almost any physique—even that serious postholiday, prediet sag. Regular paddling sessions will help burn it off, and the scenery is much better than the view from your stair machine.

Unless you're a swimmer or kayaker, canoeing is going to exploit some muscle groups that you don't often use. So start slow and short, and work up as the normal stiffness of a new activity diminishes. Some tenderness across the upper back and shoulders is to be expected, and your fingers will be stiff after paddling, until you learn to lighten up on your grip.

The most common injuries faced by canoeists are wrist tendinitis and shoulder strains. "Weekend warriors," who push themselves in a frantic attempt to *recreate* on their limited schedules, are prone to injuries. Common sense and a knowledge of one's limits are the easiest preventatives.

Off-season (or midweek) exercises can help you avoid problems. Wrist curls with either a barbell or individual dumbbells help strengthen the lower arms, and hand squeezers (you can buy commercial ones at climbing shops) build grip strength. For upper-body work, cross-country ski or rowing machines are good. An excellent workout for paddling can be had using an unweighted barbell. Sitting astride a weight bench

with your feet held down, use the bar as if it were a kayak paddle, rotating it through a paddling motion on both sides. Count your reps and work up slowly—and remember that the bar is far heavier than any paddle.

Be cautious when lifting your canoe. Most aren't really heavy, but they are fiendishly awkward, and the combination can result in strained or pulled muscles. Get help to lift the boat onto the roof rack when possible. Use your legs, not your back, to lift the boat off the ground.

Where to Go

The canoe is a tremendously versatile craft, and its popularity has far preceded more recent fads such as sea kayaking and river rafting. As a result, a healthy network of information sources and organizations is available to paddlers.

Perhaps the most intriguing way to plan a canoe tour is to read a few history books about the area to which you wish to go, then retrace a path that might have been used by earlier paddlers, whether explorers or trappers. Particularly in the north and northeastern parts of the United States, and in Canada, some of the old waterways have been protected for just such uses. *The Whole Paddler's Catalog* by Zip Kellogg lists some excellent books that can help you plan just such a trip (see resources section at the end of this chapter).

The ultimate North American canoe adventure might be an expedition to one of the remote lakes or rivers in the far north of Canada, accessible only by aircraft. A bush pilot can drop off you and your gear to utter solitude, with arrangements to retrieve you in the same place, or at some rendezvous 50 or 100—or even 500—miles distant. As an antidote to the frantic world of the late twentieth century, such a journey is the closest you can come to duplicating the experiences of the earliest travelers on this continent.

Where Can Canoeing Lead You?

As you become proficient with your canoe, you might find yourself being drawn one of two ways. The call of the Voyageurs could be strong, tempting you with dreams of remote wilderness journeys. Or perhaps your blood sings at the sight of a furious stretch of whitewater, and your eye automatically searches for the best

TOP 5

CLASSIC NORTH AMERICAN CANOEING TRIPS

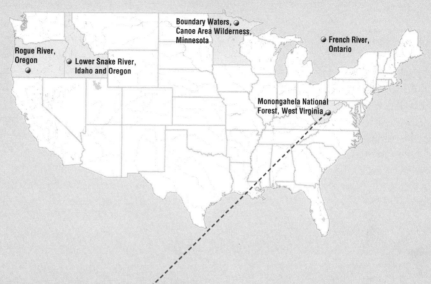

Summit Lake, in West Virginia's Monongahela National Forest.

- *French River, Ontario.* The oldest French Canadian trade route in North America, along which trade goods and pelts were ferried in 35-foot-long birchbark canoes. A 70-mile stretch is now a waterway provincial park.
- *Monongahela National Forest, West Virginia.* Streams such as the upper Blackwater, the North Fork of the Cherry, and the South Branch of the Potomac are among the crown jewels of this system, which offers something for both casual and whitewater canoeists. Tiny West Virginia boasts over 29,000 miles of rivers and streams.
- *Lower Snake River, Idaho and Oregon.* Ride the Snake on relaxing but fun class II runs. Choose three or four days on the river as it slithers through arid portions of Idaho and Eastern Oregon.
- *Rogue River, Oregon.* The Rogue offers classic Western canoeing, with 40 miles of protected wilderness paddling through the coastal mountains in easy class II and III water. Expect to see lots of wildlife, including bears.
- *Boundary Waters Canoe Area Wilderness, Minnesota.* Restricted to non-motorized boat travel, the Boundary Waters is the premier canoe experience in the United States. Conservation support is needed, however, because every few years groups try to open this pristine area, where wolves still serenade campers, to powerboats.

line. Many canoeists, of course, have a foot in both worlds, and keep two calendars. Spring might find them bouncing down fresh snowmelt on a stretch of rapids, while summer mandates a switch in boats and a break from civilization, with two or three weeks spent exploring a fly-in lake in the Northwest Territories.

Touring

As our civilization grows increasingly frantic, the time we can make to get away becomes more and more precious. The best antidote to the noise, pollution, and impersonality of the city is an immersion in wilderness—and there is no more intimate way to experience a wilderness than by canoe. You can travel within the landscape making no more noise or impact than the animals that live there.

There's no more intimate way to experience the wilderness than by canoe.

Loading

A touring canoe makes traveling and camping easy. Even a solo model can accommodate a couple hundred pounds of gear, and loading and access are simple. If you already own backpacking equipment, you'll have everything you need, but even gear more associated with car camping can be brought along by canoe. Many people take standard two-burner camping stoves, folding chairs, and large tents. Just keep in mind the recommended load limits for your canoe (check with your dealer or manufacturer). Even more important, keep in mind whether or not your route calls for portages, during which you'll be a backpacker rather than a canoeist.

Needless to say, all gear carried in an open boat must be protected from water. Dry bags of the type used for kayaking work well for clothes, sleeping bags, and tents. Dry boxes are useful for first aid kits and for storing such things as journals and books, repair items, flashlights and spare batteries. (See p. 64 for more on dry storage suitable for small boats such as canoes.)

For portaging, some kind of backpacks are necessary to consolidate and comfortably carry all the gear. Since it is inconvenient to carry a sophisticated internal-frame backpack in the canoe, most people use simpler packs designed specifically for portaging. Although these packs lack frames, they fold and stow compactly, or they can be used as nonwaterproof storage in the boat. A few companies make large dry bags with shoulder and waist straps. Pack baskets are still popular, as well.

As with any other small boat, the load in a canoe should be kept low and centered. Pack heavy items first, in the bottom middle of the boat. Don't forget to pay attention to the side-to-side balance of the canoe. Make doubly sure the gear that rests on the bottom of the boat is well waterproofed, since even on a calm paddle, water can splash in and pool here. Once the heaviest items are in place, load the other gear around them, making sure that things you might need through the day, such as jackets, rainwear, snacks, and lunch foods, are accessible.

All the gear should be well secured with line; cargo nets offer too much surface area in which a paddler or debris can snag in a capsize. Just make sure nothing can shift during a capsize. The only exception to this rule is in extreme whitewater canoeing, where items are often tied to the thwarts with lines long enough that they will float to the surface in the event of a capsize. This way, if the canoe is trapped in rocks, items such as safety gear,

PERFECTING PORTAGING

If you do any extended touring, sooner or later you'll cover a route on which you have to portage your canoe between two bodies of water. If you're a whitewater paddler, you're certain to run into stretches of rapids that call for the better part of valor: a walk around.

Perhaps surprisingly, for long portages it is generally easier for one person to carry the boat, upside down with a proper portage yoke. If two people carry a canoe this way, the person in front usually does not have a very good view forward, and unless movements are perfectly synchronized the variations in gait can set up an uncomfortable bouncing on the shoulders.

Some canoes come factory-equipped with portage yokes; many independent companies offer sophisticated models that can be added later. The original yoke was simply made from two paddles lashed to the thwarts so that the blades rested on the portager's shoulders. An even more expedient system was simply to arrange one's PFD so that it padded the shoulders and to rest a thwart across them.

Whichever system you use, it must be positioned to balance the boat properly, with the stern just a bit heavy, so the bow isn't constantly dipping in front of your vision.

A solo paddler can lift the canoe several ways. The most straightforward is to stand next to the upright boat and grab it by the near gunwale. Lift the boat straight up so that the hull is resting on your thigh, then lean over and grab the thwart on the opposite side of the boat and flip the entire craft over your shoulders. If done with the entire body, not just the arms, this maneuver is very efficient—and impressive to onlookers.

If there is a tree with a horizontal branch at head level nearby, you can turn the boat over and rest the bow on the branch, with the stern still on the ground, then crouch under and lift it off. This is also a good way to take a break during a long carry.

A second paddler can take the place of the tree branch, and also help steady the canoe during the portage. If there are very rough sections to cross, it is usually easier for two people to carry the boat across upright, one at each end.

clothing, and food can be retrieved easily, before the boat is rescued.

Paddling a Loaded Canoe

Almost every facet of canoeing technique will take a bit more effort when the boat is loaded with a couple hundred pounds of gear. One exception is straight-line track-

ing, at which a loaded canoe is better than an empty one. Turning and stopping, however, will take longer in both time and distance; plan your maneuvers accordingly.

Landing a loaded canoe is much more abusive to the hull than is landing an empty one. If possible, jump out before you touch bottom and guide the canoe gently to shore. When you stop for the night and unload the boat, turn it upside down and store the paddles underneath. Beware in porcupine country, though—wood paddles with a tasty salt finish from sweaty hands are tempting to them.

Finally, don't try to re-create Mackenzie's route across Canada for your first expedition. Do a number of weekend trips until you feel comfortable with all the aspects of paddling and camping, then extend your time out to a week or 10 days. This will give you the experience to know what you'll need for truly epic journeys.

For more information on camping, see Chapter 10. For route finding, see Chapter 9. And see Chapters 10 and 12 for more on camping and cooking.

Whitewater Canoeing

A couple of decades ago, if you wanted to paddle serious whitewater you bought a kayak. That situation has changed with the development of radical canoe designs intended specifically for the roughest stretches of the wildest rivers.

JOHN SHEPARD

Running whitewater in a canoe is challenging, but the rewards are high.

☞ **KID QUOTIENT**

If you rated kid quotient on a 1–10 scale, with 10 being top-notch for compatibility, canoeing would easily make a 10. Combine kids' natural attraction to boats with a stable, safe craft that one or two adults can easily manage with a couple of children riding along, and you've got a recipe for lifelong fun and adventure.

Any child old enough to properly fit into a PFD is old enough to go canoeing, providing you take a few precautions.

☞ PFDs should be worn whenever the child is near the water. Buy good-quality, comfortable models that will make this rule easier to enforce. Look for PFDs with a flotation collar and a sturdy grab loop at the back.

☞ The child should know how to swim, or at least have experience floating in the water wearing a PFD. That way if there is an unexpected dunking it won't be an unfamiliar and frightening event.

☞ Make sure kids are well-dressed for both water and air temperature. Children are more susceptible to hypothermia than adults are. Conversely, protect them from sun exposure with sunscreen and hats.

☞ Don't launch them on an epic trip their first time out. Try some day paddles and picnics to see how they take to the experience first.

☞ There's no need to keep all the kids piled in the center. The bow is a great place for a toddler to ride now and then, as long as an adult is close at hand.

☞ When they're old enough, give them their own paddles and let them help.

☞ Finally, resist the idea that you're bringing them on *your* experience. Make it theirs instead. Don't be discouraged if they get bored and want to read or play—it's normal for a child's attention to stray.

(See Chapter 11 for more tips on adventuring outdoors with kids.)

A true whitewater canoe is as different from a touring canoe as a sea kayak is different from a squirt boat. The whitewater canoe is designed with significant rocker and little, if any, keel, to maximize maneuverability in the tightest chutes. Whitewater canoes can even be Eskimo-rolled if—or rather when—they are capsized. With float bags taking up every cubic inch of interior volume not occupied by the paddler, even extended subsurface excursions have little effect on buoyancy.

If you're attracted to the idea of river running but lack any firsthand experience, it's possible to get a feel for the sport in a standard daytripper canoe, as long as you restrict yourself to class II rapids (see Chapter 5, p. 122, for a description of whitewater difficulty classifications). If you feel the pull of bigger water, it's time to buy a real whitewater boat and get serious.

Whitewater Canoeing Basics

Scouting. Never run a stretch of whitewater you have not first scouted. Scouting can be done from shore or, in mild rapids, from eddies. Never be afraid to portage around a rapid, no matter how many other paddlers you see running it comfortably. Use your own judgment and skill as your guide, not the actions or opinions of others. A good technique for running any rapid is to break it up into a number of segments, eddy to eddy. The eddies offer a chance to rest and plan the next section. Practice using eddies until you can pop into and out of them easily.

Avoiding pinning. One of the chief dangers of river running is broaching sideways to the current and getting the boat pinned against a rock or tree. The first time this happens to you in a mild rapid will convince you of the extraordinary power and weight of moving water. A canoe pinned against a boulder or trunk and allowed to tip upstream, so that the full force of the current can flow into the boat, can be folded in half around the

Any child big enough to fit properly into a PFD is big enough to go canoeing.

JOHN SHEPARD

object like a piece of limp pasta. Once in this position, recovery is extremely difficult if not impossible. Worse, the paddler can be easily trapped in the boat in this situation. If you find yourself broached and swept down on a boulder, lean the boat (not just yourself) aggressively into the rock, lifting the upstream edge of the canoe well out of the water. This allows the current to spill off the hull and gives you the chance to pry the boat forward or backward, so the water carries you off the obstruction. If the boat remains stuck, you are in a much better position to exit the craft and call for help.

Eskimo rolling. Yes, it is possible in a canoe. In a short, round-hulled whitewater canoe it's actually pretty easy. The technique is similar to that described in Chapter 3 (see p. 72), except you're working with a single-bladed paddle, which is in many respects easier to control.

Advanced whitewater paddling. If you've mastered class II and III rapids and still want more, consider joining a club or taking some classes at one of the many river-running centers across the country (contact one of the canoeing and whitewater associations listed below). Not only will you learn the techniques for handling really big water, you'll also be taught the rescue and boat recovery procedures that are a necessity for safely conquering such conditions.

Racing

There are many levels of canoe racing across the country, from fun "rodeos" to serious Olympic-class slaloms and long-distance marathons.

For information on canoe racing of all kinds, contact the American Canoe Association (listed under "Organizations" on this page).

Further Resources for Canoeing

Books

Path of the Paddle, by Bill Mason (Toronto: Van Nostrand Reinhold, 1980).

Canoeing Made Easy: A Manual for Beginners with Tips for the Experienced, by I. Herbert Gordon (Old Saybrook, CT: Globe Pequot Press, 1992).

The Whole Paddler's Catalog, edited by Zip Kellogg (Camden, ME: Ragged Mountain Press, 1997).

Periodicals

Canoe & Kayak, 10526 NE 68th, Suite 3, Kirkland, WA 98033; (206) 827-6363.

Paddler, P.O. Box 697, Fallbrook, CA 92028; (619) 630-2293.

Wooden Canoe (published by the Wooden Canoe Heritage Association), P.O. Box 226, Blue Mountain Lake, NY 12812; (518) 327-3259; quenelj@paulsmiths.edu.

Organizations

American Canoe Association, 7432 Alban Station Blvd., Suite B-226, Springfield, VA 22150; (703) 451-0141; acadirect@aol.com.

North American Paddlesports Association, 12455 N. Wauwatosa Road, Mequon, WI 53097; (414) 242-5228.

Schools

Nantahala Outdoor Center, 13077 Highway 19 West, Bryson City, NC 28713; (704) 488-6737, (888) 662-1662.

There are many other fine canoeing schools all over the country. Contact one of the organizations listed above for assistance finding one.

"I have never seen Mrs. Hopkins so hearty in my life . . . canoe traveling agrees with her."

—Comment made by Mr. Edward Manley Hopkins, husband of Voyageur artist Frances Anne Hopkins, to a friend in 1864

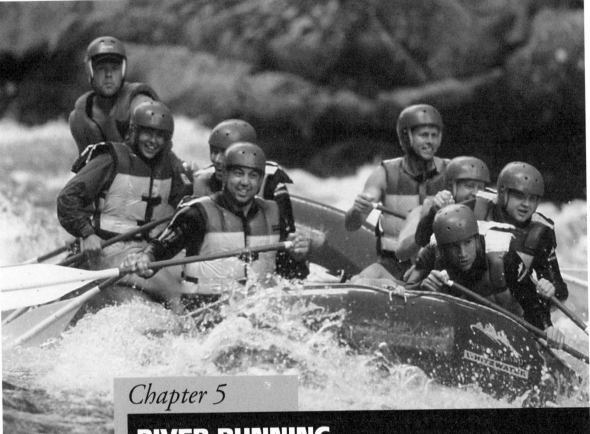

Chapter 5

RIVER RUNNING WITH INFLATABLES —*Wildwater Fun*

"No matter how many times I board a raft, I find myself captivated by the river, enraptured by whitewater, and consumed by the experience of running rapids."

—Jeff Bennett, *The Complete Whitewater Rafter*

Fast, Furious, and Fun

For thousands of adventurers, the recipe for fun goes something like this: take one part scenic wilderness with one free-flowing river; add one inflatable boat and mix in two parts lazy floating with equal parts starlit camping, then blend furiously with one part frothing whitewater.

Recreational river running in inflatable craft has been steadily building in popularity for the past 50 years, like a stream slowly gaining volume and speed as it runs toward the sea. The first known use of a rubber raft to explore a river occurred over 150 years ago, during John C. Fremont's descent of the Platte River with the U.S. Army. During World Wars I and II rubber craft were resurrected as life rafts. After the end of the World War II, surplus rafts found their way into the hands of explorers and adventurers, and by the 1950s, people such as Bus Hatch, Georgie White, Don Harris, and Amos Burg were charging down rivers on their own and with paying customers. Many early river runners also got their start taking conservationists down Western rivers to build support for fights against dam-building projects.

Today river sports are among the hottest outdoor pursuits in the country, resulting in a vast choice of guided trips for all ages and abilities, a renaissance in inflatable craft and gear technology, and a surge of support for protecting our threatened waterways.

River running with inflatables has many facets and faces: young and old, fast-and-furious and slow-and-serene, singles and families, novice and expert. For some boaters, river running means peaceful camps and relaxing floats down majestic desert canyons or past pine-covered slopes. For others, adrenaline-pumping first descents mark the apex of whitewater adventures. For still others, paddling ties friends and family together during lively river outings.

Piloting inflatable craft on rivers does not take immense strength and complex skills. Instead, river running takes a solid knowledge of moving water, its dynamic relationship with the objects it flows over and around, and how floating craft react when they are plunged into the middle of that relationship. Eddies and tongues, keepers and souse holes, rooster tails and boils—these are just some of the hydraulic results of moving water you will need to learn. But you don't need to learn everything at once. River running with

FIRST TIME OUT

You will probably never forget the thrill of launching your own boat into a river, on your own, for the first time. It is at that moment, when the current snatches at, catches, and pulls your boat into the heart of the river, that you feel the spirit-elevating reward of months of preparation and have your first taste of the sweet addiction to river running.

For your first river outing, whether in an inflatable kayak or in a raft, plan on a half-day run—no more than a few miles, depending on the velocity of the river flow—to give yourself plenty of time for a relaxed prelaunch prep and postrun breakdown. Look for a river that is easy, such as class I or II, and not too crowded. The last thing you want to do on your first day out is contend with the hazards of other boats or swimmers. Ask your boat dealer and other river runners for advice.

Relax! You will learn more if you relax, go with the flow, and absorb your surroundings—especially the way the water and your boat behave together. By all means experiment with your oar or paddle strokes, spin your boat, ferry it back and forth across the river—have fun! You might want to choose a short river stretch with easy take-out and put-in access so that you can repeat the run a second or even third time. It is amazing how much you will learn.

In your eagerness to get on the water, don't forget to take sunscreen, drinking water, hat and long-sleeved shirts, bug repellent, lunch, maps and guidebooks, and a boat repair kit.

inflatables is an endless process of learning, in which experience is piled atop experience and ever-evolving skills soon correct the misplaced strokes and ill-chosen routes of past trips. Inflatable rafts and kayaks are stable and forgiving when used properly, and are designed to support first-time river runners safely even in moderate whitewater. If you give it your best, you can acquire enough skill in your first day or two of river running to carry you comfortably from easy class II rapids to more-powerful class III rapids (see sidebar on river-difficulty classifications, p. 122). Then, as your confidence and ability grow, those same basic skills will help you navigate more-challenging rivers with only slight modification.

Choices for running rivers in inflatables include

- *Inflatable kayaking.* One- and two-person inflatable kayaks have become extremely popular craft for river running in the last decade.
- *Paddle rafting.* A crew of two or more paddlers work together to maneuver a raft with single-bladed paddles.
- *Oar rafting.* One person uses two long oars to guide the craft, which can hold just the pilot or a number of passengers.
- *Catarafting.* These double-pontoon catamarans are becoming more popular every year. They are most commonly rowed by one person using two long oars or paddled by two paddlers, although some outfitters convert large catarafts to paddle-and-oar combos.

If you have never floated rivers in an inflatable craft and are a little nervous about taking the plunge, you might first want to take a guided river trip to see if you and rivers are compatible. With so many river-running possibilities existing in North America, you should be able to find anything from a serene float to a churning whitewater run within a day or so of your hometown. Paddling experience in sea kayaks or canoes will translate to an accelerated comfort level on whitewater rivers, but soft-shelled craft behave differently from those with hard shells. A commercial trip will help you feel the difference first hand.

Taking a guided river trip is one of the ways to get a taste for whitewater thrills.

Whatever type of trip you take, you will get a feel for the gear, the nature of free-flowing water, and the skills necessary to undertake rafting or inflatable kayaking on your own. Then, when it comes time to set up your own outfit, you will be able to better answer some important questions prior to plunking down the bucks:

What kind of river experience are you after? Do you seek serenity or thrills? A little of both? This may influence the design of the raft you choose, or steer you more toward kayaks than rafts.

Will your trips be daytrips, or will wilderness camping be a big part of the experience? Many daytrips warrant small, light craft, while multiday camping trips demand cargo haulers.

Will your trips be solo, or will you add family and friends? One person can pilot a small raft, although certain designs are easier to handle solo than others. If it's just two of you, a pair of kayaks or one small-to-medium raft is plenty, but if you want to include friends, kids, or extended family, plan for one larger or several smaller craft. A core of two or three cargo- and passenger-hauling rafts with two or three kayaks makes for a fun flotilla—people can trade off rowing, relaxing, or paddling kayaks.

Much of the information for this chapter was adapted from The Complete Whitewater Rafter, *by Jeff Bennett (Camden, ME: Ragged Mountain Press, 1996) and* The Complete Inflatable Kayaker, *by Jeff Bennett (Camden, ME: Ragged Mountain Press, 1996).*

What You'll Need

Once you've settled on a type of craft, it's time to take the plunge and outfit yourself. Inflatable craft run the gamut of price, from inexpensive $100 kayaks to state-of-the-art self-bailing rafts that cost nearly as much as a new car. If you are careful and shop at a river-running specialty store, it is hard to get stuck with really poor quality, even at the lower-end prices. Many stores offer "test drives" of models as well. In addition to talking with salespeople, ask local river runners which craft is best suited to the areas in which you wish to paddle—a rig that's right for the big rivers of the Southwest might not be suitable for the small creeks of the Pacific Northwest, for example.

If you plan to get out on the river often and constantly upgrade the difficulty of your runs, do yourself a favor and invest in a top-quality boat that can withstand the rigors of river running. If you just want to putter down easy rivers a few times a year, you can get away with the moderately priced boats. The same general rule applies to oars, paddles, helmets, and life jackets (or PFDs—personal flotation devices). In a sport such as river running, your life often depends on the quality and condition of your gear.

Inflatable-Boat Hull Materials

The material from which inflatable boats are made comprises two parts: the *base fabric* and the *coating.* The base fabric provides tear and puncture protection; the coating provides abrasion resistance, air retention, and protection from ultraviolet (UV) rays.

Base fabrics. Base fabrics consist of cloth sheets made from woven or knitted polyester or nylon threads. Most whitewater rafts and inflatable kayaks are constructed of materials with a minimum of 420 denier (denier measures the weight of one 9,000-meter-long thread, in grams; the heavier the thread, the higher the denier), the more durable fabrics feature deniers of 1,000 or more.

Coatings. Most fabric coatings fall into two general categories: *rubber coatings* and *plastomers.* The most popular rubber coatings are Hypalon (polyethylene chlorosulfone) and neoprene (polychloroprene). Popular plastomer coatings include PVC (polyvinyl chloride) and urethane (ether-based polyurethane). Each coating can have many variations—for example, there are more than 20 neoprene compounds.

- *Hypalon.* Hypalon is a lightweight rubber coating that stands up well to abrasion and UV rays, is fully cured when applied, and bonds securely to the base fabric. In top-quality rafts and kayaks, Hypalon makes up almost 80 percent of the coating. Cheaper craft, on the other hand, might contain as little as 25–50 percent Hypalon. Although Hypalon is durable, long-lived, easily repaired, and deflates and stores compactly, Hypalon boats can be more flexible than PVC or urethane boats and tend to "stick" to obstacles more often. However, some manufacturers use stiffer base fabrics and higher-quality Hypalon coatings to give their craft a more solid, slick feel.
- *Neoprene.* Neoprene, once very popular in whitewater rafts, is not as common today. It is similar to Hypalon but heavier and less abrasion-resistant. Its best feature is its ability to hold air. Top-quality, carbon-

black neoprene holds air extraordinarily well, is highly resistant to UV degradation, and is easy to repair.

- *PVC.* While comparable in abrasion and UV resistance to Hypalon, PVC (a plastomer) is a much lighter and stiffer coating—especially when used with polyester base fabrics. PVC's light weight and increased rigidity lets boats glance off rocks and hold their shape in powerful hydraulics (a catch-all word to describe the surface features of a river, such as waves and holes) a little better than the softer Hypalon boats. Another advantage of PVC is that it can be welded rather than glued, thereby creating an inseparable bond between panels. The tradeoff for this added stiffness is that PVC boats don't wrap up as tight and can crack if rolled up in very cold temperatures. Also, PVC isn't fully cured when applied to the base fabric; its plasticizers leach out slowly, leaving the coating brittle and weak after many years of use.

- *Urethane.* Polyurethane—another plastomer—is particularly durable and appears on many state-of-the-art boats. It is extremely rugged and long-lasting (perhaps more so than Hypalon and PVC), it recaptures some of the *hand* of Hypalon, and it can be welded like PVC. Urethane can be used alone (without any other coatings) or sprayed over other coatings as a protective outer layer.

- *Reinforced vinyl.* Strictly an inexpensive kayak coating, reinforced vinyl's only advantage over other coatings is its low price.

Rafts

Most rafts fit into one of three categories: standard-floor rafts, self-bailing rafts, and catarafts.

Fully assembled standard-floor and self-bailing rafts consist of many independent components, each of which is important to the raft's performance. The list of components includes *tubes, baffles, seams, panels, thwarts, valves, floors, pressure-release valves* (primarily on self-bailing rafts), *D-rings, rubbing strakes, chafe pads,* and *carry handles.* In the accompanying illustration you'll see that most of these

parts show up in a typical self-bailing raft. Standard-floor rafts differ from self-bailing rafts only slightly, and catarafts, though unique in shape, display many of the features common to other rafts.

Tubes. All high-quality self-bailing whitewater rafts have one continuous outside tube that gives the raft its distinctive oval shape. The tubes are divided by baffles or bulkheads into multiple chambers. The independent air chambers keep the raft afloat even if one chamber is punctured. They also add rigidity by holding the internal air in place.

Bladder. The bladder system is similar to that of a car tire and inner tube—a bladder is inserted into the outer tube and filled with air. If the inner bladder is damaged, it can often be removed and patched, or replaced, faster and more easily than can a more conventional, single-layer tube.

Panels and seams. Tubes are constructed from many separate pieces of material, or panels, welded or glued together. Their overlapping joints are sometimes concealed and strengthened with welded or glued strips of seamtape. Thermo-welding is a process that actually fuses the panels together without the use of toxic glues or solvents. Welded rafts tend to be more bombproof than glued rafts, since there is no possibility of a seam delaminating on a hot day. Nonetheless, glued joints and seams rarely separate and can be repaired.

Valves. Each air chamber of a raft's tube or tubes has its own valve. Most rafts feature one of three types of valve: military-style, Halkey-Roberts, and AD-1. Military-style valves open and close by twisting the

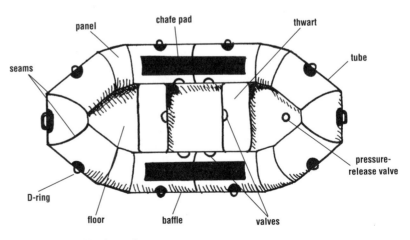

Anatomy of a self-bailing raft.

outer assembly. When they are open, air flows freely in either direction. Halkey-Roberts and AD-1 valves have spring-loaded center posts that let you pump air one-way into the raft. To release the air, you depress the post. Valves should be durable, maintenance-free, and easily accessible.

Thwarts. Thwarts are the inflated cross-tubes that run at right angles to the main tubes. Whether glued, welded, clipped, or strapped in place, thwarts help the raft maintain its shape by holding the main tubes an equal distance apart. Thwarts also give paddlers more surface area to brace against. If you will be using a rowing frame, removable thwarts can be detached to free up valuable storage space without compromising the raft's structural integrity. Removable thwarts should have a bombproof binding system.

Floors. Raft floors are generally described as *standard* or *self-bailing.* (See individual sections on standard-floor and self-bailing rafts for more information.)

Accessories. The most common raft accessories are *D-rings, rubbing strakes, chafe pads,* and *footcups.* D-rings are heavy-duty steel rings attached to a fabric patch that can be glued or welded to the raft. D-rings provide points for strapping down frames and gear, tying your raft to a trailer, or retaining a bow line. Rubbing strakes and chafe pads are extra layers of fabric that are bonded to the outer tubes to protect the raft from collisions and abrasion. Footcups are welded or glued to the floor of paddle rafts, where passengers can wedge their feet in deep and lean far out of the raft with total confidence—even in heavy whitewater. Properly mounted footcups should fit any paddler.

Design Characteristics

Many factors affect a raft's performance, from the type of material used in its construction to the size and shape of its floor, tubes, and thwarts. The most apparent differences among traditional rafts are in length, width, tube size, thwart size and attachment, number of thwarts, number of chambers, type of floor, and bow and stern shape (including the amount of bow and stern rise). Each of these factors can enhance or hinder a raft's whitewater performance, depending on the type of river traveled.

For more on these details, refer to *The Complete Whitewater Rafter* (Ragged Mountain Press, 1996) and your boat dealer.

THE ESSENTIALS—AN INFLATABLE PADDLING START-UP KIT

- Inflatable raft or cataraft, 12'–16' long ($550–$7,000) or Inflatable kayak ($100*–$2,000)
- Pump ($35–$150)
- Paddles (1–2 for kayak; 4–6 or more for paddle raft) ($35–$200 each) or Pair of oars, and one spare ($200–$400)
- Rowing frame, if you choose an oar raft ($200–$1,200)
- PFD ($50–$100)
- Helmet ($20–$100)
- Wetsuit top and/or bottom, or farmer John ($85–$225)
- Footwear ($0–$80)
- Dry bags ($10–$100)
- Safety kit of line, rescue hardware, first aid ($100–$200)

*Minimum cost essential rafting kit (paddle): $990***
*Minimum cost essential kayaking kit: $435***

*(The cost of a reinforced-vinyl kayak; some experts, including Jeff Bennett, discourage their use on rivers.)

ADD-ONS

- Water bottles
- Maps and guidebooks
- Cooler
- Cooler frame
- Dry suit
- Dry boxes
- Special river clothing (synthetic)

**The essentials list above is intended to give you an idea of minimum start-up costs, from scratch, for moderate entry into a sport using new equipment. Other options include borrowing gear from friends or renting from retailers, YMCAs, or church activity clubs, as well as buying used gear—see Appendix A.

DENNIS WELSH

Standard-Floor Rafts

The standard-floor raft is a tried-and-true design that has been used successfully and happily by generations of boaters. Standard floors are durable, and although it means your paddle crew has to bail religiously, some boaters swear that a little extra water in the cockpit goes a long way toward making the boat more stable in rough water (note: a *little* extra water, not a boat-full!). Also, standard-floor rafts are usually well priced—a plus for beginners. Do keep in mind that standard-floor rafts are best as oar (rowing) boats for moderate rivers. Because of their need for constant manual bailing, they are not the best choice as paddle rafts on difficult whitewater.

Standard floors are welded or glued to the main tubes, in effect creating a giant bathtub. Some standard-floor rafts are built with wrapped floors, which merely means that the floor continues upward around the outside of the main tubes. Wrapped floors generally extend up to a rubbing strake—an additional piece of thick, durable material bonded to the perimeter of the tubes to act as a bumper.

Self-Bailing Rafts

Self-bailing rafts, with their remarkable water-shedding capabilities, perform well in almost any type of whitewater. On small, technical streams the self-bailing raft remains light and nimble. On large-volume rivers the self-bailer's quick reactions let rafters turn quickly into

> **◆ EXPERT TIP: KEEP YOUR FLOORS TIGHT**
> Floor design can have a profound effect on a raft's handling characteristics. Standard-floor rafts capture water in the passenger compartment like a giant bathtub, rendering the raft heavy and unwieldy once it gets waterlogged. To keep the standard-floor raft light and maneuverable, the water must be bailed out manually. The best standard floors are very taut when the raft is inflated. Floppy, loose floors sag and hold more water, making bailing more difficult. If there isn't a pool or eddy close by to pull into and bail, the extra water could be a real hazard. However, on rivers with short, steep drops and long pools, the standard-floor raft works just fine.
>
> Before you settle on a standard-floor or self-bailing-floor raft, paddle or row both in a variety of whitewater, so you can get a feel for each style's pluses and minuses.

oncoming waves and deftly ferry around big holes and pourovers.

Self-bailing raft floors are buoyant, designed to float the floor's upper surface higher than the surrounding river level. When water enters the raft, it lands on the floor's top, then pours off the floor and out of the raft through holes or slots. Most self-bailing floors have either an I-beam or a drop-stitch construction. In I-beam construction, indented pleats run the length of the floor, giving it the appearance of a common air mattress. In drop-stitch construction, thousands of tiny threads hold

Raft Length (in feet)	Raft Width (in feet)	Tube Size (in inches)	Rowing/People	Paddle/People
10	5	16	1–2	2–3
12	6	18	2–3	3–4
13	6	18	3–4	3–6
14	6.5–7	20	3–5	4–8
15	7	21	4–5	6–8
16	7.5	22	4–6	6–10
18	8	24	5–6	8–10

Raft size selection table for standard-floor and self-bailing rafts: The chart above provides a useful starting point for selecting the proper raft by its capacity rating. Keep in mind that rafts aren't all the same shape and size, as described earlier. Also, factors such as the amount of gear you plan to carry and the type of rivers you will be rafting will affect your choice of raft.

the floor's surfaces an equal distance apart. A drop-stitch floor has a smooth top and bottom, as opposed to the deeply channeled surfaces found on I-beam floors. Either type of floor can be attached to the raft by welding or gluing, or by lacing the floor to the main tubes with guy-lines that run through matching slots or grommets.

The advantages of removable laced-in floors are that they can be replaced if damaged, can be separated from the raft for long portages, and can be cut loose to free pinned rafts. Only rarely do the ropes or straps holding the floor in place snap. Glued-in floors, on the other hand, are simpler, have no ropes that could fail, and can be built with a lower, faster profile. However, they sometimes bail more slowly and are difficult to replace.

Self-bailing rafts handle very differently from one another. For example, self-bailing rafts with smooth, flat-bottomed, drop-stitched floors are highly maneuverable and easy to turn, but they may not track as well as those with deeply furrowed I-beam floors. I-beam floors, on the other hand, track quite well but tend to take a little extra effort to turn.

Catarafts

Made up of two to six pontoons and a frame, the cataraft displays some distinct differences from other types of rafts—such as its lack of a floor. Because catarafts have no floor, there is no passenger compartment to bail. This cuts down on drag on shallow rivers and lets the tubes pierce all but the most stubborn hydraulics. If the cataraft ever *does* find itself wrestling a sticky hole, the river will pour through the open tubes, and the boat will be less likely to flip. The decreased

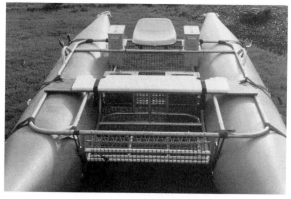

Some cataraft frames include safety nets. This helps the rower stay aboard if bounced from the seat, but makes it impossible to climb back through the center if the raft flips.

ROW-ROW-ROW OR PADDLE-PADDLE-PADDLE YOUR BOAT?

When choosing a raft, you have to decide if you will set it up as a paddle raft (with four or more paddlers for power) or as an oar raft (with a single person for propulsion).

Outfitting a paddle raft costs less (no frames and long oars), but in general, paddle rafts are best suited to daytrips, since your cargo-hauling ability is limited by the number of passengers taking up valuable cockpit space. Paddle rafting is great for families with older kids (big enough to paddle without falling out of the boat); an active part in a sport instills early confidence in kids. If you have young kids, or plan to undertake longer trips, an oared raft may be the best way to go. If you are not certain what type of raft to get, buy one suitable for both oar-rafting and paddle-rafting.

Almost any cataraft can be rowed or paddled with the right gear. Oar frames take great advantage of the cataraft's light weight by placing the weight of the rower and gear over the middle of the raft, creating a central pivot point. To paddle a cat you've got to outfit it with saddles, quick-release straps, or paddle frames.

drag also makes cats faster to row and paddle than regular rafts.

The flip side of all this added mobility and stability is a big loss in buoyancy. Without a floor to provide added lift, all the weight of the frame, passengers, and gear rests on two to six tubes. This makes it a tougher craft to outfit and use as a paddle boat and means that rafters on multiday trips must pick a cat big enough to haul all their gear. Also, a good frame in a cataraft is critical, because a broken frame cannot be repaired in the field.

Outfitting Your Raft

In order to use two oars to guide your raft, you will need a rowing frame. Constructed from aluminum, steel, or other metals, rowing frames secure gear, stiffen the raft, support a rower's weight, and provide a fulcrum for the oars.

Basic rowing frames consist of side rails that rest atop the tubes, crossbars to keep the frame square, oarlock stands to hold oarlocks or pins, and a seat for the rower. Foot braces, various seat types and mountings, and other additions—such as dry-box wells, cooler retainers, movable oarstands, and breakdown frames—are options that add to your rowing comfort and pleasure.

Raft frames provide a fulcrum for the oars, seats for rowers and passengers, and lash-points for cargo.

Frames can be built to fit in the center of the passenger compartment or in the stern. If there is only one guide, and no one else around to assist with paddling, the center frame works best, since it puts the pivot point near the middle of the raft. Stern (rear) frames, on the other hand, are often used in conjunction with paddle teams to provide some extra power when the guide really needs it.

Inflatable Kayaks

Dubbed "rubber duckies" shortly after they appeared on the river scene (the first popular inflatable kayaks were bright yellow), these versatile craft run the gamut from inexpensive reinforced-vinyl bobbers that are great for easy rapids to expensive PVC and urethane rockets that will take you down the most challenging class V waterfalls.

Inflatable kayaks, sometimes called I-Ks, share most of the features of rafts, only scaled down, and are made from the same materials (with the exception of inexpensive vinyl). Most kayaks incorporate two independent main tubes; only a few manufacturers use a single tube divided into chambers, and some use bladders. You will find thwarts, valves, and D-rings. Floors are similar as well (including self-bailing), although some of the better kayaks have foam flooring inserts, which help stiffen the kayak and protect your hind end from collisions with rocks. Usually the kayaker sits on the floor, braces his lower back against the thwart (sometimes these are adjustable), and uses thigh straps and footwells or braces for added security. A few manufacturers offer seat arrangements for canoe-paddling style, so the paddler can kneel.

Some boat makers build two-person inflatable kayaks, called K-2s. About 1–3 feet longer than one-person kayaks, they provide a fun alternative for daytrips. They are perfect for carrying older kids and teaching novices how to paddle, and can be used as a gear-hauler for one person on a multiday trip.

Another option in inflatable kayaks is the catyak—a

Features like open cockpits and stable tubes distinguish inflatable kayaks (top two) from hardshell kayaks (bottom).

scaled-down version of the cataraft. The advantages and disadvantages are basically the same for the smaller cousin as they are for the big one: less drag and more stability, but less lift and harder turning. Frames are steel, plastic, or fiberglass.

Oars and Paddles

Whichever type of propulsion device you need—oars, single-bladed raft paddles, or double-bladed kayak paddles—they all have one thing in common: a baffling array of materials and shapes, not to mention even more opinions about which is better for any given whitewater run, boat, or paddler.

In general, oars and paddles are made from wood, aluminum, or composite materials, such as graphite.

Wood. Many river runners swear by their wooden oars or paddles—usually crafted from ash, fir, oak, and spruce—for beauty, for strength, and for "feel." However, wood does flex, and it requires regular maintenance (a winter ritual of sanding and varnishing that many river runners say they can't live without).

Aluminum. Oars and paddles made from aluminum are popular for their sturdiness, easy maintenance, economy, and versatility. Also, the blades used on aluminum oars—almost always made from durable plastic or composite—can be changed, while many of the shafts can be extended or pulled apart for transport.

Composites. The lightest, strongest, and most expensive oars and paddles are made from materials such as fiberglass, carbon-fiber, and graphite (a form of carbon). When properly laminated, these materials can mimic the feel of a wooden paddle or oar while providing much of the durability of aluminum. Because they are so light and strong, they are also easier on joints such as wrists and shoulder, and thus make a good choice for frequent or long-distance paddlers. Composite oars and paddles are available in break-apart models or those with replaceable blades.

INFLATABLE REPAIR

In an ideal world, inflatables would never tear, or they'd magically mend themselves without any human assistance. In the real world, the Ram Patch is the closest thing to magic for making on-river repairs.

This amazing little tool seals small tears by squeezing the raft or kayak fabric between two rubber-faced disks—one for the inside of the tube and one for the outside. The Ram Patch kit includes a specially designed key for tightening the patch in place, as well as a miniature razor blade for making small holes large enough to accept the disks.

Carry a Ram Patch in your repair kit. If all goes well you'll never use it, but if you ever do need it you'll be glad to have it.

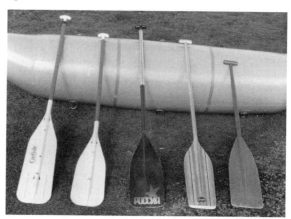

Make sure you buy paddles with the right length and blade-shape for your body size and boat type.

HARD-SHELL KAYAKS

Hard-shell boats comprise a whole separate dimension of whitewater river running. For the past 15–20 years, these boats have dominated the field for single-person river running. Fitting to the lower body like a glove, these small, sleek boats provide the best control and maneuverability on the water. On the other hand, you need more skills and a more aggressive approach to running whitewater in a hard-shell kayak. Once you're dialed in, however, you'll be able to squeeze a lot of dance and dynamics out of a classic hard-shell kayak.

Somewhat new to the whitewater scene are plastic sit-on-top kayaks. Instead of being sealed *into* these kayaks with a spray skirt, the paddler sits in a molded seat on top of what looks like a puffed-up surf board and uses thigh straps and foot braces to stay on the boat. Sit-on-tops are great for novices and experts alike and offer forgiving behavior and good maneuverability.

Choosing a hard-shell boat over or in addition to an inflatable boat is simply a matter of personality: control and finesse vs. simplicity and comfort. Many paddlers end up with a small fleet of boats to suit their moods or their destinations.

Which is best? There is no clear-cut answer. Talk to other river runners and assimilate their opinions as much as you can. Consider especially what is most important to you for the type of river running you will be doing: light weight for fast and fun daytrips, heavy-duty for serious class IV and V runs, break-apart ease for packing down, or the strength and esthetics of renewable materials. And don't forget to buy a spare of the same quality as your primary. Should you need it in the middle of a hairy run, you won't want second-rate quality.

When you purchase your raft or inflatable kayak, make sure you buy the correct-size oars or paddles for your boat. Many factors influence the correct size, including boat width, tube size, seat configuration, and of course, your size. Consult the manufacturer of your boat and your retailer for some recommendations.

Personal Safety Gear

While you cannot help but think of your boat as the most important piece of gear—and rightly so, for where could you go without one?—don't discount the importance of having good, well-fitted life jackets (PFDs), helmets, and clothing such as wet suits and river shoes.

PFDs

All river runners should wear PFDs at all times (accidents can happen in calm water, too). PFDs not only increase your buoyancy in the event of a swim, but their foam-filled shells provide some extra insulation on cold days and even some welcome body armor against rocks. A properly fitted PFD is comfortable enough to wear all day and doesn't interfere with rowing, paddling, or swimming. It will cinch snugly around your torso and won't ride up over your face or head in rapids.

♦ EXPERT TIP: PFD FIT

How is a PFD supposed to fit? Try on a PFD and cinch it up tight; then, have a friend yank upward on the shoulders. If the PFD fits properly, it will budge only slightly while remaining comfortable. Remember to account for the bulky layers of riverwear under the PFD when choosing the size that's best for you.

The main purpose of a PFD is to keep your mouth and chin above water long enough to let you breathe. To accomplish this feat on varying human bodies, PFDs come in varying degrees of flotation capabilities. In general, the heavier you are, the more flotation you will need—and the same holds for wilder water. Because of the increased likelihood that river runners might smack rocks or lose consciousness, many people opt for "high-float"–style PFDs that have extra flotation in the torso or a collar to hold the head up (but see the section on swimming, p. 119).

Before you can decide how much flotation you'll need on your next river trip, you'll need to evaluate your own abilities and your paddling plans.

What type of water will you be paddling? If you plan to take on some challenging class III or IV whitewater, make sure you have a PFD that will float you reasonably high in rough water. For mostly easy water, you can do with less flotation.

How much do you weigh? An average person is surprisingly buoyant, weighing only 10–12 pounds when immersed in water (less if you're thin, more if you're heavy).

What type of clothing do you intend to wear under the PFD? A wet suit can add 6–8 pounds of buoyancy, and an air-filled dry suit can add more.

Are you a strong or weak swimmer? If you're a weak swimmer or about to embark on a very difficult run, a PFD with maximum flotation may increase your safety during a swim. However, the more foam added to the PFD (to increase its buoyancy), the more it will interfere with your ability to swim, row, or paddle. Also, high-flotation PFDs might make it tougher to escape holes or reversals. Strong swimmers on gentle rivers may be able to get away with slim, low-flotation models. (For a discussion of the U.S. PFD rating system, see Chapter 4, p. 91.)

Since there are so many factors involved in choosing a PFD, ask your dealer to help you select one, or get a couple of types so you'll be ready for any type of river.

PFD RX

Most river runners take pretty good care of their boats (the pain of forking out a lot of cash helps), but consider what your life *really* depends on in a true emergency: your PFD. Equipment expert Annie Getchell, author of *The Essential Outdoor Gear Manual*, offers the following advice.

All your PFDs should be subjected to an annual dunk test, since the sun cooks the life right out of both shell fabrics and flotation fillings. To test: put on life jacket and jump in some deep water—it should still float your head and nose out of the water. But even if you float, the fabric may be so rotted from sunny fun that it's ready to give up the ship. In this case, buy a new one.

Always rinse your PFD with fresh water after every outing. Body salts from perspiration, plus other unknown contaminants found in our less-than-pristine rivers, can degrade the fabric. Two excellent ways to delay UV damage is to coat your PFD fabric with 303 Protectant at least twice a season and store it out of the sun when not in use. Occasionally lubricate the zipper with dry graphite or beeswax, used *very sparingly.*

Helmets

Helmets have become *de rigeur* for rafters on many whitewater rivers, and they are mandatory on any class IV or V outing. Helmets consist of a sturdy outer shell, a shock-absorbing liner, and a chin harness to keep the helmet on your head. Outer shells can be made of plastic, fiberglass, Kevlar, or other strong, rigid materials.

A properly shaped and fitted helmet covers the entire head—including the top of the head, temples, and ears—but remains unobtrusive to the wearer. Some helmets even have face guards to protect against injuries caused by rocks, flailing paddles, or collisions with other paddlers. Make sure the helmet fits your head comfortably: the chin strap should hold the helmet securely in place so the helmet won't ride up and expose your forehead or slide down and block your vision.

Clothing

Novice rafters are often astonished when they first discover how cold most rivers are. Whether fueled by snowmelt, rainfall, or dam releases, most rivers are cold enough to require some form of outerwear on even the warmest days. And although rivers look bouncy and fun, remember what creates those bouncing waves: rocks.

When choosing riverwear, select garments that provide
- Comfort
- Flexibility
- Sufficient insulation to ward off hypothermia

You may be able to get away with shorts or bathing suits when the river is forgiving and the air is warm, but such conditions are the exception to the rule. Experienced rafters consider river and air temperatures, the type of river they'll be rafting, and their expected level of activity in determining their clothing requirements. Novices, on the other hand, can follow the "120-degree rule:" If the combined air and water temperatures equal less than 120 degrees F, don wet suits, dry suits, paddle jackets, and booties to stay warm. You can always peel off layers during the trip if you get *too* warm.

Wet suits. Body-hugging neoprene wet suits have been a favored form of insulation for many years. The wet suit works by shielding unprotected skin from direct splashes and trapping a thin film of water between the suit and your skin during swims. Once water fills the suit, it is warmed by your skin and insulated from the river by the suit itself. Wet suits also provide some extra flotation and padding—nice to have if you're swimming a boulder-strewn river. Try not to get the same type of suit worn by scuba divers; a rafter's higher activity level and increased range of motion demand a thinner wet suit—⅛-inch (2–3 mm) neoprene provides both warmth and flexibility. Also check for proper fit: a wet suit should follow the contours of your body without being too tight. The most popular style for river runners is the farmer john, which leaves the arms and shoulders uncovered. For added warmth and protection you can wear a synthetic shirt or sweater and a paddling jacket or dry top.

Paddling jackets and dry tops. Paddling jackets and dry tops are high-tech rain jackets similar in design to the upper half of a dry suit (described below). The main difference between paddling jackets and dry tops is in their ability to shed water. The more affordable paddling jacket combines loose layers of waterproof cloth with water-resistant neoprene or Lycra closures at the neck and wrist. The dry top, on the other hand, incorporates waterproof latex closures at the neck and wrist. Both paddling jackets and dry tops are effective when you're sitting in the raft, but they let water in through the waist opening when you're swimming. They're usually used as an outer waterproofing layer with wet suits, to help prevent chilling blasts of cold water from finding their way down the front of your suit. On warmer days, however, paddle jackets and dry tops can be enough to keep hearty boaters warm with nothing more than a synthetic shirt or sweater underneath.

Dry suits. Dry suits differ dramatically from wet suits in both appearance and function. Instead of trapping water near the skin, the dry suit keeps water off your body by enclosing it in a loose-fitting layer of waterproof fabric. The suit has a large waterproof zipper or flap closure for entry and exit and is made totally waterproof with tight-fitting latex gaskets at the neck, wrist, and ankle openings. Though dry suits lack the insulating qualities of wet suits, they are baggy enough to fit over inner layers of clothing. As with other outdoor sports, the best way to choose clothing that will keep you warm is to follow the *layering* concept. The innermost clothing layer should wick sweat away from your skin, and the next layers should be warm and absorbent. Since the dry suit will seal in body moisture, it is important to choose inner layers made of synthetic materials such as nylon or polypropylene fleece.

Other clothing accessories. Booties, gloves, and insulating caps vastly improve the quality and safety of your boating experience on cold rivers. Thick neoprene booties with semirigid soles keep feet warm and provide decent traction during slippery portages. In warmer climates, river sandals (with extra straps to hold them securely on your feet) and water shoes work great. Neoprene caps help the body retain an enormous amount of body heat by providing another layer of insulation over your head. Hands can be kept comfortably warm with neoprene gloves.

Stowing Your Stuff
Waterproof Containers

You will want to pack your gear in waterproof containers, whether you are going on a daytrip or a two-week jaunt. Your choice includes old Army surplus ammunition boxes, hard-sided plastic or aluminum dry boxes, and rubberized dry bags. The latter two are available at specialty retailers and are worth the investment. If you take care of them—lubricating the O-ring seals and avoiding undue abuse—they will last you for years. (Tip: Pay extra for heavy-duty dry bags and boxes, and in the long run you'll be much happier.)

Ammo cans are cheap and work great if you pad their sharp corners with glued-on neoprene or dense foam. You will find a wide selection of sizes and prices at Army surplus stores; inspect them well, and avoid any that have traces of petroleum products, which can degrade your expensive rubber equipment.

Totally Tied Down

Enough can't be said for properly placing and *tying down* the dry bags, boxes, and coolers in your boat. It may not be on the first trip, or the second, or the tenth, but you will flip your boat some day, and you want your gear to stay with the boat not only for convenience' sake, but for safety, too—an airborne metal ammo box can be as deadly as the missiles it once stored.

Some tips for stowing gear:

- Place gear near the bottom of the raft to keep the boat's center of gravity low.
- Consider packing your gear on suspended cargo platforms to keep it out of the water and to protect the floor.
- Keep the weight in the boat balanced side-to-side.
- Store heavier gear toward the center, lighter gear toward the bow and stern, and keep it balanced bow-to-stern as well.
- Don't overload your boat.
- Use buckled nylon or polyester straps (not bungee cords) to lash down gear via D-rings, an oar frame, thwarts, and drain holes (make sure the straps are the correct length so there are no long "tails" that can entangle people; and don't use cargo nets to lash items down—people can get tangled in them if the boat flips).
- When you think everything is well secured, add a few extra straps for good measure, and jiggle everything to test security.

Getting There

An oft-overlooked (at least until departure day) detail when learning to outfit for running rivers is transportation. How will you carry your boat or boats, frame, oars, paddles, pumps, bags, coolers, and food? Rivers are one-way streets, so how will you get back to your put-in site?

If you own a pickup truck, then you're most of the way home. If not, there are several options. Deflated boats can sometimes be packed on sturdy roof racks if the boat is not too heavy, but frames are fairly bulky, and so are oars that don't break down (remember your transportation options when purchasing gear). Many people opt for trailers on which fully assembled but slightly deflated boats may be strapped, with plenty of room left underneath in the trailer and on the roof rack of the car for ancillary gear. Whichever transportation option you choose, make sure your boat does not rub against sharp corners and other abrasive objects on the way to the river. (See Chapter 15 for further resources for transporting outdoor gear.)

Unless you have several cars in your paddling group—several that can handle hauling gear and people—you will need to arrange with a shuttle service to pick you up at your take-out point and return you to your put-in. (You can also hire a shuttle service to drive your cars to the take-out for you, so you won't have to hassle with the long shuttle drive after a tiring day on the river.)

All About Water

For anything but smooth, flat rivers (on which boats from inflatable mattresses to inner tubes can be easily maneuvered), you will need to learn the basics of hydrology: the characteristics and behavior of water as it flows down a rivercourse. In addition, you will need to understand how a boat reacts to hydraulics in order safely and successfully navigate rivers.

Tips to remember. As river difficulty increases, the danger to swimmers becomes more severe. As rapids become longer and more continuous, the challenge increases. There is a difference between running an occasional class IV rapid and dealing with an entire river of this category.

Allow an extra margin of safety between skills and river ratings when the water is cold or if the river itself is remote and inaccessible.

Remember to take into account that rivers change

Class III whitewater is fun and challenging. Moderate rapids with irregular waves and powerful hydraulics give boaters a good run for their money.

RATING RIVERS

Of the two systems used by river runners to classify the difficulty and intensity of rapids, the most popular is the International Scale of River Difficulty, which grades rapids on a scale of I–VI. In the southwestern United States, another system, known as the Deseret Scale or Grand Canyon System, is often used (rating rapids on a scale of 1–10). Unfortunately, neither system is perfect. Rapids change constantly and are affected by water-level fluctuations and shifts in the riverbed. Rafters might rate rapids differently depending on their attitudes or skill levels. Also, the successful pursuit of more-difficult whitewater has resulted in a downgrading of many rapids. Rapids that used to be considered class VI (extreme) have been downscaled to class V after many successful descents. So river classifications are little more than a starting point for finding out about any river. You should gather as much additional information about rapids as you can—always consult a guidebook and obtain accurate firsthand descriptions prior to any run.

The American Whitewater Association's River-Rating Scale (based on the International Scale of River Difficulty):

Class I. Easy. Fast-moving water with riffles and small waves. Few obstructions, all obvious and easily missed with little training. Risk to swimmers is slight; self-rescue is easy.

Class II. Novice. Straightforward rapids with wide, clear channels that are evident without scouting. Occasional maneuvering may be required, but rocks and medium-sized waves are easily missed by trained paddlers. Swimmers are seldom injured and group assistance, while helpful, is seldom needed.

Class III. Intermediate. Rapids with moderate, irregular waves that may be difficult to avoid and that can swamp an open canoe. Complex maneuvers in fast current and good boat control in tight passages or around ledges are often required; large waves or strainers may be present but are easily avoided. Strong eddies and powerful current effects can be found, particularly on large-volume rivers. Scouting is advisable for inexperienced parties. Injuries while swimming are rare; self-rescue is usually easy, but group assistance may be required to avoid long swims.

Class IV. Advanced. Intense, powerful, but predictable rapids requiring precise boat handling in turbulent water. Depending on the character of the river, it may feature large, unavoidable waves and holes or constricted passages demanding fast maneuvers under pressure. A fast, reliable eddy turn may be needed to initiate maneuvers, scout rapids, or rest. Rapids may require "must" moves above dangerous hazards. Scouting is necessary. Risk of injury to swimmers is moderate to high, and water conditions may make self-rescue difficult. Group assistance for rescue is often essential but requires practiced skills.

Class V. Expert. Extremely long, obstructed, or very violent rapids that expose a paddler to above-average endangerment. Drops may contain large, unavoidable waves and holes, or steep, congested chutes with complex, demanding routes. Rapids may continue for long distances between pools, demanding a high level of fitness. What eddies exist may be small, turbulent, or difficult to reach. At the high end of the scale, several of these factors may be combined. Scouting is mandatory but often difficult. Swims are dangerous, and rescue is difficult even for experts. Proper equipment, extensive experience, and practiced rescue skills are essential for survival.

Class VI. Extreme. These runs often exemplify the extremes of difficulty, unpredictability, and danger. The consequences of errors are very severe and rescue may be impossible. For teams of experts only, at favorable water levels, after close personal inspection, and taking all precautions. This class does not represent drops thought to be unrunnable but may include rapids that are only occasionally run.

from season to season: For example, high water during spring runoff, or low water during fall drought—each poses different challenges.

Avoid running difficult rapids late in the day; if there is a serious problem (such as a wrapped boat), it is best to have plenty of daylight left to deal with it.

The International Scale's six classifications work well for making basic comparisons between rivers or rapids, but rafters have had to fine-tune the descriptions to keep up with the vast spectrum of rapids being run today. Some rafters have suggested using a decimal and a number from 1 to 10 in addition to the International Scale when rafting class V rivers—each increment implying a greater degree of difficulty in that level. For example, a class V.1 is an "easy class V," while a class V.10 is a "very challenging class V."

Always rely on your own skills and judgment, and don't let anyone—or any system—tell you what you can or can't do.

Water Basics

It's amazing how little we know about the wet stuff of which the world is made. Before launching your boat successfully down a local river, you'll need to learn about water in general and river water in particular.

Water weight. Water is amazingly heavy: 1 cubic foot of water weighs 62.4 pounds. Multiply this by many thousands of cubic feet moving rapidly along, and you get an idea just how much force you and your boat will be battered with.

Volume. River volume is measured in cubic units per second. In the United States, the foot is used for the cubic unit, and the correct term is cubic feet per second, or cfs. Simply stated, cfs measures the amount of water that passes a specific point on the river each second. However, the proper formula is the river's width, times its depth, times the speed of the current (velocity). For example, a river 20 feet wide by 10 feet deep, with a current flowing 5 miles per hour, has a flow of 1,000 cubic feet per second ($20' \times 10' \times 5$ mph = 1,000 cfs).

In general, "small" rivers are those up to about 1,000 cfs; "medium" rivers, from 1,000 to 6,000 cfs; and "large" rivers, from 6,000 to over 100,000 cfs. Over the course of a season, or even a week, a river can swell from small to large to medium many times.

Trying to correlate changes in water volume with the river's difficulty rating is nearly impossible. On some rivers, rapids become more difficult as water level lowers. On others, rapids disappear beneath gentle blankets of swift water at higher flows. No matter what happens to the river you plan to run, remember that larger volumes and faster currents can turn gentle rivers into powerful hazards.

One problem with gauges is that many agencies monitor water levels on a gauge-height basis. Rather than simply announcing the flow in cfs, the agency will give you a gauge height in feet. All this tells you is how high a river has climbed up an oversize ruler placed in the river at a set location. To use this information you'll have to know the river intimately or be able to correlate the gauge height with river flow. Many of the guidebooks explain how to do this. If that doesn't work, the agencies themselves usually maintain a correlation table.

Water velocity. Using the basic formula for volume (width $\times$ depth $\times$ speed of the current), you can see that the addition of more water—say, from a recent rain

---

GAUGING RIVER VOLUME

Before heading toward your intended river, you need to know its volume of flow. Many government agencies monitor river flows. In turn, river runners can obtain water-level information by contacting the agency that monitors the river they plan to run. Here are a few places to start:

- Hydrological Information Unit, United States Geological Survey, 419 National Center, Reston, VA 22092; (703) 860-7531.
- National Weather Service, National Oceanic and Atmospheric Administration, Department of Commerce, 8060 13th Street, Silver Springs, MD 20910; (301) 427-7622.
- United States Army Corps of Engineers, Public Affairs Office, 20 Massachusetts Avenue, NW, Washington, DC 20314-1000; (202) 272-0010.

Or, try Waterline National River Gauge Reports, a 900 (toll) phone service. Before you call Waterline, call (800) 945-3376 to order lists of river gauge codes (six-digit numbers) for the rivers that interest you. When you call (900) 726-4243, a recorded message will tell you the cfs, and the time and date it was last updated. The reports are current, and the cost is around $1.25/minute of connection time.

Another source is the American Whitewater Affiliation's Internet web page. Their River by State listing is updated frequently and will give you the latest information on access and dam release schedules. Look for

http://www.awa.org/awa/river_project/states.html.

---

or a tributary—to a 20-by-10-foot river running at 1,000 cfs will increase the speed of the current. For example, double the flow of the river, making it 2,000 cfs instead of 1,000 cfs: since the river's depth and width haven't changed, the additional water must move twice as fast to make the formula work. Instead of moving 5 miles per hour, the velocity jumps to 10 miles per hour ($20' \times 10' \times 10$ mph = 2,000 cfs).

Changes in volume or river velocity have some important effects that river runners need to understand. Since water is heavy (see above), the addition of a few cfs or an increase in river velocity causes a huge increase in the amount of force that water exerts on a raft or a swimmer. It works like this: for every doubling of the current's velocity, the force exerted by the water quadruples. This added force can exert itself on anything in the water's path, or it can be used to support debris suspended in the river's current. (That is why flooded rivers can displace boulders and transport giant logs like overgrown corks.)

Gradient. In the U.S., gradient is described in feet per mile (fpm), the measure of a river's average descent over a given distance. To figure out the gradient of your intended river run, you will first need to know three things: the elevation at the put-in, the elevation at the take-out, and the distance between the two points. For example, if the put-in is at an elevation of 3,000 feet and the take-out is at 1,200 feet, the river drops 1,800 feet in that section. If the section to be rafted is 36 miles long, the river drops 50 feet per mile (1,800 ÷ 36 = 50). Here's the formula:

(put-in elevation–take-out elevation) ÷ miles = gradient

Rapids appear where the gradient of one section of river exceeds the river's average gradient, and pools form where the gradient dips below the overall average.

The Dynamics of Running Water

When we were kids most of us probably spent some time throwing leaves, sticks, or toys into creeks and watching how they bobbed and turned and got sucked under "rapids," only to shoot out again a few feet or yards away. It was fascinating entertainment.

Now here you are planning to throw *yourself* into much larger rapids. Since you, too, can get bobbed, turned, and sucked under rapids, it's a good idea to learn something about the medium on which you're going to travel.

Water flowing down a rivercourse is not one unit, as you might now imagine it. For example, in *laminar flows,* which are found on straight, unobstructed rivercourses, the fastest-moving water is just below the surface in the center of the rivercourse, while the slowest-moving water is near the riverbed and riverbanks, where friction acts as a slowing agent. In between those layers are many layers (currents) flowing independently of each other and at different speeds. *Turbulent flows* arise wherever obstacles such as boulders or narrow cliffs change the course of the currents, forcing too much water into too little space. And *helical currents* flow outward from the bank along the surface until they collide with the main current, where they spiral downstream, dive, and work their way back toward the bank under the surface. At the extreme end of the spectrum you will find "chaos."

At high flow levels, rivers can become unpredictable and more dangerous.

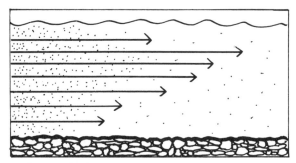

In this example of laminar currents, the longer arrows represent faster currents that appear just below the surface. The currents near the riverbed are slowed by friction.

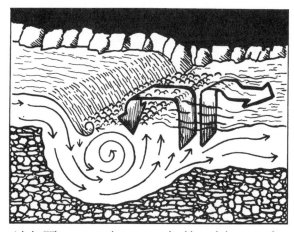

A hole: When current plunges over a boulder or ledge, some of it sneaks downstream beneath the surface while the rest of it recycles upstream to fill in the cavity. You can judge the intensity of some holes by the size and power of the backwash—the bigger, the meaner. Small holes are fun to crash through, but giant holes can flip rafts or even trap swimmers.

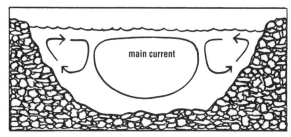

Helical currents flow away from the bank on the surface, meet the main current, then dive. Next, the water works its way back to the bank, then rises along the shore to repeat the cycle.

The perfect example is a hole—where the current scatters in so many directions that it effectively cancels itself and remains stationary.

Think of flowing water as a dynamic, multifaceted creature: it adapts, splits up, changes from moment to moment—predictably in some cases, unpredictably more often.

Surface Features

The surface features of flowing water are what river runners are most interested in—slide into a hole or under a breaking wave and you're in the rinse-and-spin cycle; or, if you're getting good, you *intentionally* jump on a standing wave and surf like crazy (this is what many river runners consider *real* fun).

When you're just starting out you will be experimenting with gentle rivers and class I and II rapids, which will introduce you to smaller and tamer versions of the surface features found on class IV and V rapids. For now, familiarize yourself with the features; later, you will need to delve in-depth into each feature's dynamics and the best ways to run them in your chosen craft (books such as Jeff Bennett's *The Complete Whitewater Rafter* and *The Complete Inflatable Kayaker* provide excellent in-depth information).

Boil. Ascending current that rises above surface level unpredictably.

Chute. Narrow, constricted portion of the river.

Eddy. A pocket of water downstream of an obstacle that flows upstream or back against the main current.

Eddy line. The interface between the eddy current and the main current (a high eddy line is called an *eddy fence*).

Funny water. Anything but funny; this describes a region of unpredictable currents and boils near eddy fences.

Haystack. A large, unstable standing wave.

Hole or *reversal.* A swirling vortex of water wherein the river pours over an obstacle and drops toward the river bottom, leaving a pocket behind the obstacle into which an upstream surface current flows. A *keeper* is a large hole or reversal that can keep and hold a raft or swimmer for a long period of time—sometimes with fatal consequences. A *waterfall* is really just a very tall hole.

Hydraulics. Changes in currents that cause surface features that can deflect, slow, or speed up a raft's descent (e.g., holes, waves, and eddies).

The best way to navigate unavoidable features like this hole is to use momentum to punch straight through it. Pool-drop rivers like the one shown here alternate between calm pools and plunging rapids, while continuous rivers descend smoothly and gradually.

This paddle captain is giving the "thumbs up" because his team avoided the dangerous undercut rock (upper left).

Roller. A big curling wave that falls back upstream on itself.

Rooster tail. A fountain of water that explodes in a fan pattern off a submerged obstacle.

Stopper. A hole, reversal, or breaking wave capable of stopping, holding, or flipping a boat or a swimmer.

Strainer. An obstacle, such as a tree, that lets water flow freely through it but catches swimmers, rafts, and debris (a.k.a. *sweeper, logjam, boulder sieve*).

Tail wave. Standing wave that forms at the base of a rapid.

Tongue. A smooth V of fast-moving water that frequently appears at the top of a rapid.

Getting on the Water

It's time to launch—but before you spin off downriver with your stern where your bow should be, you will need to learn the basic oaring or paddling techniques seasoned river runners use to navigate safely through those surface features with which you've become familiar.

Different Strokes for Different Boats
Oar Rafting

Using two 10-foot-long oars to maneuver a raft down a whitewater river takes considerable skill, which will come with practice. The best way to practice is to make easy runs as often as possible, watch more experienced rowers, and gradually increase the class of the rapids you run. There are four basic oar strokes and maneuvers you will need to learn.

Backrowing. Backrowing, which is *pulling* on the oars, is the foundation of many raft maneuvers for two reasons: it slows the raft down in relation to the current, and it provides the starting point for more advanced ferrying techniques. (For this and all of the following strokes and maneuvers, the person at the oars sits facing the front of the raft and is positioned either in the center or stern.) Each backstroke involves four phases, known as *reach, catch, power,* and *recovery phase.* The feet should be firmly braced, especially during the power phase, to maximize pulling force. Put your whole body into the pull: legs, back, torso. When rowing, concentrate on economy of movement: don't dip the oars too far into the water or arc them too high out of the water when setting up for the next stroke in the recovery phase. Also, during the catch phase, strive for a silent stroke (don't slap the water).

Portegee (pronounced *port–uh–GEE*). The opposite of the backstroke, the portegee might just as easily be called frontrowing. To execute the portegee, the rower leans back, pulls the oar handles close to the torso, and lifts the handles. This plants the blades into the river toward the bow. The rafter then begins the stroke's power phase by leaning forward, pushing the handles outward, and straightening both arms.

To backstroke, plant the oar blades in the water behind you, and pull your hands toward you. The blades will swing forward while the raft moves backward.

The portegee is less powerful than backrowing because it relies on the weaker muscles of the front torso. However, it is very useful in gentle rapids and is frequently used to give a raft the last bit of push up a steep wave or through a strong hole. To make the stroke a little stronger, put one foot on the floor or frame close to your body and push with your legs.

Single- and double-oar turns. Oar turns are based on a simple theory: one-legged ducks swim in circles. Pull on one oar and the bow will turn toward that oar. Push on the same oar, and the bow will turn away from it. Whether you pull or push this oar, the raft will turn. Whenever you need to execute faster, more powerful turns, push on one oar while simultaneously pulling on the opposite oar. This technique, called the double-oar turn, causes the bow to spin quickly toward the oar being pulled without any loss of forward motion.

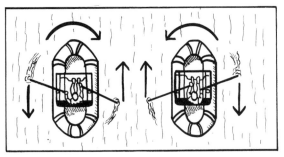

You can turn your raft with single-oar turns, but double-oar turns (shown here) are more powerful. Either way, the bow will always spin toward the backstroking oar.

Shipping oars. In narrow or rocky channels there will sometimes be more rock than water lapping against your oarblades. Sometimes, just lifting the blades out of the water will protect your oars, but at other times you'll have to pull the oars inboard to avoid hitting rocks. This is called shipping. Oars can be shipped forward by tucking the blades against the side of the bow, or shipped backward by tucking the blades against the side of the stern.

Paddle Rafting

It's quite a thrill to be part of a finely synchronized team in a paddle raft. To accomplish synchronicity, each paddler needs to know both basic and advanced paddle strokes. Canoeists will immediately recognize these as their own.

Grip. Before you take a stroke, make sure you're holding the paddle correctly. Paddles have a T-shaped grip at the top of the shaft. Firmly but gently grasp (no white knuckles) the top of the T, like you would to shift an automatic car transmission, with the thumb underneath. Your other hand wraps around the paddle shaft with the palm facing the boat (this is always the arm on the *outside* of the boat).

Forward stroke and *backstroke.* The forward stroke—the most important stroke in the paddler's arsenal—uses the powerful muscles of the torso. Lean forward and thrust the paddle toward the bow; the lower arm (shaft) becomes straight as the paddle reaches its maximum comfortable extension, and the upper arm remains slightly bent at eye level. From that position, keep the blade at a right angle to the tube, pull it toward you with your lower hand, and push forward with your upper hand. End the stroke just forward of your hips and start over again.

The *backstroke* is, for the most part, just the opposite of the forward stroke. You hold the paddle in the same manner as for forward strokes, but you plant the paddle behind your hips and drive it toward the bow.

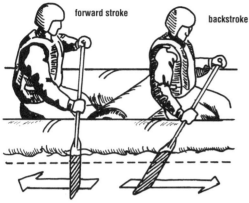

In the basic forward stroke you plant the blade ahead of you, then simply pull your shaft hand toward your hip while pushing away with you upper hand. To backstroke plant the blade behind you and rotate forward while pulling your upper hand toward you. You can use your hip as a fulcrum, but beware of submerged rocks and powerful hydraulics.

During the backstroke's reach and catch phases, you rotate your outside shoulder backward and plant the paddle in the water slightly behind the hips. Starting there, move through the power phase by rotating your outside shoulder and waist forward. If you need more power in heavy hydraulics, use your hip as a fulcrum or bracing point for more pulling power; take care, however, that rocks or strong currents don't launch you out of the boat.

Basic paddle turn. Turning a raft with paddles works the same way as with oars: the bow always turns toward the side applying the backstroke. Backstroke on

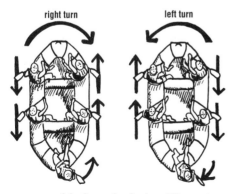

You can turn a raft by forward or back paddling on just one side, but it's faster to get everyone in on the action.

SAVE THE YIPPEE! FOR LATER

A very important concept in paddle-rafting medium and large rapids is that *paddling actually increases the likelihood of the paddler staying aboard the boat.* Tempting as it may be, the desire to raise your arms and paddle over your head and cry *Yippeeeee!* when plunging down a rapid is best resisted. When paddling, the upward pressure of the water on your paddle blade provides a push or brace that keeps you in balance and in the boat, not to mention keeping the boat in control.

Bracing. Two types of bracing are often used to steady a careening raft. The *low brace* is used when your raft bucks or tips violently, sending your side of the raft dipping precariously downward and exposing you to the grasp of an overly amorous river surface. If your tube sinks low enough, not even a powerful sphincter will help you maintain your grip on the seat. What you need to do is low-brace. Think of low-bracing as using your paddle as an outrigger. Start out by cocking both your wrists and knuckles downward so you can slap the river surface with the back side of your paddle blade and hold the shaft almost horizontal to the river's surface. As your paddle hits the water, push down with your shaft hand while lifting up at the T-grip. Keep your body weight low and shift it horizontally into the passenger compartment, bringing the paddle in with you as you go.

The *high brace* comes into play when the river has shot your side of the raft skyward. Before you lose your seat or go for a swim, lean way out over your tube and do something akin to a draw stroke. Hold your paddle with your knuckles pointed upward, your elbows bent slightly, and the shaft pointing almost underneath the raft. Rather than drawing, try to shovel some water back toward you.

the right and the bow goes right. Backstroke on the left and the bow goes left. Of course, if you forward-paddle on either side, the bow will spin away from your strokes. Paddlers can add speed and power to their turns the same way rowers do, by paddling in opposite directions on either side of the raft. To turn the bow to the right, the right side back-paddles while the left side forward-paddles; to turn the bow to the left, the right side forward-paddles and the left side back-paddles.

Sweep stroke. Properly executed, the sweep stroke done in the bow or stern turns the raft *and* moves it forward (*forward sweep*) or backward (*reverse sweep*).

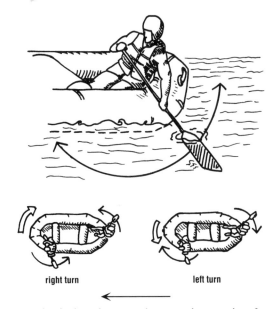

right turn   left turn

Forward or backward sweep strokes are used to turn the raft. A wide arcing paddle path is essential.

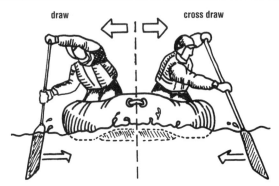

draw   cross draw

To draw stroke, reach directly out to the side of the raft and pull the blade back toward you. Keep the paddle vertical throughout the stroke and finish the stroke before the paddle hits the tube. The cross draw works the same way, but you reach across your body before planting the paddle.

To do a forward sweep stroke, hold your upper hand lower than usual, so that the paddle shaft angles downward, across the tube, and into the water at a 45-degree angle. (This position allows maximum extension in the reach phase of the stroke while keeping the paddler safely inside the raft.) In the catch phase, plant the paddle as far forward as possible with the blade parallel to the tube. With your shaft arm comfortably straight, start the power phase by pulling the paddle through an arc away from the boat. If you're sitting in the right-side bow position with the paddle in front of you, at 12 o'clock, trace the paddle through a path from 12 o'clock to 3 o'clock or 4 o'clock before beginning the recovery phase. Remember to rotate at your waist and use the powerful muscles of the torso, not your arms. If you have executed your stroke properly the bow will turn *away* from you.

Stern and center paddlers will discover that their forward sweeps have little effect on the raft. For stern paddlers, the reverse sweep stroke is a powerful tool. As you may have guessed, the reverse sweep is the same as a forward sweep, but in reverse. The critical difference between the two strokes is in paddle position. During the reverse sweep, the catch phase begins at 6 o'clock (directly behind you) and, if you're sitting on the right side of the raft, ends at 3 o'clock

or 2 o'clock. Also, the reverse sweep spins the bow *toward* the paddling side.

Draw stroke. Draw strokes excel in difficult rapids when you have to move your raft laterally without turning it. To start the draw stroke, rotate your torso outward (toward the river) until you're facing 90 degrees away from the raft. Next, reach both hands out and plant the paddle parallel to the raft; then pull the blade directly toward you and the side of the raft while keeping the shaft as vertical as possible. If the stroke is done correctly, the raft will actually move toward the paddle.

THE PADDLE CAPTAIN

By now you're probably wondering how four or more people on a paddle raft coordinate their strokes into a synchronous action that gets the boat through tough whitewater. It may be synchronous, but it's not synchronized swimming—there's no script or New Age music—it's a raging, changing river, and what worked on a run yesterday may not work today.

What you need is a paddle captain. The captain is equal parts coach, navigator, choreographer, cheerleader, and drill sergeant. Learning to captain a paddle raft takes time and skill. If you're into it, read up on the art in Jeff Bennett's *The Complete Whitewater Rafter* (Ragged Mountain Press, 1996). With practice and patience, a well-captained paddle raft can be one of the premier river-running vessels around—and, when the kids get old enough to wield paddles, this is a great way to get whole families involved in river running without the hassle of separate boats for everyone.

A sweeping or sculling brace allows you to confidently lean your kayak.

Kayak Paddling

Paddling an inflatable kayak is a little like a combination of raft paddling and oaring. The same basic concepts apply, and power strokes, turning strokes, and braces are used. The manner in which the boat behaves on the water is similar, except that kayaks are far quicker and more responsive to each stroke than are their larger brethren.

Because you more or less *wear* a kayak—your hips are touching the side tubes—you will add a dimension to paddling that isn't part of rafting: leaning. Once you get the feel for your kayak—once you feel *balanced* in it—you need to learn to rock your kayak side to side with your hips. When you can do this, you can then apply bracing strokes, as described above, with a lean to improve maneuverability and safety.

The blades of a feathered paddle are cocked at angles to each other. Although this arrangement decreases the air drag on the blade that is not in the water, you need to learn how to rotate your wrists and the paddle shaft when planting each blade in the water for the power stroke. It takes a bit of practice. Curved blades allow more "bite" in the water, but you need to make sure they are facing the correct direction for your power strokes, or you will lose much bite and power.

Once you learn to execute a powerful, smooth forward stroke by keeping your body erect, turning your torso throughout your stroke, rotating your shoulders, and drawing your power hand completely back to your hip, you will notice a number of things.

- Your kayak will want to spin around or waggle from side to side as you take each stroke. To counteract this tendency when you want to paddle in a straight line, make sure you are not planting your paddle too far away from the boat and pulling in an arc instead of straight (this is actually your sweep stroke for turning. It helps to keep your hands from crossing the centerline of your body to complete each stroke.
- When you sweep your paddle in an arc to turn your boat, you will notice that the boat has a point on which it naturally turns—the pivot point. The far-

Rotate your shoulder forward during the reach phase of a forward stroke to wind up your torso and extend your reach. Note the feathered blades.

ther your turning stroke begins from the pivot point, the more effective your turns will be.

- Just as in rafts, you can use backstrokes, sweep strokes, and draw strokes to move your boat around on the river, and high and low braces to steady yourself.
- You can learn a lot about your kayak and its motion in the water by playing in easy (class I–III) rapids. Later, you can add more complicated techniques.

River Moves

There are five basic categories of whitewater maneuvers, each of which is divided into two components: the boat's *momentum* and its *angle* in relation to the current. Some maneuvers—such as ferries and eddy turns—rely heavily on current to drive the boat across the river's surface. Others—such as turns and sideslips—have to overcome currents to be effective. The same current that assists one maneuver, then, may hinder another. Each of the maneuvers is described for rafts; but in general, you can use similar techniques when river running in inflatable kayaks.

RIVER DIRECTIONS

Four terms are used to describe river directions: (1) *upstream* is where the current is coming from; (2) *downstream* is where the current is flowing to; (3) *river left* is to your left as you face downstream; and (4) *river right* is to your right as you face downstream.

When first trying out class I and II rivers, a knowledge of these maneuvers should help keep you out of trouble, and you can experiment with and perfect each of them. A solid grasp of these skills will be your foundation for expanding your runs to more and more challenging whitewater.

Staying Parallel to the Current

The first technique any river runner should learn is how to keep the boat parallel to the current. Mastery of this technique not only will help you when it's time to slow the boat down, but will also expand your understanding of river currents and provide a solid basis for most other river-running techniques. There are bends to contend with, eddies and slack water that try to spin your raft, and obstacles that interfere with your strokes. Using subtle backward and forward corrective strokes will ultimately be able to keep your boat parallel to the flow.

Ferrying

As the name implies, ferrying is a maneuver used to scoot your boat from one side of the river to the other. You can execute a back or front (indicating stroke-type) ferry. In a back ferry, with your bow pointed downstream, begin backrowing or backpaddling; you will feel the boat's descent slow down significantly. Now, begin ferrying toward the left bank by turning the bow 30–45 degrees to your right. If you continue backrowing or

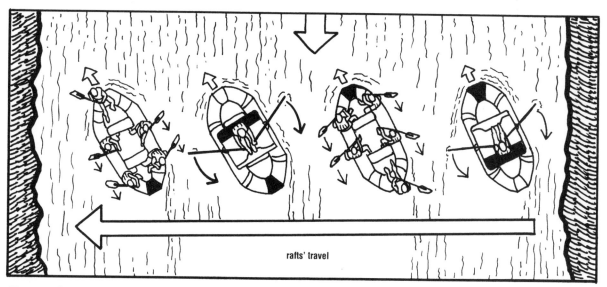

rafts' travel

The two rafts on the left are back ferrying and the two rafts on the right are forward ferrying.

backpaddling while maintaining that angle, the raft will either slow or cease its descent (depending on the power of the current) and will move sideways toward river left. To reach the right bank, simply point the bow toward the left bank and use the same backstroke.

If back ferries sound confusing, just think of one easy concept: *Pull away from the danger.* If you want to get away from the left bank, point your bow toward it and pull away . . . you'll move to river right. If you want to move away from a rock as you approach it, point your bow toward it and pull away, and you'll ferry away from the rock in the direction of your stern.

It takes a little practice to really get the feel of ferrying; stick with it until it becomes second nature. As you become more attuned to proper angles and trajectory, start experimenting with your oar and paddle strokes. Do long, slow strokes work better for you? Or short, fast strokes? Also try adjusting your cross-river speed. The more angle the boat maintains in relation to the current,

the faster the boat will move across the current, but the faster it will also proceed downriver.

In the forward ferry simply turn the bow upstream and portegee (push on the oars) or frontpaddle to push against the current. Keep in mind that the portegee, or forward stroke, is not as powerful as the backstroke, so the forward ferry is more energy-consuming and difficult to maintain than is the back ferry.

Turns and Pivots

Turning a boat in whitewater rapids differs little from turning a boat in flat water. Unlike ferrying, turning doesn't call upon river currents for assistance; it just requires some powerful oar and paddle strokes. Rafters should remember that the raft's inertia will keep it turning after the strokes have ended, resulting in a spin. Most turns require little more than one or two quick strokes. Front pivots (turning the bow downstream) and back pivots (turning the stern downstream) are usually used to straighten and narrow a boat's profile when approaching a tight slot, to align the boat with oncoming hydraulics, or to free a partially snagged boat from exposed obstacles.

Sideslips

In some boulder- or hole-riddled rapids, there simply isn't enough time to execute a turn or ferry around an obstacle. Some rapids will wrap or flip any boat that gets turned broadside. In those kinds of situations, a quick horizontal sideslip—moving the boat laterally across the river—may be the only way to find safe passage. The fastest and most efficient sideslipping strokes for paddle rafters are the draw, the cross-bow draw, and the pry stroke. Oar rafters can sideslip by planting one blade against the bow and pushing it away from the tube (to move the raft away from the oar), or by planting it a foot or two from the bow and pulling it toward the tube (to pull the raft toward the oar). Since the oar strokes are limited in their application, good rowers recognize their shortcomings and try to avoid getting themselves into tight situations in the first place. Kayakers can also use draw strokes to move horizontally.

As this raft enters a tricky rapid, a front pivot narrows its profile so it can squeeze through a narrow slot. A back pivot then helps it slide off a rock. One last front pivot lines up the raft with the current again.

Eddy Maneuvers

Eddies—pockets of water downstream of an obstacle that flow in the opposite direction of the main current—are often used as pull-outs when you want to stop or slow down your boat. (There are large, tumultuous

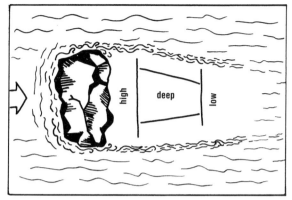

When entering most eddies, aim both high and deep. That is where the eddy is the strongest.

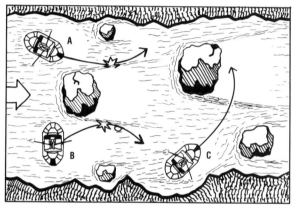

Raft A tried to enter an eddy with too little angle and was deflected downstream by the eddy line. Raft B came in too sideways and missed the eddy because it was caught on the main current. Raft C approached the eddy at about a 45-degree angle and made a perfect entry.

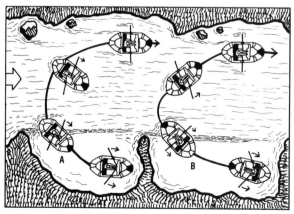

Raft A is ferrying out of its eddy and across the river. Raft B is executing a peel-out.

eddies, which should be avoided.) Boats traveling downriver have a lot of inertia, so eddies used this way are very important features.

The best way to enter an eddy is to paddle or row into it *high* (upstream, where the maximum current differential is located) and *deep* (directly behind the center of the obstacle). There are two factors to think about when entering an eddy: the speed of the boat and the angle of entry. Both concepts tie into one goal: to get across the eddy line quickly. To stay in the heart of the eddy, use small correction strokes or nestle the raft against the wall or boulder that formed the eddy and hold on.

There are three ways to exit an eddy: (1) ferry across the eddy line, (2) *peel out,* or (3) exit downstream. Downstream exits are only used in mellow eddies with weak currents—all you have to do is paddle or row downstream until the eddy releases your raft. Ferrying out of an eddy is little different from ferrying across the main channel, except that the moment the bow or stern hits the main current, the boat will try to spin downstream. To avoid this, build some upstream momentum as you work the boat to the top of the eddy, and cross the eddy line pointing more upstream than usual (10–25 degrees to the main current). A *peel-out* is an exciting maneuver that spins the boat downstream as you exit the eddy. To start your peel-out, accelerate the boat upstream and across the eddy line just as in the ferrying exit, but point the upstream end of the raft 30–45 degrees to the main current. As the boat crosses the eddy line, the main current will pile against the upstream tube and spin the boat to face downstream.

When a boat exits a fast-moving eddy, its upstream tube is exposed to the main current. The main current

Lean toward rocks and boulders to avoid being pinned.

drives against the upstream tube, then *under* the raft, trying to drag the upstream tube under with it. Paddlers can be tossed overboard as the tube plunges downward, and powerful currents can be strong enough to flip the whole boat. Whether entering or exiting eddies, paddlers can avoid tilting and flipping by shifting their weight to the far side of the raft, away from the diving current. The general rule is, Shift weight *upstream* when entering eddies, and *downstream* when exiting eddies.

FLOAT WITH THE TWO Cs AND BE SAFE

The Two *Cs* of river running are *currents* and *contingency plans*. First, think of rowing and paddling as the means of changing your boat's speed and direction in relation to the current, not in relation to solid obstacles such as rocks and cliffs. Second, always have a contingency plan in case you miss a stroke, bounce off a rock, or pop an oar loose. Finally, remember that whitewater is ever-changing and that your ability to *adapt* is more important than learning the name or category of each technique. If you keep these mental footnotes handy, the following techniques will make more sense and your boating success will increase.

Many boaters follow the SAFE System (*scout, analyze, formulate,* and *execute*), developed by Jeff Bennett.

1. SCOUT rapids fully before entering them. This can be done from either bank or, if there is an eddy or slow pool, from your boat. Make sure that every trip member observes difficult rapids from a variety of angles, looking both upstream and downstream. Also, select visual guideposts—such as uniquely shaped boulders—that will guide you as you're running the rapid. Finally, remember that rapids look different when you're floating toward them in a raft than when you're standing alongside them on the bank.

2. ANALYZE the rapid and your group's ability to run it. Where are the obstacles? Where are the safest channels? Is there a safe line through the rapid? Which way will you swim if you fall out? Are your team and equipment capable of running the rapid safely?

3. FORMULATE a plan. Which route will you follow? What is your backup plan? What maneuvers will you have to execute? Should you portage instead? Should a rescue team be stationed along the banks?

4. EXECUTE your plan. Run the rapid, carry the boat along the bank, or line the boat to safety.

Rapid Relief

While running rapids, there are two additional techniques rafters can use to get an added edge: bailing and highsiding.

Standard-floor rafts hold an amazing quantity of water, which makes the raft heavier and less maneuverable. Every standard-floor raft should have at least one bail bucket securely stored and available for quick use. In pool-drop rivers (rivers with calm pools following short, steep rapids) it is usually easier to wait for a calm eddy than to bail the raft in the middle of a rapid. On rivers with continuous whitewater, on the other hand, stopping may be difficult or impossible, making fast, effective bailing very important. In an oar raft, it's nice to have a *swamper* along—someone who will bail while the rower concentrates on the oars.

When a raft rides up onto a small rock or an exposed boulder, crew members can usually free the raft by shifting their weight to the side of the raft that will swing free, pushing off the rock with their feet, bouncing up and down, or using pivot strokes to loosen the raft. If the current is strong enough, though, the raft may keep sliding up the obstacle while the lower tube dives deeper into the main current. Left to its own devices, the river will bury the lower tube and pin the raft against the obstacle, causing a *wrap*.

To avoid a wrap, the entire crew highsides by leaning on the downstream tube (the tube riding up on the rock). This unweights the upstream tube, allowing its tremendous buoyancy to lift it free of the river's currents.

This raft has slid up onto a rock and the upstream tube is about to dive underwater. To avoid a wrap, the crew is highsiding.

Health and Safety

Risk is an elemental part of running rivers, and as in any outdoor sport, uncontrolled risk invites accidents. Accordingly, safety should be the primary concern on any river outing, whether it involves a peaceful scenic float or a heart-pounding class IV descent.

Preparation is the key to a safe river trip. A few rules must be followed prior to any trip.

- Select a river run based on the experience and capabilities of the *least experienced* member of your party.
- Always have a pretrip meeting to discuss your trip and rescue plans, then have a prelaunch talk on the riverbank, again going over everyone's roles, the upcoming day's run, and standard rescue procedures.
- Gather all the data you can regarding running that river or stretch of river, even if it's "only a short daytrip." This includes obtaining river gauge information (see section on river volume, p. 123) and weather information for the watershed region (you don't want any surprises, such as a river attaining flood stage while you're on it), having the proper maps and guidebooks, and talking to others with experience on that section.
- Allow plenty of time for your river trip—on multi-day trips, you might even add a day or two to what a guidebook recommends for trip length, as padding against unexpected delays. You can figure roughly the time on the water by dividing the river distance by the river's average velocity, but remember to factor in scouting, exploration, and leisure time.
- Make sure you and your party are up-to-date on rescue techniques and equipment. See resources at the end of this chapter for information on rescue technique manuals and schools.

Safety Gear

River runners should carry an assortment of essential safety items. If you're fortunate, they will just collect waterspots while you enjoy the river; but if an emergency arises, their presence will bring you essential aid.

Carabiners. Aluminum-alloy carabiners are the river runner's multi-purpose tool: they can be used to clip in gear and attach lines to rafts and can be substituted for pulleys in rope rescues.

Knives. A river rescue knife should be kept razor-sharp and easily accessible—a number of companies, such as Spyderco, make plastic-handled folding knives

> ## WHAT TO DO IF YOU GO FOR A SWIM (UNINTENTIONALLY)
>
> There are several good techniques for swimming rapids.
> - Feet downstream and hands out to your side
> - Rolled over on your belly and swimming toward shore
> - Balled up and protecting your limbs
>
> The position you use depends on the situation, but three rules always apply: don't go downriver headfirst, don't get between your boat and any downstream obstacles, and do whatever the river demands. If there is a huge waterfall coming up, get to the first safe, dry spot you can find. If you're getting battered on rocks using one position, change positions—try to swim around obstacles. If canyon walls have locked you into a quarter-mile of nonstop, churning rapids, try to reboard your raft. If rescue is possible from shore or by a boat upriver from you, make a powerful attempt to swim into an eddy. Try to stay calm and think things out before acting.

that clip to a PFD or belt and can be opened with one hand. A knife might be used to cut the floor out of a hopelessly pinned raft or to sever a rope quickly before it puts anybody in danger.

Whistles. Many groups use whistles as attention-getters or to signal the need for help (usually three short blasts together). However, it is very surprising how little the sound of a loud whistle will carry even in calm conditions, let alone in a roiling rapid. Brightly colored PFDs, helmets, and alert crew members should be primary to safety, whistles secondary.

Pulleys. A pulley is one of those items you'll be really glad to have the first time you wrap your raft. Pulleys reduce rope friction in Z-drag rescues and increase the efficiency of any rope-rescue system. For river use, select sturdy aluminum-alloy pulleys designed to accommodate ½-inch (11-millimeter) rope.

Throw bags. Also known as *throw ropes, rescue ropes,* and *rescue bags,* these are rope-retaining tools designed to spool out rope freely when the bag is tossed to a swimmer. They simplify rope throwing and make it easier for swimmers to see the rope coming—especially when the bag is filled with brightly colored, high-flotation rope.

Static ropes. Wraps and entrapments are two of the greatest perils facing whitewater rafters. Either situation demands a rope with superior strength and minimum stretch. High-quality static lines have incredible tensile

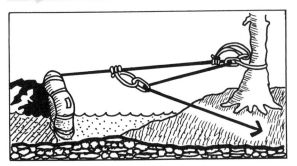

The basic Z-drag system using ropes and carabiners to free a pinned raft.

strength—far more than found in most throw-bag ropes—and very little stretch. Rafters should carry at least 100 feet of neatly stored ½-inch (11-millimeter) static rope for unwrapping rafts and freeing stranded or trapped swimmers.

Nylon webbing slings. Slings made of 1- or 2-inch-wide nylon webbing will serve all sorts of purposes. They can be used as anchors in Z-drag systems and rappels, and can even be used to make seat harnesses for vertical extrications. Carry a few slings of varying lengths (10–20 feet long) in your rescue kit and you'll be prepared to set up anchors in most any type of canyon environment.

First aid kits. A first aid kit should be standard equipment on any river trip. Minor injuries are inevitable, even on easy rivers, but they can often be treated immediately by someone trained in first aid. Take the time to consider the type of trip you're undertaking and the location of the nearest medical assistance when you assemble your first aid kit. Several companies sell first aid kits tailored for different outdoor sports; Adventure Medical Kits' river-running first aid kit comes in a waterproof case.

Also, see Chapter 13, p. 289, for a few more items you might add to a "personal essentials" kit to carry with you on all outdoor adventures.

Where to Go

While it seems that, at least in some parts of North America, there are runnable rivers all over the place, it can be a challenge finding runnable sections that are not only free from dangerous hazards such as wire fences or diversion dams, but also open to public access.

In general, accessible day-use river runs close to major metropolitan areas on which rafters and kayakers can spend a quick afternoon honing skills are often overcrowded because of their accessibility. On the other hand, wilderness rivers that run through government-controlled land can be blissfully free from crowds, but you may need to follow somewhat obtuse procedures to obtain permits. Often, they are long enough to warrant multiday trips.

If you want to find good rivers, ask around river-running circles—retail stores, clubs, and popular day-use areas are a good bet. There are also plenty of river guidebooks, at least for the more well-known runnable rivers.

The Permit Game

Of all the outdoor pursuits in this book, river running provides some of the most remote wilderness experiences possible, as well as some of the most regulated access systems in the world.

Take the Colorado River through the Grand Canyon as an example. Over 25,000 people raft down its 200-plus miles every year, most of them with commercial trips. A certain number of permits are issued each year to the commercial companies, and they must run their trips according to fairly tight schedules in order to piggyback each trip smoothly down the river. Even fewer permits are open to privately organized groups, which means that once you apply for your permit to run through the Grand Canyon, you could wait an average of six or seven years. Occasionally cancellations will push the schedule up (you need to be ready to head out with sometimes just a few months' notice), but that is the exception.

When you are looking into a river run, consult the available guidebooks and always check and double-check government regulations regarding access and permits. At times all you will need is an open backcountry river permit, or parking permits for put-ins and take-outs, but always check and follow procedures. Overcrowding on rivers and negative human impact on river corridors increasingly encourage land managers to restrict river access. Unpermitted groups just add to the problem and give river runners a bad name. Never use private property for access, landing, or camping unless you have explicit permission from

TOP 5

CLASSIC NORTH AMERICAN RIVER TRIPS

Frazier River, Northwest Territories

American River, California

San Juan River

Colorado River, Grand Canyon

Nantahala River, North Carolina

RICHARD FERRIES/BLUEPLANET IMAGES

Colorado River, Grand Canyon.

- *Colorado River, Grand Canyon.* Perhaps *the* classic North American "big water" run, this stunning one- to three-week run (225–279 miles) through the spectacular Grand Canyon is a lifetime trip.
- *American River.* A classic run through the high country of the Sierras.
- *Nantahala River.* This great run charges through the heart of the Appalachian Mountains, a place to experience vestiges of America's first frontier and down-home Southern hospitality.
- *Frazier River.* Barrenland grizzlies, tundra camps, and a midnight sun are what this wild river offers in one of North America's wildest reaches, the Northwest Territories.
- *San Juan River.* The smooth-water cousin (actually, a tributary) of the famous Colorado River, this river offers relaxing float trips through the heart of the Southwest's canyon country.

No-Trace River Running

Because of the growing numbers of river runners and increased urban development pressure on nearly all river corridors, many of North America's most special rivers are in danger. The danger can come from industrial pollution, from water pumping, and also from excessive recreation. Although river runners love their rivers, they do have an impact on the land through which they pass, however unwittingly—whether by trampling vegetation or by disturbing nesting birds. Consult Chapter 13 for a discussion of Leave No Trace wilderness tips. Also, send away for the Leave No Trace how-to booklet "Western River Corridors" and the regional booklet for whatever area you are heading to, from the Southeast to the Rocky Mountains to the Alaskan tundra. These easy-to-read, 75-cent booklets offer tips on how to leave the least impact in specific ecosystems, including the all-important universal, What do we do with human waste? (See Chapter 13, p. 297, for contact information for ordering Leave No Trace booklets.)

Where Can Inflatable Paddling Lead You?

River running is so multifaceted that options for expanding your skills and experiences are quite broad, from acquiring a fleet of different boats or increasing the difficulty of your whitewater runs, to planning long wilderness trips or becoming a professional guide.

Wilderness Camping

After honing your skills on day runs, the most natural progression will be to expand to multiday runs that include wilderness camping. To many river runners, this is a primary goal and *raison d'être*. River camping is a culture unto itself: most river runners develop elaborate, customized camp setups with full kitchens—roll-up tables and chairs, stoves, Dutch ovens, coolers, cooking kits—and screen tents, cots, lounge chairs, even river saunas. See Chapter 10 for more on camping, including equipment and set-up ideas. Chapter 12 is your resource for camp cooking, and Chapter 13 provides further information on camping health and safety, including water filtration.

RACING

Raft and kayak racing are dynamic and exciting sports for competitors and spectators alike. From downriver to slalom races, from rescue competitions to river orienteering events, the thrill of running rivers is magnified when every move becomes critical. In their effort to go fast and minimize errors, racers become totally focused. All the skills learned before—from raft and kayak control to route finding—come to a head. Sound skills shine and deficiencies become glaringly apparent.

It is in this process that another aspect of raft racing appears: good racers make good river runners. The same precision that goes into running gates carries over to running rapids, and despite philosophical differences as to what river running is all about, racing and recreational rafting accent each other magnificently.

To investigate river races in your area, contact your local clubs, the American Canoe Association, and the American Whitewater Affiliation (see end of this chapter for contact information).

Playboating

Waves and holes wisely avoided by beginning river runners can provide an endless source of amusement and challenge to boaters with advanced skills and a sense of adventure. Whether gently gliding their craft down the face of a wave or doing 360s on the shoulders of a hole, "playboaters" develop and hone their boating skills while connecting with some of the river's most exciting hydraulics.

A kayak, self-bailing raft, or cataraft is a must for playboating. With a standard-floor raft, the river will flood the passenger compartment and the boat will become difficult to maneuver. Bare paddle rafts make better playboats because they have no dangerous frames or oarstands to injure you if the raft flips. However, frames work fine on cats since these boats are harder to flip.

Before you think about playing around on waves and holes, learn to distinguish forgiving hydraulics from perilous keepers. If you know what the river is likely to do to your boat ahead of time, you'll be able to anticipate the river's actions and adjust accordingly. Since flips are common in playboating, you must be comfortable righting a flipped raft, rolling a kayak, and swimming out of holes. Finally, you should be adept at maneuvering your boat in powerful hydraulics.

Whitewater racing combines skill and endurance!

PUSHING THE ENVELOPE: BACK IN THE U.S.S.R.

The former Soviet Union comprised one-sixth of the world's landmass. Its republics still boast some of the most spectacular—and dangerous—whitewater in the world. Soviet rafters often determined success not by the length of the trip but by the number of survivors. It's possible still to see the marks etched by comrades on canyon walls above thundering rapids—final memorials to rafters who didn't make the trip home.

Professional Guiding

Another logical progression for a surprising number of river runners is to turn pro. There are many work opportunities across North America, as well as internationally, with river running companies. Most likely you will start at the bottom—probably as a swamper or grunt (doing the dirty work)—then slowly work your way up to assistant guide, full guide, and perhaps trip coordinator or even business manager. Plan on long days, hard work, frustrating clients, seasonal work—as well as some of the most rewarding and fulfilling experiences of your life.

Further Resources for River Running
Books

The Complete Whitewater Rafter, by Jeff Bennett
(Camden, ME: Ragged Mountain Press, 1996).
The Complete Inflatable Kayaker, by Jeff Bennett
(Camden, ME: Ragged Mountain Press, 1996).

These two books will tell you what you need to know to get out on whitewater rivers in inflatable craft. They're concise, useful, often humorous, and always wise. Much of the material for this chapter was adapted with permission from the two books, above.

Whitewater Rescue Manual, by Charles Walbridge and Wayne A. Sundmacher, Sr. (Camden, ME: Ragged Mountain Press, 1995).

☞ KID QUOTIENT

Most kids take to river running like, well, ducks to water. The ever-changing scenery, the thrills of mild whitewater (class I and II for younger kids, maybe class III for older kids), and the adventure of boating creates the perfect atmosphere for family fun.

☞ Always make sure the kids wear top-quality, high-flotation PFDs on any class of river, at all times.

☞ Kids as young as toddlers (maybe younger) have been taken on easy float trips, their playpens strapped onto an oar frame. Kids too young to paddle do best in oar rafts. Older kids can have a blast in a paddle raft (but there should always be at least two adults on the boat, as principle paddlers). Because you'll be traveling mostly on slow water, mix in some variety to keep things interesting: switch seats often, let kids sit with the rower, add an inflatable kayak to your raft fleet so everyone can take turns playing.

☞ Orchestrate safety "drills" in which everyone practices swimming across the river in their PFDs, throwing and grabbing a rope for swimmer rescues, pulling swimmers back into the boat, and so on.

☞ Keep your expectations in line with your passengers: small. Expect only to have a great time. Don't plan on long river miles, or think that the kids won't long for their Game-Boys occasionally, and everyone will be a lot better off.

☞ Bring along hats, sunscreen, and bug repellent (for kids, avoid repellents containing the chemical DEET, which can cause serious health problems), and kid-friendly snacks.

(See Chapter 11 for more tips on adventuring outdoors with kids.)

Easy class I and II rivers provide lots of fun for kids and adults.

The Whitewater Sourcebook: A Directory of Information on American Whitewater Rivers, by Richard Penny (Birmingham, AL: Menasha Ridge Press, 1991).

The Whole Paddler's Catalog, edited by Zip Kellogg (Camden, ME: Ragged Mountain Press, 1997).

Paddle America: A Guide to Trips and Outfitters in All 50 States, by Nick Shears (Washington, DC: Starfish Press, 1992).

Periodicals

American Whitewater (the journal of the American Whitewater Affiliation), P.O. Box 636, 16 Bull Run Road, Margaretville, NY 12544; (914) 586-2355.

Canoe & Kayak, 10526 NE 68th, Suite 3, Kirkland, WA 98033; (206) 827-6363.

Currents, National Organization for Rivers, 212 W. Cheyenne Mt. Blvd., Colorado Springs, CO 80906; (719) 579-8759.

Paddler, P.O. Box 1341, Eagle, ID 83616; (208) 939-4500.

Whitewater and Paddling Organizations

The American Whitewater Affiliation, P.O. Box 636, 16 Bull Run Road, Margaretville, NY 12544; (914) 586-2355; www.awa.org.

The National Organization for Rivers, 212 W. Cheyenne Mt. Blvd., Colorado Springs, CO 80906; (719) 579-8759.

The North American Paddlesports Association, 12455 N. Wauwatosa Road, Mequon, WI 53097; (414) 242-5228.

Conservation Organizations

American Rivers, 1025 Vermont Avenue NW, Suite 720, Washington, DC 20005; (202) 547-6900.

Schools

For a school in your area, check the guide *Paddle America* (listed above).

(Unless otherwise noted, all art in this chapter is by Jeff Bennett.)

"A river is more than an amenity; it is a treasure."
—Oliver Wendell Holmes

Chapter 6

CLIMBING—*The Vertical Dance*

"Climbing is about having fun. It is about pumping adrenaline, exposure to the outdoors, ascending impossibly vertical or smooth walls, viewing space beneath our feet . . . sitting quietly on a ledge reflecting on nature."

—Jerry Cinnamon, *Climbing Rock and Ice: Learning the Vertical Dance*

SPORT FILE

Couch potato quotient: 4 (couch to rockmaster requires serious fitness)
Coordination factor: 4 (brain-body coordination high)
White-knuckle rating: 5 (no guts, no glory)

The Vertical Dance

The fluidity and ease with which an expert rock climber ascends a seemingly glass-slick wall of rock is breathtaking—skill, fitness, grace, and intelligence come together in what many people feel is the embodiment of what an individual human can achieve. For many aficionados of this very popular sport, the art of rock climbing is a parallel for the art of living—the skill, fitness, grace, and intelligence necessary to scale a rock face are indeed the same qualities necessary to succeed in life. And the thrill of topping out after a challenging climb is among life's best rewards for hard work.

A visit to your local indoor climbing gym or a popular suburban rock climbing crag may reveal a startling abundance of young, very strong-looking climbers. But nearly anyone can climb—you don't need to be young and muscular to be a good climber. Nor do you need to be a woman—men are excellent climbers (in a nice turnabout, perhaps more than in any other athletic outdoor pursuit, women are often the rule rather than the exception). And children are often amazing as climbers because they haven't convinced themselves or been convinced that they *can't.*

What you do need to begin climbing rock (or ice) is an average level of physical ability and fitness, time to learn a few key skills, and a willingness to practice diligently. As rock climbing instructor and author Jerry Cinnamon says, "Dancers are not born as masters with the gift of springing into the air and landing softly again on their toes. . . . Like dancers, climbers start as apprentices; we rehearse our steps time and again to move fluidly and develop grace."

Rock climbing as we know it began as a Victorian pastime of donning hobnailed boots and using hemp ropes and grappling hooks to claw up mountainsides. A climbing renaissance in the 1960s and 1970s ushered in vast equipment improvements, such as lightweight rubber-soled climbing shoes, aluminum carabiners, and forged metal devices to affix ropes to the rock face during ascents (from early advances in drive-in wooden wedges and metal pitons, to later removable chocks that stuff in cracks).

FIRST TIME OUT

Your first rock climb will be exhilarating, fun, and terrifying—and hopefully leave you craving more. To minimize the impact of a first rock climb on your brain and body, follow these tips.

- Choose a relatively short climb, perhaps no more than 50–65 feet, with an easy rating—around 5.5 to 5.7 (see The Rating Game, p. 158).
- Choosing easier and shorter routes will allow you to repeat the climb over and over, so you can test and alter your technique.
- Limit your climbing time so you don't injure any tendons or lose concentration—and become careless—because of fatigue. A couple of hours of start-and-stop climbing (alternating belaying and climbing with your partner) will probably be pretty tiring, even if you are in top physical shape, if only from the mental workout.
- Unless you are particularly fearless, expect to feel "the grip" or "gripped" (climber's lingo for fear) at a certain point on your climb, usually near the crux (hardest part). If this happens, resist the urge to look down; take a couple of deep breaths, blink hard, focus on your goal, and force yourself to continue. Particularly gripped climbers have been known to freeze, paralyzed with fear, when they let the panic overwhelm them. Relax, trust your partner, and concentrate on your real goal: having fun.
- Your arms and legs may feel like rubber after the climb.
- Take power food with you, either in the form of fruit or commercial bars, and drink lots of water; a small amount of electrolyte-replacement drink would be good as well, but water is what the body needs most.

Today there are many different forms of climbing, and while some climbers may focus on just one, most do all, or at least several.

Traditional rock climbing. Traditional rock climbers ascend natural rock faces, from little more than boulders to huge cliff faces that may take more than a day to climb. The crags they climb may be within an urban area or a day's hike into the wilderness ("backcountry climbing" is a subculture all its own). Traditional climbers use ropes, harnesses, and substantial collections of protective gear (usually just called "protection," and the set is called a "rack") that the lead climber of a group uses to set the rope.

There are various forms of traditional climbing, although many people consider each of the following to be separate from "traditional" climbing: *free climbing,*

Children are often amazing climbers—they haven't convinced themselves they can't.

in which the protective devices are "clean" (removable, without damage to the rock) and the climber ascends without putting any weight on the protection; and *aid climbing,* in which the protective devices are affixed to the rock permanently by bolts, or in which the climber uses removable or fixed protection as an aid (that is, by putting weight on it), and *top-rope climbing,* wherein the rope is preaffixed to the top of the route and the climber does not need to set any protection during the climb. (Beginning climbers learn on top-ropes.)

Bouldering. Using just climbing shoes—no harness, rope, or protection—a climber who is bouldering traverses around a large boulder or across a rock face no higher than is possible for jumping down safely. Bouldering focuses on rock movement skills, stamina, and sometimes application of strength, rather than completing a vertical climb.

Sport climbing. Within the last decade or so, sport climbing calved off traditional climbing into its own niche. The objectives of sport climbing are ever-increased speed and challenge. A climbing route is preset with hangers permanently bolted into the rock; as the climber ascends between resting places as rapidly and smoothly as possible up the face, the rope is clipped into the preset hangers. Sport climbing is often a lively cultural scene, especially in areas where there are many routes.

Gym climbing. What started as a way for urban climbers to practice their moves and stay in shape for the rock the very best way—by climbing—during their lunch hours or after work, has become a form of climbing unto itself. Most sizable cities have rock climbing gyms, some privately owned, some at public recreation centers, universities, or YMCAs. Usually they are built in warehouses or gymnasiums because of their high ceilings, although in the Midwest there is at least one gym built into an old grain silo. Wooden walls are affixed with removable, hand-size resin grips to create routes of all difficulty levels; safety ropes are hung over beams. Most gyms host at least one annual climbing contest. Many nonclimbers are lured to climbing gyms by the excellent alternative workout style, and in summertime and on weekends most gyms are overrun with kids. Many of these latter never will venture out onto real rock.

Ice climbing. When the temperatures plummet, many climbers turn to the frozen wilderness, affixing crampons to their boots and using ice axes, ropes, and

ZIGY KALUZNY/TONY STONE IMAGES, INC.

Climbing gyms are an excellent alternative for practice and staying in shape.

With all these great choices, you can jump into a climbing activity suited perfectly to your personality and lifestyle. If you rarely have time to trudge off into the wilderness for long, challenging rock climbs, and just aren't thrilled about bugs and thorn bushes and dirt, then gym climbing is your thing. If you are competitive and enjoy a lively social life, sport climbing offers both in spades. And if backcountry solitude, interactions with nature, and hard rock challenges beckon, then traditional rock and ice climbing offer opportunities limited only by how much vacation time you have.

What You'll Need

For bouldering, you need little more than climbing shoes, and perhaps a bag for hand chalk; for gym climbing, add a harness, a helmet (sometimes required in gyms), a couple of locking carabiners, and a belay device. But for sport climbing and traditional climbing, you will need a bit more—a rope, for one, and more carabiners, slings, and protection devices, although the latter really only come into play when you begin to lead traditional climbs. For the most part, this chapter will deal with getting on the rock and learning basic skills that later can be applied to advanced climbing ("lead climbing" refers to the ability to ascend first, choosing the route and securely placing the protection, which is best learned with an experienced partner and at a reputable climbing school).

Climbing Shoes

Some people say that you *really* don't need special climbing shoes to get started. But the truth is that climbing shoes enhance your ability to feel the rock so much that you really ought to consider them basic equipment. The big drawback is that they are expensive—usually over $75 for little more than ballerina slippers on steroids—but if you shop around for sales or used shoes, you can find good deals. The good news is that most climbing shoes are resolable, either by professionals (ask your retailer) or with do-it-yourself kits.

Climbing shoes are usually made from leather, or sometimes synthetic materials, are soled with sticky rubber, and come in several different types.

Over-the-ankle booties. These higher laceup shoes are usually used for longer routes on which you will want maximum support as well as comfort. Some are more

various ice screws and pickets to aid their ascents of ice formations. Ice climbing is rooted in mountaineering, and requires the highly technical skills of alpine climbing under threat of avalanches and whiteouts. Recently, ice climbing has become popular as a parallel of sport climbing—many people now ice climb on iced-up roadside cliffs or on man-made ice formations (commercial operations), where movement skills, and in some cases extreme gymnastic movement skills, are emphasized.

Much of the information for this chapter was adapted from Climbing Rock and Ice, *by Jerry Cinnamon (Camden, ME: Ragged Mountain Press, 1994), who also provided expert technical and editorial review.*

THE ESSENTIALS—A ROCK CLIMBING START-UP KIT

- Climbing shoes ($75–$150)
- Harness ($25–$100)
- Large locking carabiner ($10–$20)
- Standard carabiner X 12 ($5–$10)
- Belay device ($15–$100)
- Rope ($100–$200)
- Helmet ($50–$75)
- Slings X 10 ($5–$8)
- Chalk bag and chalk ($10–$25)

Minimum cost essential rock climbing kit: $395*

Minimum cost rock gym visit: $20

ADD-ONS

- Assorted protection—chocks, camming devices, etc.
- Rope bag
- Climbing tights or pants
- Water bottles
- First aid kit

*The essentials list above is intended to give you an idea of minimum start-up costs for moderate entry into a sport using new equipment. Other options include borrowing or renting gear from friends, retailers, YMCAs, or church activity clubs, as well as buying used gear—see Appendix A. Boots are the only used item that climbers should buy, however.

helmet

locking carabiner

chalk bag

harness

climbing shoes

CLIFF LEIGHT

articulated—preshaped in the manner of a pointed foot—than others.

Demi-boots. Most popular today are laceup shoes that come to just below the ankle bone, and are a good compromise between support and slipperlike fit. These are good sport climbing or gym shoes, or for difficult traditional routes with gymnastic sections, on which every advantage is desirable. The disadvantage of demi-boots is that your exposed ankle bone will get skinned up when jamming in wide cracks.

Slippers. Very tight-fitting slip-ons became popular for bouldering years ago, but today you'll see more and more people wearing them on sport routes or in gyms.

Harness

Your harness—a system of nylon straps with leg loops and a belt by which you secure yourself to the climbing

ON CLIMBING-SHOE FIT

In the beginning, climbers stuffed their feet into shoes so small—for superior feel and control on tiny rock edges—that there was a malady called the EB Toe or Black Toe (named for a narrow-lasted, popular early-model European climbing shoes, the EBs).

Today, improved lasts with toe boxes shaped more like toes have cut back the occurrence rate of EB Toe, but there are still some good fit tips to go by.

- Consider first what type of climbing you intend to do; if it's only big-wall climbing, go for comfortably snug; but if you intend to do very difficult sport routes that require you to feel ⅛-inch-wide nubbins with your pinkie toe, go for tight.
- Make sure your foot contacts the shoe snugly all around and that when you articulate your foot, the shoe moves with it. (Remember that the tight fit will feel uncomfortable in a standing position—but on vertical rock, the shoe will feel like part of your foot.)
- If the arch area bags too much, look for another type of shoe.
- Take into account that the width of most shoes will stretch a little bit.
- Decide if you're going to wear socks or not before you buy shoes. Long days on hard routes might necessitate thin synthetic socks, but "flashing" a few routes in a morning might mean going without (sweat will hasten degradation of shoes, however).

rope—is essential to your safety while climbing. A harness that fastens around your waist and has leg loops that help hold your weight is a "sit" harness; in mountaineering or big-wall climbing, a sit harness is often used in combination with a chest harness for added security (if you fall backward with just a sit harness, you can turn upside down).

It is essential that your harness fits correctly (comfortably snug but roomy enough to add pants and jacket) and that you secure your harness's buckle properly each and every time you put it on. All harnesses these days have a double-buckle system through which you must pass the belt-end twice, in order to ensure that it does not open in the event of a fall. (Always read and follow the manufacturer's instructions; people have died from falls after not securing harnesses properly.) Harnesses range from simple and inexpensive to elaborate and expensive, with gear loops and fleece padding. One feature you might look for is adjustable leg loops, so you regulate their size to accommodate the thickness of your clothing. Tip: Buy from a reputable climbing retailer whose clerks are climbers, and choose a well-known brand name.

Carabiners are the foundation of a serious rack.

WILLIAM PELANDER

SHE BOUNCES

A few years ago national outdoor magazines were running an advertisement for Timex watches that featured world-famous rock climber Lynn Hill in a sexy black dress. Eye-catching, to be sure. But the real story in the text was about how she had just survived every climber's nightmare: while nearly 75 feet off the ground, Hill had leaned back from the ledge on which she stood, to get a better look at the route above; unfortunately she had neglected to tie in to her belayer's rope and she plummeted to the ground. Amazingly, she suffered only a severely bruised posterior. *It takes a licking and keeps on ticking. . .*

(And the moral of the story: Always tie-in properly, always double check your tie-in, and never untie during any part of a climb, unless you are safely clipped-in to an anchor.)

Basic Hardware

Carabiners. You will need several locking carabiners, to set up belay stations and for many other exigencies. Carabiners with large gates (the hinged opening) are easiest to clip. You will also want an assortment—a dozen is a good start—of standard nonlocking carabiners. These can be used for anchors, for clipping chalk bags to your harness, and for other uses. Carabiners come in a variety of shapes, the most common being oval, with variations ranging from pear- to D-shaped. If confused, start with standard ovals or Ds until you work up to more advanced climbing.

Belay device. Except in bouldering, you climb with a partner who handles the other end of the rope to which you are attached. As you ascend, your partner pays out more rope; and if you fall, your partner arrests the fall using a belay device (the person handling the device is the *belayer*). Some people still teach a waist belay technique, in which the rope is wrapped around the belayer's waist and the body is used as a brake; while it's good to learn this technique (or the Munter hitch belay, using a carabiner) for contingencies, good, inexpensive belay devices are highly recommended over a body brake for gym or top-rope climbing or lead climbing with good protection.

The rope is passed through or around the belay device, which you employ as a brake on the rope against the force of falling weight. There are several types of belay device—plain slot plates, sprung "Sticht" plates, and tubes—and the best one for you depends on the type of climbing situations you will be in (see sidebar, above). Some devices allow the belayer to apply too little force when the lead climber falls, allowing the leader to continue falling; conversely, if too much force is applied (a "static" belay), the stress may cause protection to pull loose in a lead climb. A highly recommended device, because of its versatility, is the Sticht plate with a spring. The spring provides a more dynamic belay than an unsprung slot plate, making the Sticht plate better suited for moderate-to-severe falls on climbs with a medium amount of friction in the system (friction in a system is a result of a variety of factors, including number and type of protection, and path and angle of the rope as the leader climbs). However, Sticht plates are also good for easy, low-fall-factor climbs without much friction in the system (such as gyms or easy top-roped climbs).

Rope

Climbing ropes are known as dynamic kernmantle. *Dynamic* describes the ability of the rope to stretch as it absorbs the force of a fall. *Kernmantle* (literally, "core-jacket") describes the construction of the rope: the kern, a high-strength inner core of twisted nylon threads, is covered by the mantle, an outer braided jacket or sheath. The twisted strands of the core behave like miniature springs, lengthening as they absorb the energy of a fall. They provide most of the rope's strength; the jacket protects the core and determines most of the rope's handling characteristics and abrasion resistance.

The most popular rope lengths are 50, 55, or even 60 meters long (165, 180, or 195 feet, respectively), and 10–11 millimeters in diameter. The 50-meter length was first used extensively in Yosemite Valley, where belays were protected by bolts, but this length is becoming essential in other areas where bolt-protected routes have been established. An 11-millimeter kernmantle rope is a good choice for general climbing, although many climbers prefer a 10.5-millimeter rope because it is slightly lighter, combining good abrasion resistance with moderate weight. Some experienced climbers use an even lighter 10-millimeter rope, but 9.0- or 8.8-millimeter thicknesses are never used as single climbing strands. (These ropes are used in *double-rope* or *twin-rope* techniques to help reduce the friction or rope drag that occurs when ropes turn right angles. Two ropes also allow easier rappelling.)

Coiling Your Rope

The two common methods of coiling a rope are the *mountaineer's coil* and the *butterfly coil*. The mountaineer's coil creates a continuous circle that you can carry over your shoulder and neck and allows you to carry a number of ropes at one time. For a single rope the butterfly coil can be formed more quickly even if the rope is encrusted with ice, and it is less likely to tangle during uncoiling.

The mountaineer's coil. Many people form the mountaineer's coil by wrapping the rope around their feet and knees when sitting, but this procedure normally creates irregular-length coils. If the rope has been badly twisted, however, this may be the only way you can achieve the mountaineer's coil. To form the mountaineer's coil while standing, hold an end of the rope in your *off hand* and with your *control hand* (normally the right hand for right-handed people) stretch out the standing part of the rope two arm lengths across your chest. With the rope stretched out, grasp the rope between the thumb and fingers of your control hand. To remove twist from the coil, give the rope a half-twist and bring the newly formed coil over

to your off hand. Use your off hand to grasp and enclose all the loops formed by this process.

Finish the coil by whipping the ends tightly. You need to tighten each wrap of the whip to gain enough friction to keep the wrap from falling apart. If you do it properly, you will not need to wrap extremely long ends around the coil to secure it. Long ends are unnecessary—and even undesirable if you need to use the rope quickly.

The butterfly coil. To make the butterfly coil, take both ends in one hand and stretch the doubled rope full-length across your chest. Measure out two and a half or three lengths and drop them on the groundcloth: you

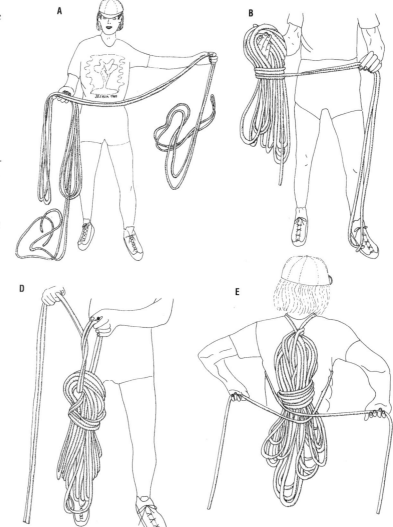

Forming the butterfly coil.

will use this rope to tie the coil together when you finish. Now you are ready to form the *butterfly wings*. Continue as before, stretching the doubled rope arm-to-arm-length across your chest, moving away from the dropped ends. Double this arm-to-arm length and drape it over the palm of your hand, forming a loop on either the left or right side of the hand. You form the next wing by draping the next doubled length of rope across the same palm with the loop facing the opposite direction. Do this until all the remaining rope is in the palm of your hand. Now use the lengths of rope you dropped to make three or four wraps around both wings. Form a bight (a doubled section of rope, formed in the middle section of the rope, that does not pass over itself) in the standing part of the rope and pull it partway through the loop at the top of the wrapped coil. Take the remaining end of the rope and place it over the body of the wrapped coil and through the last formed loop. Tighten to finish the butterfly coil. You can form a backpack from the coil by placing it on your back and passing the free ends over your shoulders. Wrap these ends across your chest and waist, and tie them together.

Other Necessities and Niceties

Other items you will want to have include a helmet—some climbing gyms require them—slings, hand chalk and a bag in which to put it, and perhaps some climbing pants or tights.

Helmets. Few rock climbers use helmets, but the risks in choosing to go bare must be acknowledged: during a fall a climber may swing wildly around as if on a pendulum and smack against the rock face, or the climber may dislodge loose rocks that the belayer cannot avoid. Ask any climbers you see wearing helmets, and they likely will tell you about scary close-calls that showed them the light. Climbing helmets should carry a UIAA certification that they are tested for such use. Many styles, weights, and sizes are available.

Slings. Eventually you will want to acquire an assortment of nylon webbing slings, either ready-made or tied by hand from cut webbing, that will have myriad uses, such as belay and rappel anchors.

Chalk and chalk bags. To combat sweaty (and thus slippery) hands, many climbers use inexpensive magnesium carbonate gymnast's chalk, sold in blocks at climbing shops. However, chalk's powdery consistency gives it some disadvantages; the fine, airborne dust may be a health hazard and is often banned at gyms, and the white residue can be such an eyesore on wilderness climbs that some land managers are also banning it. A dustless alternative called Bison Balls (egg-size bags of rosin) is highly recommended over loose chalk. You can make your own ball of chalk by placing loose powder in a cotton sock secured with a rubber band. If you use chalk you will want to get a chalk bag to hang from your harness or a separate belt.

Clothing. All you really need for climbing is comfortable clothing that allows you to stretch and bend freely. Avoid baggy garments that can interfere with movement. At the local crags you will see a lot of Lycra and stretch-cotton tights, shorts, and sport bras or tanks, or in cooler weather, stretchy long underwear or fleece tops. Specialty climbing pants or knickers made from very tough stretch gabardinelike polyester or nylon resist the abrasion of rock climbing much better than thin Lycra (especially when you are first learning and will be more prone to unintentional contact with the rock).

Dancing Lessons

Rock climbing certainly *looks* hard. How do you beat gravity and haul a body up a vertical face with few apparent hand or foot holds? You will probably make it if you just fling and thrash yourself up any face with decent holds, but it will be hard and brutal. The question is how to do it without killing your tendons and losing yards of skin—how to move with ease rather than pain.

The answer is finesse, not force. Rock climbing is a delicate combination of point and counterpoint of your weight shifted via your hands and feet as you move up the face of the rock. Rarely do you touch the rock with more than those four points—indeed, you try to maintain three points of contact while moving the fourth. Most beginners take a while to get over the tendency to hug the rock rather than relax and lean back. Advantages are gained in holding your balance just right, and in combining series of moves hand-to-hand, foot-to-foot, or hand-to-foot. Strength certainly plays a part—especially when a difficult route requires that you lean back on a lay-back crack or have to pull yourself up between very long reaches—but for the most part, finesse is the key.

But before you learn the dance, you need to build on some solid basic skills: knots, tying-in to the rope, belaying, moving on rock, and using the body as aid (finger, hand, and body jams).

All Dressed Up and Nowhere to Go

Properly tied knots are the most important safety element of climbing. You should learn these and other knots so well you can do them quickly during bad weather, in failing light, and under stress.

A knot is not properly tied until you dress and set it. *Dressing* means orienting all parts of the knot so that they are parallel to each other and do not overlap, making sharp bends. (When two different knots will serve the same purpose, the stronger knot is the one in which the rope has broader, more symmetrical bends.) Dressing a knot tied in webbing requires special attention because webbing easily folds over onto itself, preventing the smoothness you want in all parts of the knot. *Setting* a knot means tightening the parts of the knot so that they touch each other, creating friction that prevents the knot from untying. Some, but not all, knots are not considered complete until they are *backed up* with a second knot that prevents the load-bearing knot from untying. You jam the second knot tightly against the first. A well-dressed, set, and backed-up knot is a secure knot.

Parts of a knot include a *bight,* which is a doubled section of rope, formed in the middle section of the rope, that does not pass over itself; a *loop,* which is a doubled section of rope that crosses over itself; a *free end,* which is the short end left over when a knot is tied in the end; and a *standing part,* which is the end of the rope that is stationary (a knot is often formed by passing a rope around a standing part).

In learning to tie knots, nothing beats personal instruction. Begin here, consult a book such as *Climbing Rock and Ice* by Jerry Cinnamon, get hands-on advice from an experienced climber—and then practice, practice, practice.

Overhand knot and water knot. The overhand knot is the most basic knot and is frequently used to back up another knot. The water knot is a retraced overhand knot tied in flat webbing. Due to the slippery nature of nylon webbing, the water knot requires a backup to ensure its security.

Figure-eight loop. The figure-eight loop is useful when you wish to tie into the middle of a rope. It is very secure and easy to inspect. To tie this knot, begin with a

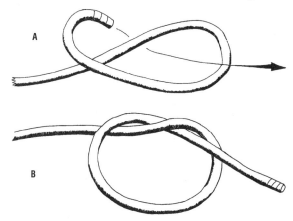

The overhand knot.

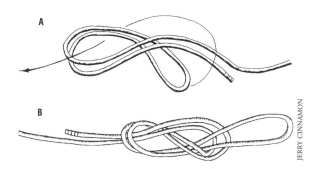

The figure-eight loop.

JERRY CINNAMON

bight of rope and make a loop of the bight. Then twist this loop around the standing part of the rope and pass it back through the first loop formed. Usually you clip a carabiner into the bight of the knot and attach it either to an anchor or yourself.

Figure-eight retraced or follow-through knot. Figure-eight retraced knots are used to tie the rope around an object. You might use this knot to make an anchor around a tree or to connect the rope to your harness. The knot is tied by a retracing process, a technique used in tying many different knots.

The clove hitch. The clove hitch is an adjustable knot that you can tie in the middle of the rope, and it is particularly useful when you set up a cliff-top belay stance near the edge. Clove hitches provide safe, easily adjustable tie-ins to anchor points for belaying. Back them up with a figure-eight knot to be absolutely safe.

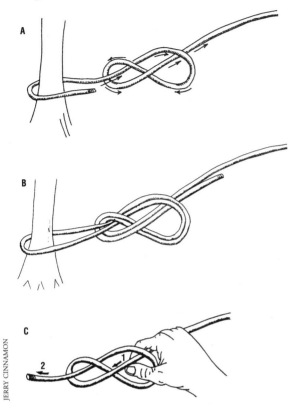

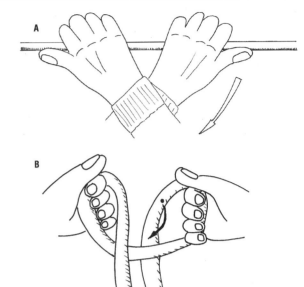

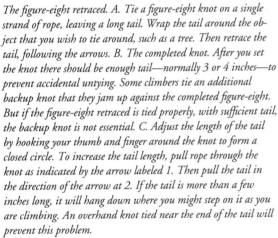

JERRY CINNAMON

The figure-eight retraced. A. Tie a figure-eight knot on a single strand of rope, leaving a long tail. Wrap the tail around the object that you wish to tie around, such as a tree. Then retrace the tail, following the arrows. B. The completed knot. After you set the knot there should be enough tail—normally 3 or 4 inches—to prevent accidental untying. Some climbers tie an additional backup knot that they jam up against the completed figure-eight. But if the figure-eight retraced is tied properly, with sufficient tail, the backup knot is not essential. C. Adjust the length of the tail by hooking your thumb and finger around the knot to form a closed circle. To increase the tail length, pull rope through the knot as indicated by the arrow labeled 1. Then pull the tail in the direction of the arrow at 2. If the tail is more than a few inches long, it will hang down where you might step on it as you are climbing. An overhand knot tied near the end of the tail will prevent this problem.

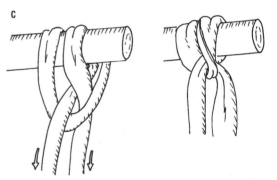

JERRY CINNAMON

The clove hitch—hand held horizontally—viewed from above. Step 1. Cross hands with the right hand above the left, palms down and horizontal, thumbs along the rope, as shown in A. Step 2. Hold the right hand steady and move the left hand beneath the right hand in an arc on the horizontal plane, as indicated by the arrow shown in A. This should result in two vertical loops (B). Make sure that the two vertical ends of the loop are touching the horizontal connecting strand between the two loops. Step 3. Hold the left hand steady and bend the right loop toward you. Then move it to the left, as shown by the arrow in B, and place it over the fingers of your left hand, on top of the left loop. Step 4. Transfer these overlapping loops to the anchor point (C). Step 5. The finished clove hitch in both loose and set forms (C). To set, simultaneously pull the two ends as shown by the arrows.

The Life Line

Your life is literally tied to your rope. With this in mind, you can see how important it is to attach yourself properly to the rope, to set up a bombproof belay and top-rope station, and to care for your rope.

Tying-In

The safest way to attach yourself to your rope system is to tie the rope directly to the harness. Since the advent of sport and gym climbing, many people clip the rope to a locking carabiner that is clipped into the harness. The advantage to tying the rope directly into the harness is that you are eliminating a possible weak link—a carabiner that theoretically could come open—with a direct tie-in. The rope, secured by a retraced figure-eight knot,

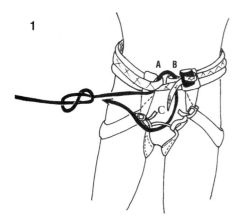

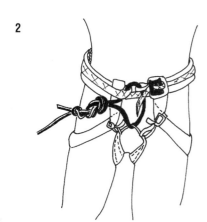

Tying into the harness. 1. Tie a figure-eight knot and pass a long tail through ears A and B and then through the leg-loop strap at C. Finish the knot by following back through. 2. Tighten the figure-eight knot to complete the tie-in. Leave a 3- or 4-inch tail or use an overhand as a backup.

becomes the primary attachment and the buckle is a secondary backup—a very strong system. The disadvantage for beginners is that you must absolutely, positively tie in correctly and know your knots perfectly—which actually is a hidden advantage.

To tie-in to the harness directly, tie a figure-eight in the rope end (leaving a long tail) and pass the tail through the tie-in loops on the waist harness, then through the leg-loop portion of the harness. (In older harnesses with two "ears," it is important to tie into both ears so that in the event of a fall, the impact forces will be distributed correctly. To avoid this possibility, it's best to buy a harness without ears.) Other types of harnesses depend more heavily on the buckle for primary security—always read and follow the manufacturer's directions for tying in to your harness. Retrace the figure-eight, and always finish off with an overhand knot backup.

ROPE ETIQUETTE
Treat your rope as if your life depends on it.
- *Never* step on your rope.
- Keep it clean, which means out of the dirt (sharp quartz or other mineral grains can abrade and cut rope fibers), away from thorn bushes, and so on. A smart climber carries a clean tarp on which to spread everything while gearing up, and also stores the rope in a stuff sack or rope bag.
- Inspect your rope for cuts and debris each time you put it away and each time you take it out.
- Never store your rope wet.
- Take special care to protect your rope while top-rope climbing: secure chafing pads under it if it runs tautly over sharp rock edges, for example.
- See sidebar Putting Your Rope Out to Pasture, p. 150.

Belaying

Belaying is the foundation of safe climbing—as a team, you and your partner combine your skills to work on one goal as a single unit. You must trust one another implicitly, so choose your belay partner well. It is worth noting that even after acquiring good belay skills, not all couples make good climbing teams, so take it slowly and don't be disappointed if you need to seek other climbing partners. Learning to climb can be stressful; if you and your partner-in-love turned out to have

JERRY CINNAMON

less-than-harmonious climbing experiences in the beginning, wait and try climbing together again after you move beyond beginner status.

In a belay system for beginners, the climb is usually "top-roped," whether in a gym or out at the crags. In this case, the rope is taken to the top of the climb (by a route other than the intended climb, unless other people in your group are capable lead climbers who can take the rope up to the top of the climb and set up the belay). The middle of the rope is anchored at the top of the climb with slings and carabiners in a manner that allows the rope to move; the other ends of the rope are tossed down the climb face. One end is tied in to the climber, while the other end is used by the belayer. (You can also belay from the top of the climb, but it is easier for beginners to learn belaying while watching the climber from below.) This chapter does not explain belaying for climbers who are lead-climbing (without a top-rope, setting their own protection as they climb), though the basic techniques are the same.

The belay concept is fairly straightforward: the belayer pays out or takes in rope as the climber moves, so as to catch the climber with as little slack in the rope as possible in case of a fall. To check a fall, the belayer instantly pulls the rope sideways against the belay device to create friction and stop the fall.

Before learning how to belay your partner, first consider your body position and the location of the belay, collectively termed the stance. At stake is your ability to remain in control at all times to prevent injury to yourself and the leader. Always do the following.

- *If using a belay anchor, make sure there is no slack in the system.* If the climber falls and there is slack in your belay anchor system (the belayer is "tethered" to a solid object if possible while belaying a climber), you will be abruptly pulled to the end of the anchor and experience shock forces as the anchor rope suddenly stops your forward motion. You may even be pulled off the ledge if belaying from the top. Besides causing injury, the shock of the sudden stop could cause you to drop the rope and lose control of the falling leader.
- *Couple natural terrain features with body position to brace against a potential fall.* For example, you can brace against a low wall with a leg extended on the helping-hand side of the body to counteract the force of a falling leader, or sit in a well-braced

position. In alpine climbing, there are times when no artificial anchor can be set up and you have to depend on a strongly braced body position alone to hold a fall.

- *Aim the belay, so you do not rotate during a fall.* Reduce the potential rotation by decreasing the distance between you and the anchor as much as possible. Sometimes, depending on the location of protection in relation to belay geography, you can aim a belay more effectively by using either your right or left hand as the braking hand. Learn to belay effectively with both hands.

To be ready to apply friction instantly, you use your *braking hand* and your *helping hand* in a coordinated manner to move the rope through the belay device. You begin with the helping hand extended to pull in rope from the climber and the braking hand grasping the rope close to the belay device. The braking hand pulls the rope through the belay device. The helping hand winds up next to the belay device and the braking hand is extended away from the device.

To keep pulling in rope as the climber ascends, there is a critical step you *must always make:* when you extend

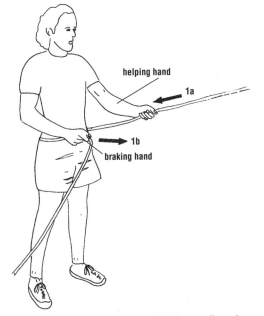

helping hand
1a

1b
braking hand

JERRY CINNAMON

Rope manipulation in belaying. The belayer pulls in the rope from the climber with the helping hand (1a) and pulls it around the friction braking surface with the braking hand (1b).

your helping hand to grasp more of the rope as you draw it in, you must also move your braking hand to also take in more rope. To do so, grasp both strands of the rope with the helping hand, so that your braking hand remains on the rope between your helping hand and your belay device. Now slide the braking hand along the rope to your body. *Never let go of the rope with your braking hand.* If you do, and the climber falls at that instant, you will not be able to hold the climber with only your helping hand. Release the braking side of the rope with your helping hand. This returns you to the starting position, ready to repeat the cycle.

SPEAKING THE SAME LANGUAGE

Good communication, which is required in climbing at all times, becomes more critical in difficult situations. When your climbing partner is nearby and in sight, you can talk normally and do not need special jargon. But when separated from your companion by overhangs or bulges that muffle sound, or in situations of stress when you must get a request across quickly and unmistakably, you need a bombproof communication system.

Climbers have developed a shorthand communication system that relies on one- and two-word phrases to communicate fundamental requests for rope management. To prevent misunderstanding, these phrases include questioning signals that are always followed by a response acknowledging the original signal. In crowded areas, climbers may use each other's name to differentiate their signals from identical signals being used by other teams. The generally accepted terms are

Climber. "On belay?" Question to belayer.

Belayer. "Belay on!" Response to climber.

Belayer. "Climb" or "climb when ready." Tells the climber it is okay to climb.

Climber. "Climbing." Indicates that the climber is starting up; sometimes the belayer is not ready yet and tells the leader so. "Climbing" can also mean that the climber is moving again after stopping for an extended period of time.

Climber. "Up rope." There is loose rope in the system and the belayer should take in some of it. There is no spoken response, since it is obvious to the climber that the rope is being taken in. When you are at a top-rope site with several ropes of different colors, it is helpful to mention the rope color in the signal: "Up on blue."

Climber. "Slack." The rope is too tight and the climber wants slack. If the belayer pays out rope without the rope becoming slack at the climber (because of friction in the system), the belayer may tell the climber to pull out what is needed. Once the climber starts up again, the signals "Climbing again" and "Up rope" should be given if necessary.

Climber. "Tension." This signal urges the belayer to make the rope very tight, because the climber is in danger of falling or needs to rest for some reason. A second climber may have difficulty getting out a piece of protection from a difficult stance, for example, and ask for tension.

Climber. "Falling." The climber is falling, and the belayer should lock off the belay.

Belayer. "[Number of] feet." This tells the leader how much rope is left and gives the leader a chance to set up a belay. Break the number up into its components—such as "two-zero" instead of "twenty"—to make the communication more clear.

Climber or *belayer.* "Rock, rock, rock!" Shouted at the top of your lungs, this tells anyone below to get out of the way of a falling rock, carabiner, nut, etc.

Climber. "That's me." This tells the belayer that the rope is not hung up in a crack or bush but has come tight on the climber. This situation often occurs just before the "Belay on" call, as the former leader initiates the belay out of sight of the second.

Climber. "Watch me." Not a traditional signal, this term now is used when climbers are doing a particularly hard move, to warn the belayer to be especially attentive.

Belayer. "I am with you." This response reassures the leader.

Climber. "Off belay." The climber is secure and tells the belayer to break the belay apart.

Belayer. "Belay off." Confirms that the belayer has broken the belay apart and tells the climber that the rope can be managed without interference from the belayer. The question "Belay off?," with the word *off* accented, is not a good way for the belayer to ask the leader if the belay can be taken off, since it may be mistaken for a statement. It is usually posed by an impatient belayer whose leader is not setting up the upper belay anchor fast enough for the belayer. The belayer may be cold or hungry, or have other personal needs. If the leader has forgotten to tell the belayer "Off belay," however, the belayer is justified in the question.

Rappeller. "Off rappel." The rappeller has not only taken the rappel apart, but has walked away from the area to avoid rock fall that might be caused by the next rappeller.

You will learn to do this quickly and efficiently, without looking at the belay device and rope.

A common mistake occurs when you begin normally but bend at the waist and straighten the elbow on the braking arm in order to take up a maximum amount of rope. In this extended position, it is difficult to reach beyond the braking hand, and you may use your helping hand to grasp the two ropes between the braking hand and the body. Since you cannot slide your braking hand to the original position, you must remove it from the rope, and thus you cannot apply effective, instantaneous braking action. To avoid this problem, leave the elbow of your braking arm bent, do not bend over at the waist, and take in a smaller amount of rope during each cycle.

THE RATING GAME

Nearly the first thing beginning climbers want to know is, "What's that climb rated at?" It's only natural to measure your ability against that of other climbers, or to compare the difficulty of climbing routes.

In North America, there is a fairly good standard rating system called the Yosemite Decimal System, which was developed from an early Sierra Club rating system. The initial system began with class 1 (a scramble, for which hands are not needed for aid) and ended with class 5 (a climb, for which rope and protection are required). Decimals were later added to refine the classifications of difficulty, from 0.1 to 0.9 (at that time—several decades ago—no climbs were rated harder than 5.9).

As climbers got better and better, the ratings were extended further and further. Today, 5.14 is the current envelope. Many climbers are also applying another grade level, from *a* through *d*. So the current envelope might be a 5.14d climb. Typically, beginners should stick with 5.5 to 5.7 climbs and work their way up the scale. Advanced climbing begins around 5.10.

Two other rating systems apply in climbing. Aided climbs are rated A1 to A5, and you might also see "commitment" grades, denoted in Roman numerals I through VI. A commitment grade describes the time that experienced climbers can expect to spend on a route (including approach and descent) as well as the number of pitches—one pitch being the length that can be climbed using one rope. So, a grade I climb may be a couple of pitches that should take 1–3 hours, and a grade VI climb may be 15 or more pitches and should take two or more days.

Setting Up for Top-Roping

Top-roped climbing is a good, safe instructional technique for beginning climbers. The climber is securely protected against a fall and can lean back against the rope if tired. The belayer can assist the climber with tension on the rope at difficult spots, as well as spot the route well, to advise the climber of the best route.

Stopping falls with a top-rope system is easy, since there is never an excess of slack in the rope. The belayer, however, must concentrate on the climber to manipulate the rope properly, and to apply the brake immediately in the event of a fall. The belayer is also in a good position to learn by observing and comparing how both beginner and expert climbers use holds and apply technique at different points of the climb.

Although top-roping is inherently safer than lead-climbing, the system must be set up properly to ensure security.

The self-equalizing anchor. The critical component for a top-roped climb is the anchor—the carabiner, webbing sling, and securing points to which it

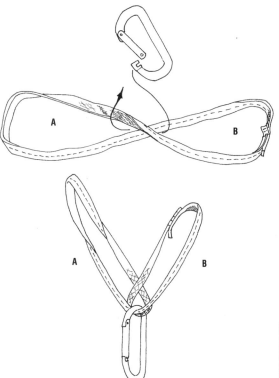

Basic self-equalization.

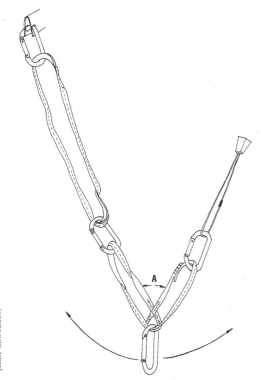

Two self-equalized anchor points. The load-bearing carabiner can travel through an arc and remain equalized. This carabiner is physically limited in its arc of travel by the length of the sling to which it is attached. Angle A determines load multiplication of the system and should be less than 60 degrees; if necessary, add slings to one or both anchor points to reduce the angle.

attaches—through which the rope runs for the belay. The anchor must be immensely strong to take the weight and shock of a falling climber safely, and the belaying rope must slide freely through the carabiner to prevent friction. At least two, and preferably three, attachment points should be used for the sling, with the weight of the climber equally distributed among them.

If you are starting out at top-roped climbing, you will probably be using an established climbing area. In such places, permanent protection often is already in place on the summit of the face, in the form of bolts. Sometimes substantial trees are employed, as well. The simplest belay anchor to set in this situation is the two-point, self-equalizing system.

To set up an equalizing anchor, lay a climbing sling on the ground and twist it into a figure-eight. Clip a locking carabiner across the **X** in the center, so that it joins the two loops of the figure-eight. Your belaying rope will run through this carabiner. Now choose two secure anchor points as close together as possible and, using slings and carabiners, clip in each loop of the figure-eight into an anchor, so that the system forms a narrow **V**. With the sling tied in this way, the carabiner through which your rope runs can slide back and forth on the sling, to equalize the stress on the anchors, yet if either anchor fails the system will still be secure—the carabiner cannot fall out of the sling.

Load multiplication. To understand the importance of the narrow angle, you need to know a little about the forces that are involved with a multiple-anchor setup.

Imagine hammering two picture hanger hooks into your living room wall, a couple of inches apart horizontally. Tie one end of a string to each hanger, so that it forms a loop hanging down a foot or two. Now suspend a 10-pound weight from the loop, and you'll have a model of a belay anchor.

If you could measure the force exerted on each hanger, you'd find it to be close to 5 pounds—in other words, each hanger is supporting half of your 10-pound weight, keeping the stress in the system low.

Now imagine moving the picture hangers a couple of feet apart, so that the loop supporting your weight forms a broad angle. Measure the force now, and you'll find that each hanger is supporting 7 or 8 pounds. Move the hangers still farther apart, and the load each supports will approach the full 10 pounds of the weight, so that your two-hanger system gives you no mechanical advantage at all. To avoid this load-multiplication effect, the angle in a two-point anchor system should always be kept narrow—less than 60 degrees. This can be accomplished two ways: by using anchor points that are close together, or by using longer slings to reduce the angle between points that are farther apart.

Further backup. It's virtually impossible for a well-placed two-point anchor to fail completely. On the other hand, it *never* hurts to use extra anchor points. The more points you have, the lower the stress on the entire system, as long as each component can equalize itself.

To rig a three-point anchor, you begin with the figure-eight sling. One loop of the eight, however, is clipped to a carabiner, which is in turn clipped into *another* figure-eight sling. The ends of this sling are then clipped to two anchor points, giving a total of three

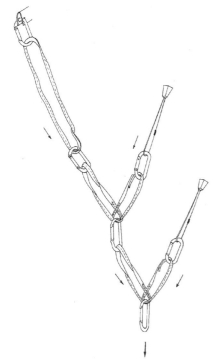

Equalizing three anchor points.

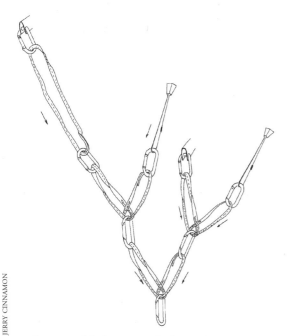

Combinations of the basic system for four anchor points.

points for the system. This can be expanded to four points simply by adding an additional figure-eight sling to the other loop of the primary sling.

To return to the picture hanger analogy, a properly set up four-point anchor would reduce our 10-pound weight to just 2½ pounds at each hanger. In the real world, a multipoint anchor both reduces the stress at each point *and* makes it even more unlikely that any one point will fail.

Anchor points. It's hard to beat a big, solid oak or pine tree for a reassuring anchor. Well-placed bolts in solid rock are nearly as secure, but there is no real way to test an existing bolt short of hanging a car off it. You must judge the bolt by eye and experience. First, reject any bolt that is rusted or otherwise corroded, or even one that just *looks* old. Older bolts are often ¼ inch in diameter, whereas newer ones are a stronger ⅜ inch—the difference is apparent when they are placed side by side. Also, stay away from bent bolts or hangers, and hangers that spin freely. Look for solid placement in clean rock, with no stress fractures radiating from the placement. Don't tap or bang on the bolt to test it; such treatment will only weaken it.

Although bolts can be extremely strong even when the pull on them is straight out, they are designed to use the immense shear strength of the bolt shaft for maximum security, so always keep the load as perpendicular to the axis of the bolt as possible. Never use fewer than two bolts as a belay anchor for top-roping; "three or a tree" is a better rule.

You can also utilize rock projections for belay anchors, but extreme care must be taken so that the sling cannot slip off the projection.

Preventing abrasion and friction. Abrasion is the deadly enemy of nylon ropes and slings, and friction is the enemy of smooth belay systems. Too much friction (heat) can damage slings and ropes.

The belay rope should not run over the top of the face through the anchor carabiner, as it will abrade against the edge of the rock and create a great deal of friction for the belayer. The belay anchor should be set up so that the carabiner hangs just over the edge. It's a good idea to use two figure-eight slings at this point for safety, and to pad the edge with a piece of Ensolite foam or anything handy. It's also a good idea to use two carabiners to run the rope through, to prevent its running over too sharp an angle. Be sure the carabiners don't hang too far below the edge, or the climber might not be properly belayed while making the crux move over the top.

Rappelling

Rappelling began as a simple and fast way for a climber to get back down a route just climbed, or for cavers or people working in high places to descend safely. Then, oddly, it metamorphosed into its own sport—many people went out with the sole intent of rappelling *off* rock faces, as an activity unto itself, with speed and daredeviling as a principle goal. The result was a slew of accidents involving people unfamiliar with basic rope and rock technique.

Rappelling must be considered a facet of rock climbing, not a substitute. You should be familiar with rope handling, belaying, and anchoring techniques before learning to rappel. Even among experienced climbers, many accidents happen on rappel because the participants are tired from a long climb or just complacent because the "dangerous" part of the day is over. Treat your rappel with the same care as you would a lead climb, and you'll stay out of trouble.

Rappelling involves running the rope through a braking device attached to your climbing harness, allowing you to control the speed of your descent (you can also run the rope around your body to create friction, but mechanical devices are safer, more comfortable, and easier to control). You can use a figure-eight descender or rig a brake from several oval carabiners.

Rappelling is usually done on a doubled rope, since after you're down you want to be able to retrieve the rope by pulling it through the anchor. A double rope doubles friction at the rappel device, and makes it easier to control your descent. The attachment point for the rope can be the same one you used for a top-roped climb, but the carabiner needs to be moved back from the edge, since you need room to clip in. Make sure the rope hangs free and untwisted all the way to the bottom of the face, and, of course, that it *reaches* the bottom. Don't laugh—an astonishing number of climbers have met an embarrassing demise by rappelling off the end of their rope.

It will help to practice clipping in to a rappel harness before you're standing at the cliff edge. At the site, you face the anchor (with your back to the edge), straddling the rope. Make sure your shirt is tucked in and that no other loose clothing or hair can become caught in the brake. Using a figure-eight descender, clip in. If using carabiners, care must be taken to set up the arrangement shown in the illustration, with the gates of the two horizontal carabiners opposed and reversed, and those of the braking two simply reversed.

Your braking hand holds the rope across your hip, where it can control the amount of resistance (if you are rappelling off a single rope, you might need to run the rope around behind your back to the braking hand, to add friction).

A
two attachment carabiners

double-rope bight

two platform carabiners with gates opposed and reversed

sling attached to harness

B
sling attached to harness

two attachment carabiners

double rappel-rope bight

two platform carabiners with gates opposed and reversed

two braking carabiners

JERRY CINNAMON

The carabiner brake in perspective.

Rappelling is a part of rock climbing—not a substitute.

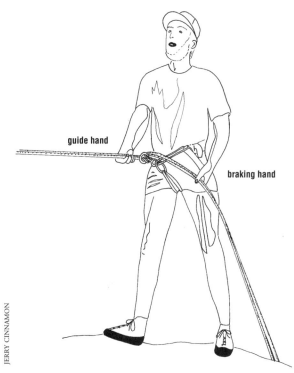

guide hand

braking hand

JERRY CINNAMON

The edge stance.

The guide hand is just that—it rides on the rope above the brake but provides no resistance. As you back toward the edge, you may actually have to help the rope through the brake, since without weight on it the resistance will be stiff.

The most difficult part of the rappel is backing off the edge. The temptation is to stand straight up, but you must stay perpendicular to the surface at all times. That means leaning back as you go over the edge, so your feet stay firmly planted on the rock.

It's popular to portray rappels as wild, free-falling rides, but the safest technique is to walk slowly backward down the face, keeping your stance wide to avoid swinging into the face and staying nearly perpendicular to the rock. Make sure you follow the natural fall line of the rope, so you don't get pulled sideways. You can twist your stance a bit to see below you, keeping your feet as far apart as possible. When you're down, you can step back from the face and pull slack through the brake before unclipping.

Moving on Rock

Whether you are climbing with a top-rope and belayer or working out alone on a boulder, you will use virtually the same techniques for moving on the rock.

There is no "basic recipe" to follow for successfully climbing a rock face, simply because no two rock faces are alike and no climb is the same for climbers of differing physiques and strengths. However, some basic techniques and moves for both foot and hand should be learned, along with some tips for weaving together a combination of those moves into a smooth ascent.

Foot Moves

Edging. When small positive edges or the tops of partially detached rock flakes are available, place the inside edge (either the big toe or ball of foot) or the outside edge (below the pinkie) of your foot on these. In general, the outside-edge placement feels less secure and is used as a transitory move on small holds while trying to get to better holds where you can rest.

Smearing. If the available holds are rounded and thus

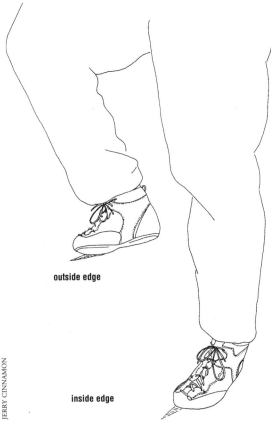

outside edge

inside edge

JERRY CINNAMON

Edging. The left foot, at the lower right corner of the figure, is edging on the inside. This places body weight directly over the inside of the big toe. The right foot, at the upper left corner, is edging on the outside of the foot. Body weight is over the outside of the ball of the foot.

don't offer good edging surfaces, you place your entire foot on the hold at a right angle to the fall line (the most direct line up and down the cliff); the object is to create the maximum contact area between the bottom of the foot and the rock.

Friction foothold. On low-angle faces, apply the same concept as above but point your toe up the fall line.

Under overhangs. Beware of using ledges under deep overhangs as footholds: if you place your foot too far back into them, as you reach up and around the overhang for a handhold, your balance will be compromised. Place your weight on your toes as far to the outside of the ledge as possible.

Jamming. One or both feet are jammed into wide cracks to offer a stable foothold; beware that your feet

do not become stuck. For more on crack climbing, see p. 166.

see p. 166.

Tips:

- As a general rule, the steeper the rock face gets, the shorter you should make your steps (to maintain balance).

- Try to stand upright on your feet, always placing your center of gravity (somewhere around your navel) above them. Lean out from the rock, and gravity will help you stay there; lean in to the rock, and gravity will pull you off.

- Moving directly up a friction slope is easier than moving sideways, during which a pronounced weight shift is necessary to transfer from one foot to another. If you must move sideways on a friction route, plan ahead and do so as diagonally as possible.

- If you need to change feet on a hold to get a better start on the next hold or move, be careful to maintain your balance on the rock. If there is not enough room on the hold for both feet, allowing a smooth weight-shift, you might have to do a quick hop—a seemingly easy move that actually takes a little practice.

Hand Moves

Open grip. Use the open grip on large, rounded holds; apply friction with your palm to increase security.

Cling grip. This is used when just the pads of the fingers fit on the hold; stabilize the grip by placing your thumb over the first finger.

Vertical grip. On narrow positive holds, use the vertical grip by forming your hand into a claw (fingers together) and using your hand as a hook to hold your weight. (This grip is very powerful on small holds but can cause tendon pain and damage, so use it sparingly.)

Pinch grip. By squeezing your thumb and side of your forefinger together you can create a strong grip for nubbins with no top edges.

Finger grip or finger cam. Insert one or more fingers in a thin crack, piton scar, or small pocket, and twist (cam) your finger while pulling to the side to enhance the effect of the cam. You can stack fingers or put them side by side.

Finger wrap. On protruding rounded knobs or large crystals, wrap your small finger and as many other fingers as you can around the knob; maximize contact between the side of your small finger and the rock, and

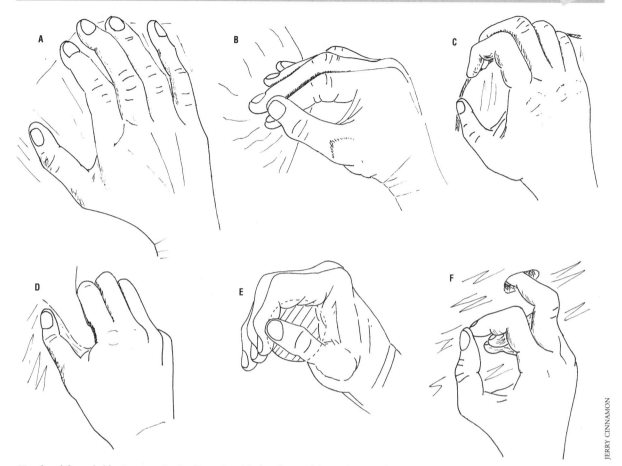

Hand and finger holds. A. open grip; B. cling grip with thumb as stabilizer; C. vertical grip;
D. pinch grip; E. finger wrap; F. finger grip.

JERRY CINNAMON

press your thumb against the other fingers or the knob
to help stabilize the hold.

Jamming. In crack climbing, your fingers, hands, and
even arms can be literally jammed into small and
medium cracks to provide friction and holds. See the
section on crack climbing, p. 166.

Tips:

- Remember that handholds should help you maintain
  balance, while footwork actually moves you up the
  rock face. Pulling up mostly on your fingers can be
  not only tiring but injurious.
- To execute a successful hand traverse, for which you
  have adequate handholds but must use smearing and
  edging for foot placement, maintain your center of
  gravity by squatting over your feet and leaning back
  on your arms. This keeps your body weight over

your feet, helping to keep them from sliding out
from under you. You may have to cross your hands
over one another while you shuffle your feet rather
than cross them.

Body Moves

Mantling. When you encounter a mantleshelf (just
like it sounds—a shelf in the rock face) you will need to
climb up and beyond it while maintaining your balance,
a feat that can be difficult if the shelf is narrow or slopes
toward you. Mantling requires that you first hoist yourself up onto the shelf on your hands (using the powerful
muscles of your triceps to push your body upward), rotating them to bear the weight and increase friction on
the palms; once you're balanced, you swing one foot up
and stand. To complete a successful mantle, you must

commit to a forceful, dynamic motion. (On small shelves, you can complete a mantle by turning sideways and placing one hand over the other to make room for a foot.)

Counterforces: underclings, liebacks, and stemming. Counterforce is a technique applied to many types of climbing. In general, you generate forces that act in opposite, or counter, directions to create friction and thus balance. You can create these forces by opposing your hands or your feet, such as you do in a right-angle inside corner when you push against holds on opposite walls with your feet *(stemming)*. You can also produce a counterweight to help balance your body over your feet, by leaning off holds. In *underclinging,* you grasp a horizontal crack palm-up and pull upward while pushing down with your feet. To *lieback* a vertical crack, you wrap your hands around the edge of the crack and pull while pushing against the rock with your feet, making sure

JERRY CINNAMON

The undercling to a long reach. The climber uses the bottom of a rock flake as an undercling hold. His hands pull upward on the hold while his feet push downward onto a friction slab to create opposing forces. Then he can walk his feet up the slab, while maintaining opposition, and reach up with one hand to gain a high handhold. Small downward-pointing flakes can also be used to create opposition.

> ◆ **EXPERT TIP: ALL TAPED UP**
> While learning to crack climb, you will want to protect the backs of your hands and knuckles against painful skinning. You can use commercial mitts (made from climbing shoe rubber), or you can tape up your hands with medical cloth adhesive tape. For good adhesion, clean your hands with alcohol prior to tape-up; if you have hairy hands, you can shave them first to avoid having your hair ripped out by the roots when it comes time to untape.

that your foot placements are close enough to your hands to produce the counterforce.

Tips:

- On steep climbs with few large holds, ideally you will move through swiftly and smoothly, but the reality is that you may need to rest. To do so, place one foot higher than the other and move your midsection (your center of gravity) closer to the rock (over your feet) while holding your head back to survey the next section of rock; you are holding on with one hand (opposite to the upper leg) stretched out straight above your head. This tripod of two feet and a hand (the other arm hangs free) is a surprisingly restful position.

Crack Climbing

Many routes will follow natural crack systems in the rock because the face offers virtually no other holds. Crack climbing ability does not come naturally, as some other aspects of climbing do. It requires experimentation, guidance, and experience—and it can be strenuous and painful. Why, then, do some climbers prefer crack climbing to all other forms of climbing? It provides good holds, good protection, and challenging routes up otherwise smooth rock.

Crack climbing involves inserting fingers, hands, feet, arms, or even knees into a crack and camming them so that they lock (this is *jamming*). Once you have jammed your feet and hands, you are secured to the rock and can remove one hand or foot at a time to move upward.

Cracks are classified by their width: *thin cracks* (finger size), *hand cracks, fist cracks,* and—for anything bigger than a fist—*offwidth cracks.* As you become adept at climbing, you will no doubt encounter these various cracks and learn to experiment with different jamming techniques.

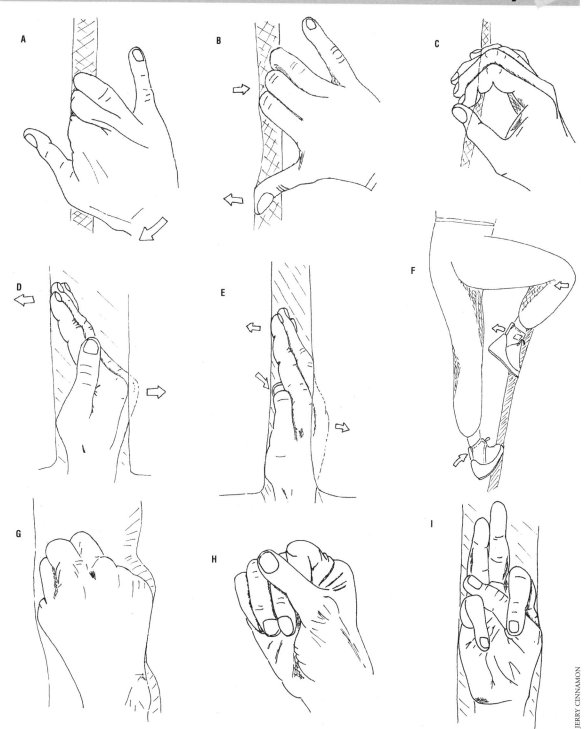

Thin-crack jams with the thumb down: A. finger lock; B. finger lock with counterpressure by the thumb; C. ring jam. Hand and toe jams. D. wide hand crack; E. narrow hand crack; F. toe jams. Fist jams. G. fist jam with palm facing into the crack; H. view of the fist position with thumb over the fingers; I. hand position for a narrow fist jam.

Lead Climbing

After you practice movement skills and gain initial proficiency climbing rock faces while top-roped, your next step is to learn the art of lead climbing. Although too involved to cover extensively in this chapter, a few tips will help you begin the learning process.

- Accompany an experienced team doing short lead climbs. Ideally, you should join two experienced climbers who will do the leading and belaying while you—climbing between them—learn about the process.

- Read up on how the lead climbing system works (see the book list at the end of this chapter), so that the instructions you receive from the experienced team will be more understandable.

- If the leader uses established bolt protection, you can concentrate on movement techniques, since you only have to unclip carabiners from the bolts and hang them from your harness. If the leader places protection, you will need to understand more about how the leader thinks in order to communicate and work well together.

- The leader initially solves physical movement puzzles and route-finding problems that confront the team in climbing sections of rock, or pitches, between belay points. When the leader arrives at the top of a pitch and sets up a fail-safe belay, it becomes the second's turn to climb.

- Many leaders store a map of the pitch in their head and use it to communicate with the second. The leader may tell the second how to overcome potential problems with removing protection, managing rope, or climbing difficult sections.

- A leader might sketch out a route "topo." It is important to remember that the symbols of the men-

tal topo remain as an image in the leader's mind even if guidebooks to the area are written in a descriptive essay style. In this particular mental topo, standard guidebook symbols are used for face climbing, corners that face left or right, overhangs, straight-in cracks, liebacks, belay stations, degrees of difficulty, and so on. On the map in the leader's head, pitons or bolts become more than just shaped bit of metal—they become landmarks of the climb, along with overhangs and other rock features that mark specific locations.

WILLIAM PELANDER

The lead climber places bombproof protection

Fitness and Health

Although climbing requires a keen mind and an adventurous heart, it will certainly do you some good to hone your body in a number of ways, including aerobic and muscular endurance, flexibility, strength and power, balance and coordination, and diet.

Conditioning

Aerobic endurance. Aerobic endurance will allow you to function at peak form, pitch after pitch. And aerobic endurance is a prerequisite for muscular endurance, so it's best to start here. One of the best ways to increase aerobic endurance, as well as enhance both upper- and lower-body strength, is mountain bike riding on rough trails. Intense hiking and cross-country skiing are also excellent conditioners for aerobic endurance. Good results in any activity require that you train for 8–12 weeks at about 75–80 percent maximum effort prior to beginning climbing.

Muscular endurance. An excellent way to build muscular endurance for face climbing is to boulder on large holds two or more times a week for hour-long sessions (climbing gyms can be great for this). Vary the intensity of each workout by varying the size of the footholds. Vary the duration of each workout as well. Traditional gyms also offer alternatives: push-ups, sit-ups, curls, squats, dips, pull-ups, and chin-ups are excellent, as are repetitive weight-lifting sets.

Flexibility. A program of regular stretching will greatly increase your flexibility while climbing. Before commencing a stretching session, warm up your muscles first with a few minutes of aerobic activity. Then work on specific muscle groups, progressing slowly and gently—do not bounce or force muscles into stretching.

You can build your own backyard climbing wall for about $200 and a little sweat-equity.

Consult a book such as *Stretching,* by Bob Anderson, or take a yoga class.

Strength and power. Weight training is an excellent way to increase your strength; however, the method differs from that used to increase endurance. To stimulate strength development, use a weight that you can lift 6–12 times before momentary failure. It is best to work with a professional weight trainer at a gym when working with heavy weights.

Balance and coordination. Some of the world's best climbers are also professional dancers, so it's no surprise that a few serious climbers take modern dance, Tai Chi, or gymnastics lessons to help improve their overall balance and coordination. In lieu of lessons, you can devise your own balance and coordination drills, such as balance beam work (use curbs in a parking lot) or standing on your toes while alternately raising one leg and then the other in various positions. You will learn much about finding and controlling your center of gravity.

Fuel

Diet is another factor to consider if you want to perform at peak levels on the rock. Not surprisingly, a low-fat (not no-fat) diet is best. A few days before a challenging day or weekend at the crags, tank up with a few high-carbohydrate meals—you'll double your glycogen stores (necessary for aerobic activity) and thus your performance. Carbohydrate-rich foods include pastas, root crops, dried fruits, bagels, muffins, pancakes, rice cakes, energy bars, and cookies. In your quest to reduce fat, don't remove it entirely—add a little fat in the form of cheese, butter, or some nuts. And don't neglect protein, found in foods such as beans, cereals, nuts, and meats.

BACKCOUNTRY TIPS
If you venture into the backcountry to climb, you will want to take all the usual precautions taken by dayhikers or backpackers.

For a good list of personal gear to take with you, see Chapter 1, p. 45, and in the same chapter, read the section on pretrip planning for emergencies, p. 19.

See Chapter 13, p. 289, for a few more items you might add to a "personal essentials" kit to carry with you on all outdoor adventures.

Beware of consuming too much of your carbohydrates in energy bars (also known as "power" bars), which often contain a lot of high-fructose corn syrup. Digestion of this form of fructose requires a lot of water—at least three times as much as does fructose from fruit juice or rice dextrin. See Chapter 12 for a more in-depth look at nutrition outdoors.

Where to Go

The recent climbing boom is matched only by a parallel boom in the production of guidebooks. There is a guidebook for nearly anywhere there is climbable rock, from California to Switzerland, and from the Arctic to the tip of South America. Visit your local climbing shop; or if you don't have one, peruse the advertisements in *Climbing* and *Rock & Ice* magazines for booksellers specializing in climbing and mountaineering titles. These magazines also feature climbing destinations each month, often with route topos and very detailed descriptions.

Word of mouth continues to be an excellent source for new climbing areas. Climbing gyms and popular weekend crags are good spots to hang out for the latest news. Climbing shops used to give out lots of free advice and even topos of new climbs, but in this age of liability, most shops now refrain from giving route advice.

Backcountry Fever

Once you are a proficient lead climber, you may go the way of those few adventuresome souls who seek out new climbs far in the backcountry. Armed with topographical maps and knowledge of an area's geology, these explorers scout possible candidate crags first on paper and then either on foot or, as do a few well-heeled backcountry enthusiasts, by small plane. The adventures are high in exploring unknown rock, but the rewards of first-ascents are equal.

When exploring in previously unclimbed areas, be mindful of private property, and contact the land management agency for their rules on climbing (ask for the backcountry ranger or manager). Many agencies are outlawing the use of bolts or pitons, white chalk, or even, in extreme cases, the act of climbing. And many crags are closed from early spring through mid- or late-summer, to minimize disturbance to breeding birds or mountain sheep.

TOP 5 CLASSIC NORTH AMERICAN CLIMBING AREAS

Gunks,
New York

Yosemite Valley,
California

Eldorado,
Colorado

Joshua Tree,
California

Santa Catalina Mountains,
Arizona

Joshua Tree, California.

CLIFF LEIGHT

- *Joshua Tree, California*. Interesting plants and more rock than you can climb in a lifetime characterize this beautiful desert oasis.
- *Yosemite Valley, California*. A world rock climbing center featuring short climbs to big walls, and the world's best-known camp for climbers.
- *Santa Catalina Mountains, Arizona*. A smorgasbord of lovely granite from 3,000 to 7,000 feet awaits climbers in this beautiful range of mountains rising from a desert sea—and the cool summers and moderate winters are an added bonus.
- *Gunks, New York*. The Gunks, near New Paltz, offer white, layered quartzite, with big holds on miles of steep faces in a unique land preserve. Features a lively social scene in a midstate village.
- *Eldorado, Colorado*. This hot spot outside of Boulder is a climber's idea of heaven—lots of challenging climbs all within a hop, skip, and jump of a road. Totally rad social scene, too.

The Grand Tour

During the winter months the climbing areas of the American Southwest seems literally overrun with climbers from the northern United States and Europe. Escaping from their frozen homes, these sun- and warm-rock–seekers have turned climbing into a year-round sport by migrating like birds. A sort of Grand Tour has evolved, beginning in winter in Hueco Tanks, Texas, moving leisurely to southern Arizona's Catalina and Dragoon mountains, then to Joshua Tree in Southern California, and ending up in spring in the Valley (Yosemite, that is) in California or points north and east such as Eldorado, near Boulder. For many, the tour has become a rite of passage in their dedication to climbing.

Check out Tim Toula's *Rock 'n Road* for excellent climbing road trip information across all of North America (see Resources listings at end of this chapter).

Where Can Climbing Lead You?

As you become proficient on the rock, you will soon learn that climbing can easily be a lifelong passion. Sport climbing and its progeny, the competitions of the American Sport Climbers Federation, seem to hold the attention of the young and ambitious, while backcountry lead climbing may beckon the more experienced and adventuresome climbers. A natural progression might be a turn to ice climbing, and mountaineering (see p. 47). Mountaineers don't seem to reach their peak until they are well into or past their third decades.

Competition

The booming popularity of rock climbing gyms set the stage for a well-organized, easy-to-manage world rock climbing competition circuit.

The competition committee of the American Sport Climbers Federation (ASCF) chooses gym or on-the-rock sites, sets up routes according to ASCF competition standards, and oversees the competition. Prizes are getting rich—sometimes in the thousands of dollars. Corporate sponsorship of competitions and climbers is getting to be big-dollar because images of hot rock climbers are creeping into mainstream advertising, especially in Europe, where rock climbing stars enjoy popularity similar to tennis or golf stars.

PUSHING THE ENVELOPE: LYNN HILL

They said it couldn't be done. "It" is a free-climb of the infamous Nose on El Capitan in Yosemite Valley. "They" is never quite clear, but suffice it to say a lot of guys had tried—and failed—to climb this awesome class VI 5.13b route without fixed aid. On September 16, 1993, Lynn Hill, a small and soft-spoken woman from Southern California, who at the time was considered among the world's top climbers, free-climbed The Nose.

"They said it couldn't be done," Hill reportedly said. "It goes, boys."

The competitions themselves are exciting to watch; most have bleachers set up for comfortable viewing, and you'll often see ESPN cameras at the ready. All ages and backgrounds seem to enjoy the competitions, regardless of climbing experience—kids, grandmothers, students, or business professionals.

Most competitions have amateur classes and bouldering classes, so you can get an early taste for the competitive scene. For more information about North America and Europe's climbing competitions, contact the American Sport Climbers Federation (see the Resources section at the end of the chapter).

Ice Climbing

In winter, many rock climbers turn naturally to the most available medium on which to climb—ice.

Although ice climbing is similar to rock climbing—ropes, harnesses, belays, and various carabiners are used—the similarities end there. If you are in shape from climbing rock all summer, on the other hand, you will be in shape for climbing ice in winter.

In order to climb solid ice or ice-encrusted rock, you do not use rock handholds or footholds or use smearing and jamming techniques. Instead, you use ice axes and crampons—toothed cleats that strap on to your mountaineering boots—to create holds in the ice. And you use ice screws, snow pickets, flukes, snargs, and warthogs as protection when lead climbing.

The hostile winter environment adds a particularly sharp edge to ice climbing. You need to be properly dressed, in rugged waterproof parkas and pants, insulated midlayers, and long underwear, and you should always protect your extremities with good gloves or

Good axe placement is essential for ice climbing.

☞ KID QUOTIENT

Most adults look pretty wobbly on their first rock climb. The fear, the pressure to succeed, the unnatural vertical movement—they all conspire to make us doubt and fail.

But kids haven't yet learned that they *can't* scale cliffs, that it's nothing more than just pure fun—so most end up scurrying up the rocks like squirrels, and they can almost never get enough.

Climbing with kids is pretty simple, because you won't take young ones on lead climbs, you won't take risks that you might take on your own, and you will restrict their top-roped climbs to fairly short crags. Begin with simple climbs—perhaps scrambling but with roped protection (you are always the belayer)—or easy 5.3 or 5.4 climbs with large and plentiful holds. Then, you might consider letting them try slightly more difficult climbs if they want to.

☞ Invest in the excellent book *Climbing with Children,* by Gary Joyce (Birmingham, AL: Menasha Ridge Press, 1996).

☞ A few manufacturers make climbing harnesses and rock climbing shoes for kids. If these aren't in your budget, consult Joyce's book for good tips on tying your own webbing harnesses and converting old tennies into climbing shoes (he resoles theirs with climbing shoe rubber using resoling kits sold at outdoor shops). Ask around for kid-size helmets, a very important precaution.

☞ Start with short climbs—just 10–20 feet.

☞ If you have several kids, don't let competition spoil the fun; make it a team effort, with the nonclimbers giving verbal encouragement, rather than an I've-got-to-beat-my-older-sister race.

☞ Take lots of snacks, water, and juices.

☞ Take lots of breaks to enjoy all of the above.

☞ Stop before everyone gets tired and cranky. In the same vein, keep a sharp eye out for frustration if someone's having a hard time or is scared. Back off and set up easier climbing routes. (This is good advice for all ages.)

(See Chapter 11 for more tips on adventuring outdoors with kids.)

DOUG BERRY/OUTSIDE IMAGES

mitts and insulated double boots. To ward off glare, sunglasses are a good idea, and a helmet is mandatory. In addition, the extreme weather and weather-related conditions of ice climbing in the mountains require that you thoroughly learn about avalanches, mountain rescues, and alpine weather forecasting. And then there is learning about ice: glacier ice, alpine ice, rime ice, water ice.

Jerry Cinnamon's excellent *Climbing Rock and Ice* (Ragged Mountain Press, 1994) is a thorough primer on learning the vertical dance on ice.

Further Resources for Climbing
Books

Climbing Rock and Ice, by Jerry Cinnamon (Camden, ME: Ragged Mountain Press, 1994). A well-organized, clearly illustrated and fully modern treatment of learning the "vertical dance." Much of the material for this chapter was adapted and excerpted with permission from *Climbing Rock and Ice,* and Jerry Cinnamon contributed excellent editorial consultation as well.

Ice World, by Jeff Lowe (Seattle: The Mountaineers, 1996). Already *the* book on ice climbing from the master.

Rock 'n Road: Rock Climbing Areas of North America, by Tim Toula (Evergreen, CO: Chockstone Press, 1995). This amazing tome covers just about every possible climbing area in the 50 states, the provinces of Canada, and much of Mexico. Designed for road trips, it concisely rates each area, in atlas-style, for types and quality of climbing and rock, land ownership and status, seasonality, access, and camping.

Periodicals

Climbing, 1101 Village Road, Suite L-1-B, Carbondale, CO 81623; (970) 963-9449.

Rock & Ice, P.O. Box 3595, Boulder, CO 80307; (303) 499-8410.

Climbing Organizations

American Alpine Club, 710 10th Street, Golden, CO 80401; (303) 384-0110.

American Mountain Guides Association, same address as above; (303) 271-0984.

American Sport Climbers Federation, 2100 SW 3rd, Corvallis, OR 97333; (888) ASCFROX; janesky@Roguewave.com

The Access Fund, P.O. Box 17010, Boulder, CO 80308; (303) 545-6772.

Schools

National Outdoor Leadership School, P.O. Box AA, 288 Main Street, Lander, WY 82520; (307) 332-6973.

Colorado Outward Bound School, 945 Pennsylvania Street, Denver, CO 80203; (800) 477-2627.

Contact the American Mountain Guides Association, above, for a complete listing of their members in your area.

Other Resources

Don't miss Tim Toula's *Rock 'n Road* web page if you're planning a climbing road trip (or any climbing trip)—www.rocknroad.com.

"You are a team, connected by a rope. Teamwork requires prolonged attention, positive verbal and nonverbal communication, and emphatic commitment to the project at hand, as well as to each other."

—Author and climbing instructor Jerry Cinnamon, on the relationship of the climber and belayer

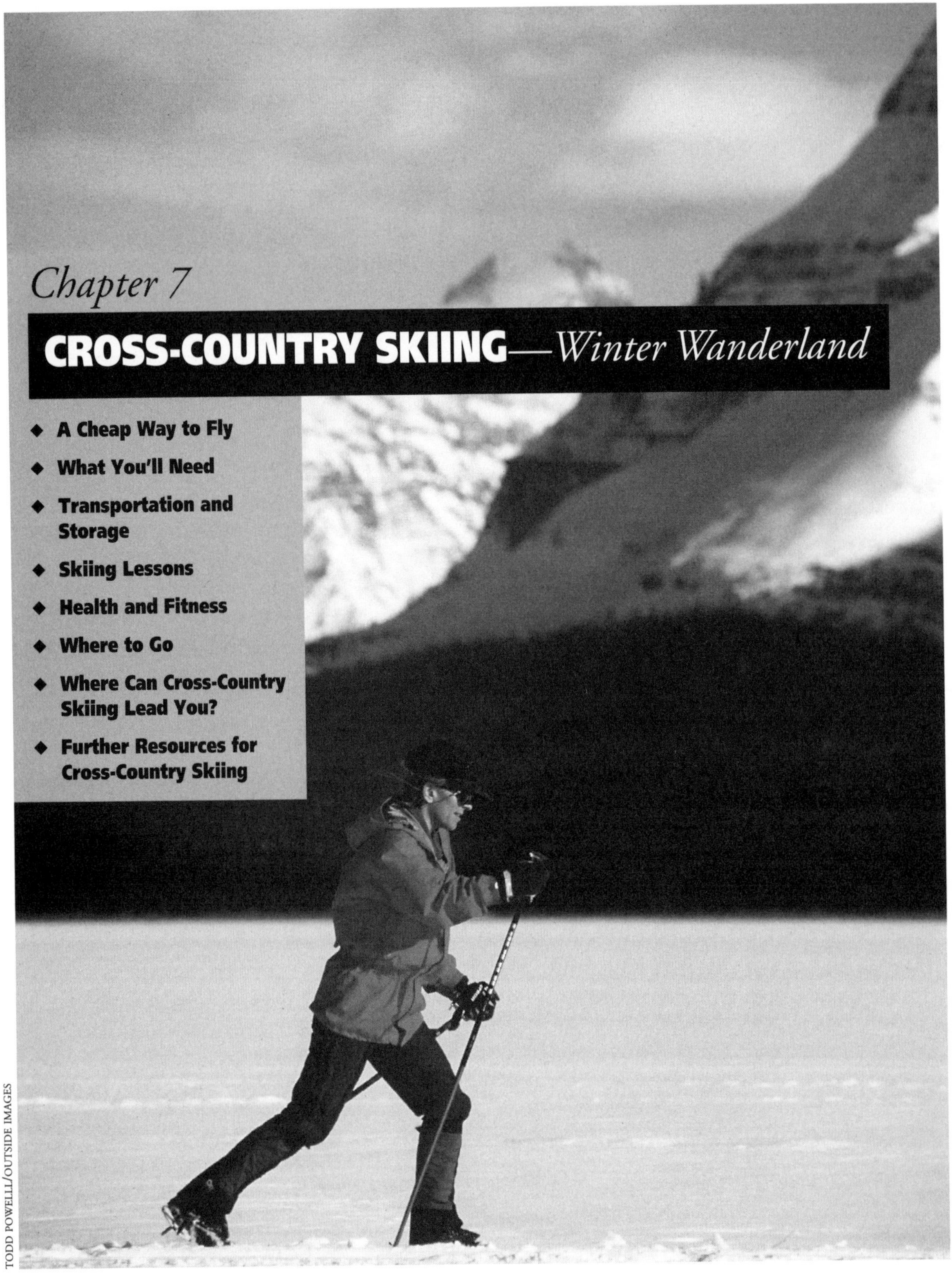

Chapter 7

CROSS-COUNTRY SKIING—*Winter Wanderland*

- A Cheap Way to Fly
- What You'll Need
- Transportation and Storage
- Skiing Lessons
- Health and Fitness
- Where to Go
- Where Can Cross-Country Skiing Lead You?
- Further Resources for Cross-Country Skiing

TODD POWELL/OUTSIDE IMAGES

"Snowflakes fall gently from a soft, gray sky, slowly blanketing the land. The scars of summer—eroded paths, flattened campsites, scraps of litter—disappear, and the wounded mountains recover their wild glory. . . . wilderness lies silent. But soon a soft, rhythmic sound can be heard, barely loud enough to disturb the peace. The first skier is venturing out into the winter hills."

—Chris Townsend, *Wilderness Skiing and Winter Camping*

SPORT FILE

Couch potato quotient: 3 (couch to happy kick-n-glide takes moderate-high fitness)
Coordination factor: 3 (pat your head and rub your tummy)
White-knuckle rating: 2 (at least the snow's soft)

A Cheap Way to Fly

The sensation of *schussing* swiftly over sinuous mounds of billowy snow with the chill wind pressing against your face and a crystalline white wilderness beckoning endlessly before you, is as close to flying as you can get without leaving the Earth.

Freedom, speed, and simplicity are the essence of cross-country skiing—that is, skiing on skinny skis with the heel "free" for kicking and gliding—making it one of the most exhilarating and rewarding outdoor pursuits of all. Sharing with sea kayaking and canoeing a birth from utilitarianism—a way for people to get around in a world without cars or airplanes, and particularly in a world covered by snow eight months of the year—cross-country skiing not only has retained its original simplicity, but that simplicity has been enhanced by modern technology, making the art of skiing cross-country easier (not to mention lighter and faster) than ever before.

Most historians place the origins of free-heel, or cross-country, skiing in Scandinavia some 4,000–5,000 years ago, but cross-country skiing as we know it today can be dated to 1863, when a Norwegian tenant farmer won a skiing competition using innovative new equipment he had designed and built. These innovations included twisted (cabled) bindings that wrapped around the heel for improved toe-to-ski control, side-cut skis for fast turning, shorter skis, and a shorter pole (at that time skiers used one long pole to aid propulsion, turning, and braking). He also introduced innovations in

---

FIRST TIME OUT

Your very first time on skis will be like learning to walk all over again—a process that, thankfully, most of us have forgotten and are willing to try once more. Unless you possess incredible natural talent for mastering the two slippery boards attached to your feet, expect to fall . . . and fall again . . . and then fall some more.

After you've fallen enough to get the hang of it and have practiced some basic skiing techniques (such as how to *stop*), try a day tour, either at a ski center with groomed trails (tracks) or on a trail you know is relatively flat and smooth (or look for designated ski trails, often marked in forests and parks). Here are some tips for your first ski day.

- If you're in good all-around physical shape, expect to be able to cover 3–5 miles in a surprisingly short time, if the terrain is not overly difficult. For a first tour, you'll probably want to turn around in time to make your total tour reasonably short—5 or 6 miles. You don't want to have to deal with skiing in the dark or confronting a storm front on your first day out beyond the roadside field. Remember that winter days mean shorter days, so get an early start.
- Unless your primary autumn activities have kept your upper body—shoulders and arms in particular—in top shape, expect to be sore after your first few outings. Poling will tax your muscles more than you think. And if you haven't been fitness walking or running, take it easy on your first tour—no more than a couple of miles—or you'll really pay for it.
- Make sure you take along good maps and a compass on your first tour, and pay attention to trail markers and landmarks.
- Always carry an essentials kit for personal safety (see Health and Fitness section, p. 199, and also Chapter 13, p. 289).
- Don't forget to relax and have fun!

technique: the telemark turn, the parallel turn, and the herringbone step. The telemark turn—named for the farmer's home, the Telemark region of Norway—is an elegant, bent-knee style that remains the classic image of moving in the wilderness on skis.

Today we ski for pleasure rather than for survival, although in some northern climes a few people do ski to their nine-to-five jobs. The great advantage of cross-country, or "nordic," skiing over downhill skiing is that once outfitted with skis, poles, bindings, and boots, you're ready to go anywhere there is enough snow—no need for crowds, lift chairs, expensive tickets, and forest clearcuts. Pick a goal and go—it's that simple.

Styles of cross-country skiing style, however, are varied:

Day touring. Day touring on untracked hiking trails, backroads, or through virgin forest is a very popular choice for the majority of cross-country skiers. The preferred skis are moderately skinny, to float on un-packed snow; sometimes the skis have partial or full metal edges, but usually they lack metal edges; poles are rugged enough to withstand collisions with trees or rocks; and boots offer light-to-medium support.

Track skiing. Across North America, commercial operations offer groomed tracks for cross-country skiing. A track machine or snowmobile fitted with special equip-ment is used to lay down twin grooves in the snow—tracks in which you ski—while simultaneously com-pacting a nice wide and smooth lane; sometimes the lane has several sets of tracks. Speed, fitness, and technique are usually the focus of track skiing, which is not true *cross-country* skiing, although many facilities offer groomed trails through woodlands for a taste of cross-

country without the work of breaking trail. Track skiing is also the choice for skiing families; the going is much easier for kids, and many ski centers offer special kids' events and lessons. The preferred skis are skinny and light, and both boots and poles are pared down for weight as well.

Backcountry touring. Mate backpacking with cross-country skiing and the progeny is backcountry ski tour-ing, to many enthusiasts the epitome of skiing cross-country style, because you can sortie many miles into otherwise-inaccessible snowbound wilderness and experience ultimate solitude and beauty. Backcountry ski touring requires more general outdoor skills than either day touring or track skiing—in addition to basic backpacking and wilderness skills, you must be profi-cient at winter travel, including avalanche knowledge—as well as more skiing skills, such as ascending and descending wearing a heavy pack. The equipment is naturally more robust: wider skis with metal edges are used, along with sturdy mountain boots and bindings and strong poles that are sometimes adjustable and serve double duty as avalanche probes.

Cross-country downhill skiing (XCD). This style of skiing is certainly an oxymoron by title, and perhaps by style. However, many skinny-ski, free-heel enthusiasts

Track skiing offers speed and aerobic fitness in beautiful forest settings, such as here at North Rim Nordic Center at Grand Canyon.

Uncertain weather and challenging terrain are part of the experience in backcountry skiing.

like to head to downhill ski areas, where they can carve telemark-style turns all day long without the work of hauling themselves uphill over and over. The equipment is hybrid: wide metal-edged skis that look more like downsized downhill skis than cross-country skis; the boots and bindings are similar to backcountry style but not quite so stiff; and the poles are slightly taller than downhill poles but not as long as touring poles. Most downhill ski areas require telemark skiers to add "leashes" (also called safety straps) between their skis (bindings) and boots, because boots can pull out of cross-country bindings more easily than downhill-style boots and bindings, sending a heavy ski spinning dangerously across a crowded slope.

Much of the information from this chapter was adapted from Wilderness Skiing and Winter Camping, *by Chris Townsend (Camden, ME: Ragged Mountain Press, 1994).*

Whichever type of cross-country skiing tugs at your fancy, rest assured you will experience one of the purest forms of outdoor activity—just you and the winter world—one that all ages and abilities can enjoy, at many levels. Virtually anyone who can put one foot in front of the other can cross-country ski—all you need is a good sense of balance and a moderate level of fitness. Choose your style, or several styles, and then your intensity. Many people never venture more than a few miles each year down the wooded paths near their homes, while a few may plan weeks-long expeditions in the Rockies or the Alps. Some skiers prefer quiet wilderness explorations in a season few people experience intimately, while others crave the whooping thrill of a seemingly endless downhill run linked by perfect telemark turn after turn after turn.

And the good news is that you can teach yourself most everything you need to know for simple day touring, and in just a morning's lesson you can learn to carve a decent telemark or stem turn. Many people can teach themselves to turn on cross-country skis, but often an instructor can help head off bad habits or give the most simple tips that would take a beginner weeks to teach themselves. Practice and perfection are up to you.

What You'll Need

Skis, boots and bindings, poles—that's it. If you've never indulged in wintertime outdoor activities, you might need to add some lightweight-but-warm clothing that allows good freedom of motion, but otherwise your basic cross-country ski kit is very simple.

As indicated above, cross-country ski equipment can vary depending on which type of skiing you wish to do: wider, metal-edged skis for backcountry touring, for example, or very narrow, lightweight skis for track workouts. Some serious skiers end up with several sets of ski equipment, each of which optimizes performance in each type of skiing. But for beginners, there is a happy medium: if you choose a basic day-touring setup carefully, it can take you on easy backcountry jaunts or do you justice at a track center.

The Skis

Although the art of cross-country skiing is simple, the dynamics of what makes a ski, well, *ski,* are somewhat complex. A few hundred years ago, skis were nothing

THE ESSENTIALS—A CROSS-COUNTRY SKIING START-UP KIT

- Cross-country skis ($100–$300)
- Boots ($50–$300)
- Bindings ($20–$200)
- Poles ($25–$150)
- Hat, gloves or mitts ($0–$50)

Minimum cost essential cross-country skiing kit: $195*

head and
hand
protection

poles

skis

boots

binding

ADD-ONS

- Fanny pack or daypack
- Water bottle
- Repair kit
- Lightweight, waterproof/breathable jacket and pants
- Stretch tights or knickers
- Stretch long-underwear top (zippered turtleneck)
- Synthetic or wool socks
- Gaiters
- Glider and klister waxes

*The essentials list above is intended to give you an idea of minimum start-up costs, from scratch, for moderate entry into a sport using new equipment. Other options include borrowing gear from friends or renting from retailers, YMCAs, or church activity clubs, as well as buying used gear—see Appendix A.

more than planks of wood with upturned tips, and it was the talent and hard work of the skier that got the things to work. However, modern technology has crafted sleek, ultralight runners of such precision that in order to make a wise choice for yourself, you should first learn a little about those technological advances. These include design attributes such as *camber, sidecut* or *waist, overall* and *tip flex, torsion,* and *central groove,* and features such as *construction materials, "fishscale" waxless bases, waxable bases,* and *metal edges.* No one attribute or feature bears more importance than another; it is the combination of many attributes and features that determine which ski is right for you.

Camber

Camber is what gives a cross-country ski its ability to propel the skier forward over flat or even upsloping terrain. The camber is the arch in the middle of a ski; when laid unweighted on the ground, a classic cross-country ski rises an inch or so in its midsection. The arched midsection is called the wax pocket (cross-country skis all used to be waxed; today there are "waxless" bases as well), and it comes into contact with the snow only when the skier applies pressure—a kick down—onto the ski. The rebound from the kick then propels the ski forward on its tip and tail sections.

On waxable skis, grip wax is applied to the wax pocket (to keep the ski from slipping backward when the skier kicks down onto the pocket) and glide wax is

♦ EXPERT TIP: THE PAPER TEST

While stiff camber is good, too much of a good thing means you'll spend as much time sliding backward as you do pushing forward.

Before you buy, set the skis on the floor and stand on them with your toes where the bindings would go (for information on proper ski lengths, see p. 184). One at a time, unweight a foot and have someone slide a sheet of paper under each ski at the wax pocket. With your weight applied evenly while standing on both skis, the paper should be loose enough to pull out; but when you put weight on one foot, the paper should be impossible to pull out.

If the camber is too stiff for touring, the papers can be pulled out with weight on either foot.

If the camber is too soft for touring, the papers can't be budged at all.

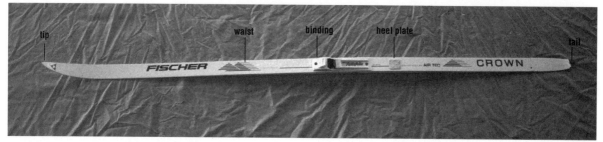

A typical cross-country touring ski.

applied to the tip and tail. On so-called waxless skis, the wax pocket has a fishscale-type pattern cut into it that is grippy without the need for wax; however, glide wax is still applied to the tip and tail of the ski.

Cross-country ski camber is called nordic camber; it is sometimes referred to as "double-camber," which is a misnomer, because skis can only have one camber. Compared to downhill ski camber, nordic ski camber is robust and stiff, because the skis' purpose is to move cross-country (although among cross-country skis the stiffnesses of camber varies).

You must pay for the ability to move over flat or uphill terrain—it's the classic "can't have your cake and eat it, too" trade-off. A ski that has stiff camber moves along quickly; but because it is stiff, it is harder to turn on downhill runs. Conversely, a ski that has soft camber turns beautifully but is slower on the flats and does not climb with alacrity. When looking at skis in the show-room, grasp one by the tip and, with the tail planted firmly on the floor, push hard into the midsection. A stiff nordic-cambered ski will bend at the tip and tail, leaving a flat section in the middle. A soft, alpine-cambered ski will form a smooth arc (called reverse camber). You will see both extremes in cross-country gear—racing skis that are very stiff and pure telemark skis with an alpine camber—and everything in between.

Sidecut

Sidecut describes the amount of "waist" on a ski. In order to turn more easily, a ski is made more narrow at the midsection. When the ski is set on its edge, as in the beginning of a turn, the curve formed by the sidecut is what helps draw the ski through the turn, allowing more of the ski to contact the hill. A ski with no sidecut remains straight when placed on edge, and only the midsection of the ski makes contact with the hill. So,

in general, more sidecut means easier turning. As with camber, however, too much of a good thing. . . . For touring, medium sidecut is desirable; for serious lift-assisted telemark, or XCD, skiing, go for maximum sidecut; and for racing, very little sidecut if any.

Overall Flex

Overall flex describes the total stiffness of the ski. In general, if the snow is hard-packed or icy, you want a stiff ski, so that the edges can "bite." Soft-flex skis on hard-packed snow are very unstable—kind of "wishy-washy," which can cause very annoying chatter (when the skis literally jitter up and down rapidly). If the snow is very soft, softer skis will perform better. For touring, go for softer (but not too soft) flex; for XCD, a stiff ski; and for track or racing, you'll want to lean toward stiff, but not too stiff.

Tip Flex

Like overall flex, the softness or stiffness of the tip of the skis will make a difference in how easy or hard it is to turn the ski. Stiff tips are good for hard-packed snow or icy conditions, but in soft powder they tend to dive under rather than float over the snow, causing a lot more work for the skier. A medium-to-soft tip is the best choice for touring. Test the tip flex in the show-room by grasping the tip and pulling it toward you—a soft flex will be very easy to curve, a stiff flex quite hard. And look at where it curves; best for touring is a curve that is gradual and extends well into the body of the ski, rather than bending abruptly at the top.

Torsion

To perform well, any cross-country ski should be tor-sionally rigid—that is, it should resist twisting side-to-side. To test for torsion, grasp the ski with both hands

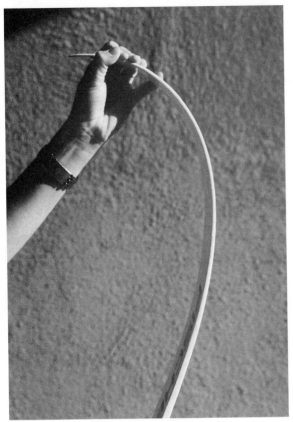

A good all-around touring ski has smooth tip-flex: Look at where it curves—you want a curve that is gradual and extends well into the body of the ski, rather than bending abruptly at the top.

Construction Materials

Camber, sidecut, flex—those are the attributes to look for in how a ski performs. But what about what they're made from? Originally, skis were carved from single staves of wood, and some companies still do so for the traditionalists out there. Modern composites are much lighter and stronger for the weight, so most good skis today have fiberglass enclosing various foam or wood cores. Types of core materials are diverse: beechwood, poplar, fiberglass, polyurethane foam, ABS plastic, Kevlar, and aluminum. Production and material *quality* probably matter more than actual material details. However, *type* of construction should be taken into account:

Sandwich construction. Layers of material laminated together, with structural layers on the top and bottom and sidewalls added to protect the core, is the preferred construction for touring and backcountry skis, as it is stronger for the weight. The big drawback is delamination, which can occur at the tip or tail in a lesser-quality ski.

Box construction. The structural layer is wrapped around the core. Flex and stiffness are much harder to produce precisely in this type of construction, making it a less desirable choice for backcountry and telemark skis, but you will see it in touring skis, where such attributes matter less.

You will do well to look for good name-brands. Look for a high quality of finish—does the fiberglass

far apart and, with the ski's tail on the floor, try to twist the ski. If it twists easily, skip it.

Central Groove

All cross-country (nordic-cambered) skis have shallow grooves running down the center of the base, to help them glide better in a straight line. Some telemark enthusiasts believe that this groove hinders a ski's ability to turn, and so you won't see many alpine-cambered telemark skis with central grooves. Backcountry ski expert Chris Townsend, author of *Wilderness Skiing and Winter Camping,* says that he can't perceive any difference in tracking in a straight line or downhill turning between grooved and ungrooved skis. He does point out, however, that ungrooved skis are easier to wax.

TIPS FOR CHOOSING SKIS
Choosing skis can be a difficult task: potentially expensive mistakes can be made in buying the wrong equipment for the intended type of skiing. Here are some rough guidelines for beginners to use when choosing skis.

	Track/Touring	Backcountry	XCD
camber	medium/stiff	medium/soft	soft
overall flex	medium	medium	stiff
tip flex	medium/stiff	medium	soft/medium
torsion	rigid	rigid	rigid
metal edges	no	yes/partial	yes
tip width (mm)	52–85	60–85	60–80
waist (mm)	50–70	52–70	55–70
tail (mm)	50–80	55–80	60–80
weight (lbs.)	2.5–4	5–5.5	6–8

look polished and smooth? Are the edges sharp and clean of burrs or nicks? It would be wise to steer clear of super cheap bargains—they could leave you miles down a trail with a couple of broken boards and a long slog back to the car through deep snow.

To Wax or Not to Wax

The big question many people start with before even looking at ski types is, Waxless or waxable bases?

Skis have come a long way since the days when they were handmade from hardwoods and the bases were treated with a variety of substances, from pine tar to beeswax to spermaceti (wax made from sperm whale oil). The bases of any skis—traditional and modern, waxable and so-called waxless—have to be treated with some substance, now usually made from sintered polyethylene, to make them glide, grip, or resist the formation of ice balls or crystals. What differentiates them is the degree to which they must be waxed.

Skis having "waxless" bases need only be treated periodically with hot base wax (also called universal glider wax; there are two types of wax—those that are applied hot, usually at home or in a shop, and those that go on cold, in the field) on the tips and tails. Waxable skis require not only glider wax on these areas, but also different types of grip wax in the wax pocket, depending on where or when you ski. Waxes come in a wide variety of blends and must be matched to snow temperature and type; sometimes a ski wax must be changed en route if conditions switch from ice to slush. For this reason, many novices choose waxless skis for their first setup, which is probably a wise decision. You will have enough to think about without worrying about the mysteries of waxing. Many skiers, as they become expert, will switch

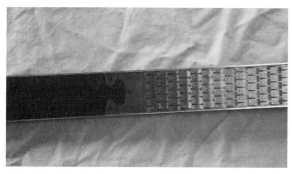

The bases of "waxless" skis are cut with fishscale-type patterns in the midsection.

WHEN TO WAX YOUR WAXLESS SKIS

The term *waxless* is definitely a misnomer that has caused no end of troubles for novice skiers who buy waxless skis, have them set up at the shop, and then promptly ignore the bases season after season.

So, succinctly put: Waxless skis need wax! When to wax and with what?

- When you first buy your skis, a universal glider (hot waxing) for waxless bases must be applied to the tips and tails. There are some liquid waxes that can be applied over the fishscales without the worry of clogging them. This allows for free gliding on the tips and tails, and helps keep the fishscales from icing up.
- When you ski often—a couple times a week—check your bases. They may need rewaxing with universal glider; wipe-on waxes that don't require heat, such as MaxiGlide, are popular.
- When you ski in very icy conditions, even waxless skis will slip, and you will want to apply klister wax to the wax pocket (a good tip: always carry klister). See p. 198 on how to apply klister.
- When you store your skis for the summer, apply a liberal coating of glider wax and don't scrape (after you clean them, of course). This will help protect your bases from drying out.

to waxable bases in order to squeeze the most performance out of their skis, since a waxable base is much quicker, turns better, and is quieter than a waxless base.

What allows a waxless ski to go waxless in the "wax pocket" is a fishscale-type pattern cut into the grip area (pocket). Each ski manufacturer has a proprietary type of waxless pattern; in general, all work well. However, make sure the pattern is cut *into* the ski base, rather than molded and raised *above* the ski base. The latter catches and drags on the snow.

If you plan to ski only occasionally or mostly in temperatures around freezing and not below, then waxless skis are your best bet, because under these conditions you will encounter widely varying temperatures and consistencies of snow (ice to slush, and everything in between) and waxing can be difficult. If you will be skiing in very cold conditions, or where optimum performance is desired, such as on a long tour or racing, then waxing is the way to go. Many backcountry tourers might be tempted to forgo waxing because of the weight and hassles of waxing paraphernalia, but many experienced tourers feel that the increased efficiency is worth the weight and hassle.

Today, most touring skis come with waxless bases and most telemark skis come with waxable bases. A few touring skis, especially backcountry skis, are available with either. For information on the how's and wherefore's of waxing, see the technique sections later in this chapter.

Types of Skis

Once you get a feel for the all the characteristics and features that make a ski, you can begin to match those with your intentions and choose your best ski. Listed below are the four basic types of cross-country-style ski available today and the uses for which they are best suited.

Track or racing. Skis for racing and recreational track-use get lighter and skinnier every year. Track skis have very little, if any, sidecut, since traditional turning is not a technique used on tracks. Track or racing skis do not perform well on untracked snow because they are so narrow, providing very little flotation.

Touring. General touring skis are of light to medium weight, have nordic camber, usually don't have metal edges, and are medium-width, so that they float well in untracked snow. They are suited best to undulating terrain (no really steep slopes) in soft snow. General touring skis make excellent choices for the day or weekend lodge skier who wishes to use skis for exploring the woods in a similar manner to hiking in spring or summer. A few companies make skis with general touring dimensions (see chart) but with metal edges in the middle part of the ski only. These skis are good for general touring in areas where you are more likely to encounter steep or icy conditions and want the added bite and thus security of metal edges without the weight of a full-length set. If you think you'll primarily be doing day touring but would like to try an easy overnight backcountry tour or two, these skis are an excellent choice.

Backcountry. Backcountry or mountain-touring skis are medium-weight, have nordic camber and a decent sidecut for ease of turning, are medium-to-high width for flotation, and have full metal edges. Although they are slower than day-touring skis, backcountry skis will glide reasonably well along flats, and they will handle all but the hairiest descents. Most importantly, however, they will handle a skier loaded down with a full backpack, because

they have the weight and width lacking in general touring skis. The most useful backcountry skis have a softer nordic camber than touring skis have (though stiffer than XCD), because in the wilderness it is more important to turn easily than to speed along, as well as medium overall flex to handle both soft and icy conditions.

XCD. If you live for the thrill of descent on cross-country-style skis, then you need XCD, or "telemark," skis. Designed to turn easily, they have alpine camber and lots of sidecut, are wide and soft at the tip, and are heavy in overall weight. Some XCD skis are designed with very stiff flex, being specifically for telemark racing and lift-assisted downhill skiing. Softer-flex XCD skis are better for touring. Because they are alpine-cambered, you'll need to use climbing skins for ascents (see sidebar, p. 196).

SIZING SKIS

European metric sizing is still the standard for measuring skis. For adults, you will find sizes from 180 cm through 220 cm, typically in 5 cm increments.

Skis should be sized so that your weight and height are both taken into consideration—no single sizing formula will work best, although some are better than others.

The old way to size cross-country skis was to raise your arm and pick a ski that reached to the palm of your hand. This only works for a few people, however. For example, if you are tall but lightweight, you will end up with a ski that has too much camber and is too stiff for your weight. Or, if you are short but heavy, you can end up with a ski that is too soft and not cambered enough.

In general, if in doubt, err on the short side. For a novice, a too-long ski is difficult to control. For greater stability, go wider, not longer or shorter.

The following is a rough guideline from Fisher for fitting track and day-touring skis. In general, for backcountry skis, find your weight and then back down one size. (Always consult the manufacturer's recommendations for fit.)

Weight (lbs.)	Recommended Ski (mm)
90–105	180
105–120	190
120–135	195
135–150	200
150–165	205
165–190	210
190+	215

Because of the advanced skills necessary to ski the conditions where XCD-style skis are suitable, these skis are best used by only the most experienced backcountry tourers.

Bindings

Bindings not only attach your foot to the ski, they are the means by which you translate the desire to turn, stop, slow down, or go faster from your brain through your foot and onto the ski—a very important relationship indeed. Not realizing how important bindings are for these motions, many novice skiers buy lesser-quality bindings, a mistake they will pay for on the trail or slopes when sloppy bindings impart only partial commands from the brain to the ski, or the bindings break altogether.

Since the late 1920s the standard way to attach ski boots to skis has been the three-pin binding, called the *rottefella,* or "rat trap," in Norwegian, because of it resemblance to that household tool. Beefy versions of the three-pin binding are still the choice for backcountry and XCD skiers. Only since the 1980s have great advances been made in cross-country ski-binding systems for racing, general touring, and easy backcountry touring. These bindings, described at right, are easier to use and are quicker for track, racing, or day touring. Relatively recent innovations in XCD bindings, particularly cable bindings that lock the heel down, have improved boot-to-ski control but can also be more injurious to a skier if the binding and boot don't separate during a fall.

Three-pin bindings. The old standard three-pin binding is both simple and effective. The boots' soles

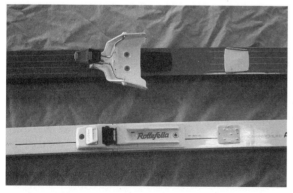

Traditional "rat trap" three-pin bindings, top, are still the choice for many backcountry skiers. The narrower-profiled New Nordic Norm (NNN), bottom, binding is popular for day-tour skiers.

are slightly extended in front, and three reinforced holes are drilled into the extension. Those holes correspond with three upright pins on a plate that is screwed into the ski (three-pin bindings are now standardized throughout the world to a specific size and width, so that any three-pin binding fits any three-pin-style boot). The boot is placed onto the pins, and a clamp, or *bail,* is lowered onto the boot extension and secured.

NNN and SNS bindings. The Rottefella New Nordic Norm (NNN) and Salomon Nordic System (SNS) bindings are the latest improvements in binding systems for racing, day touring, and easy-to-moderate backcountry (called the NNN-BC). Both systems are modifications, albeit radical, of the three-pin binding. Instead of pins and holes, the boots have bars imbedded in the extended toe; the bar slides over a slot on the binding plate and locks down. A nice feature is that the plate on the ski is long—almost as long as the boot—and has ridges running down the plate that mate with grooves in the boot sole for added control. The bindings are also very lightweight.

When you move your foot in a three-pin binding, the pivot point is at the ball of the foot, because the front part of the boot is pinned down by the bail; when using an NNN or SNS binding, the pivot point is at the toe. This feature allows for very stiff boots, because they don't need to flex in the middle—excellent for control in a variety of skiing conditions, from racing to backcountry.

The biggest drawback of both NNN and SNS systems is that the boots and bindings must be purchased together, and they cannot be used with any other system. If the company changes or discontinues the binding, you must buy new boots and bindings if one part wears out or you wish to upgrade. Otherwise, these bindings are an excellent choice for all but the most strenuous, long-distance backcountry touring. Chris Townsend, author of *Wilderness Skiing and Winter Camping,* tested the NNN-BC bindings extensively and found the only major disadvantage to be that they ice up easily—there are a lot of grooves and crevices (spraying silicone on the bindings would help). Also, they are not as easily repaired in the field as simple bails-and-pins. Carrying a spare binding and screws would be the best bet for long tours with the NNN-BC.

Cable bindings. Bindings that incorporate cables around the heel predate three-pin bindings by three-quarters of a century but fell out of favor for most touring when three-pins came on the scene. Lately, however, cable bindings have become popular again for XCD skiing and serious backcountry touring with heavy loads in steep terrain. In a cable binding, the front of a three-pin-style boot fits into a sturdy toe compartment similar to a three-pin plate, but without the pins. There is a spring at the back that fits into a groove cut into the heels of the boots (all serious backcountry and XCD boots have these grooves), and a front or rear adjustment lever or "throw" for tensioning the cable.

The advantages for XCD are many: there are no pins to ice up; torsional stiffness and thus control are excellent; and they are not only durable, but cause far less damage to expensive ski boots. The disadvantages are serious: because the foot is more tied to the ski, it may not pull out in a fall, and the flailing ski can cause serious knee injuries. Concerned about liability, some U.S. ski shops won't sell cable bindings for XCD use.

Other XCD bindings. A few companies make cable bindings that are used in conjunction with three-pin bindings. Usually they are both mounted on a plate, then mounted on the ski. The advantages of these are that if the cable fails, you have the three-pin backup, or if the three-pin fails, you can get by with just the cable. You can also remove the cable for short day tours. (For an excellent discussion of all bindings systems by brand name, see Chris Townsend's *Wilderness Skiing and Winter Camping.*)

Another option for those skiers concerned about injury caused by cable bindings are releasable bindings for both serious XCD enthusiasts and tourers. These bindings are complex, sophisticated, heavy, expensive, and not widely available yet. They are, however, recommended if you are concerned about injury.

Boots

Rule number one in choosing your ski boots is to decide on your preferred binding system before buying your boots—this will save you a lot of hassle and expense if you end up with a pair of bargain three-pin boots but later decide you want NNN bindings.

Rule number two: Buy the best boots you can afford. If you need to make allowances for price, it's highly recommended to go for best-quality boots and medium-quality skis, rather than the other way around. This is because your boots, and your bindings, are the translators for your body movement and skis. If your boots are

---

♦ EXPERT TIP: SKI BOOT FIT

Author and backcountry skiing expert Chris Townsend offers the following tips for ski boot fit.

"The fit of your boots is crucial, much more important than the make or model. A nordic ski-touring boot should fit like a hiking boot. Check in particular that your heels are held firmly in place. If they aren't, you will have less control over your skis, and you will probably develop sore heels and blisters. A boot that is too short will be very painful; your toes should not be pressed up against the end. There should be just enough room to slide a finger between the back of the boot and your ankle when the boot is unlaced. Look for a snug-fitting boot with room to move your toes—a tight boot will be painful and could cause cold feet and frostbite.

"Try on boots with the socks you intend wearing, and try several models until you find a good fit. Take your time. Walk around the store to see how the boots feel. Mimic a few ski positions, going down into a telemark stance, rolling your ankles sideways to put the boots on their edges."

---

mushy, not only will you have a hard time turning or skating (a racing and track skiing technique), you will experience greater fatigue and possible injury. For all types of nordic skiing, buy good, stiff boots.

For racing, track skiing, and easy day touring, light-weight but stiff synthetic boots make a good choice. However, these usually are not completely waterproof, having been designed for ideal conditions (nice, dry powder and smooth tracks). Many boot makers offer waterproofed boots made with a Gore-Tex or other waterproof/breathable liner. Also, some of the lighter boots are not easily resolable. Gaining popularity are boots that claim to be able to handle track skiing, day touring, as well as backcountry and light XCD skiing. If versatility and fun are your goals, rather than ultimate performance, then you might do well with the latter boots.

For day touring in variable conditions, and for backcountry touring, your best bet is a full-grain leather boot (you need the stiffness of good, thick leather—at least 2–2.5 mm—so reject any split-grain leathers). Full-grain leather boots can be treated with various waterproofing agents (follow the same care procedures as for all-leather hiking boots, although you will want to apply your treatments more frequently to keep the leather in good condition as well as waterproof; see Chapter 1, p. 7, for recommendations). You can get away with a slightly less beefy boot for day touring than you will need for backcountry touring with a heavy pack. Many full-grain leather boots with three-pin soles are resolable—a plus, since backcountry boots take a lot of abuse.

XCD skiers use either very stiff full-grain leather boots or the newer all-plastic telemark racing boots. The latter are best for lift-assisted skiing, rather than backcountry, unless your goal is using climbing skins to ascend steep mountains and then ski back down.

A few more features to look for when boot-buying:

- *Insulation.* Look for some sort of insulation, whether EVA foam, Thinsulate, or some other source of heat retention.
- *Gusseted tongue.* Foam-padded tongues with side gussets to keep out the snow are essential. Even better for backcountry are double-tongues.
- *D-ring closure.* D-rings on the front with hooks at the ankles provide the best closure system for day touring and backcountry skiing. Buckles and zippers ice up. For track skiing you might find that hook-and-loop tape closures over laces work well.
- *Stiff midsoles.* For the stiffest, longest-lasting boots, look for styles that have polyurethane, nylon, or thermoplastic midsoles (rather than leather).
- *Bombproof construction.* Particularly for backcountry touring boots, look for welt-sewn boots with double- or triple-sewn toes. NNN-BC boots cannot be welt-sewn; however, most of these are of excellent construction quality for touring. For rugged use, avoid any boots that are only glued, not stitched.

♦ EXPERT TIP: PROTECT YOUR PINHOLES

On three-pin boots, one of the first things to get loose and cause problems can be your pinholes. Widened or even torn pinholes can cause your boot to pull out while skiing, and sloppy pin-fit will make for hard turning and control.

- Inspect your pinholes often; have your boots resoled if the holes are cracked or torn, or switch to a cable binding.
- Frequent crashes will accelerate pinhole widening and tearing.
- When your bindings or boot tips become iced up on a tour, don't force the boots into the pins and bails. This will cause pinhole damage. Take the time to de-ice your boots and bindings, even if conditions are nasty.

Poles

Your poles—each comprising shaft, handle, wrist strap, basket, and tip—are the last essential item for your cross-country skiing outfit. In general, once you have the correct size, all you need to look for in poles is light weight and reasonable strength. Tip design, basket shape and size, and handle shape are primarily features of personal style rather than high performance, although baskets and tips for track and touring are different (see comments below).

Tempered aluminum alloy is the material of choice for lightness and strength (beware of really cheap aluminum poles, which are not tempered and will bend or snap readily). Fiberglass is cheap and popular, but it breaks very easily in even moderate falls under the right conditions, and it splinters, making it very hard to jury-rig with a patch kit in the field (a relatively easy task with aluminum).

The proper way to use a ski pole wrist strap is to enter the loop from below, so that when you grasp the handle of the pole the strap lies between your thumb and forefinger. Just be sure to take your hands out of the straps when descending, in case a pole snags something.

Sharp pole tips (which are replaceable, as are baskets, grips, and wrist loops) are a must for secure purchase in all types of skiing. Tungsten carbide steel tips are the sharpest and most durable. For touring, baskets should be wide—around 4–5 inches—for flotation in powdery snow, and soft, for flexibility on icy snow. For track skiing, baskets should be smaller, and may be a little more rigid or have teeth for grip on packed snow. Wrist straps should be adjustable and of break-away design for safety (tip: Don't use wrist straps when descending through forests or other areas where you could snag a basket and dislocate a shoulder or elbow).

Sizing Up

Size your poles for touring by choosing a pole that fits under your armpit with the tip on the ground (it should press up into your armpit). To fine-tune:

For track skiing. You will want a slightly longer pole than touring length for skating and maximum reach during vigorous kick-and-glide.

For XCD. Downhill enthusiasts prefer shorter poles, sized so that when the basket is on the snow, the forearm is horizontal.

For backcountry touring. A touring-length pole is best, unless you know you will be doing a lot of downhill runs. In this case, consider adjustable poles, some of which can be taken apart and screwed together to make an avalanche probe—a must if you plan to ski in areas where this is a danger.

Other Necessities and Niceties

Gaiters. These nylon or Gore-Tex boot-and-leg protectors are indispensable for day and backcountry touring, as well as for XCD skiing. Not only do they keep your laces from icing up, they keep your legs and feet drier and warmer. Look for gaiters with neoprene rubber underheel straps instead of plain nylon, which is not as durable under the strain of freezing.

Heel lifts. During long ascents, especially using skins, your heels and Achilles tendons are put under a great amount of strain. To help alleviate this, several manufacturers offer heel lifts. Some attach to your heel plate on the ski and can be flipped up and down. Others attach to your boot and can also be flipped out of the way.

TOURING REPAIR KIT

Even with top-of-the-line equipment, you will break stuff. For day or backcountry tours, you should always carry a repair kit—it's amazing how hard it is to hike in deep snow, 10 miles back to the truck. In poor conditions, a long walk can even be dangerous. Some good items to include in your touring repair kit:

- Posidrive screwdriver for tightening ski-binding screws. Different bindings have different-size screws, so make sure you have the right-size screwdriver or one with interchangeable bits.
- Vise-grip for use as pliers and to hold ski edges together after gluing.
- Strong wire for jury-rigging bindings—thin wire can even be used for stitching split boot soles.
- Quick-drying epoxy for gluing delaminated skis is essential. Swix manufactures packets called Ski Rep.
- Duct tape—strong and waterproof, it is useful for all types of repairs, especially broken poles.
- Fine sandpaper, for smoothing rough edges.
- Binding screws, in case of loss.
- Hose clamps, small and large, for holding together repaired poles and skis.
- Empty aluminum drink can—ideal as a splint for broken poles when cut in two (store it flat).
- Section of wooden dowel, for jamming inside broken poles.
- Steel wool packing, for binding holes.
- Spare binding and/or cable.
- Spare basket.
- Spare plastic slip-on ski tip.
- P-tex (polyethylene) candle, for filling in gouges in ski bases.
- Lighter and backup waterproof matches.
- Swiss Army knife or multi-tool, with good scissors.

A good repair kit can help save a tour, but don't skip a thorough inspection of your gear *before* you leave. Check binding screws, ski bases for delamination or gouges, boot soles for delamination and pinhole or bar wear, pole grips and baskets for tightness, poles shafts for damage, and the moving parts of your bindings for wear and tear.

Clothing

The keys to successful dressing for cross-country skiing are flexibility and breathability. Skiing generates tremendous heat and moisture output, so you need clothing that wicks your skin dry, allows the moisture to evaporate, but keeps you warm when you stop. A tall bill to fill? Not really. Advances in fabric technology have given us exceptionally effective clothing for the foulest weather conditions nature can throw at us. (For a thorough discussion of fabrics and clothing types, see Chapter 14, p. 299.)

Begin at the Bottom

For any type of cross-country skiing, begin with an underlayer of high-stretch wicking fabric (you want a fabric that has the ability to stretch-and-recover repeatedly without sagging). For track skiing or racing, lightweight fabric is best; for day touring in mild conditions, go for light- to medium-weight, depending on how well you handle the cold; and for day touring in harsher conditions or for backcountry touring, go for medium-weight to heavyweight fabric. A plus for skiing would be zippered turtleneck tops, which allow you to ventilate

For backcountry skiing, a waterproof/breathable jacket-and-pants set is invaluable for protection from the elements. Good gloves or mitts, a warm hat, and gaiters, if they are not built into the pants, are also necessary.

when you're working hard and to bundle up when it gets chilly. Also, invest in good sport-specific synthetic or wool socks that wick moisture well.

Warm and Dry

Your next layer will be a warmth layer. Stretch fleece works very well for this, especially vests, simple pullovers (without heavy wrist, neck, or waist bands), and tights. For tours in harsh conditions, you may want a down vest with waterproof/breathable fabric. A light stretch-fleece vest is often all you need for track skiing, to keep your torso warm, although many track skiers blaze around on mild-to-moderate days in nothing more than thick Lycra suits.

To keep you dry in the event of a blizzard, or to block warmth-stealing wind, you will also need an outer layer of waterproof/breathable fabric, such as Gore-Tex. Make sure both the jacket and pants are comfortable for the vigorous motions of ski touring: striding, reaching, and kneeling, as well as while wearing a pack. And make doubly sure there is plenty of ventilation, via armpit zippers and/or mesh chest pockets that zip open widely. Side zips on the pants shouldn't be overlooked; although they are more expensive than pull-ons, the zippers make it much, much easier to answer the call of nature while on skis (and many fleece pants come with zippered crotches, for the same reason). Finally, a hood is mandatory; make sure it zips off or tucks out of the way, so you don't get pummeled by it on those long, windy descents.

For touring, waterproof gloves, or waterproof overmitts and fleece or wool gloves, are a must. If you are on a backcountry tour, backup gloves are a good idea as well. For track skiing, fleece or thick Lycra gloves might be all you need, depending on the temperature.

And don't forget your head—a snug-fitting fleece or knit cap or balaclava (a sort of hood with a face hole) will be necessary for touring where harsh conditions are possible. In milder conditions or for track skiing, headbands to cover your ears will increase your comfort level immensely, especially if there is any wind.

Transportation and Storage

Unless you've got a pickup truck into which you can place your skis and poles, these long implements of winter fun can provide quite a challenge for transportation, even if the distance to your favorite trail is only 10 miles.

Cartop and Other Racks

Some of the best cartop ski racks are accessories to the system racks, such as those made by Thule and Yakima. These rack systems are purchased in various stages. First you invest in the towers that clamp on to the top of the car, either in rain gutters (which very few new cars have these days) or through door channels; the towers come with crossbars, which are available in various lengths. After this basic system is set, you can add all sorts of sport-equipment-carrying accessories that clamp securely onto the crossbars: from bikes and boats to skis. The ski carriers lock securely and come in various sizes, to accommodate as many as six pairs of skinny skis (fewer as the skis get wider). Don't forget the pole-carrying accessories as well. These systems aren't cheap (well over $150 to get started), but they are worth it for the peace of mind and versatility.

Other options include relatively inexpensive (under $75) ski carriers that strap directly to the top of your car on their own foam blocks. Also, if you have a built-in luggage rack on your car, check with your automaker—some offer accessories such as ski racks that bolt on to the rack. If your sport utility vehicle has a swingaway spare-tire rack on the back, use ski racks that strap on to the tire and hold the skis and poles vertically. (Keep in mind that this system does not protect your skis from road grime, including harmful salts, or worse, a fender-bender.)

When the Fun's Done

When the last powder gives way to spring's flowers, it's time to tend to your skis, bindings, poles, and boots. Here are some tips for storing your skis.

- *First, clean your equipment.* For skis, this means cleaning off all the old waxes or pine sap with either commercial ski wax solvents (which are pretty toxic) or citrus-based solvents for a nontoxic solution. Gently scrub any mud from your boots, and wipe down your poles with solvent in case they got any wax or pine sap on them. Clean any old wax or mud out your bindings as well.
- *Inspect all your equipment for signs of damage.* Check poles, including their shafts, tips, baskets, handles, and straps; inspect skis carefully, including bases, side-

> **♦ EXPERT TIP: WATCH YOUR TAILS**
> Delamination of ski tails is a common malady caused by stuffing skis into a crusty snowbank at every rest stop. Prevent delamination by leaning your skis gently against a tree or hut.

walls, tips, and tops; make sure the bindings are not cracked or showing signs of loosening at the screws; and inspect your boots, especially where the sole joins the binding (see tips, p. 187, on three-pin boot holes).

- *If you find any damage to your equipment, repair it before you store it.* If you wait (like everyone else) until the weekend of the first good snow, and you need to repair the gouges in your bases and replace a bail on a binding, expect a week or more delay as the ski shop gets overloaded. Or, if you do your own work, you might be tempted to ski on damaged equipment rather than spend the time while the sweet, new powder beckons.
- *Apply protective coatings before storage.* Apply a liberal coating of universal base wax to your ski bases (on metal-edged skis, run the wax over the edges) and don't scrape it off. Spray a little silicone on your bindings' metal parts, especially any moving parts (be careful not to put on too much silicone, however, as it can attract dirt). Dab a little silicone on your pole tips as well.
- *Attend to your boots.* Clean your boots of any mud and apply a sealer such as Nikwax (see Chapter 1, p. 7, for a discussion on how to care for leather boots). Replace your laces, if necessary, and apply a little silicone to any metal hooks or D-rings.
- *Store all your equipment in a place that is dry, cool, and dust-free.* Mildew will be your greatest boot enemy, but heat can be the worst ski killer, causing warping and delamination. Metal storage sheds are not only dusty, they can attain amazingly high temperatures on sunny days. The best way to store skis is to bind them base-to-base, at the tails and where the tip curves meet, with nylon or rubber straps (invest in a pair at your ski shop—they're cheap); some people put a wooden chock between the bases at the wax pocket. Shelve the skis on edge, or hang them from the V formed by the tips in a slot between two wall pegs set about 2 inches apart.

Skiing Lessons

For first-time skiers, the most frustrating thing is watching experienced skiers *schuss* off effortlessly, while they slip, slide, and flail a few feet before executing the only perfect maneuver they can: a face-plant.

Relaxation is actually the key to learning to move with a very long, slippery board strapped to each foot. If you are uptight and anxious, that will translate to your skis and you'll spend more time on your hind end than you will gliding across the snow.

After you relax, the best thing to do is to put down your poles. That's right. First practice the following skills, as outlined by touring expert Chris Townsend, without your poles, so that you learn to keep your balance by placing your center of gravity over your feet without the help of poles.

Positioning Your Body

Before you move the skis, think about your body position. Are you standing stiffly, with every muscle tense, because you know that if you relax for a second your skis will shoot away from you? Quite probably—but you can't ski like that. Instead, adopt a more relaxed yet athletic stance, with your stomach pulled in, your shoulders down, and your knees and ankles flexed forward. If you keep your ankles straight, you will sit back onto an invisible chair, an uncomfortable position that puts your weight too far back. You should be able to bounce up and down on your skis, using your knees as shock absorbers.

Avoid developing the habit of watching your skis. You can't control them with your eyes, though many beginners try to. Apart from preventing you from seeing where you are going or admiring the scenery, watching your ski tips also tilts your body forward and puts you in a position where you are more likely to fall.

Warming Up

It is best to move in place at first. Slide the skis backward and forward, then pick up each one in turn. Speed up the movements as you begin to feel more confident. If this makes you feel unstable (at this stage, just being on skis is bound to make you feel a little wobbly), flex your knees more. Stiff, straight legs make any ski technique—from slow shuffles on the flat to the fastest downhill turn—very difficult. To ski well, you need to be relaxed.

Falling

Oddly enough, one way to relax is to fall deliberately. All skiers fall, and if you learn to fall safely you will be far less likely to hurt yourself. Flex your knees and slowly sit down sideways, keeping your hands out in front of you. Try it again with your poles, keeping them out of the way. When you are skiing and you know you are going to fall (more often than not during a descent), it is better to fall deliberately than to lose control and do a painful and potentially injurious face-plant over the tips of your skis.

Getting Up

Falling is very easy—getting up again is difficult. First get your skis parallel to each other and at a right angle to the slope, if you are on one. Otherwise, on even the slightest slope, your skis will slide away from you as soon as you start to stand. If you fall on a slope with your body below your skis, swing yourself around on the snow and plant your skis below you. Once your skis are parallel and close together, simply push yourself up with your hands into a kneeling position and then stand up, using the slope to help you. If the snow is soft, cross your poles on the surface of the snow and push down on them for better support. Do not try to heave yourself up on your poles; it is very hard work, and you may easily bend or break a pole.

Star Turns

Once you have fallen over and gotten up a few times, try a star turn; leave your poles to the side so you are depending on balance. Lift up the tip of one ski (just the tip, not the whole ski) and move it out a little from the other ski. Then move the other ski parallel with it. Keep repeating this until you have turned a full circle. Look at the pattern you have made in the snow, and you will see why this is called a star turn. If you find yourself crossing the tails of your skis, your steps are too big; if you are crossing the tips, you are moving the wrong ski first or moving it the wrong way. If you feel very insecure and keep falling over, try flexing more at the knees and placing the ski down more firmly after moving it. Don't lean back or sideways—keep your weight over your feet.

The elements of a good turn: knees flexed, torso centered, and weight over the feet.

Kick Turns

Star turns are slow and require a wide, flat area. Imagine trying to do one on a narrow forest trail or, even worse, a slope. You can turn directly from front to back with a kick turn, using your poles as supports. Retrieve your poles and place them almost at arm's length on either side of your skis, and then kick one ski forward and up, so it is upright on the snow. Next, pivot it away from you and turn it until you can put it back down on the snow facing the other way. This position is very awkward, so as quickly as possible (but carefully, carefully!) swing the other ski around next to the first one. The kick turn may at first seem possible only if you are a contortionist, but it is an important maneuver, so it is worth persevering until you can do it readily in both directions.

Sidestepping

Sidestepping is normally used for ascending or descending slopes, but practicing it on the flat at this early stage helps you learn to transfer weight from one ski to the other. To sidestep, stand with the skis parallel, then pick up one ski and move it a short way directly to the side, following it with the other and keeping them parallel. You will find that you have to put weight on the stationary ski and then transfer your weight to the ski you have just moved. Do a few steps one way and then a few the other. If you keep your knees flexed, you will be less likely to fall and better able to react quickly if one of the skis slips. Remember that stiff legs make it difficult to ski well.

Time to Move Out

Moving forward on your skis is simple—just slide each one forward in turn. (Tip: Stay relaxed, keeping your knees loose.) If you find that your forward ski shoots off ahead, leaving you behind, flex your knee and push it forward as you glide, so that your weight stays over the ski.

One basic principle underlies all ski techniques: *your weight must be over the lead ski if you are to stay in balance.* It is better to exaggerate this stance than to edge the ski forward with your toes.

Once you have made a track in the snow, ski up and down it a few times, to get used to the feeling of moving. As you relax, you should feel a flow developing, a feeling of moving effortlessly with the skis and the snow rather than against them. Like your first balancing skills, practice moving without poles first. Then add poles to the movement.

To hold your poles correctly, put each hand through the pole strap from below (see photo, p. 187), so that when you grasp the handle of the pole the strap lies between your thumb and forefinger. Using the strap this way allows you to relax your fingers and hold the pole loosely. This in turn will allow you to relax your arms and shoulders and reduce the tension in your whole body.

A First Descent

The thought of a descent fills many nordic skiers, including some experienced ones, with trepidation, yet this experience can be the most enjoyable part of the day.

To get used to the sensation of sliding effortlessly down a slope, try some direct descents on short gentle slopes of soft snow with good, long run-outs. Push off with your poles and allow gravity to bring you slowly to a halt. As your confidence grows, practice from higher up and on steeper slopes and try changing your body position to see how it feels: stand up straight, then flex your knees and sink down. Which feels most stable? To get used to balancing on one ski, lift one off the snow, then the other.

Your next step is to practice these basic maneuvers as much as possible—it's probably easiest to do so at a cross-country ski center where there are easy tracks to ski, as well as practice areas cordoned off (to protect everyone else from out-of-control beginners). If your area lacks a ski center, find a nice flat field with a few gently sloping hills.

See p. 197 for snowplows and other techniques for slowing down and stopping.

Speeding Up: The Diagonal Stride

The fast, athletic diagonal stride—the kick and glide of the track skier—is not something you will do often when touring. That stride doesn't go with unbroken snow or a heavy pack. The basic technique is the same, however, and the better you are at the diagonal stride the easier you will find touring on flat and gently undulating terrain. The diagonal stride is much more

PAUL PETERSON

These racers are skating, using the herringbone technique. Note the pattern in the snow made by previous contestants.

dynamic than the sliding walk you have probably been doing so far. The idea is to glide as far and as fast as possible on each ski.

To perform the diagonal stride, push off with one foot and then put all your weight on the leading ski (the other foot) as it starts to glide; now push your knee and your hip forward over the leading ski, keeping your weight centered there, and glide as far as possible. The more tentative you are at getting your weight over the front ski, the slower you will glide and the less distance you will travel. Let the skis do the work. As you slow down, push off on the other foot. If you hear your ski making a slapping sound on the snow just before you kick down, your ski may be coming down on the snow too soon and too far behind the other ski. Concentrate on pushing your hips over the gliding ski, so that the rear ski hits the snow as your feet pass each other.

Practice at first without your poles, so you can concentrate on the leg and foot actions and not be confused by trying to do things with your poles at the same time. You will probably find that your arms swing back and forth naturally as you ski along. If not, swing them from your shoulders like pendulums, keeping them slightly bent at the elbows and letting them drift well

back behind your body. Force isn't needed. Your arms should be relaxed.

Once you are happy with your basic glide, you can pick up your poles again. For maximum efficiency, each pole should be planted almost at arm's reach out in *front* of you, with the basket no more than 6–10 inches from the edge of the ski (resist the urge to plant your poles too far out to the sides, like outriggers). When you lead off with your right foot, it is your left pole that should go forward (vice-versa with the left foot). The pole should be planted with the tip to the rear, so that when you push down on it you are pushed forward. (If you angle the pole away from you it will act as a brake.) To gain the most power from each pole plant, let your arm go back past your hip. Remember how your arms swung when you skied without poles: they should be moving in just the same way now. If you stop your arm at your hip, it will act as a check and result in a shorter glide.

When carrying a backpack you will need to modify your pole technique slightly. Keep your arms lower, to avoid tiring your shoulders, and plant your poles not quite so far in front.

Double Poling

Double poling is very useful for gaining speed when you are on hard snow or in other skiers' tracks, especially on slight downhill slopes. The technique also gives your muscles a break from diagonal striding. To double-pole, keep your skis parallel, plant both poles almost at arm's length—angled to the rear—and push the handles away from you forward and downward, bending forward from the waist and almost falling onto the poles as you do so. Again, let your hands go back past your hips for greatest efficiency. If you are double poling with a heavy pack, it is easier if you do not bend quite so far forward. Double poling is common on tracks, when you encounter long, sloping downhill sections.

V-1 Skating

Skating, a track technique that can be used occasionally when touring, is estimated to be twice as fast as diagonal striding. The key to effortless skating is rhythm, which is important for all skiing but is absolutely essential for skating. If you know how to ice skate, the easiest way to learn to skate on skis is to pretend you are on ice skates. If you are not an ice skater, you have to start from scratch.

There are many different styles of skating, and even more names for them. The most versatile form of skating, and the best one for touring, is known variously as V-1 skating, two-skating, or asymmetrical skating. This technique involves double poling over just one ski, and it is an easy, relaxing, and fast way to skate while wearing a pack. As with the diagonal stride, when skating you glide on one ski, pushing off with the other ski. Because your skis are at an angle to each other, one has to be set on its edge, making a platform that you can push off against. (Most people find when they try skating that the ski goes onto its edge automatically when they push on it without conscious effort.) Because skating is so efficient, the forward ski is quite likely to shoot out ahead of you. To counter this movement, flex your knee and really throw your hip over the ski. Make sure all your weight is over the gliding ski.

Try V-1 skating by pointing your ski tips out in a V, then pushing off one ski with both poles, making sure that they are outside your skis, and throwing your weight over the other ski. As this ski slows, shift your weight back to the first ski and, without using your poles, glide. Then, with a double-pole push, shift back to the ski you started with. Because your skis are farther apart and at an angle to each other, moving from one ski to the other feels much more dynamic and positive than is the case with diagonal striding.

What Goes Down, Must Go . . . Up

You can diagonal-stride straight up short, gentle slopes by leaning forward, picking up your skis, and slapping them down harder on the snow. You will slow down and glide less, but for a time you can keep going. On most slopes this technique doesn't work for long, and whether waxed or waxless, your skis will soon start slipping. For long climbs the solution is to use climbing skins. For short ascents you do need to know some uphill techniques, which you will also need for slopes too steep to ascend directly even with skins.

Herringbone Climbing

The herringbone technique works well for very short, steep climbs. You can change to the herringbone position without stopping, as soon as your skis start to slip. Simply angle your skis outward, placing the skis on their edges to form platforms that you can push off from. If

this sounds similar to skating, it is—a good skater can skate up quite steep hills. When the skate slows to a walk and the glide fades away, it becomes a herringbone. Your poles are important when herringboning (use them as you would skating, or diagonal striding, but more aggressively), and you need to keep moving. Most backsliding, a literal description, is due to a lack of aggression and commitment. Don't hesitate! If you fail to get your weight over the leading ski while on the flat, you simply go slower and have to work harder; if you fail to do so while herringbone climbing, you will start to slip and will probably find yourself down in the snow. You can't tiptoe up a slope. Put the whole weight of your body on each ski as it hits the snow, throwing your hips over the ski to get your whole weight on it quickly. Leaning your torso forward puts your weight ahead of your skis, so try to keep upright, bending at the knees and ankles rather than the waist. Look ahead rather than down at your skis.

Sidestepping

Sidestepping is a less strenuous, slower, and more relaxed way to climb short, steep slopes. On all but the steepest slopes you can stop to catch your breath, take photographs, or watch the snowshoe hare that has just appeared.

To sidestep up a hill, stand with your skis parallel and at right angles to the slope, then step sideways up the slope one ski at a time, using your poles for balance and to help pull slightly with the upslope pole. To prevent your skis from slipping, keep them tilted on the edge nearest the slope (the inside edge), to make a platform on which to stand. As you roll your ankles and knees into the hill, the skis will move with them. You also need to ensure that your weight is over one ski when you place it on the snow. Keep the steps short to avoid overbalancing, especially on steep slopes. If you find the skis slipping forward or backward, it is because they aren't at 90 degrees to the fall line (the direction a snowball would take if rolled downhill).

Another technique for climbing steep hills, using climbing skins attached to the ski bases, is discussed in the sidebar on p. 196.

Traversing

You can climb long slopes by traversing them—sliding forward at an angle at which your skis won't slip. At the end of each traverse, do a partial kick turn—you want to end up at an angle to the way you have come. A

The Downhill Stance

Body position is even more important for downhill skiing than it is for skiing on the flat or uphill. Your knees and ankles should be flexed forward, and your torso should be upright. Check this position by seeing if you can feel pressure from the tongue of your boot on the front of your ankles. If you can't, bend your ankles more. Alpine ski boots force you into this position, but nordic touring boots do not, so you have to concentrate on maintaining it.

Straight Running

When the slope isn't too long or steep and you can see a good, long run-out at the bottom, the simplest, fastest, and most exciting way to descend is to point your skis down the hill and go. If the snow is soft and even, a

partial—say, two-thirds—kick turn is usually enough. At the end of an upward traverse, kick the uphill ski around and place it on the snow in the direction of your next traverse, then follow with your other ski, placing it ahead of the first ski so you can keep moving. On gentle-to-moderate slopes, you can climb continuously by this method. On steeper slopes you may need to stop and stamp out a platform before you can do a kick turn. Traversing may be necessary even when using skins on a long, steep climb in which going straight up is either too tiring or simply impossible.

And What Goes Up . . . Comes Down

In the mountains, being good at downhill skiing means being able to stay in control and choose the best turn for the snow and the terrain, rather than to swoop at full speed into the unknown. While the function of turns is to check your speed, making fast, linked turns down open slopes or powder-filled bowls is always exciting and satisfying—and the goal of most touring skiers. For novices, however, it's best to start by learning some basic cross-country downhill techniques, then work up to the more difficult wedge, stem, and classic telemark turns.

Described below are some basics of nordic-style turning; the scope of this chapter is too narrow for a full discussion of the classic backcountry technique. For an excellent how-to session on downhilling free-heel style, see *Wilderness Skiing and Winter Camping* by Chris Townsend (Ragged Mountain Press, 1994).

PAUL PETERSON

Body position is even more important for downhill skiing than it is for skiing on the flat or uphill: knees and ankles flexed forward, and your torso upright.

straight descent may be quite easy. Where the snow varies, however, and where there are bumps and dips on the slope, a little more technique is needed. In particular, the knees should be well flexed, so they can absorb bumps. On very bumpy terrain, pushing one ski a little ahead of the other and raising the rear heel in a hint of the telemark position will aid stability.

If you feel yourself starting to fall or if your weight moves back over your skis, flex your knees even more and lower your center of gravity. Also, push your hands forward—if your hands start to drift behind you, you will straighten up, and your weight will go back too.

Slowing Down and Stopping

The next thing to do is to add the snowplow, or wedge—so-called because of the V-shape made by the skis—to your straight-slope repertoire. Before you can learn to link turns, such as in a telemark, you need to be able to snowplow, controlling your speed as you go. Snowplows applied firmly will also stop you on surprisingly steep slopes.

To execute a snowplow, push outward on your heels to force the tails of your skis apart. Your ski tips should be about a basket width apart, while your knees should have enough space between them to hold a basketball. A knock-kneed wedge will set your skis too much on their edges, and they will run as though on rails and probably converge, picking up speed as they do so. Keep your body upright, flexing your knees and ankles rather than bending at the waist. Look ahead; if you look down at your ski tips, your body will tip forward, becoming unbalanced. You also need to keep your weight over your heels. Your hands should be out in front where you can see them, roughly where they would be if you were riding a bicycle, with your poles pointing backward along the line of the skis so they don't catch on trees or bushes or stab other skiers as you go past.

Traverses and Kick Turns

The easiest and safest, but often the slowest, way to descend a slope is by traverses and kick turns. In breakable crust, where the snow collapses as soon as you put weight on it, or on slopes where the snow is thin and there are many rocks visible, this may be the only sensible way to descend. It is certainly the best method to use on any slope on which you don't feel confident.

Ignore what others do. If you feel best being cautious, then be cautious. On a wide slope you can pick up quite a bit of speed in a traverse, and with kick turns you can sometimes get down quite quickly this way—certainly faster than if you keep falling over as you try to link turns on the move.

The key to traversing is to keep most of your weight over the edge of the downhill ski. On steep slopes this means you will feel as though you are leaning away from the hill. If you lean into the hill you will fall. Keep your torso upright, angling your knees into the hill. The idea is to put the skis onto their uphill edges, to prevent them from skidding downhill. Push the upper ski slightly ahead of the lower ski; this stance makes it easier to stay in balance and to keep the skis on their edges. In soft snow or on gentle slopes, edging isn't really necessary, and you won't need to push your knees into the hill so much, either.

Many people prefer to kick-turn facing upslope, so they don't have to look down the hill. However, this maneuver can be difficult on a really steep slope, where your skis may catch on the snow; a downslope-facing turn is preferable in this case. If your kick turns are a little wobbly or the slope is very steep and the snow hard-packed, you might want to stamp out a platform first. In mixed snow, look ahead as you traverse for softer patches where it will be easier to turn.

On a fast traverse you have to stop before you can kick-turn, and some people have a problem stopping. If you twist your knees up into the slope, the skis will pivot and the tips will turn in to the hill. Practice stopping traverses on easy slopes before you venture high into the mountains and onto terrain where it could be dangerous not to be able to stop at will. Step turns and telemark turns (described below) are used when you link traverses without stopping.

Step Turns

A step turn, which is basically a star turn done on the move, is an extremely useful movement. You can use it to turn downhill across the fall line on gentle slopes, to stop a traverse, to round corners on trails and in narrow corridors in forests or rocky terrain, and to avoid rocks, trees, fallen skiers, and other unexpected objects that may leap in front of you.

To step-turn, lift the tip of the inside ski—that is, the ski that will be on the inside of the turn—point it in

WAXING POETIC

Many serious cross-country ski enthusiasts insist that waxable skis are *ne plus ultra*—offering superior glide, grip, performance in diverse conditions, and silence (waxless bases do make a loud *zithering* sound, especially in hard snow). But many novices are put off by waxing—it is complicated, sometimes cumbersome in the field, and downright mysterious. However, as with many other things that are difficult, if you take the time to learn about waxing skis, you won't be disappointed.

Modern ski wax is made from petroleum distillates, whereas for years it was made from beeswax, whale oil, or various other natural substances. Glide waxes, which are put on the tip and tail, are fairly universal in type and duty. Grip waxes come in little film-canister-shaped containers (just right for your pockets) and are labeled in a wide variety of "temperatures"—that is, the temperature of the ice for which they are rated to offer maximum performance.

Wax works as a gripping medium because ice crystals, which have sharp edges, cut into the grip wax of the wax pocket and hold as you push off. In order to choose the right wax for the right snow, you must be familiar with all the choices. Choose too hard a wax, and you will slip slide and away; choose too soft a wax, and you will charge up hill, and stay there, because you won't be able to glide down.

Performance track skiers and racers use the most complex range of waxes—14 or more different waxes applied for very slight incremental changes in temperature and conditions, from 5 degrees F/15 degrees C and below to 41 degreesF/ 5 degrees C.

For touring, you need no more than four or five wax types, although in some conditions you can get away with the two-wax system. Swix labels theirs red and blue, the first being for snow at above freezing, the second for snow below freezing. (Tip: Compress a handful of snow into a ball; if it balls up and leaves your hand wet, use the red wax; if it crumbles into powder and feels dry, use the blue.)

If you want to fine-tune your waxing, you will need to know more about air and snow temperature, so carry a thermometer. Experienced skiers can often carry just three or four waxes with them, adjusting the amount and type of wax on their ski bases as the tour progresses. Which waxes depends on your local conditions, but in general Blue Extra (32 to 20 degrees F/0 to –7 degrees C) and Red Extra (37 to 41 degrees F/3 to 5 degrees C) cover most conditions except extreme cold, in which Green Extra (21 to 14 degrees F/–6 to –10 degrees C) comes in handy (these are Swix waxes). Some quick tips:

- If you find your skis slipping or sticking during the day, check the temperature. If it is much the same, you probably need only to scrape off or add to the wax you are already using. If the temperature has changed, you probably need a different wax or, in the case of the two-wax system, perhaps a thicker layer.
- When temperatures stay below freezing, you can often ski for days on end without rewaxing at all.
- Apply the wax as you would crayons. Several thin layers are better than one thick one; be careful to keep wax out of the central groove. Cold waxes should then be smoothed with a wax cork. Warm, sticky waxes are better smoothed in with the heel of your hand. Smoothed-in wax stays on the skis longer but doesn't grip quite as well; wax left rough grips better but is rubbed off faster. For better grip, you can also wax a longer section of the ski.
- For ice, very wet snow, or snow that has changed consistencies a lot (all of which are abrasive and have rounded crystals), use klister—the word means *glue* in Swedish, which tells you what it is like and how carefully it needs to be handled. Klister comes in a tube, and it is wise to keep it in a plastic bag. Klister needs to be warm before it can be used; apply it indoors or warm it close to your body. Universal klister, as the name suggests, has the widest range and is the one to choose if you want to carry only one klister (klisters, like hard wax, vary with the temperature).
- The biggest problem with klister is removing it if the snow changes. If you expect to move into colder temperatures, use climbing skins (described in the section on climbing techniques) rather than klister to get you there. To remove klister, cool the skis by placing them in the shade, then use a scraper to peel off the wax. This isn't as easy as it sounds; try carrying a rag soaked in wax remover in a plastic bag to aid removal. If you are carrying white gas (a solvent) for your stove, you can also use that. If you don't have any wax remover and can't scrape all the klister off, an alternative is to rub it in until it is really polished and then simply apply a harder wax on top.

If you really wish to learn the full art of ski waxing, ask your local ski shop for a recommendation—most ski wax companies offer excellent instructional booklets, sometimes for free, as well as workshops.

the direction you want to go, put your weight on it, and then step the other ski next to it. The steps should be kept short, so you don't cross the tails of your skis. For sharp turns, several steps are necessary. It is quicker, more efficient, and less tiring to lift just the tip, rather than the whole ski: pull your toes upward toward your knees and press down on your heel, then turn your shoulders in the direction of the turn, so you can use your upper body to help steer the skis.

Other Turns

There are several other nordic-downhill techniques: the wedge or snowplow turn, which uses the above-described technique to link traverses; the stem turn, which begins as a wedge turn but ends with the skis parallel; the parallel turn, which involves literally turning both skis aggressively together around a turn; and of course the classic telemark turn, which smoothly links traverses with one ski forward and one back, kneeling-style. All these turns require a good instructor and lots of practice to perfect.

Health and Fitness

Because cross-country skiing uses nearly all your body—from your shoulders to your toes—you must be in good shape to enjoy it to its fullest. Throughout the snowless season (although there is always snow somewhere in the world!), if you rock-climb and maintain good aerobic fitness, such as you gain from strenuous hiking, running, or mountain biking, you will be in great shape when the first snow hits. If not, a cross-country ski machine isn't a bad idea, or try roller blades or roller skis. Consult a book such as Steve Ilg's *The Outdoor Athlete* (Evergreen, CO: Cordillera Press, 1989) for sport-specific exercise programs.

As with all outdoor sports, a good diet is essential. Like mountain biking or running, skiing is a high-energy-output sport—except you use even more energy, because of the harsher conditions. So make sure you are properly fueled up before you head out; also, carry along more fuel to feed your body as you go. For a few days before a week-end out in the snow, tank up on carbohydrate-rich foods. While on the go, snack often on lots of simple carbohydrates (candy bars, cookies) as well as complex carbohydrates (dried fruit, granola bars, trail mix). Just make sure you don't overdose on too many simple carbos, which have a lot of refined sugar, because you won't get long-term energy out of them. Carry more food than you think you'll want, in case you get delayed by bad weather. See Chapter 12, p. 276, for details on nutrition outdoors.

Whether you head out across a few rolling meadows for a half-day or across the Rockies for two weeks, you should always have a full complement of safety skills and equipment. A very minimum safety kit for day tours would include

- Lightweight Mylar emergency blanket or bag
- Spare long underwear and socks
- Spare food, waterproof matches, lighter, small metal cup
- Full repair kit (see equipment section for a list)
- Small flashlight
- Map, compass, guidebook
- Whistle, flares
- First aid kit
- Altimeter
- Sunscreen, sunglasses, lip balm

Always leave your itinerary with someone before you leave on any outing. Winter weather can change quickly for the worse, and bad conditions will often be life-threatening if you are caught unawares. Checking the current weather forecasts before you head out is a good habit. Being prepared and skilled is always your best protection.

If you really get into cross-country skiing and plan to do long day tours or backcountry expeditions, consider taking both a backcountry first aid course that includes cold-weather first aid, such as treatments for hypothermia, and a mountaineering course that includes winter safety training, such as evaluating

---

PUSHING THE ENVELOPE:
A JAUNT ACROSS A CONTINENT

Ski touring for Norwegian Boerge Ousland doesn't mean a day jaunt around Oslo. In January 1997, Ousland arrived at Scott Base, Antarctica, after having crossed the entire continent. Alone. The grueling 1,675-mile journey took 64 days. Ousland is the first person to make the journey alone and unaided.

PAUL PETERSON

There are races for just about every level, and even if you don't get out and race, you can learn a lot just by watching.

avalanche danger, recognizing hazards such as semi-frozen ponds, and building snow shelters. (See Appendix B, p. 329, for a list of schools offering first aid and mountaineering courses, and Chapters 2, p. 49; 10, p. 263; and 13, p. 292, for more on alpine environments, and for tips on snow camping.)

Where to Go

Depending on your home region, great cross-country skiing can be just minutes away—even in your city parks. If your city doesn't get snow, chances are still good that you can find skiable snow within a few hours.

Start at your local ski or outdoor specialty shop, especially one that rents skis. Most shops will print up lists of places to go for day tours. Even at outdoor shops that do not sell or rent ski equipment, you can almost always find one or two salespeople who are ski enthusiasts who can help you find the information you need.

If your town lacks a ski shop, check mountain towns within a few hours' radius of your home; keep in mind that many ski shops close down for summer, unless they have an alternate-season business such as bike rentals. Many larger cities have regional outdoor sports magazines or newspaper sections, which are great sources for information about skiing, rental shops, and nordic ski centers with groomed trails. Also, contact the Cross-Country Ski Areas Association for a listing of members (see contact information at end of this chapter).

Other good sources of information are your regional or city parks department, and federal land agencies such as the U.S. Forest Service, the Bureau of Land Management, the Park Service, and the U.S. Fish and Wildlife Service. Many agencies maintain marked or even groomed ski trails and publish free guides. Before heading out onto any public land, be sure to call ahead

TOP 5

CLASSIC NORTH AMERICAN X-COUNTRY TRIPS

Gooseberry Falls State Park, Minnesota

The Catamount Trail, Vermont

Tenth Mountain Division Hut System, Colorado

Royal Gorge Cross-Country Ski Area and Resort, California

North Rim of the Grand Canyon, Arizona

VERMONT TOURISM AND MARKETING

The Catamount Trail, Stowe, Vermont.

- *The Catamount Trail, Vermont.* Ski this classic northeaster—280 miles through the forests of the Green Hills, beginning at Readsboro on the Massachusetts border and ending at North Troy, on the Canadian border. Ski it all backcountry-style, or stay at inns and huts along the way.

- *North Rim of the Grand Canyon, Arizona.* Backcountry skiing to the very rim of a snow-shrouded Grand Canyon is about as breathtaking an experience as you can get. Stay at the comfortable North Rim Nordic Lodge, just outside Grand Canyon National Park (which is closed to vehicular traffic in winter), and enjoy 1,500 square miles of winter wilderness, backcountry skiing, as well as groomed trails, rentals, instruction, and guided yurt-to-yurt tours along the North Rim.

- *Tenth Mountain Division Hut System, Colorado.* Ski the legendary hut-to-hut system put in by the Army's Tenth Mountain Division in the heart of the Rocky Mountain wilderness—the epitome of backcountry ski touring in North America.

- *Royal Gorge Cross-Country Ski Area and Resort, California.* Billed as North America's largest cross-country ski resort, this 9,172-acre spread at 7,000 feet in the northern Sierra Nevada offers an incredible 88 trails, 328 kilometers of groomed track, four cafes, two on-trail lodges, lifts, rentals, instruction, and more.

- *Gooseberry Falls State Park, Minnesota.* Just 12 miles north of Two Harbors, on Lake Superior's scenic, rugged shoreline, with short trails through quiet birch forests and spectacular frozen waterfalls.

for information about permits and winter dangers such as avalanches or ponds and lakes.

Marked winter trails and ski centers provide the best and safest opportunities for novices. Once your day touring and general winter skills are honed through courses or outings with experienced skier friends, venturing through the backcountry is the next step. Groups such as the Sierra Club and Appalachian Mountain Club often sponsor back-country skiing excursions (see the resources sections at the end of this chapter and Appendix B for contact information), and many adventure travel agencies book backcountry ski trips all over the world. There are also many guidebooks for ski trips. See Appendix B, p. 328, for a few good outdoor and adventure travel book sources.

WINTER CAMPING

Backcountry touring is more than just skiing—it's learning to ski across rugged terrain, and up and down steep slopes, with a heavy backpack on your back. It's learning to choose safe campsites out of danger of avalanches and high winds, building snow caves, and staying warm in subzero temperatures.

Author and backcountry skiing expert Chris Townsend has this to say about exploring the mountains in winter by ski:

"The joys of ski touring are many and varied. For me the appeal lay initially in making travel easier in deep snow. Plodding through the spring snow of the High Sierras during a walk along the Pacific Crest Trail, I watched two skiers swooping down wide snowfields and gliding rapidly across frozen meadows. I vowed then never again to exhaust myself struggling on foot through soft, deep snow when I could be skimming over the surface. After a few days on skis I realized that skiing offered far more than the solution to moving over snow-covered terrain. The pleasure of a new physical discipline, a new physical sensation overwhelmed me.

"Whether you like exploring the mysterious silent world of the winter forest or climbing high into the mountains to top some winter summits, you can go faster and more easily on skis. . . . The most exciting places to ski are high above the cut tracks."

But Townsend also offers this advice: "Winter is not the time for beginners to start camping or traveling in mountain wildernesses." An important prerequisite for backcountry touring is a basic knowledge of backpacking and navigation skills. Refer to Chapter 2, on backpacking, and the chapters of Part Two, for various outdoor skills.

☞ KID QUOTIENT

Cross-country skiing can be great fun for kids, but as parents you will need to greatly modify your approach to the sport when you take the little ones.

The first challenge will be finding the gear—because kids' boots and skis are outgrown so quickly, they don't sell well, and consequently many ski shops don't sell them. Your best bet is rental gear, especially at ski centers that have special programs and package deals for families.

Kids' skis should have very soft camber, so kids can enjoy a little more control. They won't go fast anyway—just a shuffle—so stability and control are more important.

Kids will get bored faster than you will with just *schussing* down a trail or on tracks, which is why ski centers can offer more diversion. Also, you'll have the advantage of nearby restaurants and restrooms—the latter being a bigger plus than you think.

If you can't locate a ski center that has family programs, such as kids' "ski rodeos" or parades, you can create your own fun. Find a snow-filled meadow with a few small hills and try the following.

☞ Set up a rope-and-pulley system on a hill to pull kids up, so they can have fun skiing down without the frustration of climbing back up.

☞ Create an easy obstacle course using thin and flexible sapling poles on a gentle downhill slope.

☞ Go on a mini-expedition (take a picnic)—just far enough so it feels like a challenge for the smallest of your skiers—and build a snow fort. Don't forget to have a siege!

With a little imagination, you can have a lot of fun with a family on skis. A few other pointers to maximize your fun:

☞ Dress the kids in long underwear, warm mid-layers, and good waterproof outer layers, and you'll all be a lot happier. Don't forget the hats and mittens, too.

☞ Sunscreen is very important, as is lip balm.

☞ Take plenty of water or hot chocolate, to replenish fluids used up while playing hard (make sure it's well insulated against freezing).

(See Chapter 11 for more tips on adventuring outdoors with kids.)

Where Can Cross-Country Skiing Lead You?

Do you like to go fast? Are you competitive? If you're lucky enough to live in a region with substantial snow, check out your local nordic racing scene. Like road-running in fair weather, nordic racing is well-organized and includes novice to expert levels, across varying distances. Even if you don't get out and race, watching the skiers can be fun and educational. There are also telemark races, if XCD is your thing.

Winter biathlon, another aspect of competitive cross-country skiing, is a very exciting, highly skilled combination sport involving skiing for miles, stopping at stations and firing .22 rifles at a series of targets, skiing for miles, stopping at more firing stations—all for combined shooting scores and skiing times. For contact information on nordic and XCD racing and biathlon, see the resources section below.

Further Resources for Cross-Country Skiing

Books
Wilderness Skiing and Winter Camping, by Chris Townsend (Camden, ME: Ragged Mountain Press, 1994).
Cross-Country Skiing, by Ned Gillette and John Dostal (Seattle: The Mountaineers, 1988), 3d edition.
Avalanche Safety for Skiers and Climbers, by Tony Daffern (Seattle: Rocky Mountain Books, 1983).
The Best Ski Touring in America, by Steve Barnett (San Francisco: Sierra Club Books, 1987).

Periodicals
Cross-Country Skier Magazine, 1832 Fremont Avenue S, Minneapolis, MN 55403; (612) 377-0312 or (800) 827-0607.

Ski Trax Magazine, 2 Pardee Avenue, Suite 204, Toronto, ON M6K 3H5; (416) 530-1350. Covers all of North America skiing.
Great Lakes Skier Magazine, 9973 E. Grand River, Brighton, MI 58116; (810) 227-4200; www.michiweb.com/glskier/.

Organizations
American Birkebeiner Ski Foundation (racing), P.O. Box 911, Hayward, WI 54843; (715) 634-5025 or (800) 872-2753; birkie@win.bright.net.
Backcountry Skiers Alliance, P.O. Box 134, Boulder, CO 80306; (303) 444-3722.
Cross-Country Ski Areas Association, 259 Bolton Road, Winchester, NH 03470; (603) 239-4341; ccsaa@xcski.org; www.xcski.org/. Information links to other sites of interest to skiers are excellent.
U.S. Biathlon Association, Olympic Training Center, 421 Old Military Road, Lake Placid, NY 12946; (518) 523-3836.

Schools
American Mountain Guides Association, P.O. Box 2128, Estes Park, CO 80517.
Wilderness Medical Associates, RFD 2, Box 890, Bryant Pond, ME 04219.
Wilderness Medicine Institute, P.O. Box 9, Pitikin, CO 81241.

Other Resources
The best place to start searching on the Internet is with one of the search engines, such as YAHOO; also, the Cross-Country Ski Area Association has an excellent link page.

"You are one with your skis and nature. This is something that develops not only the body but the soul as well, and it has a deeper meaning for a people than most of us perceive."

—Fridtjof Nansen

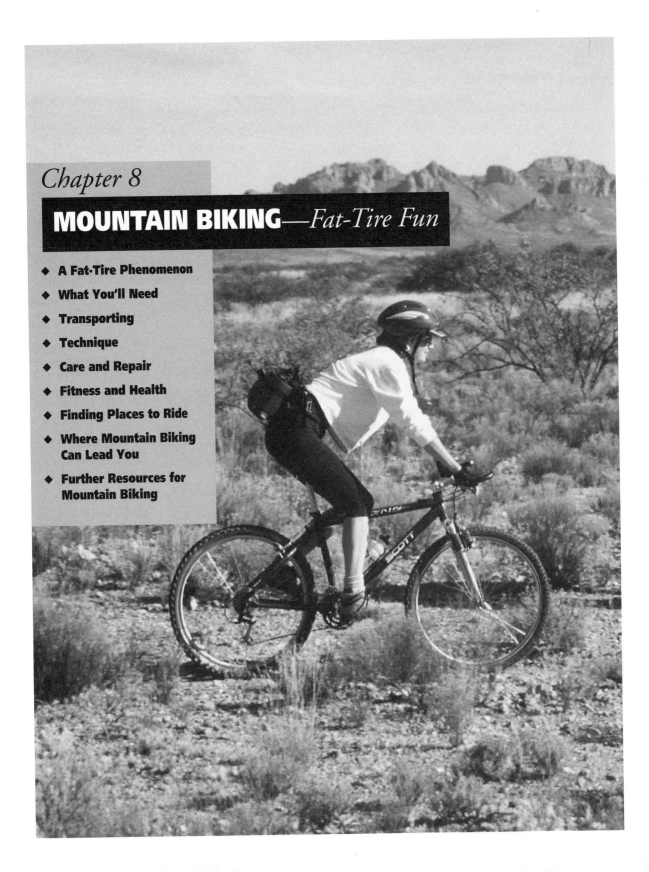

Chapter 8

MOUNTAIN BIKING—*Fat-Tire Fun*

◆ **A Fat-Tire Phenomenon**

◆ **What You'll Need**

◆ **Transporting**

◆ **Technique**

◆ **Care and Repair**

◆ **Fitness and Health**

◆ **Finding Places to Ride**

◆ **Where Mountain Biking Can Lead You**

◆ **Further Resources for Mountain Biking**

> *"Like all the best things in life, mountain biking scares the hell out of you and seduces you at the same time. This is true especially if you're a beginner."*
>
> —Bill Strickland in *Mountain Bike Magazine's Complete Guide to Mountain Biking Skills*

A Fat-Tire Phenomenon

It's amazing to think that, barely 20 years ago, no one had ever heard of a "mountain bike." In the mid-1970s, Russ Mahon, Gary Fisher, and a couple of other adventurous California bicyclists began experimenting with multispeed gearing and fat tires on stout old Schwinn Excelsior frames—and started the most spectacularly successful revolution in the history of bicycling.

In 1981 the first production mountain bike, the Specialized Stumpjumper, was introduced. Five years later, mountain bikes were outselling road bikes. In 1995, over 60 percent of all new bicycles sold in the United States were either mountain bikes or hybrids, designed to be ridden on pavement or dirt.

Like so many four-wheel-drive sport-utility vehicles, a lot of mountain bikes never see a dirt road. People just enjoy the rugged looks—and maybe the idea that they *might* someday chuck it all and move to Moab. Even if you never leave the city, mountain bikes are fun: blasting down alleys, jumping off curbs, leaping potholes. But to get the full potential out of the machine, you really need to get it out of town. You can cruise along backroads enjoying fresh air and nature, careen down a logging trail at insane speeds, or anything in between. Among the hundreds of models of mountain bikes available are designs suitable for

- Casual cruising
- Cross-country performance riding
- Downhill and slalom racing
- Long-distance touring

Perhaps the most astounding result of the mountain bike craze has been an enormous progression in technology without a corresponding escalation in price. Fifteen years ago the Stumpjumper, a steel-framed bike with a solid fork and basic components, sold for $750. Today the same money will buy an aluminum-framed model with a suspension fork and index shifting, which allows you simply to click to the next gear. Imagine going out tomorrow and buying a brand-new Toyota Celica for the price of a 1981 Corolla, and you'll have some idea of how lucky today's mountain bikers are.

Not only are we lucky, we are smart as well. Bicycling is one of the healthiest, least expensive, and most

Organized races are a great way to test your mettle, and metal—and a good opportunity to meet like-minded riders.

environmentally friendly ways of getting around that has ever been invented. Every time you ride, you'll be increasing your fitness, saving money, and reducing pollution.

What You'll Need

You'll need a bicycle.

Unlike in many other sports, in bicycling the central piece of equipment represents about 90 percent of what you must spend to get started. Still, there are a few other necessities, as well as one or two valuable extras.

The Bicycle

Let's face it—many riders who are attracted to the idea of a mountain bike have only a remote chance of ever encountering a dirt road. For this reason, manufacturers build lots of inexpensive "mountain bikes," which, while rugged in appearance, lack the strength to handle rough conditions without risking eventual damage.

So how do you tell a "real" mountain bike? To be blunt, price is one way. Very few new bikes under $400 or so are made to stand up to extended trail use. But there are exceptions, and you might also be looking at used bikes. So learn how to recognize quality frame materials and components.

Frame Materials

Somewhere on just about every bicycle is a little sticker telling you what the frame is made of. It's one of the first places to look (besides the little sticker with the dollar sign on it) to judge the quality of the bicycle.

Hi-tensile steel. Most inexpensive bikes have frames labeled *Hi-tensile steel.* While perfectly serviceable for road use, this relatively low-strength alloy is marginal for serious dirt riding. That's not to say that some such bikes aren't being utterly thrashed and holding up just fine, but the margin of safety before something bends is definitely lower.

Chromoly steel. Better steel frames are labeled *Chromoly.* Frame tubes made from this very high-strength alloy (containing chromium and molybdenum) have thinner walls than hi-tensile tubes have, resulting in reduced weight and better rigidity. Chromoly steel offers an excellent compromise among cost, strength, lightness, and resiliency. The latter is the ability of the material to flex just enough to absorb a bit of shock on rough trails or roads (that's why steel is used to make springs).

Steel also has the advantage of easy repair. If you're thinking of a bike tour through Africa or across Asia, it's reassuring to know that any village blacksmith can weld a cracked steel frame. Bust up a monocoque carbon-fiber bike in Benghazi and you'll be out of luck.

The best, and lightest, chromoly steel frames are "butted": that is, have thicker walls near the frame joints, where the most strength is needed, and thinner walls near the middle of the tubes, where less stress occurs. Variations such as "double-butted" refer to the relative thicknesses of the middle and the end of the tube.

Steel hasn't the cachet of newer, space-age materials, but its combination of strength, durability, light weight, along with the ease with which it can be worked, means that even many custom builders still use steel in their top-quality bikes.

Aluminum. Ten years ago, aluminum was considered advanced technology in bicycle construction. Today, over one-third of mountain bike frames are made from aluminum alloys, including more and more low-priced models.

Aluminum has the obvious advantage of lightness over steel. However, it lacks the tensile strength of steel, so most aluminum frames incorporate large-diameter tubing (instead of just thicker-walled tubes of the same diameter) to compensate for the difference. The technique works just fine—in fact, aluminum frames have a reputation for being *too* stiff at times, offering a very unforgiving ride over washboard and rocks. The upside is that more of your pedaling energy goes toward moving the bike, not flexing the frame.

THE ESSENTIALS—A MOUNTAIN BIKING START-UP KIT

- Bicycle ($400–$2,000; up to $5,000!)
- Helmet ($40–$110)
- Gloves ($15–$40)
- Pump that fits on bike ($15–$30)
- Tube repair kit ($3)
- Water bottle ($3–$5)

Minimum cost essential mountain biking kit: $476*

ADD-ONS

- Speedometer/computer
- Tool kit
- Handlebar or seat bag
- Shoes for clipless pedals
- Light
- First aid kit
- Lycra bicycling shorts (with padding) and top

*The essentials list above is intended to give you an idea of minimum start-up costs, from scratch, for moderate entry into a sport using new equipment. Other options include borrowing gear from friends or renting from retailers, YMCAs, or church activity clubs, as well as buying used gear—see Appendix A.

Suspension, of course, can reduce this inherent harshness.

Like steel, aluminum comes in different grades, or alloys. Lower-priced bikes are usually made from 6061-T6 aluminum; higher-priced models might utilize 7000 or 7005 alloy, or a proprietary variation.

Just as with steel, aluminum tubes can be butted to further reduce weight. Aluminum/ceramic composites are said to be stronger and more resilient than pure aluminum, so frames can be made lighter while still being cheaper to manufacture than those made with more exotic materials.

A possible downside to aluminum is the lifespan of the frame before it begins to develop stress cracks. Some engineers think steel, because it flexes more, is more durable. While this could be a concern to racers (who often go through several frames each *year*), most aluminum frames are built with enough excess material that an average rider would spend decades trying to wear it out. If any material threatens to take over from steel as the standard for bicycle frames, it is certainly aluminum.

Carbon fiber. Even more so than aluminum, carbon fiber was wildly exotic 10 years ago. Today it still occupies a rarefied niche (less than 5 percent of the market), but the technology is becoming considerably more mainstream.

Carbon was touted as the ultimate frame material when it was introduced. Certainly it has many amazing properties. Extremely light in weight, it is nevertheless immensely strong and durable. It can be laminated to specific requirements, combining stiffness where necessary with more resiliency where desired. Some carbon frames are formed in one large piece, with no separate tubes; these are called monocoque frames.

One downside is cost. Although aluminum frames are showing up on sub-$500 bikes, the cut-off for carbon is still up around $1,000. Carbon fiber frames are virtually impossible to repair; if you crunch one, it's time for a new frame. And carbon is somewhat vulnerable to impact damage, such as from flying stones.

Thermoplastic. Recently, a new frame material has appeared on the market: thermoplastic, which is formed from a plastic, such as nylon, with reinforcements of carbon fiber (often graphite, which is a form of carbon). The two materials are combined in a heated mold to produce the finished frame, which is very strong and lightweight, resistant to stone impacts, and quite resilient. Often, aluminum-alloy bottom-bracket shells and head and seat tubes are molded into the frame to provide precise bearing surfaces for the crankset, fork, and seat. Although it is a cutting-edge material, thermoplastic has the potential to be used in inexpensive bicycles, since it is easy to form and the ratio of plastic and reinforcements can be altered to save money.

Titanium. Combine the resiliency of steel and the light weight of carbon fiber, and what do you get? Titanium, which might hold the title of ultimate frame material. A titanium frame can look just like a steel counterpart, while weighing up to one-third less. It is utterly corrosion-free; in fact, many titanium frames are left unpainted, simply polished to mirror brightness to show off the metal.

Titanium might be the magic material—it will definitely make your money disappear. Expect to pay at least $1,500 for a titanium bicycle that might have components that could be found on a $900 aluminum bike. Go for the works and you'll part with three grand or more. But the frame will last you the rest of your life, if you choose.

Components

Your bike's components essentially comprise all the little, complicated moving parts: the brakes and brake levers, the crankset and pedals, the bottom bracket (the axle and bearings on which the crankset revolves), the drive chain, the front and rear derailleurs (which move the chain to different gears), the shifters (which control the derailleurs), the hubs (the axle and bearing assembly at the center of each wheel), and the headset (the bearings on which the handlebar and fork pivot).

Look at a $300 bicycle and a $2,000 bicycle side-by-side. Although the components will appear virtually identical, there are big differences in weight, strength, function, and, of course, cost.

The largest component manufacturer in the world, Shimano, offers nine complete ranges of component groups just for mountain bikes (fully three-quarters of all bikes sold—mountain and road—come with at least some Shimano parts). The mountain bike component sets are named, in ascending order of price, Tourney, Altus, Acera, Alivio, STX, STX-RC, Deore LX, Deore XT, and XTR. The Tourney components are very economical and simple and are found strictly on low-end bicycles. At the other end of the scale, the XTR group incorporates every technological innovation known to

Shimano's engineers. Each part functions superbly and is immensely strong yet as light as it can be made without compromising structural integrity. For example, the arms on the crankset are not only cold-forged—the strongest way to form an alloy part—but also hollow. Titanium parts reduce the weight of the shifters by a few grams without affecting durability. And the Shimano-designed V-brake is considerably more powerful than ordinary cantilever brakes.

All this technology costs. You can buy an entire bicycle equipped with Tourney components for under $200. Just the XTR group by itself—without a frame, fork, wheels, or anything else—is around $1,500. The other groups span the range in between.

For the prospective mountain bike buyer, this component grading might seem confusing, but it actually makes shopping easier. With very little exposure, you'll be able to recognize the grade of components that should go with a bike in a particular price range, and thus know what to expect from that bike in terms of function and weight. For example, an aluminum-framed bicycle with a suspension fork, in the $1,000 range, might be equipped with STX-RC, Deore LX, or even some Deore XT components (manufacturers frequently mix groups, but the name of the group should be stamped on each component). If you're looking at two bikes for the same price, one of which has all Deore LX components and the other mostly LX but with XT derailleurs, you can be pretty sure that the latter bike will shift just a bit better and thus may be a better buy for the money, all else being equal.

Recognizing good components is also useful because some makers will put name-brand parts in the most obvious places but substitute cheap generic pieces where you might not notice—for example, on the hubs. The presence of such parts, while not necessarily cause to reject the bike, should be factored into your buying decision.

Other factors affect which components will appear on a bike. As mentioned in the materials section, a titanium-framed bike with a $1,500 price tag might have parts that could be found on a much cheaper aluminum bike. Also, a company with a high-profile name might get away with charging more for a model with lower-end components.

Although Shimano dominates the component market, the German company Sachs is fighting back hard, and industry veteran Campagnolo is working on a component group for mountain bikes. In addition, dozens of small companies produce individual components using low-volume machining techniques.

Suspension

In 1988, many of us snickered at a new gimmick on the mountain bike scene: a heavy, ugly fork replacement called a Rock-Shox. The idea of suspension on a bicycle seemed like ridiculous overkill—until we tried it. The increase in comfort and control on a rough trail was amazing. Now suspension forks are common and growing increasingly sophisticated, and some bewilderingly complex rear-suspension systems have been added to confuse things further. Glancing through catalogs might leave you with the impression that a mountain bike without some sort of suspension is hopelessly *déclassé*. But, for all the advantages it offers, suspension isn't for everyone.

Any suspension adds weight to the bicycle. A full-suspension model might weigh as much as 6 pounds more than a nonsuspended equivalent, and even just a suspended fork adds a couple of pounds. Much of the technology that goes into suspensions is centered around racing—especially downhill racing. Full-suspension bikes, in particular, are advantageous for

RICH ETCHBERGER

Because weight isn't crucial, full-suspension bikes are great for downhills.

downhills, since the weight penalty is not crucial (some full-on downhill race machines weigh well over 30 pounds).

Rear suspension. A problem inherent in some rear suspensions is the tendency of the bike either to bob up and down or to "bio-pace," causing a jerky back-and-forth sensation, when the rider stands up to pedal. This has led to the development of different types of linkages that are compliant when the rider is seated but stiffer when the rider stands. Some are set up to be more compliant in higher gears, which you would use on fast downhills, and stiffer in lower gears, which you would use for powering up hills. The downside of many of these systems is that the bike handles differently depending on the position of the rider. "Fully active" suspensions feel basically the same at all times, but you need to learn a smooth pedal stroke to mitigate the bobbing. As rear suspension systems become increasingly sophisticated, more and more bikes designed for cross-country use are sporting them, although many cross-country racers still favor the rigidity, simplicity, and weight savings of a "hard-tail."

Front suspension. Front suspensions—that is, suspension forks—are much more common, and increasingly so on inexpensive bikes. Even a few sub-$500 mountain bikes are equipped with simple front suspensions.

Suspended forks incur few of the problems of rear suspensions. They add much less weight and complexity, and they react essentially the same whether you're in the saddle or out of it. The cheapest ones lack some of the structural rigidity and ride suppleness built into the best models, but that's not likely to be a problem for a recreational rider. And any suspension fork really takes the sting out of rough roads or washboard surfaces.

Until recently, most suspension forks used elastomeric disks as the "springs." These are simple, durable, and can be easily replaced with firmer or softer disks to suit the rider's weight and riding style. Simple elastomer forks rely on the friction of the disks against the fork tubes for damping (keeping the fork from continuing to bounce after a bump); more-sophisticated models add oil or air damping to increase control. The latest move in suspension forks has been toward coil springs, which, though heavier than elastomers, are more responsive (techno-weenies with big allowances can even substitute titanium coils). Some radical forks intended for downhill racing use motorcycle-style dual crowns for ultimate rigidity and long travel.

If you're thinking of getting into downhill racing, then by all means buy as much suspension as you can afford—front *and* rear. If you contemplate riding cross-country on rough trails, you could buy a fully suspended model designed for such use, or you could take the several-hundred-dollar premium and get a lighter and better-equipped hard-tail with a really good suspended fork. If, on the other hand, most of your riding is going to be on smooth dirt roads or well-maintained trails, you might be better off skipping suspension altogether and aiming your budget at higher-quality components or a lighter frame. Many such bikes have frame geometry that will allow you to add a suspension fork later, if you decide you can't live without one.

Gearing

Thirty years ago, people thought bicycles with 10 speeds were pretty advanced. Today, if you see a bike with 10 speeds, it probably means something is broken. Even road bikes, with only two chainwheels up front, commonly have seven- or eight-speed cassettes in the rear, giving them 14 or 16 gears in all. And a mountain bike with three chainrings and an eight-speed cassette has a total of 24 gear combinations from which to choose. It might seem like overkill, especially if you've ever seen pictures of Tibetan peasants riding over 18,000-foot passes on single-speed clunkers—but we soft Westerners need all the help we can get. As mountain biking has grown as a sport, so has the variety of terrain riders are willing to tackle. On one trail you're

likely to find yourself blasting along a flat at 30 miles per hour in top gear, then crawling up a rocky slope in low-low.

The top gear on a mountain bike is typically lower than the same gear on a road bike, since you're unlikely to need a super-high top speed with knobby tires (factory-sponsored downhill racers, who regularly top 50 miles per hour, are singular exceptions). It's in the low gears where mountain bikes really shine.

Chainrings and cassettes are sold by the number of teeth they have, which can vary depending on what type of riding is planned. A bike with typical all-around gearing might have 26, 36, and 48 teeth on the chainrings, and a spread of between 12 and 32 teeth on the rear cluster. Recently, compact drive trains have become popular, to save weight and increase ground clearance. A compact drive set could have 22, 32, and 42 teeth up front and 11 to 28 in the back, but the overall ratios would be about the same as the traditional larger setup.

Tires

All the different parts of a mountain bike combine to give it its cross-country ability, but the tires are what actually connect it to the trail. The best titanium-framed full-suspension wonderbike is worthless without correspondingly competent tires.

Just as on automobiles, tires on bikes come in

THE PHYSICS OF GEARING

The tricycle you had when you were four years old had a very simple drive arrangement. The pedals were attached directly to the front wheel, so that every time you moved the pedals one complete revolution, the wheel also moved one revolution. That's fine for sidewalks but unsuited to riding up and down hills or going over two miles per hour. The gearing on a bicycle allows variation in the torque you can apply to the rear wheel. In a "large" gear—a combination of a big chainring in front and a small cog in the rear—the wheel will make several revolutions for each revolution of the pedals. This makes the bike go fast, just like a high gear in a car, but is no good for climbing steep hills or picking your way through rocks. In a small gear—small chainring, big rear cog—the pedals might turn faster than the wheel. This allows much more torque to be transmitted to the wheel, just as if you were in the low range gears in a four-wheel-drive vehicle.

different sizes: for example, 26 x 1.95. The first number is the wheel diameter in inches (virtually all mountain bikes have 26-inch wheels); the second is the tread width. Most mountain bike tires come in a fairly small range of widths, between 1.95 and 2.1 inches, although some tires designed for mostly road use are a bit narrower. Within that narrow range, however, are big differences in tread design and pattern. Tire makers are continually striving for better traction, puncture resistance, and durability, so designs change frequently. When it's time to buy new tires, or if you're not happy with the ones that come on your bike, look for advice in a bike shop or pick up a magazine with a tire comparison test. One good rule, as mentioned in the Losing Weight sidebar, p. 220, is to spring for Kevlar beads rather than steel, to save rotating weight on the bike.

Tubes, which actually hold the air inside the tire, range from the lightest, gram-pinching latex models to heavy-duty, flat-resistant bruisers. Take your own riding style into account when buying tubes—reducing rotating weight is great, but repairing flats every 20 miles isn't worth a couple of ounces saved. A medium-weight tube is probably fine for most riding, but always carry a patch kit.

Fitting the Bicycle

At the risk of horrifying connoisseurs, it must be said that fitting a mountain bike isn't normally as exacting as fitting, for example, a road-racing bicycle. In fact, some mountain bike manufacturers have gone to a simple "small, medium, and large" sizing system. But that doesn't mean you shouldn't pay attention. Getting the right frame size will greatly increase your riding comfort and efficiency; after that, it's possible to fine-tune the fit with aftermarket components, if need be.

The frame size of the bike refers to the distance from the bottom bracket axle to the top tube and is usually given in inches: 16", 17.5", 19", and so forth. On a mountain bike, you want good clearance when you stand straddling the top tube—at least a couple of inches (some bikes have sloping top tubes, to increase this clearance). For this reason, most people ride a smaller mountain bike than they would a road bike.

Seat height is the single most important variable on a properly sized bike. To adjust the seat, have someone hold the handlebars while you sit on the bike and rotate one pedal all the way down and then a little forward, so the crank arm is in line with the seat post. You should just be able to plant your heel (*not* the ball of your foot) on the pedal in this position, with a straight leg, and sitting normally on the saddle. Set this way, when you place your foot normally on the pedal, your leg will be slightly bent at the bottom of the pedal stroke, which will help prevent knee problems.

If you look at the spec sheet for a bicycle, you'll see measurements given for such things as the seat tube angle, head tube angle, and top tube and chainstay length. These are collectively referred to as the bike's geometry. Altering these factors affects the handling of the bicycle, and various combinations are used to induce particular handling traits in a bike designed for a certain purpose, such as downhill racing or slalom riding. The trend in mainstream mountain bike design today is toward a quick-handling geometry suitable for cross-country performance riding—something close to this combination: a 71-degree head angle, 73-degree seat angle, 16¾" chainstays, and a 22½"–23" top tube. Altering these dimensions slightly will affect different factors of the bike's performance. For example, longer chainstays move the rear wheel farther out from under the seat, increasing comfort and downhill stability but reducing climbing ability, since less of your weight is over the tire.

Components also affect how a bike fits and feels. Handlebars can be nearly straight (for performance) or swept up and back (for comfort or downhill racing). Likewise, a long handlebar stem with little or no rise places the rider low over the bike for better control in cross-country situations, while a short, high-rise stem is more relaxed and better on steep downhills.

In general, inexpensive mountain bikes have components that encourage a fairly upright, relaxed riding style. More-expensive bikes tend toward a stretched-out, performance-oriented posture, with more of the rider's weight on the handlebars. You can alter the standard setup on your bike if it proves uncomfortable for you, with a new stem or handlebar. Be cautious, though—such modifications will affect the handling to some extent. Don't change any components until you've ridden the bike for several weeks and gotten used to the riding position.

Women are often uncomfortable on bikes designed for men. Some manufacturers make models with dimensions and geometry especially suited to female body proportions. Consult your bike shop for advice.

Helmet

Don't leave home without it. Many people still fool themselves into thinking that helmets are unnecessary for bicycling, but they're wrong. You wouldn't think of running across your living room headfirst into the opposite wall, but that would represent a fairly mild bicycling accident. Even a simple tipover can be serious if your head hits a rock or curb.

Today's helmets leave little room for the old excuses not to wear them: "too hot," "too heavy," "too bulky." Modern designs are well ventilated, very light (some are under 10 ounces), and radically styled. When you shop, look for a snug, but not tight, fit and an easy-to-adjust chin strap. Newer helmets offer extra protection for the back of the head—a good trend.

Gloves

You can ride without gloves, but you'll be much more comfortable with them. They provide padding, a better grip, and protection in the event of a fall. The classic string-back gloves are still around and work just fine, but newer designs with resilient gel padding absorb more shock.

When shopping, lean toward a pretty tight fit, since the gloves will stretch in time. But try them by gripping a handlebar and working the brake levers, to be sure you've enough freedom of movement.

Other Necessities and Niceties

Sometimes half the fun of a new sport is adding gadgets. Here are a few that will be really useful as well as entertaining.

Speedometer/Computer

These little devices, no larger than a wristwatch, are an astounding source of information. All will tell you your current speed and distance covered; most add tidbits such as average speed and cumulative mileage. Some even include heart rate monitors for serious training.

The computer works off a sensor that attaches to the fork and reads a magnet clipped to a wheel spoke. Inexpensive computers send the signal up a small wire to the display; fancier models use a wireless transmitter.

Clipless Shoes

Inexpensive mountain bikes come with plain "beartrap" pedals, which have teeth to grab your shoe soles (or your shins if you slip off them, hence the nickname). Better pedals use toeclips, which locate your shoe more securely and increase pedaling efficiency immensely, since you can pull *up* as well as push down. Of course, they are also harder to get out of in the event of a tumble, and so take some practice.

The most advanced pedals are clipless. Very light and compact, they are designed to clip into a special cleat screwed into the sole of your shoe. Once you rotate the shoe in and the mechanism locks, the shoe and the pedal

Many riders swear by the increased performance offered by "clipless pedals," which snap directly to the bottom of specially designed shoes rather than slide into a clip on top of a traditional pedal.

become one. This is great for efficiency, but placement of the cleat is critical to avoid knee problems (some clipless pedals allow the shoe to rotate side to side a bit, which helps). And since releasing the shoe from the pedals requires a conscious twist and pull, you will inevitably suffer a few *WHUMPS!*, as a patch of sand sucks you to a stop and you flail futilely to get your shoes out of the dang things while toppling slowly sideways. Use caution at first. Once the motion becomes second nature, you won't even notice the release sequence.

Shoes made for clipless pedals are designed to accept the cleat properly, with reinforcements to stiffen the sole and offer good support for your foot. They are much more comfortable to walk in than the old style roadbike cleated shoes, which forced you to hobble like an arthritic gnome.

Lights

The first time you see a bicycle headlamp with a price tag of $200, you'll probably think (or *hope*) someone misplaced a decimal point. Like many other facets of bicycling, a technology race has transformed the science of lighting. Those horrendously expensive lamps put out a beam that most automobiles would envy—white, consistent, and incredibly bright.

Don't worry, though; you don't have to spend the money if you don't need to light up the night like a Baja racer. Other headlamps start at under 10 bucks. If your headlamp is strictly a backup, in case of a delayed ride home, an inexpensive model will do okay. If you're going

to be out often, you might consider more of an investment. The brighter lights don't just make it easier for you to see; they make it easier for others (in cars) to see you.

Even more useful for safety's sake is a rear light, to alert motorists coming up behind you. Some headlamp systems come with a taillight, but the most effective light is a strobe, which flashes continuously and is almost impossible to miss. Strobes are available separately, and they run off a standard battery.

Handlebar and Underseat Bags

An underseat bag is a zippered pouch that attaches to the seat rails and the seatpost. It's the perfect size for carrying all the tools you need, plus a patch kit and even a spare tube.

A handlebar bag is useful for snacks, cameras, and anything else small you might want along. Make sure you buy a well-made model with a really strong handlebar attachment, not just a warmed-over road bike version. The extra vibration of trail or backroad riding will quickly loosen a less than stout mount.

Another good place to carry tools is in a shoulderstrap bag, a triangular-shaped pouch that attaches to the junction of the top and seat tubes. A strong webbing strap functions as a convenient shoulder pad when it's necessary to carry the bike.

Clothing

Let's be honest: you can probably do everything you want to do on a mountain bike in Levi's and a T-shirt. But clothing designed especially for cycling will add to your performance and comfort.

Mountain bike clothing has morphed into two entirely different lines. You can choose either the slick and aerodynamic-looking Lycra shorts and top, similar to the "roadie" clothing that's been around for ages, or its direct opposite, the grunge look, with baggy shorts and baggier tops. Both styles benefit from essentially the same modern, high-performance fabrics.

The two enemies to comfort and performance on a bike are friction and sweat. The first occurs largely in the seat area, while the second occurs everywhere. The ideal bike clothing reduces friction while wicking sweat away from your body. These requirements usually demand a synthetic material.

Most bicycling shorts are made from either a 100 percent synthetic fabric, such as Lycra, or a blend of synthetic and cotton. Many are lightly padded in the seat area, with a material that helps transport moisture to the surface of the shorts. Many baggy-style shorts also have an inner liner of tighter-fitting Lycra, to reduce chafing. Shirts are usually synthetic as well, although some can be all-cotton.

Apparel designed for cold-weather cycling uses thicker material and longer sleeves and legs but is otherwise similar. For rain and wind protection, lightweight Gore-Tex shells are perfect, since they allow body moisture to evaporate while keeping the elements out. (See Chapter 14 for more on fabrics and garments for the outdoors.)

Transporting

A bicycle is, at best, an awkward item to mate to a car, so it makes no sense to spend a lot of money on a nice bike, or two, and then drive down the interstate with them strapped to some flimsy discount rack.

For most vehicles, whether sedan or sport-utility, you can choose between roof-mounted racks or those that attach to the rear, on the trunk, the hatch, a receiver hitch, or a swingaway spare tire (a popular option on sport-utility vehicles). Rear racks are more convenient for access to the bikes, but often less so for access to stuff in the back of the car. Some receiver-mounted racks (which slide into the square tube that takes a hitch ball for towing) hinge the bikes down to get them out of the way. Similarly, swingaway mounts simply swing with the tire.

Mounting the bikes on the roof is less convenient, particularly in the case of tall sport utilities, but it keeps the bikes completely out of the way until needed, out of most road grime, and out of the reach of passersby. The bane of roof-mounted bicycles is the garage—or rather, the absent-minded owner who forgets the bikes are on the roof when entering the garage.

Technique

Okay—you already know how to ride a bicycle. If all you're going to do is ride your mountain bike around town, like the urbanites who drive those spotless Range Rovers, you won't need any practice. But riding in dirt, through sand, up and down rocky hills, and along steep-

---

◆ **EXPERT TIP: PRERIDE CHECK**

An easy seven-step check before every ride will help ensure a safe outing.

◆ Check the frame for cracks, especially around the joints.

◆ Grab each wheel at the top and try to wiggle it back and forth. Slop means the hub bearings need adjusting.

◆ Similarly, straddle the front wheel and grab the handlebars. Push straight back and forth to check for play in the headset.

◆ Make sure the quick-release skewers on the wheels are really tight.

◆ Make sure the brake shoes aren't rubbing against the wheel rim; spinning the wheel allows you to check this, as well as wheel trueness. Apply the brakes and make sure they're functioning.

◆ Do a quick check for tightness of major bolts, stem and seat post, and pedals.

◆ Check to make sure your tires are inflated to their recommended pressure.

---

sided slopes requires some new techniques. Everything you learn will increase your confidence and ability—even when you're just blasting through city traffic, past that poor guy stuck at the light in his $50,000 four-wheel-drive vehicle.

General Technique

The salient, ever-present characteristic of trail riding is that you're on a loose surface. Only on solid rock does traction approach that of pavement. It's not a problem—in fact, you don't even have to think of it as *worse* than pavement—it's just different. The simple axiom for loose-surface technique is, If you don't want to slide, ride slowly; if you want to ride quickly, be ready to slide. After some practice, sliding will become fun.

Skidding. On a flat, loose surface, you're most likely to slide, or skid, when turning or stopping. If you're riding in a straight line and suddenly attempt to turn, often the front tire will "wash out": that is, it will break loose and slide straight on, and you will fall over toward the inside of the turn. However, if the front washes out and then suddenly catches traction, you can be pitched forward over the bike. The easiest form of prevention is to slow down *before* you turn, then accelerate as you leave the turn. As you gain experience, you'll be able to balance the bike on the edge of sliding. If you feel the front start to wash out, steering into the slide and applying more rear brake can sometimes correct it.

Braking. If you're riding straight and suddenly grab both brake levers, the tires will lock up and skid. A front wheel that isn't rotating has no directional control, so you have little say about what happens next. Usually the front will grab dirt and pitch the bike sideways, and over you go. Again, the best solution is to avoid sudden stops—easier said than done at times. But remember to squeeze the brake levers rather than grabbing them. A smoothly applied brake will be able to grip *past* the point where a grabbed brake would lock. After some practice, you'll actually be able to tell by the sound the tires are making if they're about to lock up.

Unlike in a car, on a bike you have to modulate the braking force front to rear, since you have one lever for each brake. The front tire usually provides the majority of your stopping force, since the weight of the bike shifts forward under braking, but you must at all times retain steerage. If you're braking hard but starting to lose steering, you need to back off on the front brake.

As a kid, you probably remember performing wild skids by locking the rear wheel alone; it was fun and utterly controllable. You can do the same thing with your mountain bike, even using rear wheel skids to steer into a turn once you've practiced. However, such maneuvers should *never* be done on trails, since rapid erosion will result. Stick to dirt roads for hot-rodding.

Shifting. Selecting the right gear combination for the terrain will become second nature after a while. But a couple of guidelines will give you a head start. First, watch your chain alignment: you should never have the chain in the outer chainring and the inner rear cog, since this forces the chain to run at an angle, stressing the links and the derailleurs. The same thing happens when the inner chainring is combined with the outer cog. Second, always try to shift just before you have to. Down-shifting in the middle of climbing a steep hill stresses the driveline, and leaving the bike in a low gear while coasting down a hill will result in wild spinning of the pedals at the bottom unless you shift up first.

For much trail riding, you can leave the chain in the middle chainring in front, using the seven or eight (whichever your bike has) rear cogs to vary your gearing and speed. For smooth, fast roads or pavement, use the big chainring, and for steep hills or rough, slow sections, shift to the small chainring.

ETIQUETTE FOR MOUNTAIN BIKERS

Although bicycles are much less invasive than ATVs or giant four-wheel-drive trucks, they do introduce the sounds of machinery to many otherwise quiet corners of our world. To a hiker, a bicycle can be a pretty jarring sight careening down the trail, and many trails have been quite rightfully closed to mountain bikes. Others, however, which could easily be shared, are under intense scrutiny because of the selfish behavior of a few riders. This antagonism is bad, because we are in danger of losing many wild places *altogether*, not just to a few special-interest groups.

Mountain bikers should always yield to hikers and horseback riders (yes, horses create their own problems, but that's another issue). Go out of your way to promote good will, and you're more likely to see it returned.

Help keep trails in good shape. Don't ride off them or cut switchbacks, and don't plow furrows with your new V-brakes. Save hot-dogging for established race courses. If a steep trail section looks like it's getting torn up by spinning tires, get off the bike and walk it.

Finally—get involved. Join, vote, call, and write letters. See the list of organizations in the resources section at the end of this chapter.

Hills

Hills are the yin and yang of cycling: going down is fun, but getting up can be excruciating. Yet cresting a killer hill you previously had to walk up is exhilarating. Fortunately mountain bikes are designed to deal with both yin and yang as efficiently as possible.

Going down a big, smooth, gradual slope is generally a matter of hanging on, whooping loudly, and watching you don't run into anything at the bottom. When the slope gets steeper and rougher, it's time to slow down and concentrate on control. With proper technique you can ride a bike down a slope you'd have trouble walking.

When edging over the lip of a serious drop, shift your weight all the way back on the seat and crouch over the bike. This maneuver keeps your center of gravity low and behind the front axle, so you won't hurtle over the bars if you hit a rock. Ride both brakes, to keep your speed to no more than a fast walking pace. The front brake can take quite a bit of force under these conditions, but your steering will be slow—so if you have to avoid a rock or make a sharp turn, you might need to ease off the brakes, steer as the bike accelerates around the obstruction or curve, then quickly squeeze again to slow down. If you have to cross a rut, try to do it at as close to perpendicular as possible, get off the brakes so the bike rolls quickly across the gap, then re-brake. If you hit an obstruction at too low a speed, the bike will jerk to a stop and unbalance you instantly. Remember to shift to a higher gear before you start down.

If you're faced with a short, but *really* steep drop-off, such as a rock ledge, you can sometimes ride it by exaggerating the above technique: slide all the way off the back of the saddle, so your stomach can rest on it, to shift your weight as far to the rear as possible. Ride the brakes, but don't actually brake as you drop off the lip; wait until your rear wheel has cleared the ledge to slow the bike. Keep the pedals level with each other, so neither catches on the lip.

Climbing a steep hill is physically harder than descending one, but not so fraught with the danger of a faceplant. The key is a smooth ascent, rather than a mad dash toward the base followed by tractionless spinning halfway up.

Approach the hill in the small chainring, but in a middle rear cog so you can keep a medium speed without frantic pedaling. Just as the hill steepens, shift into low gear and crouch over the bicycle, arms bent to weight the front wheel sufficiently, but *stay seated* on the front of the saddle, to maintain traction on the rear wheel. You are seeking a balance—if you unweight the front wheel it will lift and lose steering control, but if you move too far forward or stand up the rear wheel will spin.

Try to avoid staring at the ground right in front of your tire; you should be watching the hill ahead to pick the smoothest line. If you lose your line or start to spin, try an alternate line or a last few pedal strokes before putting a foot down—it's almost impossible to start again in the middle of a steep hill.

Side Slopes

Trails that traverse the sides of hills are, in some ways, the trickiest of all special terrains. Nothing can put you on your side faster than having the bike go *zip* out from under you on a canted trail covered with ball-bearing gravel.

Riding on a trail section that slopes steeply sideways involves much of the same physics as leaning into a turn. The bike is riding on the edges of the tires, at the limit of its sideways traction. Obviously, then, you don't want to do anything to upset that delicate edge. That includes braking, pedaling, sneezing, or *anything*.

The first mistake many people make is staying as far toward the uphill edge of the trail as they can. While it may be comforting psychologically, this is usually where the slope is steepest, and it increases the likelihood of sliding. Better to stay in the middle, or even toward the outside of the trail, where it's a little more level. If you can coast through the off-camber section, keep the outside (downhill) pedal down and most of your weight on that. Stay in the saddle.

If you absolutely have to brake, gently apply the rear brake to maintain steering in the front, and be ready to plant your uphill foot instantly to avoid a spill.

Often, the inside of sharp turns on slopes or even flat trails will develop a similar off-camber nature. Take the outside line to avoid it; if you can't, try leaning your body into the turn while keeping the bike more upright.

Rocks

One of the trickiest, though usually least risky, situations is a dry stream bed or other area covered with loose, smooth stones, from baseball- to basketball-size. The secret to a successful crossing of such a stretch is a little more speed than you think you'd need. Momentum is the ticket to overcoming the medium-size rocks into which your front wheel will inevitably stray, and which would stop you if you lacked the speed to bounce right over them (by the way, these are colloquially known as baby heads). Don't even try to pick a particular line through the rocks; stay loose and go with the bounces, trying to avoid only the biggest boulders and keeping up the momentum. If you do get bounced straight into a foot-tall rock, punch the pedals and lift the front wheel to ride over the rock (or, if it's too big, over the side of it), rather than getting bounced violently at a right angle.

Riding Through Water

We're talking about *shallow* water, of course.

Although it's fun and harmless to blast through puddles and stream crossings if they are only a few inches deep, keep in mind that water makes an extremely effective brake as it gets deeper. If you don't know exactly what the depth is, or what the bottom conditions are as you approach a crossing, get off the bike and scout first. Slow-moving water up to about a foot deep can be ridden through easily if entered at a walking pace in a low gear, as long as the bottom is firm. Your feet will get wet, of course, but resist the temptation to try to get across on momentum with your feet in the air—a lot more of you will get wet if you do.

Soft Sand and Mud

If you've seen an old adventure movie in which some hapless extra gets sucked to his death by quicksand, you'll know what it's like to ride a bike into a patch of soft sand: it just seems to suck the bicycle to a stop and bury it to the hubs. While there is a limit to what you can pedal through, a couple of things will help for

To ride through sand successfully, start with good momentum. Pedal strongly, with a firm grip on the bars, and keep your weight to the rear to anticipate the braking action of the sand.

shallow sand or dry, sandy creekbed crossings.

First, try a little momentum. Not a lot, but hit the sand at a jogging pace, pedaling strongly, with a firm grip on the bars. Keep your weight to the rear to anticipate the braking action of the sand. If the front tire slews off course—which it almost certainly will—don't try to jerk it back on line; carve a gentle turn back in the right direction while still pedaling. If there are previous ruts through the sand, take them—the surface is likely to be a little more compacted there.

For extensive sand crossings, the trick is to "air down" the tires: if you normally run 50 pounds, try deflating them to 40 or even 30 pounds. This increases the width of the tread and helps the tire to float on a soft surface; it also, however, makes the tires much more prone to pinch flats, which occur when an impact pinches the tube against the rim. Never ride on a hard surface with underinflated tires.

Hitting a patch of mud often results in the same swift stop as with sand, but the effects are messier. Gooey mud quickly fills the tread of your tires, rendering them utterly tractionless, and you go nowhere. You have to put your foot down and—*splorp.*

Similar techniques are called for in both mud and sand: a little momentum, a firm hand on the bars, and determination. Airing down tires, however, is rarely effective in mud. The only possibility for traction is if your tires can bite down through the mud to firmer ground. For this reason, tires designed specifically for racing in muddy conditions are fairly narrow, with aggressive tread.

Extra consideration for the trail is called for after a rain. It's tempting to go around a new mud puddle, but the result is a wider, uglier trail that is more susceptible to erosion.

RAILS-TO-TRAILS

All across the country, groups are getting together to convert old railway lines to foot and bike trails. Overseen by the parent nonprofit Rails-to-Trails Conservancy are some 700 currently open trails, with many more in the works. The conservancy offers a number of publications, including *700 Great Rail Trails.* Contact them at 1400 Sixteenth Street, NW, Suite 300, Washington, DC 20036; (202) 797-5400.

Care and Repair

Although infinitely simpler than an automobile or even a motorcycle, a bicycle is a fairly complex machine compared to, say, a canoe or kayak. Some people are happy to pump up their own tires, letting the bike shop do anything else (usually after something breaks). But they're missing the satisfaction and confidence that comes from being able to maintain and repair your own equipment. And a bicycle that is maintained, rather than just repaired, will break less often and work better all the time.

The nice thing about maintaining your own bike is that you can start simple, then work up to more-complex operations. For example, just keeping your chain in good shape will eliminate about 50 percent of common bike maladies. The other nice thing is that you can experiment with working on various items, knowing that you can always run sheepishly to the bike shop if you have two springs and a pulley left over after overhauling your own derailleur.

What You'll Need

The one item that will make working on your bike effortless is a good repair stand, which holds the bike at a comfortable working height so that you can spin the wheels and work the pedals, shifters, and brakes. They start at around $60, but really sturdy models begin at about $130. If you hesitate to spend that much to begin with, a decent substitute is to hang a couple of straps from the rafters in your garage, or even from a tree. They can be hooked over the handlebars and seat to suspend the bike at a convenient height.

Although you can get by with the multi-tool you carry on rides, it's nice to have real tools for the shop. A good starter set would include:

- Hex wrenches in 2-, 3-, 4-, 5-, and 6-mm sizes
- Box wrenches in 8-, 9-, and 10-mm sizes
- Chain removal tool
- Spoke wrench
- Screwdrivers
- Two nylon tire levers
- Floor pump with gauge
- Wire cutters
- Solvent-bath chain cleaner

A good bike stand is invaluable for thorough washing and repair of your machine.

Chain Maintenance

The chain has the most moving parts of any component on your bike—over 100 tiny little axles in the links, each of which must move freely and cleanly to avoid squeaking, poor shifting, jumped cogs, and the dreaded "chain suck," which occurs when the chain, as it is coming out the bottom of the chainwheel, gets sucked up into the frame and jams.

The best way to avoid all these problems and extend the life of your chain is to keep it clean, preferably after every ride. The minimal approach is to spray degreaser on the chain, wrap a rag or sponge around the top length of the chain, and rotate the pedals backward, then use a toothbrush to remove grit. Much better are the inexpensive plastic chain cleaners (around $20), which run the chain through a solvent bath and a set of brushes, thoroughly removing debris and grease. Allow the chain to dry, then apply a chain lubricant sparingly but thoroughly to each link. Let it soak in for a few minutes, then run the chain through a rag once more to remove excess lubricant.

General Cleaning

You might or might not be a fanatic about appearance, but a clean bike is a better-working bike. After a muddy or dusty ride, or every couple of months (whichever comes first, as they say), try this quick procedure.

Put the bike on the repair stand outside, or hang it from a tree. Clean the chain as described above, but don't lube it yet. Release the brake cables at the brakes to open the calipers, and remove the wheels. Fill a bucket with warm water and a good car wash concentrate. With a big sponge, drip the soapy water over the bike, then scrub from the top down; first the nice parts, such as the frame, seat and bars, then the dirtier areas. Use a soft toothbrush for small grimy areas. Clean the wheels separately. To rinse, use a gentle flow from a hose. Most bikes today use sealed bearings on the hubs, bottom bracket, and headset, but you don't want to shoot water too forcefully at them.

Dry the bike with a towel, then take a rag and scrub in between the chainrings and cogs with a brisk back-and-forth motion. If your wheel rims show signs of gummy brake deposits, use acetone or a similar solvent to remove it. Replace the wheels in the frame, making sure they are centered and completely seated before clamping the quick-releases and reconnecting the brakes. When the chain is dry, lube it; also lube the pivot points on the derailleurs and brakes.

Shifters and Cables

Whether your bike is equipped with grip-type shifters or levers, it should shift crisply to each gear. After some use, the cable might stretch, resulting in slow changes, especially when moving to a larger cog or chainring. On the back of the rear derailleur, where the cable housing connects to it, is a barrel adjuster that can be used to take up the slack; for the front derailleur, use the adjuster on the shifter end of the cable. Turn the adjuster counterclockwise a bit at a time and retry the shifter until it works properly again. Look at the cassette from behind and make sure the chain lines up straight from each cog through the derailleur pulleys.

Periodically the cables should be lubed where they pass through the cable housings. To do this, shift to the smallest cog and the smallest chainring. The cables should have enough slack so you can pull or pry the cable housing ends from their sockets in the frame.

Slide the housing sections up the cables and apply a light coat of lubricant to the cable.

Brakes

Your brakes should work easily and smoothly, without chattering or squealing. If you have to pull the levers almost back to the grips to stop, the brakes need adjusting. Look at the brake pads; they will likely be riding too far from the rim. Use the adjusters at the levers to take up slack until the pads ride just clear of the rims. The lever pull should now be short and taut.

If the brakes squeal when you apply them, the pads might not be "toed in" properly. Ideally, the brake pads should contact the rims squarely, except that the trailing end—that is, the end of the pad toward the front of the bike—should angle in a bit, so that it contacts first. You can adjust the toe-in using the proper-size Allen and box wrenches (usually a 5 mm and 10 mm, respectively) to loosen the pad and rotate it slightly. Make sure the brake doesn't rub the tire sidewall as it's applied, or it will quickly destroy the tire. Your pads also have grooves in them to serve as wear indicators—when the grooves are gone, it's time to replace the pads.

Incidentally, Shimano originally said that their V-brakes needed no toe-in at all, but riders with V-brakes that began howling loudly soon discovered that a bit of toe-in stopped the noise.

Wheels

Although they combine light weight and resiliency with extreme ruggedness and durability, your wheels are subject to a constant, delicate balance of tension. They rely completely on the spokes for their integrity. Each spoke must be maintained at the proper tension to ensure that the wheel stays "true," meaning it spins without wobbling.

The easiest way to check your wheels is to put the bike on the stand and spin a wheel while looking along the rim. A brake pad makes a good reference point, or you can brace a fingertip close to the rim. The wheel should spin evenly; an out-of-true spot will show up as a "blip" as it goes past the pad or your finger. Slow the wheel and locate exactly where the spot is. If the wheel is bent to the right, use your spoke wrench to tighten the spoke nipple on the left side of the wheel. Tighten only a half-turn at a time, and loosen the opposite spoke the same amount. You might have to adjust several spokes along the affected area to true it. It helps to mark the out-of-true spot with chalk, so you don't have to relocate it every time you spin the rim to check it. Go slowly and check your progress often. If the wheel doesn't respond to minor adjustments, take it to a repair shop.

Tires and Tubes

Pssssssssst. Uh-oh. Depending on where and how hard you ride, that can be an all-too-familiar sound. Although you can minimize flats, you'll never eliminate them completely. Might as well learn how to deal with them as efficiently as possible.

You should use tire levers to ease the process. Remove the wheel from the frame and, starting opposite the valve stem, hook the levers under the bead of the tire and pull it over the rim (you can also just pull it over with your hands, although on narrower rims this may not be possible). Work around to the stem; as you progress the tire will come free readily. At this point you can leave the other bead on the rim and pull the tube out, freeing the stem last. If no leak is obvious, inflate the tube a bit (it will blow up to an alarming diameter very quickly, but don't worry). If you can, submerge the tube in water to look for escaping bubbles; if not, just listen closely and, when you hear a hiss, rub a little saliva on the spot to pinpoint it. Deflate the tube, and follow the directions in your patch kit to repair it, unless of course you are replacing it.

If no cause for the flat is obvious, carefully feel inside the tire casing to find any minuscule thorns or stickers. Inflate the tube just enough to give it some shape, and reinsert it into the wheel, stem first. Then hook the bead

When repairing a flat, use a tire lever to pry one tire bead loose in order to remove the tube.

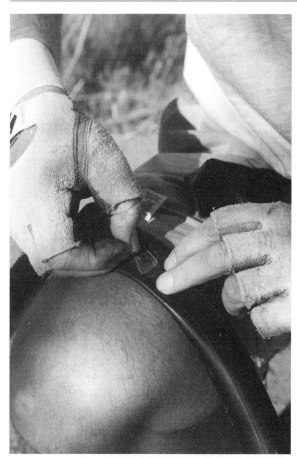

Once you've located the hole by immersing the tube in water (look for bubbles) or listening for that all-telling hiss, dry the tube and cover the hole with a patch from your patch kit. If adhesion is a problem, roughen the tube with a little square of sandpaper first.

back over the rim, this time starting at the stem and working both ways around to the opposite side of the rim. Make sure the tube doesn't get pinched between rim and tire bead. Reinflate the tire, and you're finished.

◆ EXPERT TIP: THE DOLLAR-BILL TIRE FIX
The worst thing that can happen far from home is a split in the tire casing itself when you have no spare tire. Here's a tip: Insert a folded dollar bill behind the split, to protect the exposed tube. Paper money is very tough, and such a temporary fix will often get you home. Note: A $50 bill is no stronger than a $1 bill, so save your money.

Fitness and Health
Getting in Shape
Bicycling is so convenient, so accessible, that there is really no need for substitute exercises to prepare yourself for it. Just get out and pedal. Start slow and short, and work up speed and distance gradually. When something feels sore, lay off for a few days.

Sports such as running or swimming translate well to biking, mostly because of the cardiovascular advantage runners and swimmers enjoy. But never assume that because you run 10 miles a day, you can jump on a bike and do 100. Your heart and lungs will be ready, but bicycling stresses different muscle groups.

Bicycling shares with swimming the advantage of being extremely low-impact: it is easy on joints and cartilage. Since the motion is smooth, if you pay attention to your body there is little risk of sudden or serious muscle or tendon injury. Do be careful of your knees, though—especially if you're using clipless pedals. Proper alignment is critical to avoid problems there.

First Aid
The statement that bicycling is low-impact has one exception—if what you impact is the *road*.

Bicyclists use the rather benign-sounding term *road rash* to describe the most common cycling injury— a nasty, ugly scrape caused by using portions of one's body to stop by means of friction against the surface on which you were riding. Road rashes seem to be most common on thighs, calves, and forearms, and they can turn many square inches of skin into hamburger.

Male cyclists have for years been ribbed about shaving their legs. While a small part of the reason behind the practice lies in aerodynamics, the major benefit is to make it easier to clean out bloody scrapes. The best-accepted treatment for road scrapes is to thoroughly clean the wound with antiseptic soap and plenty of clean water, being sure to remove all debris, then just leave it open to heal. If it is really deep, the scrape can be covered with a sterile gauze pad.

Take a look at first aid kits especially for biking— they include road rash ointments, for example, and some of them are made to strap onto the bike frame.

Sore knees are not uncommon for new cyclists. If the problem persists more than a couple of weeks, first check the bike. Make sure the seat is properly adjusted

◆ **EXPERT TIP—THE DISPOSABLE HELMET**
Bicycling helmets are getting lighter and more comfortable all the time, yet the level of protection they offer is actually rising. One thing to keep in mind, though: after a single hard fall, one in which your helmet plays a significant role in saving your head, it's time for a new helmet. The structure of modern helmets is not designed to stand up to repeated impacts (this includes motorcycle helmets). Sure, you could gamble after a nasty whack that the next one might involve the other side of the helmet, but is your head worth it?

(see Fitting the Bicycle section, p. 211). If you have clipless pedals, they should be checked at your bike shop for proper fit, which is critical. Try going back to regular pedals and toe clips for a while if you're not sure. Still no relief? Time to see a doctor—preferably one who specializes in sports medicine.

Finding Places to Ride

The advent of mountain biking caught land-use managers completely by surprise. Suddenly there were bicycles where none had been before. Complaints soon followed, from hikers and equestrians who were used to having trails to themselves. The result was that bicycles were banned from many areas altogether.

Recently, bicyclists have become more organized at advocating their sport, but the issue is still sensitive. It doesn't take many selfish bikers racing down quiet mountain trails to spoil the experience for others. Keep this in mind when you ride.

Contact your local land agencies to find out where you can ride in your area. Guidebooks are helpful too, but rules can change, so double-check before you go.

Where Mountain Biking Can Lead You
Touring

Touring by bicycle is an immensely fulfilling way to see the countryside. Shunning the noise and pollution of the automobile, you experience the landscape on a vastly more intimate level. Yet considerable distances are feasible—many average cyclists have completed tours across the United States.

Cycle touring is versatile. You can load up a full set of camping equipment and be totally self-sufficient, or carry just essentials and go inn to inn. Cycle touring by mountain bike is that much more versatile, since both city and country are within your grasp.

Weight-obsessed road bicyclists used to joke about doing "charge-card tours"—carry nothing but a credit card, charge your food, charge the hotel each night, charge a new set of clothes each day. . . .

That's going a bit far; however, a great introduction to bike touring is the inn-to-inn ride. You carry the basics on the bike—clothes, toiletries, and so forth—and stay in B&Bs or inns each night. Such tours are easy in the more-populated areas of the United States and are an enjoyable way to experience other countries, such as Great Britain, France, and Switzerland.

Another good way to get started is to go with an organized group tour. The logistics are taken care of for you—even the bike is provided if you prefer—and the tours usually provide a "sag wagon"—a van and crew that carries the heavy gear, picks up pooped riders, and provides repairs. The tour operators know where to go for the best experiences, and many people enjoy sharing the ride with new friends.

When you're ready to try your own fully loaded tour, pick an overnight destination to gain experience. Once you have honed your equipment list and gotten proficient at packing, you can begin extending your tours. Depending on how much water you need to carry, it is easy to stay out fully self-contained for a week or more.

There are two ways to carry luggage with a bicycle. You can install racks on the bike itself and use panniers, or you can tow a lightweight trailer. Each system has advantages and disadvantages.

With racks and panniers, everything is on the bike—you don't have to worry about clearance on tight trails or in traffic, and there are no extra tires to puncture and fewer parts to maintain or repair. A bike with racks will fit on a standard bicycle carrier, and the whole setup is lighter than a bike and trailer. On the other hand, the handling of the bicycle is definitely affected when you add all the gear weight directly to the bike. That extra weight also puts extra stress on the tires, bearings, and other components.

A trailer puts most of the weight on a separate set of wheels, reducing strain on the bike considerably. A bicycle towing a properly designed trailer will handle

TOP 5

CLASSIC NORTH AMERICAN BIKING TRIPS

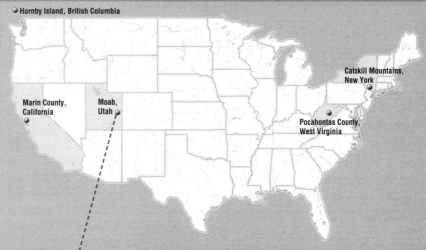

Hornby Island, British Columbia

Catskill Mountains, New York

Marin County, California

Moab, Utah

Pocahontas County, West Virginia

CLIFF LEIGHT

Moab, Utah.

- *Moab, Utah.* It may seem obvious to the initiated, but the awesome slickrock country of southeastern Utah is still Mecca to mountain bikers.

- *Marin County, California.* There's a reason this was the birthplace of the mountain bike. Spectacular coasts and forests, great cafes, and the infamous Repack downhill run.

- *Pocahontas County, West Virginia.* Tired of biking in areas hostile to mountain bikes? West Virginia *loves* mountain bikers. Begin at the Snowshoe or Silver Creek Mountain biking centers, with over 100 miles of trails and lots of services, including rentals and lodging. And don't miss the nearby West Virginia Fat Tire Festival each August, hosted by the Elk River Touring Center.

- *Catskill Mountains, New York.* From Ski Plattekill, where you can enjoy unlimited use (for a small fee) of the ski lifts for endless downhill fun, to Minnewaska State Park, where carriage roads lead to spectacular vistas, the Catskills offer incredible riding variety.

- *Hornby Island, British Columbia.* Hornby is an entire island singularly devoted to the subculture of mountain biking, with its epicenter at the summertime Hornby Island Bike Fest. A network of single-track trails webs the island—you can bike from one shore to the other without leaving dirt. Nude beaches offer riders the chance to compare road rash.

better under most circumstances than a rack-equipped bike. If you already own a bike with no rack attachment points, a trailer is a painless way to get into touring. Keep in mind, though, the added complexity of another set of wheels, hubs, and frame parts.

No matter how you decide to carry the load, remember that more weight means longer stopping distances and reduced maneuverability.

Racks and Panniers

Bicycles designed to be used with racks have attachment points built in to the frame. These are threaded holes that take the proper-size Allen-keyed bolts. While it's possible to mount a rack to a frame that isn't so equipped, by using clamp-on fittings, the latter won't be as secure—particularly considering the extra vibration they can be subjected to on a mountain bike.

A bicycle designed for racks won't have suspension. There's just no way to carry a lot of weight on a wheel that's designed to move up and down. On the other hand, touring bicycles typically have very relaxed frame geometry, which helps soak up bumps using the resiliency of the frame material.

Rear pannier racks for bicycles have changed very little over the years. They incorporate a platform over the rear wheel with an attachment to the seat stays and a triangulated frame extending down to the dropouts (where the wheels mount) on each side. Front pannier racks used to be similar, but carrying weight so high over the front wheel seriously affected a bike's handling. Now the standard front rack is a low-mount, which is centered at about the level of the wheel hub, with a brace arcing over the wheel to connect the two sides of the rack. This system lowers by several inches the point at which the weight of the front panniers balances.

Panniers come in many sizes; rear ones, for example, start at around 800 cubic inches and go up to nearly

---

PUSHING THE ENVELOPE: GETTING STARTED TOURING

Steve Bellemaire and Pierre Bouchard, two average French-Canadian guys just out of college and ready for some new scenery, decided to do a little bicycle touring. They left home in Quebec and headed west to see what they could find. Five years, 18 countries, and thirty-five *thousand* miles later, they are still out there.

3,000 cubic inches. You'll need to have an idea of your goals for touring to pick the right size—weekenders don't need the space demanded by continent-crossers. Do make sure you get bags designed for mountain bikes, with strong attachment systems to resist bouncing off the rack.

Bicycle touring is similar to backpacking in terms of the space available for gear. A set of front and rear panniers plus a handlebar bag, along with a stuff sack carried on top of the rear rack, can add up to around 5,000–6,000 cubic inches—about the capacity of a full-size backpack. If you have backpacked, you will probably have everything you need to head out on your bicycle. If not, Chapter 2 has some excellent tips on selecting gear for backpacking, many of which—tents, sleeping bags, stoves, and other accessories—are the same for bike touring. And see Chapter 12, p. 279, for tips on single-burner cooking, as well as food and nutrition tips for outdoor activities.

When you pack the bike for a tour, remember to keep most of the weight over the rear wheels, which don't carry the stress of turning. Usually, somewhere between 60 and 70 percent of the total load should be in the rear. Load too much back there, though, and the bike will handle like a pickup truck with 2 tons of bricks in the bed. Also remember to keep heavy items low in the packs; the top of the rear rack should be reserved for your sleeping bag or other bulky but light gear.

Remember that your center of gravity will inevitably be higher when loaded, even with low-rider front racks. Don't try to corner like you do with an empty bike.

Trailers

Perhaps the greatest advantage of trailers is that they can be used with almost any bike. If you've sunk a bunch of money into a full-suspension racer and suddenly get an urge to bicycle across Canada, you can find trailers that will work with your bike. Since the trend in mountain bikes today is toward performance and low weight, very few come equipped with rack attachment points—but with a trailer, you can have your high-performance and touring bike rolled into one.

Traditionally, most bike trailers have used two wheels, but a new design specifically for mountain bikes uses just one. The BOB (Beast Of Burden) has a single wheel in the back of the trailer, which reduces

RICH ETCHBERGER

Bicycle touring provides an intimacy with the landscape you don't get sealed in a car at 60 miles an hour.

☞ KID QUOTIENT

Are you kidding? This section should be titled "Adult Quotient." Kids and bikes were made for each other. In fact, let's be frank: kids invented mountain bikes decades before adult marketing wizards thought of them, by simply thrashing whatever they had over hill and dale.

Do keep in mind, though, that serious mountain bike riding demands a well-developed sense of balance, so take it easy on young children—stick to pretty smooth dirt roads rather than single-track. Once kids get past eight or nine years of age, your only problem is going to be getting them to take it easy on you. Some tips for mountain bike riding for kids:

☞ For kids too young to ride, consider a trailer. A trailer does limit the terrain you can cross, but the child is well-protected, comfortable, and close to the ground. Also available are child seats that attach to the bike behind you—but keep in mind that these will affect your center of gravity.

☞ A really neat idea for kids on the cusp of being able to pedal their own bike is a "third wheel" trailer: an extra wheel with its own seat, handlebar and pedals that attaches to your bike seatpost, allowing the child to enjoy the sensation of participating.

☞ Just as full-size mountain bikes have become more sophisticated, so have those intended for children, up to and including suspension models. You now have the option of spending several hundred dollars on a bike your kid will outgrow in about six months. Let your budget be your guide.

☞ One thing you should never scrimp on, of course, is protection: buy the best child's helmet you can afford, even if you're using a trailer. And once your child starts riding, supplement the helmet with knee and elbow guards, if possible.

☞ When riding with young kids on their own bikes, keep it short—a mile or two at most.

☞ Take along plenty of snacks and water.

(See Chapter 11 for more tips on adventuring outdoors with kids.)

Wind them up and let them go: kids and bikes were made for each other.

the overall width of the trailer and helps it follow directly in the bike's own track. The front of the BOB attaches to the rear dropouts on the bike—even on a full-suspension design—and swivels in two directions, to follow dips and ridges. Tubular chromoly steel and an expanded mesh bottom hold the cargo in place; an optional nylon bag further protects your gear. The BOB will easily carry 50 pounds, thus bringing long-range touring within reach of almost any bicycle.

Two or one, the wheels on any trailer will probably differ in size from those on the bike, so you'll have to carry the correct spare tubes.

When traveling with a trailer, remember that although the weight isn't riding directly on the bike, it will affect you. You won't be able to lean into turns as much, and rough going will hamper even the most agile trailer. Experiment before you go to determine how far your trailer articulates; you might have to walk the rig through steep washouts to avoid bending the connections.

Pack the trailer just as you would panniers: heavy items on the bottom, light ones on top. If you're using a two-wheeled trailer, keep most of the weight centered over the wheels.

Tips for Touring

First, try to avoid setting rigid goals for each day's ride. The idea is to have fun, so detours and extra stops should be part of the plan. An intrinsic facet of bicycle touring is the amount of interest you'll get from passersby; be ready to answer a lot of questions (and be invited for a lot of drinks). Even jaded residents in heavily touristed areas seem curious about bicyclists; it's a refreshing change for them from the Winnebago-and-video-camera set.

Preventative maintenance takes on a new importance when you're far from home. See p. 214 for a preride checklist, which must be followed carefully each morning. Many cycle tourers install heavy-duty tubes before trips; the additional rotating weight is not critical when the bike is heavily loaded anyway.

Racing

Since the early days of clunkers sliding down the Repack Trail in Marin County, mountain bike racing has evolved into a sophisticated, multifaceted sport. Factory downhill racers ride one-off prototype bikes that cost $10,000–$15,000 to build; even serious production full-suspension bikes can top $5,000.

However, you don't need to drop big bucks to get started racing—bicycles suitable for cross-country competition start at under $1,000. And since regional races are divided into classes, you will compete against those of similar ability right from the start. See the resources section below for organizations that sponsor races.

Further Resources for Mountain Biking
Books

Zinn and the Art of Mountain Bike Maintenance, by Lennard Zinn (Boulder, CO: VeloPress, 1996).

Mountain Biking North America's Best 100 Ski Resorts, by Delaine Fragnoli (Bishop, CA: Fine Edge Productions, 1996).

Periodicals

Mountain Biker, P.O. Box 53666, Boulder, CO 80322-5833; (800) 462-0206.

Dirt Rag, 181 Saxonburg Rd., Pittsburg, PA 15238; (412) 767-9920; Dirtrag1@aol.com.

Mountain Bike, P.O. Box 7347, Red Oak, IA 51591-0347; (515) 242-0291; MtnBikeDM@aol.com.

Organizations

International Mountain Bicycling Association (IMBA), P.O. Box 7578, Boulder, CO 80306; (303) 545-9011; IMBA@aol.com; www.outdoorlink.org/IMBA/.

American Mountain Bike Association (AMBA), Box 278, Chandler, AZ 85244; (602) 496-4124.

National Off-Road Bicycle Association (NORBA), One Olympic Plaza, Colorado Springs, CO 80909; (719) 578-4717 or (800) 726-6722; norba@usacycling.com; www.adventuresports.com/asap/norba.htm.

WOMBATS (Women's Mountain Biking and Tea Society), Box 757, Fairfax, CA 94978; jacquie@wombats.org; www.wombats.org.

Schools

Nantahala Outdoor Center, 41 Highway 19 West, Bryson City, NC 28713; (704) 488-6737.

"Look how nuts these guys are."

—Anonymous bystander at a mid-1970s cyclocross race, viewing the first homemade mountain bikes

PART 2 OUTDOOR SKILLS

Chapter 9
MAP AND COMPASS MAGIC

The Zen of Navigation

There is actually no great trick to navigating in the wilderness, whether on land or at sea—it's just a matter of knowing where you are.

And the trick to knowing where you are is paying attention to where you've been.

Perhaps this sounds like an over-simplification. Maybe. But that's what makes navigation so beautiful. There are no complicated theorems and there's nothing to memorize. Just pay attention to the world you travel through. Be aware of details, and your chances of getting where you want to go, and back, are pretty good. The "sixth sense" of direction that we hear tales about is simply the ability to combine this constant awareness with applied good judgment.

So before you buy a map, compass, and Global Positioning System device and charge off into the wilderness, the first thing you need to do is work on that "sixth sense," and to do that you need well-honed standard senses: those of sight, smell, hearing, and relative timing. These

are the tools that are most important to navigation; you can lose a compass, a map can be completely wrong, and a GPS can go kaput, but you'll always have at your disposal at least one or more of your natural senses.

The information in this chapter was adapted from The Essential Wilderness Navigator, *by David Seidman (Camden, ME: Ragged Mountain Press, 1995).*

Senses and Sensibility

A good sense to start with is the ability to judge time relative to distance. Although defining a distance as 20 miles can be just as useful as saying it's a two-day walk, time is sometimes a handier way to express distance, because we all have a natural sense of rhythm. We sense time with an internal pulse, and it is the one "extra" sense that has been substantiated. Humans are just one of many species having a sense of the passage of time. A bee, for instance, not only knows its travel times but can share this information with other bees. Many of us can tell the time with fair accuracy without looking at our watches, or estimate how long we have been at a job. It's a good, built-in measuring system, though it can be distorted by fatigue, heightened physical effort, or low blood sugar.

Sight is an obvious sense to develop for navigation skills, but don't neglect sounds and smells—while

most of our information for direction finding is gathered by sight, studies show that smells and sounds can also be useful. Smells, in particular, imprint themselves in our memories. Some people claim that smell is the most sensitive sense, and the last to leave us in death. So open your ears and nose as well as your eyes when observing landmarks on the trail.

We all have the ability to remember these details and apply them to finding our way, although some people seem better able to do so than others. One person might remember routes previously traveled by relying on specific landmarks. In driving to a friend's house, he would turn left at the faded blue building, right at the park with broken swings, and left at the dry cleaners.

But someone else might use a different method, keeping track of how

---

JUST FOLLOW YOUR NOSE

"A researcher at the University of Manchester, in England, found that when magnets were placed on the right side of a person's head the subject would tend to veer, by an obvious amount, to the right. Magnets on the left side drew the subjects to the left. This proved, or so the researchers claimed, that we are affected by magnetic fields."
—David Seidman on the discovery that we all have traces of iron located in the ethmoid bone (between the eyes). From *The Essential Wilderness Navigator* (Ragged Mountain Press, 1995).

long she's traveled and in what direction. To get to that same friend's house, she might use her internal clock to drive in one direction for three minutes, turn left, go a short distance at 40 miles an hour, turn right, and then drive for 30 seconds before making a final left turn.

Neither system is superior, and neither navigator gets lost more often than the other. There are different ways of navigating, and very often the two methods overlap. The former navigator's affinity for distinct landmarks may be the reason some people have trouble reading maps. Since they respond better to complicated chains of landmarks, and not to distances and direction (the defining parameters of a map), they may be at a disadvantage when the only navigational help is a map. Or maybe it's just that some people are less likely to be exposed to map reading when young. Certainly, anyone can become an expert map reader.

Basic Pre-Compass Skills

You will learn soon enough about the technical methods of finding your way—with a map, a compass, and perhaps a GPS—but the next step is learning a few basic nontechnical navigation skills that you will need before you learn the ways of magnetic and true north.

Find a Reference Point

When you enter a situation in which you might get lost—such as starting a hike or sea kayaking trip—go no farther until you have picked out an easily identifiable feature that can be used as a reference. This can be a single point, such as a mountain, or a line, such as a coast, river, or road. It can be something that is always visible to you as you travel, or something whose existence is known only from a map. Without delay, locate yourself in terms of direction and distance to

"Good judgment is no less present in the art of getting around without getting lost—more often known as navigating—than in other fields of endeavor. Technique is fine and necessary, but it's a foundation of good, informed judgment that keeps you out of trouble."

—David Seidman, *The Essential Wilderness Navigator*

this reference. Now you know where your starting point is, and your journey can begin. Your job is to keep track of your reference and where you are in relation to it (you don't necessarily have to know which way is North, South, East, or West). You will do this whether you navigate naturally, with just your own senses, or mechanically, with a map and compass (using a map, compass, and GPS always involves your natural senses anyway).

If the reference is a point, your routes will radiate from it, spiral around it, or vector past it. If it is a line, think of it as a tree with branches leading out from and back to a central trunk, or with vines hanging parallel to the trunk.

A line is the handier of the two references because it lets you set up crossing lines (the tree's branches),

giving you four primary directions. With a compass, the main reference line is the north/south axis, from which you also get a perpendicular east/west line. You can do the same with any other reference line, such as a river, a range of hills, a coastline, a logging road, or a valley.

Repeating patterns offer another type of reference line. These can be used in place of one central line, or for keeping yourself on course when not in sight of your main reference. A pattern could be any series of features. This could be a series of rivers running parallel—or roughly so—to your main reference line. Or it could be streams running into your reference line.

Pick a Route

When traveling toward a goal, as from a cabin to a lake, decide on a route and try to stick to it; if midcourse corrections are necessary, make them deliberate, definite, and retraceable. This way, even if you can't find the lake, you'll at least be able to retrace your steps to the cabin. If you just go out there and wander aimlessly, you might miss the lake *and* the cabin.

A lake is a good target to aim for because it's big. In contrast, a campsite by the lake would be a poor target, for it is relatively small and therefore harder to find. If you aimed for the campsite, how would you know in which direction to turn if you missed it? You wouldn't.

When you intend to wander about rather than strike off toward a specific goal, you won't be able to stick to a set route. For this sort of traveling, an easily recognizable reference is even more important, because it's all you'll have. You can use either a point or a line. With a point, head out and back over ever-increasing distances, gathering information and improving your knowledge of the area on each excursion. Or, if the point is always visible, like a tall mountain or building, you can wander as you will. As long as it stays in sight, you're okay. When you're working with a line, stay to one side of it while walking generally in a direction that is parallel to it.

Imagine the Big Picture

While underway, think of what you and the world around you would look like to a bird overhead. Envision the larger picture and your place in it. This is your mental map. Do this by constantly updating your position through the use of sequential landmarks, or by keeping track of how far and in what directions you have gone.

Experiment with your internal rhythm, your natural ability to judge time. Experiments show that many animals can measure time to an accuracy of 0.3 percent. In other words, they would be no more than three minutes out after a period of 16 hours, 40 minutes.

Humans do not have such extraordinary accuracy in judging time. But with practice, we can come to within 10 minutes (although not consistently) in 12 hours—which is good enough in a pinch. Sharpen your skills at estimating time by trying to guess what time it is, or how long you have been doing something. By all means take your watch with you on the trail, but tune in your innate sense of time as you tune in your other senses.

Above all, pay attention to the world you are moving through. Every once in a while, stop talking on the trail or listening to that cassette player. Watch where you are going and don't just follow the boots or boat ahead of you. Look around continually.

Problems can arise when our mental maps are influenced by our prejudices, imagination, and unique perceptions. For instance, you might

> **WHEN IN DOUBT . . .**
> It's always safest to stay on marked roads or trails, not leaving them unless you are positive you know where you are and how to reach your destination. Trails may seem boring, but they offer the best chance of taking you where you want to go and back. (In many wilderness areas, we are requested to stay on marked trails for another reason: to minimize disturbance to surrounding areas, which may include nesting sites, thin soil vulnerable to erosion, or scarce habitat.)

read a guidebook that comments on landmarks on a trail, or on sights along the way. From the written words, you'll build an image of what you expect to see. But it's not always what you'll find. If you force yourself to be objective, though, you'll probably have to agree that what was written was an accurate description, and that it was you who read something else into it. This is perfectly normal. We concoct images not so much from the way things are, but the way we think they are, or should be. The two are often very different. Be prepared to revise your preconceptions when they no longer fit your surroundings.

Learn to Get Lost Properly

It's human nature to deny that you're lost. The coverup urge is stronger in some of us than others. Yet it is important to recognize this shortcoming and acknowledge it when you feel the slight twinge of being disoriented. Don't wait for the twinge to develop into the full-blown panic of being lost. Ignoring the reality that you *may* be lost is a good way to get thoroughly lost.

CHRISTINE ERIKSON

Identifiable patterns are a big help in orienting yourself, and your map, with the surroundings.

"Asking for directions and picking up local knowledge is half the fun of getting lost. You get colorful advice and meet lots of new folks (whom you will never be able to find again, of course). Don't be too anxious to believe what others tell you. Integrate local knowledge with what you know for sure from your map or compass. And be wary of asking strangers to pinpoint a place on your map. Many are not familiar with maps. They'll jab a finger down anywhere, just to save face and get rid of you."

—David Seidman, *The Essential Wilderness Navigator*

What to do when you forgot to mark your reference point, yammered too much on the trail, and suddenly you get that twinge—*Where am I?*

- *The first thing is to stop.* Don't keep on walking and making things worse.
- *Admit that you are lost* and that it's probably only going to be a small inconvenience, not a life-threatening episode.
- *Calm yourself.* Sit down, have a bite to eat, clear your head.
- *Begin looking for clues.* Try to remember where you have been during the last half-hour. Envision the last point where you were sure of your position. Look around for features that might provide a reference.
- *If nothing registers,* but you think that you are not far from somewhere familiar, start navigating from scratch. Identify a landmark, or make one, for your current position so you can find it again. Head out from there to explore a little at a time, returning if unsuccessful.

We often have no control over the causes of our getting lost. But there is no excuse for getting lost when it can be prevented—that is, when it is only our failure to use good navigational techniques that gets us into trouble.

Cartography 101

Like books, maps are meant to be read, but a map gives you all its information at once instead of doling it out a page at a time. The trick is to learn how to absorb it in small doses.

The first thing to learn about maps is that no map can be taken at pure face value. Maps have been called "truth compressed into symbols," and they need to be interpreted. They're not exact replicas, and therefore imagination is required to get out what has been put in. So don't take any map literally, particularly with regard to road and trail systems, which tend to change between map editions. Look for significant features within the general pattern of details. Good navigators will plan ahead for alternative routes and landmarks, in case what a map shows doesn't seem to be there.

Types of Maps

The most useful maps for outdoor recreation are topographic maps. These describe the terrain—the shape of the landscape, its ups and downs—as well as some man-made features. Topographic maps are ideal for hikers, campers, fishermen, cross-country skiers, and anyone else who may forsake the beaten path. They are of value even if you stick to the trails; by painting a more accurate perception of the landscape, they offer you a better chance to keep track of your position. Planimetric maps, such as road maps and maps of forests printed by the U.S. Forest Service, will often show trails and roads that are not on topographics, and topographics will show natural features you won't find on a planimetric. If you can, carry both types, or transfer information to your topographic map before leaving.

There are topographic maps, or "topos," covering almost every square inch of the United States, U.S. territories and protectorates, Canada, and a good part of the remaining world. In the United States they are compiled by the U.S. Geological Survey (USGS), which now has a library of about 54,000 topos. You can purchase topos directly from the USGS, by mail or phone, or from local outdoor shops (see the resources section at the end of this chapter for map sources).

To make ordering easy, each state has been subdivided into quadrangles—commonly known as "quads"—based on lines of longitude and latitude. Simply choose the quad you want from a free state index. Quads are named for towns or prominent geographical features. USGS maps are made to extremely high standards: at least 90 percent of all points surveyed must be accurate to within one-fiftieth of an inch on the map. You won't miss much with a USGS topo for your guide. Costing only a few dollars, the maps are true bargains.

If you're traveling by water, maps are properly called charts. Nautical charts carry very little information about the land (usually only along the shore) but a lot about the water and what is under it. They show depths, bottom features, what the bottom is made of, and the positions of navigational aids, such as buoys and lighthouses. The National Ocean Service compiles charts for coastal waters and the Great Lakes. The Army Corps of Engineers covers the navigable inland waterways, lakes, and rivers. For camping by canoe or kayak you can get by with just a topo, but when heading into open or coastal waters, carry a nautical chart, too. (For sources, see the resources list at the end of this chapter.)

Map Symbols

If we are successfully to interpret a map's message, we must first understand its language. And the language of maps is symbols. It's a purely visual and very descriptive means of communication that is done with a surprisingly modest vocabulary of lines, colors, and forms.

Since cartographers try to make symbols look like what they represent, most are self-explanatory—a campsite is a tent, a school is a box with a bell on top, a church has a cross, a well is a windmill. This is why the symbols used in USGS topos are so similar to those found on maps from private companies, as well as those from other nations. Canadian topos are very handy in that a complete list of symbol descriptions is printed on each

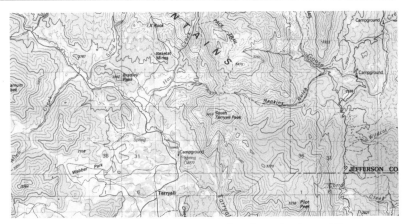

A USGS topographic map, covering South Tarryall Peak in Pike National Forest, Colorado.

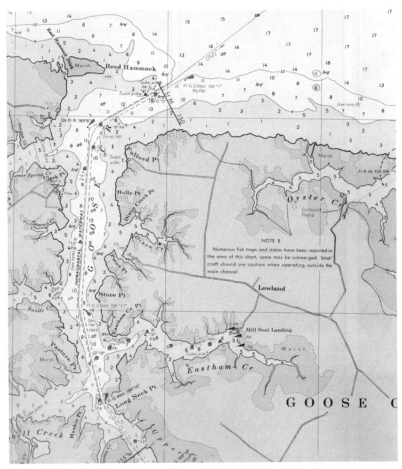

A nautical chart covering a portion of Goose Creek Island, North Carolina.

map. U.S. maps have only a few listed. Definitely send away for the free pamphlet *Topographical Map Symbols.* For U.S. nautical charts, a complete book of symbols can be found in the NOS publication *Chart No. 1.* (For sources for these booklets, see the resources list.)

Color is used to enhance information or make it more obvious. The USGS has standardized its use of color as follows:

Black: Man-made features, such as roads, trails, railroads, or buildings. Names are always in black.

Blue: Waterways, such as lakes, rivers, canals, swamps, and marshes. The contour lines of glaciers and permanent snowfields are also blue.

Brown: Contour lines and elevations.

Green: Substantial vegetation, woods, scrub, orchards, or groves.

White: No vegetation, cleared land, or areas with sparse or scattered foliage.

Red: Larger, more important roads and surveying lines.

Purple: Overprinting. Revisions added from aerial photos but not yet field-checked.

Map Series

The USGS categorizes maps by "series" according to how much land is covered—or more precisely, how many degrees of latitude and longitude. The most common is the 7.5-minute series. This means that each side of the map is 7.5 minutes, or one-eighth of a degree, long. Navigators divide the world into degrees. Each degree consists of 60 minutes. A 7.5-minute-series map is 7.5 minutes of latitude high by 7.5 minutes of longitude wide. There is also a 15-minute series covering 15 minutes (one-quarter of a degree) of latitude,

and 15 minutes of longitude, although this series is getting less common.

Every 2.5 minutes of latitude is marked by a fine black line along the right (eastern) and left (western) borders. Latitude in the northern hemisphere increases as you go north, toward the top of the map. Degrees are usually omitted, with only minutes and seconds shown. There are 60 seconds in a minute. Every 2.5 minutes of longitude is marked by a fine black line along the top and bottom borders. Longitude in the western hemisphere increases as you go toward the left (west) side of the map—again, with only minutes and seconds shown.

Scale

In order to make the most use of any map, you need to know its scale, or how the distances on the map relate to true distance. For example, in a map with a scale of 1:24,000, one unit of measurement on the map equals 24,000 units full-sized. The USGS uses the 1:24,000 scale for most of its 7.5-minute series. One inch equals 2,000 feet—about three-eighths of a mile. The 15-minute series maps use a scale of 1:62,500—1 inch equals a mile. The third common scale for U.S. topos is 1:250,000 (1 inch equals 4 miles), which gives you the "big picture" you need for expedition planning. Most maps will include a graphic bar scale showing the inch-to-miles ratio.

A common confusion arises over whether a map is properly called "small-scale" or "large-scale." Which is which?

Here's an easy way to remember:

Small scale = little detail (bigger number, such as 1:250,000; good for the overall picture).

Large scale = big detail (smaller number, such as 1:24,000; good for precise route planning).

Contour Lines

Features such as roads, towns, lakes, even rivers and streams, are pretty easy to spot on any map. Look at a topographic map, and you will see not only those obvious features, but also a lot of squiggly brown lines. Pretty soon it will be easy to decipher representations of hills, mountains, canyons, cliffs, and plains from all those lines.

The lines are called contour lines, and they are not randomly drawn to approximate a hill or cliff or sinkhole. Each line follows an exact *elevation*. Elevations are measured in feet or meters above a constant. Originally this constant was the mean (average) level of the nearest ocean, which was not always easy to determine. Now we use the "National Geodetic Vertical Datum of 1929," a preset sea level that works everywhere. But don't worry about the details; just think of elevation as "height above sea level."

If a contour line on a topo map is labeled 800 feet, every point on that line has an elevation above sea level of 800 feet. If you put together a lot of these contour lines, with each indicating a different elevation, stacking them or working them around each other, you'll have a fair depiction of the land around you. To keep such a map from getting too crowded with numbers, only every fourth or fifth contour line is labeled with its elevation. This line is a contour index, and is double the thickness of the other, intermediate contour lines. You may have to follow the contour index with your fin-

ger for a while to find the printed elevation, but it's always there.

All contour lines (including contour indexes) are separated by a uniform vertical distance. Each line is an equal change of elevation from the next, and this standard interval, the contour interval, is noted below the bar scale in the map's margin. If the contour interval is 20 feet, consecutive contour lines will increase or decrease in height by 20 feet from their nearest neighbors. Using the contour interval, you can tell the elevation of intermediate lines. Just add or subtract the intervals to or from the closest index. Contour intervals vary from map to map.

HIGH ELEVATION OR ALTITUDE?

A common confusion arises over nomenclature regarding attaining high elevation and altitude. Here's the rule:

If you're at high elevation, you should have your mountaineering boots on. If you're at high altitude, you'd better be in an airplane.

Estimating Distance
For Walkers

Maps show distance as if the world's surface were flat, which it isn't, and can lead you into underestimating how far you might have to travel. There's a big difference between

SOME RULES FOR INTERPRETING CONTOURS

- There is no beginning or end to a contour line. It is an irregularly shaped closed loop. If you could walk along a contour line you would go neither uphill nor down. You would eventually arrive at your starting point.
- The steeper the slope, the closer the spacing between lines. An extreme example of this is a vertical cliff, where contour lines fall right on top of one another on the map.
- Your trail is going uphill if it regularly crosses contour lines of increasing elevation. Conversely, it's going downhill if it crosses contour lines of decreasing elevation.
- Valleys (ravines or gullies) usually show up as a series of V-shaped lines pointing toward higher ground. Sometimes the V rounds into a U if the valley is gentle.
- Ridges or spurs can be shaped like a series of Vs (sharp) or Us (rounded) pointing toward lower ground.

- To determine if a group of U-shaped or V-shaped contours shows a ridge or a valley, check the elevation of contour indexes to see which way the ground is sloping, or check to see if a stream runs down the middle or side of the Vs.
- A pass or saddle in a ridge has higher contour lines on each side, giving it a characteristic hourglass shape.
- Contour lines running up one side of a river or stream, crossing it, and then running back down the other side form a U or a V that points upstream. If the lines are U-shaped, the valley through which the river flows is reasonably broad and flat-bottomed. If the lines are V-shaped, the valley is fairly narrow and the ground rises steeply on each side of the river.
- A peak is depicted by the innermost ring of a near-concentric pattern of contour lines. It is often marked with an × and its elevation.

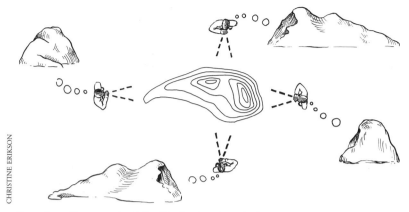

Four views of a mountain. A familiar landmark can look very different when viewed from an unfamiliar perspective.

CHRISTINE ERIKSON

Navigating with Your Map

To successfully use a map or chart as a direction-finding tool, you'll have to correlate it to the world it represents. Luckily, it is very easy to orient a map—all you have to do is look around and align the map with the surrounding landscape. Once this relationship is established, you can plan routes and explore with confidence. Begin by looking for easily identifiable features, such as peaks, clearings, buildings, and roads, that are also on the map. Compare what you see to what is on the map, turning the map until it relates to what you see. If something is ahead of you, it should be ahead of your position on the map. If something is to your right, it should be to the right of your position on the map. Once this is done, you're oriented. By keeping the map oriented as you travel, with the direction of travel forward, you will find it easier to relate what you see to what

uphill (or downhill) miles and level ones, and the steeper the slope's gradient, the greater the difference becomes.

How far can you go in a given time? Back in 1892, W. Naismith, a Scottish mountaineer, came up with the following rule: An hour for every 3 miles on the map, with an additional hour for every 2,000 feet of ascent. (See Chapter 1, p. 3, for further information on hiking pace.)

That works out to 20 minutes per mile on an easy trail with no pack, which is probably only feasible for an athletic hiker on level terrain. Most people can average only 2 miles per hour (30 minutes per mile) under good conditions, without constant hurrying. With a full pack, or on a difficult trail, this can increase to at least 40 minutes per mile, and a full pack on a tough trail will push your time up to 60 minutes. A hike that measures 15 miles on the flat map and ascends 4,000 feet in the real world will take about nine hours nonstop, and you'd need at least an extra hour for rest stops. That's a reasonable estimate, but the variables are endless. Marshy or rough terrain,

thick undergrowth, dense woods, elevation, fatigue, snow or rain, extreme heat or cold, wind, darkness, and pack weight all take their toll. You also lose speed on descents, although only about half as much. And groups of hikers move more slowly than solo hikers.

You'll find, though, that distances to be covered tend to be underestimated before starting out, and distances traveled are overestimated when walking them. To work out your rate of progress, measure elapsed times and distances covered whenever you can. Write these figures down for use later, when all you have is your sense of time and a few pebbles in your pocket.

For Boaters

Sea kayakers and canoeists on large lakes can estimate their distance to an object appearing just over the horizon by the method shown in the illustration at the top of p. 236. You need only know the height of your eye above the flat surface between you and the horizon, and the height of the object on the horizon (for that you will need to consult your chart).

(See illustration at the top of p. 236.)

READING BETWEEN THE LINES

When interpreting a map for planning purposes, be careful not to expect too much exact detail from the map. For example, maps with wide contour intervals, such as 50 feet, often won't show a feature such as a 30- or 40-foot cliff, which may be totally impassable to a hiker. Or conversely, a series of tightly compressed contour lines on the map may be a sheer cliff, or a navigable if steep scramble.

The important thing to remember is that no matter how good your map is and no matter how good you are at reading maps, some things you can't know until you get there, so try to leave yourself options and backup routes along the way.

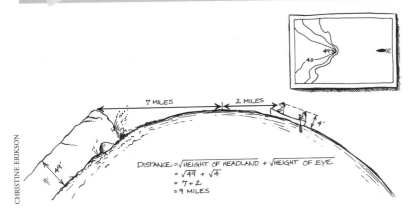

$$DISTANCE = \sqrt{HEIGHT\ OF\ HEADLAND} + \sqrt{HEIGHT\ OF\ EYE}$$
$$= \sqrt{49} + \sqrt{4}$$
$$= 7 + 2$$
$$= 9\ MILES$$

7 MILES   2 MILES

Estimating distance to an object just over the horizon.

is on the map, and thus reduce the risk of getting lost. Orienting the map will also give you an approximate idea of your location, although not as accurately as with a landmark or crossed lines of reference.

The only problem with keeping a map oriented is that you might wind up holding it at an angle, or even upside down, making it difficult to read names, notes, or symbols. So some folks hold their maps right side up (that is, north on top; on almost all maps, geographic north will be at the top), regardless of the direction they are facing. This can take a lot of visual juggling, because when heading south, for example, anything to your left on the map is actually to your right. Interpreting the world in reverse can be very disorienting, but some people can and prefer to do it. In general, orienting the map is the better and more reliable method, allowing you to determine directions directly.

For trail hiking in fair weather, a map and a good "sixth sense" is all you'll need for successful navigation. But for off-trail, backcountry exploration, for winter and harsh-condition wilderness travel, and for ocean excursions, you will want to use a compass, with or without a map.

Compass Work

The golden rule is, Trust your compass. It's one of the most reliable manmade tools ever invented. If its case is intact, and you're not holding it or (on a boat) haven't mounted it too close to any ferrous metal or electronics, chances are your compass is correct.

Most of us have owned a compass, and many of us have been lost at least once while carrying one. So, as you can guess, merely being able to find

north won't, by itself, keep you from getting lost. You have to keep track of north (and therefore south, east, and west) from the very start of, and all through, your journey. A compass shows only directions, not position.

What else will a compass do?

- By checking the compass to find your intended direction of travel when first heading out, you'll be able to tell later (when you're not quite sure of things) whether you're coming or going.
- A compass will keep you pointed in the right direction in the absence of a trail or markers.
- If you know your general direction of travel, a compass can help you make the right choice at a fork in the trail.
- We tend to veer to one side as we walk, but a compass will keep you headed in a straight line.
- A compass can help you walk toward something you can't see because it's either too far off or obscured by trees, fog,

Orient your map to match what you see.

snow, or darkness.

- When you deviate from your direct course to get around an obstruction, a compass will help (only help) get you back on track toward your destination.

- If you walk a direct compass course to somewhere, you can return by following that course in reverse.

- You can return to your starting point even if you followed no fixed outward route by keeping track of each change of direction and distance traveled.

- A compass will get you back to a line of reference, like a road or river, after you've been wandering haphazardly.

The workings of a compass could hardly be simpler. The needle pivots in response to the earth's magnetic field and stops when it's aligned with the forces. The needle's north end

then points to an encircling ring marked in degrees, thereby enabling us to determine directions.

But although the workings of a compass are straightforward, when you choose a compass you need to consider a few points. For instance, how good and accurate an instrument will you need? Compasses vary in price (and accuracy and quality), from under $6 to over $200. In general, go with a compass that will give you directions within 2–4 degrees (one degree of error will put you only about 100 feet off your mark after a 1-mile walk; a 4-degree error will put you off by 400 feet, an acceptable margin for most navigation by foot in the wilderness). And be sure to buy a compass that is rugged enough to take abuse, compact enough to fit in a pocket, and simple enough to use easily. Spending more money for a compass will not necessarily get you greater accuracy. Anything over $20 means paying for extra options, not precision. The desired accuracy can be found in all but the cheapest models.

Declination

Compasses are simple—they point north, right? Well, yes, and no.

The most important thing to learn when navigating with a compass is the phenomenon of declination, which is the varia-

tion between "true north" and "magnetic north." True north, or geographic north, is the "top" axis of the world, its exact geographic center (also known as the North Pole). Magnetic north is at the northern end of the planet's magnetic core, which is west of Baffin Island. Maps and charts use geographic north, but the compass is attracted to magnetic north. On land maps the difference in degrees between the two is the declination, and the amount you must therefore compensate for when using both a map and compass varies with your position on the globe.

Declination is measured in degrees and designated either east (E) or west (W). There are places where declination is greater, places where it is less, and places (such as parts of Michigan, Indiana, Ohio, Kentucky,

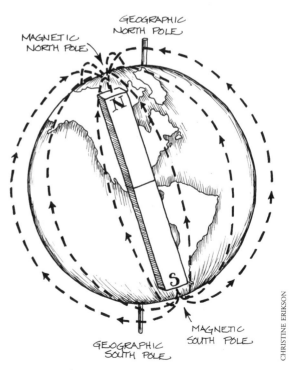

Declination is the variation between "true" and "magnetic" north.

Tennessee, and North and South Carolina) where it doesn't exist at all, because those points are aligned so that the magnetic pole is directly between them and the geographic north pole. You must consult the most current topo map available—no more than a decade or so old—which will have the region's declination marked in the legend (declination gradually changes over time as magnetic north shifts). When you take a bearing and translate it to your map you will need to compensate for the declination if your compass does not have a declination-compensation feature.

Types of Compass

There are three basic types of compass.

Fixed-dial compass. In these simplest of compasses, a needle is free to pivot on a bearing and rotate within a case marked in degrees running clockwise around its circumference. They are good basic tools, and because there is not much to them, they tend to be cheaper than other types. They are not used for serious navigation, however.

Baseplate compass. A baseplate compass is nothing more than a simple fixed-dial compass mounted so that it rotates on a transparent baseplate. The rotating case is marked in 2- or 5-degree increments running clockwise around its dial. The clear center portion of the case has north-south orienting lines, as well as an orienting arrow that makes it easy to align the needle with the "N" mark (north). What makes the baseplate compass so practical is that it gives you a choice of indicating directions either with or without the use of numbered degrees. The base doubles as a protractor for determining bearings from a map, and its edges are inscribed with map scales or a ruler to measure map distances. Almost all include an adjustment you can use to compensate for declination, converting magnetic bearings to geographic ones that can be used directly with a map. Other nice but unnecessary additions are a magnifier to help read small map details, a clinometer to see how steep a slope is, and a sighting mirror. This last item is a flip-up mirror with a vertical line inscribed down its center. You raise the mirror, hold the compass so the line on the mirror crosses the needle's pivot point, look across the notched sight, and read the dial's reflection where the mirror's line crosses it. Baseplate compasses are simple to use, easy to refer to in the field, extremely versatile, and relatively inexpensive—which is why they should be your first choice when purchasing a compass.

Magnetic-card compass. In the magnetic-card compass, needle and dial are joined (on a card) to rotate as one unit. The advantage is that "N" (north) on the card is always aligned with magnetic north, so there are no extra steps needed to orient the compass before taking a reading. The disadvantage is that you can't compensate for declination. Conversions

An inexpensive fixed-dial compass that will hang from a zipper pull.

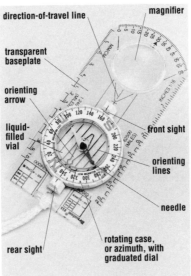

Baseplate compass.

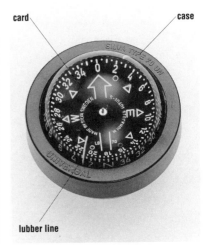

Auto/marine magnetic card compass.

from magnetic readings to geographic, or back, must be done by arithmetic. If all your route finding will be done with compass alone, and no maps, the magnetic-card type will work quite well. Compasses that mount to sea kayaks are usually this type. No matter what direction the kayak is pointing, the lubber line, a mark on the forward part of the case in line with the sights, will show that bearing. All you have to do is mount the compass so you can view the lubber line directly, and so that the central pivot of the compass and the lubber line are parallel to the kayak's centerline. This ensures that both compass and boat point in the same direction.

Following are some basic tips for navigating with only a compass both with and without landmarks, as well as basic navigation using a map and compass together. For space consideration, the methods are described for baseplate compasses only. Consider these only brief introductions to the art of navigation. For an excellent treatment of all types of navigation, see *The Essential Wilderness Navigator,* by David Seidman (Ragged Mountain Press, 1995).

Basics of Compass-Only Navigation

After you set your baseplate compass for local declination following your manufacturer's directions (although for compass-only navigation you don't need to necessarily worry about declination, it's a good idea to get in the habit so you don't forget about it when using a map) you are ready to take your first bearing. A bearing is the direction of one object from another, measured as a horizontal angle from a fixed baseline.

To take a direct bearing at a landmark, hold your compass level at your waist or chest. Point the direction-of-travel line at the landmark. Turn the case until the orienting arrow is aligned with the north end of the needle. Read the bearing where the direction-of-travel line intersects the case's dial (careful navigators always use a three-digit notation for bearings, such as "060 degrees").

A direct bearing relative to your starting point, or baseline, is used to accomplish point-to-point navigation, following landmarks. Another useful bearing to shoot at the same time as your direct bearing is the back bearing, which is simply the exact opposite bearing of your direct, or forward, bearing. You can take your back bearing off your compass, or use arithmetic (if the direct bearing is 180 or greater, subtract 180 degrees; if the direct bearing is less than 180 degrees, add 180 degrees).

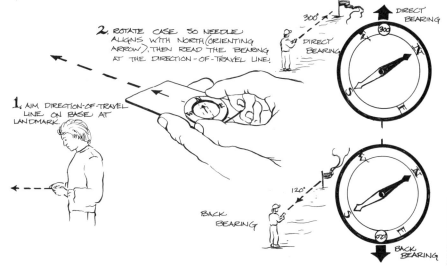

Use of baseplate compass to take direct and back bearings.

CHRISTINE ERIKSON

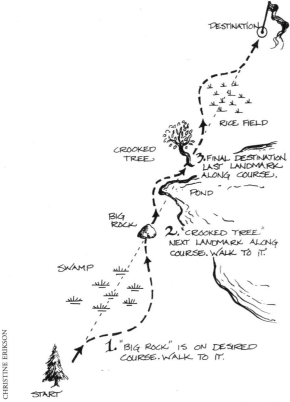

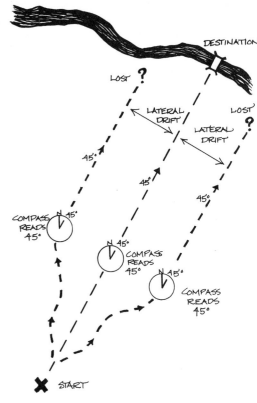

Divide long trips into short segments. Pick landmarks that will not be obscured, and try to keep your intermediate goal and starting point in view as you walk.

To avoid lateral drift, continue to check both direct and back bearings.

Point-to-Point Navigation Using Landmarks

If you want to get from point A to point B, and you have a landmark in sight from which you can take a bearing, you might be able get to point B using just your landmark. But because as you travel to point B you will have to move around obstacles such as trees, rocks, or ponds, you might lose sight of your landmark, and thus your natural point of reference. Before you start, take a direct bearing off your landmark (tip: write it down). Then, look ahead to the limit of your vision and pick a distinct intermediate landmark on that same direct bearing.

Walk to that landmark (you don't need to watch your compass as you walk—you might get hurt!) by the easiest route. Once there, look back to your original starting point to check your orientation, then find or make a recognizable landmark at your new location (so that you can refer back to it after the next leg).

Now take out your compass and sight along your original bearing (toward your final destination landmark, which you may not be able to see), look along that sightline for another intermediate landmark, and walk to it by the easiest route. Getting the picture? Continue making intermedi-

ate legs, checking your positions fore and aft following each leg. To return to your baseline, you repeat the process using your back bearing.

Lateral Drift

All that sounds rather complex. Why not just shoot a direct bearing and walk in a straight line to it without stopping? Because while walking a "straight line" you will invariably stray to one side or the other—"lateral drift." This is why you make intermediate legs, and check your position fore and aft. If while trying to walk a straight line you stray to one side, you will continue to walk to your direct bearing position, but because your have strayed to one side, your new back bearing will differ from your original back bearing. To correct your line of travel, you must shift sideways until your compass reads both your original direct *and* back bearing.

Point-to-Point Navigation Without Landmarks

If while navigating point-to-point you find yourself at an obstacle, but without good landmarks to guide you around to the other side and meet up with your direct bearing (such as in dense swamps, or foggy weather), you can make a series of short, right-angle turns (see illustration, top right).

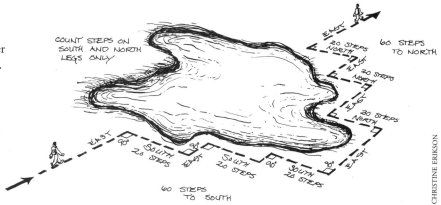

Point-to-point navigation.

CHRISTINE ERIKSON

MAKING AN EMERGENCY COMPASS

Take any piece of iron or steel that is long, thin, and light. Aluminum or yellow metals won't work; only things that rust will do. A pin or needle is perfect, but a straightened paperclip, piece of steel baling wire or barbed wire, or the clip from a pen (careful, some are chrome or aluminum) could also work.

Now, you want that piece of metal to rotate easily. If you are sure that absolutely no drafts will influence it, you can suspend it from a thread. You will get more reliable results, though, if you float the metal on still water using balled-up paper, a wood chip, or a leaf. Gather some water in a *nonmagnetic* container or use a puddle. Place the float on the water, then the metal on it. It will slowly turn to orient itself with magnetic north.

An obstacle may require more elaborate series of "steps," but the principle is the same; just make sure you keep track of the number of steps you take when traveling directly perpendicular to your original course (your distance out from the original course must equal the distance back, no matter how many intermediate doglegs you had to take to get free of the obstacle).

Map-and-Compass Navigation

To make life easier and, indeed, accurate navigation possible, you will need to set your compass for the declination, the number of degrees that your area differs from magnetic north (you must do this, remember, because all maps are based on geographic north; the use of two different northern reference points will cause your navigation to fail, because the true and map versions of north will not match). You can also convert your map to magnetic north, using a protractor

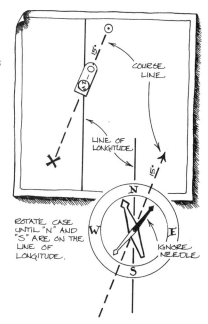

Determining your course.

CHRISTINE ERIKSON

and ruler (see a book such as *The Essential Wilderness Navigator* for instructions).

The first two map-and-compass tasks are based on the assumption that you know where you are on the map. But what if you don't know where you are? A simple explanation of using lines-of-position transects follows. These just tap the surface of map-and-compass skills; with diligent practice and good instruction, you will soon be a master of the art of navigation.

Finding a Course from a Map

On your map, use a pencil and straight edge to draw a course line from your position to your goal; extend the line through them until the line intersects a line of longitude or a vertical border.

Place the compass's baseplate along the course line and its transparent case over a vertical line. Rotate the case until North and South on the dial (not the orienting arrow; for now, ignore the arrow) are parallel to the vertical line. Read the course at the point where the direction-of-travel line intersects the dial.

Hold the compass in front of you and turn your whole body until the needle is enclosed within the orienting arrow's outline. Follow that course.

Locating an Observed Object on the Map

Mark your position on the map. Take a bearing of the object you wish to find on the map. Place a side of the baseplate on your marked position, with the pivot over a geographic north line such as a map border line or a line of longitude. Turn the entire compass by the baseplate until North and South on the dial (not the orienting arrow or lines; ignore the needle) are parallel to the geographic north line. The direction-of-travel line (which you marked when you took the bearing) should be pointing toward the object. Draw a line along the baseplate outward toward the object; you will probably have to extend the line with a ruler or other straight edge.

Locating Yourself on a Map

If don't know where you are on a map, but you can shoot bearings of easily identifiable landmarks around you, you can use them to find yourself on the map.

First, you must take back bearings of two or more landmarks around you (ideally the imaginary lines drawn from those objects to you should intersect at about 90 degrees of angle; angles of more than 120 degrees or less than 60 degrees will not give you an accurate fix on where you are). Then mark those bearings on the map using the same method as in the above two examples, except that when you rotate the case while sighting the bearing, align the orienting arrow with the South end of the needle. Mark the two bearings on the map by placing the baseplate alongside each object to draw the lines (see example). When the lines are drawn, your position should be reasonably close to where the lines intersect.

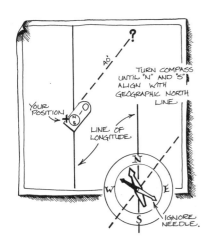

Finding a course from a map.

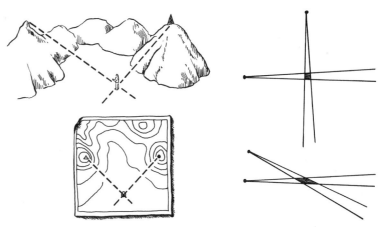

When two bearing cross at an angle near 90 degrees (top) you get a close read (shaded area) of your position. A poor crossing angle (bottom) yields a sloppy position estimate.

Natural Clues

In the lines to the right, Mr. Long-fellow was writing of North America's pilot weed (*Silphium lacinatum*), which does indeed orient its leaves more-or-less north-south when in direct sunlight (apologies to the poet—the plant is not responding as a magnet to magnetic north, but to geographic north).

Like pilot weed, there are hun-dreds of examples in nature, true and false, to which you can look for clues about direc-tion, but be wary of folklore, such as the famous old saying that moss grows on the north side of trees in the Northern Hemi-sphere. Go for a walk in the Pacific Northwest, or in any dense, damp

"Look at this vigorous plant that lifts its head from the meadow, See how its leaves are turned to the north, as true as the magnet . . . "

—from "Evangeline," by Henry Longfellow

forest. You'll see moss on the north, all right. And some on the south, some on the north *and* south, and some on all sides.

Stick with proven facts and with common sense. Consider these com-mon-sense tidbits, and learn to ob-serve similar natural events in your own stomping grounds.

- Game trails often lead to water.
- Swales showing signs of carrying water during storms should lead to brooks, and these should lead to feeder streams, and these should lead ultimately to the stream or river that drains the local watershed. Careful reading of the topo map will tell you roughly where the watershed lim-its are.
- Gulls and other shorebirds seen winging overhead at dusk are probably returning to rookeries on the shore or a near-shore island.
- Locally, the vegetation changes with elevation. (In the Southwest, there is a dramatic example: low-elevation saguaro cactus and mes-quite trees yield to mid-elevation juniper and piñon trees, then oak and ponderosa pine at mid-to-high elevation give way to Dou-glas fir and aspen, and finally spruce and fir at the highest elevations.)

Such knowledge brings its own reward of connection to the land-scape around you. But use such

ALTIMETERS AND GPS RECEIVERS

Sometimes it's difficult to take bearings of or from a shrouded summit. Wouldn't it be nice if there were some other instrument to help mountaineers find their way? Actually, there are two.

An altimeter is nothing more than a portable barometer, an instrument that measures air pressure. The principle is that as you go up, air pressure (the weight of the air) decreases at a uni-form rate. As you descend, it increases. So if you calibrate a barometer to read these changes in pressure as feet (or meters) you can always tell your eleva-tion. For example, if you're sure you're at 1,800 feet, then you must be some-where along the 1,800-foot contour line—which eliminates a lot of real estate. That contour line provides an excellent line of position that can be crossed with a bearing or a natural feature (such as a trail, ridge, stream, or notch) to give you a fix. Unfortunately, uncontrollable factors can throw off an altimeter's readings. These are changes in temperature and variations in air pressure caused by weather.

The best way to get accurate readings is to keep your altimeter at ambient temperature, and reset it as necessary each time you are at a known position—ideally every hour.

For not much more than a good altimeter, you can buy a Global Positioning System (GPS) receiver, which will fix your position *and* your elevation and can be used in fog, darkness, or your tent. Essentially a computer that takes continuous readings from a global satellite position-fixing network, a GPS can tell you: your position by latitude and longitude, or Universal Transverse Mercator (UTM) coordinates; elevation; average speed; direction, distance, and time to your destination; how far off course you are; and the path you've taken so you can follow it back, or retrace it in the future.

Sound great? Well, it is. But don't throw away your map and compass. It's still a gadget made up of microchips, circuit boards, and wire, and it can go wrong. In addition, satellites can be a little off, or their signals may be affected by atmospheric conditions. Overall, the potential for errors within the GPS system is remarkably low. But if you are depending on this alone, that small probability can become a disaster when it happens. The prudent navigator should never rely on a single source for determining position and always verify results by other means.

indicators only as rough guides, looking for confirmation from other sources whenever you can. Signs in the heavens are always dependable. So look up—learn to navigate with the sun and the stars. See *The Essential Wilderness Navigator* for a good start.

Further Resources for Navigation

Books

The Essential Wilderness Navigator, by David Seidman (Camden, ME: Ragged Mountain Press, 1995).

Fundamentals of Kayak Navigation, by David Burch (Old Saybrook, CT: Globe Pequot Press, 1993).

The Map Catalog: Every Kind of Map and Chart on Earth and Even Some Above It, by Joel Makower (New York: Tilden Press, 1992), 3d edition.

Maps

Earth Science Information Center (the map sales branch of the U.S. Geological Survey); (800) USA-MAPS. Topo maps are also widely available at specialty outdoor retailers and map stores.

National Ocean Service, Riverdale, MD 20737; (301) 436-6990. Nautical charts for coastal waters, Great Lakes, and offshore.

Organizations

United States Orienteering Federation, Box 1444, Forest Park, GA 30051.

"Now we return to camp. While eating supper we very naturally speak of better fare, as musty bread and spoiled bacon are not palatable. Soon I see Hawkins down by the boat, taking up the sextant— rather a strange proceeding for him—and I question him concerning it. He replies that he is trying to find the latitude and longitude of the nearest pie."

—John Wesley Powell, *The Exploration of the Colorado River and Its Canyons*

Chapter 10

THE ART AND JOYS OF CAMPING

Into the Wild

Back when tribes were nomadic, "camping" was a full-time activity, a necessity rather than a choice. We've come a long way, certainly, but many people still think of camping as a primitive, uncomfortable, dirty activity to be endured when venturing outdoors for recreation.

But far from a disagreeable necessity, camping can become the most enjoyable centerpiece of your outdoor explorations—indeed, with a little gear and forethought, it can become a high art.

For the purposes of this chapter, we'll span the extremes of camping. At one end of the spectrum is the kind of camping done when traveling into the wilderness by foot, ski, or bike. Though minimalist by nature, camping while exploring solely by muscle power can still be comfortable, even luxurious. Add a small boat, such as raft, canoe, or kayak, for explorations and you've expanded your space and weight-carrying capabilities by quite a bit. At the other end of the spectrum is the kind of

camping people probably do the most because it's easy, it's accessible, and, let's be honest, it's often all we have time for—car camping. Don't worry about being apologetic to the "purist" wilderness campers—car camping is a lot of fun and offers endless possibilities for creative comforts and adaptations to living in the great outdoors.

Some of the information from this chapter was adapted from The Backpacker's Handbook, *Second Edition, by Chris Townsend (Camden, ME: Ragged Mountain Press, 1997);* Simple Tent Camping, *by Zora and David Aiken (Camden, ME: Ragged Mountain Press, 1996); and* Wilderness Skiing and Winter Camping, *by Chris Townsend (Camden, ME: Ragged Mountain Press, 1994).*

The Art of Camping

Camping—living outdoors without a permanent structure for an extended time—is elevated to an art when you move beyond just throwing a bedroll down on a rocky slope and using your boots as a pillow. All it takes is a little creativity and some good gear. The idea is that comfort leads to greater relaxation, and more energy can be spent pursuing such lofty outdoor joys as wildflowers, elusive wood warblers, wild trout on the fly, or a nap. Some outdoor ascetics decry comforts, claiming they diminish the experience of the wilderness. There may be a little bit of truth in that (after all, a motor home with satellite

reception and a diesel generator clanging away is hardly a wilderness experience), but the reality is that opening one's heart and mind to the best parts of the wilderness experience goes far beyond being uncomfortable.

Below are some basic tips on camping, and some not-so-basic tips on camping comfortably. The quality of wilderness experience is up to you.

Choosing a Campsite

This is perhaps the most critical step for making any camp—perhaps less so in a car-accessible campground, but definitely so in the wilderness. And the crucial elements—safety and low-impact—are often lost on most campers, because scenic value is usually considered first.

Some good general tips to consider for campsite selection include

- Use preexisting campsites whenever possible.
- If there are no old campsites, look for open areas with durable ground cover (preferably mineral soil, sand, small gravel, or short grass).
- Groups should split up as much as possible (although in grizzly country, safety dictates staying closer together; see p. 247), form a central camp-kitchen, and take care not to create paths in between (take different routes each trip).
- Never clear any vegetation, or dig any trenches or tentsites, to set up

When camping in desert areas, place your tent on durable surfaces such as rock or sand.

• Always restore any campsite to pristine condition (as if you had never been there) after you strike camp. It only takes a few moments.

Certain ecosystems or areas require particular forethought when setting up camps.

• *Woodlands and forests.* Take care setting up camp under tall or big trees whose falling branches might pose a hazard. Check for and avoid shrubs such as poison ivy or poison oak, or fruiting berry bushes, which might attract bears.

• *Rivers, streams, lakes.* Tempting as it may be, don't camp along the banks of water sources; camp at least 200 feet away. Bankside vegetation provides critical wildlife habitat and erosion control, and camp-related activities trample seedlings and cause soil compaction. Also, there is the obvious flooding danger, and the presence of mosquitoes around standing water (such as lake or river backwaters, and ponds).

• *Deserts.* Look for durable surfaces, such as rock slabs or dry wash beds (but beware of flash floods!), for campsites; in many North American deserts, steer clear of open unvegetated areas with crusty soil, which might be tracts of biologically rich and very delicate cryptobiotic soil—literally, "living soil." Vegetation in desert areas is delicate and slow-growing, and any soil disturbance will eventually lead to erosion. In many parts of the country (not just deserts, although they seem most conspicuous there), watch for scorpions under tents or other camp structures that are being moved or taken down.

camp. If you move any rocks or logs, remember where they were so you can put them back, although for the lowest impact on an ecosystem, campers shouldn't move anything but small rocks (lots of critters that are eaten by bigger critters live under rocks and logs).

• Set up camp at least a quarter-mile from solitary water sources during dry periods; some animals won't come in to drink if you are too close.

- *Timberline and above.* Treat above-timberline ecosystems as you would deserts—essentially, that's what they are, because most of the moisture is locked away in snow most of the year. Harsh winds and deep cold keep growth of plants to a minimum, so trampling any vegetation should be avoided.

- *Ocean or inland sea coasts.* Search carefully for the highest high-tide or storm-tide lines (strips of flotsam), and camp well above them. If in doubt, always camp high. In spring and summer, many species of shorebirds nest in the flotsam of the storm-tide lines, so care should be taken to keep activities away. Also, rocky shores and tide lines are often full of small, hungry arthropods, such as sand fleas.

- *Bear country.* In bear country, the widely held wisdom is to set up the camp kitchen as far from the tents as possible—and in grizzly country, to group the sleeping tents fairly close together, to discourage inquisitive bears and have help close at hand. More tips on bear-country camping are covered on pp. 262–263 and p. 288.

LIGHTNING SAFETY

It's a good idea to avoid camping under the tallest tree in the area: lightning can travel through tree roots, or side-flash if the tree is struck. The good news: occurrences of *tents* being hit by lightning are rare enough to qualify as almost unheard of. (For more lightning safety tips, see p. 269.)

Primal Light: Campfires

Our love of the campfire is strongly atavistic, going back to the times when it provided our only warmth, cooked food, and much-needed security.

Alas, in many wilderness areas campfires are completely banned or severely restricted during certain seasons. And it has become in many respects politically incorrect to build a campfire; with so many millions of people venturing into North Amer-

> *"A thing is right when it tends to preserve the integrity, stability, and beauty of the biotic community. It is wrong when it tends otherwise."*
>
> —Aldo Leopold, *A Sand County Almanac*

ica's wildernesses each year, important forest resources such as deadwood are quickly disappearing, and fire rings in the backcountry are a real eyesore. Certainly, in some ecosystems, such as above-timberline, canyonlands, and deserts, fires have no place at all (at least fires burning local woods).

But campfires are among the joys of camping. What are some ways to enjoy campfires, while still minimizing impact?

- *Car campers should bring their own wood.* Better yet, the wood should be waste-wood, such as lumber from construction sites or from renewable sources such as pruning remains.

- *Never create a new fire ring.* If your campsite has a preexisting fire ring, use it and leave it for the next party. (It's tempting to sanctimoniously destroy existing fire rings, but if each backcountry party on popular routes used the same campsites and fire rings instead of creating new ones at

every hill and dale, wilderness impact would be greatly reduced.) If there are no fire rings at your campsite, use the following formula for a low-impact "Zen fire," courtesy of the National Outdoor Leadership School's Leave No Trace program.

Do not use rocks to make a fire ring; instead, make the fire on a mound of mineral soil that you have built up on a tarp or fire pan (to keep the heat from sterilizing the soil). Use only dead and downed wood, and compromise with a small fire. The last morning, crush and widely scatter the cold ashes with your hands and sweep away signs of the fire site with branches or disguise with debris. Pack out any fire remains that can't be crushed and scattered.

The Kitchen

It is said that the heart of the home is the kitchen, and it's no different at camp. And it's surprisingly easy to make a great camp kitchen, even while backpacking, biking, or boating. Tips that follow concern setting up a great camp; for food and cooking information, see Chapter 12.

Chilling Out

Keeping the food cold is basic to a good camp kitchen. For backpacking or bike touring, most of your food should not need refrigeration—or you can take frozen foods such as cheese or meat, if you use them up in the first day or two. Lightweight, soft insulated cases can hold such items as fruit, Roma tomatoes, celery, carrots, and other produce, keeping them cool; make sure you pack them deep in the pack, where the sun won't heat things up. Eggs in special plastic egg holders (from backpacking stores) will keep well if kept cool.

When kayaking or canoeing, your options expand quite a bit. Soft insulated coolers are indispensable, providing the benefits of regular coolers without the hard, unpackable edges. In kayaks with fore and aft bulkheads (or in some doubles, a center hatch), you can invest some time, money, and ingenuity by lining one compartment with foam and using it as a permanent cooler by utilizing dry ice. (This works only if you're traveling with a group, and other camp gear, such as tents and kitchen necessities, is shared; never let bare dry ice contact your fiberglass or plastic hull.)

Most oar-rafting setups include rowing frames that integrate luxuriously large coolers—even car campers usually don't go for the monster-size 200-quart versions (the average car-camping cooler is about 50-quart). Another rafting tip: You can float your beverage cans (never glass) in mesh bags behind the boat in calm water.

If you use a cooler, here are some good tips for boating as well as car camping.

- Block ice and prefrozen foods work the best; since cold sinks, try to elevate ice and frozen foods if possible.
- At camp, keep the cooler in the shade and leave melted water inside as long as it stays cold; a filled cooler retains cold better than empty air space.
- If space permits, use two coolers, one for beverages and snacks (this will be opened often) and one for the food to be kept cold for meal-

time (less opening, longer cold-keeping).

- Cool your cooler the night before your trip with some ice cubes, and cool everything that goes into it.
- Freeze water (or lemonade or other fruit drinks) in plastic bottles to use as "ice"; you'll have ice to start the camping trip, and cool drinks as it melts. Don't fill containers completely; allow space for expansion.
- For the cooling benefit, and to save at-camp cooking time, prepare and prefreeze food items: chili, meat loaf, pasta sauces, and so on.
- Experiment with dry ice, especially if you take along frozen meat. Wrap the dry ice in layers of newspaper and then plastic (taped up well) and place it on top of your prefrozen food. Don't let bare dry ice come into direct contact with the cooler—it could warp the plastic.

At campgrounds with electric outlets at each tent site, car campers can enjoy another way to keep food cold. Cooler-size portable refrigerators can be operated on 12-volt DC or 120-volt AC. As you drive to camp, connect it to the car's 12-volt system (cigarette lighter plug-in); at camp, switch to the 120-volt cord. You won't have a separate freezer compartment, and it may not hold as much food as a comparable-size cooler, since some interior space is taken by the cooling mechanism and the walls are thicker, for insulating. Still, refrigerators definitely provide a more consistent cold than ice does. (Tip: These refrigerators are designed to chill only a certain number of degrees—usually about 40—below outside air temperature; if it's 95 degrees, your cooler may not get below 55.)

Sinks and Sumps

So-called wilderness camping areas have different levels of amenities. Some have water available at a few central sites. Some have no improvements; your water source is the nearest stream, river, or lake.

For those places where you'll be ferrying water, whether from a tap at the bathhouse or from a natural water source, bring easily carried jugs, preferably 3-gallon square or rectangular bottles (the 5-gallon size is too heavy for most people when full). If you don't have room to pack these, look for soft, collapsible containers at camping stores, although you'll have to treat them carefully, because they do puncture. The 2½-gallon size is a good choice for sea kayaking in Baja or other arid areas where you'll need 5 or more gallons (the general rule is a gallon per person per day, minimum). For backpacking or biking, use good-quality plastic water bottles, such as Nalgene, from outdoor stores; 1- and 2-liter sizes are the most usable. Cheap water bottles always break—a potentially dangerous event when water is scarce.

Kitchen chores require some special attention to water usage and disposal. First rule: Dirty dishwater (gray water) does not drain onto the ground; use a bucket to collect it. At some campgrounds, you'll be asked to empty the bucket into the appropriately named "slop sink," usually outside the bathhouse. In the wilderness, scatter it far from the tent site, where it can filter naturally through sand or soil; you can also dig a "sump" pit in which you can pour your gray water. Remember that animals will be attracted by the smell, so make sure it's far away.

The key to efficient camp cleanup is to wash dishes as quickly as possible with a simple substitute sink/drainer/drain arrangement: make up a container (pot or plastic tub) of soapy water, scrub up your dishes and set them on towels or plastic, then rinse with hot water (for sterilization) from a teapot or pot, pouring over a bucket, other pan, or your sump to collect the gray water. Car campers and rafters may use inflatable sinks, or plastic sinks that incorporate a reservoir of water, a pump and spigot, and a drain. Groups should think about using the three-tub dip system (see sidebar, p. 250).

Sea kayakers have a unique option when there is plenty of wave and tidal activity at the camp. Choose a spot down the beach from your camp, and wade out into the water to scrub out your dishes with salt water and sand (don't use soap); do a final rinse of freshwater out of a small water bottle or kettle. This is an especially good option for areas where freshwater is scarce. Do not use this technique if there are other camps near you or if you plan to stay more than a few days—excessive food debris can wash up downshore.

> ### ♦ CLEANUP TIP FOR CUTTING THE CARBON
> To ease cleanup when cooking over a fire, coat the outside of your pots with liquid dish soap, or a paste of bar soap and water. Black soot will wash off more easily.

In wilderness areas, it's especially important to use the right soaps. Buy the most mild, natural, nonpolluting, and biodegradable products you can find, to keep contaminants out of the water source that ultimately catches your dishwater. And for easy rinsing, greatly dilute your soap. For a whole catalog of "green" products, call Seventh Generation at (800) 456-1177, or look in natural-foods markets. You can also follow Jacques Cousteau's lead and use Shaklee products; look in the White Pages of your local phone directory for a distributor in your area.

Water Purification
Once upon a time, you could dip water from a wilderness stream and drink it safely, but those times and places are mostly gone. In most places, if you're using found water for drinking, cooking, or dishes, you must first treat it in some way, to make it safe. Without some kind of water treatment—boiling, purifica-tion tablets, or filter—you risk severe stomach cramps, vomiting, and diarrhea that can lead to dehydration.

For a discussion of different types of water purification systems for camp use, see Chapter 13.

Pots, Pans, and Utensils
You *could* stick to cold cereal, sandwiches, and finger-food dinners from the grill; then you don't need pots, pans, or plates. That's actually fun for a couple of weekends, but eventually you'll want to fix other foods—really *cooking* outdoors becomes part of the fun. Car campers can bring almost as much kitchen stuff as they like, initially taken straight from cabinet to car; boaters may need to be a bit more conservative; and backpackers and bike tourists, as well as minimalist kayakers and canoeists, can refer to the setups in Chapter 2.

With the exception of cooking over a campfire, cooking outdoors is really not much different from cooking at home—you just have one or two burners instead of four, and your baking might be done in a Dutch oven or a special outdoor baking oven instead of a big, standard convection oven. And of course, the views are better.

So at first raid your pantry for gear, but when camping becomes a regular thing, it's practical to have a "camping only" inventory of pots, utensils, and dishes; ideally, you can keep them packed and ready to go in their own "chuck box" (see p. 251). To outfit your own box, head for the camping store, browse the garage sales, or shop a local flea market. Look for

- Pots with bucket-type bail handles if you want to hang them over a campfire. Camping pots are often sold in sets of graduated sizes; handles either come off or fold in, so pots nest completely into one another for the most compact storage.

- Pots whose lids become frying pans—you just invert them and attach a handle or use a pot lifter.
- Nonstick-coated aluminum cooksets—for easy cleanup.
- One or two medium-to-large frying pans (covers aren't essential; you can always use aluminum foil) and/or a long griddle.
- A cast iron or nonstick-coated aluminum "sandwich cooker" (sometimes called a pie iron), to cook single burgers, meat pies, or dessert mini-pies.
- "Fire sticks"—one giant fork holds six hot dogs at once, and smaller forks or skewers can be used for traditional marshmallow toasting.
- Long-handled spoons, forks, tongs, and spatulas. Look for those with non-heat-conducting handles, and keep a pair of thermal quilted elbow-length mitts for insurance.
- Mismatched stainless flatware found at garage sales, which makes excellent campware, as do plastic or metal plates and old (thick) ceramic or plastic insulated mugs. (Many campers use paper plates, but the cost in the long run is much higher than buying reusables, and if weather or forest conditions preclude a fire at camp, you're stuck with a bunch of smelly garbage; for easy utensil cleanup tips, see sidebar on this page.)

Other essentials: a good Lexan cutting board (thinner, lighter-weight, easier to sanitize than wood), plastic tablecloth, several sharp knives, plenty of paper towels for napkins as well as mop-up, assorted plastic bags (zip-top and garbage-size), matches—and don't forget a mechanical can opener, a bottle opener, and a corkscrew.

♦ GROUP CAMP CLEANUP TIPS

For backpacking, biking, or ski touring, you will want to carry only a few utensils and pots (see Chapter 2 for tips on backpacking kitchens and gear), and washup will often consist of just a hot water rinse and wipedown of a spoon and a pot. But for sea kayaking, canoeing, rafting, and car camping, you can add such nice touches as plastic or metal plates, dinnerware, mugs, and even tumblers. To cut down on dish duty, especially for groups, consider these shortcuts.

Make up one place setting per person (plate, bowl, cup, knife, fork, and spoon), and sew or buy nylon mesh drawstring ditty bags in which each person stores his or her utensil set (label the bags with masking tape or other personal "markers," such as differently colored cord locks or drawstrings).

After each meal, everyone washes their utensils in the handy "dip" system: line up three plastic tubs, the first containing hot soapy wash water and a brush, the second containing a clear water rinse, and the third filled with a mild bleach solution. After running through the dips, the utensils are placed back in their ditties and hung from a line to dry.

Your bleach solution tub may last one or more days' worth of dishes, depending on the number of campers. The other two will need to be changed after each meal session.

Organizers

Bag it up. For easy no-rattle carrying and convenient use, put utensils in their own "bedroll"—make one from a rectangle of canvas with cloth pockets sewn to the one side (one pocket for each of your cooking utensils). When cooking, untie and unroll the holder, so everything is reachable; you can hang it from your awning or the side of your chuck box or stove stand.

Chuck box. Anything that helps to organize the kitchen area is good, whether it's a basic packing box, a few plastic milk crates, or a chuck box—a counter-and-cabinet arrangement that folds up and out to hold a whole miniature kitchen (see sidebar, opposite). Whichever you choose, it's most helpful when things are visible (at least, after lifting one lid), so no searching or rummaging is necessary. Visibility not only prevents the constant "where" queries, but it helps your camping companions help themselves.

Other keepers. Organize your food in plastic bins, cardboard boxes, dry bags, or other handy containers. As much as possible, remove cardboard packaging, especially baking or stove-top mixes. Repackage the food in freezer-quality zip-top bags (cut off the cooking instructions and place in the bags); this saves space and garbage volume at the campsite. Some campers like to have separate bins or bags for breakfast, lunch, dinner, and snacks, while others like to organize by food type, such as baking items, canned food, cereals, etc. Just keep it consistent and maybe even labeled, to help guide kitchen helpers.

Dutch Ovens

The cast-iron Dutch oven could be your ticket to one-pot cooking for car camping, canoeing, and rafting (possibly for sea kayaking, if there is a communal kitchen and plenty of storage space). For entrees you have the option of stewing, roasting, or frying; you can cook meats and vegetables together in a sauce or separated by foil wraps, even though it all cooks in the same pot. Use the Dutch oven for baking, too: prop cake or muffin tins on a few small rocks placed in the bottom of the oven (or on an upside-down cake pan) for even baking without bottom-burning.

Cooking in a Dutch oven takes a little practice—try it at home a few times for a fun change—to master the temperature control (charcoal briquettes offer more reliable, even heat than wood coals). If you've never savored dumplings steamed over sumptuous stew, or hot and spicy apple cobbler, you are missing out on some of life's greater pleasures.

Some tips on Dutch ovens:

- Don't be tempted by lighter aluminum varieties, which burn food more easily.
- A true Dutch oven will have legs and a slightly domed, lipped lid with a handle.
- Dutch ovens are sold by inches-in-diameter. Common sizes are 10 (4 qt.), 12 (6 qt.), 14 (8 qt.) and 16 (12 qt.). Twelve- and 14-inch ovens are most useful, and cost between $25 and $50.
- Season by coating a new oven (after washing with soap) with vegetable shortening or bacon fat, then heating it in a 400-degree oven for about an hour. Wipe down, cool, and repeat.
- Never use soap or harsh scouring pads on your oven again (it takes the seasoning off); just wipe down while still warm. A properly seasoned and cared-for Dutch oven will last nearly forever.
- Start learning to cook with a Dutch oven by using charcoal

briquettes; they provide even, easy-to-manage heat. A rough guideline for guestimating temperature in a 12-inch oven is as follows: for 350 degrees, use 8 coals under, 16 on the lid; for 450 degrees, use 10 coals under, 20 on the lid. (Dutch oven recipe books tell you how many to use; once you get the hang of it, you can adapt your home recipes in the field.)

- Every time the lid is removed, cooking time should be extended by 5–10 minutes.
- Useful accessories: a "gonch" hook to lift the oven and lid (a pair of sturdy pliers will do); a lid stand, to keep it out of the dirt when checking on dinner (try a ring cut from a coffee can); and a pair of tongs for handling coals.
- A few good Dutch oven cookbooks: *Outdoor Dutch Oven Cookbook* by Sheila Mills (Camden, ME: Ragged Mountain Press, 1997) and *The Old-Fashioned Dutch Oven Cookbook* by

MAKE YOUR OWN CHUCK BOX

You can buy ready-made aluminum chuck boxes for around $50, or you can make your own from quarter-inch plywood or even solid hardwood. The beauty of do-it-yourself is that you can custom-design to fit not only your own needs and desires, but also the shape and size of your van, car, or truck storage area. Usually, chuck boxes hold your pots, pans, utensils, gadgets, towels, and a few condiments; food goes in other containers. Use your imagination, but here are some ideas from some great custom-made chuck boxes.

- Don't make it too big to carry

easily—about 24" wide by 15" deep by 15" tall seems good for exterior dimensions; don't forget carrying handles.

- Sand and varnish well inside and out, so it can withstand some weather and spills.
- Make the door fold-down style, attached at the bottom with a piano hinge, and with retainer-chains at the sides to hold the lid horizontally.
- Line the inside of the lid (the "kitchen counter") with a Lexan cutting board or Formica; you could do the same with the top of the box,

thus doubling your counter space.

- Line the shelves with thin cork, to cut down on rattles and slippage.
- Split the box into two sides—one unshelved, to store pots, pans, and plates (get creative with nesting), as well as paper towels; and the other divided into shelves, for mugs, bowls, and spices, with a drawer for silverware (size it for a plastic silverware divider).
- Include a way to hang your large-utensil roll from one side.
- Attach a foldaway paper-towel holder or towel ring on one side.

Don Holm (Caldwell ID: The Caxton Printers, 1970).

Camp Stoves

Most car campers, and a lot of boaters (when in a group), use a two-burner camp stove. When folded for transport, the stove is about the size of an attaché case and is similarly equipped with a convenient carrying handle. When set up, the lid stands at a 90-degree angle to the cooking surface, to provide a back-wall wind block. Side panels can be popped into position if a breeze continues to threaten the flame. Camp stoves sit conveniently on a picnic table, a level rock, or the ground (under the tent's awning when it's raining). Prices for two- to three-burner camp stoves range between $35 and $90. Single-burner backpacking stoves are covered in Chapter 2.

Regardless of their fuel source, all two-burner camp stoves have a similar compact shape. Those that burn liquid fuel (kerosene, unleaded gas, or white gas) have an attached cylindrical fuel tank. Those that burn propane use disposable propane bottles, or are connected to a larger, refillable propane tank.

Propane. Propane stoves are clean and efficient, and they are the easiest camp stoves to use because they are most familiar, especially if you are used to a gas stove or grill at home. While you may need to use a match or other spark to light the burner, from then on it is cooking as usual: the knob adjusts for high or low heat, and cooking times will be fairly close to what you expect on a home stove. (Some models do have a built-in sparkmaker, eliminating the step of lighting the burner, but these have a way of breaking.) A few campers shy away from carrying pressurized fuel because of the potential hazards, and disposable fuel is quite expensive (however, propane in refillable cylinders is extremely cheap and efficient).

Liquid fuel. Most popular liquid-fuel stoves burn white gas (also sold as Coleman fuel, after a popular stove brand name); some dual-fuel models accept either white gas or plain, readily available automobile unleaded gas. These stoves are just as easy to cook over once they're burning, but they are not quite as easy to start as the propane stoves (keep in mind that while white gas is relatively "clean," automotive fuel is smelly). While propane is already pressurized in the cylinder, liquid fuel must be pressurized. This is accomplished with a simple pumping mechanism built into the tank. If you've followed the manufacturer's instructions carefully, you simply pump up pressure, turn the knob, and light the burner with a match. (A common problem with lighting these stoves stems from simple overfilling—if the tank's too full, you can't get enough pressure into the tank to vaporize the fuel for combustion). Once you become comfortable with using a liquid-fuel stove, you'll find they provide the best heat.

Propane, white gas, and automobile fuel are all commonly available. As with all combustion appliances, use common sense when operating them: follow the manufacturer's directions carefully, especially regarding the fuel type and source; don't use stoves inside the tent or in any unventilated place (all fire uses oxygen and produces odorless and deadly carbon monoxide).

Be wary of the advertised amounts to determine how much fuel you should take. On your first

CAMP STOVE TIPS

- Although not a necessity, folding stands (around $20) made to hold camp stoves offer the convenience of cooking at a familiar standing level. (Some stands have a pot-or-food-holding shelf about midway between base and stove platform.)

- Propane is also known as LPG or liquefied petroleum gas.

- When pouring liquid fuels, use a funnel for less chance of spillage. Coleman sells a filter/funnel, to help keep impurities out of the stove.

- Don't store liquid fuel for any length of time (not in the can, and especially not in the stove), or it may get gummy. If you use the stove every week or two, there's no problem, but burn out all fuel before seasonal storage.

- Liquid-fuel stoves sometimes need help. Carry spare parts and whatever tools you'd need to put in the parts. (Kit could include gasket and/or O-ring, spare jet, cleaning pad, and jet-cleaning needle.) The pressure-pump plunger should be lubricated regularly with a light-grade machine oil. Reread stove instructions and maintenance tips before each trip, and bring troubleshooting instructions with you.

- Carry an inexpensive backpacker's one-burner stove with you as a backup (for example, the Scorpion stove folds up into a small bag and costs less than $25 with a fuel cartridge), in case your big stove goes on the blink and a campfire is not possible or practical.

- For tips on buying used stoves, see Appendix A, p. 324.

trips, take a lot; then keep track of what you use in a typical weekend. Some people drink lots of coffee or cook long, complex meals, while others use stoves a lot less and thus burn less fuel.

Campfire Cooking

Once you have the desired hot coals in your Zen fire (see p. 247), you can use the fire to cook directly (as in hot dogs on sticks, kabobs on skewers, or steaks on a grill) or indirectly (as the heat source for Dutch oven stewing, frying, baking, or steaming).

Even for this kind of camp cooking, you can use an assortment of stout pans from the home kitchen, the exception being the hang-over-the-fire meals. These require sturdy top handles that ordinary pots from home do not have. Look for cooking kettles with lids as well as handles in camping stores; Dutch ovens, hung from a tripod, work great as regular pots. Good campfire cooking accessories include

Cooking platform. Buy or make a simple grill—recycle a grill from a burned-out barbecue, for example. Bend some V-shaped metal legs to hold it up, or prop it up on rocks.

For car camping and river running, a Dutch oven can be one of your most versatile cooking pots: use it as a slow cooker, a baking oven, or a regular over-the-fire pot.

Then cook directly, by broiling (grilling); or indirectly, with frying pans or pots, or by heating the food right in the can (open all lids first). Adjustable legs are very handy for uneven or rocky ground.

Tripod. The classic camp "bean pot" hangs from a tripod. To make a tripod, use three 4-foot lengths of half-inch or three-quarter-inch metal electrical conduit for the leg. Clamp them together at the top; an electrical-fitting J-clamp works well. Use an appropriate length of lightweight chain to hang the bean pot, with an S-hook at each end. You can also add a grill to the tripod—square or round, whichever you find first. Attach pieces of chain to the corners of the grill, if square, or to the north, east, south, and west marks on a round grill. Connect the chain ends with one S-hook, and use another piece of chain and a second S-hook to hang the grill.

Ovens

Camp baking takes a bit more practice than grilling a slab of steak over the coals, but the effort is worth the gastronomic pleasure.

Most camping stores sell square, folding ovens that sit on top of a camp stove or next to a fire. The oven collapses into a flat package for transport. The advantage of commercial camp ovens is that they are large-volume; the biggest drawback of these is their high price (around $50 or more) and bulk, even folded.

Smaller and less expensive are the BakePacker and Outback Oven units available at backpacking specialty stores for under $45. A single unit's product is enough for two people, but too skimpy for a growing family or group of hungry

boaters (the obvious solution would be to take several bakers).

Experiment with baking in your large Dutch oven, in a large coffee can converted to an oven (see the instructions for a great one in Don Jacobson's *The One Pan Gourmet*), a converted heavy-gauge aluminum ring-style bake pan (see the August 1996 issue of *Canoe & Kayak* magazine for instructions and recipes) or try an even easier and more portable creative alternative—a large roasting bag, or a length of roasting wrap or aluminum foil, placed over any makeshift framework to confine heat.

See Chapter 12 for more on baking.

HEALTHY HELP FOR CHARCOAL FIRES

Charcoal lighter fuel works, but it's unhealthy for people and the environment. Alternative fire starters exist; they just require a little more effort than standing in the checkout lane (self-starting charcoal is just presoaked with starter fluid, so it doesn't count as a reasonable alternative).

One alternative is to make a reusable chimney from a large can. Using tin snips, cut away the bottom as well as the lid, and scallop the bottom edge to allow air to flow through. Place the chimney on the fire mound or in the barbecue, then rumple up some sheets of newspaper and put them into the bottom of the chimney. Put briquettes on top; light the newspaper, and it lights the charcoal. Later, remove the chimney with tongs or pliers, and spread out the coals.

If you run out of time, commercial chimney-type starters are available for around $20 to $30.

Let There Be Light

Endlessly black skies dotted with dia-mondlike stars surely are one of the great joys of camping. It's often sur-prising how bright just plain starlight can be. Alas, you will want some arti-ficial lighting to avoid cooking up too many bugs or bumbling over logs, into bears, or over a drop-off. Car campers can choose from many dif-ferent gas or electric lanterns, while backpackers, bikers, and boaters can opt for candle lanterns and head-lamps. (For information on buying used lanterns, see Appendix A, p. 324.)

Classic Camp Lanterns

The classic camping lantern has been updated and upgraded and made for use with various fuels, but it still looks at least somewhat old-fash-ioned, with the traditional shape, glass globe, and flame glow. Prices range from about $40 to $100.

The kerosene model is the only one that still requires preheating (done by pouring denatured alcohol into the burner cup and lighting it). Kerosene is economical, readily avail-able (often from gasoline stations), and, unquestionably, the safest fuel to use. A minor disadvantage is carrying the alcohol as well as the kerosene; also, some people object to the smell of kerosene, especially if it's not burning properly.

Many camping lanterns burn white gas. Some are "dual-fuel," with ordinary unleaded gasoline as the sec-ond choice. These lanterns need no preheating or priming. Just pump up the pressure, turn the knob, and light with a match or butane lighter. Fuel for these lanterns is easily found but highly flammable, so it must be han-dled and stored with care.

Next on the list of fuel options is propane. These lanterns can be used with disposable propane cylinders, or can be connected to a larger, refill-able tank via handy poles that also elevate the lantern above work areas. Familiar, convenient, and clean-burning, propane might be the lantern of choice.

Because all gas lanterns work by pressure, all emit a constant, charac-teristic hiss. Some people find the noise annoying, disrupting the sought-after quiet of nature. If you can live with less light but more quiet, use a hurricane lamp instead. Small (about 10" high) and practical, with the charm of form-and-func-tion, hurricane lamps burn quietly, using a wick to carry the fuel. They'll burn kerosene, lamp oil (your choice of scent), or citronella oil (an insect repellent). Few things can go wrong: fill it, lift the globe, and light.

Camp lighting choices include simple and effective candle lanterns (left), and pressur-ized white-gas lanterns (right), which are very bright and efficient.

They're even reasonably priced, sometimes under $20; you can find them in basic black or red-painted metal, or a gleaming brass finish.

Alternatives

Candle lanterns. At camping stores you can find a number of different mini-lanterns, about 6 inches tall and under about $20; some burn lamp oil, some use candles. A glass globe brightens the flame and keeps it out of the wind.

Do-it-yourself candle lights. Punch some holes in the side of a juice can (or other small can that is tall rather than squatty), and set a candle in it. Melt a bit of wax onto the can bot-tom to hold the candle—just like a Halloween pumpkin. Loop a wire handle into the top rim (but handle it cautiously when the candle's lit). As with all flame-lights, never use in a tent.

Fluorescent lanterns. Battery-oper-ated (either 12-volt or flashlight-size batteries) or rechargeable fluorescent lanterns are efficient, although re-placement bulbs can be hard to find. Prices vary widely, but may start around $25.

Flashlights and headlamps. Flash-lights have come a long way from the basic beam-pointer. They've stretched out in both length and di-ameter; the same flashlight can give you a focused spot or a wide-angle circle of light. They may be water-proof (some float) or PVC-coated for bump and drop protection. You can find flashlights with a clip-on handle, a stand-and-tilt base, or a wrist-tie strap. Some flashlights have two sides, with a choice of fluorescent and incandescent beams. One small flash-light becomes a headlamp when in-serted into a loop on a headband. A real headlamp is much more useful than an ordinary flashlight; hands are free to put up the tent, fix dinner, or hold the map you're trying to unfold and read. Flashlights and headlamps cost from $5 to $80.

The Bedroom

A comfortable place to sleep at your campsite is key to a great camping experience. From backpacking to bike touring to canoeing to car camping, the range of options for shelters is vast. The choices for sleeping bags and pads is fortunately not so wide but does require a little bit of investigation as well.

Shelter

Before you run out and buy the first sale tent you find, you need to ask yourself some questions: *What constitutes adequate shelter? How do tents provide it? How much space is enough? How will I use a tent? And, which tent designs, construction techniques, and detailing should I look for or avoid?*

First, your primary sport interests will determine which designs you should look for.

Car camping. Cargo space and weight-carrying ability is greatly expanded when car camping, so you can choose larger tents than a backpacker or bike tourist would choose. Choices for car campers range from simple nylon domes and modified A-frames, to nylon or canvas cabin or wall tents, to special sport-utility tents that attach to your truck or 4×4, converting it to a mini-RV. Keep in mind that when car camping at campgrounds, sometimes you can't pitch your tent right at your car. If you choose a sport-utility tent, be prepared to have to "camp" in the area for motorhomes (some of which

Car camps can provide many amenities, including shade, a shower, lighting, and comfortable seating.

run generators) at some organized campgrounds.

Rafting. River runners can use just about anything a car camper would use, except, of course, a sport-utility tent.

Canoeing and sea kayaking. Most people on canoe or kayak trips will want their own tents, for comfort and privacy. For space considerations, smaller nylon backpacking-type designs are most efficient for packing in a boat. Some canoeists still use the traditional "baker's tent," a canvas shelter that combines a cooking awning with a small sleeping cubby at the rear—a great, compact, and versatile shelter most easily found in the north country, where traditional canoeing remains popular. Baker's tents are not as compact or lightweight as backpacking tents, but they sleep two and obviate the need for a separate cooking tarp.

Backpacking, ski and bike touring. Lightweight and compact are the two tent features most desirable for these

activities. See Chapter 2 for a discussion of good tent designs for backpacking. One option for bike tourists is the "pyramid" design—a floorless nylon tent shaped like a pyramid, with one center pole, a zippered door on one side, and standing headroom at the center. A bike and a camper would easily fit inside out of the weather.

When shopping for any tent, consider the following factors.

Durable materials. Is the nylon tough, or does it feel thin and flimsy? The zippers should be stout and work smoothly, and the seams should be flat and smooth, with strong stitches. Heat-tempered aluminum poles are the strongest and the easiest to repair, with a simple sleeve and duct tape; fiberglass poles break much more easily and are impossible to repair. (Incidentally, "ripstop" nylon was a great marketing product of the 1970s, but today it's no more or less prone to stopping rips than good modern nylons.)

The $100 rule. With a lot of outdoor equipment the old adage "You get what you pay for" holds true. Really cheap tents won't hold up, even for one outing. What's really cheap? Those $29.95 specials at the low-price warehouse, for one. Stick to good tents that sell for around $100 and up. A leaking, sagging, flapping tent with splintering poles is just no fun at all. (If you want to save money by buying used tents, see Appendix A, p. 324; if you want to save even more money, buy a good tarp and poles for $30 and learn how to set up a taut lean-to.)

Tough, waterproof floors. The floor must halt any upward absorption of ground moisture. Floor-to-wall side seams should not rest on the ground (the elevated seam creates a "bathtub" floor, standard in good tents). Any center seams on the floor should be factory-sealed or taped. You can do it yourself with a tube of sealer, but it won't last as well as a factory job.

Full-coverage rainfly. Except for canvas cabin tents and a few specialty tents such as the pyramid, any good tent has two parts: the tent body, made of uncoated (breathable) nylon, and the rainfly, made of polyurethane-coated (waterproof) nylon. Less-expensive tents will have partial rainflies, which in a gullywasher will leak. A rainfly should cover all the way to the ground, and it should not touch the body of the tent except at the poles (this causes condensation). Tip: Leave your rainfly on all day, to protect the uncoated tent body from harmful ultraviolet light and to keep it cooler.

Good ventilation. The tent should have openings (doors or windows) on all sides, if practical, to catch breezes from any direction and carry condensation away. Fine-meshed screens on all windows and doorways let air in and keep bugs out.

User-friendly. Ideally, a tent should be fairly easy to put up (pitch) or take down (strike), even in the dark and especially in the rain. It should fold into a compact, easily

carried package, usually in its own storage bag, ready to stuff into a car or boat. You'll find lots of different pitching styles, many of which claim to be the "fastest" and "easiest." Test them before you buy—don't take someone else's word for it. Keep in mind that the strongest (and slowest) way to attach poles to a tent is via sleeves; clip or ring systems are speedy and easy, and so are umbrella designs, but eventually those clips or rings will break.

Freestanding vs. stake-out. The advantages of freestanding tents are usually strength (although a number of strong winter-quality tents are stake-outs) and mobility—you can pick it up to move it or shake out debris.

Three- or four-season? Many backpacking tents are sold as either three- or four-season (the latter sometimes called "winter tents"). This is just a simple way of letting you know for what degree of weather-harshness the tent is designed—four-season being for extreme weather conditions such as heavy snowfall in winter, and high wind and driving rain, which are not winter-only events. In some areas you may desire a winter tent all year, such as withstanding Arctic gales in summer on the Alaskan coast, or fall windstorms sea kayaking in Baja. So don't pass up a good "winter" tent if security and peace of mind are important to you.

Buying a first tent can be a little

Severe winds, such as this fall Baja wind called an elefante, *can make you wish you'd spent an extra few bucks on a good-quality tent. After 12 hours of plus-30 mph winds, about half the tents in this picture suffered broken poles or ripped fabric.*

confusing, but if you take your time and try before you buy—look especially for outdoor retailers that rent the tents they sell—you should come out of the process with a great shelter for your car or wilderness camping. Tip: Outdoor retailers not only are staffed with folks who know all about outdoor gear and have used it, but also service and warranty what they sell; whereas at discount stores and with some mail-order companies you are on your own.

After your purchase, resist the temptation to head straight for the hills. Take some time at home to do the following.

- Unpack it, lay out and check off all the parts, then set it up again. Never go camping without having done this; it's the only way to be sure you understand the setup.

- If the tent needs to have seams sealed (instructions will tell you "if" and "how"), set it up and leave it for a few hours before applying the sealer. This way, the stitching holes will stretch as much as they can, so the holes will be filled completely. After sealing, let the tent dry standing up, out of direct sun, for at least two days.

- Make up, or buy, a tent repair kit for about $15. Include some nylon repair tape for the tent and some vinyl tape for the groundcloth. If a kit isn't sold with the tent, try to get a swatch of matching fabric to use for patching. Besides sewing supplies, take a pole repair kit: a short length of pole makes a temporary repair sleeve; slip the sleeve over the broken pole section, and tape together. Also include spare zipper sliders, some spare netting (in a pinch

you can use a piece of fiberglass window screen), a length of shock cord, duct tape, and snap-on grommets.

MORE TENT TIPS

- ◆ Always, always, always stake out your tent well with ground stakes and guylines—even "freestanding" tents. Any breeze can turn a tent into a colorful kite. Use strong heat-treated metal stakes; plastic stakes chip and splinter (dangerous for your eyes). Follow your tent manufacturer's directions for guylines, which can greatly reduce annoying flapping if a breeze picks up at 2:00 A.M.

- ◆ Your tent floor is most prone to wear and tear—and is very expensive to replace. Carefully clear your tentsite of sticks and small sharp rocks. Use a lightweight nylon or plastic groundcloth inside your tent to catch potential hole-producing debris—just roll it up and shake it out occasionally. (A no-shoes policy is always good in a tent.)

- ◆ Poles are delicate—treat them carefully and they will reward you with years of service. Especially make sure the joints are fully seated in each other before bending any poles in a dome tent, or the joint ends will split.

- ◆ Don't spritz stiff or sticky zippers with an oily lubricant; it will stain the fabric and possibly damage it. Instead, use plain wax or bar soap. Ditto for pole joints; use a tiny bit of silicone.

- ◆ Don't spray the tent with insect repellent; most repellents can damage the fabric or waterproof coating. One exception—Duranon repellent, with Permethrin, is made for use on clothing and tent fabric.

Taking care of your gear properly will extend its life by many years. Consult the excellent *Essential Outdoor Gear Manual* by Annie Getchell (Ragged Mountain Press, 1995) for in-depth how-to's on gear care and repair. See also p. 269 for a discussion of aftertrip gear chores.

Sleeping Cots, Mattresses, and Pads

Nothing is fun if you haven't slept well. No matter how much you may want to enjoy the pleasures of sun rising, wood fire smoking, coffee steaming, and bacon sizzling, you won't even recognize them if you're still in sleep mode. All the jokes about grumpy-in-the-morning can't change the way you feel.

You can help ensure a great night's sleep while camping with a number of great bed products, from cots to air mattresses to foam pads. Remember that besides comfort, one of the things a bed should do is help keep you warm when the nights turn chilly. Some thoughts on each:

Cots. Car campers and rafters can go for the luxury of camp cots, which will work only if you have a tent with sufficient headroom and near-vertical walls or if you're not using a tent. Also, they are best in warm weather. Before buying, check the way the cot is made: bent, rounded tubing for legs is easiest on the tent floor, although other styles could be cushioned to protect the fabric; at the very least, it should fold in half for carrying and packing, but roll-ups are more space-efficient; look for sturdy, mildew-resistant fabrics, and consider the convenience of removable covers. Cots cost between $40 and $100.

Standard air mattresses. Most air

mattresses are variations on two styles: the full-length, tubular-shaped I-beam construction, or the non-chambered fake-button-quilt-look in a square-cornered, flat mattress. They're made in an assortment of materials, but the rubberized canvas seems most favored; even though it may be heavier, it has a softer touch. (The heavier weight also means heavier-duty—it lasts longer.) Air mattresses sound like a perfect solution for maximum comfort for minimum size. Deflated, they are small and light; when filled, they provide a large, fairly thick mat. Prices are reasonable as well—from $15 to $50. If you've got weak lungs, take along a foot or hand pump.

Self-inflating air mattresses/pads. Self-inflating foam pads cushion with both foam and air and are the most efficient heat-insulators of all the bed types. Several variations are available. The Equalizer has separate chambers, so you can adjust the amount of air for different parts of the body. Three of the chambers are connected, so air flows through; three are independent. Therm-a-Rest is a popular mattress for good reason. Its open-cell foam compresses to a smaller package—the choice for backpackers up to boaters, even car campers. Therm-a-Rests are made in full and three-quarter length, and in several thicknesses; two can be connected to form a double bed. Self-inflating mattresses aren't cheap; expect to pay from $40 to $100.

Foam pads. There are two types of foam pad—dense, efficient (keeps you warmer) closed-cell foam, and thicker, softer, and more airy open-cell foam. The former is more water-resistant (actually, open-cell foam is essentially a sponge). A full-length pad is very comfortable, but it makes a big bundle to pack and carry, so many campers settle for a three-quarter length. A thickness of ⅜ inch is the minimum—and it is truly minimal for comfort. Maximum comfort may be had from 2-inch-thick egg-crate foam mattress pads cut to fit the floor of your tent or the back of your pickup truck. Buy pads as thick as you can pack and carry. Prices range from under $10 to around $60.

Don't forget the pillows—it's surprising how much better you sleep with a good pillow. Car campers can take their home pillows. Other campers should look around camping stores for a variety of creative outdoor pillows: down- or polyester-filled; inflatable; or pile-covered stuff sacks that you fill with clothing.

Sleeping Bags

Bags are most practical for camp bedding. They're cozy for sleeping, and even young children can roll them up and out of the way come daylight.

A lot of sleeping bag features are built-in for cold-weather camping, designed to keep sleepers warm in near-freezing temperatures. Summertime campers don't need all the extra detailing and super-tech materials; they may want to be covered, but not cocooned. Families may already own sleeping bags for the kids, from bring-your-own-bed slumber parties. Car campers can buy a similar, lightweight basic bag from a discount or department store and take along a few old wool blankets to pile on top if the weather report calls for chilly nights.

Backpackers, bike tourists, and boaters may want to invest in serious sleeping bags, and since they are an investment ($100 and up), multiplied by how many family members camp, they require some prior study. See Chapter 2 for more discussion of backpacking-quality sleeping bags, their fabrics, and insulations; and Appendix A, p. 323, for tips on buying used bags.

Bags are made in two basic shapes—rectangular and tapered—but there are several variations:

- *Rectangular* is the roomiest, so you have the most freedom of movement. They sleep the coldest, but that's not a problem for summer campers.
- *Semirectangular* tapers at the feet, and a bit at the shoulders; with less space inside, it warms up faster than a rectangular bag.
- Shaped and tapered, a *mummy bag* has the least space to heat; made for cold-weather camping, it also has a head-covering hood. If you move around a lot when you sleep, you won't like the confinement of a mummy bag.
- A *modified mummy* shape tries to ease the claustrophobia without sacrificing too much heat-keeping ability.

DOUBLE-BAGGING

Two of the same-model rectangular bag can often be zipped together into a double-bed bag; this also works with semirectangular bags. You can use two of the same length, or put a longer bag on the bottom.

Most sleeping bags are made for an average-size adult, but if you're above average height, look for extra-long. If you're otherwise oversized, or simply like more room to move, look for extra-wide or jumbo (and ignore the label). A few bags are made in children's sizes, too. Sierra Designs

is its loft—that is, how thick the insulation is (this is particularly true with down; newer synthetic insulations can offer more warmth for less loft). For example, a down sleeping bag with a 4-inch loft is generally considered a spring-summer bag, while one with an 8-inch loft is a full wintertime bag. Talk with salespeople who have used the type of bag you're looking at, and read the manufacturer's information carefully.

For practical reasons, frequent car campers, especially families, should get sleeping bags with an easy-care fabric and synthetic insulation, so they can throw them into a washing machine when need be.

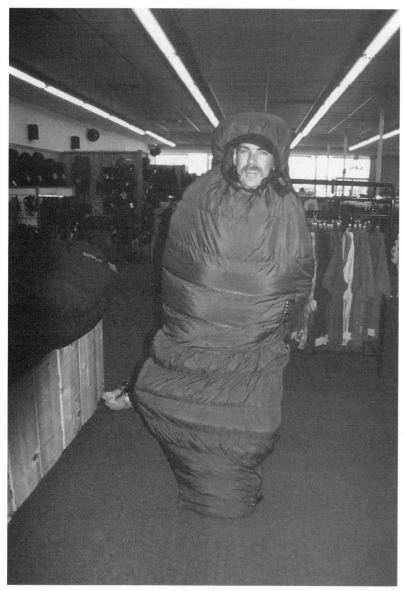

Some manufacturers are making mummy bags, which are snug-fitting and thus efficient, with elasticized sides, which help alleviate feelings of claustrophobia.

HAMMOCK HAVEN

A hang-anywhere bed lets you loaf in the nicest places. Beachfront is a favorite: the cooling touch of a steady sea breeze, the lullaby of endless waves, and the gentle swing of your private cocoon put your world on hold—*and* give you something to call on for future stress management.

A cotton woven hammock is probably the most comfortable, although it will mildew and rot eventually. You can also find hammocks in nylon or polyester twine, or in a solid canvas fabric. Wooden spreader bars, inserted at the ends of some hammocks to hold the shape, must be well padded, or they will destroy the feeling of unhampered freedom.

You can forget the tent if you sleep in a jungle hammock. With mesh net sides, a fabric top, and a cotton canvas floor, this is a self-contained, functional, elevated shelter with all the fun of a hammock. Look for them at military surplus and supply stores.

and possibly a few other manufacturers make bags designed just for women.

Sleeping bags are given temperature ratings, which indicate the range within which they are likely to keep you warm. Unfortunately, there is no industry standard for these ratings, so use them as a guideline only; in general, a bag rated at 20 degrees will be the most versatile for the generalist spring-summer-fall camper, backpacker, and boater. A better way to judge a bag's warmth-keeping ability

The Bathroom

Most commercial, and many public, campgrounds have nice toilet and shower facilities, so you don't have to worry about it.

But backcountry campgrounds and wilderness campsites won't have such amenities, so here's how to set them up yourself (although for some people, part of the "fun" of camping is seeing how long they can stand it without bathing).

Wilderness Showers

Weekend campers seldom worry about showering. Some may use a lot of moist towelettes, but a full shower is hardly a necessity in a back-to-nature experience. When you set up camp for a week or two, however, part of the setup should include a way to bathe. Whatever method you choose, don't use the nearby lake or stream for a bathtub. No soap degrades instantly. And make sure your shower is at least 70 adult paces from any water source or does not drain off into one.

SunShower. Pour water into the black, heavy-duty plastic bag, leave it out in the sun until the water's warm, then hang the bag so gravity feeds the sprayer hose attached to the bottom of the bag. You control water flow by the foolproof hose-up or hose-down method. (Hurry the warming with stove-heated, but not boiling, water.) Look for SunShowers at camping or boating stores for around $25.

People sprayer. For car campers with enough space, another portable shower setup uses a $20, 2-gallon garden bug sprayer (buy a new one that hasn't had chemicals in it). Either fill it partway with cool water and add heated water, or wrap a black plastic garbage bag around the filled con-

SunShowers are wonderful camping luxuries. Privacy enclosures (around $25) are also available.

tainer and leave it in the sun all day. When the water's warm, pump up the pressure and shower away. (Tip: If you replace the attached spray hose with a kitchen sink sprayer hose, you'll get better water flow.)

Dry shower. When camping in places where water is hard to get or unavailable, you can still wash your hair and your body with products that don't need to be rinsed away. Appropriately called No Rinse, both shampoo and body-bath make washing suds using only a small amount of water. You wash with a cloth or sponge, but after washing, you don't rinse; just towel yourself dry. It may sound strange, but it worked for NASA astronauts as well as for more down-to-earth expeditionists. (Find it in camping stores, or call the company for information: 800-223-9348. You'll find other specialty products, too, such as liquid soaps that work in hot or cold water, fresh or salt; or dry shampoos that you brush in, then brush dirt out. Sailing supply stores are good places to look for these products.)

Toilet

There are a few schools of thought out there for how to best deal with wilderness toilet duty. The currently accepted method is to dig a shallow "cathole" (about 5 inches deep) at least 70 adult paces from any water source in an area that gets maximum sun exposure. Pack out your toilet paper in zip-top bags; because of fire danger, burning is no long recommended, and burying it is not ideal, because critters almost always dig it up. (Likewise, pack out all toiletries associated with menstruation.) Recover the cathole with soil. Groups may want to dig a long, shallow trench, to be used and filled in successively from one end.

Along heavily used river or ocean corridors, all waste should be packed out in airtight plastic-lined ammo cans or in portable toilets. At one time it was recommended to deposit waste in the beach intertidal zone, the theory being each high tide would wash it clean. However, this has proved to be a poor practice, especially in popular areas.

Put together a toilet kit to hang in a handy spot in camp: trowel, toilet paper, plastic bag, antibacterial soap, small bottle of water.

For a recommendation on kids and the outdoor potty, see Chapter 11, p. 274.

More Necessities and Niceties

What else is there that can augment your camping comfort?

- *Reading light.* A personal "bedside" light can be a nice touch if you enjoy the latest John Grisham before snoozing.
- *Seating.* From folding lawn chairs and camp stools, to covers that adapt your self-inflating mattress into a very comfortable camp chair (sling-style) for minimal space and weight—any camper can find comfortable seating.
- *Tables.* The classic fold-up picnic tables, the ones with the integrated seats, worked great and are still made, albeit of plastic rather than sturdy metal. Many rafting and kayaking groups take along roll-up tables, which really increase the ease of kitchen work. If you lack space for a table, get creative—logs and rocks make excellent tables (just make sure you replace anything you move, and watch for insects).

Safe and Happy Camps

Our ancestors huddled around the campfire, a safe haven from hungry wild animals. Today, the animals that wander into popular camping areas are not nearly as wild as their ancestors once were. The resident raccoons have probably been foraging in trash cans and bins since their parents

taught them how to pry off the covers. Local squirrels are practically domesticated in many campgrounds; even deer lose much of their shyness after constant exposure to people.

Despite this gradual taming (and no matter how much we might want the storybook picture of nature to be real), the truth is that these animals are not trying to be friendly—they are simply trying to take our food. Understandable though that may be, giving them food does not help them in the long run; they will become dependent on (and later, demanding of) handouts, when they should be practicing the self-sufficiency that is *their* nature. Finally, wild animals can carry and transmit diseases that also affect people. Tick-related diseases and rabies are just two of the most commonly recognized.

Regardless of how pretty, cute, fluffy, or sweet a forest creature may appear, think wild, and try to send them on their own, wild way.

What about domestic animals? For tips on taking Fido outdoors, see Chapter 1, p. 17.

General Critter-Proofing

Animal-proof your campsite by leaving no food out unattended during the day and putting the fresh food inside the vehicle at night, not in the tent; you don't want to attract night visitors.

If your food boxes or coolers aren't well hinged and clamped, tie them shut with a buckled utility strap, or the raccoons will be enjoying your cookout food. Raccoons are *very* strong, clever, and persistent.

Rodents such as squirrels and chipmunks are eager to try people food, too, and while it's tempting to offer them some tiny morsel, remem-

Backpackers and boaters can enjoy camp seating comfort with products such as the Therm-a-Lounger, which converts a self-inflating air mattress from sleeping pad to camp chair.

ber they can, and sometimes do, bite the hands that feed them. While rabies is the most serious concern about squirrels, any rodent can be pesky; they'll chew their way into your food supply, given half a chance, which is why you don't leave any flimsy food packages around camp.

Discourage bird beggars, too. It may be fun, at first, to watch them catch food you toss, but the downside is they just become bigger pests. Crows, seagulls, and jays are especially bad; they're not at all timid.

Bearing Up

When you head out to camp, either by foot, boat, or bike in the back-country, or by car, check with the land agency's rangers regarding the presence of "problem bears" and ask advice on bear-avoidance tactics. Remember that bears range all up and down a mountain, so you might find bears as low as the oak-covered foothills or even in the valleys between mountains.

At night, and when you leave the camp, be prepared to bag your food and hoist it high, out of reach of a bear standing on its hind legs. First pack your fresh and dried food, and secure everything in one or more heavy-duty plastic bags or stuff sacks. To hang your food bag, find a usable tree limb—about 15 feet high, and extending out from the trunk far enough to prevent a small bear from crawling out to it. Tie a rock or other weight to the end of a line, so you can toss the line over the limb. That done, tie the food bag onto the line, haul it up, and tie if off securely to the tree trunk.

IF YOU GET SKUNKED

If a surprise encounter with a skunk results in your worst camping nightmare, be prepared with Skunk-Off, which claims to remove all traces of skunk smell (look for it at outdoor retailers). Old stand-by solutions are tomato juice, or a vinegar/water mix of about 1 to 10.

You can also buy bear-resistant containers, made specifically for backcountry camping, at outdoor retailers. The tight-sealing containers are designed to save your food, even if the bear gets to the container, as well as to prevent the animals from becoming problem bears.

Remove all food and toiletries—anything that smells, including bug repellent, sunscreen, lip balm, toothpaste, lotion, and so on—from your sleeping tent.

As an added precaution in bear country, locate your cooking area as far from your sleeping tent as possible, and group your sleeping tents fairly close together.

If you're fishing and consuming your catch, be prepared to attract curious and hungry bears—the smell carries a long way. Clean your fish far from camp, and wash up both your dishes and yourself extremely well.

If you come across a small bear along the trail or near camp, leave as quickly and quietly as you can, before the big bear knows you're there. Mama bear stories are true.

Dealing with Insects

On the basis of numbers and pesterability, the smallest pests win. Biting insects—whether flying or crawling—seem the constant enemy. But while the campsite is the first line of defense, don't be overly aggressive about insect-killing. Try to remember that most insects are good: they pollinate flowers and food plants, and are the first link in many a food chain. Even the majority of the biting/stinging group are more often annoying than threatening. Only a few—fleas, ticks, and mosquitoes—actually carry human diseases.

COUGAR COUNTRY

Recent attacks by cougars (also called mountain lions or pumas) on people—some with fatal results—have increased some people's fear of this normally very secretive animal. But all such attacks have occurred near urban or suburban areas, where cougar habitat (and thus cougar prey, such as deer) is increasingly shrinking under the blades of bulldozers. In most wilderness camping situations, you will never even see cougars, even if they are present.

If you do happen to meet up with a cougar and it doesn't immediately run away, try to stand tall and raise your jacket or shirt over your head to look bigger. Make noise as you back away slowly. Never run—it triggers the chase instinct, which few cats can resist. (If you sing or whistle as you hike, such a meeting is less likely to occur.)

So, focus on insect-deterrence rather than killing bugs. Never use "bug-bombs"—one study in a national park along the Río Grande in Texas showed that enthusiastic campground use of bug bombs resulted in extremely high levels of pesticides accumulating in the soil, plants, and animals (as much as 38 pounds of DDT accumulation over one season in four campgrounds).

Citronella. Citronella is a nonchemical repellent, made from a plant commonly called lemongrass. Of all the bug-chasing preparations, citronella is easiest on the humans using it—although, unfortunately, not always hard enough on the insects. You can buy citronella oil to burn in a lamp, or you can light a bunch of citronella candles. You'll also find it as an ingredient in insect repellents applied directly to skin.

Mosquito coils. Other burnable deterrents include inexpensive mosquito coils, although these are treated with a repellent that sometimes bothers people as much as insects. With one brand, the coil sits inside a short, metal canister; holes cut into the sides allow the smoke to escape. Another holder leaves more space for smoke to exit; a fiberglass netting material over the coil keeps ashes in if the container should be knocked over.

Permethrin. An insect repellent in a water-based formula, Permethrin is EPA-approved for use on clothing and tent fabric. One application will remain effective for two weeks, even if it rains on the tent (or you wash the clothes).

Insect repellents and other insect-deterrence strategies. For tips on "bug juice" and a few natural insect-deterring strategies, see Chapter 13, p. 286.

For more information on health and safety in the outdoors, see Chapter 13.

Snow Camping

A whole new world awaits those who venture out into the backcountry in winter. In order to camp comfortably in the snow, however, you need a few more skills and specialized equipment than you do for warm-weather camping.

For starters, good group organization is essential when camping in the snow. Deciding in advance who will stamp out the tent platforms, who will pitch the tent, who will hold it down in a wind, who will set up the stove and start melting snow or go to collect water if available, and in what order these and other tasks should be done, will make setting up camp much quicker than if no plans are made. Even when alone, think out what needs doing and what order you will do it in. Decide where gear will go and make sure none is cast aside on the snow, where it could soon disappear.

Pitching Tents

It is not enough for comfortable snow camping that you have a good winter tent; you also need to know how to use it to the best advantage. To start with, care has to be taken with the choice and preparation of the campsite. If any shelter, such as trees, cliffs, or banks, is available, it should be used, as long as there is no danger from avalanches. For warmth, remember that cold air sinks. Valley bottoms, basin floors, meadows, and lakes will be chillier than the surrounding slopes or forest.

Camping on deep snow has little effect on the landscape, so you can camp anywhere without worrying too much about harming the environment. One point is worth thinking about, however: if there are signs of much animal activity in an area, particularly in forested areas, it is best to camp elsewhere. Wildlife has a hard enough time surviving the winter without being disturbed by people.

Thin snow cover is a different matter. Camping on it will compress the snow, causing it to take longer to melt, thus shortening the growing time for the plants below. Bare ground may be saturated with snowmelt and even more easily damaged, so greater care must be taken in spring camping. Choose sites where you know that the terrain below the snow can stand compression, such as vegetation-free areas of gravel and stones or, in the forest, conifer

needles. Alternatively, climb up to areas of deeper snow or drop down to find dry areas in the valley.

If the snow cover is very thin and the ground below is suitable for low-impact camping, it is often worth shoveling the snow away before pitching the tent. This isn't practical in deep snow, and unless you can find an area of hard snow, a flat platform must be stamped out. If you are ski touring or snowshoeing, it is easiest to do this with your skis or snowshoes on. Remember to make the platform much bigger than your tent, so there is room for guy lines and for walking around the tent. The platform should be smoothed flat and, if possible, left to harden before you pitch the tent, otherwise you will find the floor rather lumpy.

Main guys and staking points can be anchored securely with skis, ski poles, and ice axes. Large curved or T-shaped stakes designed to hold in soft snow are available but tend to be heavy. Nonetheless, carrying half a dozen on long winter-camping tours is probably worthwhile, especially if you intend to make day tours from a base camp and thus can't use your skis and poles to stake out the tent.

Stakes can be buried horizontally with guy lines tied around the middle, then stamped down in the snow. Once the temperature drops below zero they will freeze into place, and you will probably need to hack them out (carefully!) with a shovel or ice axe in the morning. Tie short guy lines to the staking points of your tent before a tour, or else carry plenty of cord and add them when necessary. An alternative to burying stakes is to fill stuff sacks with snow, attach the guy lines, and bury them. If there are trees or large boulders near the

site, it is worth running a line out to them for added security.

If your tent has snow valances—ground-level flaps running around the edge of the flysheet—then pitching is much easier: you just pile snow on them. However, valances severely limit ventilation and are a nuisance when not camping on snow, so overall they are not recommended. If your tent doesn't have valances, stability in high winds can be improved by heaping snow against the edges of the tent.

When the wind is really strong and a sheltered site isn't available, a wall of snow blocks can be built as a windbreak. However, drifting may occur on the leeward side and bury your tent, which can also happen if you dig a pit in which to pitch your tent. One solution to this problem is to build two walls, a high one some 15 feet or so away from the tent and a smaller one half that distance. If you build only one wall, pitch your tent the same number of feet in front of it as the wall is high, so that snow buildup will occur between the tent and the wall.

If snow builds up around the tent, someone has to go out and shovel it away. Do this as often and as carefully as possible—it is easy to damage the tent with the shovel blade. Snow pressing on the walls could cut out ventilation when cooking and lead to asphyxiation, and so could a collapsed tent. Tents with ventilators are a help.

A pit about a foot deep dug right in front of the tent can make getting out much easier; you can sit with your feet in it while you put on boots and clothing and then simply stand up to leave the tent. Such pits work best in tents without vestibules. If your tent has two vestibules, a pit can be dug in one of them, leaving the other for gear storage and cooking. An alternative is to dig a pit outside the vestibule and use a large stuff sack or other item as a seat while you put your boots on. If you do dig a pit, don't forget it is there when leaving the tent after dark!

All walls and pits should be dismantled and filled in when you leave a camp, so other visitors will not be aware you have been there.

Ventilation and Condensation

Dampness is a major enemy in snow camping. Because drying out wet gear is almost always difficult and often impossible, you need to be careful to keep snow out of the inner tent. A light brush or whisk is useful for brushing snow off clothing and for removing the snow that inevitably finds its way inside despite the best precautions. Wet clothes should be left in the vestibule or even outside, preferably in a plastic bag or stuff sack. Don't leave boots outside; they will freeze. Instead, brush off the snow, then store them inside the tent in a waterproof bag. If it is really cold, wrap the bag in spare clothing to help keep the boots from freezing. Some people put their boots in their sleeping bag.

Cooking in the vestibule requires as much ventilation as possible, to prevent steam from condensing on the flysheet and dripping back onto you and your gear. Ideally, cooking should always be done with the flysheet doors wide open. If this isn't possible, you should at least leave the top section of the zipper undone. In severe storms, even this may not be possible, and cooking with the doors

shut may be the only option. Then all you can do is try to minimize the inevitable condensation by keeping lids on your pans and, when you have finished cooking, leaving the stove running for a few minutes to dry out the air a little.

Wet, often dripping, flysheet walls are almost unavoidable in calm conditions—another reason for having a roomy tent in which you can keep well clear of the sides. It is also a reason for using either a sleeping bag with a water-resistant shell or an overbag or bivy bag made of waterproof/breathable fabric inside the tent. A small sponge is useful for wiping up drips and condensation.

Bivy Bags

If someone is injured or you have to spend an unintended night out, a bivy (bivouac) bag or sack (sometimes called an emergency bag or overbag) is the best and quickest way to gain protection from the weather. Even if you are able to dig a snow shelter, a bivy bag is useful for keeping your sleeping bag or clothing dry, and it can serve the same purpose in a damp tent. And when the stars shine and the wind dies and you decide to sleep under the vast winter sky ringed by shining peaks, a bivy bag can add several degrees of warmth to your sleeping bag, keep off stray breezes, and protect it from frost.

Bivy bags made from breathable waterproof fabrics such as Gore-Tex perform best; nonbreathable ones will leave your sleeping bag wet with condensation if you spend a night in one. There are various styles and weights, the most basic designs weighing and costing the least (around $100 or sometimes less). Those with nonbreathable coated-

nylon bases are adequate but can result in considerably more condensation than ones made entirely from the breathable fabric, especially if you roll over during the night so the nonbreathable section is above you. Some form of hood with a zippered or drawcord-fastened closure is needed. While you can seal yourself entirely into a microporous-fabric bag, such as one made of Gore-Tex, you must not enclose your head in one made of hydrophilic fabric, because it isn't possible to breathe through these fabrics. However, hydrophilic bags are cheaper and lighter than Gore-Tex, some weighing as little as 13 ounces; Gore-Tex bags start at around 20 ounces for the simplest designs. There is also growing evidence that hydrophilic bags work better than microporous ones in really cold temperatures—around 0 degrees F.

Double bags are available, which could be useful in emergencies when two people warm each other, but single ones can be used for solo trips without having to carry the extra weight and as sleeping-bag covers for extra warmth. The main thing is to ensure that your sleeping bag will fit easily inside. Roomy ones can also be used for storing clothing, boots, and even water bottles overnight.

Tarps

Not all winter campers spend their time above timberline. If you camp regularly in forests, a tarp may be all you need for shelter. Using a tarp saves on weight and makes ventilation easy. They are also worth carrying on day tours in forested country, for making emergency shelters or even just to use as a wind shelter. They are not as warm as tents, so a warmer sleeping bag and more clothing will probably be needed. Nylon tarps are the lightest. Moss Tents produces a sophisticated ripstop-nylon tarp called the Parawing, which has "hyperbolic paraboloid compound curves" to aid the shedding of wind and snow. Whatever the style of tarp, you will need a few stakes and some cord for tying it to trees.

Tarps are used in winter in exactly the same way as in summer, only your ingenuity and available anchoring points limiting the shapes of shelter you can construct. Steeper-roofed constructions are better if snowfall is likely, and it is advisable not to erect the tarp under branches bearing particularly heavy burdens of snow, in case it falls and crushes your shelter.

Groundsheets

If you use a tarp you will need a groundsheet, which is also useful in the snow shelters discussed next. A bivy bag will protect your sleeping bag, but it won't provide a place to put other items. Nylon tarps can be used as groundsheets, but the thin fabric isn't very durable and may not be sufficiently water resistant under pressure to prevent snowmelt from coming through.

The best groundsheets are the laminated sheets of aluminized polyethylene, polyester, and fiberglass sold under the names Sportsman's Blanket and Allweather Blanket. They are very durable but crack at the seams if always folded the same way. Rolling them up is a better idea.

Avoid the thin silver space blankets often promoted for survival use. The material tears easily and is very difficult to handle in a wind. A bivy bag is much better for emergency use

and a tougher material for a wind shelter or groundsheet.

Snow Shelters

High winds and blizzards can make tent use difficult or even impossible at times, so winter campers need to know how to dig snow shelters; even hut users may need one in an emergency.

But snow shelters aren't just for emergency use. Snow is an excellent insulator, and a snow shelter is warmer than a tent. A nice roomy one can make an excellent base for day tours, and they are better than a tent in snowy or blustery weather because they are absolutely quiet and still inside. Small ones can even be dug for lunch shelters in stormy weather.

Snow shelters range from basic trenches and slots to complex igloos. The possibilities are limited only by your imagination, snow being a very malleable substance. Building snow shelters requires a fair amount of knowledge and practice. See *Wilderness Skiing and Winter Camping* for excellent how-to instructions on building them (see the resources section at the end of this chapter for publisher's information).

Snow Trenches for Emergencies

A good snow-shelter will take at least a couple of hours to build, so it isn't really a practical proposition in an emergency. However, a slot or sentry box big enough for one person to get out of the wind can be shoveled out in a matter of minutes. It can always be enlarged if you decide to stay put. But the best emergency shelter is a snow trench or snow grave, which

can be built very quickly and will shelter two people. At least 5 vertical feet of reasonably level snow is required, so this is a technique for places where the snow falls heavily and lies deep.

Start by digging a slot about shoulder width and a little shorter than your skis. While one person digs, another can build a wall around the windward end with the excavated snow. Dig straight down until the trench is 4–5 feet deep. There will now be room for two people to sit in the trench. Insulating mats can be used as the floor. To roof it, lay two ski poles across the trench, then slide a pair of skis into a plastic tube tent, bivy bag, or folded-over tarp (the open sides can be tied together with cord—don't worry about bunching of the material, it doesn't matter) and lay this bundle across the poles. Use snow to hold the ends down. You can get in and out of the trench by lifting one corner of the roof and sliding in. If this is only a temporary shelter while you lunch or rest out of the wind, no more needs to be done. However, if you are going to spend more than a few hours in your trench, perhaps even the night, dig out the sides at the bottom to make slots you can slide your legs into so you can lie down.

A small trench will be warmer than a big one, and quicker to dig. Overall, if your need is to get out of the wind quickly, several snow "graves" are better than one large trench. If it looks like your stay will be prolonged, a more solid roof can be put on a snow grave by using snow blocks to make an A-frame-style roof.

When you leave a snow trench, fill it in and stamp the snow down. Apart from leaving as little sign of your presence as possible, this also ensures that other skiers won't have an accident by skiing into it.

If there isn't enough snow for digging a trench or cave, you can still make a shelter by piling up a huge heap of snow, compressing it as you go to help set the snow, leaving it to set, and then tunneling into it.

Natural Shelters

Where possible, use the terrain to help you build emergency shelters. Big snow scoops often occur under the roots of fallen trees, under steep riverbanks, and around large trees and big boulders where the snow has melted or been blown away by the wind. These can be quickly dug out to make lunch shelters and even roofed with tarps or tent flysheets for longer stays.

Traveling in winter wilderness requires many special skills, and more health precautions. See Chapter 13, pp. 292–296, for information on hypothermia, frost bite, acute mountain sickness, snow blindness, and avalanches. Chapter 14 provides information on dressing properly for extreme conditions. And for more on winter camping and skiing, see *Wilderness Skiing and Winter Camping,* by Chris Townsend (Camden, ME: Ragged Mountain Press, 1994).

More Joys of Camping

Camping is more than just being "out there" or conquering the wilderness. By living in one place for three or four days, or several weeks, you begin quite quickly to become part of the natural web of life.

There are many ways to enhance your sense of place, including studying and recording the plants and animals, observing weather, and tracking the stars and planets. Include the whole family, especially the youngest kids.

A Sense of Place

Begin by consciously observing, and then recording, what you see, hear, touch, and smell each day, from the moment you get up until you go to

---

BABY BINOCULARS

You can greatly enhance your outdoor experience with a pair of small binoculars—use them for bird or butterfly watching, star gazing at night, scanning across the valley for good campsites, and on and on.

Binoculars come in a variety of magnifications: very light, tiny "subcompact" binoculars usually have around 7 x 25 optics (the first number refers to the magnification, the second to the diameter of the front, or objective, lens, in millimeters), while "compact" binoculars are generally 7 x 30 or so. More-powerful binoculars, such as 10 x 40s, can be a little harder to hold steady and have a shorter field of view (although what you see is more magnified, you see less area in the lenses); bigger binoculars, such as 8 x 50s, are quite heavy.

The low end for decent binoculars is around $60 for a pair that will do the job—high end is $1,000. Go for a reputable brand. U.S. and Asian companies make good optics for less money; hardcore nature nerds will usually be found with something from Germany or Austria. Many outdoor suppliers carry binoculars. Birdwatchers (try your local Audubon Society, especially if it has a retail shop) are excellent sources of reliable information about binoculars and can direct you to good suppliers.

---

bed that night. Eventually the observation process becomes automatic—subconscious—and it will seem normal to take a few moments each morning and evening recording the day's natural events.

The best medium for recording your nature observation is your own field notebook, which can be anything from a 95-cent spiral notebook to a custom-made, leather-covered blank book. It doesn't matter what it is, so long as you keep it with you and use it.

What to record:

- Dates.
- Location of your camp (as detailed as possible).
- High and low temperatures of each day (bring a high/low thermometer to hang in camp out of direct sun).
- Weather highlights of each day.
- When you get to a new campsite, spend some time doing a "biological inventory" around camp; make lists of all the plants, insects, birds, and mammals you see. Look up what you don't know (keep a box or bag of field guides handy), and draw and make notes of things you can't identify, so you can ask someone later.
- Make notations when something interesting happens—you watch a tree squirrel raiding the nuts from a woodpecker granary, for example—and don't forget to mark the time and weather.

Eventually you will learn patterns in the natural web of life around you: birds are active in the morning, mammals are more active at night, butterflies become more numerous at midday, mountain lions often walk down trails and backroads at night (from track sightings), foxes and coyotes often poop on trails or on rocks, and so on.

Experiment with creative writing in your nature book, too. You'll be surprised at how inspiring just being outdoors can be.

Your nature notebooks will become invaluable resources for looking up information about favorite old campsites, reminding yourself of bad campsites, tracking natural events, and just fun nostalgic reading for when you are city-bound.

Meteorology

In North America, weather generally moves from west to east, so storm systems are seldom a surprise. Storms and clearing tend to follow an overall pattern, but with so many variables over a vast area, the weather defies consistently accurate predictions.

Most Americans have seen enough weather reports on television to be able to visualize the approach of bad weather. The colored lines on the TV map represent locations of cold or warm fronts, or areas of high or low pressure. Cold fronts displace warm fronts, creating unsettled weather conditions as they move. To the camper, it means clouds and warm rain, with the wind out of the south-southwest; then more clouds and possibly cold rain as the wind shifts to the west-northwest. This typical pattern may be punctuated by random thunderstorms, or preceded by a line squall filled with thunderstorms and possibly tornadoes, in some parts of the country.

Thunderstorms usually come with the cold-front portion of the storm system, but in summer they may occur independently, like the afternoon storm rising out of the classic anvil-shaped cloud.

CLOUD LORE

Watch the clouds: they are good forecasters, and they can help you plan best- and worst-case camp days.

Clouds are concentrations of moisture in the air. There are three main types—cirrus, cumulus, and stratus—but given their indistinct and overlapping nature, clouds often show characteristics of more than one type. Like modern marriages, combination clouds are described by two connecting family names, as in cirrostratus or stratocumulus. In addition to the family names, cloud titles may incorporate *alto* (to indicate high clouds) or *nimbus* (to indicate rain).

- When clouds become generally heavier and lower, wet weather is probably on the way.
- When clouds start to show holes, or lose their definition, weather will improve.
- A mackerel sky (the high, rolling wave pattern of cirrocumulus) warns of possible severe weather in an approaching front.
- "Red sky in the morning": weather is likely to turn bad (or you're in an area with a lot of air pollution).
- Before the arrival of a thunderstorm, wind may be steady or variable. As the cloud mass nears, the wind weakens or may quit (calm before a storm), but once the storm passes overhead, strong wind shifts and downdrafts can be expected, along with rain and possibly hail.

Air Pressure

Barometers are good indicators of changing weather; they are easy to read, and information is immediate. Barometric pressure may be expressed in "inches of mercury" and/or in millibars; barometers frequently have

both scales. Initially, you set the barometer's indicator according to a known reading from a NOAA or comparable report. After the reading is set, a succession of readings tells you what the weather is about to do.

Rapid changes in pressure probably mean the weather being forecast won't last long. If the barometer is falling, bad weather is on the way. If it's rising slowly but steadily, go camping. (You can buy a barometer the size of a pocket watch, if you want to take one along. They cost as little as $25.)

Weather Radio

The National Weather Service broadcasts continuous weather reports from nearly 400 places throughout the United States. When you're in the outback, take along a nifty little gadget called the Weather One (available at most outdoor stores for about $30), and you'll get frequently updated reports that may make your trip safer and more comfortable because you can plan for severe weather. The reports are broadcast 24 hours a day on seven frequencies, all at about 162 MHz (FM).

Astronomy

Watching the night sky is a favorite pastime for campers. With the clarity of cleaner air, and the absence of distracting city lights, you can see more stars and recognize constellations more easily. To make viewing more comfortable, pull your sleeping pads out of the tent to a clear area.

Binoculars—especially those with large, light-gathering lenses—are excellent for augmenting your star gazing. Galileo made his great discoveries 400 years ago using an instrument as simple as a pair of today's

lars, like 10 x 40s or 10 x 50s, will just show a crescent shape as the planet is sidelit by the sun.

- In winter, the great nebula in Orion is a beautiful sight. Look in the hunter's sword; the nebula will show as a bluish or greenish glow. This is an enormous region of ionized hydrogen where stars are literally being born, about 1,500 light years distant.

Without binoculars, in middle to high latitudes, look for the elusive and spectacular *aurora borealis,* or northern lights. The display of shifting, glowing, often colorful light patterns cannot be described.

And of course the common constellations are always fun: the Big Dipper, Little Dipper, Draco, Cassiopeia, and so many more. Buy an inexpensive star chart or Planisphere, usually available at outdoor stores, to guide you.

After-Camping Chores

To make your next trip as easy as buying food, checking some lists, and loading up the truck, make sure you clean up, inspect, and repair your gear—whether for car camping, backpacking, biking, or boating—after every trip, then stow it in a cool (but not cold), dry place where you can get to it easily (keep it all in one place, so there's no last-minute treasure hunting).

Tents and Tarps

If you weren't able to clean and dry the tent at camp before packing up, set it up in the yard. If it needs cleaning, hose it down or use a sponge to get rid of mud and leaves, taking special care to remove spots from

bird droppings or tree drippings. Use warm water and a mild soap, such as Ivory flakes, Dr. Bronner's soap, or the liquid hand soap you buy in pump bottles. Don't use detergents or bleach; they may damage the fabric or waterproof coating. (When in doubt, refer to the care label of your tent.)

It is most important that the tent be completely dry before packing, so mildew doesn't have a chance to form.

Some campers keep the tent in its carry bags; others accordion-fold it loosely and hang it over a padded hanger, or lay it on a shelf.

Look for any places where the fabric is starting to get thin from chafing, and reinforce it before it becomes a hole. Nylon tape can help, but patching with tent fabric will be most permanent.

When zippers don't work smoothly, the first step is to wash with warm, soapy water; it may be an attack of killer grit. Also try rubbing them with trusty old bar soap or a wax candle. Spray lubricants might help a stubborn zipper, but they can also stain the fabric.

Watch pole ends for corrosion or scratches. Sand them with a fine wet or dry paper and spray *lightly* with silicone lubricant. Replace bent poles before the weak leg causes others to buckle.

When the shock cord in your poles starts to lose its spring, buy a replacement kit and restring the poles. Put a leader on the cord so it threads through without bunching.

If one style of tent peg seems to bend too readily, consider replacing them all with stronger stakes, before it becomes necessary.

Not surprisingly, major repairs (on tents, sleeping bags, packs) are

birding binoculars. Books such as *Exploring the Night Sky With Binoculars,* by Patrick Moore (Cambridge University Press, 1986), and *Touring the Universe Through Binoculars,* by Philip Harrington (John Wiley and Sons, 1990), will guide you in detail.

What can you see with binoculars?

- Consult your monthly chart (buy a current *Astronomy* magazine) to see which planets are visible when you're out. Jupiter is the prime goal, because with 7×35 or larger optics you should be able to spot one or all of the Gallilean moons: Io, Ganymede, Europa, and Callisto. Jupiter actually has 16 moons, but these four are the only ones visible through small magnification.
- Mars will clearly show its red tinge, and when Venus is near us in its orbit, sharp and powerful binocu-

done at shops that specialize in outdoor gear.

Sleeping Bags

After each use, air the bags inside out, out of direct sunlight, for a few hours. (Or toss them into the dryer on very low heat, one by one.)

When sleeping bags need to be washed, it's easiest to take a trip to the nearest laundromat (make sure the washers are front-loaders).

Down bags can be washed—carefully—in a large washer with mild soap on a gentle cycle (check label instructions). Hand washing is also suggested, but to call that tedious is an understatement. Dry the bag at a low-heat setting, for as long as it takes. Or, take your bag to your local outdoor retailer—they can send it to a down cleaning service. Don't dry-clean down.

For storage, roll or fold the bag loosely, and keep it in a laundry bag or a big pillow sham.

Mattresses

Sponge-wash with mild soap and warm water; then rinse with a hose and leave outside to dry thoroughly, out of direct sun. Partially inflate and store on a cool shelf.

If your inflatable mattress springs a leak, buy an appropriate sealer to plug the pinhole. Manufacturers usually offer repair products and kits.

Stoves

The orifices on liquid-fuel stove burners get clogged after a while and

> **FOR GEAR CARE AND REPAIR**
> Every camper should have a copy of Annie Getchell's *Essential Outdoor Gear Manual* (Ragged Mountain Press, 1995), which is full of excellent do-it-yourself tips for tents, bags, stoves, boats, climbing gear, boots, and more.

need to be cleaned out with the tiny wire device in your maintenance kit. (Kerosene is a quicker clogger.)

Some liquid-fuel stoves are made to be self-cleaning. If this doesn't seem to be working, and it's possible to take the burner apart, soak the jet in some of the fuel the stove burns. When all cleaning attempts fail, replace the burner.

The pressure pumping handle will need a new O-ring or gasket sometime.

Lanterns

Treat liquid-gas lantern burners the same as stove burners. Also, burn out the fuel rather than let it sit for any length of time. If you didn't buy a lantern case, leave the light in its "wastebasket" travel holder. Check your supply of spare mantles and add to the "buy" list when needed.

Packs

Backpackers should give their packs a thorough going-over. See Chapter 2 for some good posttrip tips for getting your pack up to speed for your next adventure.

Further Resources for Camping Information
Books

Simple Tent Camping, by Zora and David Aiken (Camden, ME: Ragged Mountain Press, 1996).

The Backpacker's Handbook, by Chris Townsend (Camden, ME: Ragged Mountain Press, 1997), 2d edition.

Wilderness Skiing and Winter Camping, by Chris Townsend (Camden, ME: Ragged Mountain Press, 1994).

Woodall's Campground Directory, 13975 West Polo Trail Drive, Lake Forest, IL 60045; (800) 323-9076.

Periodicals

Family Camping, 33 East Minor Street, Emmaus, PA 18098; (215) 967-5171.

Outside Magazine, 400 Market Street, Santa Fe, NM 87501; (505) 989-7100.

See also resource listings in chapters on specific sports for magazines that specialize in backpacking, bicycling, skiing, canoeing, sea kayaking, and river running.

Other Resources

See Appendix B, p. 328, for more outdoor resources.

Chapter 11
HALF-PINT ADVENTURING

Big World,
    Small Adventurers

Kids Afield—Practical Tips
    and Advice

Further Resources for
    Half-Pint Adventuring

Big World, Small Adventurers

Many of us can trace our love of the outdoors to time spent with a special adult—an aunt, a parent, a brother—hiking, canoeing, camping, or just exploring. And so, as a parent or eager aunt or uncle today, you can't wait to introduce the kids in your life to the great outdoors.

What does it take? A common thread you'll read in all books about adventuring with kids is, Relax, slow down, take it easy. Keep that in mind, and things are bound to go great. And you're likely to learn something along the way as well—a new way to look at frogs, how to build a stick fort, how interesting ordinary pebbles can be, or the value of a completely open mind, for starters.

START YOUNG
According to a recent public opinion poll (as reported in *Family Camping* magazine, Summer 1996), 63 percent of Americans began their favorite recreational activity while growing up, with 31 percent starting before they were eight years old.

How Old?

Some dedicated outdoor enthusiasts can hardly wait until baby is home from the delivery room to ask their mate, When's the first camping trip?

Cautious parents might ask, How old do our kids have to be before we can take them on trips with us?

The answer is, It depends—or perhaps, it depends on what you are prepared for. One extreme is illustrated by a well-known couple who work off the coast of Antarctica as researchers on their steel-hulled sailboat: she gave birth twice at sea, once in a storm in between helm duty while her husband was sick. Needless to say, that baby started having "outdoor adventures" from hour-one. Common wisdom says to wait until the baby can hold its head up on its own. Then begin cautiously. Certainly, the sooner camping and hiking and boating become part of the "normal" life of a child, the happier and more comfortable that child will be in the wilderness throughout childhood. By all means consult your doctor if you have any doubts.

A wonderful story of a baby's first river trip, in Ken Wright's *A Wilder Life: Essays from Home* (Durango, CO: Kivaki Press, 1995), is all about the decision to try it, the mental and physical preparations, and the joy and the agony of taking a one-year-old on a four-day raft trip on the San Juan River. (The essay is also reprinted in Ragged Mountain Press's *Whole Paddler's Catalog.*)

Much of the information in this chapter was adapted from the wonderful book, Simple Tent Camping, *by Zora and David Aiken (Camden, ME: Ragged Mountain Press, 1996).*

The Zen of Kids in the Outdoors

As mentioned at left, the most important thing to do as an adult introducing kids to the outdoors is to take it easy. If you are new to an activity and are still uneasy with it, you might want to wait to introduce kids to it until you are confident and secure yourself. Kids will pick up your uneasiness. Choose an activity you know well, and then pare it way down to kid level, which means about a tenth of what you normally would do. Do you cruise a five-mile hike regularly and with ease? With small kids (under 12), stick to a half-mile foray—or better yet, just head out with fun in mind and pay no attention to any time or distance goals.

Seasoned outdoor educators who work with kids say that adults often have preconceived ideas about what kids *should* be doing or experiencing in the outdoors and get frustrated when after an hour of walking, the kids get bored and ask for their GameBoys or want to go home. The problem is not that kids get bored with the outdoors, but that perhaps they get bored with the adult conception of the outdoors. Ideally, we could let kids run free in the wilds, to discover their own sense of the

DEALING WITH GENERATION Y

The thing most likely to drive you crazy while introducing kids to a new activity is the nonstop litany of *why's*. Why do we have to camp here? Why do we have to wear a helmet? Why can't we feed the birds?

The trick is to explain to kids what you do and why you do it *as* you do it, rather than just issuing a seemingly endless series of nonsensical orders that are guaranteed to go in one ear and out the other. For example, you could explain

- Why you pick a certain tentsite—away from tall trees with branches that could fall on the tent, or in a site with no baby trees or plants growing in it.
- Why you locate a fire in a particular spot, or why you choose not to have a fire—there is not enough natural wood, or you want to keep the fire from scarring the land.
- Why wild animals shouldn't be fed by people—wild animals need to eat wild food; some animals, such as deer, will eat human food and even the wrappers the food comes in, and this can kill them.
- Why the latrine is placed far from water—you don't want human waste getting into the water.

Kids may not show immediate cosmic connections to all the explanations, but some day it will click, and you'll have raised a conscientious camper and lifetime lover of the outdoors.

Kids might have a different idea of what's fun and interesting than you do.

DENNIS WELSH

outdoors. But because we can't do that, here are some suggestions from outdoor educators on how you as an adult can work with kids in the outdoors.

- Let kids be kids—don't overlay your agendas on their own way of seeing the world around them (so don't try to force them to learn something—let nature teach them in its own way).
- Make sure the pace is slow; kids like to stop and look at things, and they also get distracted easily.

That's okay—it's only natural.
- Kids need plenty of fuel to keep up their energy; make sure you pack plenty of carbohydrate-rich food (peanut butter crackers, bagels, granola, bananas, and so on) and drink lots of fluids. Stop-

ping often to snack and look around is the best plan.

- Provide kids with their own packs and "outside kits": field guides especially for kids (the Golden Guides are great), blank notebooks or diaries, several small plastic bottles for briefly collecting insects or tadpoles for a closer look, a plastic magnifying glass, kids' binoculars, a compass, and so on.

- Offer guidance but don't be overbearing. This is a hard one for an anxious parent, but try to put yourself in the child's place—do *you* like having someone tell you what to do all the time?

- Put a twist on the planning process: let kids pick the place, plan the day, be "in charge" (within reason, of course).

- Plan some games to keep the activity level up if you are out for an extended time, such as a backpack or canoe trip, since kids won't be as happy as you just lolling around after a week at the office. The books listed in the resources section at the end of this chapter offer some great nature and outdoor game suggestions. Do keep your travel time short each day— a few hours at most, until kids get the hang of wilderness travel.

- Young kids especially love to find their own "secret places"; help them find shallow cubbies or caves under boulders or build a secret fort under a shrub where they can do whatever they like— eat, nap, read.

- See the Kid Quotient sections of the chapters in Part One for tips for specific sports, including hiking, backpacking, sea kayaking, canoeing, river running, climbing, mountain biking, and cross-country skiing.

- Refer to Chapter 13 for good tips on health and safety outdoors, including important information about insect repellent chemicals and first aid for kids.

Highly recommended reading for adults who are interested in children's interactions with wild places is *The Geography of Childhood: Why Children Need Wild Places* by Gary Paul Nabhan and Stephen Trimble. The authors share their own and their friends' parenting experiences, as well as refer to interesting studies about children in nature. (See the resources section at the end of this chapter for more information on books.)

Professional environmental educators highly recommend books by Joseph Cornell, including *Sharing the Joy of Nature: Nature Activities for All Ages* and *Sharing Nature With Children* (both Dawn Publications).

Kids Afield— Practical Tips and Advice
Sleeping Arrangements

Babies sleep like babies in a portable playpen, which also serves as a useful safe haven during the daytime. On backpacking trips, rig a temporary "sleeping pen" out of packs and other soft gear in your tent. Later, they'll use a sleeping bag and mat of their own.

For safety, let a small child sleep between two adults, or at least on the side of the tent opposite the entrance, so there's no chance of an attempted moonlight stroll without your being alerted by the crawl-over.

REMEMBER TO THINK SMALL

When venturing outdoors with kids, remember to think small. You see grand, postcard-pretty vistas and the awesomeness of nature; they see the colorful pebbles along the trail or the squirrels playing on the rocks, the way leaves get trapped in whirlpools or the industrious work of an ant colony. You want to climb to the highest ridge; they want to find secret hideouts.

Gary Paul Nabhan in an essay in *The Geography of Childhood* remembers: "In retrospect, it is amusing to me that when I wished my children to have contact with wildness, I sent them 'out,' to climb high upon ridges and to absorb grand vistas. Yet when they wished to gain a sense of wildness, of animal comfort, they chose not the large, but the small. In doing so, they may have been selecting a primordial connection with the earth and its verdant cover."

Little children can share a grown-up's sleeping bag; just unzip it and use it as an under-and-over comforter. (If you wait till they're exhausted to put them to bed, they'll be less inclined to have a giggle-fest playing footsie.)

"Middle-aged" children can share an adult-width bag—a good sleep setup when they are also sharing a separate small tent.

Children's sleeping bags are made in a couple of lengths. These are fine hand-downs, but if no second child is waiting, they're outgrown too soon.

To bring an adult bag down to size, roll up the unused foot portion, clamping it shut with a long bag clip or giant clothespins. (Or, fold it underneath for extra protection from the ground.) You may lose some of the insulating property due to compressing the bag where it rolls; if feet are cold, you can always toss a small blanket over the end of the bag.

Latrine Duty

Introducing a toddler to camping is challenging enough, but finding an easy way to deal with potty duty can be too much of a challenge. For car camping, try the flower-pot potty:

Take along an extra-large plastic flowerpot and base. Before you leave home, cut out the bottom of the pot, leaving no sharp edges—this is your toilet seat. At your "wilderness" bathroom, dig a small pit at least 12 inches deep and turn the flowerpot upside down over it. Use the flowerpot base for a lid. Each time you use the flowerpot, cover the waste with a scoop of dirt. When leaving the campsite, refill the hole completely.

Any collapsible toilet seat—or a jury-rigged seat on a frame—can be used over the wilderness pit.

Young children are often fascinated by new options in the world of toilet training and will want to use them more often than necessary. A few may be nervous about a toilet that has no reassuring flush; this attitude is the greater problem. In either case, introduce the portable toilets at home, long before the first camping trip and when you *have* an acceptable alternative.

Children may not be the only ones to experience initial problems with a changing toilet scene. Attitude adjustment is easy to suggest, less easy to accomplish, but creating a sense of privacy makes a good start. Extra effort in setting up a wilderness bathroom should not be considered a waste of time.

In lieu of a bathroom sink, put some antibacterial liquid hand soap or a soap-on-a-rope near the outdoor toilet. Keep a bottle filled with water nearby for rinsing.

Safety Inspection

When the tent is up, everyone should go on a walkabout to look for anything that could be regarded as a serious hazard, especially after dark. Note the location of sharp rocks, large roots, messy mud, or problem plants such as poison ivy and nettles.

Remind the children of safe-camping rules:

- Mind the tent guylines (have kids tie bandannas to the lines).
- Don't play with the campfire!
- If camping near a river or lake, never go near the water alone, and always wear a flotation vest in boat or canoe.
- Don't leave camp without telling an adult.
- If you chance upon an animal, leave it alone: no feeding, no chasing, no bothering.

GETTING THERE

Many children (and some adults, too) are prone to motion sickness, which can really spoil a trip, as well as put a damper on the desire to ever go on a trip again.

Prevention starts the day before you leave. Eat a light supper—no fried foods, no hot spices. Pack the car with boxes of pretzels and crackers, vanilla wafers and ginger snaps—all easily digestible settlers for unsettled stomachs. Good drinks to have handy are apple juice, ginger ale, or flavored seltzers. (Ginger itself may be a nausea preventive; get pills from a health food store.)

Sitting in the front seat, properly belted, lessens the queasy feeling for some people; it's better to watch the scenery than the interior of the car.

BOB ALLEN/OUTSIDE IMAGES

Once you're set up, remind the kids of the basic rules of safety.

First Aid

Head to your local outdoor retailer to check out the first aid kits especially for kids. Specialty outdoor first aid companies such as Adventure Medical Kits and Atwater-Carey offer kits with children's-strength medications and first aid booklets with advice on child first aid. These are definitely worth the cost (around $15 to $30).

Further Resources for Half-Pint Adventuring
Books

Simple Tent Camping, by Zora and David Aiken (Camden, ME: Ragged Mountain Press, 1996). This well-illustrated guide includes great tips for being outdoors with kids.

Kids Outdoors, by Victoria Logue, Frank Logue, and Mark Carroll (Camden, ME: Ragged Mountain Press, 1996). A book *for* kids, this is a must for kids 9–14 to whom you want to introduce the great outdoors (lots of how-to information).

Tom Brown's Field Guide to Nature and Survival for Children, by Tom Brown (New York: Berkeley Publishing Group, 1989).

Canoe Tripping with Children, by David Harrison and Judy Harrison (Merrillville, IN: ICS Books, Inc., 1990).

The Geography of Childhood, by Gary Paul Nabhan and Stephen Trimble (Boston: Beacon Press, 1994).

Periodicals

Family Camping, 33 East Minor Street, Emmaus, PA 18098; (610) 967-5171.

Chapter 12

CAMP COOKERY AND ADVENTUROUS FARE

Beyond GORP

Basic Nutrition Background

**Preparation and
Cooking Tips**

**Further Resources for
Camp Food and Cooking**

Beyond GORP

Most of us imagine outdoor foods as variations on a theme of that old standby, GORP (believed by some to stand for granola-oats-raisins-peanuts)—GORP for lunch, with milk for breakfast, and for snacks. And for dinner we can't seem to get beyond freeze-dried stews or macaroni and cheese. Ho-hum. No wonder some people don't want to try backcountry overnight trips.

But with only a little planning and time before a trip, whether it's a dayhike in the Sierra Nevada or a week canoeing in the Boundary Waters, you can enjoy delicious, fresh, varied foods. In fact, you can spend less time—and much less money—getting trip food ready if it's mostly grocery-store-bought than if you have to run around to the outdoor store, the health food store, and the import food store to amass all the freeze-dried and dehydrated foods you think you need.

Eating good, fresh food in the outdoors also means being safer. If you become malnourished because you've been surviving on jerky and GORP, you might become sick, de-

hydrated, and disoriented—and who knows what could happen. A safe outdoor trip means a well-fed backpacker, bicyclist, or boater.

This chapter won't provide recipes—there are many good books offering up sumptuous camp fare (see resources section at the end of this chapter). Rather, it will focus on how to plan what foods to use, including how much food you need to consume for certain activities, which foods offer the active outdoorsperson the best energy and nutrition value for the weight, and which foods store and travel well in packs or boats.

Freeze-dried and dehydrated backpacking foods, at one time passed over by finicky eaters, are worth a mention now because they have gotten much better over the last few years—especially those from a small southern company called Adventure Foods. If saving weight is your most important consideration, then by all means go dehydrated or freeze-dried—although keep in mind that they are somewhat costly, because of the expensive drying methods. Dehydrated food is dried slowly in a special drying chamber (to retain nutritional value); freeze-dried food is flash-frozen under vacuum at low temperatures. Most campers feel that dehydrated foods taste better than freeze-dried, but dehydrated foods are slightly heavier and take longer to cook. But cost is still the main reason why many wilderness campers search out their own alternatives to foil

packets, including drying their own food and inventing good, lightweight outdoor dishes from grocery store findings.

Much of the information in this chapter was adapted from Chris Townsend's The Backpacker's Handbook *and* Wilderness Skiing and Winter Camping *(both published by Ragged Mountain Press). And, Townsend cites the excellent book* Food Facts, *by David Briggs and Mark Wahlquist (Penguin), as his source for many of the food charts.*

Another excellent book with lots of good tips on outdoor food and cooking (a few of which are mentioned in this chapter), especially for car and family camping, is *Simple Tent Camping* by Zora and David Aiken (Camden, ME: Ragged Mountain Press, 1996).

Basic Nutrition Background
Fats, Proteins, Carbohydrates

Food consists of several components, each of which the body needs. The main ones are fats, proteins, and carbohydrates. All three provide energy but also serve other functions.

Fats release their energy slowly and can be stored in the body to be used when required. Because fats are digested gradually, they aren't a quick source of energy. Your body cannot

HOT OR COLD?

According to Chris Townsend, hot food provides no more energy than cold food does, and cooking food can destroy some vitamins. (Exceptions are certain starches, such as potatoes, beans, and lentils, which need to be cooked to make them more digestible and, in the case of the last two, to destroy substances that make utilizing their protein difficult.) One way to cut the weight of your pack, bike, or boat significantly would be to eat only cold food, and thus dispense with stove, fuel, and cookware. However, on short trips, the extra weight is so slight that it doesn't matter; on long trips, the psychological boost of hot food is essential, especially if the weather turns cold and wet. And in winter, a stove and fuel can be important survival tools.

Why suffer? With a little planning, meals on the trail can be something to look forward to.

CLIFF LEIGHT

easily digest food while exercising, either, so it's best to avoid eating a lot of fat during the day. When eaten as part of your evening meal, however, fats release their energy during the night, which helps keep you warm. Sources of fat include dairy products, margarine, eggs, nuts, and meat. The current wisdom is that you should cut down on foods high in saturated fats (butter, animal fat margarine, cheese, whole milk, lard, chocolate) and replace them with those high in polyunsaturated fats (vegetable margarines, low-fat spreads, vegetable oil) and monounsaturated fats (olive and canola oils). Nutritionists also recommend cutting down the total amount of fat in the diet, anyway, since fat can have other unwanted health effects. The body needs some fat, but nothing like the amount most people in developed countries eat. However, fats are an important part of the ac-

tive outdoorsperson's diet, especially in cold weather.

Protein renews muscles and body tissue. During digestion, proteins break down into the amino acids from which they're made. The body

then rebuilds these into muscle and tissue protein. Complete proteins contain a full complement of amino acids; they're most commonly found in meat, eggs, and dairy products. Incomplete proteins, which lack one or more amino acids, are found in grains and legumes and can be combined to create complete proteins: for example, a stew with beans and barley provides all the amino acids you need. The body either burns protein as fuel or stores it as fat if it isn't immediately used for muscle regeneration, so protein is best eaten in small amounts at every meal.

The body quickly and directly turns *carbohydrates* into energy, so these are the foods most needed by the backpacker. Carbohydrates may be simple or complex. Simple ones are sugars (sucrose, dextrose, fructose, glucose, and honey); complex ones include starches (grains, vegetables, legumes). Generally, you should try to rely more on complex carbohydrates, because they provide more energy over a longer period of time. They also provide fiber, vitamins, and minerals. Fiber is essential in your diet to prevent constipation—a potential problem for the outdoorsperson living on dehydrated food for a long period. Sugars give you a quick boost when you're tired, but it won't last, and it can lead to fatigue when the carbohydrates are used up.

Determining what constitutes a proper proportion of these components in your diet is a nutritionist's basic reason for being. The current advice is to eat less fat and protein, and more carbohydrates. Most serious backpackers, skiers, boaters, and bike tourers, especially those who undertake long expeditions, come to this conclusion naturally, because it's carbohydrates that speed you along and that you crave when food runs low.

Vitamins and Minerals

Vitamins and minerals are also food components, but not ones you need

worry about on trips of less than one month. Even if your diet is deficient in them for short periods, you shouldn't be harmed. On long trips, however, the lack of fresh food could mean that you need to add a vitamin and mineral supplement to your diet.

Calories and Weight

A calorie is the measure of food's energy value. The calorie measurement used in reference to food is the kilocalorie (kcal)—it represents the amount of heat needed to raise 1 kilogram of water 1 degree Celsius. (Although *kilocalorie* is the proper term of measurement, *calorie* is the term used on most food packets.) Sometimes kilojoules are used instead of kilocalories; there are 4.2 kilojoules to the kilocalorie.

How many kilocalories a person needs per day depends upon the person's metabolism, weight, age, sex, and level of activity. Metabolism, an extremely complex process that is not fully understood, defines the body processes that transform foodstuffs into usable elements and energy; any surplus is stored as fat. If you eat more kilocalories than you use, you will put on weight; if you eat less, you will lose it.

Each person's metabolic rate differs, although in general, the fitter and more active you are, the faster you will burn up food, whether you are working or at rest. Figures are available for the kilocalories needed for "everyday life" for people of different sizes: for someone 5 feet, 8 inches tall who weighs 155–160 pounds, it's around 2,500 kilocalories a day. Of that, 1,785 kilocalories make up the basal metabolism (the energy required simply to keep the body functioning), based on 1,100 kilocalories per 45

kilograms of body weight. To be able to expend more energy without burning body stores, that person needs to consume more than 2,500 kilocalories per day.

You can calculate roughly your kilocalorie needs based on figures that give kilocalorie demands of different activities. Using the information on p. 279 as a guideline (note that the figures are for *kilocalorie used per hour*), calculate your kilocalorie demands for different activities; don't forget to include all 24 hours of the day, including sleeping. Adjust your trip food accordingly (see the section on kilocalorie content of certain foods, p. 280). These figures are adapted from *Food Facts*.

Keep in mind that on longer trips, your appetite will go up dramatically after the first couple of weeks, and that in cold weather, you will need more kilocalories.

See p. 280 for figures for kilocalorie content in common foods. The figures in the table are adapted from a variety of sources, including *Agricultural Handbook No. 8: Composition of Foods* (U.S. Department of Agriculture), reproduced in *Mountaineering: The Freedom of the Hills* (4th edition); *Food Facts;* and manufacturers' specifications.

Based on calories only, these figures suggest that you should live solely on margarine, vegetable oil, dried eggs, nuts, and chocolate in order to carry the least weight. But you wouldn't feel very good or travel easily, since all these are very high in fats. In fact, fats contain 9 kilocalories per gram, while proteins and carbohydrates have just 4.

A diet of complex carbohydrates (dried skimmed milk, dried fruit, dried vegetables, pasta, rice, oat

	Kilocalories per hour	
Activity	128-pound woman	154-pound man
Sleeping, resting, fasting	30–60	60–90
Sitting–reading, desk work	60–90	90–120
Sitting–typing, playing piano, operating controls	90–150	120–180
Light bench work, serving in store, gardening, slow walking	120–210	180–240
Social sports, cycling, tennis, light factory work, light farm work	180–300	240–360
Heavy physical labor, carrying, stacking, cutting wood, jogging, competitive sports	240–420	360–510
Very hard physical labor, intense physical activity, heavy lifting, very vigorous sporting activity	600+	720+

crackers, muesli, and granola bars) plus a little fat (cheese, margarine) gives around 400 kilocalories per 3 ½ ounces. This works out to 2.2 pounds of food for 4,000 kilocalories per day. This diet should also provide enough in the way of protein. Only a sugar-based diet runs the risk of insufficient protein.

It's worth checking the caloric content of any food you intend to carry—there are significant variations between brands, and high-calorie carbohydrate-based foods mean less weight than low-calorie ones. For example, canned fish, a popular outdoor staple, has a high weight-per-calorie ratio (including the can); and coffee lovers should note the low score there, too—cocoa's a much better choice.

On backpacking trips, Chris Townsend carries 35 ounces of food for each day on the trail. Powdered drinks, condiments, and other odds and ends are included in this total, which roughly divides into 5 ounces for breakfast, 14 ounces for dinner, and 14 ounces consumed during the day. The main evening meal usually

weighs around 7 ounces, the other 7 ounces made up of soup, margarine, herbs and spices, milk powder, coffee, and sugar. These figures yield approximately 800, 1,600, and 1,600 kilocalories for the three meals. Bike tourists, canoeists, and kayakers will find similar breakdowns useful, while rafters and campers might do with less, unless the weather is very cold or they plan a few days of hard hiking or rapids-shooting.

Preparation and Cooking Tips

Cooking food outdoors, as discussed in Chapter 10, can take many forms: single- or double-burner stoves, grilling and roasting over campfires, baking, Dutch ovens, multicourse, or single-pot.

Just plain old experimentation and experience will be your best guides to learning the art of outdoor cooking. The information on p. 280 will help you choose the best foods, but only you can perfect its preparation in the dark during a rainstorm

on a rocky mountaintop in subfreezing temperatures.

One-Pot Cooking

Certainly cooking with just one pot, Dutch oven, or skillet makes the most sense—easy fix, easy clean.

It's surprising how many meals you can come up with just on your own for one-pot meals, such as

- Soups
- Stews
- Rice-based casseroles and stir-fries
- Cheese-based casseroles
- Pasta dishes
- Roast meat with dumplings steamed on top

Make your favorite stews and casseroles from scratch, or start at the grocery store and see what you can find: tuna helpers, cheese and noodle packets (and not just macaroni and cheese, but really good sauces, such as Alfredo and garlic-and-butter), flavored rices with dried vegetables, dried soup mixes, simmer sauces for meats, and much more. Augment your backpacking pantry with freeze-dried or dehydrated foods such as tuna or vegetables.

And consult a book such as Don Jacobson's *The One Pan Gourmet* (Ragged Mountain Press, 1993) for a wide variety of one-pot, one-skillet, or one-oven recipes for backpackers, boaters, and bikers.

BOIL INSTEAD OF TOIL

At home, freeze leftover soups, stews, casseroles, and other meals in boiling-safe plastic bags, such as those sold for Seal-A-Meal; make sure you label the contents and include the date.

At camp, just heat the bag in boiling water—no prep, no cleanup.

Food	Kilocalories per 3½ ounces	% fat	% protein	% carbo-hydrate
Dairy products, fats, and oils				
Margarine	720	81.0	0.6	0.4
Low-fat spread	366	36.8	6.0	3.0
Vegetable oil	900	100.0	—	—
Instant dried skim milk	355	1.3	36.0	53.0
Cheddar cheese	398	32.2	25.0	2.1
Edam cheese	305	23.0	24.0	—
Parmesan cheese	410	30.0	35.0	—
Eggs, dried	592	41.2	47.0	4.1
Low-fat cheese spread	175	9.0	20.0	4.0
Dried fruit				
Apples	275	—	1.0	78.0
Apricots	261	—	5.0	66.5
Dates	275	—	2.2	72.9
Figs	275	—	4.3	69.1
Peaches	261	—	3.1	68.3
Raisins	289	—	2.5	77.4
Vegetables				
Potatoes, dehydrated	352	—	8.3	80.4
Tomato flakes	342	—	10.8	76.7
Baked beans	123	2.6	6.1	19.0
Nuts				
Almonds	600	57.7	18.6	19.5
Brazil nuts	652	66.9	14.3	10.9
Coconut, desiccated	605	62.0	6.0	6.0
Peanut butter	589	49.4	27.8	17.2
Peanuts, roasted	582	49.8	26.0	18.8
Grain products				
Oatmeal	375	7.0	11.0	62.4
Muesli, sweetened	348	6.3	10.4	66.6
Pasta, white	370	—	12.5	75.2
Pasta, whole wheat	323	0.5	12.5	67.2
Rice, brown	359	—	7.5	77.4
Rice, white	363	—	6.7	80.4
Flour, plain	360	2.0	11.0	75.0
Flour, whole meal	345	3.0	12.0	72.0

Food	Kilocalories per 3½ ounces	% fat	% protein	% carbo-hydrate
Baked products				
Granola bar	382	13.4	4.9	64.4
Crispbread, rye	345	1.2	13.0	76.3
Oat crackers	369	15.7	10.1	65.6
Bread, white	271	—	8.7	50.5
Bread, whole meal	243	—	10.5	47.7
Cookies, chocolate	525	28.0	6.0	67.0
Fig bar	356	5.6	3.9	75.4
Cake, fruit	355	13.0	5.0	58.0
Meat and fish				
Beef, dried	204	6.3	34.3	—
Beef, corned, canned	264	18.0	23.5	—
Salami	490	45.0	19.0	2.0
Salmon, canned	151	7.1	20.8	—
Sardines, drained	165	11.1	24.0	—
Tuna, drained	165	8.2	28.8	—
Sugars and sweets				
Honey	303	—	0.3	82.0
Sugar, brown	373	—	—	96.4
Sugar, white	384	—	—	99.5
Chocolate, milk	518	32.3	7.7	56.9
Custard, instant	378	10.2	2.9	72.6
Drinks				
Cocoa, mix	391	10.6	9.4	73.9
Coffee	2	—	0.2	—
Tea	1	—	0.1	—
Complete meals				
Pasta and sauce	384	4.7	13.1	77.1
Vegetable goulash and potato mix	375	11.9	15.9	54.4
Vegetable cottage pie	391	3.0	16.3	66.5
Thick pea soup	333	5.3	17.0	58.0
Bean stew mix	349	2.9	17.5	67.3
Fruit-and-nut bar	420	28.0	17.0	56.0

(from Food Facts, by David Briggs and Mark Wahlquist)

No-Pot Cooking

One way to cook outside is to forget the pots altogether. Think aluminum foil; wrap and steam food over any heat source.

In addition to being easy to cook, steamed foods are healthy for you. Not to suggest they will be tasteless: country-style ribs foil-wrapped with your own barbecue sauce will have flavor steamed through the meat, not just sitting on top in a surface glaze.

Using heavyweight foil, wrap each packet securely, rolling up and folding in the side edges to seal in juices. Wrap food with the shiny side of foil facing in, so heat won't be deflected back to the fire. Double-wrap any items that tend to burn easily. Steam vegetables for dinner and fruit for dessert (add a little water).

Cooking corn-on-the-cob in its own husk is fairly common around campfires (soak the corn in water first), but other foods benefit from a natural wrap, too. Wrap meats or sliced vegetables in grape or cabbage leaves and steam/broil a subtle flavor into the food as it cooks.

Outdoor Baking

A few years ago the BakePacker and Outback Oven hit the scene and changed the lives of outdoor cooks forever. It's truly amazing what you can do with these gadgets, and many others (including homemade) like them. The BakePacker (under $20) works on the steam-in method, so the baked items are quite moist; the Outback Oven ($45, for deluxe model that includes nonstick baking pan) and others work on traditional convection heat, so the end products—including chocolate cake and pizza—taste like they came out of your GE range.

Batter up! With the right equipment, such as this multiburner stove, there are very few limits on what you can eat.

Outback Oven and BakePacker sell their own meals and cake mixes, a good idea if you don't have time to experiment with adapting home recipes and grocery store cake mixes to the right proportions and substitu-

tions (such as dried milk and egg). They happen to be delicious, as well (the pizzas, especially).

But if you have the time to experiment with outdoor baking, it's well worth it. First, don't start without reading Jean and Samuel Spangenberg's *The Portable Baker* (Ragged Mountain Press, 1997). They will tell you which ovens work and how to

adapt recipes for them, as well as give you their own great recipes. (Incidentally, they include recipes for Dutch ovens, which are, after all, the original camp oven.).

Here are some camp baking and baking-prep tips.

- Pack muffin, cornbread, pancake, or other dry mixes in zip-top bags (double up for extra security). When you're ready to cook, add liquid ingredients and use the sealed bag as a mixing bowl (or bypass the dirty spoon—close the bag and mix and massage ingredients with your fingers). Write the recipe on the bag or cut it off the original container and stash inside the zip-top bag.
- Look in the grocery store for egg powder. The boxes usually indicate how many teaspoons equals one egg for baking recipes. (You might need to increase the water a little if more than two eggs are called for.)
- Dried milk or buttermilk is also a handy baking substitute; mix up as needed in a Nalgene at camp.
- Make a trip to the grocery store to investigate new ideas for camp baked foods (as well as stovetop mixes). There are a lot of easy-to-fix mixes that can be adapted to camp cooking—biscuits, muffins, strudels, pie dough (make meat and vegetable pies), pizza dough, stuffing, and more.

Dry Your Own Camp Foods

From a weight-and-space perspective, the best food to take camping—especially backpacking, bike touring, and boating—is dried food. Instead of buying commercially prepared and packaged meals, many backcountry campers dry their own.

WANTED: EXPERIENCED TRAVELING COMPANIONS

If you want to include more fresh foods in your camp fare, you need to stick with foods that travel well in terms of both spoilage and durability. Here are some good ones.

- *Bagels.* For sandwiches, toast, and dinner rolls, nothing beats the durability and tastiness of bagels.
- *Limes or lemons.* Add a couple of limes or lemons to your pantry and you'll appreciate the pep they give to meat dishes, vegetables, rice, even your drinking water.
- *Roma tomatoes.* These plum-size fruits are just the right size for one serving or dish (no leftover tomato halves floating around), and are very tough and tasty.
- *Cabbage.* A small cabbage keeps well, makes great salad with a little oil and vinegar, and is great shredded over soft-tortilla tacos or chicken stir-fry.
- *New potatoes, baby carrots.* These root crops keep well, are an easier size to manage while camping than their grownup counterparts, and can add a lot to many soups, rice dishes, and stews, or be eaten as side dishes.
- *Granny Smith apples, tangerines.* Like their vegetable cousins above, these fruits are small and tough, keep well, and are versatile for both cooking (add tangerine sections to your morning cream of wheat) and snacking.

TOP 10 CAMP KITCHEN MUST-HAVES

In no particular order,

1. Sharp knife (knives)
2. Plastic cutting board, as large or small as you have room for (doubles as a card table, bedside light stand, splint, emergency paddle, etc.)
3. Heat diffuser (makes slow simmering possible on cantankerous stoves)
4. Nonstick pot(s) and/or griddle (the Outback Oven Deluxe, a baking setup, comes with a nonstick pan and lid, heat diffuser and pot risers, *and* cutting board)
5. Well-stocked spice kit (oregano, garlic, basil, dill, cumin, curry, chile, cinnamon, and so on)
6. Boil-in plastic bags and zip-top plastic bags, for leftovers
7. Precut squares of aluminum foil (at least 10; they can be washed and reused a number of times)
8. One or more PackTowls, a thirsty cellulose wonder that can be used to wash *and* dry
9. "Survival" lighter, and lots of backup matches in a zip-top bag
10. Small Nalgene bottle (the only kind that won't leak) of vegetable oil—a little rubbed in your pots before you cook will greatly ease cleanup (change oil after each trip; it gets rancid)

Fruits and vegetables, meats, cheese, even eggs can be home-dried. Think about which foods you would use the most for camp cooking.

- For pasta and stir-fries: dried mushrooms, garlic, green and red peppers

- For soups or stews: beans, potatoes, carrots, onions, meats, turnips
- For Italian food: tomatoes, mushrooms, zucchini

A commercial food dryer may provide the most efficient means, but once food is appropriately cut, diced, or sliced, it can be dried in other ways, too. With all methods, timing will be "until dry." Store all dried foods in the most airtight containers you own.

Sun

Place all food on screens in direct sun. Screens should be raised about 8 inches off the ground, so air circulates. Cover with netting, to discourage bugs or birds. Turn the food a few times during the day, and bring it inside at night.

Oven

Set at lowest temperature (probably 140 degrees F); prop door open a bit; set food directly on racks, or on trays or cookie sheet.

Room

Some items (such as herbs, green beans, pepper strips, apple slices) can be hung out to dry.

Dried food can be enjoyed as snacks, but it can also be used in recipes that call for fresh foods, including fruit, meat, and vegetables. It takes some practice to use dried foods in cooking. You want to be sure to rehydrate them enough so you don't end up with hard lumps of blue jerky in your blueberry muffins, for example; soak dried foods for at least an

hour in hot water before using in a recipe and test before using. And get creative—dried fruit and vegetables can be added to rice, stews, soups, cereals, salads, flambéd with brandy for dessert, sautéed with olive oil and pasta, marinated in oil and spices, and so on.

Tips on drying your own outdoor food are from Alan Kesselheim's *The Lightweight Gourmet* (Ragged Mountain Press, 1995).

THE PERFECT SNACK

Beware of chewing on a hunk of meat jerky as a trail or boating snack—it can make you very thirsty.

Instead, buy or make your own fruit leathers. They're much better for you, and won't leave you parched. Puree your favorite fruit or fruit mix with a little lemon juice (to keep it from turning brown) and honey, then spread on a greased baking sheet; cook very low, at 140 degrees, until it is pliable but not sticky. See *The Dayhiker's Handbook* (Ragged Mountain Press, 1996) for a complete recipe.

Further Resources for Camp Food and Cooking
Books

The Lightweight Gourmet, by Alan S. Kesselheim (Camden, ME: Ragged Mountain Press, 1995). A must-have book for outdoor cooks. It includes instructions on drying your own food (and a build-it-yourself dehydrator), plus

preparation and packing tips and recipes for fresh, healthful, delicious, and economical meals.

The One Pan Gourmet, by Don Jacobson (Camden, ME: Ragged Mountain Press, 1993). A simple, honest, and likable book that deals with camp food for the ordinary backpacker, canoeist, kayaker, or bike tourist—no fancy pretrip preparations, no difficult recipes, no super-ultralight spiels, just lots of familiar and filling food (but not much for vegetarians).

The Portable Baker, by Jean and Samuel Spangenberg (Camden, ME: Ragged Mountain Press, 1997). This wonderful and timely book will change the way you think about camp cooking. Includes reviews of baking ovens, 120 recipes, and substitution and nutrition guides.

Good Food for Camp and Trail. All-Natural Recipes for Delicious Meals Outdoors, by Dorcas S. Miller (Boulder: Pruett Publishing Company, 1993).

Simple Tent Camping, by Zora and David Aiken (Camden, ME: Ragged Mountain Press, 1996).

Other Resources

Agricultural Handbook No. 8: Composition of Foods, U.S. Department of Agriculture, Food and Consumer Services, Public Information, 3101 Park Center Drive, Alexandria, VA 22302; (703) 305-1492; www.usda.gov.

Chapter 13

SAFE AND SOUND ADVENTURES

Ensuring Sound Adventures

Water Purification

Basic First Aid

On Animals

Basic Outdoor Safety, Search, and Rescue

Hot and Cold Extremes

High-Elevation Adventures

To Explore and Protect

Further Resources for Safe and Sound Adventures

Ensuring Sound Adventures

Whether we venture into the wilderness for a day or for a month, we face the same challenges: contaminated drinking water, poisonous plants and insects, heat or cold exposure, and the possibility of getting lost or severely injured. If we cataloged every possible danger that could befall us when we head off on an outdoor adventure, we'd probably opt to stay home with ESPN instead.

But consider the challenges of everyday life in an average American city: carjackings, muggings, armed robberies, automobile accidents, drugs, gangs. Put in perspective, poison ivy and bears sound better all the time.

Another aspect of outdoor adventuring that weighs heavily on our minds is impact. As more of us venture forth into the wilderness, the greater the chances of altering the land in less-than-ideal ways.

To head safely and soundly into the wilderness, you need only two things: preparation and knowledge.

Prepare your gear by inventorying and inspecting it before you leave on your trip, giving yourself plenty of time to repair or replace anything.

Prepare an itinerary carefully and leave a copy of it with a friend.

Prepare for the worst possible weather and accidents.

Know your sport well before you head off on advanced trips, or go with someone who does know.

Know the lay of the land and a little of the natural history—plants, animals—of your destination before you leave.

Know basic first aid and evacuation procedures.

You'll find that the more prepared and knowledgeable you are, the more relaxed you will be, and thus the safer you will be. An extra bonus is that, because you are confident and relaxed, you'll have more fun. Following are some tips on outdoor health and safety. For more information, refer to the resources section at the end of this chapter, and to the chapters in Part One on specific sports.

Some of the information for this chapter was adapted from Simple Tent Camping, *by Zora and David Aiken (Camden, ME: Ragged Mountain Press, 1996);* The Backpacker's Handbook, *by Chris Townsend (Camden, ME: Ragged Mountain Press, 1997), 2d edition; and* Wilderness Skiing and Winter Camping, *by Chris Townsend (Camden, ME: Ragged Mountain Press, 1994).*

Water Purification

Unfortunately, the good old days of dipping a Sierra cup into an icy mountain stream to slake your thirst are gone—unless you want to risk acquiring an unfriendly microscopic hitchhiker in your digestive tract. Such widespread (throughout North America, in most waters) waterborne biota as *Giardia* sp., *Cryptosporidia* sp. (both protozoans), and *E. coli* (a bacteria) can cause diarrhea, vomiting, cramps, dehydration, and weight loss, along with more serious health problems if left untreated. So it's best to treat your water, by boiling, adding chemicals, or filtering.

Heat. Boiling is still a reliable way to kill waterborne biota, including *E. coli* bacteria and *Giardia.* The most cautious time recommendation is now 20 minutes. Boiling, of course, takes time and uses stove fuel. Plan accordingly for fuel supplies. (At high elevations, lower boiling temperatures may not kill biota, so chemicals or filters are preferred.)

Additives. Water purification tablets sold at outdoor or travel stores are usually iodine-based. While noses turn up at the mention of iodine, the manufacturer of one such product—Potable Aqua—offers a second additive, P.A. Plus, to take away the bad taste; always follow the directions closely to avoid health problems. Some health experts recommend that you do not use iodine for "extended periods," but the exact definition of "extended" is unclear. If you have concerns, ask your pharmacist or doctor. Occasionally, chlorine-based purification regimens are available, but household bleach is not a substitute for a regimen that chemically neutralizes chlorine after it purifies the water (chlorine in the wrong form and dilution is a health hazard). A few dollars will buy enough water treatment tablets for a few weeks of average water consumption.

Portable filters. Small, water-filtering pumps (such as those made by Katadyn, PÜR, MSR, Sweetwater, and Basic Designs) are another way to purify water, removing bacteria such as *E. coli* and *Salmonella,* and many protozoans such as *Giardia.* Some filters also claim to screen out chemicals or some viruses, although the latter are not a major concern in the United States or Canada. Don't be tempted by the simplicity of gravity filters; pumping water through fine mesh and charcoal or iodine matrices is the best way to get out germs. Portable filters from the companies listed above are very easy to use and worth their weight and cost (from about $50 to over $150).

Basic First Aid

A prerequisite for any outdoor activity, whether a quick two-mile hike or a two-week mountain bike tour of the canyonlands, is a well-stocked first aid kit that you know how to use.

To acquire a good kit, take a trip to your local outdoor retailer and see what they stock; look for prepacked kits or modular kits from Adventure

---

◆ **BASIC FIRST AID TIPS**

◆ *Blisters:* Wash with soap and water; cover with a bandage or moleskin to protect. Don't prick the blister; the fluid will be absorbed as the blister heals, and you don't want to invite infection. If the blister has broken, wash and apply 2nd Skin (a gel, available at outdoor retailers), then cover with a bandage.

◆ *Bruises:* Apply cold packs for 10- to 15-minute periods for a few hours, to reduce pain and swelling.

◆ *Burns:* If hair or clothing is burning, use a towel or blanket to smother the fire; roll the victim on the ground if necessary. For first- or second-degree burns (red, possibly blistered skin; resembles a bad sunburn), run cold water over the area for 15 minutes, or immerse in a basin with cold water. Wash, rinse, and keep site elevated. Cover burn area if it needs protection from dirt or friction. Give aspirin for pain. See a doctor if bad blistering develops. For third-degree burns (deep, very serious): Do not hold under cold water. Cover with a clean dressing or sheet, and go to a doctor.

◆ *Cuts and scrapes:* Minor bleeding usually stops in a few minutes. If not, press a gauze pad over the wound for about five minutes. Wash with soapy water, disinfect, and cover.

◆ *Eye injury:* If something is embedded in the eye, cover it with some thing, such as an inverted paper cup, to prevent further problems, and go to a doctor.

◆ *Fish hook:* If the barb is still visible, back it out. If the barb is too far into the skin, push it all the way through; cut the barb off, then pull the rest of the hook out. (Also, check date of last tetanus shot.)

◆ *Nosebleed:* Sit down and lean head forward. Pinch the nose and hold 10 minutes; if it's still bleeding, try an ice pack over the nose for 10 minutes. Or, soak a cotton ball with water and place in nostril (not too far in).

◆ *Punctures:* Wash well and disinfect. These are very susceptible to infection. See a doctor; you may need a tetanus shot.

◆ *Splinters:* If you can see the end, sterilize the tweezers and remove. If you can't see it, put some adhesive tape over the site, and pull.

◆ *Sprains and strains:* A joint may be sprained, a muscle strained; symptoms are the same: pain, swelling, bruising. Apply ice; support the area with an elastic bandage. In case of a suspected fracture, fabricate a splint with anything that will restrict movement of the affected area.

From *Simple Tent Camping,* by Zora and David Aiken (Camden, ME: Ragged Mountain Press, 1996).

Medical Kits or Atwater-Carey. This is not a good piece of gear on which to scrimp, so plan to spend from $25 (dayhiking) to $75 or more (full backcountry). Choose an appropriate kit—a mountain bike–specific kit might contain first aid items for road rash, for example, or a river-running kit might come in a waterproof container; and there are family first aid kits with remedies especially for children. The next step is to learn how to use your kit, as well as how to administer basic first aid, such as CPR and treatment for broken bones, hypothermia or hyperthermia, and shock. One can learn much from an excellent first aid book (see the resources section at the end of this chapter), or better yet take a class from your local Red Cross, at the very least. But the very best route is to learn from a school that specializes in wilderness first aid (see the resources section)—hands-on, in a wilderness setting. It's one thing to practice in a classroom, but are you sure you can handle an emergency in the middle of nowhere?

On Animals
Arthropods

From some human perspectives, bugs have no redeeming qualities (although they do—as pollinators and sources of food for billions of animals). Mosquitoes are pesky and persistent. No-see-ums are sneakier, because you almost cannot see them. Blackflies are just plain mean: one bite and you bleed. Chiggers literally get under your skin. To deal with the arthropods, you have two remedies in your arsenal: one is active (repellents) and the other passive (clothing coverage).

Insect Repellents

There are many insect-repellent products, but most contain the same basic chemical ingredients—DEET is common. All-natural repellents, such as those containing citronella, are easiest on you but less effective on some bugs. DEET-based repellents are the most effective on the worst flying insects, such as mosquitoes and flies, and, according to some repellent manufacturers, on ticks. (For more on ticks, see next page.)

DEET is the acronym for N, N-diethyl-meta-toluamide, a chemical that really is as nasty as its name

sounds. Full-strength DEET (concentrations vary from manufacturer to manufacturer) will damage varnish, plastics, and some synthetic fabrics, and there have been confirmed reports of DEET-related illnesses in adults, including confusion, irritability, and insomnia. DEET repellents should not be applied to synthetic clothing.

Heavy use of full-strength DEET (over several weeks, applied liberally at a camp) caused the deaths of three young girls due to toxic encephalopathy, or swelling of the brain, though this is very rare. Read label warnings, and use only as necessary. DEET-based repellents come in varying strengths. Adults should use repellents with concentrations of no more than 30 percent DEET; use concentrations of no more than 10 percent for children.

Non-DEET insect repellents include Green Ban, Natrapel, Bygone Bugs, and Buzz Away. Skedaddle and DEET-Plus contain nonabsorbent agents. One repellent, Permethrin can be sprayed on your clothing and tent (Duranon is one brand name).

Avon's Skin-So-Soft skin moisturizer is used by many outdoor enthusiasts, reportedly as an effective repellent against mosquitoes, no-see-ums, and (some say) blackflies. Now bottled and labeled for antibug use, the familiar scent was—and still is—found on the most unlikely wearers.

Deterrents

You can always choose to skip bug repellents altogether and go for cover and disguise. Denim, canvas, and twill jackets and pants are too tough for small biters. Rubber bands around sleeves and pant legs will discourage up-bound crawlers; or you

could tuck pant legs into the tops of heavy socks. Cloth shirts are better than knits (the stingers will find those tiny holes). Wear heavy socks and leather shoes. Light colors seem less attractive to bugs than do dark colors. Fragrances attract bugs, so don't use anything scented.

The Original Bug Shirt is a hooded pullover style made of cotton so densely woven, bugs can't bite through it. Mesh inserts help keep you cool (800-998-9096). Or you can buy a head net or an entire outfit—jacket, pants, and hat—made of bug-deterring mesh.

Insect Sting and Bite First Aid

Despite the best repellents, be prepared for bite treatment. After Bite is a popular product; its ammonia-in-mineral-oil formula neutralizes the effect of a bite, and its pen-type applicator is neat. Many other products can ease the itch: Bactine, Solarcaine, Sting-Eez, first aid creams, calamine lotion, or home remedies such as vinegar or baking soda.

Chigger bites might need special treatment. Chiggers burrow under your skin and raise itchy welts, often around a waistband or wherever clothes are snug. Some people claim a coating of clear nail polish suffocates them.

Bees, wasps, and hornets are everywhere. Really, they're good guys who go about their pollinating business until we get in their way. If you get stung, you may find the actual stinger stays in your skin after the insect has gone. First, scrape the area with a dull knife, to ease the stinger out without releasing any more venom. Then, remove the stinger with tweezers; wash, and apply ice and something to ease the stinging (any bug-bite treatment, or alcohol). Benadryl—pill or ointment—may help.

Any stinging thing can trigger an allergic response in sensitive people. If you develop hives, headache, nausea or vomiting, wheezing, dizziness or fainting, swollen face or tongue, get medical help quickly. People who know they're allergic carry a special treatment kit wherever they travel.

The black widow spider has a painful bite; she can be recognized by a red/orange hourglass shape on the underside of the abdomen. A bite *is* nasty and can cause pain, sweating, and intense abdominal pain, but all victims recover.

A bite from the brown recluse or "violin" spider produces severe pain and local swelling, sometimes weeks after the bite; there may be chills, nausea, or fever. In the area where the venom was injected, tissue may be destroyed.

At one time, the name *tarantula* conjured up a terrible threat (or a terrible movie plot). Now people keep them for pets, also regarded as terrible by others in the household. While tarantulas *can* bite, they seldom do, and the bite is not significantly venomous.

As with any bite, wash and disinfect. For severe pain, apply ice or a cold compress, and see a doctor.

Scorpions are related to ticks and spiders, but they don't bite: scorpions inject venom through a stinger in the tail. In addition to causing severe pain, a sting may bring nausea, abdominal pain, and possibly shock or convulsions—all good reasons to shake out sleeping bags, shoes, and clothes when camped where scorpions live. Also, be careful if you pick up a rock to pound in a tent peg.

Tick Tonics

Ticks can carry human disease, and thus it's a good idea to guard against them. One of the most serious diseases is Rocky Mountain spotted fever, carried by the ordinary dog tick. If you've been bitten by a tick, and develop a rash along with headache and high fever, see a doctor. Untreated, the disease can be fatal.

Lyme disease is spread by the bite of the tiny tick commonly called a deer tick, but which is just as likely to be found along with field mice or other mammals as deer. "Tiny" means about the size of a fat pencil point; they're hard to spot on clothes or skin, though sometimes you feel the tickle of tiny legs as they crawl. Their bite usually (not always) shows as a circular red spot. Diagnosed early, Lyme disease can be cured with oral antibiotics. Untreated Lyme can produce many problems, including neurologic or cardiac abnormalities,

joint inflammation, and more. Once considered a threat only in the northeastern United States, Lyme disease is now found all over the country.

The newest tick disease to worry about is ehrlichiosis. Originally identified in the Midwest, it is now believed to be found wherever the Lyme tick lives. Curable with tetracycline, its nonspecific symptoms make diagnosis difficult. Always tell the doctor if you've been in tick territory; otherwise, you may be treated (or not) for flu.

Even if you catch a tick in midbite, you can't brush it off; they burrow partway into the skin. Use tweezers and try to remove the tick with a steady tug. (You'll need the smallest needle-nose tweezers you have to remove a deer tick.) Many people think a tick will relax its grip if touched with alcohol, kerosene, or nail polish. Official recommendations either ignore the practice or deny that

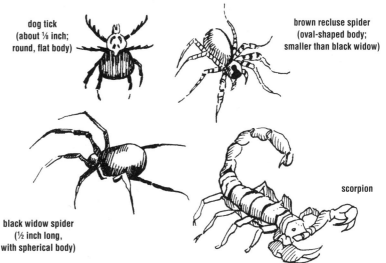

dog tick
(about ⅛ inch;
round, flat body)

brown recluse spider
(oval-shaped body;
smaller than black widow)

black widow spider
(½ inch long,
with spherical body)

scorpion

DAVID AIKEN

Knowing how to react to—and treat—unexpected bites will eliminate a great deal of anxiety.

it helps. Many outdoor stores carry tick-remover kits. Once the tick is out, wash and disinfect the bite. Save the tick, to show the doctor if the bite becomes infected.

Snakes

Contrary to popular belief, snakes don't lie around waiting to attack people. Bites usually occur because the snake was startled, hurt (as in stepped-on), or harassed. Only four genuses of North American snakes are venomous. Three—rattlesnakes, cottonmouths (water moccasins), and copperheads—are pit vipers: head shaped like an arrowhead, with an indentation, or pit, between eye and nostril on each side. Fourth is the diminutive coral snake, a distant relative of the cobra, with a very tiny, blunt head and round eyes. Other snakes, such as kingsnakes, have similar markings, but on coral snakes, the color order is yellow, red, yellow, black (and repeat). Remember: "Red on yellow, kill a fellow" or "Red on black, venom lack." Coral snakes are nocturnal and extremely secretive, as well as very small—you are as unlikely to be bitten by one as you are to see one.

If a (suspected) venomous snake bites someone, it's best to seek qualified medical help. Identify the snake if possible, but don't try to chase and kill it; don't risk another bite.

The best treatment for snakebite is said to be the keys to your car: get to a hospital calmly but quickly. If you are too far from quick evacuation, stay calm, send someone for help, and use a Sawyer Extractor (never use the old cut-and-suck kits, and never, ever the electric-shock treatment—you'll do more harm than good). If used properly within a few minutes of a bite, the Extractor can remove much of the injected venom. Only a very small number of snakebites are fatal.

Lions and Bears

Exploring the wilderness means that you might meet up with one of the larger natives—namely, bears and cougars. For tips on camping in bear or cougar country, see Chapter 10, pp. 262–263.

Black bears and cougars by nature are extremely secretive and forage and hunt under thick cover. It's unlikely you will even see one, or if you do it's likely to be a view of its backside disappearing over the nearest hill. Black bears and cougars that are not accustomed to people will flee at first scent or sight of you. However, with expanding suburban growth and therefore shrinking habitat for large predators, as well as in frequently used campgrounds or campsites where people directly or indirectly feed bears and other animals, "problem" bears and cougars are becoming more common in recreation areas near urban centers.

Unlike black bears and cougars, grizzly bears tend to forage in open areas, and although grizzlies generally don't want much to do with people, they aren't that afraid of humans, either. And some grizzlies are becoming accustomed to camp food, unfortunately.

If you encounter a cougar or bear that shows no fear of you, you likely have a problem animal, and a slight safety problem as well. It is recommended that you try banging pots together and generally making noise; if this does not scare them off, don't run. Back away slowly, trying to remain calm but also confident; some people recommend raising your jacket over your head to appear larger. In the unlikely event you are attacked, there are two very different schools of thought: play "dead" or fight back. Every situation will be different; certainly, you should try one tactic, and if it does not seem to work, by all means try the other. Pepper sprays have been proven very effective against animals attacks. Many outdoor shops carry pepper sprays (which is not Mace, but a compound made from the natural chemicals found in chile peppers) marked as "bear spray"; hunting and gun shops also stock pepper spray.

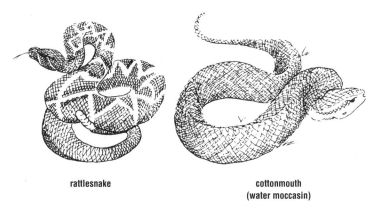

DAVID AIKEN

rattlesnake   cottonmouth
(water moccasin)

The rattlesnake and cottonmouth, two of the venomous North American snakes. If you're bitten seek qualified medical help. Identify the snake if possible, but don't try to chase and kill it; don't risk another bite.

ROSEMARY CALVERT/TONY STONE IMAGES, INC.

Camping in bear country requires some extra precautions to ensure you won't have unwanted—and close—bruin encounters. One of the simplest ways is to keep your kitchen area away from sleeping areas, and to make sure food is well secured or hung out of reach.

Poisonous Plants

Everyone knows they should not touch poison ivy, but there ends the common knowledge. People expect to see a climbing or creeping vine, but it also grows as a shrub. Deer and other animals eat it, so it's not universally "poisonous." While some people aren't sensitive to the plant, most are; the standard reaction is an itching rash that must usually run its irritating course.

Poison oak and sumac raise the same kind of lumps as the ivy. Try not to scratch the lumps—that will only spread the rash. Try using a top-

ical cream, such as Sting-Eez, which contains cortisone.

Basic Outdoor Safety, Search, and Rescue

Most wilderness accidents occur because of two things: carelessness (or, perhaps better phrased, loss of carefulness) and inexperience—for example, The Mountaineers in Seattle reports that the majority of mountaineering and climbing fatalities are due to loss of footing in steep places. It does not take a lot of extra effort to be careful and to choose adventures within your experience level.

One way to be careful is to always be prepared for the worst possible turn of events, even if only on a dayhike or day paddle—read the accident reports in *Sea Kayaker* magazine, and you'll notice that many fatalities involve paddlers who venture out in cold water without proper protective clothing or who do not wear their life jackets because the day *started out* calm.

Prepare your list of essential safety gear, using the following list as a guideline, and always carry it with you—even for just a short hike or bike ride. For watersports, you will want to add a few items, such as flares and a rescue knife (for cutting lines). See individual sports chapters in Part One for further suggestions.

Essential Safety Gear

Map/chart and compass
Matches in waterproof container, and
  fire-starter kit
Sharp knife
Spare clothing
Emergency food (a few power bars)
Extra water

Light (twist-on, to avoid accidental
  turn-on)
Spare bulbs and batteries
Emergency blanket or bag

What to Do in an Emergency

Anyone planning a trip, whether solo or a group of 12, should establish, prior to leaving home, an emergency plan for contingencies such as a member of the party (or yourself) getting lost or injured, or an unexpected turn of weather. Everyone should know the plan, which should include

- Designating a leader and a backup leader (in case the leader is hurt) who will direct any actions in an emergency
- Determining several fast, safe evacuation routes throughout the course of the trip
- Determining the proper agencies to contact if assistance is necessary (such as Park Service or Forest Service rangers, or sheriff or Coast Guard agencies) and acquiring the phone numbers
- Compiling an information and contact list for each participant (including emergency contact, medical conditions or allergies, and age)

The trip leader, who should have at least basic first aid training, should be responsible for keeping the group calm but functioning efficiently during an emergency. And remember that if you have filed an itinerary with someone (always a good idea), you should be aware of the dangers of abandoning that itinerary in case of an emergency (the rescue party may look for you in the wrong location).

See *Wilderness Search and Rescue,* by Tim J. Setnicka (see the resources section for publication information), for excellent information on dealing with emergencies in wilderness situations.

Following are some basic tips for dealing with a common outdoor problem—a lost group member.

When Someone's Lost

1. Establish where the person was last seen.
2. Station someone there in case the lost person returns to that location, and determine a communication process for letting the rest of the group know if the person shows up; in the absence of two-way radios (a good idea for larger groups), arrange for search members to report back to the central location at regular intervals.
3. If someone in the party is experienced in search techniques—and *only* if someone is experienced—then send out a group of two or more to run search patterns using maps and compasses. Never send people off on their own, and never send out anyone who is not a very experienced navigator.
4. At a time to be determined by the group and leader, call for help if a search is unsuccessful. In poor weather, that may mean as little as an hour or two; in fair weather, perhaps longer. Every situation is different (for example, is the lost person experienced in the outdoors, or a novice?).

If You Are Lost

1. Stay where you are when you finally determine that you are lost. Moving around will only hamper rescue attempts if you were with

a group and are confident someone will be looking for you.
2. Don't light signal fires—more often than not, these just become out-of-control forest fires.
3. Don't panic. Hopefully you have been carrying the proper safety essentials (see above) and can survive 24 or more hours until help arrives.
4. If no one knows where you went and when you were due back, and therefore no one knows you are lost, you are on your own to get yourself out. Try to retrace the terrain in your mind; sometimes, getting to a high spot will help you see where you need to go, or you may need to try following watercourses down to "civilization" if you are in the mountains. All situations will be different. The important thing is to turn off the panic and turn on your brain. (See Chapter 9, p. 228, for more tips on navigation, including what to do if you lose your way.)

How to Avoid (or at Least Mitigate) Getting Lost

1. Always tell someone where you are going, and don't deviate from that route; at least that way if you're missing, a search party can get to you and then you won't really be lost, just un-found for a while.
2. Learn how to navigate before you head out on your own (see Chapter 9).
3. Stick to the trails until you learn number 2.

Hot and Cold Extremes

Sometime during your outdoor adventures you will have to contend

with extremes of heat and cold. Each requires different preventions, as well as treatments if overexposure occurs. And remember that you can get a sunburn in the snow or suffer snow blindness in hot sand—temperature is not always the culprit.

Sun Sense

It's no secret that excess sun is bad for your skin. Despite persistent denial by sun worshipers, "tan" is a signal that your skin is calling for help. You could hide from the sun all day, but that defeats your purpose of being outdoors, and, fortunately, isn't necessary. Sunburn prevention, however, is a priority. Wear light-colored but opaque clothes, to reflect rather than absorb the sun's rays. Long-sleeved shirts and long pants cover more skin. Wear hats with wide brims, to shade your face, neck, and ears. Watch out for reflected sun—rays bouncing back from a boat deck, water surface, or sand (see p. 293, for information on preventing and treating snow blindness as well).

Sunscreens are rated with SPF (sun protection factor) numbers, which tell you how long you can stay in the sun without burning. If you'd normally burn in 10 minutes, and you apply a sunscreen with an SPF of 30, you should be protected for 300 minutes (10 minutes multiplied by 30 SPF). Sunscreens don't have a cumulative effect; two coats of SPF 10 won't equal one of a 20. They're waterproof for a time, but excessive perspiration can take away some of the protection. For ordinary activity, reapply every two hours—more often when swimming or exercising.

A *sunblock* will stop the sun's rays, preventing both UVA and UVB from reaching your skin. Sunblocks use either zinc oxide (the original opaque white nose protector) or titanium dioxide (newer blocks may be translucent or skin-colored).

Children's skin is extra-sensitive. Unfortunately, sunscreens should not be used on infants. Keep babies out of direct sun; shade with umbrellas, canopies, sunbonnets. With older children, start the sunscreen habit as early as the pediatrician recommends, using sunscreens or sunblocks made especially for kids.

Burn Soothers

Despite your precautions, you may get burned. Be prepared with aloe-vera gel or an aloe-based ointment; take aspirin or other pain relievers to ease the burning, and drink lots of water to prevent dehydration. Cool compresses will soothe the skin temporarily; and, of course, further exposure to the sun should be avoided.

Hydrating

The rule for desert or arid conditions, including high elevation, is

Drink a minimum of 4 liters or quarts a day. More is better.

This may seem like a lot, but you will need it. Sports drinks may be absorbed a little more quickly into the body, but don't drink all your fluids as sports drinks—take the majority of your fluid intake in good old-fashioned water. (See Chapter 1, p. 16, for more on sports drinks.) If your urine is dark, or you are not urinating normally, you are not drinking enough.

If you can't remind yourself to stop and drink frequently, wear waistbelt bottle holders, or check out water carriers that have a tube through which you can draw water while you walk or paddle or ride. Re-

A sensible approach to sun and heat protection: a wide-brimmed hat and light, opaque clothing.

member not to guzzle a lot at a time—drink smaller amounts more frequently, so your body can absorb it gradually (and avoid that lead-stomach feeling).

Heat Exposure

Sun can do more than burn your skin. On a hot day, overexertion can prompt excessive perspiration that could result in heat exhaustion. The symptoms are extreme thirst, heavy sweating, headache, dizziness, and possibly nausea. Anyone with all or some of these symptoms should sit in the shade, drink water, and hope the feelings subside. If they don't, the problem might be more serious: heat stroke. Initially, heat exhaustion and heat stroke symptoms are similar (both are levels of hyperthermia); the big difference is that in heat stroke, skin is usually hot and dry. Breathing may be alternately deep and shallow, the pulse alternately weak and strong. Muscles may twitch; the person may become disoriented. Heat stroke can be fatal if the condition is ignored, so get to a hospital as quickly as possible. If a doctor isn't immediately available, splash victims repeatedly with water, to cool them off as quickly as possible. Give them water to drink (assuming they're conscious).

Prevention

To prevent both conditions
- Drink lots of water (see Hydrating section, p. 291).
- Wear a sun hat that has a full-coverage wide brim.
- Minimize skin exposure to direct sun by wearing lightweight, long-sleeved shirt and pants. Wear light but opaque colors.
- Try tricks such as a moistened bandanna around your neck or draped over your head (under your hat). Some stores sell bandannas that are sewn into a tube and filled with hydrophilic synthetic beads: dowse it in water and tie it around your neck; it will stay damp and cool for a long time.
- Avoid alcohol and caffeine when exercising (they are diuretics and thus increase the flow of urine,

which could speed up symptoms of dehydration and heat exhaustion).
- Eat properly. In extreme heat, your appetite may wane; make sure you continue to eat the minimum number of kilocalories necessary for maintaining your body through your activities. Poor nutrition will speed up the onset of hyperthermia. (See Chapter 12, p. 280, for charts listing kilocalorie content of various foods and suggested kilocalorie requirements for a variety of activities.)

Plan activities for cooler times of day, and if it's really hot, stay in the shade as much as possible.

Cold Exposure

When your body can no longer keep warm on its own and your core temperature begins to drop, you are experiencing *hypothermia,* a dangerous condition if not remedied as quickly as possible. Sometimes hypothermia is sudden, precipitated by a sudden event such as a fall in freezing water, but more commonly it builds up over the long term, such as when walking for hours in freezing sleet wearing inadequate clothing.

The greatest danger of hypothermia is that once you begin to realize you are suffering from it, your mind is becoming groggy enough that subsequent decisions might be poor and could actually get you in more trouble. Mild hypothermia begins with shivering, stiffness, lethargy, and irritability; as it progresses, the skin begins to cool down and turn pale or gray, because the body is shutting down circulation in its extremities to save its core. Severe hypothermia moves into disorientation, lack of coordination, collapse, coma, and ultimately death.

In cold conditions, be on the lookout for signs of hypothermia. If you or someone in your group begins to show signs, stop immediately, pitch a tent if possible, and put the person inside in a sleeping bag, preferably with someone else for extra warmth. Replace all wet clothing, and feed the victim hot liquids and food.

Never rub the skin of a hypothermia victim; this will stimulate blood flow to the skin and away from the core, where warmth is needed. And don't apply alcohol to the skin, for the same reason.

Prevention

Avoid hypothermia by
- Dressing properly for cold conditions. Many people have died with their jackets in their packs (see Chapter 14, p. 299).
- Don't wait until you're uncomfortably cold to put on sweaters, hat, jacket, and pants; it might be too late.
- Always carry spare clothing in winter, as well as a stove, spare fuel, and adequate shelter.
- Eat properly. On long trips in cold conditions, increase the amount of fat in your diet, usually by adding more margarine and cheese to evening meals. Polar explorers often consume appallingly large amounts of fat daily, since it's the only way they can consume the 7,000–8,000 calories they need. Eating that amount in carbohydrates would mean huge loads and never-ending meals.

Frostbite

Frostbite occurs when flesh becomes so cold that it freezes. Exposed parts of your body, such as ears, nose, and cheeks, are most at risk, plus your

WINDCHILL FACTOR CHART

When the wind's blowing, the extra cooling effect of the wind on your skin serves to *increase* the intensity of the actual air temperature—that is, if it is 20 degrees but the wind is blowing at 20 miles per hour, the effective temperature to exposed skin is −9. The higher the wind speed, the lower the *windchill factor*.

CHILL FACTOR (EQUIVALENT TEMPERATURE ON EXPOSED SKIN)

wind speed (mph)	air temperature (°F)												
	35°	30°	25°	20°	15°	10°	5°	0°	−5°	−10°	−15°	−20°	−25°
40	1	−4	−15	−22	−29	−36	−45	−54	−62	−69	−76	−87	−94
35	3	−4	−13	−20	−27	−35	−43	−52	−60	−67	−72	−83	−90
30	5	−2	−11	−18	−26	−33	−41	−49	−56	−63	−70	−78	−87
25	7	0	−7	−15	−22	−29	−37	−45	−52	−58	−67	−75	−83
20	12	3	−4	−9	−17	−24	−32	−40	−46	−52	−60	−68	−76
15	16	11	1	−6	−11	−18	−25	−33	−40	−45	−51	−60	−65
10	21	16	9	2	−2	−9	−15	−22	−27	−31	−38	−45	−52

fingers and toes if they become wet or are not adequately insulated. Signs of frostbite are a colorless appearance and tingling pain. If your feet or hands feel very cold or painful for a while and then go numb, it is a very serious situation. The tissues may die, leading to infection and possibly need for amputation.

The solution to frostbite is prevention. Minor frostbite or frostnip of the extremities (tips of fingers and toes, nose, face) isn't serious if dealt with promptly; deep frostbite can be very serious. All frostbite should be taken seriously. In the authoritative *Medicine for Mountaineering*, editor Dr. James A. Wilkerson says that "the extent and severity of frostbite are notoriously difficult to judge accurately during the early stages, particularly when the tissues are still frozen."

As with hypothermia, frostbite shouldn't occur if you are adequately equipped and take action as soon as any part of your body starts to feel cold.

Don't rub the injured area with or without snow. You may damage the underlying tissue.

If part of the body starts to feel very cold, don't ignore it; stop and warm it. Move the affected part vigorously to create heat. A good remedy for cold hands is to whirl your arms around and around. After a short while you will feel the blood flowing back into your hands. They may ache painfully with the returning heat, but that is better than frostbite. You can stamp your feet and flex your ankles and jump up and down.

Don extra clothing. Frostbite occurs because the body shuts down some of the blood supply to the extremities in order to conserve heat in the core. Keep the trunk warm and you are less likely to have a cold nose.

Eat food and a hot drink. Just hugging a mug of steaming hot liquid can warm up cold hands.

Cold feet can be warmed on someone's stomach, hands warmed in armpits or crotch. You could even pee on cold fingers. Warm breath can be blown on facial frostbite or a hand cupped over it. If a serviced lodge can be reached easily, a warm (not more than 108 degrees F) bath works wonders.

Tight boots can be a cause of frostbitten feet. In extreme cold don't wear too many socks—they can constrict the feet, reducing circulation. For more warmth it is better to use an insulated supergaiter or even pull socks on over your boots.

Finally, if someone's feet do become frostbitten and there is no other option such as rescue or retreating to a road or lodge, ski out before you try to warm them (in fact, get medical help before thawing them if you can), as they will suffer more damage (and the victim experience great pain) if they are thawed out and then refreeze.

For information on snow camping, see Chapter 10, p. 263.

High-Elevation Adventures

The mountains provide some of our most spectacular wild experiences—trekking, telemark skiing, snowshoeing, climbing, and mountaineering. But they can also dish up some severe conditions for which adventurers need to be prepared. Some conditions, such as avalanches, are mountain-specific, but keep in mind that other conditions, such as cold temperatures and windchill, can occur anywhere. These latter topics are discussed above.

Snow Blindness

The reflection of the sun off snow can cause snow blindness, which is why wearing sunglasses is essential at high elevations and in all but the dullest weather at low ones. Snow blindness is caused by ultraviolet radiation burning the cornea and is reputedly extremely painful. A halfway stage can lead to sore eyes that feel as though they have grit in them. Don't rub them, this may cause further damage. Analgesics can help relieve the pain, as can cold compresses (tea bags are sometimes suggested). Otherwise, rest and wait. Healing can take several days.

Prevention is much better, so always carry spare sunglasses. In an emergency, you can cut slits in an eyemask of cardboard or other stiff material and strap it to your head with a piece of cord.

"Snow blindness" can also occur when your eyes are exposed for long periods to glare from sand or water. In these conditions, the same preventative measures are called for.

Avalanches

Avalanches are probably the greatest and most-feared hazard in snow-covered mountains. Immensely powerful, they can destroy anything in their path.

In many areas avalanches are not a problem. Where the snowpack has consolidated steadily throughout the winter without any sudden changes in temperature, it is likely to be very stable. A freeze-thaw cycle can also lead to very stable snow, but very warm temperatures can cause the snow to become wet and rotten. The nature of the terrain under the snow is important too. Regular smooth surfaces, such as steep grass and rock slabs, hold snow less securely than rough broken ones with plenty of boulders and shrubby plants. Cirques with steep back walls can be dangerous, and convex slopes with snow pulled tight over the curved terrain are more prone to avalanche formation than are concave slopes.

Although avalanches are not fully understood, and predicting them is

an inexact science, there are many precautions that can be taken. To start with, understanding something of how and why avalanches occur is important. Every alpine explorer should read one of the many books on the subject. Start with Chris Townsend's *Wilderness Skiing and Winter Camping* for an easy-to-understand introduction. Tony Daffern's *Avalanche Safety for Skiers and Climbers* is particularly good, as is *Mountaineering: Freedom of the Hills.* (See resources section at the end of this chapter for publication information for these books and others.)

Avalanche Warnings

Most popular ski areas where avalanches are a danger put out regular avalanche warnings, which are usually posted at ski resorts, ranger stations, and local mountain-equipment stores. Warnings may also appear in newspapers and may be available as recorded phone messages. Your first line of defense is to heed such warnings. They are based on fieldwork by experienced skiers and climbers who know the history of the season's snowfall. The scale of risk usually runs from low through moderate to high and very high. If it is either of the last two, potentially dangerous slopes should be avoided. Even if the risk is low it is not nonexistent, and you should make your own observations while you are out. Local information can also tell you where notorious avalanche areas are located.

Danger Zones

Avalanches occur on steep slopes, usually between 25 and 45 degrees. Such slopes are far steeper than most nordic skiers or trekkers feel happy

descending, but they often traverse them. The angle of a slope can be measured with your ski poles. Put one stick upright in the snow, then hold the other pole at a right angle and slide the tip down the snow until the handle touches the vertical pole. If the second pole touches the first at the handle, the slope is 45 degrees; if halfway down, 26.5 degrees. Stay off steep slopes unless the avalanche risk is low. Narrow canyons are dangerous. Ridges and buttresses are much safer than the backs or sides of bowls. Avalanches often follow the same track. They can be identified by debris at their base or by the absence of trees on the lower hillside or in the valley below. Gullies are particularly prone to avalanche. Lunching or camping at the bottom of one is not a good idea.

Danger Times

Most avalanches occur during or soon after heavy snowfall, so dangerous terrain should be avoided for the 24 hours following a blizzard. Storms that start cold with dry snow but finish with warmer temperatures are more likely to lead to avalanche conditions than the opposite, because dry snow doesn't adhere to or support the wetter, heavier snow on top of it very well. In spring, heavy rain can be a problem, saturating and destabilizing the snowpack. Warm temperatures can have the same effect. Strong winds blow snow around, dumping it on lee slopes to form potentially dangerous windslab, and building cornices on the sides of steep ridges and cliffs. Even when skies are clear, snow plumes blowing off summits and cliffs are signs that the wind is moving snow around.

Windslab

Windslab is a very dangerous type of avalanche that may occur whenever strong winds have been blowing. Because windslab forms on lee slopes, knowledge of the wind direction for the period preceding your trip is useful. In a slab avalanche, a huge block of snow breaks away and slips all at once. Slab avalanches leave behind them a fracture line known as a crown wall.

Windward slopes usually hold less snow and tend to be safer. If the snow settles or sounds hollow under you, or cracks appear, windslab is probably present.

Crossing Dangerous Slopes

At times your party may have no choice but to cross a dangerous slope. Before you do, think hard. Are there really no alternatives? What lies below? If there are cliffs or big boulders, turn back. If you do cross, stay well apart from each other and aim for rock "islands," slight ridges, or flat areas. Watch each other cross, and watch and listen for signs of an avalanche starting. Fasten clothing but unfasten pack hip belts, unfasten ski safety straps, and take your hands out of the wrist loops of your poles. If you unclip your bindings, or at least loosen cables and put three-pin bails on the top notch, your skis can be kicked off if necessary. It is safer to go straight up or down a dangerous slope than to traverse it. Your skis slicing neatly through the snow could be the trigger for an avalanche. Remember that most avalanches are caused by the victims themselves. If you do have to traverse a suspect slope, do so as high as possible, above most of the snow.

◆ EXPERT TIPS FOR HIGH-ELEVATION ADVENTURING

When you venture high into the mountains—above 8,000–10,000 feet as a general rule—you may have a hard time adjusting to the increased stress on your body, depending on what elevation you are acclimated to (your hometown). Below are listed some of the side effects of high-elevation hiking, climbing, or skiing (sometimes erroneously called high-altitude; if your feet are on the ground, it's elevation, and if they're in the air—such as in a balloon or plane—it's altitude) and some tips for dealing with them.

◆ *Nosebleeds.* Dry alpine air can cause tissues in your nose to desiccate, and you may get nosebleeds. (Tip: Drink plenty of water.) Pinch your nose about halfway up and lean forward for about 10 minutes.

◆ *Acute Mountain Sickness (also called Altitude Illness).* AMS is the result of your body reacting to the decrease in available oxygen at high elevations. Symptoms include shortness of breath (especially during exertion), fatigue, headache, light-headedness, dizziness, nausea, decreased appetite, and difficulty sleeping. These symptoms will often appear within the first 24 hours of arriving at high elevation. The best thing to do is acclimatize for two or three days before exerting yourself (and after symptoms subside). Avoid alcohol, eat carbohydrates and reduce fat intake, and drink lots of water. Consult your physician about medications that can reduce the effects of high elevation on the body.

◆ *High Altitude Pulmonary Edema (HAPE) and High Altitude Cerebral Edema (HACE).* These are progressive forms of AMS. Symptoms to look for include shortness of breath, cough, and headaches that become severe and persistent. If you suspect HAPE or HACE, a physician with mountain-illness experience should be consulted immediately and evacuation carried out at his or her suggestion.

◆ Hypertension. It is believed, though not conclusively proven, that high-elevation activity causes an increase in blood pressure. This can definitely be the case in people currently taking medication for high blood pressure. Consult your doctor if you have problems associated with high blood pressure.

There are different types of tests used to determine avalanche danger levels, as well as specific gear used for avalanche country—snow shovels, probes, snow-crystal magnifying glasses, and electronic beacons in case of burial—and anyone venturing into avalanche-prone country should familiarize themselves with these techniques and gear. Contact the schools and organizations listed at the end of this chapter about classes, and refer to the excellent books listed there as well.

To Explore and Protect

Because most of us who head out regularly to hike, mountain bike, climb, canoe, or run rivers are careful to carry out our trash and are quiet and respectful, it's tempting to think that, as only one person or one small group, our impact is not so great in the grand scheme of things. After all, we're so unlike the archetypal outdoor abusers, hacking up trees for firewood and zooming cross-country on ATVs.

But one set of footprints leading off-trail might lead another explorer over the same path, and another, and another, until a trail is born; erosion sets in and a gully is born; and so on. One way or another, we are all causing an impact on the wilderness we love so much.

It's not all gloom and doom, though—we don't need to stay home and subscribe to the Discovery Channel to adhere to low-impact backcountry experiences. It's important to keep our connections to the land, because a love of wild things is born of spending time in the wilds, and a love of wild things hopefully leads to stewardship.

It takes very little foot traffic to set the stage for conditions prime for erosion.

DENNIS WELSH

Some easy tips to follow, adapted from the National Outdoor Leadership School's Leave No Trace code of outdoor ethics, provide surprisingly simple ways to walk the land and leave nary a trace of our passing.

Think of it as the practice of three principles (the three *P*s): preparation, path-awareness, and preservation.

Preparation. Believe it or not, the most important way to ensure "leaving no trace" happens before you even leave home. Planning ahead by looking over a topographic map of your destination will help you choose the best trails, and calling ahead to the governing land agency will help you pick good campsites and determine any sensitive areas to avoid, such as zones of cryptobiotic soil or breeding areas of sensitive wildlife—bighorn sheep or peregrine falcons, for example.

Once you know where you're going, you can make sure you have the appropriate equipment you need to take care of yourself if something goes wrong; hikers who lack proper clothing to stay warm in an unexpected storm, for example, usually end up building a fire, which leaves scars and destroys resources. If you get lost and Search and Rescue is called out, this means perhaps a dozen or more people combing a large area, which creates a great deal of disturbance.

Path awareness. Being aware of the paths you take is another important tool for lessening our impact. On existing trails, walking single-file inside the use zone is best; shortcutting causes erosion, and walking around rocks or mud puddles widens trails (another good preparation: weatherproof footwear or gaiters, so you can walk through water rather than around).

If you must travel off-trail, stick to durable surfaces; groups of two or more should spread out, taking different paths to avoid creating a permanent "trail" others might follow. In desert, canyon, and alpine country, where vegetation rebounds very slowly, it is best to avoid off-trail walking unless there is plenty of rock or sandy washes to travel over. Finding a lightly used trail creates a dilemma;

a decision to avoid semi-used trails might allow nature to reclaim them.

Path awareness also translates to campsite awareness. See Chapter 10, p. 245, for tips on locating campsites.

Preservation. Preserve water resources in all areas by not bathing in streams or ponds (sunscreens and bug repellents are nasty chemicals), and by keeping all camp activities at least 200 feet (or 70 adult paces) from water.

By not collecting flowers, seeds, rocks, bones, potsherds, or other such things we all love to take home with us to remind us of our explorations, we allow others the same sense of discovery we enjoyed. This is the hardest one for a lot of us. Sketching in a nature journal and taking photographs are great ways to remedy itchy fingers and beckoning pockets.

Preserving the essence of wild lands is also important. Choosing natural-colored clothing and equipment lessens visual noise, while talking softly maintains the legendary quiet of the wilderness.

Fires burn wood, which is an important natural resource for soil ecology, so if at all possible it's best to limit your campfires (although in desert and high alpine country, you should never build fires). See Chapter 10, p. 247, for tips on how to build a great "Zen" fire.

(There's one more *p* word that some people might be wondering about. Human waste certainly leaves an impact. See Chapter 10, p. 261.)

If you would like to find out more about the Leave No Trace program, call (800) 332-4100. Ask about ordering their excellent booklets in the Leave No Trace Outdoor Skills & Ethics series, including *Desert & Canyon Country, Rocky Mountains, Southeastern States, Backcountry Horse*

Use, Western River Corridors, Temperate Coastal Zones and Pacific Northwest, and the bilingual *Minimum-Impact Camping Techniques for Desert & Coastal Mexico.* NOLS also offers classes for outdoor guides and educators in Leave No Trace techniques.

Further Resources for Safe and Sound Adventures
Books

Avalanche Safety for Skiers and Climbers, by Tony Daffern (Seattle: Cloudcap, 1992).

Commonsense Outdoor Medicine and Emergency Companion, by Newell Breyfogle (Camden, ME: Ragged Mountain Press, 1994), 3rd edition. Small enough to carry along but chock-full of everything you need to know to deal with outdoor illness and injury.

Desert Hiking, by Dave Ganci (Berkeley: Wilderness Press, 1993), 3d edition. A very valuable book written by a long-time desert rat.

Mountaineering: Freedom of the Hills, edited by Don Graydon, (Seattle: The Mountaineers, 1991), 5th edition. The best book available on safety and rescue in mountainous terrain.

The Onboard Medical Handbook, by Paul G. Gill, Jr., M.D. (Camden, ME: International Marine, 1997). Though intended for sailors, sea kayakers will appreciate this book for the marine-injury-specific information.

Wilderness Search and Rescue, by Tim J. Setnicka (Boston: Appalachian Mountain Club, 1980).

Wilderness Skiing and Winter Camping, by Chris Townsend (Camden,

ME: Ragged Mountain Press, 1994). An excellent book that is informative and also very user-friendly. Much of the information on winter travel and camping was excerpted and adapted with permission from this book.

Three publications chronicle accidents in climbing and mountaineering, canoeing and river running, and sea kayaking; these are worth reading as lessons in how to avoid such accidents, as well as how to deal with them if you find yourself in similar situations.

The American Canoe Association's River Safety Anthology, by Charlie Walbridge and Jody Tinsely (Birmingham, AL: Menasha Ridge Press, 1996).

American Alpine Club's *Accidents in North American Mountaineering,* published annually by the American Alpine Club (710 10th Street, Golden, CO 80401; 303-384-0110).

Sea Kayaker's Deep Trouble, by George Gronseth and Matt Broze; edited by Chris Cunningham (Camden, ME: Ragged Mountain Press, 1997).

Schools

American Mountain Guides Association, 710 10th Street, Golden, CO 80401; (303) 271-0984. Contact AMGA for a complete listing of their members, which includes schools, in your area.

Colorado Outward Bound School, 945 Pennsylvania Street, Denver, CO 80203; (800) 477-2627.

National Outdoor Leadership School, P.O. Box AA, Lander, WY 82520; (307) 332-6973.

Wilderness Medical Associates, RFD 2 Box 890, Bryant Pond, ME 04219; (800) 742-2931.

Wilderness Medicine Institute, P.O. Box 9, Pitkin, CO 81241.

Other Resources

Princeton University operates a fine department for training professionals in outdoor recreation. The Outdoor Action Program is recognized as one of the finest sources in the world for wilderness health and safety information. The best way to peruse their program is via their excellent Internet web site, at http://www.princeton.edu/~rcurtis/oa.html.

Chapter 14
HOW TO DRESS OUTDOORS

This chapter was excerpted and adapted with permission from The Backpacker's Handbook, *Second Edition, by Chris Townsend (Ragged Mountain Press, 1997)*

Keeping Warm and Dry in the Outdoors

Choosing lightweight, low-bulk clothes that keep you warm and dry in wind and rain, warm in camp when the temperature falls below freezing, and cool when the sun shines, requires a fair amount of care and consideration. Before looking at clothing in detail, it's useful to have some understanding of how the body works when exercising, and what bearing this has on what you wear.

Heat Loss and Heat Production

The human body is designed for a tropical climate, and it ceases to function optimally if its temperature falls more than a couple of degrees below 98.4 degrees F. In nontropical cli-mates, the body needs a covering to maintain that temperature, because the heat it produces is lost to the cooler air. Ideally, clothing should allow a balance between heat loss and heat production, so that we feel nei-ther hot nor cold—easy if we are sit-ting still on a calm, dry day, regardless of the temperature. Maintaining this balance when we alternate sitting still with varying degrees of activity in a range of air temperatures and conditions is much more difficult. A body actually creates heat and moisture, which has to be dispersed, but it seeks to conserve heat when exercise stops.

The body loses heat in four ways, which determine how clothing has to function to keep the body's tempera-ture at an equilibrium.

Convection, the transfer of heat from the body to the air, is the major cause of heat loss. It occurs whenever the air is cooler than the body, which is most of the time. The rate of heat loss increases in proportion to air motion—once air begins to move over the skin (and through your clothing), it can whip body warmth away at an amazing rate. To prevent this, clothing must cut out the flow of air over the skin—that is, it must be windproof.

Conduction is the transfer of heat from one surface to another. All mate-rials conduct heat, some better than others. Air conducts heat poorly, so the best protection against conductive heat loss is clothing that traps and holds air in its fibers. Indeed, the trapped air is what keeps you warm; the fabrics just hold it in place. Water, however, is a good heat conductor, so if your clothing is wet next to your skin, you will cool down rapidly. This means that clothing has to keep rain and snow out, which isn't difficult; the problem is that clothing must also transmit perspiration to the outer air to keep you dry—a characteristic known as *breathability,* or moisture-vapor transmission.

Evaporation occurs when body moisture is transformed into vapor—a process that requires heat. During vigorous exercise, the body can respire as much as a quart of liquid an hour through the skin. Clothing must transport it away quickly so that it doesn't use up body heat. Wearing garments that can be venti-lated easily, especially at the neck, is as important as wearing breathable materials through which moisture vapor can pass.

Radiation is the passing of heat directly between two objects without warming the intervening space. It is the way the sun heats the earth (and us on hot, clear days). Radiation re-quires a direct pathway, so wearing clothes—especially clothing that is tightly woven and smooth-surfaced—solves most of that problem.

The Layer System

The clothing *layer system* is versatile and efficient if used properly, which means constantly opening and clos-ing zippers and cuff fastenings, and

Dressing properly outdoors goes beyond fashion—good outdoor clothing can mean the difference between being warm and comfortable, or cold, uncomfortable, and potentially in danger.

removing or adding layers, including on legs, hands, and head in severe conditions.

The Inner Layer

Sometimes described as "thermal" underwear, the prime purpose of the inner, or base, layer is to keep the skin *dry* rather than *warm*. If perspiration is removed quickly from the skin's surface, your outer layers keep you warm more easily. Conversely, if the layer of clothing next to your skin becomes saturated and dries slowly, your other clothes, however good, have a hard time keeping you warm.

No fabric, whatever the claims made for it, is warm when wet.

While on the move, your body can generate heat even if your inner layers are damp, as long as your outer layer keeps out rain and wind and your midlayer provides enough warmth. But once you stop, wet undergarments will chill you rapidly, especially if you've been exercising hard. Often—after a climb to a pass or a summit—we want or need to stop. Once you stop, however, your body heat output drops rapidly, just when you need that heat to dry out your wet underwear. But your under-

garment's warmth-trapping properties are impaired, because its fibers hold less air and more water—which conducts heat from the body much more rapidly than air. The result is known as *after-exercise chill.* The wetter the clothing, the longer such chill lasts, and the colder and more uncomfortable you will be. Thus, the inner and outer layers are important because they can minimize after-exercise chill; what goes on in between these layers matters far less, and this is where compromises can be made.

The one inner material to avoid is cotton, since it absorbs moisture very quickly and in great quantities and it takes a long time to dry, using up a massive amount of body heat in the process. To make matters worse, damp cotton also clings to the skin, preventing a layer of insulating air from forming. Short-sleeved, wicking, synthetic tops work as well as cotton in the heat.

Fabrics remove body moisture in two ways: either by transporting, or *wicking,* it away from the skin and into the air or the next layer of clothing or by *absorbing* it deep into their fibers, to leave a dry surface next to the skin. Generally, wicking is a property of specially developed synthetic materials; traditional, natural fibers absorb.

Synthetics wick in four ways: by being nonabsorbent (hydrophobic) and having an open weave through which the moisture quickly passes, pushed by body heat; by having hydrophilic (water-attracting) outer surfaces, which "pull" moisture through the fabric and away from the skin; by absorbing moisture and passing it along the fibers to the outside; and by both pushing and pulling moisture along blends of hydrophobic polyester and hydrophilic nylon, known as *push-pull fabrics.*

However, while the best-wicking fabrics are very good, they can become overloaded with sweat and end up very damp on the inside. What is important is how long they take to dry when you're not producing body heat to push the moisture through the fabric. The best are those that have brushed or raised inner surfaces, so that there is a minimum of material in contact with the skin. If the outer surface can absorb moisture, it will draw it from the inner and then allow it to spread out through the

fabric or over its surface, where it will evaporate more quickly. This can be achieved by using different materials on the inside and outside, as in push-pull polyester/nylon fabrics, or by having one piece of fabric with different inner and outer surfaces, as in Malden Mills' BiPolar Technology and Paramo's Parameta S clothing.

Other requirements influence fabric selection, however. All these modern fabrics are fairly lightweight. Most come in three weights or thicknesses, some in four. Lightweight fabrics are thin and fast-wicking, ideal for aerobic pursuits such as running, but also good for warm-weather backpacking and under other layers in cold weather. Midweight underwear is slightly heavier and thicker, and usually has a tighter weave. It's warmer, but often slower-wicking— good for all but the warmest weather. The heaviest weight and thickest constructions are known as *expedition* or *winter weight.* Some of these don't wick moisture or dry as fast as the lighter-weight fabrics and are better suited as midlayers. A few of the latest expedition fabrics work even better than thin ones, however. Most lightweight and midweight underwear is reasonably inexpensive, certainly when compared with mid- and outer-layer garments.

Designs are usually simple; most tops are available as either crew neck or crew- or turtleneck with zipper, button, or stud fastenings at the neck. Most have long sleeves, though some short-sleeved tops, usually crew necks, are available.

Figure-hugging "tights" are the norm for long pants. Briefs made from wicking synthetics are far superior to ordinary cotton or nylon. Close-fitting garments help trap air

and wick moisture quickly, and also offer an easy fit under midlayer clothing. Long underpants need to have a particularly snug fit—there's nothing worse than baggy long johns sagging down inside other layers; elasticized waists are essential. Wrist and ankle cuffs need to grip well to keep them from riding up under other garments. Stretch fabrics often wick fastest due to the close fit. They're generally more comfortable, too. Seams should be flat-sewn to avoid rubbing and abrasion. Colors are usually dark, probably because dirt and stains show up less, but it is worth your time to consider white or pale-colored garments, because they reflect heat better when worn alone in warm weather.

Choosing a wicking synthetic fabric can be difficult because there are so many, each claiming to work best. Actually, there are only a few base fabrics, and they're all derived from petrochemicals. Regardless of the fabric, open-knit garments absorb less moisture, wick faster, and dry more quickly than close-knit ones. The three main choices are polypropylene (polypro for short), polyester, and chlorofiber. Blends of these materials are also available.

Polypropylene

Polypro, the lightest and thinnest of the three wicking synthetics, won't absorb moisture, which is quickly passed along its fibers and into the air or the next layer. Polypro wicks away sweat so fast that after-exercise chill is negligible. However, after a day or so, polypro stinks to high heaven—a stench that can be hard to get rid of. Apart from the odor, if you don't wash it every couple of days, polypro ceases to perform properly, and it will leave your skin feeling clammy and cold after exercise. So you have to carry several garments or rinse out one regularly and learn to live with the smell of stale sweat.

Polypro's drawbacks are mostly overcome in Helly Hansen's Lifa Prolite. This has a softer, less "plastic" feel than the early polypro, and it can be washed at 200 degrees F, a heat that rids it of noxious aroma. Lifa Prolite polypro comes in three types: thin, stretchy Lifa Super; slightly thicker Lifa Super Net, a fishnet weave; and Prowool, a polypro/wool blend. In warm weather, Lifa Super works very well. A crew-neck Lifa top weighs 4½ ounces, bottoms 3¾ ounces.

Polyester

Polyester repels water and has a low wicking ability—not ideal for underwear. However, it can be treated with a chemical so that the outer surface becomes hydrophilic. The result is that moisture is drawn through the material to the outer surface, where it spreads out and quickly dries. The drawback is that after repeated washings the treatment wears off. When this happens the material stops wicking. Most polyesters are treated with an antibacterial agent to prevent odor.

Patagonia's Capilene was the first treated polyester. It was quickly followed by others, including REI's MTS, Acclimate, and Comfortrel and the very popular Malden Mill's Polartec 100, available in plain and BiPolar constructions, which is used by many companies.

Unlike polypro fabrics (except Helly Hansen's Lifa), treated polyester can be washed and dried at relatively high temperatures. Both Capilene and Polartec 100 work as well as polypro and are effective for weeks at a time. It takes a week or so before treated polyester really reeks—though once it smells it's nearly as bad as polypro.

Polyester fabric structure can be altered so that it absorbs moisture, drawing water from the skin through the fabric to the outer surface. Weights and performance are much the same as for treated polyester, though with these fabrics there is no chemical to wear off. Tops made from DuPont's Thermax and Thermastat (both made from hollow-core polyester), and Thermal Dynamics (used by The North Face and other companies) can all be worn for several days before starting to smell, and they all wick moisture, even when dirty. Underpants made from CoolMax, also a DuPont fabric, are very efficient and not as clammy as polypro. Another structurally altered polyester is BTU, from Hoechst Celanese.

Weights for both tops and bottoms in the lightest polyester weaves range from 5½ to 6½ ounces; midweights can run up to 12 ounces for zippered turtlenecks.

Polyester-based push-pull fabrics, such as Hind's Drylete or Nike's Dri-F.I.T., often get positive reviews. Malden Mills' BiPolar Power Stretch, which works on a somewhat similar principle, seems to wick moisture faster than any other material except Parameta S, and it dries extremely quickly. Power Stretch is used by many companies; average top and tights weights are 10 and 7 ounces, respectively—less than some expedition-weight underwear that isn't as warm or as efficient at removing moisture. There are other lightweight stretch fleeces, including Patagonia's Activist Fleece and Helly Hansen's nylon ProStretch, which probably perform much like Power Stretch.

Chlorofiber

Chlorofiber is made of polyvinyl chloride (PVC), and like polypro and polyester, it absorbs little water and wicks well. Chlorofiber garments are comfortable and efficient, but they shrink to doll's size if put in more than lukewarm water or draped over a hot radiator. The most well-known chlorofiber is Thermolactyl, from Damart. Rhovyl is another brand name. (Chris Townsend reports that he hasn't used pure chlorofiber since he washed a set of tops and bottoms in a machine set on a cool wash and had them shrink to half their size, leaving him with 17 days of snow travel along the Pacific Coast Trail with no long underwear.) Chlorofiber isn't as bad as old-style polypro—nothing is—but it still smells after a few days' wear. For strength, it's usually blended with nylon or polyester in an 80/20 mix.

Wool

Wool, the traditional material for thermal underwear, is not as popular now as it once was, yet it still has much to recommend it. Rather than wicking moisture, wool absorbs it into its fibers, leaving a dry surface against the skin. Wool can absorb up to 35 percent of its weight in water before it feels wet and cold, so after-exercise chill is not a problem unless you've been working incredibly hard. Wool also seems to be able to withstand heavy use with no odor problem. Wool's only limitation is its insulating capability, which makes it a cold-weather-only material. If temperatures are expected to be above 50 degrees F, opt for synthetics. Wool also is relatively lightweight; a crew-neck wool top might weigh around 7 ounces, only a little more than a synthetic one.

What puts many people off wool is its reputation for being "itchy." However, very fine wool, such as merino, is designed to be worn next to the skin and doesn't itch.

Many wools *do* cause itching, though, and people with sensitive skin may be dubious about even the highest-quality, finest wools. However, there are now several synthetic/wool, two-layer midweight garments available that keep the wool off the skin. Duofold's Thermax/wool three-button crew-neck top weighs 9.7 ounces, and it is quite effective at wicking and very warm for a garment of this weight—too warm for summer, in fact. For the rest of the year, though, it's a good garment. Norwegian company Devold also makes Thermax/wool garments; Helly Hansen makes polypro/wool combinations.

Silk

Silk is the other natural material commonly used in outdoor underwear. It can absorb up to 30 percent of its own weight in moisture before it feels damp. Silk's best attribute, however, is its luxurious texture; it's light too—a long-sleeved top weighs just 3 ½ ounces. Odor problems are negligible, although silk does stain easily with sweat and dirt. After strenuous exercise, it can also feel cold and clammy for a few minutes before warming up. Silk is not recommended for longer trips, however, because it demands special care; it has to be hand-washed and dried flat, and it doesn't dry

quickly, so it won't dry overnight in camp unless it's very warm.

Hot-Weather Alternative Base Layers

Cotton or cotton-combination shirts have always been popular for outdoor sports for warm-weather wear, although some people feel that lightweight wicking synthetic tops work better because they get less clammy and dry more quickly. If the weather turns unexpectedly cold, a wicking synthetic also works better than a shirt under other layers.

However, a growing number of both cotton and synthetic undershirts designed specifically for hot weather are available from companies such as Sportif, Ex Officio, and Sequel. All-synthetic shirts seem to work best, because they dry quickest when damp. They're also lighter (around 8 ounces) and feel more pleasant next to the skin than cotton or cotton mixes when damp. Cotton takes longer than synthetic fabrics to dry, so it's best on trips during which weight isn't crucial and it's possible to carry more than one next-to-the-skin layer. Overall, the windshirts described below might be better choices—they can be used next to the skin and also as windproofs over other layers in cooler weather.

A very popular hot-weather shirt is Sequel's Solar Shirt, made from CoolMax on the top half and Wick-Net, a wicking mesh, on the lower half and under the arms. It has a deep front opening closed by snaps; two snap-fastened, mesh-lined chest pockets that double as vents; a stand-up collar; and long tails. It's available in long- and short-sleeved versions that weigh 7.2 and 8 ounces, respectively. This shirt works as a wicking inner

layer as well as a cool outer layer. A long-sleeved one was reportedly worn for two weeks in the Grand Canyon and found to be superb in the heat, never sticky or clammy feeling, and very quick-drying. At the end of the late-fall trip, the weather became cold and windy, with frequent rain and hail showers; despite its accumulation of 10 days' sweat, dust, and sunscreen, the Solar Shirt performed well as a base layer underneath a microfleece top and lightweight rain jacket.

The Middle Layer

The middle layer of clothing keeps you warm. Midlayer clothing also has to deal with the body moisture brought up from the inner layer, so it needs to wick that moisture away or absorb it without losing much of its insulation value.

Midlayer clothing can be divided into two types: *trailwear* and *campwear*. The first category includes garments made from wool and light- and medium-weight pile. In above-freezing weather, one or two of these garments may be all you need while walking and in camp. Once temperatures fall, you will need heavyweight pile, down- or synthetic-filled garments.

Mid-layer shirts, sweaters, smocks, anoraks, and jackets come in every imaginable design. Garments that open down the front at least partway are easier to ventilate than polo- or crew-neck styles—and ventilation is the best way to get rid of excess heat and to prevent clothing from becoming damp with sweat. Far more moisture vapor can escape from an open neck than can wick through a material. Conversely, high collars keep your neck warm and hold in heat.

Pullover tops tend to weigh less than open-fronted ones.

Shirts

A lightweight shirt made from a heavyweight wicking synthetic can be an excellent intermediate shirt for weather that is too cool for no jacket but too warm for fleece. Of course, you can wear two layers of light- or medium-weight synthetics, but these will generally be heavier than a single expedition-weight one. Choose very lightweight pile tops, because these weigh no more than expedition-weight underwear and are more versatile.

The traditional alternative to a synthetic shirt is a conventional wool or cotton one. Wool is bulky, heavy, and too warm if you want your shirt to be cooler and lighter than your main warm garments. Cotton is a often thought to be a poor choice, because of its poor wet performance, but don't overlook brushed chamois cotton shirts. Chris Townsend said that on a two-week walk his chamois shirt, worn over a silk inner layer, was very comfortable and quite warm; worn under a breathable shell, it never became more than slightly damp, despite wet and windy weather. He suspected that this was partly because the silk inner took up much of his sweat. (With a synthetic inner layer, the cotton shirt likely would have become damper.) But at 17½ ounces, the cotton shirt is heavier than a much-warmer fleece or pile top, and twice the weight of synthetic shirts.

Pile and fleece can be regarded as the synthetic equivalent of animal fur and work much the same way. Pile and fleece insulate well, wick moisture quickly, are lightweight, hard-wearing, almost nonabsorbent, warm when wet, and quick-drying. These properties make them ideal for outdoor clothing. Chris Townsend says he has carried a pile top on almost every trip since he first tried pile in the 1970s. Low-loft polyester insulations such Thinsulate don't seem to provide the almost-instant warmth of pile, and don't perform as well in cold, wet weather, since they absorb more moisture and dry more slowly. Neither do they last as long or cover the same wide temperature range.

There are many different types of pile and fleece. Generally, pile describes the more loosely-knit, thicker, furrier fabrics; fleece is a type of pile, a denser fabric with a smoother finish. Manufacturers often use both terms for the same fabric, but when used generically "pile" means both fabrics in this discourse.

Most pile is made from polyester, although a few types are made from nylon. Neither material has any advantages over the other. Polypropylene and acrylic piles can be found, but neither has become popular.

Worn over a synthetic, wicking inner layer and under a waterproof/breathable shell, a pile top will keep you warm in just about any weather while you are on the move. Pile is most effective in wet, cold conditions, which is exactly when other warmwear doesn't work so well. A pile top can wick moisture as fast as synthetic underwear, so it will quickly pull sweat through its fibers. At the end of a wet, windy day, for example, you might find the outer layer of a pile jacket to be quite damp, but the inner layer dry. If you feel cold, nothing will warm you up so fast as a pile top, even a damp one, next to the skin.

Of course, pile has a few drawbacks, albeit minor ones. Most pile garments are not windproof, which means you need windproof layers over them even in a cool breeze. Although this is a disadvantage at times, their lack of wind resistance means that pile garments are effective over a wide temperature range—without a shell when it's warm or calm, and with one when it's cold or windy. Windproof pile clothing is available, but it's heavier, bulkier, and less breathable than ordinary pile, and you can't wear the two layers separately. Another drawback is that pile clothing doesn't compress well, so it takes up room in the pack—far more than a down jacket, for example.

Pile comes in different weights and in single and double versions—that is, either one or both sides has a raised or plush surface to trap air. After some use, little balls of fluff appear on the outside of single piles, making them look scruffy; this is known as *pilling*. It can be partly prevented by coating the outside of the fabric with resin or other material, but this makes garments stiff, and adds weight and bulk. If you are bothered by pilling, use a double-pile fabric, which won't pill, or put the smooth side, which is the one that pills, inside, out of sight. Most piles are double-sided. All pile fabrics work in a wide range of temperatures, but obviously the lighter ones aren't as warm as the heavier ones.

Pile garments need to be close-fitting, to trap warm air efficiently and wick moisture away quickly. They are prone to the *bellows effect*—when cold air is sucked in at the bottom of the garment, replacing warm air—so the hem should be elasticized and have a drawcord or be designed to tuck into your pants. Wrist cuffs keep warmth in best if they are close-fitting, as do neck closures. The broad, stretchy ribbing found on the cuffs and hem of many pile tops works well at keeping in warm air, but it absorbs moisture and then feels cold, and it takes a long time to dry. Better is the nonabsorbent and quick-drying stretch Lycra now found on many garments. Damp cuffs are only an inconvenience, not a serious problem.

Pile was first used in clothing from Helly Hansen and tested in Norway's wet, cold climate, for which it proved ideal. It soon became popular in Britain, another country with wet, cold weather, and throughout the 1970s, British climbers and walkers on jaunts abroad could be identified by their navy blue, nylon pile Helly tops.

In North America, pile started to become popular after Malden Mills made a smoother pile, called Polarfleece, for Patagonia in 1979. In 1983, this was replaced by the first of the Polartec fleeces, introduced as Synchilla by Patagonia, and the takeover of outdoor warmwear by pile clothing was under way. There are other manufacturers of pile, including Dyersburg, which now makes the pile Patagonia uses.

These newer pile fabrics provide the same performance for less weight than the originals. They also have smarter styling, don't pill, and are available in bright, cheery colors. Pile comes in various weights and finishes; different makers and companies use different systems for grading weight. Malden Mills lists its pile fabrics as Series 100, 200, and 300.

In warm weather the lightest pile garments, weighing from 10 to 16 ounces, should provide all the insulation you need. Midweight pile—including Polartec 200, Lightweight Synchilla and mid-weight Propile (finished garment weights of 14–25 ounces)—is arguably the most versatile, usable as campwear on cool summer evenings and as midwear while on the move in cold weather. Heavyweight piles—like Polartec 300, Original Synchilla, Patagonia's Retro Pile and Heavyweight Propile—are fine for cold winter conditions, but too warm for general use. (You could carry this weight of pile instead of a filled garment as an extra-warm layer in wet, cold weather.) Weights for heavy pile garments range from 16 to 30 ounces.

Microfleece (sometimes called *microdenier fleece*), is a soft, dense, velvet-like nonstretch microfiber fabric that's extremely comfortable. Although often promoted for next-to-the-skin wear, microfleece doesn't wick, but it makes excellent mid-wear; when worn over stretch pile the combination is warm under a windproof shell while moving in all but the bitterest winter weather. Weights run about 11 ounces. Microfleece also takes up little room in the pack.

Until recently, the only way to make a pile garment windproof was to add an outer shell or lining of windproof material, usually nylon. Shelled and lined pile garments are bulkier and heavier (20 to 40 ounces) than standard pile, less comfortable, and not quite as breathable. The best are surprisingly water resistant, though they won't keep out heavy rain; a waterproof/breathable shell is still needed. When snow rather than rain is expected, these garments are more useful. An ordinary pile top and a separate windshell are far more versatile, however.

The latest development consists of an ultralight, windproof membrane sandwiched between two layers of lightweight pile, which gives a fully windproof pile. (There are several versions, including Malden Mills' Polartec Windbloc 1000 and W. L. Gore's Windstopper fleece. Duofold and Columbia Sportswear have their own proprietary versions, while Patagonia has a variation called Performance Enhancing Film, in which the membrane is sandwiched between a Capilene mesh inner and a Light or Retro pile outer.) Weights run from 18 to 40 ounces.

Pile is nonabsorbent and quick-drying. Even so, moisture can be trapped between the fibers, especially in thicker piles like Polartec 300 or the windproof types, which slows the drying time and makes the garments feel damp. Some pile fabrics have water repellence built in during manufacture; these shed water and snow from the surface quickly and don't hold moisture in the fibers, which speeds up drying time. You can improve the water repellence of any pile by treating it with a wash-in waterproofing agent, such as Nikwax TX.10 Polarproof.

Increasingly, pile is being made from recycled polyester and plastic soft-drink bottles, which, according to many reports, significantly reduces the use of oil and natural gas (used in manufacturing polyester), and keeps plastic bottles out of landfills. Recycled pile was first introduced by Dyersburg Fabrics in 1993 in association with Patagonia, which made the first recycled pile garments. The first recycled pile actually contained about 50 percent virgin polyester, but the amount of recycled polyester is increasing. Malden Mills' Polartec

Recycled Series now contains 89 percent recycled polyester; Dyersburg makes some 100 percent recycled pile. Malden Mills is testing 100 percent recycled pile, too, so it may appear soon in Polartec garments. Currently, the choice of recycled pile is limited to mid- and heavyweight standard double-sided pile, but both Malden Mills and Dyersburg intend to incorporate as much recycled pile in their fabric as possible. Dyersburg calls its recycled pile E.C.O. Fleece; Patagonia calls its PCR (Post-Consumer Recycled) fleece; Draper Knitting Mills makes recycled pile under the name Eco-Pile. It appears in many ranges under makers' own names.

Many outdoorspeople prefer pile for warmwear—they see no point in carrying a garment that is heavier than pile for the same insulation. Wool absorbs moisture—making it even heavier—takes ages to dry, requires special care, and isn't as durable as pile. But there are still those who like wool shirts and sweaters, which are widely available. If you already have wool sweaters, you might as well wear them and spend your money on good-quality inner and outer layers, where specialty fabrics are more necessary. You can replace your woolens with pile garments when they wear out.

Insulated Clothing

Whenever or wherever a pile garment won't keep you warm on its own, you need a second insulating layer. This garment could be a second, perhaps thicker, pile one; in cold, wet weather, Retro Pile or a windproof pile is a good choice, but there are warmer items that take up less space in the pack. Down-filled clothing is preferred by many people

because it's warmer than pile and less bulky when packed.

If the need for a second layer seems marginal or weight is a factor, a sleeveless top is a good bet, because it's most critical to keep the torso warm. Generally, however, if you have the space, carry a jacket or sweater, which doesn't weigh much more than a vest and provides much more warmth.

Waterfowl down is the lightest, warmest insulation there is, despite all attempts to create a synthetic that works as well. Garments filled with down pack small and provide much more warmth weight-for-weight than pile. They are too hot to wear when walking, but ideal when resting. Down is also durable, but *it must be kept dry.* When it is wet, down completely loses its insulating ability, and it dries very slowly, unless you can hang it out in a hot sun or put it in a machine dryer. Down can absorb vast amounts of water, so a sodden down garment is very heavy to carry as well as being useless. Nonetheless, down is often the first choice for a second layer of insulation when weight and space are at premiums. Keeping down dry is rather easy if it is only worn in camp or at rest stops in freezing temperatures.

For basic backcountry purposes, a lightweight down jacket or simple sweater is all you need—complex constructions, vast amounts of fill, and heavy, breathable, waterproof shells are for mountaineering and polar exploration. Garments suitable for backpacking, ski touring, or biking and boating in cold conditions need no more than 6–9 ounces of down and should weigh no more than 25 ounces. One of the lightest is the Feathered Friends Helios jacket,

which weighs a mere 14 ounces. Lightweight nylon with sewn-through seams is adequate for the shell. Although a hood isn't necessary, a detachable one can be useful in bitter cold. Even lighter are down vests, which can weigh as little as 8 ounces, with 3½–4½ ounces of down fill. Most makers of down clothing offer one lightweight garment and perhaps a vest among expedition-weight models. Makers of good lightweight down clothing include Feathered Friends, The North Face, Marmot, Mountain Hardwear, and REI, among many others.

If you are allergic to feathers or nervous about garments that won't work when wet, polyester-filled jackets are an alternative. Although they too are cold when wet—despite manufacturers' claims—they dry quickly, so they perform better in the wet than down. Few jackets weigh much under 2 pounds, however, and most weigh more. Packed, they are bulkier than pile garments, and more than twice the size of comparable down ones. Synthetic-filled vests make more sense, as they weigh between 16 and 25 ounces. In high-loft, synthetic fills include Quallofil, Hollofil, and Polarguard. See the Sleeping Bag section in Chapter 2 (p. 33) for more details.

While polyester fills expand like down when uncompressed, and produce thick, warm-looking jackets, *microfiber synthetic insulations* provide warmth without the bulk. These now dominate synthetic-filled clothing, especially alpine skiwear, because of their slim looks and easy fit. First in the field was 3M's Thinsulate; there have since been a mass of others. The fill is made from very fine polyester and polypropylene fibers that are able to trap more air in a given thickness than anything else, including down, resulting in garments that are warm but not bulky. On the other hand, microfiber-insulation garments weigh more than a comparably warm down jacket—well over 2 pounds—and are as bulky when packed as equivalent high-loft insulated jackets. Most microfiber-filled tops, therefore, are not useful for backpacking.

An exception to the above are some very lightweight, low-bulk garments using the latest synthetic fills such as Primaloft, a high-loft insulation, and Microloft, a microfiber. These garments are alternatives to pile rather than down in terms of insulation. In fact, they're lighter than the heaviest piles and just as warm. They're also windproof and less bulky than pile. Typical are those from Patagonia (which uses Microloft in the Puffball Pullover and Vest, which weigh 14½ and 8½ ounces, respectively) and Marmot (which uses Primaloft in the Alpinist Sweater, which weighs 16 ounces).

The Outer Layer

Keeping out wind, rain, and snow is the most important task of your outer clothing. If this layer fails, it doesn't matter how good your other garments are—wet clothing exposed to the wind will chill you quickly, whatever material it's made from. In a wet outer garment, you can go from feeling warm to shivering with cold and on the verge of hypothermia very, very quickly.

There are two types of shell garments: ones that are windproof but not waterproof, and ones that are both. A windproof/waterproof shell is essential; a windproof shell is optional. Any fabric that is waterproof

is also windproof. The belief that some waterproof fabrics are not windproof is based on the misunderstanding that the reason a garment feels chilly in windy weather is because it's not windproof. There are several reasons why you might feel cold under a waterproof garment, but letting in the wind isn't one of them.

Don't expect too much from rain gear, however. In heavy showers you can expect to remain pretty dry. At the end of a day of steady rain you'll probably be a little damp, even in waterproof/breathable rain gear, because the high humidity will restrict the fabric's breathability. In nonbreathable rain gear you'll be soaked with your own condensation. If rain continues nonstop for several days and you can't dry out any gear, you'll get wetter and wetter, however good your rain gear. This is where synthetic, wicking inner layers and pile midwear are important—they don't absorb much moisture and are still relatively warm when damp.

If rain keeps up for more than a few days, heading out to where you can dry your gear is a good idea.

Waterproof/Breathable Fabrics

The moisture vapor given off by your body eventually reaches the outer layer of your clothing. If it can't escape from there, it will condense on the inner surface of that layer and eventually soak back into your clothes. The solution is to wear fabrics that allow water vapor to pass through, while keeping the rain out. These are known as *moisture-vapor-permeable* or *waterproof/breathable* fabrics. Most, but not all, rainwear now is made from breathable fabrics, but this was not always the case. Until Gore-Tex came along in the

SOME TERMS DEFINED

- *Microporous:* a material with microscopic holes in it that allows moisture vapor through but keeps liquid water (rain) out.
- *Hydrophilic:* a solid waterproof material with chains of water-attracting molecules built in, along which moisture vapor can pass through to the outside.
- *Membrane:* a very thin breathable waterproof film. *Gore-Tex* is a microporous membrane, *Sympatex* is a hydrophilic membrane.
- *Laminate:* a membrane stuck to a more durable fabric, usually a form of nylon. In *two-layer laminates*, the membrane is glued to the outer fabric, the lining hanging free. In *three-layer laminates*, the membrane is glued between an outer fabric and a lightweight inner scrim, so the finished material appears as just one layer. In *lining laminates*, the membrane is glued to the lining and the outer hangs free. In *drop liners*, the membrane is bonded to a light scrim and hangs free between the inner and outer layers.
- *Coating:* polyurethane applied to the inside of a fabric, usually nylon or polyester. Many makers have their own coatings, though they may come from the same source and there is often little difference between them.

late 1970s, the choice was between being wet from rain or being wet from sweat, unless you only went out when it was sunny. The first is far more unpleasant and potentially dangerous than the second, so standard rainwear was made of non-breathable fabric.

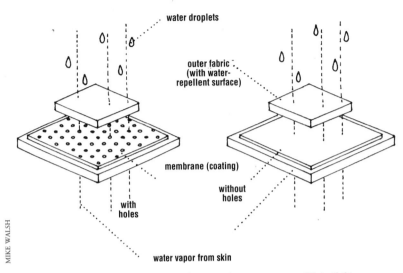

water droplets

outer fabric
(with water-
repellent surface)

membrane (coating)

without
holes

with
holes

water vapor from skin

MIKE WALSH

Breathable materials are either coated or laminated. In microporous fabric (left) water vapor passes through microscopic holes in the membrane or coating. In hydrophilic fabric, water vapor is absorbed by and then evaporated from a nonporous membrane or coating.

Since the advent of Gore-Tex, a host of waterproof fabrics claiming to transmit moisture vapor have appeared. Such fabrics work due to a pressure differential between the air inside and outside the jacket. The warmer the air, the more water vapor it can absorb. Since the air next to the skin is almost always warmer than the air outside your garments, it contains more water vapor, even in the rain. Condensation forms on the inside of nonbreathable fabrics as cooler air becomes saturated with vapor that cannot escape. Water vapor can pass through a breathable fabric as long as the outside air is cooler than that inside. (Theoretically, waterproof/breathable fabrics can work both ways, but in conditions where rain clothing is needed the outside air is always lower than your body temperature.) Breathable garments need to be relatively close-fitting to keep the air inside as warm as possible, because

this enables the fabric to transmit moisture more effectively. However, ventilating any garment by opening the front, lowering the hood, and undoing wrist fastenings is still the quickest and most efficient way to let moisture out.

Breathable fabrics aren't perfect, of course, and they won't work in all conditions. There is a limit to the amount of moisture even the best of them can transmit in a given time. This means that when you sweat hard, you won't stay bone dry under a breathable jacket, nor will you do so in continuous heavy rain, despite manufacturers' claims. When the outside of any garment is running with water, breathability is reduced and condensation forms. With the best breathables, once your output of energy slows down and you produce less moisture, any dampness will dry out through the fabric. The same happens after heavy rain.

In very cold conditions, especially if it's also windy, condensation may form on the inside of an outer garment. It might even freeze, creating a layer of ice. This seems to occur whether or not the garment transmits water vapor. What happens is that the dew point—the point at which air becomes saturated with water vapor—occurs inside the clothing in freezing temperatures. Icing is a particular problem if a windproof layer is worn under the outer garment, probably because warm air is trapped inside the windproof layer, leaving the air between the two outer shells very cold. It also occurs with windproof, nonwaterproof garments that transmit water vapor faster than the best breathable rain gear.

The best thing to wear under a shell garment when it's really cold seems to be a pile top, which keeps the air warmer throughout the clothing layers. If the clothing is too thick, though, breathability is compromised. Nick Brown of Paramo has calculated that more than $\frac{1}{15}$ inch of insulation is enough to significantly reduce breathability. Many heavyweight pile garments are thicker than this. They'd be better worn outside your rain jacket than inside.

There are two main categories of breathable materials: coatings and membranes. New coated fabrics appear constantly, although many garment makers assign their own names to the same fabrics. Generic fabrics include Entrant and Ultrex; proprietary ones include Triple Point Ceramic (Lowe Alpine), Helly-Tech (Helly Hansen), H_2NO Storm (Patagonia), Drytec (MontBell), Elements (REI), Microshed (Solstice), MVT (Moonstone), Texapore (Jack Wolfskin), Omni-Tech

(Columbia Sportswear), and Camp-Tech (Campmor).

Coatings used to be inferior to laminates in terms of breathability, although just as waterproof. Now, however, the best coatings are as breathable as the best membranes, and are less expensive. The real differences lay in the water repellence of outer fabrics, garment ventilation, whether the garment is lined, and what the lining material is. The thickness of the coating matters: the thinnest coatings are the most breathable but least waterproof; the thickest are most waterproof but least breathable. Chris Townsend reports that of the coated fabrics he has used, Triple Point Ceramic works best. It's available in two specified weights, 1200 and 1600; his Lowe Alpine Northwind Jacket in 1200, with 1600 on the shoulders and arms for greater durability, weighs 19 ounces and he feels it is excellent as a year-round rain jacket.

Membranes are arguably the most effective (and most expensive) breathable fabrics. There are far fewer of them than there are coated fabrics, with just one generally available—Gore-Tex—although Sympatex is becoming more widely distributed. There are a few proprietary membranes, such as Sierra Design's Amino Acid Laminate and Marmot's Mem-Brain, as well as several proprietary laminates that usually use a Gore membrane (Alpine Designs' Weatherstop, and Patagonia's Gridstop and Super Pluma are examples).

Gore-Tex, which started the breathable waterproof revolution, is a microporous membrane made from polytetrafluoroethylene. Sympatex is a hydrophilic membrane made of polyester. Both membranes can be laminated to a wide range of fabrics, mostly nylons, although sometimes polyester or polyester/cotton. The thicker the fabric, the more durable the garment, but the lower its breathability. In three-layer laminates, the membrane is glued between two layers of nylon to produce a hard-wearing, somewhat stiff material. The glue dots used to stick the layers together reduce breathability. However, the latest three-layer laminates with ripstop nylon outers are lighter, more flexible, and more breathable than earlier ones that used Taslan and Taffeta nylons. More breathable but less durable are two-layer laminates, in which the membrane is stuck to an outer layer while the inner lining hangs free, or drop liners, in which the membrane is left loose between an inner and outer layer. Finally, there are *inner-lining laminates,* also called *laminated to the drop,* where the membrane is stuck to a very light inner layer. This design minimizes the number of seams, which is a bonus.

Nonbreathable Rain Gear

Nonbreathable clothing is made from nylon or polyester, usually coated with polyurethane or PVC and occasionally with silicone. Its greatest advantage is that it's far less expensive than waterproof/breathable fabrics. Polyurethane is much more durable than PVC—but both eventually crack and peel off the base layer. Both will also leave you soaked in sweat after a hard day walking in wet weather, and the only way to remove that moisture is to ventilate the garment. One way to limit the soaking is to wear a windproof layer under the waterproof one and trap some of the moisture between the two layers.

While moving you will still feel warm, even if your undergarments are wet with sweat, because nonbreathable rainwear holds in heat as well as moisture. Therefore, since rain is colder than perspiration, it's better to wear a nonbreathable waterproof shell than a breathable nonwaterproof one. When you stop, though, you'll cool down rapidly unless you put on extra clothes.

Nonbreathable garments are only worth considering if you wear a windproof top most of the time; wear rain gear only in continuous, heavy rain; or for areas where prolonged rain is unlikely. Those on a tight budget should consider it, though. Remember, until the late 1970s all rain gear was nonbreathable, and people still hiked the Appalachian Trail in the rain and slogged through the wet forests of the Pacific Northwest.

Designs are much the same as for breathable garments, and include the old standby *poncho,* still popular with some hikers and backpackers and quite versatile—it can double as a tarp or ground cloth. Ponchos are easier to ventilate than jackets, although they tend to act like sails in strong winds, making them unsuitable for use above the timberline.

Weights of nonbreathable rain tops range from 4 ounces for a thin top to 2 pounds for a tough, long-lasting one. Cheap vinyl rain gear is available, but it lasts about as long as it takes to put on and isn't worth considering, despite the price.

Garment Design

Material alone is not enough to ensure that a garment will perform well—design is nearly as important. The more ventilation, the fewer condensation problems there will be, so all

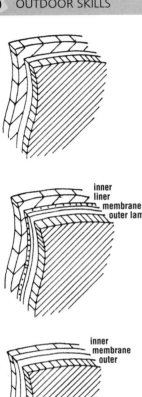

Two-layer laminates

the waterproof membrane is laminated to the back of the outer fabric

Drop liner

inner
liner
membrane
outer laminate

the membrane is laminated with an interlining material

Lining laminate
(laminated to drop liner: L.T.D.)

inner
membrane
outer

the membrane is laminated with the inner lining

Three-layer laminate

inner
membrane
outer

the membrane is laminated with both the inner and the outer fabrics

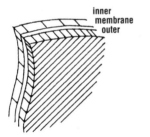

Methods of laminating waterproof fabrics.

MIKE WALSH

> **KEY FEATURES TO LOOK FOR IN RAIN GEAR**
> ✓ Waterproof/breathable fabric, to allow some body moisture out
> ✓ Taped seams—the fewer seams the better
> ✓ An adjustable hood with a peak that gives protection and allows side-to-side vision
> ✓ Adjustable cuffs
> ✓ A full-length front zip with a storm flap
> ✓ Zippered chest pockets big enough for maps
> ✓ Low weight and bulk

the most critical feature of a waterproof garment. Unless these are waterproofed (or you have a Paramo garment), they will leak. In waterproof/breathable garments and the more expensive nonbreathables, seams are usually taped, the most effective way of making them watertight. In cheaper garments, seams may be coated with a special sealant instead. If you have a garment with uncoated seams, buy a tube of sealant and coat the seams yourself. You also can do this when the original sealant cracks and comes off—which it will. Taped seams can peel off, although this is very rare. Even so, the fewer seams the better, and where the seams are located is important, too. The best garments have seamless yokes or capes over the shoulders to avoid leakage from abrasion.

The front zipper is another other major source of leakage. This must be covered with a single or, preferably, a double waterproof flap, closed with snaps or Velcro. Even so, after facing into driving rain for any length of

closures and fastenings should be adjustable. The two basic choices are *zip-front* and *pullover* garments. Zip-front jackets are more versatile and are preferable, because pullover jackets can be difficult to put on in a strong wind. The exception is with the ultralight rain gear to be carried "just in case"—a pullover design that's lighter than a front-opening one, important when weight is critical.

Aside from the fabric, *seams* are

CHRIS TOWNSEND'S PICK OF THE BREATHABLES

Which breathable fabric is best? It depends on the membrane and the materials used for the inner and outer layer, so there is no easy answer. There's also a big tradeoff between breathability and durability. Based on his extensive use of several garments, Chris has found three-layer Gore-Tex to perform slightly better than three-layer Sympatex. Surprisingly, he also found that three-layer laminates breathe better than two-layer or drop-liner constructions, despite the many laboratory tests showing the opposite. The reason may be that the tests are done on the two-layer laminate without a lining—but all finished garments have a lining, which impedes breathability. The best performer in terms of breathability is the inner-lining laminate, because the membrane is kept warmer than in other constructions, making moisture vapor less likely to condense on it. There are still times, of course, when condensation will occur, whatever the construction.

For durability, however, Sympatex has the edge. Chris reports that he has twice worn out Gore-Tex three-layer garments on walks lasting several months, and three times had Gore-Tex jackets fail during heavy rain. Sympatex garments, with more use than the Gore-Tex ones that failed, are going strong and are so far not leaking.

How the latest coatings compare with membranes in terms of durability has not been thoroughly explored. Gore-Tex garments are widely offered in many styles. The North Face, REI, Patagonia, MontBell, Moonstone, Solstice, Mountain Hardwear, Marmot, Sequel and many more all make top-quality Gore-Tex garments; Sympatex is restricted at the time of writing to VauDe garments.

Chris's picks: In Gore-Tex, a three-layer one with a ripstop nylon outer; weights should be in the 16- to 22-ounce range. In Sympatex, a lining-laminate garment; weights range from 16 to 30 ounces. However, the performance of coatings such as Triplepoint Ceramic are now so good that he's no longer sure that membranes are worth the extra money.

The problems with both coatings and membranes are that they aren't very durable, can't be reproofed when they start to leak badly, and they only allow passage of moisture vapor through to the outside, not sweat. A recent development solves these problems. Paramo clothing, from Nikwax, is very durable, can be reproofed and will allow sweat through to the outside. It does this without coatings or membranes. Instead it mimics the way animals stay dry—a unique waterproof/breathable system inventor Nick Brown calls the Nikwax Biological Analogy.

Without going into details, the fabric is said to mimic the way animal fur guides perspiration away from skin toward larger spaces; natural hair also keeps rain off the skin. Paramo utilizes a very thin polyester fleece, called Parameta, which has fibers that are tightly packed on the inside but become less dense toward the outside. To replicate the animal oils that keep fur water repellent, Parameta is coated with TX.10. Like fur, Parameta pumps water in one direction—away from the body. It does this at a faster rate than rain can fall, so moisture is always moved away from the body faster than it arrives, keeping you dry.

To be effective on its own, Parameta would have to be very thick, however. In order to keep it thin (and therefore not too warm), Paramo garments have an outer layer of windproof polyester microfiber, also treated with TX.10, which deflects most of the rain. The resulting material allows more moisture through, including condensed perspiration, than any membrane or coating. It's not dependent on humidity levels outside the garment, or on temperature inside the garment. The fabric can be reproofed with TX.Direct if it starts to leak. In finished garments, all components, such as zippers and cords, are also treated with TX.10, so they won't wick moisture into the garment.

All this sounds wonderful, but is it true? Chris Townsend says that it is. He has been using Paramo garments since the early 1990s and has found them very comfortable and efficient. Reproofing with TX.10 works, so Paramo garments should last a long time. There is one limitation: the garments are quite warm due to the two-layer construction.

time, you may find a damp patch inside the zipper where water has found its way in. Often it's at the neck, which a high collar helps prevent. The covering flap should come all the way to the top of the zipper. Most zippers open from the bottom as well as the top. These are slightly more awkward to use than single ones, and other than ease of movement in very long garments, have no advantages.

Hoods are clearly potential leak points. Good ones fit closely around the face when the drawcords are tightened, without leaving a gap under the chin. Fold-away hoods that wrap around a high collar often provide better protection than fixed hoods, though they are more awkward to use. Detachable hoods need to have a large overlap of material to prevent rain running down your neck; most are very difficult to attach in strong winds. A wired or otherwise stiffened peak or visor helps keep off hail or driving rain, and people who wear glasses tell me that such a peak is essential. The best hoods move with your head, so that you can look to the side without staring at the inner lining, which is the case with too many designs. Clearly, the best way to check this is to try the hood on, but you can make a quick assessment by looking at the hood seams. A single seam running back to front over the hood generally means it won't move with you; if there are two seams, or a single seam that runs around or across the hood from one side to the other, the hood is more likely to allow good visibility. Unfortunately, the hoods that limit vision most are the ones that give the best protection.

In cold weather, a pile-lined, waterproof/breathable cap with a large peak instead of a hood works well alone during light showers, and worn under a hood in storms and blizzards, provides better protection than any hood alone can give. This combination is too warm outside the snow season. Whether or not you wear such a cap, your jacket hood must be big enough to allow you to wear warm headwear underneath, whether a full balaclava or a lightweight knitted hat. (Many hoods now have a drawcord or adjustable tab at the back, so they can be expanded to cover a bulky hat, or reduced in size so that the peak doesn't

flop in your eyes when you take the hat off. These work well.) Front hood drawcords can lash you in the face in strong winds; some jackets have tabs to hold drawcords down or cords that tuck into the jacket at each end. These can be fiddly to use but are welcome in storms.

Sleeves need to be cut full under the arms to allow for free movement. Trying on a garment is the best way to find out how well the sleeves are cut. *Articulated sleeves,* with a built-in curve at the elbow, are worth the extra price for climbers, skiers, and kayakers. Some garments have underarm zippers, which allow better ventilation, but they tend to leak in heavy rain. The cuffs on sleeves need to be adjustable to aid ventilation; simple, external, Velcro-closed ones seem to work better than the neater but more awkward internal storm cuffs. Avoid if possible nonadjustable elasticized ones, which can make your arms overheat and run with sweat. Wide sleeves provide the most ventilation and can even be rolled up when it's warm. They're also easy to pull over gloves or mitts.

Pockets are undoubtedly useful, but making them waterproof is difficult, if not downright impossible. Backpackers might prefer two chest pockets only. Hem pockets are usually inaccessible under a fastened hipbelt when backpacking or ski touring. However, since shell jackets, particularly the more expensive ones, are often used as general-purpose garments, people want plenty of pockets. Zippered or not, pocket openings should always be covered by flaps, and the seams should be taped or sealed on the inside. The most water-resistant hem pockets hang inside the jacket, attached only at the top.

The best compromise between waterproofness and accessibility for chest pockets is a vertical-zippered entrance under the front flap but outside the jacket's front zipper. (Pockets inside the jacket stay dry, but you let in wind and rain when you open the jacket front to use them.) Pockets on the outside of the jacket that have angled flaps and zippers are the best for access but the first to leak in heavy rain. Zippers that close upward are best, because small items in the pocket are less likely to fall out when you open them. One advantage of pullover garments is that they usually have a single large "kangaroo" pouch on the chest, which is the easiest to use and very water-resistant.

Pockets don't need to be made from the same material as the rest of the garment. A lightweight, unproofed nylon is adequate (avoid cotton—it absorbs moisture). However, mesh is the best material for chest pockets, because it adds minimum weight and you can ventilate the garment by opening the pockets. Mesh is particularly effective on a garment with two outside, angled chest pockets, because with both pockets open but protected by their flaps, you can ventilate the whole chest and armpit area. Mesh is also the best material for the inner lining that most two-layer laminates and coated garments have, again because it's lightweight and because it helps moisture reach the breathable layer as quickly as possible. If the mesh is made from a wicking fabric, as many now are, all the better. Woven linings, even nylon ones, become wet with condensation, however breathable the outer layer.

Drawcords are needed at the collar for tightening the hood. They are also often found at the waist, but these are unnecessary, since the pack's hipbelt cinches around the bottom of the jacket. Self-locking toggles are a boon on drawcords; trying to untangle an iced-up tiny knot with frozen fingers in order to lower your hood is not easy or fun.

Fit

Rain jackets are more comfortable if they fit properly. When they were simply baggy waterproof sacks with sleeves this hardly mattered, but today's garments are more tailored and much closer-fitting. The jacket should be roomy enough to cover a pile top and still feel unrestricted. Remember, a close-fitting jacket will have better breathability, but a slightly large garment is far better than a slightly small one. Look also for sleeves that are long enough to pull over your hands, so that you won't need gloves if the weather turns unexpectedly cool. Until recently, women had to put up with ill-fitting garments—the so-called unisex sizes were really just men's sizes in disguise. These days, though, many companies make jackets specifically designed for women—including a Swiss company, Wild Rose, that is for-women-only and includes serious mountain wear.

Rain Pants

Rain pants used to be uncomfortable, restrictive garments that sagged at the waist, bulged at the knees, and snagged at the ankles. The introduction of waterproof/breathable fabrics made overtrousers slightly more comfortable, but it was only when designers got to work on them that they really changed. In part this is due to changes in legwear in general. Traditional overtrousers had to be big and baggy, because they had to fit over

heavy wool knickers or trousers, which were also big and baggy. Modern legwear is made from lighter, thinner fabrics and is more slim-fitting, so voluminous rain pants are simply not needed. Softer fabrics have helped, too.

The changes have been so dramatic that the best waterproof legwear is comfortable enough to be worn instead of normal outdoor trousers, either next to the skin or over long underwear.

There are two basic designs of waterproof legwear: simple pants; and bibs with a high back and chest, with suspenders. For most walking, pants are best, especially if they will spend much of their time in your pack, because bibs are heavier and bulkier. Bibs, however, are excellent for cold-weather use, especially for ski touring, ice climbing, and mountaineering—they are warmer than pants, prevent gaps at the waist when you stretch, and minimize the chances of snow getting into your clothes. They're difficult to put on in a wind, though. Because of their weight and bulk, they're best worn all day rather than carried.

Synthetic long underwear or, in really cold weather, stretch fleece pants, are the best garments to wear under rain pants. Synthetic trail pants are good too, but cotton/nylon and cotton trousers tend to feel damp and cold.

Features to look for are adjustable drawcords at the waist and knee-length zips to allow you to get them on over boots. Pockets, or slits to allow access to inner legwear pockets, are useful. If you intend wearing rain pants all the time, then full-length side zips are benefits, because they can be opened at the top for ventila-

tion; they also allow rain pants to be put on over crampons or skis, though handling long zips in a strong wind can be difficult. A drawback is that it's very difficult to make full-length side zips fully waterproof. Velcro-closed overflaps help, but they make putting the garment on a little more difficult. Gussets behind knee-length zips help to keep rain out, but they tend to catch in the zips. For men, pants with flies are worth considering. Nonelasticized hems with drawcords or Velcro-closed tabs are better than elasticized hems.

Weights of rain pants run from 4 to 32 ounces, depending on design and fabric. As with rain jackets, heavier garments will outlast lighter ones. Rain pants suffer more hard wear than jackets, though, so if you plan to wear them all or most of the time, extra weight could be better. However, if they'll spend most of their time packed away, the lighter the better. Heavier garments might be too hot in summer. Conversely, in severe winter conditions, the lightest rain pants don't give much protection.

Try legwear on before you buy, preferably over the underlayers you will wear with them—you need to be sure they don't bind anywhere when you move. Length is important, too. Unfortunately, few makers offer different leg lengths in the same waist size (REI, Moonstone, Patagonia, and Paramo do in some models). Alterations are possible, although zipped legs make this difficult (ones where the zips start a little way above the hem are easier to shorten). It's better to find a pair that fits to begin with.

Water Repellence

Eventually, the water repellence of the outer or face fabric begins to wear off and the material starts to absorb moisture. When this happens, damp patches appear on the outside of the garment, a process known as *wetting out.* This usually occurs first where pack straps have rubbed on shoulders and around hips. Moisture absorption adds to weight and drying time and impairs breathability, leading many wearers to think their garment is leaking. Fabric manufacturers are very aware of this problem and much work goes into creating better durable water-repellent (DWR) treatments. They certainly lasts much longer now than the week or so they did when waterproof/breathable fabrics were first introduced.

One way to maintain water repellence is to clean rain gear only when it really needs it; even the most gentle wash removes some of the DWR. It's best to sponge off dirt. When you finally decide you can't stand to wear your rain gear again until it's clean, it should be washed with a pure soap powder or a special treatment such as Loft Tech Wash (Nikwax). *Never* dry-clean—the solvents used strip off all DWR.

Reviving water repellence can be done by machine drying or ironing the garment on a low- to medium-heat setting, which will melt the original DWR and spread it over the outer surface. If you tumble-dry your rain gear, make sure all zippers are done up and flaps closed to minimize damage. Some tests show that tumble-drying garments often damages the coating or membrane, leading to eventual leakage—ironing is much safer.

So much of the original DWR will eventually wear off that it can't be revived. The best way to replace it is with a wash-in treatment such as

TX Direct, from Nikwax. This not only replaces the DWR, but also seals minute cracks in the membrane or coating without affecting the breathability. Spray-on treatments aren't as effective and don't last as long.

Windproofs

The advent of waterproof/breathable fabrics was hailed as a weight-saving boon, since one garment served to protect from both wind and rain. This is true, but even the best fabrics are far less breathable than nonwaterproof, windproof ones, and waterproof jackets are never as comfortable as lightweight windproof tops. Paramo garments are the only exception to this.

One combination setup is a double-layer, water-repellent, windproof jacket plus an ultralight rain jacket; another, more common combination is a single-layer, lightweight, windproof top and a standard-weight rain jacket.

Double-layer jacket designs are similar to waterproof ones, and weigh 16–50 ounces, which is why you wouldn't want to carry a full-weight rain jacket as well. The lightest are made from various polyester, cotton, and nylon combinations, which dry quickly and are very comfortable, but not very water-resistant. The standard is the hard-wearing 60/40 cotton/nylon cloth.

Single-layer windproof tops, sometimes called *windshirts,* make much more sense, since they can double as a midlayer shirt to keep a cool breeze off the inner layer, and as a shell to keep stronger, colder winds off your warmwear. They aren't as water-repellent as double garments, so you must also carry a fully waterproof top.

Lightweight nylons and polyesters, especially microfibers, are the best materials for windshirts; they're windproof, water-repellent, quick-drying, low in bulk, and durable.

Manufacturers making single-layer and even double-layer microfiber garments include Patagonia, Sierra Designs, Marmot, Lowe Alpine, Sequel, Mountain Hardwear, Columbia, REI, and The North Face—and the ranks are increasing constantly. Fabric names to look for include Pertex, Supplex, Hydrenaline, Versatech, Gore Activent (called Pneumatic by Patagonia), Climaguard, Tactel, Bergundtal, Perfecta, Silmond, and DriClime. If worn over a pile jacket, single-layer garments made from these fabrics will keep out rain surprisingly well. At the same time, they are more breathable than any fully waterproof fabric.

Most windshirts are pullover designs, which are preferable because they are lighter in weight than jackets and more comfortable when worn as a shirt in camp. They usually are short, so they won't extend below a rain jacket if one is worn over the top. The size should be adequate for wearing over all your warmwear. Useful features are hoods, map-size chest pockets, and adjustable cuffs. Windshirts can be worn next to the skin, but they may feel a little clammy when you're on the move. However, there are windshirts with wicking linings that should overcome this.

The Vapor-Barrier Theory

As always, there is a view that challenges the accepted wisdom—in this case the concept of "breathability." Our skin is always slightly moist, however dry it may feel; if it really dries out, it cracks and chaps, and open sores appear. Our bodies constantly produce liquid—either sweat or, when we aren't exercising hard, insensible perspiration. The aim of breathable clothing—to move moisture away from the skin as quickly as possible and transport it to the outside air, where it can evaporate—inevitably causes heat loss. And as we have seen, maintaining breathability is difficult in severe weather conditions.

The vapor-barrier theory says that instead of trying to remove this moisture from the skin, we should try to keep it there, so that its production and attendant evaporative heat loss will cease. This will enable us to stay warm and our clothing to stay dry, because it won't have to deal with large amounts of liquid. To achieve this result, one wears a *nonbreathable waterproof layer* either next to or close to the skin, with insulating layers over it. Because heat is trapped inside, less clothing need be worn.

Because of the way they work, vapor barriers are most efficient in dry cold—that is, in temperatures below freezing—because when humidity is high, heat loss by evaporation is less. Vapor-barrier clothing also prevents moisture loss by helping stave off dehydration, a potentially serious problem in dry, cold conditions.

Apparently, if you have a hairy body, waterproof fabrics feel comfortable worn next to the skin. People who are relatively hairless, however, report that vapor barriers make them feel clammy unless something is worn under them. Thin, nonabsorbent synthetics, such as polypro, are ideal for wearing under vapor barriers.

Wearing a vapor barrier in your sleeping bag will add several degrees of warmth to the bag.

Chris Townsend says he changed his waterproof suit for a lighter, more comfortable, vapor-barrier design made from a soft-coated ripstop nylon that weighs just 7 ounces. The shirt has a zipper front and Velcro-closed cuffs; the trousers have a draw-cord waist and Velcro closures at the ankles. Although they perform well, he says he has rarely used them since the first winter, because every time he walked in them he quickly overheated. He suspects they work best in very cold conditions.

Plastic bags, or thin plastic or rubber socks and gloves, can be worn on feet and hands as vapor barriers. If your feet become very cold and wet, an emergency vapor barrier worn over a dry, thin sock with a thicker sock over does help them warm up.

Few companies make vapor-barrier gear. The main one is Stephenson, of Warmlite tent fame, which offers shirts, pants, gloves and socks made in a fabric called Fuzzy Stuff. This is a stretchy, brushed nylon glued to a urethane film. The inner is said to feel like soft flannel and be far more comfortable against the skin than is ordinary coated nylon; it wicks moisture and spreads it out for rapid drying. It sounds as though Fuzzy Stuff should be far better than simple coated fabrics, and it is probably the stuff to try if you want to see what vapor-barrier clothing is like.

Headwear

"If your feet are cold, put on a hat." This old adage has been floating around for a long time. It happens to be very accurate.

When you start to get cold, your body protects its core by slowing down the blood supply to the extremities—fingers, toes, nose—first. However, your brain requires a constant supply of blood in order to function properly, so the circulation to your head is maintained. If it's unprotected in cold weather you can lose enormous amounts of heat through your head—anywhere from 20 to 75 percent, depending on whose figures you read. The capillaries just below the skin on the head never close down to conserve heat the way they do on hands and feet, so *you must protect your head in order to stay warm.*

Outdoor hats come in a wild variety of colors and styles and every sort of material, including pile, wicking synthetics, wool, and mixtures of everything. All of these fabrics are warm, but fleece or a synthetic are preferable—wool can be itchy, takes much longer to dry if it gets wet, doesn't have the same temperature range, isn't as durable, and is slightly heavier. Wool hats lined with a synthetic are available. Fleece and knitted synthetic hats tend to keep their shape better than wool ones do, although they can stretch and occasionally need a hot wash to shrink them back to size.

Whatever the style, hats can be divided into two categories: those that are windproof and those (the majority) that aren't. Windproof hats are made from windproof fleece such as Polartec Windbloc or Gore Windstopper, or have an outer made from a waterproof/breathable or windproof synthetic material. In a cold wind, any hat that isn't windproof will feel cold unless you put your hood up. Nonwindproof hats are more breathable, though, and they're better for milder weather than windproof hats.

How warm a hat will be is determined by both thickness and style. Whether it can be pulled down to protect the ears is an important feature. As with other clothing, the warmest hat isn't always the best—one that will keep your ears warm in a blizzard will be too hot for a cool evening at a summer camp. How much you feel the cold matters, too.

There are currently four main styles of hat, all available in windproof and nonwindproof fabrics. The basic *bob hat* (also called a *watch cap, stocking cap,* or *tuque*) is still with us, though it may have ear flaps. The *balaclava* still survives, too. A newer design consists of a tube of material open at each end. This style, known as a *neck gaiter,* can be combined with a hat to form a balaclava. Some examples have a drawcord at one end and can be worn as a hat when the this end is closed. The final style is the *peaked cap* with ear flaps and a pile lining. This is the most weatherproof design; it protects the face from rain, snow, and sun, and can be used in place of a jacket hood. There are also warm *headbands,* useful for when a full hat isn't needed but your ears feel chilly.

Some hat styles are available in several sizes, although many aren't. Because most pile doesn't stretch the way that knitted wool or acrylic does, it's important to get a good fit if you choose pile headgear. Hats that are a bit tight will be very uncomfortable after a few hours' wear. However, if the fit is too slack the hat will blow off in every breeze; chin straps are useful to prevent this.

Sun Hats

Good sun hats are essential in spring and summer, from the deserts up to the high mountains. A good hat—preferably made of opaque canvas and with a wide brim all around—not only keeps off the sun, but it also repels light rain, keeps leaves and twigs out of your hair when bushwhacking, and holds your head net in place when the bugs are really bad. Many seasoned backpackers, kayakers, canoeists, and rafters choose canvas hats, such as those from Tilley Endurables, the Ultimate Hat company, or Watership Trading Company.

Gloves and Mitts

Cold hands are not only painful and unpleasant, but they make the simplest tasks very difficult. Except at the height of summer, you should carry at least one pair of liner or inner gloves made of synthetic wicking material, thin enough to wear while doing things like pitching the tent or taking photographs, but surprisingly warm. At about 1–2 ounces per pair, they are hardly noticeable in the pack. They don't last long if worn regularly, though. Wool and silk versions are available, which may be more durable but probably not as quick-drying as synthetics.

In cold temperatures, thicker mitts or gloves are needed. Traditionalists still use gloves made from boiled wool. Boiling shrinks the wool fibers, to make a dense fabric that increases wind and water resistance. Dachstein is the most common brand name; weights are 4–5 ounces. Gloves or mitts made from Polartec Windbloc fleece are more windproof but not as warm as wool, and they are thinner, so you can do more with your hands while wearing them. Neither wool nor Polartec seem to last very long, however. Several windproof fleece gloves are now available (such as Outdoor Research's Windstopper Gripper Gloves and REI's Windbloc Gloves) and have extra-strong material at high-wear spots.

Another debate centers on whether to wear gloves or mitts. Gloves aren't as warm as mitts, because they have to keep each finger warm separately, but mitts decrease dexterity and you have to pull them off for all sorts of fine tasks. Those who suffer from cold hands usually prefer mitts, though. (If your hands do get very cold, by the way, a good way to warm them up is to windmill your arms around as fast as possible—this sends blood rushing to your fingertips and quickly, if a little painfully, restores feeling and warmth to them.)

Another feature to look for is whether handwear has gauntlet-type wrists designed to go over jacket sleeves, or elasticized cuffs designed to go inside sleeves. Gauntlets are best if you use hiking or ski poles, because snow and rain can't be blown up your sleeves. If you don't use poles, cuffs are better—water running down your sleeves can't run into your handwear.

Boaters needing insulated gloves can find pairs with precurved fingers, to make it easier to grip paddles or oars for long periods. Waterproof/windproof pogies are also popular; these Velcro over the paddle and you slip your hand in from the gauntlet-like top.

Layering systems, with waterproof/windproof outer mitts, are the best way to go for ultimate warmth. Many companies offer two-layer systems consisting of pile or fleece inners and waterproof/breathable overmitts. The great advantage of these is that the two layers are designed to fit on top of each other. The systems are available for moderate cold as well as for extreme cold. An example of a moderate cold set is Manzella's 3-Way HandGear: fleece gloves with outers made from a waterproof/breathable polyurethane laminate with a nylon shell. They have pre-curved fingers and a fabric grip on the palms. The weight is just 2½ ounces—incredibly light for overmitts or gloves. However, they're not fully waterproof, don't cover much of the wrist, and will not fit over really thick gloves. When severe cold is expected, look to a set such as Black Diamond's Shell Gloves with thick Retro Pile inners, which weigh 9½ ounces and have long, gauntlet-type wrists. The outer fabric is waterproof but not breathable, which means they can get a bit damp. Current models come with waterproof/breathable Entrant-coated outers. They're also available as mitts.

Losing a mitten or a glove in bad weather can have serious consequences. Several precautions are suggested. One is to attach wrist loops (often called "idiot loops") to your mittens, so that they dangle at your wrists when you take them off. You can use thin elastic shock cord for this. Many mittens now come with D-rings or other attachments for wrist loops; others come with the loops already attached. The second precaution, unless weight is critical, is to carry a spare pair of mittens or gloves. Always do this on ski tours and on bike rides and paddling trips in cold weather when it's inadvisable or impossible to travel with your hands in your pockets.

In an emergency, you can wear spare socks on your hands. Unfortunately, if your feet are cold, the reverse is not possible!

Bandannas

While not really clothing, a bandanna is an essential piece of equipment. This 1-ounce square of cotton can be a headband, brow-wiper, handkerchief, pot holder, dishcloth, flannel, towel, and cape for protecting the back of the neck from the sun. Carry two—one threaded through a loop on your pack shoulder straps for wiping sweat off your face, and the other in your pack for backup.

Treatment and Care

At home you should follow the washing instructions sewn into every garment. Note these carefully—many fabrics that are tough in the field are vulnerable to detergents, softeners, and washer and dryer temperature settings. Polypro, other synthetics, and pile function best if they're kept as clean as possible. Pile and brushed synthetics should be washed inside-out to minimize pilling and to help fluff the inner fabric. Some materials can be damaged by too much washing, however. Down in particular will lose some loft every time it's washed; wool loses natural oils. Sponge stains and dirty marks off the shells of down garments. Washing down is tedious and time-consuming; send your down garments away for professional cleaning (*not* dry cleaning) rather than risk damaging them by doing it yourself. Your local outdoor store should know of companies that do this. If not, ask the garment maker. Washing may shorten the life of waterproof garments, so keep it to a minimum.

Special soaps for high-tech clothing are available. Nikwax makes two liquid soaps: Loft Down Wash (for down clothing) and Loft Tech Wash (for wool, polyester, and waterproof/breathable materials, which leaves water-repellent qualities intact). Nikwax recommends Loft Tech for cleaning Gore-Tex. Avoid harsh detergents anyway, and use washing powders (like Ecover), which neither strip away water-repellent treatments and natural oils nor harm the environment.

Most outdoor clothing can be stored flat in drawers, but down- and synthetic-filled garments should be kept on hangers, so that loft is maintained; prolonged compression may permanently affect loft. Check zippers and fastenings before you put garments away and make necessary repairs. It's irritating to discover that a zipper needs replacing when you are packing hastily for a trip.

Chapter 15
HOW TO PACK FOR A TRIP

Honey, Have You Seen My . . .
Organizing
Check Lists
Hauling Gear

Honey, Have You Seen My . . .

It's eleven o'clock Friday night. You blasted out of work late, rushed over to the outdoor shop to pick up the stove that was in for repair, stopped at the health food store to buy some granola and dried fruit, scarfed some Chinese takeout, and now you're frantically stuffing gear and provisions into the back of the truck. Tempers flare as you discover . . . you can't find your headlamp and you forgot to buy batteries, your pack is missing a buckle, and you let your best friend borrow your favorite sleeping pad. Is there some way to avoid all this hassle of *having fun in the outdoors?*

Aside from the initial planning, packing for a trip is one of the more important aspects of adventuring— certainly one that if done too haphazardly can derail even the best-planned trip.

The keys to good packing are (1) organization and (2) lists.

Organizing

Packing for trips can be greatly simplified if you store your trip gear in boxes that can go directly from closet to car and if you followed the outdoor adventurer's cardinal rule: Al-

When packing for a wilderness trip, it helps to spread everything out neatly so you can sort, check-off, and pack your gear efficiently.

ways clean, repair, and resupply your gear *after* each trip and store it in ready-to-go condition (see Chapter 10, p. 269).

The box-to-car system works very well for car camping, as well as for trips that require long drives and overnight stops between home and your canoe put-in, for example. Medium-size heavyweight cardboard packing boxes from moving companies are very inexpensive, durable, and recyclable; or look at hardware stores and home improvement centers for plastic boxes with hinged or snap-on lids (keep the sizes down, so one person can easily handle them). Try to get different colors, or label them on all four sides if you plan to separate your gear by category: food, kitchen gear, sleeping gear, bathroom

gear, and clothing.

Backpackers, boaters, and bicyclists may want to pack packs, dry-bags, and panniers before leaving home, if they don't need to car-camp along the way. It is still most helpful to store your gear at home in labeled boxes by type of gear: water bottles and water treatment pumps or chemicals, lighting and electronic devices, sleeping necessities, repair kits and safety equipment, PFDs and spray skirts, and so on. When you lay out your packs or panniers, you just select what you need from the boxes as you pack, using your trip lists for reference (see below), and thus eliminating the mad-dashes around the house, tearing up closets to look for lost gear.

Because most of us use our outdoor clothing for more than just outdoor activities, sometimes finding our stretch tights, fleece pullovers, or Gore-Tex rainwear can end up a wild goose chase. The only solution is to try to keep your "outdoor stuff" in one drawer or on one shelf at least, so that you can get to it easily when packing for a trip. Remember to care for your clothing, too, when you clean and repair your gear after a trip (see Annie Getchell's *The Essential Outdoor Gear Manual* for care and repair tips).

Another important rule to remember, to help keep all your organization running smoothly: When you use something out of your gear boxes, make sure it's returned where it belongs.

Check Lists

The following master list, adapted from *Simple Tent Camping,* by Zora and David Aiken (Camden, ME: Ragged Mountain Press, 1996), is broken down into categories and should give you a good start on compiling your own lists. You will probably want to have a car-camping list, as well as lists for backpacking, biking, or boating camps, because the needs will be different. Once you've settled on those items applicable to your activities and your camping, cooking, and travel needs, make copies of the lists (one set for each trip).

Tack the master list onto a bulletin board in your "camping closet" or keep it on the family computer, so you can update it after each trip (lists are never "done"—they will evolve continuously). Families can make copies of the individual "Campers' Needs" list for each person, so everyone can do their own packing and checking.

Camp Setup

- ___ Tent
- ___ Awning
  - ___ Poles
  - ___ Stakes and spares
  - ___ Guylines and 100 feet of extra $\frac{1}{8}$-inch nylon line
- ___ Groundcloth
- ___ Sleeping bags
  - ___ Sleeping-bag liners
- ___ Sleep pads or air mattresses
  - ___ Foot pump (for inflating air mattresses)
- ___ Pillows
- ___ Blankets
- ___ 1 or 2 tarps
- ___ Repair kit
  - ___ Nylon tape
  - ___ Duct tape
  - ___ Length of pipe (for tent pole sleeve)
  - ___ Snap fastener kit or grommet kit
  - ___ Small sewing kit with safety pins
  - ___ Scissors
- ___ Folding chairs
- ___ Lantern
  - ___ Extra mantles
  - ___ Fuel (liquid gas or propane cylinder)
  - ___ Gas lighter, matches
- ___ Battery-operated lamp
  - ___ Extra batteries and bulb
- ___ Flashlight(s) or headlamp(s)
  - ___ Extra batteries and bulb(s)
- ___ Candles
  - ___ Candle holders
- ___ Radio (weather)
  - ___ Batteries
- ___ Water hose
- ___ Water bottles (for ferrying and for hiking)
- ___ Water filter or tablets
- ___ Mosquito coils
- ___ Dishwashing
  - ___ Portable sink (*or* dish pan/wash bowl/ rinse bottle)
  - ___ Bucket
  - ___ Dish soap
  - ___ Kitchen cleanser
  - ___ Scrubbing pads
  - ___ Dishcloth or sponge
  - ___ Dish towel
- ___ Clothesline
  - ___ Clothespins
- ___ Small shovel or trowel (fire, latrine)

- ___ Work gloves
- ___ Pocket knife/multi-tool
- ___ Utility straps
- ___ Short shock (bungee) cords
- ___ Block and tackle (if desired, for hanging food bag)

Food Preparation and Storage

- ___ Camp stove and fuel
  - ___ Repair kit
- ___ Firepan
- ___ Firewood
- ___ Propane or charcoal grill and fuel
- ___ Fire-starting aids: newspaper, kindling, paraffin fire starters, gas lighter, matches
- ___ Grill platform
- ___ Pots
  - ___ 1 large frying pan
  - ___ 1 small frying pan
  - ___ 2 or 3 saucepans, preferably with lids (*or* cook set of nesting pots and pans)
  - ___ Foil baking pans
- ___ Nonstick cooking spray
- ___ Coffee funnel and filters
- ___ Cooking utensils
  - ___ Aluminum foil
  - ___ Heat diffuser
  - ___ Pliers or pot lifter
  - ___ Oven mitts (pot holders)
  - ___ Spatula
  - ___ Tongs
  - ___ Skewers
  - ___ Large stirring spoon
  - ___ Ladle
  - ___ 2 sharp knives
  - ___ Mechanical can opener
  - ___ Bottle opener
  - ___ Potato peeler
  - ___ Cheese grater
  - ___ Cutting board
  - ___ Fish-filleting board and knife
- ___ Dining
  - ___ Dinner plates
  - ___ Soup/salad/cereal bowls
  - ___ Mugs
  - ___ Plastic glasses
  - ___ Silverware
  - ___ Paper towels (use as napkins, too)
  - ___ Tablecloth
- ___ Miscellaneous

___ Plastic food bags
___ Zip-top bags
___ Garbage bags
___ Twist ties
___ Extras
   ___ Bean-pot tripod
   ___ "Spit" cooking setup
   ___ Wood chips for smoke flavor
   ___ Long griddle for camp stove
   ___ Measuring cup
   ___ Mixing bowl
   ___ Dutch oven
   ___ Reflector oven or stove-top oven
   ___ Hanging bean pot
   ___ Grilled-sandwich maker/pie iron
   ___ Broiler basket
   ___ Popcorn popper
   ___ Hot dog fork
   ___ Icepick
   ___ Toothpicks
   ___ Corkscrew
   ___ Tablecloth clamps
   ___ Foam-rubber can holders
___ Cooler
   ___ Small jars for ketchup, mayo, mustard, relish, jams
   ___ Ice supplements (block ice, dry ice, or blue coolant freezer packs)
   ___ Covered plastic containers or zip-top bags for leftovers
   ___ Egg holder
   ___ Juice mixer/pitcher
___ Don't forgets
   ___ Salt and pepper
   ___ Spice kit
   ___ Salad oil
   ___ Coffee
   ___ Tea
   ___ Instant milk
   ___ Sugar
   ___ Marshmallows
___ Food list and menus, your choice (see Chapter 12)

Campers' Needs

___ Duffel or pack
   ___ Long pants
   ___ Shorts
   ___ T-shirts
   ___ Flannel shirt(s) and/or sweatshirt(s)

___ Shoes/hiking boots/climbing shoes/ water shoes
___ Spare walking shoes
___ Socks
___ Underwear
___ Belt
___ Heavy sweatshirt and/or sweater (natural or synthetic fleece)
___ Windbreaker
___ Hat (wool and/or sun-shade)
___ Gloves
___ Sunglasses
___ Rainwear
___ Swimsuit
___ Shower kit
   ___ Soap
   ___ Shampoo
   ___ Comb
   ___ Toothbrush/toothpaste
   ___ Dental floss
   ___ Razor
   ___ Mirror
___ Towel
___ Washcloth
___ Toilet tissue
___ Moist towelettes
___ First aid/health
   ___ Alcohol swabs
   ___ Cotton swabs
   ___ Bandages
   ___ Moleskin and 2nd Skin
   ___ Gauze
   ___ Adhesive tape
   ___ Elastic bandage
   ___ Disinfectants (alcohol/hydrogen peroxide)
   ___ First aid cream
   ___ Eye patch
   ___ Tweezers
   ___ Clove (oil or powder)
   ___ Insect repellent
   ___ Insect bite treatment
   ___ Sunscreen
   ___ Sunburn treatment
   ___ Calamine lotion
   ___ Aspirin or acetaminophen
   ___ Ibuprofen (anti-inflammatory)
   ___ Antihistamine
   ___ Antacid
   ___ Antidiarrheal
   ___ Extractor snakebite kit
   ___ Personal medications

Other Gear

___ Bicycles and panniers
___ Climbing equipment
___ Binoculars
___ Compass
___ Topographic maps, nautical/river charts
___ Sport watch with alarm
___ Water bottles
___ Daypacks/fanny packs
___ Reference books
   ___ Birds, animals, plants, stars
___ Writing notebook
___ Musical instruments
___ Games and puzzles
___ Fishing gear
___ Books for reading
___ Camera(s) and manual(s)
   ___ Film
___ Video camera and manual
   ___ Blank tapes

Canoe/Kayak/Other Boat

___ Roof racks (*or* foam blocks) and tie-down straps/ropes (for cartopping)
___ Paddles/oars
___ PFDs
___ Sprayskirts
___ Charts/maps
___ Compasses
___ Waterproof bags
___ Flashlights
___ Line for gear tie-in and lining canoe or raft
___ Repair kit
___ Anchor
   ___ Anchor line
___ Bailer
___ Sponge
___ Whistle

Car

___ Wood blocks (wedges to block tires)
___ Spare tire and changing equipment
___ Jumper cables
___ Flares
___ Small tool kit
___ Spare engine belt
___ Spare hoses, fuses
___ Duct tape
___ Silver reflective tape
___ Engine oil
___ Compass

___ Road maps/atlases
___ Guidebooks
___ Travel games
___ Music (CDs or tapes)
___ Picnic blanket
___ Moist towelettes
___ Whisk broom/dust pan
___ Small trash bags

Dog
___ Dishes
___ Food
___ Harness/leash
___ Identification/health certificate
___ Brush
___ Pooper scooper
___ Bedding
___ Toys
___ Doggy pack
___ Booties, jacket, other safety items

Essential Personal Safety Gear in Daypack, Fanny Pack, or Dry Bag
___ Map/chart and compass
___ Matches in waterproof container, and fire-starter kit
___ Sharp knife
___ Spare clothing
___ Emergency food (a few power bars)
___ Extra water
___ Light, with spare bulbs and batteries (packed outside the light, or with polarities reversed, to prevent accidental burnout)
___ Emergency blanket or bag

Hauling Gear

If you're wondering how you can cram all your gear into your compact car, don't worry. You won't have to cram *or* head out and buy a truck if you invest in a good roof rack or even a small sport trailer. If you plan to indulge in lots of different outdoor sports, take a look at versatile rack systems such as Thule's and Yakima's, which can handle anything from kayaks and canoes to bikes and skis.

Below are some roof and pickup bed rack manufacturers, and some trailer companies as well.

Racks
Jemb Rack Systems
(800) 272-5362

Rail-N-Rack
(800) 243-9592

Thule (pronounced "TWO-lee")
(800) 238-2388

Trailers
M.O. Trailers
605 Logan
Goshen, IN 46526;
(219) 533-0824

Trailer Lite Corporation
Camarillo, CA 93012;
(800) 854-8366

Appendix A
HOW TO BUY USED OUTDOOR GEAR

Finding a Peach, Not a Lemon

Backpacking, Hiking, and Camping Gear

Boats

Climbing Gear for Rock and Ice

Mountain Bikes

Winter Gear

Finding a Peach, Not a Lemon

You can save quite a bundle on used outdoor gear if you know what to look for. And you can blow it, too. Sometimes a seeming bargain is a hidden lemon. How to tell?

Learn as much as you can about all kinds of outdoor gear by reading current catalogs and buyer's guides in national magazines. It's an ongoing process—you can't learn it all overnight. You need to know current retail prices, old retail prices if the gear is not current, what details indicate good or poor quality for that type of gear, and the resale value of a particular item. For example, North Face four-season tents hold very high value if they are in good condition; so do Specialized mountain bikes. Sea kayaks pretty much depreciate at the same percentage of purchase price— to about 25–30 percent—but then the value holds fairly steady for a number of years, because there's not a lot to go wrong on them and kayaking is a hot sport right now.

Look for used-gear listings on bulletin boards at local outdoor shops, climbing gyms, and activity centers or health clubs. Classified ads in major daily papers are a crap shoot, but classifieds can be good in specialty sports tabloids or regional magazines. Garage sales are a real shot in the dark—check with your local hiking, boating, or biking clubs to see if they have annual swap meets. Some retail stores also host big swap meets, so ask around.

For somewhat regionally specialized gear such as sea kayaks, canoes, and skis, you may need to look farther afield if you don't live in the heart of kayaking country, for example. Plan a vacation to the coast and scout for gear. Keep in mind that prices for some items may be higher in high-demand areas, although choice will be concurrently higher; so a sea kayak marooned in the desert might sell for less than the same model on an ocean coast. But you won't have much choice either—you take what you can get. On the other hand, skis, especially slightly outdated models, may be cheaper in the North Country, where you can buy them just about everywhere. The same goes for canoes and inflatables.

Following are specific buying tips for outdoor gear, including some key questions to ask the owners. Some universal questions you might include:

Why are you selling it?

Where did you buy it? Do you have the receipt?

Has it had any repairs, and did you do it or was it done at a shop?

More often than you'd think, sellers of used but broken gear don't realize that item had a lifetime guarantee from the manufacturer (a lot of gear is bought impulsively, without much or any background research, and most people never read their owner's manuals). Sometimes you can snag a real bargain and subsequently have it repaired at minimal or no cost at the factory. This is where knowing your gear and manufacturers well will really pay off.

Happy hunting!

Backpacking, Hiking, and Camping Gear
Boots

Boots are important and personal pieces of gear, so take care when buying them used. Although you can save a quarter to half the retail purchase price, you may be buying into problems that will cost you more sooner than if you had bought them new. For example, if you buy a moderately used pair of midweight hiking boots for a bargain at $50 (they sell for $100 new) and in just a few months the soles begin to delaminate or chunk off because the rubber was dried out from disuse, the cost of resoling for some models can run

$45 to $65, including shipping—*voilà,* you have spent more and gotten less than a new pair of boots.

Buy used hiking boots only if they are barely worn (the soles will tell much about boots; also, even if they are not worn, if they have been sitting unused for a year or two, the rubber could be dried out and resoling will be needed sooner than later). You also need to be confident fitting them properly. A poorly fit pair of bargains might not be bargains at all if they sit in *your* closet and you end up selling them again for half the purchase price.

Packs

Used packs can be a great bargain. What little can go wrong on them can be easily discerned and usually repaired either for no cost at home or minimal cost at the factory. Most of what follows holds for fanny packs, day packs, or multiday packs.

- *Check for splitting seams at the bottom, and where the hipbelt and shoulder straps are sewn into the pack.* These can be sewn up at home by hand with a Speedy Stitcher or at moderate cost at a shop or factory ($25–$40), but they are a good bargaining point.
- *Check for thinning fabric or small holes or tears.* As with splitting seams, holes can be patched to an extent, but don't buy a full expedition pack that is so old and thin that it's about to blow apart—no patching will save it.
- *Avoid any packs that are greasy or overly caked in food grime.* This might indicate that the fabric is degrading in ways you can't do anything about (petroleum destroys nylon, and mold or other microscopic critters will do the

same). Plain old honest dirt and mud should be no problem.

- *Inspect the interior seams: they should be taped or sealed off in some way.* If the inside seams are fraying, this could lead to ripped out bottoms or straps. If frayed too much, a torn out seam is hard if not impossible to repair. If the seams are not taped or sealed but are in good condition, a little work on your part will set them straight—but be sure to bargain for the time and effort.
- *Broken or missing buckles can be easily replaced if they are standard sizes.* Half-inch, 1-inch, and 2-inch are standard webbing widths and buckle widths. They run about $1–$2 each.
- *On frame packs, inspect the frame carefully for cracks or dents that might turn into cracks.* Aluminum frames might be able to be welded locally, or sent back to the factory. The costs vary widely, and unless the pack is a super bargain (as in $10), steer clear of broken frames, especially if you plan to use the pack far into the backcountry. Also, don't buy a bare old pack frame and expect to be able to easily find a pack, hip belt, and shoulder straps to fit it. The time, energy, and money spent scouting them out may never be worth even the cheapest bargain.
- *On a frame pack, missing clevis pins and split rings are easily replaced.*

Expect moderately used packs to be about half of original retail; packs in good condition might be 30 percent or so below retail.

Sleeping Bags

Okay, this is where some people might be saying, *Eeeww!* Indeed you

need to decide if inheriting the former owner's body oils on a used bag is something you don't mind. Usually a good cleaning will erase nearly all traces of the former owner, so don't worry overly much.

- *Questions to ask:* What was the original temperature rating? How many times have you washed it or had it washed professionally (and which one)? How often was it used?
- *Check the loft.* This is where you will need to know new bags pretty well, so you can recognize a 20-degree bag that has lost its loft. If in doubt, take an experienced gearhead friend with you.
- *Work the zipper.* It should run smoothly and not hang up on broken teeth. A new zipper can run over $50 to have it sewn in professionally if it's not warrantied.
- *Determine how much it was used, especially a down bag.* Down bags that see daily use for long periods—such as by a guide—might be best skipped. Abused down that gets stuffed and unstuffed daily for months at a time, stored damp, and not washed will not hold its loft well. If it's a real bargain (under $100 for a 5-degree microfiber or Gore-Tex bag, for example), you can pay to have the down recharged at the factory (a $75–$100 prospect, perhaps).
- *Make sure the bag hasn't been overwashed.* A down bag that was dry cleaned or washed too often will not loft well. Again, recharging is an option if it's a bargain.
- *Synthetic bags are hard to kill.* Most rental bags are synthetic and will survive about five years; however, each year the bag, like any bag, will lose some of its loft.

Expect to pay 30–50 percent of original retail for bags in good-to-moderate condition. Down is more expensive generally, because it does have a longer life *if* properly cared for.

Stoves and Lanterns

Stoves and lanterns are pretty easy to buy used. Just light them up for a test run and put them through the paces. You need to know current models, but in general most modern stoves and lanterns can be pretty easily rebuilt or repaired at home or at your outdoor store. If in doubt, ask your shop for advice (also, you might not want to buy one that your local shop doesn't stock parts for—you might be up a creek without a paddle trying to find a dumb $2 part the day before a big trip).

- *Questions to ask.* Where did you buy it? What fuel does it run on? Where do you buy parts for it? Has it ever given you any trouble?
- *Don't buy a really outdated lantern or stove.* You might not be able to get parts such as wicks, mantles, chimneys, generators, or gaskets (the most commonly needed parts). You need to know your gear to make this determination.
- *Don't buy a stove or lantern that runs on unusual fuel.* As above, you won't be able to get fuel and your bargain might indeed be a lemon.
- *Check for dings or cracks in the fuel reservoir.* Don't buy if there is any doubt here.

Expect pretty good bargains here for even modestly used stoves or lanterns—at least half of the original retail.

Tents

Like packs, tents can be great bargains used if you just follow a few guidelines.

- *Questions to ask.* How often was it used? Where did you use it? Where was it stored? Has it ever had any repairs?
- *Set the tent up—never buy one "as-is" in its bag unless the bargain is ridiculous (under $20).*
- *Check the poles for splits at the joints or missing parts if sectional.* If a well-known brand and current model, you can get pole sections pretty readily. Worn-out bungee in shock-corded poles is pretty cheap and easy to replace at home. Reject any tent missing poles or parts that you cannot determine are easily ordered, either from the factory or at your local shop.
- *Check the floor for rips, tears, and delamination of the waterproof coating.* Rips and tears, if very small, can be repaired at minimal cost. A new coating might be done by you for the cost of a can of polyurethane (under $10), but this might not last; a factory recoated floor is well over $50, and much more for big tents.
- *Check the rainfly for rips, tears, and delamination of the waterproof coating.* Same as above, except replacement rainflies cost more than floors. As with poles, a missing rainfly might prove to be a difficult thing to deal with unless you are certain the model is current and replacement an option.
- *Check the tent body for wear and tear: zippers, bug netting, pole sleeves.* Zippers can be replaced (usually) for under $75; pole sleeves and bug netting are relatively easy to repair at home if the damage is minor.

Expect to pay 30–50 percent of original retail on moderately used tents. Good-quality tents (such as those from The North Face, Mountain Hardwear, Sierra Designs, Moss, Kelty, and others) can be used a lot without diminishing their lifespan significantly *if they were stored properly.* See Annie Getchell's *The Essential Outdoor Gear Manual* for more tips.

Boats
Inflatables

When looking for a used raft or inflatable kayak, spend enough time to adequately "kick the tires." Look for signs of damage—patched tubes, broken D-rings, marred floors—which you are bound to see unless it's been used only once or none at all. Don't despair—with some time and effort many rafts can be inexpensively reconditioned and used for many more years.

- *Questions to ask.* How old is the raft/kayak? What rivers have you used it on? and Does it hold air?
- *Inflate the boat* and listen for air leaks.
- *Inspect the material* for any fading or discoloration that might indicate too much exposure to damaging ultraviolet rays. This can't be repaired.
- *Check the seams* to see if they're intact, and see how carefully any patches have been applied.
- *Check the valves.* Do they open and close smoothly?
- *Check the integrity of the baffles* by inflating one chamber at a time.
- *Examine the floor* in good light to see if the material's outer coating

is worn away from the base cloth (the true measure of the raft's prior use and care is its floor). Expect to find some wear, but if large patches of cloth are showing through, chances are the raft has seen some heavy use.

For moderately used boats, expect to pay about half retail of that model. Be wary of killer bargains; these boats may have gotten more wear than you want to deal with, especially if you're just beginning.

Sea Kayaks

Since there are so few moving parts on a sea kayak, it is pretty easy to determine the overall condition through careful inspection.

* *Questions to ask.* Where and how has it been stored? How many miles has it seen? In what conditions primarily?
* *Inspect the hull, especially the bottom.* Most wear and abuse on a kayak occurs on the bottom of the hull, where it is dragged over rocks. But light scratches on a plastic hull don't hurt, and the same goes for fiberglass. Even scars that go through the gelcoat affect performance very little, as long as the underlying material is sound. Of course, if the hull is close to pristine, you can be sure the previous owner was careful in other aspects as well.
* *If the boat is fiberglass, check the side seam and bulkhead seams.* Avoid any boat that has separated at the main side seam. A bulkhead can be repaired, but you will need to know how to lay up fiberglass.
* *If the boat is plastic, check that the bottom of the hull is straight and unfurred.* Plastic hulls can take a

"set" if improperly stored or tied too tightly to a roof rack. A bent hull will not track worth a darn. If the bottom is too scratched up, the boat will be sluggish.

* *Inspect rudder cables, the rudder, and hatch covers.* Rudders and cables can be repaired or replaced relatively cheaply. Hatch covers should fit snugly; if not, they may leak. You can either replace them if the boat model is still made (check before you buy), or try to add new seals, depending on the type. If the boat is a current model, it should be no problem to replace the hatch covers for under $100.

It's possible to pick up used plastic boats for a few hundred dollars, and fiberglass models for under a thousand. In general, sea kayaks depreciate rapidly to about 25–30 percent of retail, and then hold steady for years.

Canoes

Even more so than kayaks, canoes are simple to buy used, because they're very simple craft—no moving parts.

* *Questions to ask.* How old is it? How often was it used? Where was it paddled? How and where was it stored?
* *Inspect polyethylene and Royalex canoes carefully.* Look for signs of aging such as minute cracks radiating from gunwale screws, and lack of resiliency of the hull (this indicates that the material is hardening). In general, you might want to avoid polyethylene boats that are older than 5–6 years; Royalex lasts a bit longer. And look for nasty gouges in the hull, particularly ones that go through the surface layer into the foam

core; this is can be a bad defect if not very well repaired. You might want to have a shop look at any repairs for a consultation if the boat is expensive.

* *Check aluminum-hulled canoes for dents with sharp edges that may turn into holes, or too many patches.* In general, aluminum canoes are ageless; as long as the hull in reasonably good shape, go for it.
* *Check wood-and-canvas canoes carefully.* You really need to know your stuff about wood-and-canvas canoes in order to judge the condition of a used one. Unless it's an obvious pristine gem, it's probably best that beginners avoid them, unless you can ask a knowledgeable friend for advice.
* *For all canoes, check the condition of the hull, and wood gunwales and cane seats.* If in poor condition, both seats and gunwales can be renewed relatively easily at home or by a shop, but be sure to bargain for the work involved. The main thing to worry about is a smooth, straight, unholed hull.

Boating Accessories

Paddles and oars are simple to buy used: just check for signs of delamination in fiberglass- or composite-bladed models, and check the shafts and blades of wood models for splitting and warping. Varnish can be easily renewed if the wood is in good shape. Check take-apart versions for any sticking or looseness.

PFDs and helmets are another matter. It's probably best to buy these items new, unless you know the person and know that the gear is relatively new and unabused. Both items incrementally lose their ability to float and protect you as they get older.

Climbing Gear for Rock and Ice

Most climbing safety experts agree: don't buy used gear. You never know what has happened to it—how many lead falls a rope has suffered, untold stress on pro and carabiners, an old helmet whose protective lining is getting brittle. The only exception might be if you know and trust the person selling the gear. Otherwise, for climbing hardware and ropes, skip it.

Climbing shoes, on the other hand, are a great bargain, and there are a great many out there, because of misfits and changes of mind. Check out climbing-shop and -gym bulletin boards. Some shops and gyms have consignment boots as well.

Mountain Bikes

Great bargains can be had in any kind of used bikes, but you can get skunked a little more easily on mountain bikes because of the rapidly changing market. Know your bikes and their prices. Some new models are even *going down* in price, because of market competition and improvements in materials production and availability.

- *Questions to ask.* How much was the bike new? How old is it? What kind of riding do you do? Has the bike been in any bad crashes? Has the frame ever been cracked and repaired and re-painted?
- *Go for a thorough test ride.* Run through all gears; make sure the brakes are smooth and powerful;

check for looseness in the bottom bracket and headset; test the wheels for trueness and the wheel hubs for slop.

- *Inspect the frame.* Look carefully for cracks around the head tube and bottom bracket especially, but also check all joints. Look for signs of crash damage: scratched up bar ends and dented or scratched frame. All bikes will have some scratches and dents, but excessively abused bikes will look trashed and feel loose.
- *Know the cost of replacing worn-out parts.* Pedals and grips can be easily and inexpensively replaced. Tires might run $60 or more, so bargain if they're really thrashed. Cranksets, derailleurs, and brakes are pricey, so keep an eye on these parts particularly.

Bikes lose value fast, so expect a two- to three-year-old bike to be half the original retail price. If it's a current model, however, check carefully to see if you can get the same bike (or a better version of it) for only slightly more money new because the price is coming down. Any mountain bike older than 6–10 years can be considered not worth much more than $100 for top-of-the-liners, less for midrange models.

Winter Gear
Cross-Country Skis

Used skis are a great bargain if they were cared for properly during their first life.

- *Check for signs of delamination,* especially at the tips and tails.
- *Check the top plate, base, and side walls of the skis for damage.*
- *Make sure the skis are straight.* You

can check them by looking along the length of the skis with the bases held together to see if they touch right across the ski at the tail and shovel. If there are any gaps, at least one of the skis is twisted. When squeezed together in the middle the ski bases should match exactly from tip to tail.

- *Look for offset bases.* Offset bases mean a warped ski that won't track properly. By running a flat edge along each base—a ski scraper or credit card will do—you can look for spots of light. If these exist the base isn't smooth, which can cause poor glide and, in a waxable ski, uneven wear of the wax. Although nothing can be done for warped or twisted skis, uneven bases can be smoothed out; this can be done at a ski shop, or at home.
- *Imperfections have different effects.* Imperfections won't affect wilderness-skiing performance as much as they will skiing on the smooth, hard surfaces of set tracks or prepared downhill runs.
- *Watch out for obsolete bindings and boots.* When buying old three-pin gear, make sure it's the modern standard of 75 mm; years ago the bindings and boots varied from 38 to 79 mm in width. If you end up with one of the latter, your boots and bindings will be useless with any new system.

Expect to pay half or less of original retail for ski sets.

Snowshoes

Old snowshoes will last forever if the wood is not cracked, dried out, or warped. You can buy or make your own replacement rawhide bases, and bindings are still available for around $25. You can pick up snowshoes absurdly cheaply at garage sales—as little as $10.

New alloy snowshoes will also last forever if the frames are not cracked or bent, so your only caveat is that each company makes specific rubber bases for their models (they won't interchange with other manufacturers' snowshoes). If worn out, and the company is no longer around, you may have to invent your own bases (not an impossibility for folks handy in the shop).

Expect to pay half or less of original retail if moderately used, half to 30 percent of original retail if lightly used.

With a little research and the right questions, you can find bargains aplenty on the used-gear market.

Appendix B
HOW TO FIND OUT MORE—
Further Resources for Outdoor Adventures

Books
Outdoor Specialty and Adventure Travel Booksellers
Conservation Organizations
Periodicals
Schools
Outdoor Organizations
Land Agencies
Weather
Internet Resources

Books

(see also individual chapter resource listings)

The Amateur Naturalist, by Gerald Malcolm Durrell (New York: Alfred A. Knopf, 1983).

Ashley Book of Knots (New York: Doubleday, 1993).

Backwoods Ethics: Environmental Issues for Hikers and Campers and *Wilderness Ethics: Preserving the Spirit of Wildness,* by Laura and Guy Waterman (Woodstock, VT: Countryman Press, 1993).

EcoLinking: Everyone's Guide to Online Environmental Information, by Don Rittner (Berkeley, CA: 1992).

How to Shit in the Woods: An Environmentally Sound Approach to a Lost Art by Kathleen Meyer (Berkeley, CA: Ten Speed Press, 1989).

Hypothermia: Death by Exposure, by William W. Forgey, M.D. (Merrillville, IN: ICS Books, 1985).

Medicine For the Outdoors: A Guide to Emergency Medical Procedures and First Aid, by Paul S. Auerbach, M.D. (Boston: Little, Brown, 1991).

Natural Health, Natural Medicine: A Comprehensive Manual for Wellness and Self-Care, by Andrew Weil, M.D. (Boston: Houghton Mifflin, 1990).

The New Wilderness Handbook, by Paul Petzoldt (New York: W. W. Norton, 1984).

The Outdoor Athlete: Total Training for Outdoor Performance, by Steve Ilg (Evergreen, CO: Cordillera Press, 1989).

Soft Paths: How to Enjoy the Wilderness Without Harming It, by Bruce Hampton and David Cole (Mechanicsburg, PA: Stackpole Books, 1995).

Sports Health: The Complete Book of Athletic Injuries, by William Southmayd, M.D., and Marshall Hoffman (New York: Perigee Books, 1984).

Stretching, by Bob Anderson (Bolinas, CA: Shelter Publications, 1980).

This Land is Your Land: A Guide to North America's Endangered Ecosystems, by Jon Naar and Alex J. Naar (New York: Harper Perennial, 1993).

The Ultimate Adventure Sourcebook: The Complete Resource for Adventure Sports and Travel, by Paul McMenamin, et al. (Atlanta: Turner Publishing, 1992).

World Wildlife Fund Atlas of the Environment, by Geoffrey Lean, Don Hinrichsen, and Adam Markham (New York: Prentice-Hall, 1990).

Outdoor Specialty and Adventure Travel Booksellers

Adventurous Traveler Bookstore
(800) 282-3963
books@atbook.com
www.gorp.com/atbook.htm

GORP (Great Outdoor Reading and Provisions)
P.O. Box 3016
Everett, WA 98203
(888) 994-4677

The Wilderness Collection
716 Delaware Court
Lawton, MI 49065
(616) 624-4410

Periodicals

(see also individual chapter resource listings)

Ecotraveler Magazine
P.O. Box 1341
Eagle, ID 83616
(208) 939-4500

Men's Journal (If you can get beyond the title, there is good stuff for all genders.)
1290 Avenue of the Americas
New York, NY 10104
(800) 926-MENS

Outside annual buyer's guide, Spring
   issue, 400 Market Street
   Santa Fe, NM 87501
   (505) 989-7100
Summit: The Mountain Journal
   P.O. Box 1341, Eagle, ID 83616
   (208) 939-4500
Women's Sports & Fitness
   2025 Pearl Street
   Boulder, CO 80302
   (800) 877-5281

Conservation Organizations

*(see also individual chapter
resource listings)*
National Audubon Society
   700 Broadway
   New York, NY 10003
   (212) 979-3000
National Wildlife Federation
   1400 16th Street, NW
   Washington, DC 20036
   (202) 797-6800
The Nature Conservancy
   1815 North Lynn Street
   Arlington, VA 22209
   (703) 841-5300
Sierra Club
   85 Second Street, Second Floor
   San Francisco, CA 94105
   (415) 977-5500
The Wilderness Society
   900 17th Street, NW
   Washington, DC 20006
   (202) 833-2300

Schools

*(see also individual chapter
resource listings)*
American Mountain Guides Association (for listings of affiliated
   schools), 710 10th Street
   Golden, CO 80401
   (303) 271-0984

Leave No Trace, Inc.
   P.O. Box 997
   Boulder, CO 80306
   (303) 442-8222 or
   (800) 332-4100
National Outdoor Leadership School
   (NOLS), 288 Main Street
   Lander, WY 82520
   (800) 332-4100
Outward Bound
   945 Pennsylvania Street
   Denver, CO 80203
   (800) 477-2627

Outdoor Organizations

*(see also individual chapter
resource listings)*
Appalachian Mountain Club
   5 Joy Street
   Boston, MA 02108
   (617) 523-0636
Appalachian Mountain Club Huts
   (AMC Reservations)
   P.O. Box 298
   Gorham, NH 03581
   (603) 466-2727

Land Agencies
National Wildlife Refuges
U.S. Fish and Wildlife Service
   4401 North Fairfax Drive
   Arlington, VA 22203
   (703) 358-1769
   http://www.fws.gov/
National Forests
U.S. Department of Agriculture
   P.O. Box 96090
   Washington, DC 20090-6090
   (202) 205-0957
   http://www.fs.fed.us/

National Park Service
Information:
   P.O. Box 37127
   Washington, DC 20013-7127
   (202) 208-4747
   http://www.nps.gov/nps

National Trails System
National Park Service 2230
   P.O. Box 37127
   Washington, DC 20013-7127
   (202) 565-1201
Army Corps of Engineers
   Regional Brochures
   CEWES-IM-MV-N
   3909 Halls Ferry Road
   Vicksburg, MS 39180-6199
   (601) 634-3111
   http://www.nosc.mil/
      planet_earth/army.html
Department of the Interior
   Bureau of Land Management
   Washington, DC 20240-0001
   (202) 208-5717

Weather
NOAA (National Oceanic and
   Atmospheric Administration)
   Network Information Center
   Weather Page
   www.nnic.noaa.gov
*Weathering the Wilderness: The Sierra
   Club Guide to Practical Meteorol-
   ogy,* by William E. Reifsnyder
   (San Francisco: Sierra Club
   Books, 1980).

Internet Resources

Please be aware that World Wide Web page addresses (URLs, or Uniform Resource Locators) change frequently. If you cannot find a page listed below, try searching for the subject in a global search engine, such as Lycos, Infoseek, or Magellan.

GORP (Great Outdoor Recreation Pages) http://www.gorp.com/

General Outdoor and Hiking Information News Group
news:rec.backcountry

Hosteling Information Page
http://www.hostels.com/hostels

Outside Online
http://outside.starwave.com/
index.html

Yahoo Outdoor Pages
http://www.yahoo.com/
entertainment/outdoors
and
Yahoo Outdoor Magazines Reference Page
http://www.yahoo.com/
entertainment/outdoors/
magazines/

INDEX